IRISH NOVELS 1890-1!

Irish Novels 1890–1940

New Bearings in Culture and Fiction

JOHN WILSON FOSTER

OXFORD
UNIVERSITY PRESS

OXFORD
UNIVERSITY PRESS

Great Clarendon Street, Oxford OX2 6DP

Oxford University Press is a department of the University of Oxford.
It furthers the University's objective of excellence in research, scholarship,
and education by publishing worldwide in

Oxford New York

Auckland Cape Town Dar es Salaam Hong Kong Karachi
Kuala Lumpur Madrid Melbourne Mexico City Nairobi
New Delhi Shanghai Taipei Toronto

With offices in

Argentina Austria Brazil Chile Czech Republic France Greece
Guatemala Hungary Italy Japan Poland Portugal Singapore
South Korea Switzerland Thailand Turkey Ukraine Vietnam

Oxford is a registered trade mark of Oxford University Press
in the UK and in certain other countries

Published in the United States
by Oxford University Press Inc., New York

British Library Cataloguing in Publication Data

Data available

Library of Congress Cataloging in Publication Data

Data available

Typeset by SPI Publisher Services, Pondicherry, India
Printed in Great Britain
on acid-free paper by
Biddles Ltd., King's Lynn, Norfolk

ISBN 978–0–19–923283–3

3 5 7 9 10 8 6 4 2

For my wife
Gail Malmo

Acknowledgements

I wish to record my thanks to the Leverhulme Trust for a visiting professorship to the United Kingdom (2004–05), and to the University of Ulster (Academy for Irish Cultural Heritages) for being my host institution, with especial thanks going to Professor Brian Graham and Dean Robert Welch. I thank also St Michael's College, University of Toronto for inviting me as Armstrong Visiting Professor (2005), and Professor David Wilson (Celtic Studies programme) and Principal Mark McGowan for their academic hospitality. Thanks are also due to the Arts Faculty of the National University of Ireland/Galway for a visiting fellowship (2006), and to Professors Kevin Barry and Hubert McDermott of the English Department.

Among other things, these academic sojourns enabled me to forage in excellent libraries and exploit their inter-library loan services. In this regard I also wish to thank (again) the librarians of the University of British Columbia, especially David Truelove of Inter-library Loans, Koerner Library. I must not forget the librarians of Trinity College Dublin (including the Early Printed Books Reading Room); Queen's University, Belfast (Henry Collection); Robarts and John M. Kelly libraries (University of Toronto); the South Eastern Education and Library Board, Northern Ireland (especially Lily Devlin, head of Portaferry Public Library); British Library (Reading Room); Linenhall Library, Belfast; National Library, Dublin, and James Hardiman Library (NUI/Galway), all of whom provided me with, or secured the loan of, copies of long-forgotten and hard-to-come-by novels. I am also grateful to the following individuals: in Ireland, Dr Dennis Kennedy, Professor Liam Kennedy, Dr Bruce Stewart, Ms Sheelagh MacCormack, Mrs Allison Murphy, Mr Rowland Murphy, Professor Gearóid Ó Tuathaigh, Mr James Ryan; in Canada, Ms Dominique Yupangco (who efficiently and sympathetically solved my computer problems) and Professors Leslie Arnovick, Miranda Burgess, and Gernot Wieland. This book grew out of my commission to write an account of Irish prose between 1890 and 1940 for the *Cambridge History of Irish Literature* (2006), and I thank the editors, Margaret Kelleher and Philip O'Leary, for that commission and the trust it implied.

J.W.F.

Vancouver, 2007

Contents

Introduction: The Shock of the Old

Irish Novels 1890–1940 is for most of its length a sampling of Irish popular and minor fiction (novels in the main) published between 1890 and 1922, and is followed by a briefer survey of women's fiction, 1922–1940. The sampling merely gestures towards a schematic critical representation, more concerned as it is with the prior task of recovering for the record largely forgotten novels and novelists. Almost all of the novels were written by writers born in Ireland, whether or not that fiction was set in Ireland and whether or not it was concerned with what in political affairs was then known as the Irish Question or with what in cultural affairs was then known as the Irish Revival. Much of it *was*, as it happens, set in Ireland, and as I read novel after novel, the picture both of Ireland and of Irish fiction that I found emerging (like a negative in photographic developer) was in many of its details, and certainly in its panorama, a strikingly unfamiliar one; to say that it carried the shock of the old is to exaggerate just a little. This portrait of Ireland in fiction certainly departs from the story we have told ourselves under the auspices of the Irish Literary Revival, and I have thought it worth bringing to the attention of students of Irish writing and Irish culture. Besides enriching my own sense of fictive Ireland before 1922, this unfamiliar story has enabled me to see unsuspected connections between the fiction written by Irish women in the 1920s and 1930s (some of it well known, some of it virtually unknown) and the popular fiction of their predecessors. The opening year of 1890 is rather more arbitrary than the closing year of 1922, when Ireland was reconstituted, but in terms of popular fiction, 1922 is fairly arbitrary, too; but chronological brackets had to be inserted. The unfamiliar story has also enabled me to see a rewarding confusion of the popular and mainstream, categories that most commentators on Irish fiction have either declined to countenance or have yet to explore. Commentators have preferred, or been preoccupied with, the notion of a ruptured or interrupted tradition in the Irish novel that perhaps too conveniently reflected the political and constitutional ruptures of the time.

An orthodox account of Irish prose fiction between 1890 and, say, the middle of the twentieth century might run as follows. The Literary Revival defined itself in part as an abstention from the English literary tradition, and this included the 'English novel', using the term in a generic as well as national sense.[1] After all, it was thought by Irish cultural nationalists that the English novel written by Irish novelists had tended to demean Ireland, especially in the form of the 'Anglo-Irish novel', which, in the middle and late nineteenth century especially, was said to perpetuate a view of the island that Yeats disapprovingly referred to as the 'humourist's Arcadia'.[2] Such fiction seemed self-consciously Irish and written mainly by southern Protestants to entertain English readers. It could be described as a branch of English popular litera-ture—no doubt an exotic graft as far as mid-Victorian English readers were concerned—and Douglas Hyde in his landmark 1892 address, 'The Necessity for De-Anglicising Ireland', warned Irish readers off English popular literature in favour of 'Anglo-Irish literature', by which he meant the serious Irish literature in the English language that he and other Revivalists intended to write.[3] As late as 1919, the Belfast essayist Robert Lynd was decrying the English view of the real-life Irishman as an irresponsible creature whose utterances one need not take seriously.[4] Because the kinds of stories, charac-ters, literary styles, and meanings that the Revivalists wished to revivify or invent did not without effort suggest the novel as their best vehicle, the novel did not fare as well as poetry and drama once the Revival got under way. The Revival regarded itself as an inauguration, one that returned to the past to achieve a beginning, so its exponents paid little attention to the Irish Victor-ian novel which continued through the 1890s and into the Edwardian decade and beyond. Literary historians of the Revival in our own day have main-tained this inattention.

The Revival, it transpired, was to be a revival neither of realism, opposed to the alleged patronizing unrealities of the 'Anglo-Irish novel', nor of Irish thought in the ordinary sense, opposed to the representation of the Irish as an emotional, unthinking people. Rather—and ironically—it was to be a revival primarily of folk-belief, folk-heroism, folk-myth, and ancient folk-courtesy: in other words, dignified and genuinely romantic versions of what had prompted English and Anglo-Irish condescension, but now tracked back to an impressive pre-Conquest Ireland that was to be resuscitated. This required a recovery of the Irish peasants as real human beings beset by life's difficulties in general and Irish rural difficulties in particular, though they were still picturesque, entertaining, humorous, and tragic by turns: figures of poetry and tale. This time around it was not an exploitative Anglo-Irish writer or even a Catholic countryman like William Carleton, intimate with the peasant, that was depicting the peasant but the Protestant or middle-class (or upper middle-class) Catholic writer engaging in a kind of cultural redress.

One can see a tentative departure in this direction in *Irish Idylls* (1892) by Jane Barlow, daughter of a Reverend Professor, Vice-Provost of Trinity

College Dublin. This was a very popular set of stories in which the Conne-mara peasant is portrayed respectfully and fairly knowledgeably (the speech-patterns and idioms are there, even if rather unlocalized), though the note of condescension is impossible to miss, likewise the feeling that the Victorian eloquence of the storyteller is itself civilizing, as it were, her quaint subjects, despite a textural density of prose that confers its own respect on its subjects. A more localized and regionalized knowledge of the peasantry came soon after with Hyde and Lady Gregory, and it was they and others who firmly established the peasant as the central figure in the reconfigured Irish land-scape. Barlow, meanwhile, followed *Irish Idylls* with numerous volumes of comparably readable stories, including *Strangers at Lisconnel: A Second Series of Irish Idylls* (1896), *A Creel of Irish Stories* (1897), *By Beach and Bog-Land* (1905), and *Irish Neighbours* (1907). Rehearsal did not deepen her fiction into a pervasive sense of social malaise of some remediable kind. In the opening sketch of *Irish Ways* (1909), Barlow identified three popular Irelands she was eschewing: pitiable Ireland, sentimental Ireland, and glamorously Celtic Ire-land. She offered instead a fourth Ireland, what we might call uniquely ineffable Ireland, its 'atmosphere, elusive, impalpable, with the property of lending aspects bewilderingly various to the same things seen from different points of view', an Ireland essentially beyond the range of real reform, even if desirable.[5] In *Irish Ways* only one practical step might be taken towards alleviating the penury of the west of Ireland: mobile lending libraries, around which she builds one story, 'An Unseen Romance'. Barlow turned—I almost wrote 'reverted'—to what she knew thoroughly, life in the country house, in such a novel as *Flaws* (1911). But as if in recompense, the unprepossessing nature of many of the characters seems at times like a nod to *The Real Charlotte* (1894) by Somerville and Ross, as if complementing the picture of an idealized peasantry with the picture of an all too realistic minor gentry. But this dull and interminable novel proved only that Barlow was at home solely at the precise distance from her characters she maintained in her peasant stories.

Hyde's firm grip on the peasant in his folk-collections and translations, strengthened by his scholarship, was loosened with extraordinary results by J. M. Synge who burst through to the other side with what could be described as his 'higher condescension' to the peasantry but one that disarmed readers and theatregoers with flamboyantly eloquent comedy or magnificently elo-quent tragedy. Here was the Irish peasant's apotheosis, though it met token resistance from Catholic cultural nationalists of a more earnest and realistic hue. All the while, the peasant held centre stage.

Meanwhile, though the English novel is hospitable to realism, ideas, and debate, it was of little use to the Revival. One might think this odd, given the necessity of the Revivalists to argue their case and cause, but the ideas thought necessary to the Revival were couched instead in a small number of manifestos, leaving the art itself freer from ideation.[6] While drama, too, can obviously accommodate debate and the play of ideas, Yeats and the Abbey Theatre under his sway proposed a different kind of Irish drama. It was as if Yeats, aware that no native (Gaelic) drama existed, took the opportunity to commence *ab ovo*, returning to drama's roots in folk and religious ritual and symbolism in order to begin; the drama of Ibsen and Shaw and its engagement with burning social and political issues of the day, the Society drama of Pinero and Jones, the mannered comedy of Wilde—all these were to be avoided.

In consequence of these vigorous predilections, prose fiction of the Revival was a diverse mingling of the traditional (i.e. what purported to be distinctively Irish) and the experimental, the latter being a re-working of the former. Conscious reaction against the Revival came in the form of realism, spearheaded by anti-heroic and anti-romantic short stories written by George Moore and James Joyce—both lapsed Catholics—and continued in the fiction of Daniel Corkery, Brinsley MacNamara, and Gerald O'Donovan. Joyce's later fiction developed under the auspices of an international modernism which he was helping to create, though at times it could suggest affinities with an odd kind of Irish modernism developed on the mythopoeic fringes of the Revival by James Stephens, Eimar O'Duffy, and even Padraic Colum.[7] The end of the Revival was signalled by a later and more recognizable modernity, deriving from modernism but different enough, and self-conscious enough, to suggest postmodernism, emerging in the 1930s and 1940s from the pens of Samuel Beckett and Flann O'Brien. During those decades, it was signalled also by a refreshed and critical realism from the pens of Sean O'Faolain and Frank O'Connor, newly exercised by the severe constraints on society after the limited Home Rule of the Irish Free State was achieved in the early 1920s.

There the matter until the 1960s has been seen to lie. The recovery of a few women fiction writers, flourishing after the Revival (Kate O'Brien and Mary Lavin chief among them) and neglected until recently, has mildly complicated the picture of Irish realism's abiding contest with Irish romanticism (counter-Revival with Revival), postmodernism's quarrel with both, and the presentation of the entire scenario as a family quarrel among cultural and literary nationalists.

There is a good deal of justice and truth in this 'grand narrative' of modern Irish fiction. Indeed, it seems to me largely true, *but only if the Irish Revival is the central focus of our investigation.*[8] I told the story myself in just this form in *Fictions of the Irish Literary Revival* (1987) and I wish in the present study to supplement it and, by doing so, cast it in a new light. It was the twin concepts of the Revival and the counter-Revival that prevented my study from being a comprehensive and recuperative survey. I believed that a revisionist account of the Revival was required, but thought then that the counter-Revival was the whole of it. I believe now that a fuller survey of the prose fiction of the period is what is required to complete the revision, and that popular and minor fiction outside the Revival/counter-Revival quarrel should be accounted for. *Irish Novels 1890–1940* is not meant, then, to supersede *Fictions of the Irish Literary Revival* but to be a companion volume, and for this reason I have not in what follows discussed at length writers treated substantially in the earlier book, including George Moore, James Joyce, James Stephens, Daniel Corkery, Brinsley MacNamara, Canon Sheehan, and Seumas O'Kelly. Nor have I dealt at length with writers treated substantially in my earlier study of regional novels, *Forces and Themes in Ulster Fiction* (1974), including Forrest Reid and Shan Bullock. And in the present study, I discuss different works by St John Ervine from those discussed in *Forces and Themes*. I should add here, too, that only occasionally have I paid attention to historical novels, a populous genre in Ireland that has often mirrored political developments and sentiments at the time of composition.

Should the Revival and counter-Revival not be our sole concern, then we can see, with help from library catalogues and second-hand bookshops, what has been omitted from this reading of Irish fiction between 1890 (an approximate beginning for the Revival) and 1922, the effective year of partition of the island into the Irish Free State (outside the United Kingdom but inside the British Empire) and Northern Ireland (inside the United Kingdom and the Empire and outside the Irish Free State). By which time, given the terrible realities of the Anglo-Irish war and the Irish civil war, overt references to an Irish literary revival would have seemed out of tune. The omissions become glaring as soon as we expand our notion of fiction to incorporate varieties of popular and 'genre' fiction. To do so is to diversify matters well beyond the jurisdiction of the Revival and its familiar opponents. As I was completing this book appeared a mammoth study of British popular and mainstream fiction between 1870 and 1918. I was struck by the applicability to the Irish critical scene of what one reviewer observed of *Writers, Readers, and Reputations: Literary Life in Britain 1870–1918*: that Philip Waller's study reminds us that 'most twenty-first-century readers, even academics who specialize in the period, scrape by on a pitifully selective knowledge of the boom he describes'.[9]

In *Fictions of the Irish Literary Revival*, I used the plural word 'fictions' (with its double sense of prose imaginations and cultural inventions, even fabrications) to suggest such diversification, and although I have once again expanded the critical purview, I have largely stayed within the boundaries of what most readers regard as fiction. *Irish Novels 1890–1940* chiefly concerns neglected novels that represent literary subgenres active during the years of the Revival but that have gone largely unacknowledged. I have formulated my project quite independently of David Trotter's *The English Novel in History*

1895–1920 (1993) but nevertheless—allowing for differences in approach—mine is a parallel project; in his study, David Trotter discusses 'all manner of fictions. My aim is to provide a more comprehensive account of the fiction of the period than has hitherto been available'.[10]

The orthodox account explains Irish literature, including fiction, on the Revival's own ground and cultural nationalism's own ground. As a result, we have accommodated a counter-Revival (see, for example, three sections so titled in the third volume of the *Field Day Anthology of Irish Writing*, 1991) but have reserved no shelf-space for creditable Irish writing that neither promoted nor repudiated the Revival and that reflected the continuities in both Irish fiction and Irish society that survived Revivalism in literature and separatist nationalism in politics, even if these continuities were driven underground in the decades after the achievement of the Free State. Two important fiction writers we associate with the counter-Revival were convinced of the unsuitability of Romantic Revival expression to the astringencies of Free State Ireland. They thought that the new Ireland was a broken world, with its sectionalism, puritanism, philistinism, anti-intellectualism, and censorship and that it could not therefore sponsor an artistic realism over the stretch of the novel. Sean O'Faolain thought in 1947 that only four realistic novels had been published since 1922, only nine since 1873.[11] O'Faolain may have been right about the suffocating nature of the Irish Free State, but, as we shall see, his scanty honour roll was to overlook many Irish novels, especially those set outside Ireland, for example Shan Bullock's London novel, *Robert Thorne* (1907), obviously ignored by reason of its setting, since Bullock's *The Loughsiders* (1924), set in Ulster, is one of O'Faolain's nine. Both O'Faolain and Frank O'Connor considered the short story the more realistic genre for the time and place and went on to achieve international reputations in it.[12]

After O'Connor and O'Faolain the idea took hold among critics that Ireland had at best a ruptured tradition in the novel; indeed, given the allegedly peculiar nature of the rollicking nineteenth-century Anglo-Irish novels, the romanticism of the Revival, and the novel drought proclaimed by O'Connor and O'Faolain in the 1930s and 1940s, it had hardly a novel tradition at all. I leave for another time and place whether this critical opinion, with its particular conception of Irish literary proclivities, influenced later fiction writers (and potential novelists) as well as later literary critics, but it is the case that in a significant essay of 1965 Augustine Martin contrasted the capacity of contemporary English novelists of the 1950s and 1960s to see life steadily and whole with the incapacity in that respect of contemporary Irish novelists. Rather than blaming the nature of Irish society, as O'Faolain and O'Connor had done, with some justification he blamed the writers themselves who he thought were avoiding the values and actualities of the society in favour of an assumed dissent inherited chiefly from George Moore and James Joyce.[13] The net critical inference has been the same: Ireland has been immensely gifted with poetic, dramatic, and short story traditions but its achievements in the novel are intermittent, disconnected (from society and from each other), and even *un*novelistic.

A recent and similar characterisation of the Irish novel by a distinguished critic has preferred to tie it to Irish society in the way O'Connor and O'Faolain had done but has pushed historical rupture and distortion in both genre and society back before 1922, indeed to before the appearance of the novel even in Britain. In this view, the ruptures and distortions of Irish history have precluded a recognizable Irish novel up until, at the very earliest, the middle of the twentieth century:

The old Gaelic aristocracy fell after 1600 but was not fully replaced by a confident native middle class until the middle of the twentieth century. In between these dates, the key works of Irish writing were collections of micro-narratives cast in the appearance of a novel but without its sense of a completely developed narrative. Swift's *Gulliver's Travels* is really four short *contes*, in each of which the protagonist starts a new voyage as if he had learned nothing from the previous ones. *Castle Rackrent* by Maria Edgeworth describes many generations in just sixty pages; and the prose trilogy of Samuel Beckett, like *At Swim-Two-Birds* by Flann O'Brien or Máirtín Ó Cadhain's *Cré na Cille*, is structured around anecdotes which never quite shape themselves into a novel. If epic is the genre of the aristocracy and the novel that of a bourgeoisie, then it is in the troubled transition period between these orders that a radical innovation of forms becomes possible. In countries like England, France or Germany that transition was managed fairly speedily, but in Ireland it lasted more than three centuries.[14]

The disappearance of Irish history as it pertains to the novel into an abyss between the Gaelic aristocracy of 1600 and the Catholic middle class of the mid-twentieth century gives one pause. Moreover, although no one could dispute the social and cultural distortions in Irish society produced by English rule, often unjust and sometimes inhuman, I for one would wish to resist the temptation to see Irish society as essentially, unavoidably, and unceasingly freakish across the centuries, a 'sport' entirely outside the development of British society.[15] Since religious differences shrink in importance as demarcators the farther up the social scale one goes, one might also question the necessity of the term 'native middle class', by which I assume Declan Kiberd means a Catholic middle class. Was there a Protestant middle class anywhere on the island before the middle of the twentieth century and if so, did it produce or inspire any novels? In either case, is it disqualified for consideration, despite the critic's recruitment of the Protestant writers, Swift, Edgeworth, and Beckett?[16] The late date at which a confident Catholic middle class is said to have appeared holds only if there is a very specific concept of what constitutes the highly various middle classes.[17] And one could wonder if the works cited are 'key' because they prove a proposition. Even if one did not hesitate at the idea, acknowledged to be O'Connor's, that novels require a 'made' or whole society in order to be written (an hypothesis that surely needs some comparative testing), the contraction of representative Irish long fictions into seven works across three centuries brings O'Connor's and O'Faolain's earlier formulation of the Irish novel to a startling terminus.

One common thread in all these denials of true novels written by Irish writers is the assumption of deep literary difference between Ireland and Britain and the assumption of Irish exceptionality. The 'English connection' in Irish literature and society is ignored. Yet despite the crucial political events of the Home Rule movement, the Irish-Ireland movement, the Republican movement (and the rebellion in Dublin at Easter, 1916), the setting up of Dáil Éireann in 1922, and the declaration of the Republic in 1937, the entwined relations between Ireland and Britain continued, with their direct and indirect literary and cultural expressions. Yet they find no place in the orthodox account. The 'emigrant' Irish trains that converged on the transatlantic port of Queenstown (Cobh) were certainly a feature of nineteenth- and early twentieth-century Irish life, but the Irish Mail train between Euston station and the port of Holyhead, and the packet steamer between Holyhead and Kingstown (Dun Laoghaire), also speed through Irish popular novels of our period and the scenes imply what was the case in real life: a steady volume of human traffic—and therefore cultural traffic—between Ireland and Britain. The train, as the name conveyed, carried letters, but it was primarily a people mover. In one of her novels, Ella MacMahon was precise in its timetable and was thinking, moreover, of the train and boat *to* not *from* Ireland: 'The Irish Mail leaves London every evening at eight forty-five and covers the distance to Holyhead in some six hours', upon which the Royal Mail steamer receives the baton, as it were, and crosses the Irish Sea.[18] George Birmingham opens *The Simpkins Plot* (1911) with a genre sketch of the Euston platform during the last week of July, with schoolboys, sportsmen (lawyers, stockbrokers), tourists, and members of the House of Lords, all crowding on to the Irish Mail in a ritual melee.

In 'Harvesters', a chapter in *A Cluster of Nuts, Being Sketches Among my Own People* (1894), Katharine Tynan gives us a bitter-sweet memory of a boat-train ride she took from Euston to Holyhead en route to Dublin (and thence home for Christmas).[19] One assumes that the passengers in her carriage would have been typical, apart from the exclusiveness of their sex (Tynan was bundled against her will into a 'Ladies Only' carriage reserved for unescorted females). The interest of the sketch takes it in one direction to the borders of the essay, and lies in the author's musings on Irish–English relations and relations between the classes. Taking it in another direction to the borders of the short story are the author's class identification with the English passengers and her class revulsion, followed by an apparent gender offendedness and then anti-Irishness, when two bilingual Irish (male) seasonal farm-workers returning to Galway from England invade the carriage. We would nowadays be tempted to recognize Tynan's anti-Irishness as a form of self-dislike, since she feels racial or national humiliation in front of the English (middle-class) passengers. However, it is likely that the deeper ensuing emotions are wounded Irish pride and then guilt at her intolerance, followed by an unsuccessful attempt to redeem herself through benign thoughts and actions. They are a surprisingly complex few pages fittingly set in the conveniently compact and telling capsule of the Irish mail train and testify, certainly from the Irish side, to the intricacy of Anglo-Irish relations cross-hatched by class, gender, language, culture, and race. Surprisingly, contemporary interest in cultural 'hybridity' does not seem to extend to those hyphenated writers whom we can call, in the most generous sense, Anglo-Irish, nor even to a Catholic writer of the archipelago like Tynan. Yet hybridity of one sort or another can be tracked through the Irish novel from the beginning to the present.

If works that seemed neutral on the question of the Revival do not find a role in the orthodox account, neither do works by Irish writers set outside Ireland (including England), since the Revival demanded on-site engagement, as we might say nowadays; for Irish commentators, Revival literature and Irish literature of the period 1890–1922 became synonymous. For example, a discussion of George Moore by an Irish critic will typically concentrate on *A Drama in Muslin* (1886) and *The Untilled Field* (1903) and ignore, say, *A Mummer's Wife* (1885) and *The Brook Kerith* (1916), though these are indubitably works by an Irish novelist of the period. A comparable synonymity has outlasted the Revival. A discussion of Elizabeth Bowen will typically devote itself to *The Last September* (1929) and an essay or two by Bowen on the Irish Big House but ignore the rest of her sizeable body of work, much of it set in England. A discussion of J.G. Farrell will typically discuss *Troubles* (1970) as though it were not one third of an Empire trilogy written by an English-born Oxford graduate.

This critical squint began with the Revival. Stephen J. Brown SJ shares with that movement an interest only in homeland fiction; his indispensable *Ireland in Fiction* (1915, 1919), as the title signals, concerns only fiction set on the island. For example, he lists but does not give bibliographical details for or summarize the novels of George Moore set outside the island. (My own treatment of Moore in *Fictions of the Irish Literary Revival* would not be atypical and follows Brown's lead in the matter of Moore's eligible works for discussion. Even when the Revival was my declared theatre of critical operation, I should have suspected that Moore's defection from the Irish Revival was probably hastened by his prior achievements in realism, particularly *Esther Waters*, 1894, a novel set in England.)[20] And to take another example (almost at random), Brown gives full details of the Irish novels of M. McDonnell Bodkin but passes over in silence Bodkin's detective fiction, which is set in England. Brown's book is a kind of 're-patriation' of Irish fiction. Much fiction by Irish authors has been discarded, therefore, which is recoverable only by our reading beyond Brown's covers. Oddly, the critical practice of, in effect, bisecting some writers' *oeuvres*, is not frowned upon. (Joyce's body of work does not challenge this procedure even in its counter-Revivalism, since he set only one work, and it a negligible one, beyond Irish shores.) The selective inattention has been retroactive, so that Maria Edgeworth's Irish novels are intensively discussed by Irish critics but not her English novels. This selectivity, unsurprisingly, has fractionally reinforced Ireland's literary self-absorption which has had cultural and even distantly political repercussions.

The exclusiveness is understandable for the Revival period, since the idea that it was only Ireland that mattered was a strategy by which a necessary native cultural recovery could happen. The problem is that the strategy became over time an exclusive policy and pespective, so that it is now no wonder the student of Irish literature should be drawn to novels set in Ireland even by English writers, more than to novels set in England even by Irish writers. The governing assumption is that a student of Irish literature is *primarily* a student, not of Irish writers, but of Irish culture, by which is meant a student of Ireland's cultural nationality either in its most or least generous senses. But it isn't merely a question of focus and priorities. Critics have neglected numerous Irish novelists who felt qualified, and secure enough in their identity, to depict and illuminate the neighbouring island of Britain. Or to depict life beyond what until recently was called the British Isles. Irish popular fiction is a reminder that many Irish were engaged with matters in the wider world, that there was in Ireland, even during the time of the Irish Revival—a necessarily self-regarding and self-interested movement—a centrifugal energy and enthusiasm. Such energy and enthusiasm were facilitated and impelled by the Empire in which the Irish participated, certainly, but also by an historical Irish interest in the New World and other parts of the globe as well. The cultural as well as political sentiment of Sinn Fein ('Ourselves') came to dominate Irish feeling as it was publicly acknowledged inside and outside Ireland, but the larger sentiment remained alive and expressive, though just as neglected by literary critics since, as well as during, the Revival.

Behind the critical practice of neglecting writers who set at least some of their work outside Ireland, is almost certainly a reluctance to countenance certain aspects of Irish literary and social reality, including the geographic

mobility of the Irish imagination and the social mobility of the Irish, especially the middle and upper middle classes even after the creation of the Free
State. The historic Irish expatriate mobility that comes readily to mind and
that has been dealt with so extensively in the critical and historical literature
that it is now a sub-field in Irish Studies, is called the Irish Diaspora, which
refers chiefly, however, to the emigration of the Catholic lower classes, out of a
perceived necessity, to England, America, and Australia. (Even when voluntary, such emigration is normally assumed to be *in truth in*voluntary.) By
contrast, the dispersal of upper-class, middle-class, or farming Protestants, be
it their eighteenth-century emigration from Ireland to the New World or their
military, administrative, or commercial sojourns in India and elsewhere in the
British Empire, has not been striking enough to attract a great deal of
scholarly attention. Since they tended not to establish ethnic urban enclaves,
and their emigration was often a voluntary and individual affair, they have not
registered importantly on the radar of economic and social historians. The
Protestant and Catholic middle-class or upper-class 'diaspora' we can find
recorded in the popular novel but it is as neglected by the critics as the reality
has been by the historians.

Presumably a literal patriotism and a class bias or even religious bias (in
varying ratios) account for the neglect of fictions by certain writers who set most
of their work beyond Irish shores. One might think of the novels of B. M. Croker
set in India, save for the fact that *all* of Croker's novels have been forgotten,
without the need for geographical discrimination: it was presumably her social
class, her unqualified Anglo-Irishness, and her popularity that already counted
against her. These would explain, too, the oblivion enjoyed in Irish critical
circles by the very readable adventure novels of Henry de Vere Stacpoole from
County Dublin, set in the South Seas, the Congo, and other far-flung places and
which we will give a second glance later. But in the case of a third writer, an
expatriation of no use to the cultural nationalist must be the main explanation
for his total neglect. Arthur Mason (1876–1955) was born in Kilclief, Co. Down
but went to sea aged 17, visiting or sojourning in Scotland, the United States,
Canada, the Andes, and Australia; six years later he became an American
citizen. His most popular books (published by Jonathan Cape in the United
Kingdom) were autobiographical fictions—episodic, picaresque tales of adventure which include the entertaining *Wide Seas and Many Lands* (1923), the
characters and incidents of which border on tall tales of the kind we associate
with seafarers. Mason was a romantic realist and can be classed with Jack
London, W. H. Davies, and Patrick MacGill from Donegal. One idea recurs
in the autobiography, namely that we are all equipped with a 'clutch', a
mechanism that allows us in tight spots to access our unconscious mind and
thereby enjoy safety and achieve wholeness untrammelled by fear and anxiety.

Mason likens the connection between conscious and unconscious minds to a narrow channel and it is interesting to note that Mason grew up beside the Narrows, that turbulent tidal flow between Strangford Lough and the Irish Sea. (We will see later how Filson Young was also influenced by this same troubled body of water.) In a second and revised version of *Wide Seas* Mason returns to Kilclief and in defiance of his conscious mind seeks the fairies, banshees, and ghosts he once saw there. The fairies are an unfortunate expatriate touch (he risks resembling poor Paddy Button in de Vere Stacpoole's *The Blue Lagoon*), but the search for ghosts is understandable enough. Back in sight of the Narrows, he tries to take soundings between two realities: otherworldly experience and worldly experience, but stands forever between them, as in their own way do Kilclief and Strangford.[21]

Missing, too, from familiar accounts of Irish prose of our period are the intriguing travel writings, informal cultural anthropology, and overseas novels of Hannah Lynch and Beatrice Grimshaw. I will return to both of these. Meanwhile, it may be convenient to record here that Grimshaw (1871–1953), who was born in a country house in Co. Antrim and educated in Belfast and Normandy, travelled widely and fearlessly in the South Seas (living the life de Vere Stacpoole imagined), and wrote forty-two books (novels, travel books, and volumes of short stories) and dozens of magazine articles. Born a Protestant, she became a Catholic at the age of 23 when she was a journalist in Dublin. After many years of travelling in the South Seas and living in Papua/New Guinea, she settled in Australia where she died, no part of the Irish Story, despite her fascinating 'New Woman' life and though a citizen of that 'greater Ireland' it is now fashionable to study.

Chiefly through the figure of Yeats—though he did not himself belong to the gentry—'Anglo-Irish' has become something of an honorific for literary critics, though in pre-Revival circumstances the term could still refer to a tyrannous alien presence in Ireland. Since in reality most Anglo-Irish were not nationalist but unionist *and* were middle class or upper middle class, Irish nationalism encouraged tacitly or overtly an animus against these classes. Yeats, Hyde, and their class-equals largely (but not entirely) escaped the odium attached to the higher orders by incorporating into their cultural nationalism an extravagant and eloquent championship of the peasantry (an ineradicably Catholic class despite the Revivalists' wish to see it as pagan), an excoriation of the bourgeoisie, and a highly selective acceptance of the gentry. This class animus seemed to extend to the Catholic middle and upper classes as well, who as the Revival proceeded endured a sinking profile in the manifestos, declarations, and criticism of that movement. Their fading visibility—and presumably, fading social influence, if not economic influence (a more complex and often indirect affair)—was, and has been, maintained by most historians of the twentieth century. And by most literary historians. Altick estimates that 'at a rough guess, 90 per cent of the characters in the Victorian fiction which is read today belong to the middle class and the gentry'.[22] In my own experience, this is as true of Victorian and Edwardian fiction, including Irish Victorian and Edwardian fiction, that is *not* read today. Such fiction is largely ignored because (one suspects) higher social class became less reputable as a literary preoccupation amidst the democratic movements of the twentieth century; but especially in Ireland, I would argue, because the upper classes, Catholic and Protestant alike, were seen as inimical to the nationalist project which swelled to claim all attention and loyalty. This swelling has hardly subsided since the heyday of the Revival, because after-shock waves of nationalism have continued to inundate the island for the past hundred years or more. Upper-class Catholics, nationalist or no, have been curious casualties of this phenomenon, at least where their cultural and social profiles have been concerned. Even contemporary literary critics have been reluctant to rehabilitate them through the medium of their own fictional productions or those of their admirers.

To this extent, such a novelist as Mrs J. H. Riddell (1832–1906) has been trebly neglected. To begin with, she was an Irish novelist, born in County Antrim, who threw her lot in with England and did not permanently return either in body or spirit to the new Ireland, being essentially a pre-Revival Victorian writer engaged in the production of three-deckers. Secondly, she was at heart an urban writer while during the last third of her career the Revival privileged rural literature to the point of exclusivity. (It is noteworthy that the greatest Irish writer of the city, Joyce, is regarded, rightly in his case, as a counter-Revival writer. True, he never permanently returned to Ireland in body, but in spirit he never left it.) *City and Suburb* (1862), *George Geith of Fen Court* (1864), and *The Head of the Firm* (1892) seem exotic productions now from an Irish pen, though they oughtn't to, given that Riddell hailed from the industrial heart of Ireland and grew up some few miles from Belfast, the manufacturing capital of the island.[23] The first two novels include hymns to London, transforming the great city into poetry and romance; see, for example, the opening pages of *City and Suburb* that offer the reader a verbal streetmap charting the excited and bewildered movements of the lonely arriving foot-traveller. In *City and Suburb* and *A Struggle for Fame* (1883), the hero or heroine pilgrimages to London (what we might call the Dick Whittington motif—Alan Ruthven in the former novel walks to London all the way from Cumberland!)—in order either to recover or make his or her fortune, mildly romanticized versions of Riddell's own pilgrimage to the metropolis as a young woman. But as the title of her 1862 novel implies, Riddell was conscious of the class and architectural varieties of urban life, particularly the distinction between city and suburb, each nonetheless suggesting a much greater social democracy than existed in the countryside. As for a third reason for her neglect: her characters belong firmly to the middle class and upper middle class, though with scope for her lowlier characters' social ascent through talent. Even when a novel of hers is set in rural Ireland, for example *Berna Boyle: A Love Story of the County Down* (1884), outside its familiar romance plot it concerns the propertied classes and would have been of no use to the Revivalists.[24] Riddell's preoccupations are few but rich in potential variation and detail: business, property, money, the city, the making and losing of fortune, rise and fall through the social ranks. In the intimate attention she paid to the operations of business, she was pioneering even by English standards but, on critical hindsight, unacceptable by Irish standards, the question of merit aside.

The way in which Irish nationalism trumped social class, urbanism, and religion in critical consciousness has meant, then, a reluctance on the part of commentators to acknowledge the existence of mobile and imaginative Catholic middle, upper-middle, and even aristocratic classes that did not throw their lot in with certain culturally disaffected members of the Protestant middle and upper class who led the Irish Literary Revival, and disaffected members of the Catholic lower middle class (disaffected politically as well as culturally) who engineered the Sinn Fein rebellion. As it was, Yeats would have preferred not to have had to countenance the Catholic lower middle class (Pearse and company), wishing to contemplate instead a superstitious, courteous, lore-bearing peasantry. The shock of the event that forced him to confess his own preference was the immediate trigger for his great poem 'Easter 1916'. The Irish Literary Revival itself was prepared to countenance upper and middle classes (Catholic or Protestant) only when they were philanthropic in the cause of Irish cultural nationality and they felt the weight of Yeats's tongue when they attempted to be anything else.

Otherwise, the tradition of Christian philanthropy, Catholic and Protestant, which we will see at work in the popular fiction, held no interest for the Revivalists and has held little interest for literary critics since. Victorian philanthropy was maintained equally, if not chiefly, by women and this has meant that female Irish philanthropists, or those who appreciated the social significance of philanthropy and charity, including several novelists, have been forgotten. Hence the neglect of educated Victorian and Edwardian women who were socially *engagée*, such as Sarah Atkinson, Hannah Lynch, Katharine Tynan, and Rosa Mulholland—all observing Catholics, incidentally, and the first three fine intelligences. There have to be further reasons, of course, for the neglect of the many popular women novelists that I intend to discuss and I will adduce some of the literary reasons later. But here and now it can be assumed that the force of male bias, even in the practice of literary criticism, has been a factor. Another would be the way in which the Irish 'grand narrative' is essentially a male narrative that does not require female novelists in order for it to be told, especially middle-class and upper middle-class novelists with a Victorian or Edwardian outlook and set of values. The tenacity of the anti-colonial, anti-British 'Story of Ireland' has queered the appreciation even of the New Woman writers I will discuss below, combined, as it happens, with the mild selective xenophobia in the matter of fictional settings: the Ulster-born Sarah Grand who set her fiction in England is perhaps the most vivid case in point. In any event, writers like Grand, Riddell, and M. E. Francis who left for England and more or less never returned, failed to appear in the Irish critical histories and surveys.

Critical selectiveness in the question of social class consorts with a reluctance to acknowledge overtly Christian (Catholic or Protestant) topics and perspectives that we find in some of the novels I wish to discuss. These topics and perspectives have been occluded in a criticism that has taken its cue not only from the secular priorities of twentieth-century literary criticism in Britain and America, but also from the agenda-driven paganism and cultural politics of the Irish Literary Revival itself. The topics and perspectives remained in the popular Irish novel but one has to engage in a bit of spadework to recover them.

Of course, Roman Catholicism is perceived by outsiders and Irish Catholics alike as such a pervasive element in Irish culture as almost to represent that culture by a kind of immense synecdoche and thus to be taken as read. There is a large degree of historical truth in this perception. Even when the (Anglican) Church of Ireland was the established church of the island, there was a hidden theocracy at work among the bulk of the populace who regarded Roman Catholicism as the true established religion. That theocracy in waiting became more overt after the disestablishment of the Church of Ireland (1869), despite continuing differences with Fenians and republicans who had been born into the Catholic faith. Certainly they had been educated in that faith. In 1907 Stephen Lucius Gwynn reminded readers that

no ordinary person in Ireland contemplates the possibility of teaching morality apart from religion...Almost every school maintained by the State is managed by a clergyman, who appoints the teacher...in any neighbourhood even a small group of families of any particular denomination is always provided with a separate school of its own....so far as Catholic Ireland is concerned, an immense proportion of the teaching both in primary and secondary schools is done by members of religious orders, and in these, of course, there is no conception of separating moral influences from religious...positive Christian belief, and the practice of religious observances, are everywhere in Ireland very general, and among the Catholic population almost universal.[25]

For the original writer of the Koran (in Jorge Luis Borges's fanciful logic), there was no need to mention camels, whereas a later forger would have had caravans of camels across its pages. Perhaps by analogy, Catholicism was, and has been, too pervasive, established, and commonplace to require attention from Irish critics except when it took the form of apostasy. In turn, the confidence and self-consciousness exhibited by such apostates from Catholicism as George Moore and James Joyce are surely an indirect measure of the orthodox nature of the religion. Apostasy was validated, as it were, for Irish writers both in the present and the past, when after 1922, and constitutionally after 1937, the Roman Catholic Church became the established Church in twenty-six of the thirty-two counties. Readers and the Irish State authorities, and the Church itself, came to expect varieties of apostasy and problematic fidelity expressed by Irish writers from Moore and Joyce onwards, and the State authorities responded with censorship laws, the Church with an invigoration of its own Index of Proscribed Publications, and many Catholic readers with revulsion. This silencing by an aggressive Church and State and by a laity turning a deaf ear, exerted their greatest force between the 1930s and the 1960s. Religion in the Irish novel came to mean just this for critics: apostasy or protest by a few beleaguered lapsed Catholics, while more orthodox expressions of Catholicism in fiction were ignored almost as roundly as expressions of Protestantism, orthodox, heterodox, or heretical. This neglect was retroactive so that religious faith in the Victorian and Edwardian novels was, I suspect, one of the reasons those novels were, and are, largely undiscussed.

Historians have charted the general retreat from Christianity during the European twentieth century. The retreat was not as pronounced in such a traditional and traditionally Catholic society as Ireland but the Irish Revivalists tried to surmount the difficulty posed by a religion inimical both to art for art's sake and nationality for nationality's sake by mining under Irish Catholicism to find and bring to the surface the aboriginal deposit (as they saw it) of elder pagan Irish faith: its folk beliefs, its folk tales, its folk songs, even its putative magic and mysticism.[26] This was so successful in the short run that the collision between the Revival and the Catholic Church that Filson Young predicted in his *Ireland at the Cross Roads* (1903) did not happen. The Church did not admit to being undermined, and in any case the political revolutionaries, Pearse, Plunkett, MacDonagh, even Connolly, could be regarded in an enlarged frame as *Catholic* revolutionaries. The Church bided its time until it could make for itself an unrivalled cultural position in the new Free State while the Revival guttered to a close in the late 1920s and 1930s, many of the Revivalists having already shown Ireland a clean pair of heels, the party well and truly over.

It was only with complicated qualifications that either Catholic Ireland or Revival Ireland had truck with the European-wide alternative and successor to

Christian culture that originated with the Enlightenment. Science was discountenanced in important ways by both the Revival and the Church and we know now that the Story of Ireland that emerged from the period 1890–1922 was a winning if unconfessed combination of nationalism, Catholicism, and Revivalism, the second of these allowing by inversion such a brilliant apostate as Joyce to become in time part of that story, though not George Moore who after all had become both a Protestant and a self-styled sensualist as Joyce had not (there were limits to the elasticity of the Story). Practical and applied science lay behind many of the major economic and social improvements and reforms that had been suggested as remedies for what ailed Ireland (and these included an extension into the rest of Ireland of Belfast's successful industrialism) but the Revivalists were interested chiefly in reforms thought to be compatible with ancient Gaelic polity and economy (e.g. agricultural cooperatives). Meanwhile, the Church was suspicious of modernization for its own good reasons but also because it was felt that modernization might loosen the Church's grip on the people. This, together with the general inhospitality extended to the English novel by the Revival, might help account for the critical neglect, then and after, of novels of improvement and reform, of what we might call Condition-of-Ireland novels. These represented their own fictive answers in what have been called problem-novels, some of which I discuss below and that I have had to exhume in order to do so.[27]

Romantic, religious (especially Roman Catholic), and rural biases against science—it was assumed even if it weren't entirely true that historically Ireland's best scientists had been Protestants—all fed into the Story of Ireland, though it was perhaps just as effectively the bias against popular (or lowbrow) fiction that operated until recently in English and American literary criticism that accounts for the neglect of Irish science fiction and the genre that also presumes the paramountcy of reason—detective fiction. It may be, too, that these two genres tend to upset the preference for Irish fiction to be set in Ireland and to be about Ireland whereas British and Irish science fiction and detective fiction have been set in what we might call a 'generic space' (which happened to be recognizably English, as in the case of, say, Bodkin), not for unpatriotic reasons but for literary-historical reasons.

The possibility of a generic space occurred to me when I recently read a novel by the Belfast writer, Forrest Reid: *Pirates of the Spring* (1919). It is a typically fluent and assured Reid achievement. The action takes place in an affluent upper-middle-class suburb (the spacious houses have servants and shrubberies), a few years, it seems, before the Great War (there are telephones and motor cars) in south Belfast near the river Lagan. The school the boys of the novel attend is in town and although it is a boarding as well as day school, it seems to be loosely modelled on Royal Belfast Academical Institution which

Reid himself went to. There is a country 'Intermezzo' which is set around Carrick-a-rede on the County Antrim coast. There is some treatment of polite sectarianism in the novel, mainly anti-Catholic feeling which under the fairly elevated social circumstances of the novel seems particularly crass on the part of the bigots. There is some snobbery expressed towards National School boys (a snobbery in which across Reid's novels one can't but help detect a certain narratorial complicity). The boys, however, speak no Ulster dialect but instead an English 'schoolboy' dialect of the Edwardian period: things are 'beastly', masters get 'into a wax', and there are 'rotters' and 'blighters' about. One possibility is that Reid was writing chiefly for an English audience and therefore anglicizing affluent Ulster so that the novel could function in the generic space of English schoolboy fiction. (Interestingly, Joyce's *A Portrait of the Artist* inhabits in part this same generic space. Dedalus and his school-friends attend boarding school, play rugby and cricket, are enjoined to aspire to the ideal of the gentleman, who would never 'peach on a fellow', etc., and represent York or Lancaster in class quizzes; the first two chapters have a distinctly English feel to them.) Another possibility is that in affluent, upper-middle-class, Edwardian Belfast, Protestants were far more 'English' (i.e. British) in speech and attitude than we now imagine. (And perhaps this was the case, too, with Catholics: an important character is Father O'Brien and the mother of the novel's hero, Beach Traill, is Catholic.) It is possible that dialect (a derivative of Irish Gaelic or Lowland Scots) was by contrast, in both parts of Ireland, either rural or urban working-class. A third possibility concerns less generic space than 'Reid space'. Reid occupied a unique niche, exclusively writing adult novels about pre-pubescent and pubescent boys; his great theme, as in *Pirates of the Spring*, was friendships among boys which in this novel takes a notably homosocial form; indeed, the novel is really a love story, a romance perhaps disguising its unacceptable variables alongside the acceptable constants inside the romance formula. It was perhaps the case that Reid's cast of boys in an apparent schoolboy genre—though boys who in this novel are precociously thoughtful and eloquent—was a way of handling homosexuality without 'outing' himself, an unthinkable thing for any Irish writer, especially a respectable Belfast middle-class novelist, to have done in those days. In any case, setting may be a more complicated affair than we might think and might not carry the immediate cultural freight we can assign to it.

A peculiar genre that can be interpreted both as the progeny and opponent of the Enlightenment, the Gothic, far from being overlooked, has recently been used to swell the Story of Ireland in fascinating ways (particularly via Stoker's *Dracula* about which I add my own more prosaic observations), but there is more orthodox Irish fiction of the supernatural waiting to be recovered that we must probably be content to read on the genre's own apparent and modest terms. The relative neglect of Irish genre fiction has been disappointing since such fiction can be read in such a way as to uncover disguised, inadvertent, or subtextual representations of Ireland that lift them above mere generic formulism; at the very least they extend our sense of the world as Irish writers saw it, even when those writers set their fiction outside the island: that, too, is a dimension of their Irishness.

So, too, is the Irish fictional engagement with the Great War that has been scanted in the criticism in such a way as to suggest a studied negligence deriving from an absence of sympathy. Only recently have cultural historians begun seriously to look at this writing, having politely refused the obligations imposed by the Story of Ireland in which participation by Irishmen in the Great War was the result of folly or infidelity, which charge extended to the literary participation of Irish writers.[28] Yeats's attitude to Ireland and the Great War, be it O'Casey and his Great War play *The Silver Tassie* (1926), or Yeats's appropriation in his poetry of Major Robert Gregory for local patriotism rather than a wider, European sense of duty, can stand as representative of the broader Revivalist attitude. But once again, it is in the popular novel that we can find a more historically faithful picture.

Any account of the popular novel must perforce include works that are interesting and worthwhile less for their literary merit than for the historical context of their popularity and for their social content. Such inclusion goes against the critical grain and requires a suspension of critical disbelief while priorities are rearranged. One outcome hard to avoid is an implied flattening out of literary merit. However, I believe that the social and at times literary pay-off makes this suspension worth the critical concession. An Oscar Wilde or Elizabeth Bowen, for example, is superior to a second-ranking writer such as Ella MacMahon or Katharine Tynan, and far superior to a third-ranking novelist such as Rosa Mulholland. Yet a prolific lower-ranking novelist, for example the ubiquitous L. T. Meade, can across a plethora of texts generate an impressive wattage of social and cultural illumination.

Moreover, we encounter in the accumulated popular fiction an Ireland busier and broader than the Ireland we see in Revival literature, an Ireland ironically closer in those respects to the Ireland we currently live in, or visit, and that has for some time outlived and outgrown the Revival. In the popular fiction we recover what fiction writers, and by extension their thousands of readers, were thinking about, and saying, at the time, and it is a universe of discourse far more populous in matter and heterogeneous in point of view than I for one ever suspected. To read the fiction is to realize to what extent we have read Irish literature of the period in the light of what came after it politically and socially.[29] There is another bonus: many of the novelists I discuss blur refreshingly what we have assumed to have always been hard-and-fast distinctions between

Protestant and Catholic, nationalist and unionist, peasant and gentry, and in ways that should not always be read as failure or evasion. Whereas it has been possible through a studied and over-frugal selection of texts, genres, social formations, historical events, and geographical areas to characterize Ireland as an essentially 'strange country', that is an idea whose exclusive aegis Irish critics and commentators no longer need, and the popular novel of the 1890–1922 period, and beyond, is an entertaining way of coming to that realization.

Since most of the fiction I will discuss has been long out of print and much of it difficult of access, it can nowadays be displayed for discussion only with the aid of plot summaries; I have therefore had to provide simultaneously the data for discussion, and the discussion itself. This too goes against the critical grain, but the plots are themselves telling, and I have tried hard to make their summaries readable and eventful.

NOTES

1. I say this despite W. B. Yeats's later (1937) acknowledgement of his personal debt to English literature and the English language: 'A General Introduction for My Work,' *Essays and Introductions* (New York: Collier, 1968), p. 519.
2. Introduction to *Fairy and Folk Tales of the Irish Peasantry* (1888; London: Pan Books, 1979), p. 7. Seamus Deane quotes Yeats in *A Short History of Irish Literature* (London: Hutchinson, 1986), p. 114. Having done so, Deane himself is of the opinion that such Anglo-Irish fiction offered 'a more winsome view of the Irish as an entertaining people rather than a people horribly mutilated and demoralized by English misrule'.
3. Douglas Hyde, 'The Necessity for De-Anglicising Ireland', in Gavan Duffy, George Sigerson, and Douglas Hyde, *The Revival of Irish Literature* (1894; New York: Lemma, 1973), p. 159. Hyde's address was originally given to the Irish National Literary Society in Dublin, November 1892.
4. Robert Lynd, *Ireland a Nation* (London: Grant Richards, 1919), p. 9. I have retained Lynd's male form 'Irishman' as it was the Irish man who suffered more from English caricature.
5. Jane Barlow, *Irish Ways* (1909; London: George Allen & Sons, 1911), p. 3.
6. The most notable artistic and cultural manifestos can be found in Gavan Duffy, Sigerson, and Hyde, *The Revival of Irish Literature* (1894); W. P. Ryan, *The Irish Literary Revival* (1894); John Eglinton, W. B. Yeats, AE (George Russell), and William Larminie, *Literary Ideals in Ireland* (1899); and Lady Gregory (ed.), *Ideals in Ireland* (1901).
7. See John Wilson Foster, 'Irish Modernism' in *Colonial Consequences: Essays in Irish Literature and Culture* (Dublin: Lilliput Press, 1991), pp. 44–59 and Adrian Frazier,

'Irish Modernisms, 1880–1930,' in *The Cambridge Companion to the Irish Novel*, ed. John Wilson Foster (Cambridge: Cambridge University Press, 2006), pp. 113–32.

8. Though whatever the focus, I would still quarrel with Yeats's attitude to Irish humour, despite the measure of justification in his cultural and even political reservations, reservations shared by two commentators separated in time by over half a century, Lynd and Deane. Since Irish humour is suspect in some quarters because it is seen to perpetuate a demeaning stereotype of the Irish, to cite Edith Somerville on the matter would possibly be unwise, despite her broad Irish nationalism, but as late as 1918, having agreed that *Recollections of Sir Jonah Barrington* (1827–32) gave the first authentic portrait of 'the rollicking Irishman of later literary tradition', she claimed (mixing life and literature) that 'the Ireland of Barrington and Lever has still its standard-bearers' and that 'the Ireland of the self-satisfied twentieth century can furnish some incidents that might challenge comparison with Barrington's most purple patches': 'Ireland Then and Now,' in E. Œ. Somerville and Martin Ross, *Stray-Aways* (London: Longmans, Green, 1920), pp. 197, 199, 198. In August 1901, 'Martin Ross' visited Coole and relayed to Somerville Yeats's admiration for *The Real Charlotte* (1894) but also his dislike in literature of humour for humour's sake. Martin, no shrinking Violet, reported her own reply: 'here Miss Martin said beautiful things about humour being a high art': *The Selected Letters of Somerville and Ross*, ed. Gifford Lewis (London: Faber and Faber, 1989), p. 252. Somerville and Ross aside, to read *Recollections of an Irish Judge* (1914) by the Catholic hagiographer, Home Ruler, and nationalist MP, M. McDonnell Bodkin, KC (for years acting editor of *United Ireland*), is to peruse some first-hand evidence for the surprising percentage of reality in the humourists' Arcadia. Bodkin remembers an intensely funny as well as put-upon Ireland in the second half of the nineteenth century. 'My father', he recalled, 'had many stories to tell of the rollicking, devil-may-care gentry of Galway and Mayo, stories which acquit Charles Lever of the charge of exaggeration'—and tells some of them. The author knew Isaac Butt, saw him in action, and wrote of him: 'To the strength of a giant he joined the amiable weakness of a child. He was Irish all over, intensely Irish alike in his qualities and his defects. If one could imagine the most genial, thoughtless, reckless of Charles Lever's heroes, gifted with eloquence, statesman-ship and genius, one could realize the strange combination of his character': *Recollections of an Irish Judge: Press, Bar and Parliament* (London: Hurst and Blackett, 1914), pp. 6, 112. The native Irish were as ready to write humorous fiction as the Anglo-Irish. Stephen J. Brown in *Ireland in Fiction: A Guide to Irish Novels, Tales, Romances and Folklore* (1915, 1919; New York: Barnes & Noble, 1969) offers 'Humorous Books' as a category (covering 'wit and comicality or broad comedy, as well as humour in the strict sense of the word', p. 333). Whereas there was a generic momentum at work in these humorous Irish works, there was also a bedrock of reality, the Irish being in fact a witty people. Moreover, it is possible to argue that wit, play-acting, banter, jocularity, even buffoonery in real life, like humour, the macabre, and the grotesque in literature were on occasion, or in part, as Deane implies, desperate reactions to unfavourable circumstances (one thinks of

Jewish humour in life and literature). Brown lists three of Bodkin's own books in the category of the Humorous. Bodkin entitles one chapter of his *Recollections* 'The Humours of Coercion' and another 'Humours of the House of Commons' (during the Parnell years). In the first he recalls the cases brought under the Coercion Bill of the early 1880s that he took part in as defence counsel (he also helped *United Ireland* spearhead the attack on coercion): serious matter but not without its 'burlesque', as he terms it. His recollection of funny episodes is meant to convey 'the comic character of the government of Ireland in those days' (p. 159) and so has retroactive political point. He writes: 'Coercion in Ireland slowly collapsed. Everywhere it is ridicule that kills; but this is essentially true in Ireland, where the sense of humour is so strong' (p. 168). Although Stephen Gwynn thought in 1901 ('A Century of Irish Humour') that good humour had diminished in Irish politics and ill humour had increased, he thought that outside politics the Irish still earned their reputation for being humorous. But he thought, too, that Irish humour in literature as in life was rather too obvious, did not hang about the brain, and was not the product of deep feeling or deep thought. He did, however, praise the Swiftian humour of *The Real Charlotte*. When he collected his essay, Gwynn was pleased to admit in his 1919 Preface that with the advent since 1901 of Synge, Lady Gregory, and (ironically) Yeats, no one could accuse Irish humour of lacking seriousness. See Stephen Lucius Gwynn, *Irish Books and Irish People* (1920; Free Port, New York: Books for Libraries Press, 1969), pp. 1, 24–43. All in all, it is past time to acknowledge without embarrassment the potency of humour, broad or subtle, in Ireland, personally, politically and literarily, and *Ulysses*, of course, is unthinkable without it.

9. Dinah Birch, 'Modest Nat: The stories we tell about the books we no longer read', *Times Literary Supplement*, 1 September 2006: 3. Indeed, another recent and pioneering compilation, *A Guide to Irish Fiction 1650–1900* (2006) by Rolf Loeber and Magda Stouthamer-Loeber, shows that critics of the Irish novel have been subsisting on the same thin diet.

10. Trotter, *The English Novel in History 1895–1920* (London: Routledge, 1993), p. 2.

11. Sean O'Faolain, *The Irish* (1947; Harmondsworth: Penguin Books, 1969), p. 130.

12. The novelist and short story writer Benedict Kiely summarized O'Connor's position while genially dissenting from it: *Kenyon Review* 30 (1968): 464. See also Terence Brown, 'After the Revival: The Problem of Adequacy and Genre,' *Genre* 12 (1979): 571.

13. Augustine Martin, 'Inherited Dissent: The Dilemma of the Irish Novelist,' *Studies* (1965): 1–20.

14. Declan Kiberd, 'Bloom in bourgeois Bohemia', *Times Literary Supplement*, 4 June, 2004: 14. This is one of the post-colonialist assimilations of O'Connor and O'Faolain that Paddy Bullard alludes to when he gives O'Connor's and O'Faolain's theory an outing during a *Times Literary Supplement* (13 May 2005) review of a volume of Irish short stories: 'a top-heavy bourgeois genre like the novel could never thrive in the provisional culture of the post-1922 Republic; only the "pure storytelling" of short fiction, with its quick-rooted sympathy for the marginal and dispossessed, would flourish among the constraints of an emerging nation.' Bullard thinks the relevance of the theory for the present is in need of review but not, apparently, for the past. Meanwhile, Kiberd rehearsed his belief in

2006, pushing the date after which real Irish novels could in theory have been written back to 1904 on the assumption that *Ulysses* (1922) took the un-novelistic form it did because of the nature of Irish society in the year in which it was set: 'Literature and Politics' in Margaret Kelleher and Philip O'Leary (eds.), *The Cambridge History of Irish Literature* (Cambridge: Cambridge University Press, 2006), vol. 2, p. 33.

15. There are ways, of course, in which the bulk (if not all) of Ireland departs from the British pattern. Indeed, Andrew Roberts points out the numerous ways in which Catholic Ireland is odd man out among the English-speaking nations, not the least of them deriving from its Catholicism, the other Anglophone countries having been Protestant in the main: *A History of the English-Speaking Peoples since 1900* (2007).

16. The missing factor in Kiberd's formulation, of course, is the Protestant bourgeoisie, even though he goes on to praise the hardheaded business sense of the Irish Revivalists.

17. Terence de Vere White for one believed that there was a Catholic middle class 'growing in self-confidence' a half-century after Catholic Emancipation, i.e. in the last two decades of the nineteenth century, and quotes Synge's disgust with 'the middle class Irish Catholic' after the attacks on *The Playboy of the Western World* in 1907: *The Anglo-Irish* (London: Gollancz, 1972), pp. 204, 206. The economic factors we associate with middle-class culture—commerce, industry, and banking—are discussed by Cormac Ó Gráda for the period 1850–1914 in *Ireland: A New Economic History 1780–1939* (1994). Half a century ago, Maureen Wall identified a Catholic middle class even earlier, one that turned economic and political disabilities into advantages. Prevented by the penal laws from owning land and entering the professions, Catholics often went into commerce: 'catholics succeeded in amassing considerable wealth in trade, in spite of, or even because of, the popery laws', and she analyses a 'catholic middle class which we find established in many of the towns and cities of Ireland by the middle of the eighteenth century'; the net result of 'the gradual rise of a wealthy catholic middle class in Ireland during the eighteenth century' was a fair amount of uniformity with Britain: 'As a class, the merchant section of the Irish population, whatever its origins, differed in no marked degree from merchants in Great Britain and in other countries during the eighteenth century': see 'The Rise of a Catholic Middle Class in Eighteenth-Century Ireland', *Irish Historical Studies* 11. 42 (1958): 91, 104, 115, 112. Wall restated her case in 'Catholics in Economic Life', in *The Formation of the Irish Economy*, ed. L. M. Cullen (Cork: Mercier Press, 1969), pp. 37–51.

18. Ella MacMahon, *The Job* (London: James Nisbet & Co., 1914), p. 219.

19. *A Cluster of Nuts, Being Sketches Among my Own People* (London: Lawrence & Bullen, 1894), pp. 63–78.

20. For this reason I restored *Esther Waters* to my survey of Irish fiction, 'The Irish Renaissance, 1890–1904: Prose in English' in Margaret Kelleher and Philip O'Leary (eds.), *Cambridge History of Irish Literature*, (Cambridge: Cambridge University Press, 2006), pp. 141–2.

21. Mason funnelled his taste for whimsy and hyperbole into children's writing, including the 1931 brace of stories, *The Wee Men of Ballywooden* (inspired by a

Strangford area townland whose Otherworld he creates), which with its delightful fairy characters and lively idiom and dialogue, bears comparison with the famous tales by James Stephens, author of *The Crock of Gold* (1912).

22. Richard D. Altick, *Victorian People and Ideas* (New York: Norton, 1973), p. 33.

23. The 'deep' historical background to Riddell's Northern Irish commercial enthusiasm can be found in Jean Agnew's study, *Belfast Merchant Families in the Seventeenth Century* (1996).

24. Riddell maintains a critical perspective despite any generic limitations and *Berna Boyle* includes pointed criticisms of British policy in the Crimea and Egypt.

25. Stephen Lucius Gwynn, *Irish Books and Irish People* (1920; Freeport, New York: Books for Libraries Press, 1969), pp. 65–6. However, Gwynn tells us that in National Schools, organised by the State, no religious (or political) picture or decoration is permitted whereas in every Catholic school not controlled by the State 'the emblems of religion are everywhere present' (p. 74). As an Irish cultural nationalist he decries this rule and calls it 'the tyranny of compromise'- what we would call today political correctness. 'Nothing must be taught anywhere which could offend any susceptibility', and he thought this meant that pupils remained in ignorance about their own country.

26. I discuss this cultural programme in *Fictions of the Irish Literary Revival* (1987).

27. Problem-novels can be put into the larger British context of didactic fiction, what Robert A. Colby describes and analyses as 'fiction with a purpose'; he relates major Victorian novelists back into a cultural and novelistic context of didacticism, of ideas, information, and education: *Fiction with a Purpose: Major and Minor Nineteenth-Century Novels* (1967). In *Ireland and the Fiction of Improvement* (2006), Helen O'Connell studies didactic or 'improvement' fiction distributed in chapbooks, tracts, and pamphlets in nineteenth-century Ireland. Such writing she sees as promoting progress and reform through a philosophy of realism, moderation, and liberalism, opposed to the aesthetics of 'high' literature (be it Romanticism or, later, the Revival) as well as the romance and fantasy of popular fiction. O'Connell's study has a useful adjacency to parts of my own.

28. One recent sympathetic account of Irish participation in the First World War is Myles Dungan's *They Shall Not Grow Old: Irish Soldiers and the Great War* (1997), which devotes a chapter to three writers, Ledwidge, Kettle, and MacGill.

29. In *The Long Gestation: Irish Nationalist Life 1891–1918* (1999), Patrick Maume believes that the two rival orthodox interpretations of the politics of the period (one privileging republican nationalism, the other privileging Home Rule nationalism) share their use of hindsight in interpreting this crucial period of recent Irish history, both viewing and reading events in the light of what came afterwards. He offers a reading at once more detailed and more alive to what was being said and thought and done at the time, and I regard my literary-historical approach as not unlike his political-historical approach.

1

'A Deplorable Facility': Popular Fiction

CONTEXTS OF POPULARITY

'To be popular, one must pay the price,' said John. 'As the artist lives in his work, the price of popularity for him is death'.

Herbert M. Pim, *The Pessimist* (1914)

Popular fiction, in all the richly suggestive meanings of the adjective, is largely missing from the standard accounts of Irish imaginative prose between 1890 and 1922. 'Popular' can denote the established fact of a wide readership; it can also signal intent: fiction offered to the public often in a recognizable genre, at a certain level of sophistication, as an intelligible narrative structure, and in an appropriate, often unchallenging prose style. Usually, but not always, the attempt to create believable plots and easily imaginable characters takes precedence over the ambition to achieve an overall literary construct, unitary effect, or testamentary vision of the world. Yet 'popular', although it qualifies literature to mean widely read by the people rather than primarily by an educated minority, can also be an unwittingly ironic category since it can imply that *un*popularity and obscurity are the usual ends of popularity once certain appetites of the reading public are satisfied and tastes and fashions change. And great popularity can suggest swift onset of the darkness. The first implication is normally justified but the second is more problematic. To take a few, almost random examples: *Far Above Rubies*, a novel by Mrs J. H. Riddell from Carrickfergus, Co. Antrim, who published at least ten novels and collections of stories after 1890, was first published in 1867 (with a second edition that year) and went into a ninth edition in 1900.[1] *Phyllis* by Mrs Margaret Argles was republished in 1906 and 1913, twenty-nine and thirty-six years respectively after first publication. Jane Barlow's *Irish Idylls* (1892) saw a ninth edition in 1908; an eighteenth edition of Canon Sheehan's *My New Curate* (1900) appeared in 1918,[2] while a 1919 reprinting of William O'Brien's *When We Were Boys* (1890) sold out in Ireland. The case of B. M. Croker from Roscommon is also convincing evidence of longevity: her novel *Pretty Miss Neville* was published in 1883, republished the following year, and re-issued in 1919; *Mr. Jervis*, 1894, had a new edition the next year, was republished in 1917, and then again in 1924; *Angel* was published in 1901, republished in 1913 and saw a thirteenth edition in 1934. These are not the champions of perseverance, however. By 1920 there were twenty-one impressions of Fisher Unwin's 1908 publication of *The Blue Lagoon* by Henry de Vere Stacpoole and at least five reissues of George Newnes's 1908 edition; and if publication slowed down after 1920 it picked up again in the 1970s and 1980s; it has been most recently published in 2006. Alexander Irvine's *My Lady of the Chimney Corner* was published in 1913 and then again in 1914, 1915, 1923, 1930, 1954, 1980, 1981, and 1993. If Irvine's tale is virtually a perennial, *The Riddle of the Sands* (1903) by Erskine Childers is genuinely such. There was a 2006 edition and innumerable editions in the intervening century. *Dracula* (1897) by Bram Stoker bids fair to be immortal like its eponymous villain.

Clearly the Irish Literary Revival did not stop the popular Irish novel in its tracks. Indeed, it may be that we have over time inflated the contemporary reputation and profile of the Revival. Writing as late as 1921 for a memoir published in 1922, Katharine Tynan referred to 'the little and memorable movement in Dublin into which came W. B. Yeats and AE and Douglas Hyde, and others who were, beyond their own actual achievements, the precursors'—and since Tynan has often been recruited into that movement, her sense of proportion ought perhaps to be trusted. She speaks of the Revival in the past tense: 'That was a pure movement, in which money and worldly success were never dreamt of.'[3]

It is true that popular novels were sometimes published in small, frequent runs. Stephen J. Brown tells us that Miriam Alexander's historical novel *The House of Lisronan* (1912) went into a sixth edition before two months had elapsed,[4] but we don't know how large or small were the print-runs, though clearly the novel was a fast-seller. Sometimes titles were bought by second and even third publishers, but this suggests marketability in a variety of niches rather than artificial life-support. In any case, a publication life of more than thirty years (reaching two generations of readers), with shelf lives at least some years longer than the latest date of publication and the span between editions, implies stamina of a sort in the work. My examples might testify to an expanding reading society in Britain and Ireland, yet the stamina is still impressive. Moreover, the readability of these novels survived both literary modernism and the Great War; and if they continued to be read by Irish readers, that means they also survived the Irish Revival and Irish independence, and these were all (in their different ways) high cultural watersheds.

By 1890, indeed, the popular novel catered to a complex demographic obtaining in Ireland as well as Britain. Whereas the circulating libraries lent bound novels to members, the weekly magazines offered for sale the 'penny novels' (or 'novelettes') that Hyde, one of the movers of the Irish linguistic and cultural revival, deprecated in his famous address and manifesto, 'The Necessity for De-Anglicising Ireland'. He has little to say about more respectable popular English (or Irish) fiction and by putting in the dock only 'penny dreadfuls, shilling shockers, and still more, the garbage of vulgar English weeklies like *Bow Bells* and the *Police Intelligence*', Hyde could be thought to evade the knottier problem of forming an opinion about popular and mainstream English and Irish novels that were not dedicated to the new Irish cultural revival and no doubt conveyed values at best useless to, at worst inimical to, the Revival he was promoting.[5] In *Lismoyle: An Experiment in Ireland* (1914), Croker depicts Parker, young Rhoda Kyle's English companion-maidservant, reading *Tit-Bits* (which included fiction, such as the story, 'Matcham's Masterstroke', that entertains Leopold Bloom at stool) while Madame Conroy, the Irish chatelaine of Lismoyle, a country house, avidly reads a novel of the kind, one assumes, in which she herself is a character, an altogether more cultivated affair.

The Education Act of 1870 set in motion an expansion of literacy and learning in the United Kingdom; by the 1890s the regular school attendance rate in Ireland was more than 60 per cent and by 1911 only 12 per cent of the Irish population could not read or write.[6] The editor of *Blackwood's Edinburgh Magazine* was scathing in 1898 about this growth of literacy in the United Kingdom since it seemed to have resulted in a deluge of penny fiction.[7] He counted thirty weekly magazines feeding the appetite for novelettes, the vast majority of whose readers he thought were women, 'the wives and sisters and daughters of our shopmen and our mechanics.'[8] The Wexford-born caricaturist Harry Furniss (who for a time owned the *Pall Mall Budget*) listed the chief readers of lower-end popular novels as 'shopgirls, factory hands, servants' and 'board-school young ladies.'[9] In ironic contrast to the world of the readers, the fictional world of the penny novel, as the editor of *Blackwood's* points out, is inhabited by peers of the realm, even dukes: 'baronets may be met with in abundance; while there is a rich profusion of the landed gentry and her Majesty's officers'; the occupants of the vicarage are permitted to associate on the same footing with these exalted beings, but below them yawns a class gulf (empty save for a 'few stray family solicitors') until the reader comes to rest with 'horse copers and other gangrel bodies'.[10] There is much dabbling in the legalities of guardians and wards, wills and legacies, with which the novelist plays fast and loose. A perpetual element is love, sensation an equally essential element, and a common element, crime. Clearly such fiction was a species of coloured daydream for readers leading grey workaday lives. (Yet bad though the novelettes were, the editor of *Blackwood's* thought them superior to 'the pedantic obscenities of an Ibsen, the unintelligible nonsense of a Maeterlinck, or the dubious rodomontade of a Ruskin. Let us be thankful for small mercies...'.[11])

However, the author of this witty skewering correctly believed that the same elements occurred in the novels of the circulating libraries and railway bookstalls though without what he saw as the moral certainties of the lower form. Many of these novels were written by Irish authors, often women. Most readers of popular fiction by women were in turn women, whether in Ireland or Britain. According to Maureen Duffy, 'there was still at this period no real rival to the novel for leisure pastime, and women in particular, who were much more restricted in their activities than men, read avidly'.[12] But surely the popular magazines of the day rivalled novels in this regard, and there were many such magazines that catered to readers of fiction, as we shall see in a moment. In any case, the period Duffy refers to was, of course, before the invention of the cinematograph and wireless as sources of indoor entertainment, and even longer before the invention of television.

Having anatomized down-market fiction in 1898, the editor of *Blackwood's* the following year performed the same procedure on middle-market fiction. Royalties, he claimed, were now regarded as the best test of merit; what the drama was to Elizabethan England, the novel is to Victorian England and the simpler the fiction the better it is liked; the popular novelist 'obeys without question the mandate of his audience' and observes the golden rule, 'never to be ahead of his public'; the public is, at the time of writing, hungry for mysticism, theology, and crime detection; the novelist's chief aim is to make money. Some of these novels enjoyed a popularity and circulation comparable to those of the penny novels; sales of Silas K. Hocking's novels averaged 1000 copies per week and by 1899 his publishers had sold a million and ninety-three thousand—sounding, the editor added, like the French national debt expressed in francs.[13] *The Heavenly Twins* (1893), a serious and ambitious work by the Donaghadee, Co. Down-born writer Sarah Grand, was described soon after its publication by Heinemann as 'a work more widely discussed and sold than any book of the day', and must therefore have sold tens of thousands of copies and made Grand a pretty penny.[14] After all, according to Marion Shaw, the novel sold 20,000 copies in the first week alone.[15] It was said to be 'one of the greatest sensations in literature', causing 'tremendous excitement in the ranks of the Feminists and the Ant-Feminists, and the upholders of the new and the old morality'.[16] Grand's novel *Ideala* (1888) was brought out in a new (third) edition of 10,000 copies by Heinemann in 1893.[17] According to Brown, *John Chilcote M.P.* (1904) by the Cork novelist Katherine Cecil Thurston sold 200,000 copies in the United States alone; *The Lady's Realm* called it 'the novel of the year', causing Thurston's name to be 'on the lips of every reader of fiction, and on the lists of every lending library for the last few months'.[18] A 1912 issue of *Newsbasket*, the house magazine of W. H. Smith, the biggest UK retailer, announced that George A. Birmingham (Revd James O. Hannay, born in Belfast) was a best-selling author in that year, alongside Hilaire Belloc, Arnold Bennett, Marie Corelli, Conan Doyle, Thomas Hardy, Rider Haggard, and Bram Stoker.[19]

If it is size of readership rather than remuneration that interests us in these statistics, then we should at least pause at the British popular magazines of the day that catered to readers of fiction. As in volume of circulation, these varied in quality and sophistication as greatly as the novels. At the high end were those magazines that published short stories or serialized novels by Kipling, Chesterton, Conan Doyle, Haggard, Hardy, Maugham, Stevenson, Conrad, and Wells. Ashley has called the period 1890–1940 'the Age of the Storytellers' and popular magazines, with *The Strand* as their flagship, were, with novels, the chief channels for the storytelling. Many of the fiction writers to be discussed in *Irish Novels 1890–1940* appeared in the popular magazines Ashley treats, including Bram Stoker, Edith Somerville, George Birmingham, M. McDonnell Bodkin, B. M. Croker, Sarah Grand, M. E. Francis, Shan Bullock, Katharine Tynan, and Dorothea Conyers. Several, however, were regarded as mainstays of the English magazine subculture. Elliott O'Donnell published in *Hutchinson Story Magazine*, *The Novel Magazine*, *The Premier*, *The Idler*, *Mystery Story Magazine*, *Weekly Tale-Teller*, *Colour*, *The Imp*, *Hutchinson's Mystery-Story Magazine*, and *Lilliput*. L. T. Meade herself edited *Atalanta* magazine (1887–1892) for 'mature girls and young ladies', and contributed to, among others, *Lambert's Monthly*, *The Temple Magazine*, *Woman at Home*, *Cassell's Magazine*, and *The Windsor Magazine*. Indeed, Ashley describes her as one of those writers 'who collectively define the Age of the Storytellers' and who was 'crucial to *The Strand*'s long-term success'.[20] Her visibility and influence were challenged by Beatrice Grimshaw, whom Ashley describes as a mainstay author of *The Grand* and the doyenne of south-sea adventure, and who appears 'inevitably' in *Lloyd's Magazine*.[21] Grimshaw also appeared in the pages of *The Story-Teller*, *Britannia and Eve*, *Tip Top Stories*, *Temple Bar*, *Pearson's*, *The Windsor Magazine*, *Adventure-Story Magazine*, *The Premier*, *Blue Book*, *Everybody's Magazine*, *Golden Book Magazine*, *Liberty Magazine*, *The Popular Magazine*, *Short Stories*, *Red Book*, *Saturday Evening Post*, *Argosy*, *The Passing Show*, *Lippincott's*, *The Novel Magazine*, and *Romance*.[22] Magazine publication often overlapped with book publication and Meade, for example, often republished her stories as what Ashley calls 'episodic novels'. The episodic *Some Experiences of an Irish R.M.* by Somerville and Ross appeared first in *Badminton Magazine* (1898–9). Grimshaw first published at least two novels in serial form: *Vaiti of the Islands* (1908) and *When the Red Gods Call* (1910–11). In Ashley's 'Chronology', the former is listed as a 'key story' and its appearance in *Pearson's* as a 'significant event'. Oscar Wilde's *The Picture of Dorian Gray* appeared first in *Lippincott's* (1890) and Hannah Lynch's *Autobiography of a Child* in *Blackwood's Edinburgh Magazine* (1898–99). Sometimes novels were serialized after book publication, as in the case of Rosa Mulholland's *Giannetta: A Girl's Story of Herself*, which as published by Blackie's in 1889, after which it was serialized in *Sheffield Weekly Independent* in 1890.[23] *Dracula* was serialized in *Argosy*—thirty years after its book form!

Profitability in novels was orchestrated by the publishers, and many of the houses identified by Sutherland as the most active between 1830 and 1870— Blackwood, Chapman and Hall, Macmillan, Hurst and Blackett, Sampson Low, Marston & Co.—were still going strong in 1890.[24] Irish novelists of the kind I wish to discuss below published with these houses before and after 1890, and after 1890 they published with other British houses just as well-known, including Methuen; Longmans Green; Hodder and Stoughton; Hutchinson; John Lane; Edward Arnold; Grant Richards; and Fisher Unwin.[25] There were Irish publishers who published mainly homegrown fiction, including Maunsel; Sands & Co.; Duffy, Sealy, Bryers & Walker; and M. H. Gill. The Irish publishers were motivated by varying degrees of patriotism, occasionally of a Catholic kind. Irish Catholic writers were assured of a kindly ear in the United States by Benziger Brothers, a New York publisher. This Swiss house opened offices in New York in 1853, by which time they were a global disseminator of Catholic literature; in 1867 they became 'Printers to the Holy Apostolic See'. Among their publications was *A Round Table of the Representative Irish and English Catholic Novelists* (1897) to which I will return.

Despite the honest sectarianism (or simply targeted readership) of Benziger Brothers, it comes as a surprise to read in Katharine Tynan's *The Middle Years* (1916), a memoir of the years 1891–1911, that 'in Ireland, if you are a Protestant you read one class of books, and if you are a Catholic you read another; and if you want to depart from this course your Protestant or Catholic bookseller sees that you are kept in it.'[26] She says this apparently to explain the obscurity in which Frank Mathew (1865–1920) was then languishing, an historical novelist she thought back in the 1890s was the novelist Ireland was waiting for, repeating her hope in her 1902 revision of Charles A. Read's *Cabinet of Irish Literature* (1879). The implication can only be that Mathew, a Catholic, was unread by Protestants through the disobligingness of Protestant booksellers. Ironically, the book of Mathew's she lauded most was *The Wood of the Brambles* (1896) which Stephen J. Brown, himself a Catholic (indeed, a priest), found to be 'a grotesque picture' of the 1798 rebellion, 'a burlesque '98'.[27]

THE CASE OF KATHARINE TYNAN

Yet Tynan (1859–1931), a popular poet and novelist, was a Catholic too and was widely published and read in Britain as well as Ireland.[28] Some of her work was approved and published by the Catholic Truth Society but more often she was published by Smith, Elder; Constable; Blackie; Lawrence & Bullen, and other big English firms. *The Middle Years*, a stylish episode of autobiography like all her memoirs, as well as a cultural history that has been stored in one woman's retentive memory, is an account of her long sojourn in England from May Day 1893 ('I said good-bye to the old happy irresponsible life, I was going to London to be married and to settle there') until 1911 when she and her family returned to Ireland. Her husband had been called to the English bar in 1902. It is true she concluded that 'though England had been good to us and was dear to us, we were not English', but there are loving evocations of the English countryside, for example of Kent in the hot summer of 1899 where in a coppice she wrote two books, and a hymn to the 'beauty of the garden-like English country', the 'ordered rich beauty' of which, 'so different from the beauty of my own land, filled me with a quiet rapture... Surrey, Sussex, Kent, Worcestershire, laid hold upon my heart'.[29] Her highly readable 1906 novel, *Dick Pentreath*, also contains a hymn to the English south-country village, with its lush English gardens and woodland, serenading nightingales, benevolent Duke, good-hearted squire, contented peasantry, and busy cricket and football pitches (on which high and low meet amicably), a bucolic world rent only, unlike Ireland, by star-crossed love-matches.

Yet Tynan regarded herself as a Parnellite (*The Middle Years* opens with visits to Glasnevin after the funeral of the Chief), and thought herself disapproved of by the Catholic Church. Later she became a Redmondite, but still a nationalist, though she lamented the fact that whereas her extreme nationalist friends barely tolerated her, her unionist friends suspected her of being a Shinner (Sinn Feiner).[30] Her nationalist coloration to the contrary, she had a warm memory of the visit of Queen Victoria to Ireland in 1900 during the Boer War (Tynan was wintering in Ireland that year) when the old queen was welcomed; Tynan watched her from the Provost's House in Trinity College, having witnessed her arrival with an escort of warships in Dublin Bay, and concluded: 'She had great qualities, the old Queen; and in their hour of grief she was the Mother of her people... There was something about her of the Divine Right, of the great days.'[31] Tynan remembers being back in London in time for Mafeking Night 'when London went mad', and the implication is of a fond memory; after all, like many Irish Catholics, she and her family were part and parcel of British colonialism, and after the Great War, one son got an appointment in the Colonial Office in British East Africa. Tynan wrote her memories of Mafeking Night in 1916 as her youngest son was going to join his regiment, the Royal Irish, adding piquancy to her affecting recollections of England, Victoria, and the Boer War. Both her sons fought in the Great War in British khaki.

The fact is that Tynan, and many privileged Catholic Irish like her, had the choice of inhabiting two overlapping or even, in some regards, superimposed countries and two overlapping, though hardly superimposed, Irish societies. The countries were Ireland and Britain and complicated enough in their interrelations, though at moments of deep political crisis something like a choice was made necessary. The two Irish societies were less tangled, perhaps, but self-presentation, as well as religion and racial membership, required at some level that the two societies be regarded as one. We are given one of those societies in *A Cluster of Nuts* (1894), an assembly of short prose pieces written, it would appear, just before Tynan moved to England, and self-consciously subtitled *Being Sketches Among My Own People*. The book's epigraph reads: 'Kindly Irish of the Irish/Neither Saxon nor Italian.' The people in question are in the main Catholic Irish of the peasant class, living in cabins and the best of them exhibiting traits of the saints or experiencing the sufferings of martyrdom. Some of the stories, including 'A Descendant of Irish Earls' and 'Cissy', overcome their inherent sentimentality in their depiction of a nineteenth-century, post-Act of Union Ireland characterized by the haemorrhage of emigration, depleted and wasted energies, loneliness, disease (especially tuberculosis), inbreeding, dereliction of habitation, and hunger. This is the Ireland that seemed to demand a cultural as well as political revival (as George Moore had intimated in *A Drama in Muslin*, 1886, and was to suggest again in *The Untilled Field*, 1903) and which might be read as, indeed, an early minor, ground-clearing work of the Irish Literary Revival. There are passages of descriptive prose-poetry that anticipate Synge but do not have the syntactical sinew of his writing.

At the same time, the vignettes (sketch-like stories) derive some of their attenuated momentum from Tynan's nostalgia for a pre-Union Ireland, given its most explicit expression in 'A Descendant of Irish Earls' which refers to a native Catholic aristocracy, but one deriving its noble nomenclature—though this is not admitted—from the English connection. The narrator, it is implied, is the author herself, just as the sketches purport to be true, each 'a transcript from life' (thereby accounting for their being sketches and not stories).[32] This lends a certain irony to the presentation. The characters are on the whole a pious and credulous folk whereas the narrator is clear-headed and rational, making common cause with the peasants but really, it would seem, unconsciously playing the role of the visitor or the condescending social superior making the rounds (always accompanied by a friend or dog), even if at some level she shares the peasants' credulousness in the matter of the supernatural.

The other Irish society, one composed of the surviving remnants of that native Catholic nobility, is depicted in *Cousins and Others* (1909), a volume of stories that appeared two years before Tynan returned to Ireland from England.

The premiss of the title novella leads the reader to assume a fictional scale-modelling of Anglo-Irish anti-Catholicism. In the eighteenth century, the elder branch of a titled family is reduced to commoner status and habitation of a mere glebe farm, all because of the apparently Roman Catholic ('Popish') officiation at the marriage of the peer and an Irish peasant woman, of which the Penal Laws (on the eve of Catholic Emancipation) could not permit legal acknowledgement. But in fact, the fifteenth Baron Annaghmore is Catholic, as are all the rightly or wrongly titled, as well as all the untitled, characters in the story. The tensions and rivalries in the story are entirely among Catholics. The current Lord Annaghmore has been brought up as an Englishman, educated at Eton and now at Christchurch, Oxford, and his English accent offends his Catholic countrymen. By contrast, the eighteenth-century Lord Annaghmore who married Molly Devine had ridden fifty miles to vote against the Act of Union and was an Irish patriot. But the current impostor will in fact altruistically admit his unwitting impostor status before the story is out (having discovered from Molly's wedding-lines in her hitherto lost workbox that there had been in fact Anglican officiation at the marriage of Molly and Lord Annaghmore), and by doing so subvert his shallow Englishness. In manipulating the romantic attraction and marriage between the current Lord Annaghmore and the descendant of Molly Devine, Clodagh Lawson, now about to be the rightful Lady Annaghmore, Tynan unites the (honorary) Irish peasant who is in reality aristocratic with the England-educated (and now honorary) Irish aristocrat. But she also legitimates the idea *per se* of the native Irish aristocrat and indeed, considers the ennobled Lawsons more authentic than Lady Kiltrasna, an Englishwoman who married an Irishman awarded his peerage for voting for the Union.

The unavoidable Anglo-Irish (or perhaps we should say, British, indeed imperial) dimension of Tynan's Irish Catholic nobility is made clearer in another story in the collection, 'A Friend of Little Sisters', and it is a dimension that Tynan obviously welcomes so long as it does not erase Irish identity and patriotism. The Honorable Violet Frant is a frequenter of the Little Sisters convent in London's impoverished East End, some of whose sisters had been titled ladies in the world but have now humbly submersed themselves in strenuous philanthropic work among the elderly. Violet herself is the daughter of a peer engaged from the Foreign Office in the running of the Empire. Violet has been more literally engaged to a worldly and high-spirited young man but has broken it off, sacrificing her love to her 'Catholic ideals', even though Anthony Hamilton has come 'of an old Catholic family'.[33] Everyone, including the sisters, is opposed to Violet's intention to join the Carmelite order of nuns, the Reverend Mother (an erstwhile Duchess in the extramural world) telling her that her vocation is to marry Anthony Hamilton, serve God in laces, silks, and linens, and bring Anthony to God. When a beautiful and highborn rival for Anthony's affections heaves into view, Violet's piety falters and when he arrives to 'rescue' her, she receives him rapturously. (That he turns out to have been the clubman-cum-angel who also rescued two sisters marooned in a week-long London fog while engaged in charity work, is icing on her cake.) Although Violet and Anthony marry quietly in the chapel of the Little Sisters, the story illustrates the belief that God can be worshipped, and Catholic ideals made flesh, in the real and fashionably-dressed world Tynan knew in England and Dublin. And these can happen in the titled world more specifically, for, as the Duchess remarks of Anthony's angelic rescue of the sisters and his subsequent donation of 'a Bank of England note for ten pounds', 'Ah! Blood yet tells' (p. 156).

COMMON GROUND

I am offering Tynan as an example of a popular Irish writer who regularly plied the Kingstown–Holyhead–Euston route (like young Yeats, then a popular lyric poet) and for whom so much of British culture, if it was a second culture, was so in the way we describe something as 'second nature'. British and Irish popular novelists shared much the same readership and nourished the same idea of what constituted the concerns and style of an effective novel. Readers of popular novels seem to have been unconcerned whether they were set in Britain or Ireland; the same indifference was at work in the novelists themselves. A popular Scottish novelist like Annie S. Swan could readily set several of her novels in Ireland while Irish novelists and storytellers like Riddell, Ella MacMahon, M. E. Francis, M. McDonnell Bodkin, and Tynan could as readily set their work in England. Mrs Hungerford from Rosscarbery, Co. Cork set the first half of *Mrs Geoffrey* (1886) in Ireland, the second half in England; E. Temple Thurston used both settings generously in *Traffic* (1906). And, of course, Irish popular novelists could set their novels farther afield: B. M. Croker with her Anglo-Indian romances, Beatrice Grimshaw with her New Guinea adventures.

While the differences between Ireland and Britain were often asserted in popular British and Irish Victorian and Edwardian novels—differences that became more dangerous as the nineteenth century progressed—common ground was tacitly asserted by publishers and readers. Whereas British writers in Ireland were usually visitors, Irish novelists often took up residence in Britain, including (in a short random list) Deborah Alcock, W. M. Letts, Riddell, Alice Dease, M. E. Francis, Filson Young, Croker, MacMahon, and Rosa Mulholland. Katherine Cecil Thurston spent three months a year at her large Co. Waterford house and the rest of the year at her house in Kensington.[34] If these writers who went to England were coming from behind, it was merely the disadvantage of the ambitious provincial who knows that opportunities reside in her cultural capital and nearest metropolis, which was, where each of these writers was concerned, London. (On one of the rare occasions on which these successful women writers have been recently discussed, it is dismaying to find their success translated into suffering and martyrdom.[35]) Such writers were as likely to be Catholic as Protestant and all violated equally the tacit 'Residency Requirement' of the Revival, most famously imposed by Yeats when he enjoined Synge, a student of French literature, to desert Paris and return to Ireland to write. Such authors were more likely to be published by British than by Irish publishers and, by so doing, reaching more British (and American, and Irish-American) than Irish readers. Setting, so important to a novel, was in fact a more casual affair to popular novelists than to writers of the Revival who believed an Irish setting was all but essential to the Revival project. For the popular writers, story trumped setting and they told it wherever it lay at hand.

Even during the time of the Revival, the assertion of difference coexisting with the assumption of similarity (sometimes rousing itself into explicit claim) was one dimension of the complicated Anglo-Irish relationship that had as another dimension the tangled nuances of Irish nationalism and unionism before and even after Partition and the setting up of the Irish Free State. For example, M. McDonnell Bodkin's lively memoirs, *Recollections of an Irish Judge* (1914), are replete with these entanglements, but I am thinking specifically of his portrait of the unionist and Irish patriot, Lord ('Mickey') Morris, Chief Justice of Ireland and whose son was Lord Killanin.[36] Another example of the rich ambiguity of a relationship verging on love-and-hate would be an extended and warm 1896 reminiscence about London and the House of Commons by William O'Brien, editor of *United Ireland*, Irish Parliamentary Party MP, quondam prisoner for his rent strike organization, author of *When We Were Boys* (1890), and opponent of the third Home Rule Bill.[37]

The Irish novelist intimate with England, setting her work there, herself living there, practising the Catholic religion, and enjoying publication by English publishers: M. E. Francis (1859–1930) fitted this bill in its entirety. Her best-known book was *In a North Country Village* (1893) which consisted of twelve sketches of life in 'Thornleigh' linked by the characters (in both senses of the word: her major fictional figures and the minor eccentrics who colour village life) who appear and reappear; they are linked too by the fitful presence of Francis herself who acknowledges herself as narrator. The sketches and stories are deliberately low-key, their topics being 'Births and weddings, illnesses and deaths, partings and home-comings'.[38] Francis depicts a yeoman and manorial England the ways of life of which still carry the stamp of folk-ways, giving her observations some mild anthropological interest.[39] The quality of life, muffled even when there is cruelty and violence, is very different from rural Irish life in almost any literary representation, and Francis's portrait of a benign squirearchy is in telling contrast to the strained landlord–tenant relationships she must have known, or certainly known about, from back home. The stoicism of the villagers in the teeth of adversity and the face of death is an aspect of the muffled quality of life; although the stories are in fact rather sentimental, Francis insists that the villagers are an unsentimental lot, a trait that is surely in tacit contrast to the Irish characters. (The two Irish villagers are a 'saint'—a tall eccentric in a perpetual wrestle with the Devil and a Parnellite—and the village poetess specializing in dirges and performing her verses with extravagant gestures.)

Francis's own dispassionate narrative tone adds to the peculiar elegiac quality of the book which fittingly ends with the probability of Thornleigh's being 'modernised beyond recognition, its old-fashioned customs forgotten, its traditions stamped out' (pp. 300–1). In one chapter of what is really a glorified journal, Francis evokes the households she visits, no doubt out of *noblesse oblige* and a philanthropic motive: clearly Francis was at least minor gentry, a notch down from the squire perhaps (but more refined). Later we will explore the role of philanthropy in the Irish novel of the period, though we can register here the social and narrative *perspective* that the philanthropic posture generated—broad but partial in its social angle and elevation. It is likely that Mrs Francis the narrator feels more at home in the village because the squire's ancestors were Catholic and Jacobite (and it is not clear that the canon is Church of England rather than Roman Catholic). In real life Francis married into English minor Catholic gentry but had herself grown up in Lamberton Park, a country house in Co. Laois.[40] The autobiography of her early years, *Things of a Child* (1918), recalls an entirely domestic Victorian girlhood of games, picnicking, and riding; of nursery and governesses and of a mother who read Scott, Dickens, and Edgeworth to her children: young Mary was infatuated by the Rosamund of Edgeworth's early children's tales and devotes a chapter to the infatuation.

CRITICISM AND POPULAR FICTION

Popularity then, like best-sellerdom today, was indifferent to borders. But what the popular novel faced, both then and until recently, was a critical coolness or even disdain. In 1939, the Belfast-born writer C. S. Lewis discussed the distinction between 'popular' and 'serious' literature in terms that were common then but became unfashionable by the 1960s: 'lowbrow' and 'highbrow'.[41] Lewis was reacting against the modernist notion that only serious literature is

Literature proper (which is an honorific). Lowbrow novels were seen as trivial or elementary and often sentimental and unliterary, whereas highbrow novels were seen as important or serious, and literary; lowbrow novels were seen as merely entertaining, highbrow as edifying and difficult. Defending 'lowbrow' or popular work by claiming a range of merit within each category, Lewis may have been indirectly defending his own romances and fantasies at the outset of his career. By 1939 his fiction included only *The Pilgrim's Regress* (1933), an allegory, and *Out of the Silent Planet* (1938), a science-fiction fable, but a trajectory of sorts had been embarked on. However, we would think of Lewis's fantasies as middlebrow rather than lowbrow, if we were to re-employ these terms; I refrained from using them when discussing the *Blackwood's* editor's onslaught on cheap fiction in 1898 and 1899 because the terms, now discarded, had not come into use at that time.

Two decades after Lewis, G. D. Klingopulos saw the gaps between low, middle, and high brows opening in Britain after 1875 and continuing to widen in his own day. He quotes Henry James from *Partial Portraits* in 1888; the Master described the recent development of the English novel as, unlike its popular and 'old-fashioned' predecessor, 'an organized, moulded, balanced composition, gratifying the reader with a sense of design and construction'.[42] The implication was that the popular novel was a rudiment, at best an unpolished ancestor. The structural transformation of the novel at the hands of the avant garde accelerated after James, contributing to the revolution of modernism. By contrast, the novelists I discuss play only variations—albeit often illuminating or even liberating variations—in familiar romance plots or the formulas of category fiction. The most gifted of them may have essayed reforms of their genre but without joining the modernist cause, for which, frankly, they lacked the intellect. It might be worth remarking—without suggesting that the literary experimentalism of modernism accompanied left-wing political or social radicalism (the opposite is nearer the truth, as John Carey and others have contended)—that almost invariably those of the novelists I discuss who broach the simmering Irish Question advocate neither revolution nor a radical constitutional departure, but reform.

It was appropriate for Lewis to exhibit Pound, Joyce, and Eliot as exemplars of real and difficult literature, for we associate an articulate disdain for popular writing with the modernists of the second and third decades of the twentieth century. It has been Carey's contention that 'modernist literature and art can be seen as a hostile reaction to the unprecedented large reading public created by late nineteenth-century educational reforms', thus inadvertently aligning the modernists in this regard with the editor of *Blackwood's*.[43] The academic purveyors of that disdain survived the deaths of the major modernists and dominated English departments in British and American universities where the literary canon that was established and maintained between the 1930s and 1960s firmly excluded popular (lowbrow or middlebrow) literature. It was as late as the1980s when the gaps Klingopulos saw opening wider in the late 1950s, began to close; certain kinds of excluded literature were invited back in, but then only as guests under the auspices of Theory inspired by notions of extratextual redress (New Historicism, Feminism, and Cultural Studies).

Modernism encouraged the idea that literature is a taxing and exiguous affair and its proper and deserving readership a select, indeed élite one. Joyce may have written millions of words but they were expressed in a very small number of texts, the last two of them unintelligible to readers of popular novels. There is some irony here in so far as Joyce had a demotic appreciation of the popular novel albeit one that combined irony, imitation, mockery, and amusement, and it may later be worth briefly relating Joyce's unpopular and respective realism, decadence, and finally high modernism to the popular novel tradition that flourished in Ireland as well as in Britain and America. Certainly Joyce's immediate contemporary readership was tiny: by the middle of 1916, *Dubliners* (1914) had sold about 550 copies.[44] Pound may also have been prolific of word but in the latter part of his career he threatened to reserve his thousands of lines for a single continuous master-work. And Eliot of course was renowned for a studied and relatively spare body of work. It was Eliot who claimed that art had to be difficult for a difficult age and who wished to define culture in such a way as to exclude large portions of the population. Samuel Beckett, often seen as Joyce's successor, also developed a reputation for scantiness through the brevity of many of his works, though of course he was prolific in his own way; the titles of his works make a lengthy list (as do Eliot's). Beckett like Eliot worked by compression, Joyce by extension; Joyce's few works described widening spirals of language and formal pattern. That other 'successor' to Joyce, Flann O'Brien, wrote more novels than either but his *oeuvre* is suitably contracted by the critics' conferring of canonical status only on *At Swim-Two-Birds* (1939), *The Third Policeman* (composed by 1940), and *An Béal Bocht* (1941; as *The Poor Mouth*, 1973); as a result he has the reputation of having been a disappointed and thwarted writer. Foreign to all of these writers, including James, and excepting, one suspects, O'Brien, is the desire to amass innumerable, full-length novels widely accessible to the book-buying and book-borrowing public.

This is exactly what many Irish and British novelists of our period did. Considered against the notion of the artist inching forward through the complexities of his art and times, the prolificness of late Victorian, Edwardian, and even post-Great War popular novelists seems vulgar and even alarming; modernism was in part a reaction against such fecundity and popularity. One online bibliography lists 169 novels by Swan; in 1902 she published eight novels, in 1935 six, in 1937 seven and in 1940 five: twenty-six novels in just four years—all with reputable publishers. These do not include the novels she wrote as 'David Lyall', seventy of which are listed by the *British Museum Catalogue pre-1956 Imprints*. The encyclopaedic *Twentieth-Century Romance and Historical Writers* (1994) lists forty-nine volumes of stories by Swan and thirteen non-fiction books. The ten most prolific Irish fiction writers published between them well in excess of 700 novels. Tynan published over 100 novels and twelve short-story collections, as well as five volumes of memoirs. Since Tynan was a poet of repute and ambition, and as such a minor ornament of the Irish Revival, it might be thought that she is only statistically put in the shade by L. T. Meade, pseudonym of Elizabeth Thomasina Toulmin Smith (née Meade) from Bandon, Co. Cork, but in fact Meade, who wrote her first book at 17, was a considerable figure. *Twentieth-Century Crime and Mystery Writers* (1985) lists twenty crime novels by Meade but also 227 other novels (a good many of them written for schoolgirls) as well as volumes of what the entry-writer calls 'mystery story-chains' by which, the writer claims, Meade is now chiefly remembered.[45] Katharine Tynan called Meade 'perhaps the most voluminous of all living writers.' Tynan's own prolificness is the more impressive since she claimed: 'I have never typed, all was written by my own hand.'[46] George A. Birmingham published close to sixty novels, as well as five volumes of stories and over a dozen volumes of mixed-genre writing (including essays and travel accounts). The combined catalogues of Trinity College Dublin (a copyright library) and World Catalog yield a total of fifty-eight novels by the Limerick novelist Dorothea Conyers, but there may be others. The *British Museum Catalogue* lists thirty-two novels under the name of M. E. Francis and twenty-one under her real name, (Mrs) Mary Blundell. Croker published at least fifty works of fiction (at least forty-two of them novels). In her brief forty-two years, Mrs Hungerford wrote something like fifty-five novels and five volumes of stories. The British Library Public Catalogue lists forty-five novels by Mrs Alexander, twenty-seven of them published in 1890 or after. Mrs Alexander (1825–1902) is not to be confused with the novelist Eleanor Alexander (1857–1939) from Co. Tyrone, daughter of Mrs Cecil Frances Alexander, the celebrated hymnist, and William Alexander, Archbishop of Armagh, nor with the (chiefly historical) novelist, Miriam Alexander (later Mrs Harold Stokes, dates unknown). Rosa Mulholland (Lady Gilbert) from Belfast wrote at least forty-three volumes of novels and stories, and Riddell at least thirty-nine books (novels and tales), as well as two novels under the *nom de plume* Rainey Hawthorne, and eight under the *nom de plume* F. G. Trafford for a grand total of at least forty-nine volumes. So it was almost reprehensible for Mrs Victor (Jessie) Rickard to have written as few as thirty-seven books (most of them novels)!

Prolificness was a British and not just an Irish phenomenon. Perhaps it could only be achieved by some with the aid of technology, and the editor of *Blackwood's* jeeringly revealed that Guy Boothby

speaks his novels into a phonograph! There is the problem solved ... Now we have it. Mr Boothby does not like the stubborn pen or the mechanical key-board to come between his invention and the popular taste, so he speaks his novels into a phonograph ... the phonograph ... enormously increases the speed of composition ... Thus he can compose a dozen books at a single *coup*, and where others are content with one public, he may buckle twelve to his heart.[47]

Furniss praises one popular novelist for not dictating her novels, 'as many busy authoresses do, nor does she employ the typist'.[48] One of the authors who apparently did dictate her fiction was Meade who according to Helen Black had a full-time staff of two or three female secretaries who took dictation and typed.[49] Riddell told Black how she wrote her novels: she observed things in the real world unconsciously, then in the borderland of sleep, images would return photographically and sentences form themselves; on waking, Riddell simply reproduced the sentences.[50] Black had it from Croker that the latter secretly drew out her pen 'to beguile the long weary days' and that, having done so, 'as in a dream, everything passed swiftly before her: fleeting visions of places, people past and present, conversations, ideas, &c. The moment of inspiration had come and was seized ... day after was spent in transmitting her thoughts to paper.' She wrote ten to twelve hours a day.[51]

WOMEN AND THE POPULAR NOVEL

Whatever the secret of furious composition, Furniss seems to be justified in seeing women as dominating the world of the popular novel in the period 1890–1920 (and perhaps beyond). James Milne's article in the *Book Monthly* for January 1907 that surveyed the previous year's fiction output was abstracted by W. T. Stead in *The Review of Reviews* as 'The Triumph of the Woman Novelist.' Milne named twelve novels by women (including novels by Mrs Humphry Ward and Marie Corelli, among the few who have survived oblivion) that he believed outsold novels by any men in 1906. According to Stead, in *Chambers's Journal* for January Milne in another article, 'The Novel of To-Day', 'refers to the demand of readers for studies of life as it appears to the woman's mind'.[52] The novelists composed a wide spectrum of ability as well as celebrity, the two sometimes converging. In *A Struggle for Fame: A Novel* (1883), Riddell offers portraits from either end of the spectrum.

Lady Hilda Hicks is a literary diva: a titled, beautiful, exasperating, self-seeking best-selling novelist whose plots and characters begin to skirt the libellous, plunging her publisher into a dilemma: he is unwilling either to forgo her lucrativeness or to risk expensive lawsuits. At the other end of the spectrum is Riddell's heroine, Glenarva (Glen) Westley, whose literary career we follow from its beginning to its mellowed and defiant end and who we assume is a recognizable version of Riddell herself. She travels from Belfast to London with her father as a 17-year-old woman determined to make it as a professional novelist. At the age of 15, her decision to become a writer has the force of an epiphany: '"I will write," she said, standing in a flood of moonlight; and, opening her little desk there and then, she began',[53] and one has the feeling that Riddell's girlhood vocation may have been as abrupt.

Furniss, recalling his lunch with Riddell, alludes delicately to the present whereabouts of her husband: 'I believe her husband through some queer way in business was resting somewhere at his country's expense.' (In other words he was languishing in gaol for debt.) Indeed, Furniss was of the opinion that many of the 'authoresses' he met 'only thought of taking up writing when their husbands had come a cropper financially, or morally—when through necessity or caprice they drowned their sorrow in the flowing ink-pot'.[54] The life of Mrs Alexander might seem to bear Furniss out. According to Black, she married Alexander Hector in 1858 'and wrote no more until she became a widow' and then wrote 'to seek distraction from bereavement'.[55] But perhaps the necessity of activity in middle-class and upper middle-class marriage was a more normal stimulation. For example, Croker accompanied her husband, a Lieutenant-Colonel of the Munster Fusiliers, to India and Burma and is said to have begun writing only after ten years of marriage and motherhood, 'to occupy the long hot days while her husband was away', often on game safaris.[56]

Despite the mild toxicity of Furniss's remark, he was impressed by the professionalism of prolific women novelists. In fact, already knowing that women writers wrote a great deal of advertising copy for popular novels, he claimed that often women novelists wrote novels for which male authors took public credit. He instanced one author at Tinsley's the publishers, though he does not name her, who told him she wrote novels over the name of Edmund Yates (1831–94), the popular novelist and editor-proprietor of the *World*, editor of *Tinsley's Magazine* and *Temple Bar*. 'So it comes to this', Furniss concluded, 'as far as I can judge—that . . . clever journalists posed as novelists with books written by literary lady "ghosts".' Furniss also claims that Florence Marryat the popular novelist (Mrs Ross Church) told him she wrote most of the criticisms published by Tom Taylor in *Punch*, which Taylor edited.[57] Perhaps the truth of such allegations provoked Mabel E. Wotton to publish 'the Fifth Edition' (1896), a troubling story about a vain novelist suffering writer's nerves while trying to follow up on his first popular success and who buys a novel in manuscript from an overworked, long-suffering, and lower-class professional woman story-writer (who wishes initially to give it to him in a stroke of misguided female altruism in thanks for what she believes to be his kindness), defaults on the payments, revises the manuscript (inserting the original author as a character), and finds himself with an instant popular hit that soon sees five editions. After several appeals to him to send her the remaining pounds, the woman writer vanishes, probably to die in poverty; in recollection he sees himself as the aggrieved party, a victim of harassment, and dismisses her memory: 'How like a woman!' he exclaims in self-exculpation.[58]

The busyness of these authors was fearsome. Mrs Hungerford told Black that she was 'over-full of work', was selling as fast as she could write, and had more commissions than she could get through in the next few years. (Hungerford wrote her first novel before she was 19.) Like Riddell she planned her fictional scenes at night and awoke to write them out without any trouble (with a faint suggestion of automatic writing).[59] In writing The Middle Years, Tynan consulted her diary for the early 1890s and describes her own industry as having been 'prodigious', despite migraine headaches. She refers to 'my industrious, exemplary English days.' Amidst her prolific journalism, she revised Read's four-volume Cabinet of Irish Literature in three months. 'Anyone else would have taken three years or a lifetime', she claimed. She schooled herself, in imitation of Alice Meynell, to write in the midst of the family circle, abstracting herself from the conversations around her: 'My deplorable facility!' she calls it.[60] (D. H. Lawrence had the same indifference to his surroundings while he wrote as fast as his hand could trot.) Tynan repeated the observation in The Wandering Years.[61] Deplorable in a sense it was, and yet one might at times see virtue in the fluency and modesty of the best popular novels, very different from the virtue of such works as Ulysses, Murphy, and At Swim-Two-Birds in which the novelist seems to be straining at the limits of his capacity for insight, design, vocabulary, character invention, and plot development. Like Tynan, Annie S. Swan had to cultivate a capacity to be undistracted amidst people since she 'grew up in a large family where it was impossible to have a room entirely to oneself.' In The Middle Years Tynan gives two sample days in the life of a prolific author and it is an impressive workload.[62] Getting time to write has been a problem for the twentieth-century woman writer, if she has been both mother and housewife. These older women writers seem not to have had the same problem, writing as they did at a time when most people had domestic help of some kind. Some were childless or single and conducted themselves like the professional writers they were, devoting a certain portion of the day to their career. Nevertheless, there were sometimes deprivation and sacrifice as well as a Victorian determination and work ethic. Deborah Alcock, unmarried and selflessly devoted to her father, and whose only real fictional theme was, fittingly, martyrdom, would rise at 5.30 a.m. and write between 6.15 a.m. and 8.30 a.m. each morning before assuming her other duties and activities.[63]

The use of pseudonyms by popular women novelists belongs to this context of large fast production. The truly prolific authors used one or two or more *noms de plume* partly in the spirit of play, partly to diffuse an effect like monopoly and to relieve possible readerly tedium, partly on occasion to assume a different overall narrative voice or authorial persona. A woman novelist who was married had a choice of course of using (or changing to) her husband's name. Annie French married Alexander Hector and on writing her first book was afraid it might not be popular so took, not her husband's surname, but his Christian name, and became Mrs Alexander. It is unclear if she thought French or Hector was the bad bet.[64] Mary Chavelita Dunne took her first husband's forenames, ignored his surname Clairmonte, and became George Egerton. But most women assumed the husband's surname. Margaret Wolfe Hamilton married Edward Argles and published at least twenty-four volumes under the name of Mrs Margaret Argles. She afterwards married Henry Hungerford (who owned 11,000 acres west of Bandon) and published under the name Mrs Hungerford. However, in the commercial fashion of the day, she also published semi-anonymously. 'By the Author of *Molly Bawn*' (1878, her best-known novel), 'By the Author of *Phyllis*' (1877), and 'The Duchess' (from the title of that novel, 1888): these appeared instead of her name. Jessie Louise Rickard published as Mrs Victor Rickard and she signed at least one Preface to a book 'L. Rickard' but her maiden name is never catalogued. Charlotte Cowan became Charlotte Riddell and published under that sur-name; indeed, she assumed her husband's forenames as well in initial form, becoming Mrs J. H. Riddell. Croker (née Sheppard) kept the initials of her own Christian names, Bithia Mary; initials sounded more masculine and it was often for this reason that women novelists used them, knowing that novel writing was still thought of as a male art, despite voluminous evidence to the contrary. Going beyond ambiguous initials, Mary Chavelita Dunne required readers to assume she was a man when she published under the name George Egerton. The women writers of the 1890–1922 period may have been the last generation to feel the need for sexual deception in their names; the use of 'Mrs' might seem on the other hand to be a clever piece of ingratiation with male condescension, or perhaps it was thought to confer a kind of respectability befitting a serious novelist.

Sarah Grand, a New Woman (indeed, co-coiner of the term), reversed the process, and just as she broke with the three-decker novel (at some risk to her sales), she broke with the alternative practices of pretending to be male or pretending to be a compliant and happily married woman. She shed her identity as Mrs Frances Elizabeth McFall (née Clarke) and refashioned herself out of the blue as Sarah Grand, the name implying the very haughtiness the refashioning required; she did not know then, she claimed later, that she shared her new name with Talleyrand's mistress. She also specified how she wished to be addressed thenceforward—'call me Madame'—which both raised the haughtiness and neatly avoided both 'Mrs' and 'Miss'; she went on to become honorary Lady Mayoress of Bath for six years. Her new name was really a *nom de guerre*, we might say. There may be clues in two of her novels as to why she chose the pseudonym 'Grand'. In *Ideala* the title heroine insists that human beings 'want grander minds, and we must have grander bodies to contain them. And it all rests with us women'.[65] This hints at Grand's sense of a mission, primarily that of being a leading women's advocate, and only secondarily a novelist. In *The Beth Book*, young Beth listens to her aunt Victoria read an inspiring religious text and jumps up excitedly: ' "O Aunt Victoria! That is—that is"—she tore at her hair—"I want a word—I want a word!" "It is *grand*, Beth!" "Grand! grand!" Beth shouted. "Yes, it is grand"'.[66] Yes, I am Grand. Since Grand's real name, Frances Clarke McFall, resembles her heroine's name, Elizabeth Caldwell Maclure, some slight immodesty may be inferred from the subtitle, *A Woman of Genius*.

But if Grand's adventure in nomenclature was ideological, Annie S. Swan's was commercial. Of Swan's exploitation of magazine serialization, the editor of *Blackwood's Edinburgh Magazine* remarks: 'Nor do we imagine that Miss Annie S. Swan and her extremely shrewd literary advisers would have entered into this branch of the business unless they had, as the saying goes, *smelt roast meat*'.[67] The name that Swan published seventy novels under, David Lyall, seems to have been shared with the novelist Helen Buckingham Mathers (Mrs Henry Reeves) who published at least thirty-six novels under the name 'Helen Mathers' and twelve under the name of David Lyall, the latter name clearly being a valuable commercial property. The arithmetic is pretty much guesswork and it is all enough to give bibliographer and critic alike migraines.

Yeats took precautions against such headaches. When he wrote his novella 'John Sherman' (1891), he wished, he told Tynan, 'to be taken as an Irish novelist, not as an English, or cosmopolitan one' but (or therefore) 'I have no desire to gain that kind of passing regard a book wins from the many. To please the folk of few books is one's grand aim'.[68] He was echoing Oscar Wilde who went even further, telling the editor and readers of the *Scots Observer* in response to a hostile review of *The Picture of Dorian Gray* that he could not have had a depraved intent in writing the novel since he, like all true artists, was unconcerned with readers' opinions, and certainly not the opinions of the people: 'If my work pleases the few I am gratified . . . As for the mob, I have no desire to be a popular novelist. It is far too easy'.[69] Yet by courting notoriety in his public appearances, Wilde was indeed concerned about public opinion, and *Dorian Gray* was written in an eloquently accessible style that allowed it to achieve popularity as well as notoriety. Yeats was more ingenuous. Addressing American audiences in 1932–3, Yeats claimed (for reasons irrelevant here) that the impulse that drove him and his fellow Revivalists to the old legends and peasant speech in the first phase of the movement (up to around 1910) also drove him and them to 'a hatred of democratic compromises'; during that phase 'our work was above the heads of the people'.[70] In dismissing popularity to Tynan, he was talking to the wrong woman. Yeats valued Tynan for his Revival as a writer of slender Irish poems but her dozens of popular novels were apparently of little use to him. Actually, the Revivalists *did* court popularity but of a certain and odd kind; Yeats himself hoped his poems would turn up as songs or poems sung or recited by Irish peasants; the Revivalists wanted to write literature *for the people*, on occasion as though *by the people*. As for the other more familiar kind of popularity: once the Revival got into stride, capturing much of the popular cultural imagination—operating as it did on many fronts—the popular novel (and there was no other kind out of Ireland in, say, 1900, save a handful of highbrow works by George Moore) was shunted into its middlebrow sidings: too English, too Anglo-Irish (in the wrong way), too neglectful of native pre-Conquest culture, too—well—*popular* in those middle-class and urban lower-class ways established before Yeats had defined popularity not as being read by the literate masses but as *acceptance by the folk*.

The marginalizing of the popular novelists was made easy and even 'natural' by the systemic sexism of the day; it was easier to ignore the productions of 'authoresses' and 'literary ladies'. (Even Wilde referred condescendingly to 'lady-novelists'.[71]) And since women dominated the world of the popular novel, to dismiss them was in effect to dismiss the bulk of popular novels, and vice versa. This sexism both survived and pre-dated the Revival and modernism and was standard operating procedure even in the literary history and criticism of the academy until a couple of decades ago; by then, however, many Irish novelists had sunk irrecoverably from sight and existed only by name in the mausoleum of Brown's *Ireland in Fiction*. In a novel by one such author, Mrs Victor Rickard, a clause occurs that ironically describes the fate of the novelist herself: when Sylvia Tracy in *The Fire of Green Boughs* (1919) peruses bookshelves 'which were a mortuary of dead and forgotten authors'.[72]

The justice of their neglect has been difficult to gauge since there has not been a comparable programme of recovery in Ireland to that in Britain and America, where it has been chiefly driven by assiduous critics and sympathetic or dedicated publishing houses (such as Virago in England). Books that are long out of print and difficult of access even in university libraries are less likely to be recovered. Meanwhile, anthologies perpetuate the existing canon more often than they alter it or establish a radically different one, since they tend to imitate each other, thereby guaranteeing the neglect of those writers not selected for the early influential compilations. (And novelists suffer particularly in this regard, since it is far easier to insert a poem into an anthology than an excerpt from a novel, which many anthologists are reluctant to do anyway.) Nor have there been in Britain and America quite the same pervasive political objections to certain perceived agendas, whereby, for example, an expressly Catholic or demonstrably unionist woman author is unlikely to be championed or even read closely by critics who themselves operate, sometimes unknowingly, from a hostile political perspective.

THE EXCLUDED MIDDLE

It should be clear by now that the distinction between lowbrow and highbrow, popular and serious fiction is entirely inadequate. The insertion of 'middlebrow' hardly helps matters. Novelists of 'high' modernism are recognizable by their radical experimentation in form; their de-familiarization of the genre through the technique of making the text more opaque, so that it cannot be read simply as though it were a window on the 'real' world; their frequent diversions of the reader from the easier allurements of plot or story; their deep interiority of character and narration; and their frequent multiplicity of perspective that encourages the relative at the expense of the essential, and flux at the expense of fixity. But such novelists were few in number even in modernism's heyday; besides, there is a group of English novelists who are modern without being modernist, and they include Hardy, Lawrence, and Forster. (Conrad seems to inhabit a no-man's land between the categories.) Both modernists and English moderns might be thought to make good on James's hopes for the new novel as primarily a formal composition, but whereas novelists of both groups express and represent the changes in sensibility and consciousness that flag modernity, the English novels, though clearly still literary fictions, might seem formally slack, with their form generated by expansiveness of idea and by diversity of experience and social reality rather than shaped into the kind of literary architecture Joyce attempted. There is another but not entirely distinct kind of English and Irish modern, the fiction writer whose aspiration is to register certain social deficits and to promote certain social ends in what have been called problem-novels, and these include the New Woman writers and the slum and underclass writers. If at the end of the spectrum are the genre or category writers whose main aim is entertainment, there are those who while seeking to entertain are also trying to illuminate society though without the aid of an agenda. Many of the novels I discuss below, particularly by novelists too prolific to have a narrow agenda, fall into this mixed category populated by works that we might at their best call mainstream novels.

In any case, the popular Irish novel continued in blithe disregard of the tendencies and agenda of the Revival. Tynan and George A. Birmingham published novels in the 1920s not essentially different in kind from those they had published twenty years before, while Shan F. Bullock's last, and possibly best Irish novel, *The Loughsiders* (1924), shows no detectable influence of the cultural ferment in Dublin. Popular novels, good or bad, remained contemporaries of the Revival and of modernism, and did not become merely embarrassing and disowned ancestors. My contention is that the term 'popular novel' covers a multitude of degrees of merit and seriousness; many good novels were published not for shop-girls, maidservants, or clerks but for what we would call the general (and therefore reasonably informed and interested) reader. Many novelists were trying their best to be on artistic par with Galsworthy or Gissing or Wells, and if they failed they occasionally succeeded at only a slightly lower level than these. Some recoverable and fine work has been allowed to fall by the wayside.

Even the middling work, if it is added to the best and both are looked at in the round, alters our notion of Irish prose, and of the culture of the period too, not merely by enlarging the body of discussible Irish writing but also by its belated contribution to the historical Irish conversation. ('Debate' might be a better word, and on occasions, 'row'.) Indeed, it is often the authors' impulse to say illuminating (and usually helpful) things about Ireland or England, or women, or marriage, or ghosts, or extraterrestrials, or whatever, that drives the plots of the popular novels. Further, it is that impulse that causes those plots, in many cases, to groan and creak as they follow the novelists' didactic urge, rather than issuing from the convincingly imagined autonomy of the characters. Not surprisingly, the plots, manipulated and manoeuvred in this wise, are frequently distorted into melodrama against, one occasionally feels, the intention of the novelists. But what is said or represented about these regions of experience often remains useful and even insightful. When Irish novelists set their novels in England and peopled them with English characters—very well then, England and the English were by definition topics of the

Irish conversation, as they remain to this day. Irish popular novels reveal that many Irish men and women, whether or not they were deeply concerned about affairs inside Ireland, were certainly concerned about affairs outside the island—about science, say, or travel, or marriage as an institution (and divorce as a controversial eventuality), the Great War, political developments in Europe, the stock market, spiritualism, the British Empire. In the novels themselves, these concerns could take the form of themes or subgenres by which the concerns are expressed and which were shared by English and Irish novelists of the Victorian and Edwardian periods.[73]

Whereas it is easy to imagine that the only alternative to a radical departure in Irish literature in the 1890s was to continue with the humourists' Arcadia, it is wrong to do so. Most of what Claud Cockburn says in 1972 about the British best-sellers of our period can readily be said of successful British and Irish popular novels in general. Having asserted the craft and skill required for bestsellerdom, he admits that best-selling fiction in the early twentieth century was satisfying the need of its readers to escape for a time from their lives, to be entertained by losing themselves in a fictional world. But following T. H. Green, Cockburn implies that it was not simply a case of escape *from* real life, but also an escape *to* life imagined as fuller, and therefore more real than the reader's working or daily life outside fiction, a life from which the reader was alienated.[74] But what Cockburn says beyond this notion of virtual engagment with life rings true: that successful popular novels are a mirror of 'the mind and face' of an age. When he makes the claim that it is difficult to write recent British history without studying them, I would echo his claim about the writing of recent Irish history, yet it has been done with, at most, a parsimonious and highly selected body of literature. If indeed a given best-seller expresses the prevailing political and social climate of which it is the product—the public sector of life—then an extraordinary opportunity to understand the Irish weather of 1890–1940 has been lost.[75] In fact, the loss has been the greater when the novel in question has not just been the product of the times but has tried to make sense of the times, sometimes even change those times, most obviously in the case of the so-called problem-novel.

Nor does Cockburn dismiss the element of love in bestselling fiction, seeing it as part of popular fiction's presentation of the 'private sector' of life, and spilling over 'to cover the general status of women',[76] something we will find to be the case in many Irish popular novels. Fictional romance, then, can illuminate as well as divert, even when women characters in the hands of male novelists—or even female novelists—are in their conception undernourished, typecast, subordinated. But where novels that address the condition of Ireland are concerned, we can go farther than Cockburn. Very often we will find in the popular novels love and romance as transposed versions of England–Ireland relations (or Saxon–Celt relations, or Protestant–Catholic relations).[77] Indeed, England–Ireland relations (chiefly in their social and cultural guises), male–female relations (love, marriage, separation, divorce, remarriage), economic relations (income, debt, wills, employment, bankruptcy) and daily cultural relations (field sports, visiting, vacations) form a set of equations or homologies. These are preferred to the hard outlines of specific political and constitutional prescriptions. To the extent that these equations are a form of substitution or sublimation, they may appear as an evasion conducted by those who do not wish to see hard political or constitutional changes. But the equations honour the language and perspectives of the novel. Besides, they also honour the aim of entertaining rather than discomfiting the reader.

The novel as primarily entertainment and the novel as primarily social commentary differ from the novel that came to dominate academic study of the twentieth century: the novel as art-form or 'literature', the twentieth-century conception of which we've already linked to modernism. They differ also from the literature of the Irish Revival, which was a special way of 'making it new' that turned away from the novel, even the art-novel when it arrived, because the aim of the Revival was not primarily aesthetic. The Revival project was not one of establishing and maintaining a special artistic space separable from society, religion, and ethics and without designs on these spheres, but rather one of specialized cultural retrieval and specialized cultural transformation. The new space for writing—equivalent perhaps to the aesthetic space of the contemporary modernist work—was a reimagined Ireland largely different from the Ireland of daily experience and as ideally autonomous as the realm of the aesthetic, a literary form of Sinn Fein (Ourselves).[78] The real-life social space imagined as its literary counterpart was one in which the middle class and lower middle class were effectively absent. It is not surprising, then, to discover Cockburn identifying the British middle class as the chief consumer of the successful popular novel, the literary form from which the theorists of the Irish Revival recoiled. If he is right in claiming that study of the best-seller (and, we can add, the aspiring best-seller) throws light on the moods, attitudes, and needs common to large sections of the middle class,[79] it made perfect sense for the Revivalists to ignore the popular novel since the Irish middle class itself, Catholic and Protestant alike, was to be ignored as studiously by them as by the modernists.

Two of the best-sellers Cockburn discusses were written by novelists born or raised in Ireland: *The Riddle of the Sands* (1903) and *The Blue Lagoon* (1908). The latter might seem a prime example of escapist fiction, since it is set mainly in that most exotic of settings beyond even the far reaches of the British Empire and almost comparable with the planets of science fiction: the remote desert island. Some editions of *The Blue Lagoon* subtitle it *A Romance* and indeed it has the outlandish setting, adventure, quest, chivalry, and love-match of classic romance. It tells the story of three (then two) castaways on a South Seas coral island somewhere east of the Marquesas, one refuge among thousands of islands, reefs, and atolls lost in hundreds of thousands of square leagues of sea. It shares with its distant progenitor, *Robinson Crusoe* (1719) the sudden involuntary return to Nature accompanied by the apparent useless-ness of material culture, the reduction of life to its literally bare essentials, and the necessity of a fresh start. But the pain is smaller and briefer than in *Crusoe*; Cockburn remarks that *The Blue Lagoon* has all the romance of Defoe with only ten per cent of the realism.[80] Young Dick Lestrange and his cousin Emmeline (both 8-year-olds from Boston), and the old seadog Paddy Button from Connemara, survive a shipwreck and are stranded on an island that initially resembles paradise.

On either side of the broad beach before them the cocoa-nut trees came down like two regiments, and bending gazed at their own reflections in the lagoon. Beyond lay waving chapparel, where cocoa-palms and bread-fruit trees intermixed with the mammee apple and the tendrils of the wild vine. On one of the piers of coral at the break of the reef stood a single cocoa-palm; bending with a slight curve, it, too, seemed seeking its reflection in the waving water.

But the soul of it all, the indescribable thing about this picture of mirrored palm trees, blue lagoon, coral reef and sky, was the light. Away at sea the light was blinding, dazzling, cruel. Away at sea it had nothing to focus itself upon, nothing to exhibit but infinite spaces of blue water and desolation.

Here it made the air a crystal, through which the gazer saw the loveliness of the land and reef, the green of palm, the white of coral, the wheeling gulls, the blue lagoon, all sharply outlined—burning, coloured, arrogant, yet tender—heart-breakingly beauti-ful, for the spirit of eternal morning was here, eternal happiness, eternal youth.[81]

The light, eternal happiness, and eternal youthfulness will return at the end of the novel, though with tremors of ambiguity set off almost from the start of the narrative. But on the surface and for much of its length, de Vere Stacpoole's novel belongs to what we might call the sunny 'coral island' branch of the genre *Crusoe* began. 'The romance of coral has still to be written,' de Vere Stacpoole asserts (p. 149) and proceeds to write it.

Yet even in that branch of the genre, paradise is skirted by evil and the promise of a Fall. The dark fin that Arthur Lestrange (Dick's father, Emme-line's uncle) sees from the ship at the outset of the journey from Boston to San Francisco (p. 18) is the same thing that resembles 'a small triangle of dark canvas' that ripples through the water and sinks from sight immediately after the passage I have quoted above. The fin returns, below or just above the surface of the story, just like the merrows Button tells the children about, and the 'gibly-gobly-ums' and 'Billy balloos' he pretends to see in the water chasing the 'albicore' (*sic*: albacore, tuna); Button is forever talking about the troubling 'cluricaunes' but in an attack of delirium tremens it is red rats Button sees sprouting from the sand. Moreover, recurring in de Vere Stacpoole's lush descriptions is a dark spot or stain of various origin, unsettling the reader almost subconsciously. And overarching all is the eternal indifference of Nature which Dick comes to realize; the island is peopled by just two beings, rather like specks themselves, and the perspective resembles that of the vast green vale that dwarfs Tess of the d'Urbervilles towards the end of Hardy's novel.

The naturalness, the freedom, the spontaneous self-reliance, the instant recovery of the dawn of civilization, the childlike innocence of Eden, the promise of a new beginning away from the busy distractions of society and the world's stain and corruption—these are the first and surprising bounty and warm consolation of paradise to those whose marooning turns out to be a fortunate fall. When the castaways are children, the idea of ontogeny repeating phylogeny, growth into adulthood repeating human evolution into civilization, is given impetus. But a true second beginning, as Defoe knew, required a reversion to the rudeness of that beginning and so we have Crusoe as a grotesque, a primitive in his goatskins. Emmeline's sixteen-year-old nakedness in the life-giving open air (the latter a Victorian touch Defoe would have found peculiar) is accompanied by Dick's return to a state of savagery, speaking in monosyllables, acquiring the instincts of the hunter but put to savage uses: 'he would kill, and kill, just for the pleasure of killing, destroying more fish than they could possibly use' (p. 148). It is hard not to see in this strand of *The Blue Lagoon*—reversion, stains, blood and death in the life of a schoolboy in ostensible paradise—the premiss of Golding's *Lord of the Flies* (1954), a premiss usually understood to be an inversion of Ballantyne's *The Coral Island* (1858).

But unlike *Lord of the Flies* and like *The Coral Island*, the schoolboy passes through the savage state. The pictures of the mirror in the early description of the coral paradise are useful since in faithfulness to the genre that *Crusoe* began, Dick and Emmeline, especially after the death of Paddy Button, begin to make seriously a mirror image, if a rudimentary one, of the society they have left behind. The first essentials of the real and fictional castaway are food, water, and shelter. (These can require gathering, preservation, cultivation, construction.) Unlike poor Crusoe until the peculiar arrival of Man Friday, Dick and Emmeline already have the next essential: companionship. Moreover, since the children are not merely friends but cousins—a kinship we will meet again in the popular novel—and since Paddy Button stands *in loco parentis*, we could read the novel at first as an update of Wyss's *The Swiss Family Robinson* (1812) in which a family maintains its survival and integrity in the wilderness. In Defoe, Wyss, Ballantyne, and de Vere Stacpoole, more than family is at stake—material culture itself is remade, using that other seeming essential of castaway life: salvage, which becomes the bricolage from which, quite quickly, nothing less than civilized society is reconstituted. Defoe is profounder and odder than Wyss and Ballantyne in this respect, since the society the solitary Crusoe remakes is as philosophical and solipsistic as it is real, hence the novel's allegorical force and complexity.

The Blue Lagoon has its own oddity. Like Golding's boys, Dick and Emmeline are initiated into death from which Lestrange had tried to keep them sheltered, and it is done with a surprising realism. When the children find Paddy lying sideways on the reef, they pull his body on to its back, the mouth hangs open and a small crab darts from the mouth and scuttles over the chin and drops on to the coral (p. 130). On another occasion they find, like Crusoe, disturbing evidence of human activity on the beach and it is obliquely identified but described with an almost gratuitously grotesque explanation.

On the right-hand side of the beach something lay between the cocoa-nut trees. He approached; it was a mass of offal; the entrails of a dozen sheep seemed cast here in one mound, yet there were no sheep on the island, and sheep are not carried as a rule in war canoes. The sand on the beach was eloquent. The foot pursuing and the foot pursued; the knee of the fallen one, and then the forehead and outspread hands; the heel of the chief who has slain his enemy, beaten the body flat, burst a hole through it through which he has put his head, and who stands absolutely wearing his enemy as a cloak; the head of the man dragged on his back to be butchered like a sheep—of these things spoke the sand. (p. 165)

But after Death, Dick and Emmeline are initiated into Love, which is what prompts Dick to reverse his decline into savagery and end his reign as a Crusoe-like 'imperial master' in a tiny feudal state (p. 157). Love leads to sex and sex to an Edenic, Miltonic nuptial sleep in edgy scenes that must have given some Edwardian readers pause. When Emmeline bears a child, she completes the nuclear family that had been broken when Button died.

Civilization lost, nature found; civilization remade, nature lost; paradise found, paradise lost: these are the positive and negative formulas of The Blue Lagoon. But the ending is in a different key from the desert-island adventure. We would anticipate the youngsters being rescued and reassimilated into the society they were torn from and which they have painstakingly reconstructed, but this does not happen. Instead, the spirit of that one stain on the novel, the character of Paddy Button, an unfortunately typecast Celt—lazy, melancholy, goodhearted, superstitious, bibulous, storytelling—returns to preside over the ambiguous conclusion in which, thanks to the crimson 'never-wake-up berries' that Button warned the children against, life and death become one, happiness is at once lost and made eternal, and likewise youth. Cockburn thought some readers might see a kind of suicide pact at work before he interprets the ending, indeed the 'steamy philosophy' of the whole novel, as a genteel, middle-class reaction to the 'fierce political revolutionary anarchism which at the turn of the century exploded in so many bombings and assassinations' (p. 73). If I cannot follow him here, I can at least see that *The Blue Lagoon* is less an escape *from* life than an escape *to* life, in all its ambiguities and ambivalences. The waters of de Vere Stacpoole's lagoon are indeed disturbed by something both archetypal and threateningly unspecified.

NOTES

1. Here and elsewhere I try to use the form of a female author's name as it always, or usually, appeared on the title pages of her novels, instead of retrieving her maiden name or supplying her own first names. *Far Above Rubies* was in fact published under a pseudonym. Mrs J. H. Riddell was Charlotte Eliza Lawson Riddell (née Cowan).

2. Catherine Candy estimates that 40,000 copies of *My New Curate* were printed between 1900 and 1958: *Priestly Fictions: Popular Irish Novelists of the Early 20th Century* (Dublin: Wolfhound Press, 1995), p. 178.

3. Katharine Tynan, *The Wandering Years* (London: Constable, 1922), p. 287.

4. Stephen J. Brown, *Ireland in Fiction* (1915, 1919; New York: Barnes & Noble, 1969), p. 18.

5. Hyde, in *The Revival of Irish Literature* (1894; New York: Lemma, 1973), p. 159. The situation was even more complicated than what I've suggested. In one story in *A Cluster of Nuts* (London: Lawrence and Bullen, 1894), Tynan offers as one of her passengers in the Ladies' Only carriage an overweight middle-class woman 'with a frivolous yellow-back and an abundance of sandwiches' (p. 64), a yellow-back being a cheap, especially French, novel, presumably purchasable at railway station stalls.

6. F. S. L. Lyons, *Ireland since the Famine* (London: Fontana, 1973), pp. 87–8.

7. Neither was Yeats pleased about the expansion of 'popular education', which he thought taught the virtues of objectivity, utility, and mechanism and which, he read 'somewhere', had reduced Shakespeare's audience: 'A People's Theatre' (1919) in *W.B. Yeats: Selected Criticism*, ed. A. Norman Jeffares (1964; London: Pan Books, 1976), p. 182.

8. 'Penny Fiction', *Blackwood's Edinburgh Magazine* 164 (December 1898), 811. Cf. Yeats: 'During an illness lately I read two popular novels which I had borrowed from the servants.' (He clearly would not wish us to think he had acquired the two novels himself.) Yeats is at pains to point out that a 'people's theatre' is not to be confused with a 'popular theatre' which he thought fit only for servants: 'A People's Theatre', *W.B. Yeats: Selected Criticism*, pp. 183, 181.

9. Harry Furniss, *Some Victorian Women: Good, Bad and Indifferent* (London: John Lane The Bodley Head, 1923), p. 39.

10. 'Penny Fiction', 805.

11. Ibid., 811.

12. Duffy's *A Thousand Capricious Chances* (a centenary history of Metheun) is quoted by Richard Dalby, Introduction to B. M. Croker, *'Number Ninety' and Other Ghost Stories*, ed. Dalby (Mountain Ash: Sarob, 2000), p. xiii. The psychology and sociology of women's readerly engagement with literature is subjected to intensive analysis in Kate Flint's *The Woman Reader 1837–1914* (1993) in which Meade is briefly mentioned but Grand is more substantially dealt with.

13. 'Fashion in Fiction', *Blackwood's Edinburgh Magazine* 166 (October 1899), 531–42. As well as Hocking, the most popular novelists of the day included Guy Boothby, C. M. Sheldon, and Hall Caine.

14. Helen C. Black, *Notable Women Authors of the Day* (1893; Freeport, NY: Books for Libraries, 1972), p. 324. *The Heavenly Twins* was privately printed in 1892 before being picked up by Heinemann. See Philip Waller, *Writers, Readers, and Reputations: Literary Life in Britain 1870–1918* (Oxford: Oxford University Press, 2006), p. 852. See also Joan Huddleston, *Sarah Grand: A Bibliography*. Victorian Fiction Research Guides I. (Queensland: Department of English, University of Queensland, n.d.), p. 14. Five of the thirty novelists Black profiles are Irish: Riddell, Mrs Alexander, Mrs Hungerford, May Crommelin and Grand. Mrs Houstoun (Matilda Charlotte Houstoun, neé Jessé) knew John Wilson Croker, a friend of her father's, and she spent twenty years in the west of Ireland ('In sheer weariness of spirit she took to her pen': Black, p. 230.)

15. Marion Shaw, 'Victorian Women Prose Writers', in *The Penguin History of Literature*: vol. 6, *The Victorians*, ed. Arthur Pollard (1969; 1987; London: Penguin Books, 1993), p. 231.

16. A contemporary commentator quoted by Amy Cruse, *After the Victorians* (London: Allen & Unwin, 1938), p. 130.

17. Black, *Notable Women Authors of the Day*, p. 324.

18. Brown, *Ireland in Fiction*, p. 293. Anon, 'The Making of a Novelist', *The Lady's Realm*, April 1905, 655. In the United States the novel was entitled *The Masquerader* (New York: Harper, 1904). The novel first appeared in serial form in *Blackwood's Edinburgh Magazine* between January and October, 1904. It was reissued by Grosset and Dunlap in 1922. Three Thurston novels, *The Masquerader, The Gambler*, and *Max*, were among the top ten annual best-sellers in the United States, in 1904, 1905, and 1910 respectively: Philip Waller, *Writers, Readers, and Reputations*, p. 647. Thurston was born Katherine Madden in Cork; her father Paul Madden was director of the Munster & Leinster Bank and was a political associate of Parnell, though his daughter was of the opinion that women ought not to engage prominently in party politics ('The Making of a Novelist', 658).

19. Waller, *Writers, Readers, and Reputations*, p. 679.

20. Mike Ashley, *The Age of the Storytellers: British Popular Fiction Magazines 1880–1950* (London: British Library and Oak Knoll Press, 2006), pp. 14, 200. Riddell was also an editor (*St James's Magazine*): see Graham Law, *Serializing Fiction in the Victorian Press* (London: Palgrave, 2000), p. 155. A recurring figure in Law's

landscape is John Maxwell, an Irishman who besides being a literary representative, owned several popular magazines that published fiction, including *Belgravia*, *The Sixpeny Journal*, *The Welcome Guest*, and *The Halfpenny Journal*: Law, pp. 27, 66, 254 n. 3.

21. Ashley, *Age of the Storytellers*, pp. 85, 212, 109.

22. See Ashley and, since some of the titles are American, see also the online FictionMags Index.

23. Law, *Serializing Fiction*, p. 147.

24. But not William Tinsley (surviving sibling of Tinsley Brothers): see J. A. Sutherland, *Victorian Novelists and Publishers* (Chicago: University of Chicago Press, 1976), pp. 4–5. Tinsley's right-hand man during the late 1870s and early 1880s was Edmund Downey, the Irish novelist, according to Furniss: *Victorian Women*, p. 11. Downey (1856–1937), who was only 22 when he went to England and entered the literary scene, wrote novels into the second decade of the twentieth century (sometimes as 'F. M. Allen') and while editor of *Tinsley's Magazine* published a good deal of Irish writing; he was a member of the Southwark Literary Club, one of the early forums of the Irish Literary Revival; he became a partner in Ward & Downey that published Irish novels (including his own): see Stephen J. Brown, *Ireland in Fiction*, pp. 91, 342.

25. These publishers 'played the market' by offering novels in variously priced editions, sometimes arranged in attractively named series. For example, Chatto & Windus in 1900 published The Piccadilly Novels (3*s* 6*d* each), The Mayfair Library (2*s* 6*d*), The Golden Library (2*s*), Handy Novels (1*s* 6*d*), and Popular Sixpenny Novels (1*s* in cloth). Methuen's 'Sevenpenny Novels' included novels by Croker and Meade, Methuen's 'Shilling Novels' included novels by Croker, Birmingham, Somerville and Ross, and Conyers. Sutherland's earlier research on fiction publishers in the Victorian period is supplemented by Simon Eliot's essay, 'The Business of Victorian Publishing', *The Cambridge Companion to the Victorian Novel*, ed. Deirdre David (Cambridge: Cambridge University Press, 2001), pp.37–60, in which he accounts for print runs, reprintings, editions, and copyright trading among other topics. Several Irish novels were published on the Continent by Tauchnitz of Leipzig as part of their Library of British and American Authors, which began in 1841 and by 1908 numbered 4,000 titles; Tauchnitz published fresh editions and new impressions of the same novel; see The British Library: 'Todd-Bowden Collection of Tauchnitz Editions,' http://www.bl.uk/collections/tauch.html and 'Tauchnitz,' http://www.75.1911encyclopedia.org/T/TA/TAUCHNITZ.htm

26. Katharine Tynan, *The Middle Years* (London: Constable & Company, 1916), p. 192.

27. *The Middle Years*, p. 192. Stephen J. Brown, *Ireland in Fiction*, p. 204. Tynan dedicated her novel *The Golden Rose* (1924) to Mathew for 'the Wood of the Brambles'.

28. According to John Kelly and Eric Domville, editors of *The Collected Letters of W. B. Yeats*, vol. I: *1865–1895* (Oxford: Clarendon Press, 1986), p. 516, Tynan was born in 1859 and not in 1861 as she always claimed.

29. Tynan, *The Middle Years*, pp. 96, 405, 201–08, 295.

30. Tynan, *The Wandering Years* (London: Constable, 1922), p. 257. The historical novelist and detective writer M. McDonnell Bodkin was an even richer compound of attitudes and identities: deputy editor of *United Ireland*, KC and QC (King's Counsel, Queen's Counsel), nationalist M.P., a hero-worshipper of Gladstone who thought the English parliament the greatest club in the world, an Irish county court judge. Political polarization in the second decade of the twentieth century simplified public attitudes, and even identities, among Irish writers and citizens as well as politicians.

31. Tynan, *The Middle Years*, pp. 212–13, 221.

32. Tynan, *A Cluster of Nuts*, p. 168.

33. Katharine Tynan, *Cousins and Others* (London: T. Werner Laurie, [1909]), p. 138.

34. 'The Making of a Novelist', 658.

35. The distinguished literary sociologists, Rolf Loeber and Magda Stouthamer-Loeber, who have put Irish critics in their debt by recovering invaluable data, think it necessary to construe the Irish women's popular literary achievement negatively, in obedience to the nationalist dogma that Irish writers, especially women writers, in nineteenth-century England must have suffered and been discriminated against. By doing this, they allow nationalism to trump gender as it trumped social class, urban experience, and religion. Against the evidence of their own data, they insist on seeing 'barriers to authorship experienced by Irish women writers', claim that any fame or fortune 'tended to be short-lived', and describe the attempts of Irish women writers to live and publish in England or the 'British colonies' as 'struggles' (that loaded Irish term). But the experiences of the middle-class and upper middle-class Irish women writers in England were for our purposes identical to those of English and Scottish women writers in England. In removing to England, the Irish women writers were not suffering cultural deficit and dislocation; their removal was not an 'exodus' (with its biblical overtones of suffering and exile) but what we nowadays call (with, if anything, less justification) 'migration' in the EU context, in this case migration towards the publishing capital. The attempt to isolate the experiences of the Irish women writers—irrespective of their geographical, class, religious, or political identities—is clearly made by analogy with the nationalist reading of all Irish experience as exceptional and lamentable. L. T. Meade, Katharine Tynan, Mrs J. H. Riddell, M. E. Francis, or B. M. Croker would be amazed, and probably angry, to find themselves recruited as Irish gender martyrs. I regard the accomplishments of the Irish women writers, in England or in Ireland, as an occasion for unalloyed celebration. See Loeber and Stouthamer-Loeber, 'Literary Absentees: Irish Women Authors in Nineteenth-Century England', in *The Irish Novel in the Nineteenth Century*, ed. Jacqueline Belanger (Dublin: Four Courts Press, 2005), pp. 167–86.

36. M. McDonnell Bodkin, *Recollections of an Irish Judge* (London: Hurst and Blackett, 1914), pp. 122–6.

37. William O'Brien, 'London Revisited', *The Contemporary Review* 69 (1896): 805–812. I discuss O'Brien's novel briefly in *Fictions of the Irish Literary Revival* (Dublin: Gill & Macmillan; Syracuse: Syracuse University Press, 1987), pp. 4–5. For biographical

facts about O'Brien, see R. F. Foster, *Modern Ireland 1600–1972* (1988; London: Penguin Books, 1989), p. 409n.

38. M. E. Francis, *In a North Country Village* (Boston: Little, Brown; London: Osgood, McIlwaine, 1893), p. 57.

39. Francis published *The Manor Farm: A Novel* in 1902 which Kemp, et al. summarise as 'about two cousins in a farming family, Beulah and Reuben, who rebel against the family order that they should marry, but then fall in love after all': *Edwardian Fiction: An Oxford Companion*, ed. Sandra Kemp, Charlotte Mitchell, and David Trotter (Oxford: Oxford University Press, 1997), s.v. FRANCIS, M.E.

40. Francis was born Mary Sweetman into a landowning Catholic family near Dublin. In 1879 she married Francis Blundell of the Catholic gentry in Lancashire and lived the rest of her life at Crosby, a village in that county. She lived at Crosby Hall with her husband's family and is buried in Little Crosby graveyard. The census record for 1881 and the text and photograph of her headstone are available at http://www.sunnyfields.freeserve.co.uk; the census record lists her husband as a land agent; there were ten servants employed at Crosby Hall. Her husband died in 1884. Besides a large number of novels, she published prayers, meditations, and other religious books, some disseminated by the Catholic Truth Society, and a couple of books on Dorset. She appears to have co-written at least two novels with her daughter, Agnes Blundell (1884–1966), at least one with Margaret Blundell (1857–1930), perhaps a sister-in-law, and at least two with her daughter, Margaret (1881 or 1882–1964). She was educated in Belgium at a convent, as were her sisters. One sister, Elinor Sweetman, published at least four volumes of verse between 1893 and 1911. Another sister, Agnes (1860–1922), married Egerton Castle (1858–1920) of London and with him she wrote at least forty-five books, many of them historical romances, often hugely successful commercially if not critically; Agnes wrote at least three books by herself while he wrote at least fifteen without her aid. For assorted biographical facts see *A Round Table of the Representative Irish and English Catholic Novelists* and *Edwardian Fiction: An Oxford Companion* (1997), s.v. FRANCIS, M.E. A biographical study of the literary Sweetmans, Blundells, and Castles would be welcome.

41. Lewis, 'High and Low Brows,' in *Rehabilitations and Other Essays* (London: Oxford University Press, 1939), pp. 97–116.

42. Klingopulos, 'The Literary Scene,' in *The Pelican Guide to English Literature: From Dickens to Hardy* (Harmondsworth: Penguin, 1958; rev. 1963), pp. 100, 104.

43. John Carey, Preface to *The Intellectuals and the Masses* (London: Faber and Faber, 1992).

44. Richard Ellmann, *James Joyce* (Oxford: Oxford University Press, 1983), p. 400.

45. E. F. Bleiler, 'L. T. Meade' in *Twentieth-Century Crime and Mystery Writers*, ed. John M. Reilly (New York: St Martin's Press, 1985), p. 641.

46. Katharine Tynan's description of Meade is in her revised version of Charles A. Read's *Cabinet of Irish Literature* (1879; London: Gresham Publishing Company, 1902), vol. 4, p.193. Tynan's comments on her lack of typing can be found in *The Years of the Shadow* (London: Constable, 1919), p. 176.

47. 'Fashion in Fiction', 535–6.
48. Furniss, *Some Victorian Women*, p. 33.
49. Seth Koven quotes Black's *Pen, Pencil, Baton and Mask* (1896) in *Slumming: Sexual and Social Politics in Victorian London* (Princeton: Princeton University Press, 2004), p. 215.
50. Black, *Notable Women Authors of the Day*, p. 20.
51. Black's observation is offered as an Appendix to B. M. Croker, *'Number Ninety' and Other Ghost Stories*, ed. Richard Dalby, p. xi.
52. 'The Triumph of the Woman Novelist', *The Review of Reviews* 36 (1907): 69.
53. Mrs J. H. Riddell, *A Struggle for Fame: A Novel* (1883; London: Sampson Low, Marston & Co., 1900), p. 102. There is a lengthy reading of this novel, together with observations on contemporary publishing practices, in Margaret Kelleher, 'Charlotte Riddell's *A Struggle for Fame*: The Field of Women's Literary Production,' *Colby Quarterly* 36.2 (June 2000): 116–131.
54. Furniss, *Some Victorian Women*, pp. 6, 25.
55. Black, *Notable Women Authors of the Day*, p. 62.
56. Richard Dalby, Introduction to B. M. Croker,*'Number Ninety' and Other Ghost Stories*, p. x. Another source identifies John Stokes Croker's regiment as the Royal Scots Fusiliers: http://home.freeuk.net/sarobpress/html/books_out_of_print.html
57. Furniss, *Some Victorian Women*, pp. 39, 10, 9, 6–7.
58. 'The Fifth Edition', repr. in *Daughters of Decadence: Women Writers of the* Fin de Siècle, ed. Elaine Showalter (London: Virago Press, 1993).
59. Black, *Notable Women Authors of the Day*, pp. 112–13.
60. Tynan, *The Middle Years*, pp. 329, 5, 73, 211, 294.
61. Tynan, *The Wandering Years*, p. 70.
62. Tynan, *The Middle Years*, p. 315.
63. Elisabeth Boyd Bayly, *The Author of 'The Spanish Brothers' (Deborah Alcock): Her Life and Works* (London: Marshall Brothers, n.d.[1914]), p. 180.
64. Black, *Notable Women Authors of the Day*, p. 64.
65. *Ideala: A Study from Life* (1888; London: William Heinemann, 1894), p. 256.
66. *The Beth Book: Being a Study from the Life of Elizabeth Caldwell Maclure, A Woman of Genius* (1897; London: William Heinemann, 1898), p. 146.
67. 'Fashion in Fiction', 803. In *A Pitiless Passion* (New York: Macmillan, 1895), Ella MacMahon has one character describe his friend's attitude to a drunken woman as an outdated pose and add, in Wildean fashion: 'No one could make it pay,— except, perhaps, a lady novelist. But then lady novelists make so many things pay, including, I understand, their own novels' (p. 4). *A Pitiless Passion* is listed in the catalogues of COPAC and BLPC as *A Pitiful Passion*, indicating a transatlantic difference of title.
68. Yeats, quoted by Tynan, *The Middle Years*, pp. 67, 71.
69. Letter reproduced in *The Essays of Oscar Wilde* (New York: Cosmopolitan Book Corp., 1916), p. 561. Among Wilde's witty dicta of the kind that made him paradoxically popular was the one that appeared in his *Soul of Man Under Socialism*: 'Art should never try to be popular; the public should try to make itself artistic.'

70. W. B. Yeats, 'Modern Ireland', an address to American audiences printed in *Massachusetts Review* 5 (1964): 256–68.

71. In his review of Rosa Mulholland's *Marcella Grace*: see *The Essays of Oscar Wilde*, p. 343.

72. Mrs Victor Rickard, *The Fire of Green Boughs* (New York: Dodd, Mead and Company, 1919), p. 162.

73. And so, for example, the chapters in *The Cambridge Companion to the Victorian Novel* (2001), ed. Deirdre David, devoted to race, gender, detection, religion, the fantastic and supernatural, throw light on the Irish novels of the period as well, and we need not regard the Irish novels as mere inflections of the English.

74. Claud Cockburn, *Bestseller: The Books that Everyone Read 1900–1939* (London: Sidgwick & Jackson, 1972), pp. 61–2. T. H. Green published *An Estimate of the Value and Influence of Works of Fiction in Modern Times* in 1862 (republished 1911).

75. Cockburn, *Bestseller*, pp. 7, 8, 13.

76. Ibid., 14.

77. Or even broader political relations. Cf. Janice Hubbard Harris' citation of Phyllis Rose's contention that an individual's sense of 'husband' and 'wife' reflects his or her sense of 'liberty' and 'authority': *Edwardian Stories of Divorce* (New Brunswick, NJ: Rutgers University Press, 1996), p. 4.

78. I discuss the Revival literary project in *Fictions of the Irish Literary Revival* (1987).

79. Cockburn, *Bestseller*, p. 4.

80. Ibid., 68.

81. H. de Vere Stacpoole, *The Blue Lagoon* (London: Fisher Unwin, 1908), pp. 72–3.

2

'When the Tide Turns': After the Victorians

POST-VICTORIAN MARRIAGE

Such works of fiction as I am discussing had no role in the evolving Irish 'grand narrative' which owes its coherence in part to their absence. Of course, many popular novels deserved no role in *any* narrative of substance. The editor of *Blackwood's* was right in identifying love and sensation as essential elements of penny fiction. But in the case of love, he is speaking of silly, hackneyed, and formulaic treatments of this subject and plot-element. Lady Halliday in Ella MacMahon's *A Pitiless Passion* (1895) remarks airily of a new and apparently artistic magazine: 'I don't see anything new about it . . . It's full of pictures and love stories like any other magazine.'[1] The narrative voice of MacMahon's *A New Note* (1894) refers to 'bridal dresses which forlorn maidens in romantic novels are continually finding in old trunks'.[2] For love in all its inflections—flirtation, wooing, seduction, sexual response and expression, fidelity, betrayal—helped compose the novel from the beginning, and Ian Watt in *The Rise of the Novel* devotes a chapter to Richardson's treatment of it in *Pamela* (1740–1) in which he charts its evolving concept and relates it to the intricately allied components of courtly love, social class, marriage, the family, and the heroine.[3]

It will be necessary to return later to love and marriage, both of which in the better Irish novels were developing into something complex in the late Victorian period, what MacMahon in her own voice in *A Pitiless Passion* describes as 'the relationship between the sexes, as we like to call it now',[4] suggesting a new contemporary perception of an old and fascinating theme in human nature. In 1913 D. H. Lawrence was sure that relations between men and women was '*the* problem of today, the establishment of a new relation, or the readjustment of the old one'.[5] In the course of outlining a pioneering case for women's rights in 1869, including the right to work and equal rights in strictly voluntary marriage, the famous English activist, Josephine Butler, nevertheless declared that whereas women had had enough of emotion and sentiment which education should lessen, 'we need—together with other and higher influences—a revival of the grave and romantic ideas of love which have prevailed in happier periods of human history, and which can never wholly perish'. Such love can only flourish when the woman is free and respected; under those circumstances marriage will itself flourish whereas it will surely decline if men continue to think of it as women's only salvation. We can view the theme of love in the best and most serious popular novels of the generation after Butler in the circumstances described by her.[6]

One aspect of the new perception was the wish to distinguish love from marriage and to scrutinize their separate identities and dynamics. Marriage itself was to come under scrutiny socially, culturally, and legally in the late Victorian and Edwardian periods and after.[7] Indeed, in 1894 Sarah Grand stated simply: 'The Woman Question is the Marriage Question.'[8] The cultural–historical evidence that the institution had not always, and everywhere, been as it was now, that it is a changeable cultural construct, was furnished by the anthropologist Edward Westermarck who published his influential *History of Human Marriage* in 1889 (a third edition appeared in 1901 and a fifth in 1921).[9] In *When the Red Gods Call* (1911), her novel set in British New Guinea, the Co. Antrim writer Beatrice Grimshaw (1871–1953) drew on her intimate knowledge of the far-flung colony to depict, among other things, a marriage between a restless and hard-bitten Irish trader, pearl-fisher, and gold-digger (Hugh Lynch from Co. Clare) and Kari, a Papuan native girl. The marriage is a mistake: 'When a white man marries a native woman, he commits the unforgivable sin—folly.'[10] The cross-cultural union ends in fatal misadventure; a white man steals Kari, provoking his own murder and Kari's drowning.

When, soon after the death of his native wife, the 30-year-old Lynch meets the 19-year-old daughter of the Governor, he realises that the 'little savage' (Kari) had not been his true wife. 'As for calling it a marriage—why, in the sight of heaven (if there be a heaven) it was no marriage at all, whatever earthly laws might say' (p. 227). Nor was he truly married to the Spanish woman who had been his mate in South America. Grimshaw does not mean Lynch to be an opportunist or hypocrite, rationalizing away a Papuan marriage that would not stand him in good stead with respectable whites and future in-laws. In fact, Grimshaw means to connect marriage with love of an intense kind; race is an issue but not the paramount factor. 'Marriage, it seemed to me,' says Lynch, 'even the shadow of marriage to come, changed life upwards from the root' (p. 189). His marriage to Stephanie is different not just because it is to a white woman, an Englishwoman (the wedding is, in any case, a rough colonial affair), but also because it is a form of soul-bonding, and induces in Lynch, normally taciturn of thought, a piece of comparative anthropological introspection on the institution. Lynch has learned his love-making in Spanish America but his love for Stephanie is deeper and wider: 'Love of the body—companionship of the mind—and of the soul, what?' It is a case of 'true marriage' (p. 190) and we will later meet numerous examples in other novels.

Despite the wildness of her settings, Grimshaw embraces a Catholic sense of the indissolubility of marriage, a sense that is passed on to the Protestant Stephanie by a Catholic priest in London, as a result of which Stephanie comes to see that her loyalty to a murderer who happens to be her lawfully wedded husband is more important than his crime. Stephanie is refused divorce from all quarters while her husband lives. She comes to accept these refusals, awaits news of her husband's death for ten years, blaming him for their predicament, seeking at length to enter a convent. Although the priest dismisses Stephanie's request to become a nun, what occurs in Stephanie is a kind of conversion, a pale reflection of Grimshaw's own conversion to Catholicism. It is the Catholic priest who shows her the error of her attitude and her mistake, indeed her sin, in not standing by her husband during his arrest, trial, and conviction. She returns to New Guinea to find the husband she deserted on their honeymoon. It is as if Grimshaw's conversion in Dublin was to a faith that survived her exposure, in primitive New Guinea and elsewhere, to other kinds of marriage and cohabitation. This conservative perception of love and marriage recurs in Grimshaw; it is typically tested not just by exotic alternatives but by the anomalies of affairs and separations in British marriages; divorce is discountenanced and affairs are abortive and, if necessary, sexual and emotional fulfilment is postponed until a spouse's death. It is this conservative perception that prevents *When the Red Gods Call* from depicting a truly Conradian heart of imperial darkness. This despite the fact that the novel is strong enough meat to prevent it from being labelled a romance, if for no other reason than its virtual obsession with cannibalism.[11]

Notwithstanding the exotic locations and unfamiliar ethnic pressures and opportunities in her novel, Grimshaw registers a change back in Britain in the protocols of marriage. When faced with the customary prospect of asking the Governor for his daughter's hand, a request certain to be denied, Lynch is of the opinion that such a custom of dependency is outmoded. 'In the latter end of the nineteenth century, a girl who is of age, and a man who knows his own mind, don't eat out their hearts and wear away their youth waiting for one another, simply because an early-Victorian parent chooses to deny that intangible "blessing" so dear to the soul of the novelist. They just manage to get on without it, and the story closes at the second chapter, which would not do at all in a three-hundred page novel, but is quite satisfactory in real life' (pp. 211–12). This is echoed in MacMahon's *The Job* (1914) by Lady Hexham who confesses to Thady Muntfort her bewilderment at young women's attitudes to marriage. In her day marriage was simply expected and was a passive affair: 'we were more "given", I think, than in these days. They ought to take that out of the marriage service. No one gives away a girl now', any more than a girl can be influenced in her choice of husband: 'Who ever heard of a girl in these days allowing herself to be influenced?'[12]

As it happened, Grimshaw, unlike her characters Lynch or Stephanie, did not assert her own independence from her Victorian parents by choosing her mate without the consent of parents; she remained unmarried, which in her day could be its own form of self-assertion, though she enjoyed (apparently) her singleness a world away from the customs and constraints of British and Irish society, some of which were in any case changing and loosening. Yet she was attracted time and again to relationships and marriages as themes, highlighting them as issues by placing them in exotic or otherwise challenging situations.

The pages of *When the Red Gods Call* in which Stephanie seeks and fails to arrange a divorce are a portion of the novel that inhabits the contemporary context of heated debate on the 'Divorce Question' in the United Kingdom. Grimshaw may have been opposed to divorce (at least for Catholics) but many Britons were for it; for some time divorce had been the rare, disturbing, and denied twin of marriage, with legal separation the common and unsatisfactory shadow between them. In the very year Grimshaw's novel appeared, a Royal Commission was conducting hearings on divorce and matrimonial causes and published its minutes of evidence in 1912. The commission recommended putting men and women on equal footing as regards grounds for divorce. As it was, a man had to prove only his wife's adultery, a woman her husband's adultery plus cruelty or desertion. This recommendation was not translated into law until 1923. A second recommendation was the addition of extra grounds for divorce. These were legally added in 1937. A third recommendation, to end discrimination against the poor who could not afford their own or witnesses' transport to the London divorce court, was not implemented until 1967, when jurisdiction over divorce trials was extended beyond London.[13]

The Divorce Question was one of the watersheds between Victorian and twentieth-century Britain and the debate it generated found its way obliquely through plot, and directly through dialogue and narratorial interventions, into novels and short stories of the day. These were fictions set in England by either English or Irish writers, since divorce in Ireland was not the same burning issue as in England. The Divorce and Matrimonial Causes Act of 1857, which many were campaigning to change, had not been extended to Ireland, nor was it protested much that this was wrong. Between 1857 and 1910, there were only thirty-nine divorces granted to Irish residents, no doubt because anyone there seeking a divorce had to submit a private bill to parliament and because the costs involved in doing so exceeded £500 in 1910.[14] But of course, many middle-class, upper-middle-class, and aristocratic Irish lived across the water (or could remove there) and so could avail themselves of divorce provisions, though in an English rather than Irish context. In her study of British 'divorce novels', *Edwardian Stories of Divorce* (1996), Janice Hubbard Harris briefly discusses three Irish divorce novels: *The First Claim* (1906) by M. Hamilton; *The Crumpled Leaf: A Vatican Mystery* (1911) by Mrs Alexander (Annie French Hector); and *The Serpent's Tooth* (1912) by B. M. Croker.

NEW NOTES

Beyond marriage, society in Ireland and Britain was changing in a variety of ways in the last third of the nineteenth century, and several Irish novels register the shared experience of those changes. The changes were seen, as in Grimshaw's novel, as the emancipatory yet troubling transition from early Victorianism to later Victorianism (and then Edwardianism); we would now see it as a transition from Victorianism to modernity. The Victorian frame of mind, to borrow the title of a well-known study of the mentality of the time, was being transformed.[15] Among Victorian preoccupations, values, and concerns, Walter E. Houghton's identification and discussion of science, doubt, evangelicalism, machinery, racism, moral earnestness, patriotism, love, womanhood, manhood, and Darwinism—all crucial issues—share a direct relevance not only to English society but also to sizeable segments of Irish society that have tended to be neglected by Irish historians and cultural commentators because those segments were not uniquely Irish.

Popular novelists paid especial attention when the changing frame of mind involved relations between men and women and the social representation of the male and female. Merton Byng in *A Modern Man* (1895) by the Dublin-born and London-domiciled Ella MacMahon is depicted as a representative of the emerging male generation.[16] The novel, set in upper-class London in townhouses and gentlemen's clubs, is a portrait of a vain, ambitious, and opportunistic barrister who is rescued and redeemed by the love of a good—and superior—woman. The modernity of the novel lies not only in the cleverness and wittiness of the 1890s narrative style (at one point a woman character fans herself with a copy of the modish magazine, *Black and White*) but in the strength of the New Woman (here it is Muriel Pomfret) who deigns to accept the finally humbled Byng. Women do not get off scot-free; amidst the novel's brisk epigrams is the arch observation that 'If women only married men who had a nice sense of honour the world would soon come to an end'.[17] And there may be some regret in the narrator's terminal remark—Byng having failed to deceive his new wife into thinking that he had rejected

Sibyl Llewellen for her when in fact Sibyl had rebuffed him—that 'to be a hero to one's wife is, it would seem, seldom permitted to the modern man'.

But MacMahon's novels convey the idea that times have changed drastically and irreversibly when it comes to relations between the sexes. If Merton Byng is a modern and therefore rather hapless young man, then Victoria Leathley in *A New Note* (1894) is a modern young woman, who suffers none of the condescension the author inflicts on Byng and, perhaps, on the cigarette-smoking young red-haired woman Byng meets on a train—'a charming specimen of the new humanity...Age I shall say about twenty-three. Sex feminine—er—at least, hybrid' (p. 89). *A New Note* is set in Berkshire, London, and Connacht, with the opening chapters taking place in 1888 and the main events unfolding in 1891. In the course of tracking the artistic career of Victoria Leathley, a young English violinist, MacMahon engages with many of the issues of the day that troubled lively or gifted women, including the conflicts between love and marriage, between marriage and career, and between all three and the artistic calling. (The conflicts between Ireland and England, gentlemanliness and caddishness, celebrity and happiness, do not affect women alone but they are part of the warp and weft of the novel.) MacMahon creates Victoria as a vivid child of 'the New Age' which preaches a 'New Doctrine', and the conflict within Victoria between the pull of the old and the pull of the new provides the chief drama of the novel. Her father, a Liberal MP (who dislikes 'the heavy-father business'—a phrase which strikes an oddly modern note), believes in the 'gradual progress of the human race' but his cousin, Victoria's Aunt Doll, is firmly 'Early Victorian' ('everything is topsy-turvy', she complains), and disbelieves in any such possibility—an earnest version of the Wildean pseudo-conservatism of the character Conway Keppel, who wishes to start a 'Society for the Disimprovement of the Human Race' and 'resolve' marriage and 'the British Parent' 'into a historic reminiscence', echoing Aunt Doll's lament that 'the feminine outlook...will soon be an historic reminiscence',[18] by which she means that strong female outlook that preceded feminism. The difficult succession from Victorianism to modernity is thrashed out in two scenes, one between George and Dora (Aunt Doll) and one between Victoria and her aunt. MacMahon's resolution of that succession as it plays itself out in Victoria's life transgresses the bounds of the popular romance, as will become clear later.

Meanwhile, Victoria's aunt finds her counterpart in Mrs Hamlyn, a character in L. T. Meade's *The Cleverest Woman in England* (1898) who would have disdained Victoria's wish for a public career as she disdains her new daughter-in-law's involvement in radical feminist politics and whom she tells: 'I am old-fashioned, I have been brought up to look upon the home as sacred, the wifely duties as coming first of all. The restlessness, the craving for publicity in the modern woman, are extremely repugnant to me.'[19] The aunts in Annie M. P. Smithson's *Her Irish Heritage* (1917) look upon the younger generation 'with a sort of surprised horror' and dislike for its class inappropriateness the social work their nieces engage in.[20] Another spokeswoman for Victorianism is MacMahon's Lady Hexham, who finds equally repugnant (though her attitude is tinged with admiration) the modern young woman's desire to be useful and practical. Ria Devereux in *The Job* is 'modern', Lady Hexham laments, 'witness the horrible type-writing business... Ria was unfortunately touched (Lady Hexham never could understand how), but she *was* touched by that dreadful spirit of independence—so-called—abroad in the present day'. But although Ria Devereux is an athletic, outdoor young woman (an exhibition swimmer)—a version of the new woman alfresco we will encounter later, though she refuses to embrace the category 'new woman'—Lady Hexham's explanation for the origin and dissemination of this spirit is medical with a Wildean flair. The press in young women to be useful derives, she thinks, from 'having a Radical Government so long in, don't you think? The air gets infested with germs of—of that sort, I can't see why it shouldn't be so, as well as with influenza, or—or—anything else; and women are susceptible to germs and—and—so Ria would go to that dreadful place to learn typewriting and shorthand. She's very clever, for I'm told that shorthand is more difficult to learn than Greek—.'[21] To Thady Muntfort, she adds: 'You know Greek, of course... but I dare say you don't know shorthand, so perhaps you can't tell me why it is harder than Greek' (pp. 126–7).

An equally graphic female embodiment of early Victorian attitudes and values inhabits *The Rambling Rector* (1904) by Eleanor Alexander (1857–1939), a trivial-sounding serious novel about an unworldly and undistinguished curate, Geoffrey Owen, who becomes a rector and is ill-fitted, both by temperament and belief, for the promotion. The setting is 'southern Ulster', a 'drowsy Cathedral town' which surely must be Armagh; the reference to 'the late Coronation' (Edward VII was crowned in August 1902) dates the action of the novel to 1902 or 1903.[22] Owen's aunt, Jane Owen, threatens to overshadow him as a character in the novel, and the story involves her frozen Victorian posture being thawed by the attentions of the returned Yank and wealthy businessman, Jimmy O'Loughlin. When the local schoolmaster makes a disparaging remark about Disraeli, Miss Owen (and her appellations 'aunt' and 'Miss' are a kind of shorthand for her Victorianism) stiffens: 'Aunt Jane belonged to the simple type of old-fashioned Conservatives who still looked on Lord Beaconsfield as nearly the saviour of his country.' Having 'all the refinement of the early part of the nineteenth century', she is outraged when O'Loughlin, a man returned from the New World with money on his lips, uses the word 'bigamy': 'Miss Owen rose and drew her shawl round her.

She moved majestically towards the fire and made as though she were warming her hands' (pp. 231, 96). O'Loughlin has the effrontery to ask for her hand with accompanying endearments and though she refuses him, duly affronted, tears come unbidden when he leaves, because her suitor is a tradesman (she snobbishly insists on believing), because his suit betrays temerity, because in any case he and it had come too late, but finally because the girl he imagines she had been—and whom he had married (only in his retroactive imagination) forty years before, walking with her lover, hearing the blackbirds sing beside a river—never existed. Her resentment dissolves into profound regret and sense of loss; his recalled endearments 'led her to realise for the first time all that she had lost in life.' It is a moving epiphany (pp. 162–3). He occupies the new world, she the old and her challenge is to make the enormous leap from one to the other.

The Rambling Rector is a species of domestic realism, as are many of these neglected novels, with a developed sense of locality (Alexander employs Ulster–Scots dialect words and phrases with discrimination). There are lingering descriptions of rooms, furniture and decor, clothes, and of physiques and facial expressions; and the work and leisure of large houses and grounds—they compose the literary equivalent of genre painting. If the observation is sometimes ponderous, advertently or inadvertently arch, there are several fine descriptive passages, for example of the Ulster countryside (pp. 37–8), and this impressionistic depiction of a smithy:

[Geoffrey] saw the great bellows moving, and the sparks flying from the furnace. Then the clang of the smith's heavy hammer fell on the silence of the night . . . The red and orange lights; the tawny shadows in the corners of the forge; the unholy blue that dazzled the eyes when the hissing iron was struck; the pose of the smith's figure bent backwards for the stroke, with every muscle in high relief; the bronze of his face, when the lifted arms had fallen, and it showed out strongly for a few seconds like an antique bust—all appealed to that artistic temperament which Mr. Owen had not the least suspicion that he possessed . . . he turned again to the white harmony of the starlight; the thick, blue shadows under the hedges; the manifold tones of grey on the road, and on the white- washed barn that stood clear of any yellow spark from the companion picture still hanging in the retina of his eye. Two matched Morelands on corresponding panels—a glowing interior, and a sombre scene of outdoor tranquillity. (p. 107)

The trysts, letters read and unread, assignations met and missed, misadventures, illnesses, and faintings—these propel the narrative and transform domestic realism into low-intensity romantic realism. But this novel has the inherited amplitude of the Victorian three-decker and demonstrates Alexander's controlling intelligence. In the scene (pp. 188–92) in which Hester Sullivan recounts by way of confession to Geoffrey her involvement with the philandering Count Eugene, Geoffrey's simultaneously growing awareness of his own inadequate worldliness is in descant to her own oblique recollections. There are echoes of Conrad's muffled indirection; it is a fine piece of narrative interiority of the kind we associate with modernism.

This novel, like many of the others, depicts a society of social barriers, constraining etiquette and manners (which Jimmy O'Loughlin flouts) and prescribed behaviour (of which he is in violation). In Riddell's *A Rich Man's Daughter* (1895), an inferior effort to Alexander's, Miss Loveland (Amabel Osberton's Aunt Dulce), though not yet fifty, belongs to the old school and holds fast to rules of decorum unlike the outspoken young who know no reverence, 'the modern want'.[23] But it is Alexander's own painstaking scenting out of honesty that makes *The Rambling Rector* a post-Victorian novel . The appurtenances of modernity make their appearance, too: it is 'the golden age of bicycles'—the chosen and readily available vehicle of the New Woman— telegraph poles cross the countryside, and a factory horn blows in the town.

The once scandalous and highly praised novel *The Sands of Pleasure* (1905) by the Co. Antrim-born writer Filson Young (1876–1938) also plots the end of an era and through one major character's eyes looks back in anger to Victorianism; the impersonal narrator is recounting events in the past, prob- ably the late 1880s (the Montmartre cemetery holds the body of Offenbach who died in 1880). The voice of the novel, two decades on, is unmistakably twentieth-century. When the protagonist of the novel, the marine engineer Richard Grey, confesses that 'I can't get on with the Early Victorians—I'm too near them, I suppose. Talk of granite', the pre-1880s Victorian age is obituar- ized by John Lauder as 'the Albert Period . . . the period of South Kensington, the Crystal Palace, the Albert Memorial; the streaming whisker and flying coat-tail period; the deadly period of English prosperity and happiness. A good man unfortunately gave his name to a whole age of silliness— Albertism . . . the age of shams and symbols . . . People had no opinions; they had beliefs . . . Look at their works, their tastes! Frith, Landseer, Mendelssohn, Cowper, and South Kensington! A long age of vaporish meditation results in—the Crystal Palace.'[24] Grey inhabits that Victorian world of hard work, stern morality, and staunch Christian belief, but in Paris on business he falls in love with a prostitute and frequents the world of pleasure, art and agnosticism, atheism and paganism. Young felt his picture of Parisian cocottes required a prefatory explanation, 'To the Reader,' because 'in this age good taste greatly busies itself about matters of social morality',[25] and it seems as if the novel provoked outrage among some in England.

In the novel, Parisian bohemia is seen from one angle, certainly by Lauder, as a desirable, seductive French future for the English present, but it is also seen as a threat, a social disorder, and Grey turns his back on Paris and Toni the *demi-mondaine* and returns to Cornwall to finish the lighthouse he is building, a symbol of confidence, work, faith, and stability in the face of flux. Young anticipates Virginia Woolf's use of the lighthouse as a beacon, destination, a fixed point amidst the waves, but his is the more real; Young after all wrote a masterly account of *Titanic* and its sinking (a ship and an event said by some at the time to form a watershed between epochs); Robert Louis Stevenson's family's hands-on involvement with lighthouses is recalled, and Stevenson and Shaw are authors whom Grey likes and who are mocked by Lauder before they travel to Paris and Grey's bohemian adventure in love and life begins.[26]

The influences suffusing the two sites of Grey's engagement with the world, the Cornish coast and bohemian Paris, are like incoming and outflowing tides, and Grey is caught as it were in that uncertain time and place between tides. This in fact is the master theme and motif of this book and others by Young, including *Ireland at the Cross Roads* (1903), *When the Tide Turns* (1908, a novel), and *Titanic* (1912). Its distant real-life origin was perhaps in that remarkable turbulent meeting of two tides between the villages of Portaferry and Strangford in Co. Down called the Narrows, an apt metaphor for the intensity of a novel that tries to harness briefly what Lauder calls 'the vital force of the world'.[27] Strangford Lough appears at length in *When the Tide Turns* (1908); the name of Lady Killard in *The Sands of Pleasure* is a nod to the vicinity (Killard Point, near the village of Strangford, across the Narrows). It is a theme—tides in the affairs of men, countries, and cultures—that either stems from, or explains, Young's strong journalistic, documentary impulse. This impulse is often not enough to quell Young's ambition to write finely—when as a result he labours and over-writes. In this respect he learned little from the famous 'scrupulous meanness' of *Dubliners*, of which collection of stories he approved and as publisher's reader recommended in early 1906 to Grant Richards for publication.[28] Young's best Irish books are the documentary accounts, enlivened by personal engagement, *Titanic* and *Ireland at the Cross Roads*, two fine prose achievements that also hymn the best of the modern age, the finest Victorian accomplishments carried over into his own day.

I will have occasion to return to the second book. As for the first, Young was not as prolific as many contemporary writers but fleeter than most, for *Titanic* was on the bookshelves three weeks after the disaster. Yet this suggests less Young's commercial opportunism than the deep feeling the wreck aroused in someone who had been born near Belfast and spent each summer as a boy in Ulster. With the pace of a novel, *Titanic* (which begins with the chopping tides of Belfast Lough) showed, as North puts it, the hierarchical layers of Victorian and Edwardian society being upended on the ship during the calamity. *Titanic* also records the alarm caused by the progress of machines in the Victorian period. This ship, earth's largest moving object until then, came to symbolize, in its death throes and after, widespread anxiety over the speed and size of machines and, more generally, over the human ambition that drove the building of such vast liners. Local pride in Belfast where the ship was built may have muffled such anxieties and alarm but as the only densely industrialized city in Ireland, Belfast participated in the troubled Zeitgeist of Victorian applied (as well as theoretical) science, as the local sermons that the sinking provoked—mixing pride with disapproval, hero-worship with Godfearingness—showed. In the building and launch of the ship, modernity reannounced itself but after the shipwreck an older orthodoxy and set of values tried to shore up the ruins, creating a turbulent cultural cross-current.[29]

THE ACHE OF MODERNISM

A New Note, The Rambling Rector, When the Red Gods Call, and *The Sands of Pleasure* are, then, four novels among many by Irish writers that try seriously to portray the competing tides of Victorianism and modernity. Thomas Hardy was famously trying the same thing, and in *Tess of the d'Urbervilles* (1891) he identified what he called 'the ache of modernism' (an early secular use of the term). Tess herself stands at the crossroads, though unaware of the nature of her predicament ('this hobble of being alive'). She is frightened of the future that is promised by the present, of the trees with prying eyes and the indifferent river, and the threatening queues of tomorrows, spoiling figures like the goblins in E. M. Forster's later *Howards End* (1910).[30] Hardy has a philosophy beyond the desire or capacity of the neglected Irish novelists I am discussing, and he explores the defining self-consciousness of advanced late Victorian (i.e. modern) humanity, in ways they do not. Yet when we set in its historical cultural context the ache of Tess and the other major characters in the novel (which is both a contemporary and a centuries-old ache) we can speak among other things of the collision of folk beliefs and customs with modern education, of Christianity with evolutionism, of nature and primitive agriculture with industrialism, of manual labour (with its direct relationship to the real world) with machinery, of natural or at least traditional behaviour with moral impositions. Versions of these collisions were happening in late nineteenth-century Ireland as well. One of the most acutely felt of them was the challenge posed to Christianity by the theory of evolution; it was felt more acutely in Protestant Ireland (especially the Presbyterian north) than in Catholic Ireland (where the laity silently took its cue from a hierarchy that was dogmatic and outwardly unruffled) and a quantity of sophisticated polemics and theory resulted from the cultural abrasion.[31]

Whereas novels that were popular in a generic sense—sensation novels, penny romances, detective novels, etc.—were written strictly for amusement, serious novels (however successful they were) were written to a purpose, to edify the reader; often they were what have been called problem-novels which dealt with social ills more specific than the difficult transition from the nineteenth to the twentieth century.[32] I have already mentioned novels in which the idea of divorce generates some of their complication. Only with James and Conrad and then with the high modernists did the idea of the novel as art (difficult art) take wider hold and the novel try to liberate itself from social obligation, which is why we do not think of *Howards End* as a modernist novel; it is, rather, a problem-novel *par excellence*. Forster's novel casts in fictional form many of the vexing issues of the day that were approaching, or had reached, a turn in the tide or even a crisis, including 'the Woman Question', the Class Question, 'the Marriage Question', the Two Nations (or Distribution of Wealth) Question, the Empire Question (though he treated this more fully in *A Passage to India*, 1924, where it is in part the Race Question or the East–West Question), the Country and the City problem (including the expanding Suburbs problem, the Nature vs. Society Question and the Folk-world vs Machine-world problem). Forster approaches 'the Irish Question' only obliquely as the gulf between Saxon and Celt; indeed, each of these 'Questions' involved a yawning gulf below which lay a dreaded abyss.[33] Hardy closed with some of these issues in *Tess* but Forster in *Howards End* broadens the scope of Hardy's foreground and gives us a veritable handbook to the troubling questions that beset the birth of our modern world, at the price, though, of the older novelist's tragic intensity.

Many of the Irish novelists were engaged with these questions too, either as English questions when their novels were set in Britain, or as Irish questions when their novels were set in Ireland. The questions when posed in Ireland had distinctive inflections. Many Irish were active participants in the Empire and so were face to face with the Race Question.[34] But in Ireland the Race Question was instead part of the Irish Question itself and concerned the power relations between the Anglo-Irish and the native (or Catholic) Irish in the south and between the Ulster Scots and the native (or Catholic) Irish in the north. In each part of Ireland, therefore, there was a version of the mainland Two Nations Question. The Irish Question also implicated the Class Question, since the simmering conflict was seen by many Irish and many English alike as a conflict between a privileged Anglo-Irish ruling caste and an underprivileged lower-class native Irishry. Of course, the issue for some was whether this was justified even if true. What is certainly true is that almost every historian and commentator who is remembered and who was conscripted into the debate simplified the conflict by ignoring the sizeable

Catholic middle class and even upper middle class, whose existence was thought, it seems, to impede a forseeable solution and thus to compose an awkward reality best overlooked.

In so engaging with such questions, the Irish novelists were essentially Victorian novelists who, as Jenni Calder reminds us, 'reflected in a peculiarly vivid and urgent way the social anxieties of their time', among these being crises and changes in the institution of marriage.[35] But the Irish novelists were also exercised by distinctively Irish social problems that were coming disturbingly into sharper focus in the late Victorian and Edwardian periods. The Irish Revival in so far as Yeats viewed it was to show scant interest in complicated foreground social issues, such as marriage and the family, that captured the attention of the Victorian and Edwardian novelists. The Revival was to concern itself instead with the aspiration towards a culture entirely different from what contemporary England and Ireland constituted. This ideal culture had political, even constitutional implications and subtexts that could be foregrounded as issues as the occasion demanded, especially the urgent, violent, or climactic occasion. Yeats's Revival also shared modernism's disdain for didacticism or purpose in literature: 'I hated and still hate with an ever growing hatred', he wrote in 1937 and thinking back to the 1880s, 'the literature of point of view.'[36] By this he would probably have included problem-novels, and yet the English novel has fictionalized social problems from the beginning, however directly or indirectly, and often from a 'point of view'. Moreover, the Irish problem-novels could be tracked back to what have been called the conservative Irish 'tales of the times' dating from the 1790s onwards (preceding the so-called national tales) which were provoked by varieties of social and moral decline and which didactically promoted varieties of moral and social restoration.[37] In any case, much Revival literature surely itself had a point of view and often thought of itself as serving the distinct purpose of national regeneration.

In 1893, Helen C. Black reconstructed a visit to a country house in England where Sarah Grand was the subject of discussion 'during the pleasant informal five o'clock tea hour'. Black reproduces the discussion from memory, giving herself the lion's role of defending Grand by explaining her, during which she claims that Grand's new novel, *The Heavenly Twins* (1893), is 'not what is ordinarily meant by "a novel with a purpose".'[38] inasmuch as Grand having created characters tried to let them develop according to principles of physiology and pathology (Black's words) as one would let creatures or cultures in a laboratory or nature reserve develop without further intervention (my words). But clearly Grand's novel had a purpose and point of view that Yeats would have detested. In her Preface to *Our Manifold Nature: Stories from Life* (1894)— her subtitle implicitly denying any purposeful manipulation—Grand said that these stories had appeared in magazines but had been mutilated for various reasons, successful magazines resisting inducements to 'air the grievances, touch upon the interests, or meet the special demands generally of the present generation'.[39] Mrs Houstoun claimed that one of her 'novelettes' not only had a purpose but also had a clear effect; she claimed that *Only a Woman's Life* (1889) succeeded in obtaining the release of a woman who had been convicted on circumstantial evidence for the murder of her child and who had already served twelve years.[40] I am sure that Dickens would have been thrilled to have had such concrete results from the campaigning portions of his novels. Perhaps a greater sense of grievance pervades Grand's pages than those of other Irish novelists I wish to discuss, but most of the novelists share a social concern. To be successful, Grand's own experiments with characters and plots in order to air her grievances nevertheless touch upon interests and meet broad contemporary demands, in her case all to do with relations between the sexes. Interestingly, neither the grievances nor the deep social concern has prevented her being hailed as a kind of modernist,[41] but this is at present a minority view and Grand is usually seen as a problem-novelist of radical if restricted purview: that of the proactive feminist.

Looking back from the other side of the Rubicon of the Great War, Sir Shane Leslie from Co. Monaghan—high-born, conservative, Catholic, fresh from active service—had a foreshortened view of 'Post-Victorianism'. *The End of a Chapter* (1918) is a memoir of the past seen through the prisms of caste, race, and religion. He tallies with distaste the symptoms of ailment in the period between the death of Victoria and the War: new movements were taken up and abandoned hastily; 'Everybody set out to break rules and supplant conventions'; patriotism came to be regarded as old-fashioned; 'To be serious was a social defect' (Wilde's mocking use of 'earnestness' chimes here); sinners were accepted: indeed, there were those who *affected* sinfulness and decadence; Browning and Tennyson were dismissed as 'grandmotherly'; instead, there was 'a feverish rechauffé of Wilde, Beardsley and Pater'.[42] This is an entertainingly ranting shopping-list but accounts for only one strain of society, one train of events, that came to pass in Ireland as well as Britain towards the close of Victoria's long reign.

NOTES

1. MacMahon, *A Pitiless Passion* (New York: Macmillan, 1895), p. 69.
2. MacMahon, *A New Note* (1894; New York: R. F. Fenno, 1895), p. 58.
3. Ian Watt, *The Rise of the Novel: Studies in Defoe, Richardson and Fielding* (1957; Berkeley: University of California Press, 1965), pp. 135–73.

4. MacMahon, *A Pitiless Passion*, p. 285.

5. Quoted by G. H. Bantock, 'The Social and Intellectual Background', in Boris Ford (ed.), *The Pelican Guide to English Literature 7: The Modern Age* (Harmondsworth: Penguin Books, 1964), p. 20.

6. Josephine E. Butler, Introduction to *Woman's Work and Woman's Culture: A Series of Essays*, ed. Butler (London: Macmillan, 1869), pp. xxxiii–iv.

7. Landmark parliamentary Acts in the United Kingdom that helped redress increasingly recognized inequalities of gender power in marriage included the Matrimonial Causes Act of 1878 (facilitating legal separation, maintenance for ill-used wives, and the award of legal custody of young children to a wife) and the Married Women's Property Act of 1882 (permitting their ownership of property and earnings). In a Chronology that she offers in her study *Women and Marriage in Victorian Fiction* (1976), Jenni Calder lists essays and books on marriage published between 1888 and 1913 by Mona Caird, Cicely Hamilton, H. G. Wells, and Elizabeth Sloane Chesser. Sarah Grand, too, was a prolific commentator on the institution. Butler's 1869 Introduction to *Woman's Work and Woman's Culture* (1869) remained pioneering.

8. Sarah Grand, 'The New Aspect of the Woman Question', *North American Review* 158 (1894): 276.

9. A more practical and intimate account of marriage was Margaret Stephens's *Woman and Marriage: A Handbook* (London: T. Fisher Unwin, 1910; eighth impression, 1923) which attempted to demystify the institution. 'Although marriage is no longer regarded by women as the sole aim of their existence' (the interest in marriage coinciding with women's rights awareness) 'the mysterious fascination of the sex-instinct . . . with the blessings and bonds of wifehood and motherhood, is in no danger of becoming extinct among them' (pp. 39–40). Stephens objected to the way the female's education 'is nothing but a concealment of the woman from herself' (p. 6). She also objected to the double standard in morality (p. 42). Among the activities and conditions that heated the blood and stirred the imagination and that could therefore lead to excess of sexual participation, Stephens listed 'novel-reading' (p. 46)!

10. Beatrice Grimshaw, *When the Red Gods Call* (New York: Moffat, Yard & Co., 1911), p. 23.

11. I refrain from speculating on the psychological origins of Grimshaw's obsession with headhunting and cannibalism. It goes beyond, though shares the slightly mischievous insouciance Mary Kingsley, her elder contemporary, showed towards cannibalism. (The well-known Kingsley and her *Travels In West Africa*, 1897, and *West African Studies*, 1899, may well have been role models for Grimshaw.) There are as many lingering passages on headhunting and man-eating in the travel book, *Isles of Adventure*, as in the novel, *When the Red Gods Call*, so many indeed, and of such casually bloodthirsty detail, that it seems ludicrous for Grimshaw in the former book to wonder at the 'morbid' interest shown by newcomers and visitors to Papua in cannibals and headhunters: *Isles of Adventure: From Java to New Caledonia but Principally Papua* (Boston and New York: Houghton Mifflin, 1931),

p. 187. Cannibalism forms the climax of two episodes in the adventure novel, *Vaiti of the Islands* (1908), one of them meant to be comic. Unsurprisingly, too, cannibals appear in Grimshaw's memoir-cum-popular anthropological work, *From Fiji to the Cannibal Islands* (1907), though since this also functions as a kind of guidebook (there is an appendix, 'How to Reach Fiji'), they are less pruriently detailed. There would have been for a popular novelist like Grimshaw a profitable shock value in depictions of cannibalism. (The shock value in the impaled heads in Conrad's *Heart of Darkness*, 1902, is diffused amidst the general and intense horror Conrad is creating.) This value would have been increased by the fact that the author was a woman. Still, the high incidence of cannibalism in Grimshaw goes beyond readerly and writerly thrill into some obscure authorial preoccupation.

12. Ella MacMahon, *The Job* (London: James Nisbet & Co., 1914), pp. 130, 128.
13. See Janice Hubbard Harris, *Edwardian Stories of Divorce* (New Brunswick, NJ: Rutgers University Press, 1996), pp. 156–7. For a contemporary reaction to the published report see 'Whom Man Would Put Asunder: The Decree of the Judge and the Plea of the Archbishop', *The World's Work* 21 (1913): 123–6.
14. See David Fitzpatrick, 'Divorce and Separation in Modern Irish History', *Past and Present* 114 (1987): 172–96. This article is available online at JSTOR.
15. Walter E. Houghton, *The Victorian Frame of Mind 1830–1870* (1957).
16. I have found biographical details about MacMahon scanty. *Who's Who 1907* tells us she was born in Dublin, the daughter of Revd J. H. MacMahon, Chaplain to the Lord-Lieutenant of Ireland. Her address in 1907 was Leeson Park, Dublin and six years later (*Who's Who 1913*) was Chelsea, London. She was unmarried at those times. According to Kemp et al., she was a British civil servant during the Great War, later contributed to the BBC, and was given a Civil List pension for services to literature: *Edwardian Fiction: An Oxford Companion* (Oxford: Oxford University Press, 1997), *s.v.* MacMahon, Ella. The Princess Grace Library EIRData website tells us she was in the intelligence service in World War II. Her birth date remains elusive but she died in 1956. A translation, *Maxims and Counsels*, was published in 1884 and *A Great Attraction* and *Diana's Destiny* in 1949. These dates seem to represent the beginning and end of a long literary career. She was a novelist but also a translator of religious texts. I have compiled a list of twenty-seven of her volumes, suggesting a fair degree of prolificness.
17. Ella MacMahon, *A Modern Man* (London: J. M. Dent, 1895), p. 164.
18. MacMahon, *A New Note*, pp. 248–9, 82, 75, 37, 105, 126–7.
19. L. T. Meade, *The Cleverest Woman in England* (London: James Nisbet & Co., 1898), pp. 190–1.
20. Annie M. P. Smithson, *Her Irish Heritage* (1917; Cork: Mercier Press, 1988), p. 146.
21. Ella Macmahon, *The Job*, p. 126.
22. Eleanor Alexander, *The Rambling Rector* (London: Edward Arnold, 1904), pp. 115, 127. Alexander was born in Strabane, Co. Tyrone. She kept alive the memory of her father, Revd William Alexander, later Archbishop of Armagh, in *Primate*

Alexander, Archbishop of Armagh: A Memoir (1913). Her mother, Cecil Frances (Mrs Cecil Alexander, née Humphreys), poet and hymnist, author of 'There is a Green Hill Far Away', died before her husband was raised to the Primacy.

23. J. H. Riddell, *A Rich Man's Daughter* (New York: The International News Company, 1895), pp. 85, 115.

24. Filson Young, *The Sands of Pleasure* (Boston: Dana Estes & Co., 1905), pp. 83–5.

25. Young, *The Sands of Pleasure*, p. xi.

26. I had occasion to excerpt Young's *Titanic* in my anthology *Titanic* (London: Penguin Press, 1999) and I discuss this creatively imagined book in *The Age of Titanic: Cross-Currents in Anglo-American Culture* (2002). It belongs in a minor way to the Irish canon and Richard D. North (see below) is right to call it 'in effect a documentary novel'. Alexander Bell Filson Young was born in Ballyeaston, Co. Antrim, son of Rev. W. Young and Sarah Filson of Portaferry, Co. Down (*Who's Who*, 1913). The Filsons had owned a house in that Co. Down village on Strangford Lough from 1810 and it passed later to the Filson Youngs who owned it until 1923: see P. J. McHenry, 'No. 8 Ferry Street, Portaferry: The History of a House', *Journal of the Upper Ards Historical Society* 1 (1977), 29–30. In one essay, 'Going Away and Arriving', Young remembered the journey to Portaferry that began summer holidays: *Letters from Solitude and Other Essays* (1912). In leaving and arriving is the rhythm once again of tidal movement. North's brief 2003 introduction to a forthcoming biography of Young sketches his colourful career as journalist, war correspondent (he covered the relief of Mafeking), novelist, broadcaster, flyer (in his late fifties). His dozen or so books cover early motoring, sensational murder trials, naval affairs, and classical music. Young was the second husband of Vera North whose third husband was Clifford Bax, brother of Arnold, the English composer who wrote Irish stories under the pen name Dermot O'Byrne. The journalist and broadcaster Richard D. North is Young's grand-nephew by marriage: see his website and 'Author's Introduction to a Forthcoming Biography by Silvester Mazzarella', http://www.richarddnorth.com/elders_betters/fy_bio.htm

27. Young, *The Sands of Pleasure*, p. 82.

28. Richard Ellmann, *James Joyce* (Oxford: Oxford University Press, 1982), p. 219.

29. I discuss the broader cultural cross-currents in *The Age of* Titanic: *Cross-Currents in Anglo-American Culture* (2002), and the late Victorian and Edwardian cultural context of shipbuilding and applied science in Belfast in *Recoveries: Neglected Episodes in Irish Cultural History 1860–1912* (2002).

30. Thomas Hardy, *Tess of the d'Urbervilles* (1891; Harmondsworth: Penguin Books, 1985), p. 180.

31. For accounts of the impact of Darwinism in Ireland, see David Livingstone, 'Darwin in Belfast: The Evolution Debate', in *Nature in Ireland: A Scientific and Cultural History*, ed. John Wilson Foster and Helena C. G. Chesney (Dublin: Lilliput Press, 1997), pp. 387–408 and John Wilson Foster, *Recoveries: Neglected Episodes in Irish Cultural History 1860–1912* (Dublin: University College Dublin Press, 2002), pp. 7–48.

32. David Trotter uses the term 'Fictional Polemics' and discusses Sarah Grand under the section of this title: *The English Novel in History 1895–1920* (London: Routledge, 1993), pp. 116–17.

33. The Woman Question, the Marriage Question and Irish Question were known as such at the time, hence my use of quotation marks.

34. For example, a surprising number of Northern Irish Protestants were involved in India: see my Afterword and Notes to Andrew James, *The Nabob: A Tale of Ninety-Eight* (2006).

35. David Daiches, 'General Editor's Introduction' to Jenni Calder, *Women and Marriage in Victorian Fiction* (London: Thames and Hudson, 1976), p. 9.

36. W. B. Yeats, 'A General Introduction for My Work', *Essays and Introductions* (New York: Collier, 1968), p. 511.

37. See Miranda Burgess, 'The National Tale and Allied Genres', in *The Cambridge Companion to the Irish Novel* (Cambridge: Cambridge University Press, 2006), pp. 41–2.

38. Black, *Notable Women Authors of the Day* (Freeport, NY: Books for Libraries, 1972), pp. 320, 324.

39. Sarah Grand, *Our Manifold Nature: Stories from Life* (1894; Freeport, NY: Books for Libraries, 1969), p. iii.

40. See Black, *Notable Women Authors of the Day*, pp. 230–1.

41. David Trotter, *The English Novel in History*, p. 117.

42. Shane Leslie, *The End of a Chapter* (London: Constable, 1918), pp. 180–1.

3

A New Theology: Protestantism and the Irish Novel

SERMONS AND SACERDOTALISM

Many country-house novels of the 1890–1922 period veer in their telling between humour, whimsy, and archness on one side, and earnestness on the other. The importance of being earnest was emphasized weekly in Victorian and Edwardian Ireland (as in England) by the Sunday sermon. Those usually ephemeral oral or written prose forms, the sermon and the tract, are nonetheless part of the Irish literary past, though mostly forgotten and unheeded despite their contemporary power and influence. Along with hymns, they were dominant forms of expression in Protestant Britain and Ireland until early in the last century, and spanned popular and highbrow taste. The power and sophistication that the sermon at its best was capable of are recoverable in two historical episodes: the reaction of Protestant ministers in Belfast to Irish-born John Tyndall's Presidential Address to the British Association for the Advancement of Science in Belfast in 1874, in which he defiantly proclaimed a materialist account of the cosmos, and the reaction of Protestant ministers in the north of Ireland in 1912 to the sinking of RMS *Titanic* which had been built in Belfast.[1]

A theme of the *Titanic* sermons was the 'splendid heroism' displayed aboard the stricken liner, as thrilling, said the Revd R. M. Kerr, as the heroism of the battlefield. The claims of heroism aboard *Titanic* were the more insistent because doubts about the possibility of heroism in the contemporary world were as freshly troublesome as widespread doubts about the truth of Christianity. Proclamations of heroism were attempts to roll back the post-Victorian world, of which Forster's liberal secularism in *Howards End*, with its 'heroes and shipwrecks' undermined by the goblins of doubt and time's mischief, was a recent expression. Kerr told his Belfast congregation: 'We are living in an age of transition; we have passed away from our standing ground in the old; we are not yet sure of our place in the new. We have a new theology, a new astronomy, a new chemistry, a new biology, and there are those who tells us that all that has wiped out our old-fashioned belief about the soul.'[2] The enlightened Protestant position was that this was not the case, and that science and progress, be they in the shape of evolutionism or technological marvel, were not threats to Christianity. (Even those of Tyndall's opponents who were science-minded Protestant clergymen denied that there was any threat from Darwin.) There is irony in the fact that the Irish Revival was unwittingly allying itself with fundamentalist Christianity in largely (if not exclusively) turning its back on science and progress and seeking to reinstate a heroism in Ireland more ancient than the chivalry said to have been exhibited on the famous ship. (Yeats seems to have entirely ignored the *Titanic* and its sinking.)

Still, the advance of science was one of several cultural phenomena that troubled Christianity—by turns Catholicism and Protestantism, sometimes both at the same time—during the late nineteenth century. There was the Evangelical fever that broke out in the United States in 1858 and spread to Ulster the following year (the Revival of '59), and thence to the rest of the United Kingdom, and that troubled many Protestant clergy in its irrational ardour. There were the deep doctrinal controversies inside the Church of England (and therefore Church of Ireland). There was the specific challenge of evolutionary theory and the general challenge of scientific materialism and material progress. There was the issue of the disestablishment of the Church of Ireland. For the Roman Catholic Church in Ireland there was the University Question to deal with.[3] And, of course, for both Protestantism and Catholicism there was the vexing relationship of politics to religion, of nationalism to Catholicism, unionism to Protestantism, the latter a relationship that was particularly vexed around the times of the Home Rule bills (1886, 1893, 1912) and that has persevered to our own day. Altick quotes Kitson Clark's opinion of the nineteenth century in England that 'probably in no other century, except the seventeenth and perhaps the twelfth, did the claims of religion occupy so large a part in the nation's life, or did men speaking in the name of religion contrive to exercise so much power'.[4] This is as true of the Irish nineteenth century as of the English nineteenth century; indeed, perhaps Ireland did keep the religious seventeenth century alive during the nineteenth and even twentieth centuries, as exasperated outsiders sometimes alleged. Certainly the religious nineteenth century is a long one, stretching into the 1920s or even 1930s when the Catholicizing and Protestantizing of, respectively, the Irish Free State and Northern Ireland accelerated.

Little wonder, then, that the sermon (which can be a focus and distillation of religious feeling and on occasion of political feeling) is heard time and again in the Irish novel of the 1890–1922 period. Joyce's *A Portrait of the Artist As a Young Man* (1916) aside, its most graphic appearance is in a peculiar and

counter-productively high-voltage novel—by turns realistic and surrealistic—
The Unpardonable Sin (1907) by James Douglas. In this novel, Gabriel Gordon from Belfast becomes a celebrity preacher known throughout Britain
and Ireland, a better-known version of the historical 'Roaring' Hugh Hanna,
who is a minor character in the novel. Another preacher, Dr Ryan, has
not entirely departed the Ulster scene even yet: 'the celebrated Orange
divine...the idol of Bigotsborough [Belfast]...By practising the arts of
the demagogue in the pulpit he had acquired an absolute ascendancy over
the Orange party. Sunday after Sunday he thundered against the Pope and the
Church of Rome...a giant in stature...his face a map of fixed ideas and
frozen prejudices...a storehouse of obsolete malignities'.[5]

Exposed too long to the white heat (without the proportionate light) of
Douglas's prose, one seeks a quieter presentation of the sermon in novels of
the 1890–1922 period. One can find it in L. T. Meade's slum-novel, *A Princess
of the Gutter* (1896) in which Joan Prinseps listens to a remarkable preacher,
the head of Balliol House in Bethnal Green, preach on the text 'Whatsoever ye
shall ask the Father in My Name, He shall give it to you', and as a result is
reconfirmed in her determination to help the East London poor with her
considerable wealth.[6] (Balliol House was one of the University Settlements
established in British slums in the late nineteenth century—there was one in
Belfast.)[7] One can find it also in *A Woman-Derelict* (1901) by May Crommelin, in which an Irishwoman who survives a train wreck at the expense of her
memory is taken in off the streets by a kindly doctor in Brighton. Early in
their relationship he advises her to attend Church and listen to a famous
preacher who is pleading for the Home Missions and who takes for his text,
'Who will go for us?' from Isaiah chapter 6, verse 8. His sermon is a call to a
life of humble religious service, Elinor Grey listens and responds, and the
direction of her life is altered, and stays so even after she recovers her memory
to find herself married. In each novel, the sermon leads to direct action.

At its most innocuous, however, the sermon was a weekly pleasant
background soundtrack for daydreams. In *The Soundless Tide* (1911) by
F. E. Crichton, Patty Maxwell, on a return visit from England, sits in her
pew listening to Rev. Bernard Hamilton but really musing on her aunt's
cousin, Randal. 'His preaching was always quiet and sensible if not very
enlightening, and the careful periods slid pleasantly across Patty's consciousness, without leaving any direct impressions.'[8] Things are slightly sterner in
The Rambling Rector where Mrs Gilliland the Bishop's wife admits that good
preaching has always appealed to her—'It certainly is a pleasant intellectual
exercise for the hearers', remarks Aunt Jane, 'when it is not too orthodox'. 'Oh,
but I think it can be interesting even then', replies the Bishop's wife with a faint
Wildean mischievousness, 'if it introduces some quite new heresy that one has

never heard of or thought of, just for the sake of argument' Later, ruminating on the diverse choice of husbands by women, the narrator observes: 'Another marries the preacher whose eloquence should be such a byword as that of Fénelon, Bossuet, or Magee ... Mrs. Gilliland had married the man of such perfect tact that she knew he ought to be Archbishop of Canterbury.'[9]

Behind this conversational sparring, so common a feature of the Irish novel of the period, lies a deeply serious predicament for Geoffrey Owen, 'a Curate of no reputation' catapulted into a rectorate of a church whose laity is vigilant on the matter of doctrinal irregularity. *The Rambling Rector* is a novel about, among other things I have already referred to, the threat posed to a newly appointed and unworldly rector in the Church of Ireland by the seduction of Anglo-Catholicism and Ritualism from one side and rebellion by a vigilant congregation from the other. 'The critical faculty is very highly developed in the North of Ireland', remarks a Duchess when one of her experiments in 'social democracy' fails, before detecting the same faculty at work in the reaction to Revd Owen's sermons (p. 136) that have seemed to skirt hetero-doxy or worse. Ritualism (or Sacerdotalism) was seen by many in the 1870s as an organized movement to undo the Reformation and although the Evangel-ical, anti-Roman Catholic wing of the Church won revisions to the Canons in 1871 and to the *Book of Common Prayer* in 1878, the issue between Evangelical and traditional Anglican was still smouldering in 1900. A commentator could claim in 1898 that 'the word "Ritualism" is in every man's mouth'.[10]

Owen has written hymns based on Thomas à Kempis's *Imitation of Christ* and this has put some of his congregation on amber alert; after all, the hymns were praised for 'a truly monastic spirit and the highest sacerdotalism'. The Bishop warns Owen about his perceived 'Romish tendencies' but the younger man is befriended by Lady Laura Sullivan, a Catholic for whom *Hymns from the 'Imitation'* is a favourite book and who 'spoke naturally and candidly of religious experiences', a departure for him. 'I know, of course', she tells him with a subtext he barely detects, 'that the Church of Ireland has extraordinary limitations. But there are many like yourself who are truly Anglican, and who will gradually spread the light' (pp. 28, 12, 55). Early on Easter Sunday morning he finds his church sumptuously decorated: 'The east-end was all a glory of white lilies, and nameless starry flowers unknown to him. The communion rails were covered and festooned with them, the plain little communion table was a garlanded altar. Above it, where was generally no decoration, there stood a floral reredos with the sacred initials wrought into the side panels, and a cross of white lilies in the centre' (p.180). The scene stirs his poetic temperament (which for the moment overrides his theology) and he imagines the parishioners have done this. He goes home to alter his sermon to pay tribute to the accomplishment, only to find the church locked against him when he returns to conduct the service and the legend

'No Popery' nailed to the front door. It is Lady Laura who has festooned the church, for bedecking by flowers was a practice of High Church ritualism.[11] 'We don't like the way you're carrying on,' Jimmy O'Loughlin's brother tells Owen— 'you and your extra services, and your sermons that has [*sic*] no straight doctrine in them that a man can lay hold of, and your ritualistic ways.' The door is unlocked, but the scene has changed, with the flowers pulled and trampled; 'the church looked like some plain saint who has been wantonly insulted'. Owen conducts the service without hymns or chants 'and he preached his sermon much curtailed' (pp. 183, 185).

Owen changes his tune. 'You just want a little ballast, old chap', he is told; 'He is not the sort of man who will ever get on', the Bishop concludes. Later to Lady Laura, Owen identifies himself as an Evangelical in doctrine and not at all a ritualist or Anglo-Catholic. 'But you spoke differently in your Lenten sermons', she reminds him. 'You are not quite *Low* Church, are you?—it came out with a gasp of horror.' In the course of the novel, Owen has become a noted sermon-izer but in his last sermon in a different church in a neighbouring parish (High Church, 'one of your English churches') he departs from the expected Anglican formula used by preachers across the land that Sunday morning and which Alexander wittily anatomizes: the use of a *Times* leading article on European politics; the endorsement or denunciation of some government policy in Christian terms; an attack on social vices of those in Society ('in the limited sense') in the manner 'least likely to correct them', i.e. by substituting for the earthly passion that has been their undoing 'a heavenly passion hardly less erotic and evanescent'. Instead, to those 'whose gracefully decorated heads marked the front row of the ducal transept like the mixed border in a garden' his sermon 'was just a little bit too religious—of the positive kind of religion that has gone so entirely out of fashion'—and sends them to sleep.[12]

Behind Alexander's sport are the deadly serious problems of the Church of Ireland. The battle to establish what was orthodoxy in the Church, the battle between the Anglo-Catholic and Evangelical wings of the Church, was being waged in Britain too, where a Catholic Revival instigated by Froude, Newman, Keble, and Pusey was seen as a threat. The issue was differently grave in Ireland because the larger war between Protestantism and Roman Catholi-cism that loomed behind it had a perennial, overt, and dangerous quasi-political urgency. The Oxford Movement, Tractarianism, Higher Criticism: these created the larger British context of unease and dispute. 'Ritualism' was the hostile epithet Evangelicals gave to Anglo-Catholic liturgy in which the pulpit no longer dominated the altar.[13] Anti-ritualist legislation in the dises-tablished Anglican churches failed in the United States but succeeded in Ireland (1871–7).[14] Sam O'Loughlin reminds Owen that it is actually *against the law* for him to put a cross on the communion table.

The disestablishment of the Church of Ireland in 1869 is the backcloth to Alexander's theological theme. The Bishop tells Owen that humility is a Christian virtue 'but in a disestablished Church it must be practised with caution by the clergy' if it means the minister refusing to seek financial help from wealthy laity. When Jimmy O'Loughlin visits her, Aunt Jane hopes he will propose to do 'something very generous for the Church' but instead he proposes marriage to her. The Duke announces he cannot lavish help upon the parishes where he owns property as his father had done when the Church was first disestablished; rents had been reduced by decisions made 'in the land court': in the latter half of the nineteenth century, Church and Big House alike were in difficulty, a repeating theme in the Irish novel of the period.[15]

Sermons are preached at key moments in *The Rough Way* (1912), a rich novel by W. M. Letts and to some extent a portrait of an artist *manqué* as a young man.[16] In a dedicatory note, Letts describes the novel as 'the story of a man who cannot make up his mind', a man having, as she describes it in the novel, 'a nature peculiar to the spectator rather than to the actor'. But this allows her to send her curious hero, Antony Hesketh, on passage through several of the cultural movements that attracted the intellectual young in the late nineteenth and early twentieth centuries (two thirds of the way through the story, one character is reading Synge's *Well of the Saints*, 1905): belated Pre-Raphaelitism, journalism, the theatre of Ibsen, feminism. As a youth he discusses Higher Criticism and is all for the art-for-art's-sake movement, and horrifies his mother with 'Modernist opinions that he had gathered in hasty glimpses of works beyond his grasp' which probably identify his advanced liberal views in religion (though Catholic modernism ought not to have horrified his Anglican mother) rather than his literary predilections. Raised in a quite ordinary and straitened household between Manchester and Oldham, son of a Church of England rector (a renowned preacher), young Hesketh attends a college founded by an Oxford member of the Tractarian movement. Hesketh early has a beatific vision and has 'an innate reverence of soul that responded eagerly both to the inward grace and to the outward signs of Catholic faith'. The novel is fuelled by the hope for the reclamation of the Church of England, of England herself, by Anglo-Catholicism. But it is a novel that gives competing philosophies a fair hearing in the presence of Letts's cultivated intelligence.[17]

In a scene that anticipates Stephen Dedalus's interview with the Dean of Studies in *A Portrait of the Artist as a Young Man* (1916), Antony has a discussion about vocation with the chaplain of the college. The chaplain is leaving the college to join the Society of Saint Andrew that runs a mission in East Africa. Young Hesketh borrows from the chaplain *John Inglesant* (privately printed 1880, published 1881), an influential novel by J. H. Short-house about religious intrigue at the time of the English Civil War and the suppression of the Molinists in Rome.[18] Molinism, a Catholic movement that originated within the Jesuits in the late sixteenth, early seventeenth centuries, attempted to reconcile diverse aspects of belief and this Shorthouse himself tried to do through his young hero, an aristocratic Jesuit-trained Englishman, and as Antony Hesketh does too. With its 'strongly libertarian account of human freedom', Molinism encountered opposition from Thomists and Augustinians. The Molinist attempt to square human freedom of choice with God's foreknowledge and predestination takes, in Letts's novel, the late nineteenth-century form of Antony's succession of free choices of vocation and enthusiasm on the one hand, and, on the other, the steadying underlying influence of his 'good heredity, and the tremendous force of good environ-ment behind him...sound middle class and clerical morality held him in grip'.[19] (Heredity is a repeated theme and concern in the Irish novel of our period, a legacy of biological and social Darwinism.) Letts clearly intends some similarities between Inglesant and Hesketh: Inglesant had a beatific vision which never deserted him; he was distracted by worldly affairs (as Hesketh is distracted by journalism and art), and visits the religious commu-nity at Little Gidding, as Hesketh is attracted to the Society of the Incarnation in London which ministers to London slum-dwellers. (Ritualist churches flourished in the impoverished East End of London, ministers using bright trappings and mysterious ritual to attract worshippers.)[20] The suggestion is of Letts taking up the torch from Shorthouse; both *John Inglesant* and *The Rough Way* connect themselves with the Anglo-Catholic movement.

Hesketh's attraction to the Anglican Incarnation society begins when he hears a socialist Lenten sermon by Father Digby and he determines to join the society. But before he does he finds himself at a crossroads, 'dark with doubt and self-disgust', tempted by journalism, art, love (for a French actress), and marriage: the relationship of celibacy to priestliness is argued out in the novel, a theme that provoked two modern Irish novels sharing the same story and characters: Moore's *Héloïse and Abélard* (1921) and Helen Waddell's *Peter Abelard* (1933). Hesketh is persuaded by the actress to marry her and forgo the Order but she returns to Paris and jilts him and taking it as a sign, he returns to Digby in London. He listens to Digby's hope not for the Church *of* England but the Catholic Church *in* England, and to Digby's quoting from a book by John Oliver Hobbes on 'the sanity of the Catholic faith'. (It was Newman who thought that the Church of England was actually 'the Catholic Church in England.')[21] Hobbes was the pen-name of Pearl Richards (1867–1906), later Pearl Craigie, an Ameri-can novelist and playwright who lived in England and changed her religion from Nonconformist to Roman Catholic.[22] (Letts nods to her also in the name of Digby's Canadian fellow missionary, Richards.) Hesketh joins the Order, travels to Canada, and publishes a book of essays. When he returns one summer to

London he preaches a sermon that discomfits his mother with its utopian socialism but it is the manifesto of a man who has found himself.

Like Pearl Craigie, Ella MacMahon is said to have converted to Catholicism later in life.[23] The religious 'problem' that such conversions demonstrated is implicit in *A Pitiless Passion*. One is tempted to see the author's later conversion adumbrated in the character of Magdalen Ponsonby who is 'very religious', according to one character, who avoids the church 'where *everybody* goes' (and where there was a spot of bother about the vicar and the candlesticks), in favour of a little church on a hill which she attends every other morning before breakfast. She also has a crucifix in her room, indeed 'a chapel, or an oratory, or whatever you call it' and has 'certain opinions about eating meat on Fridays'.[24] MacMahon has her chief character, Magdalen, accuse a friend carrying on a monologue of talking 'like a page out of a problem novel' but *A Pitiless Passion* is itself a problem-novel, the problem being Anglo-Catholicism but also alcoholism, since it is in part the portrait of an alcoholic young woman in London Society.

There is a tacit irony perhaps in an Irish novelist removing the Drink Question from Ireland to England; one character, Mr Popplewhite, delivers himself of anti-Irish remarks—' "Oh, they're a rotten lot, anyhow." Nobody contradicted his statement'—but is punished by being absurd. MacMahon also removes it from the gutter to 'Society—spelt big'.[25] MacMahon takes some pleasure in showing the underbelly of Society. When Norman Grain MP marries young and pretty Georgie Fitz-Roy he is unaware that she is an alcoholic and his painful and embarrassing discovery threatens his career and place in Society, and changes his view of life. Of his subsequent visit to Fordham Place, the country house in the Midlands Sir Anthony Chenevix lets to Mr Evanson, a millionaire from New Zealand, MacMahon remarks acidly: 'So here were some of the pleasing little undercurrents, running below the smooth surface of artificialities, which find a fitting home in Elizabethan country houses, wherein Society, led by millionaires, refreshes itself on mediæval art through the kind instrumentality of modern money.' MacMahon tries with some success to recreate the subjective states of alcoholic craving, euphoric drunkenness, and hangover while maintaining the third-person narrative and without the aid of the later stream-of-consciousness method. Georgie's alcoholism is cleverly anticipated by the drunken London street girl at the start of the novel, by the baby of the drunken mother Magdalen lifts up sympathetically when the Society figures shun it, by a painting of a drunken street woman with child (a kind of reverse or perverse Madonna and Child) by Magdalen (who like the heroine of *A New Note* is an artist), and by Grain's nightmare that confuses the real and the painted mother and child.[26]

MacMahon uses Magdalen to explore many of the repeating themes of the Irish novel of the period—love, marriage, money (poverty or riches), art, religion, types of womanhood, Society—various permutations of these forming social syndromes of concern inside and outside the novel. She, like her creator, dislikes English Society, her dislike expressed remarkably in a lengthy one-sentence paragraph in which the façade Society requires is 'without the draw-back of any problematical waiting for a world to come, as well as in some other trifling particulars'. It is a task for MacMahon to achieve the selflessness of Magdalen and still keep her character complex. Magdalen ministers to Georgie even though she loves Grain (and he her), a love she must keep submerged. Her painting too is restrained yet truthful: 'She *could* have been pitiless', Grain observes of her 'Madonna and Child', 'but she was not'; it is a painting remarkable by a man, more than remarkable by a woman. Yet she is 'very strong' and is 'a woman of her time; and the time has never been when the lust of happiness, the fierce rebellion against unhappiness, had a firmer hold on the sons and daughters of men'.[27] MacMahon's analysis of Magdalen here provides, I think, the master notion that holds together the connected themes that are repeated in these novels and prevent the best of them from being mere commercial formulae: these were the themes of genuine concern in the late Victorian period as society underwent major shifts in attitudes and laws.

Magdalen, then, is a strong woman, a kind of New Woman, whose aim, however, is not the self-realization of the familiar New Woman. Moreover, MacMahon is aware that 'it is not always the woman who is the injured party in the relationship between the sexes'. Magdalen's dilemma is resolved by MacMahon's having her character exhibit strength by trying to secure the happiness *of others*. But despite her strength she needs to pray for deliverance from the temptation of what would be the sin of adultery, and Christ answers her. She chooses Georgie's need over her love for Grain and his for her. (Grain dies anyway trying to save Georgie in a fire, Georgie being all the while safe, in that kind of perverse irony alcoholics provoke.) The novel is an attempt to resolve the competing claims of happiness and duty, self-realization and altruism, womanliness and humanity, through transcendence into a higher spiritual state. The pain involved must have been of the kind that accompanied religious lapses and conversions at that time.

ESLER AND PRESBYTERIANS

These novels depict Anglican Protestantism in internal difficulty. The equivalent difficulties faced by Presbyterians are harder to find portrayed in fiction, though E. Rentoul Esler (?1860–1924) sets her novel *A Maid of the Manse* (1895) between two manses in Co. Donegal, the First and Second Kincraigie

Churches, the Second having seceded from the First in the eighteenth century.[28] As in the case of Alexander, one imagines that Esler's fictional models are English, especially Jane Austen and Anthony Trollope.

The events of *A Maid of the Manse* take place twenty-five years or so before Esler's time of writing, i.e. around 1870. The social difficulties attending two churches of the same denomination in the same village are part of Esler's theme, and we learn something of the ordination, home-lives, and ministries of these Ulster Scots Presbyterians and the living Scottish connection. The children of the Manse, we are told, live a life 'as frugal, as pleasureless, as poverty-stricken as that of the farmers around them', though they are to consider themselves socially separated by a wide gulf, reflecting that curious combination of actual snobbery and self-attesting humility we find in Ulster Protestants, often accompanied by a smouldering self-suppression. It is an appropriately plain tale but nevertheless tries to import two romantic sub-plots into what we might think of as unpromising circumstances; it is the love entanglements more than the fruits of schism that serve to destabilize what we would otherwise think of as a community of bedrock faith.

However, the Episcopalian (Church of Ireland) wife of one of the two ministers has for Nonconformism an 'invincible disdain' and admires Catholicism and she adds to the novel a note of religious uncertainty. Even her husband, the Revd Dr Walter Hamilton, is regarded as not entirely sound on 'the Roman Catholic question'[29] and was much too cordial with Father Mathew when this Catholic priest started his temperance crusade in Ulster years before.[30] The chief crisis of faith is not theirs, however. When a personal religious crisis occurs, conversion to Anglo-Catholicism or the discovery of a vocation (neither of which seems to involve much anguish of the kind Letts's Hesketh uncommonly suffers) appear to be more common in the Protestant novels than apostasy. Or if apostasy does occur, one's impression is that it hardly seems to merit the word, either in life or literature; the Protestant typically drifts away from faith into secularism without a spiritual crisis of the kind suffered by Joyce's Stephen Dedalus. This is odd, considering that doubt was an immense cultural phenomenon in Protestant Britain in the nineteenth century,[31] and it may be that the novels in which Protestant spiritual crisis occurs have not been recovered. In *Pirates of the Spring* (1919), Forrest Reid has his young hero enlightened by his clever school pal as to the incredibility of the biblical account of the creation and the incompatibility of the ten commandments with reality. His pal has read Herbert Spencer and also *The Mistakes of Moses* (1880), a famously controversial lecture by Robert Ingersoll.[32] Still, his seems to have been a dispassionate and intellectual rather than spiritual crisis.

But in *A Maid of the Manse* Hugh, son of the Revd Walter Hamilton, undergoes a deep crisis of conscience. He is a theological student in Glasgow, where students pride themselves on liberal views, and begins to wander off from received opinions and eventually, a few months before his final theological examination, he is moved to come to his father at home to confess his loss of faith. 'I find I cannot accept our creed, cannot acquiesce in any of the dogmas it enunciates.' Specifically he can accept the concept neither of election ('it is a creed of devils') nor of an omnipotent God who sanctions suffering and sin; he believes in free grace and concludes heretically that He must be a God of limited power. Hugh must give up the Presbyterian Church since despite prayer to deliver him from 'presumptuous sins' and discussion with professors in Glasgow and Derry, he can no longer subscribe to the Confession of Faith. When his son leaves the room, Revd Hamilton with tears in his eyes thinks he had rather see Hugh dead than fallen from faith. Later he tells Hugh that he must not enter the ministry of any Church; Hugh is not only a deserter but a traitor; Rev. Hamilton will lay his embargo on his son's leading souls astray. '"To kill me would be nothing," Hugh said, half to himself, "nothing compared to striking me dumb when I have a message to deliver. Oh, it is hard, hard, hard"' (pp. 250, 252, 267). His mother is less exercised and suggests he get ordained anyway; their exchange puts one in mind, before the fact, of Stephen Dedalus's exchange with Cranly. '"What is to hinder your getting ordained?" "There are minor difficulties. You would not like me to become a Methodist, would you?" "Certainly not," was the prompt answer. "Nor an Episcopalian?" "I wouldn't say that ... If your conscience led you into the Episcopal Church, I should be content enough."' But Hugh responds to his mother: 'I have no ambition towards any form of Christianity but the one I have been accustomed to, and it is forbidden.' He will leave Ulster and go into exile, choosing medicine over religion.

When Revd Hamilton confides in the other, younger Presbyterian minister and bemoans Hugh's questioning of the Bible, John Wedderburn ventures the observation that 'Opinions are not altogether what they used to be.' And as to the centrality of the Bible: 'There is a danger of making a God of the Divine Record ... The Book is surely not greater than He of whom it treats.' Revd Hamilton, embodying an older, sterner Presbyterianism, relents after listening to Wedderburn but he is already sick, and dies after writing to bless his son who is back in Scotland. When Wedderburn's 'supply' (i.e. substitute) minister assumes that Hugh will replace his father, Wedderburn tells him Hugh does not intend to enter the Church. Why not? 'Because of some trifling points of doctrine. We need a revised Confession of Faith. It is a terrible thing to see a man like that shut out from the ministry by a mere question of dogmas.' Esler appears to be talking here about Presbyterianism of the generation of her father (Revd Alexander Rentoul of Manor Cunningham, Co. Donegal) which she laments is still alive, unchanged after a quarter century. The major theme of the novel, disguised by the unclear paternity of Rosie Wedderburn, the maid of the manse (her adoptive father took to drink and died young, unmarried) is the way in which dogma strangles life, and towards the end the book becomes a problem-novel. It ends in Esler's pessimistic voice: 'Life goes on, and the thoughts of men are modified by the process of the suns, but creeds and dogmas stand exactly where they did, and in the face of certain vital questions the lips of the Church are dumb.'[33]

DEBORAH ALCOCK

To see a depiction of Protestant faith sure of itself, conquering even when crushed, and its champions magisterial in their certainty, we need to turn to a thoroughgoing Anglican Evangelical. Evangelicals according to Deborah Alcock (1835–1913) were accused of preaching faith and doctrine over morality and duty, but the latter are portrayed in her fiction so sternly that the distinction seems otiose.[34] In a letter of 1873 or 1874, Alcock speaks of 'this day of doubt, when it is the wise men (according to the world), and not any more the fools, who say "No God".'[35] This certainty would seem to damage her pretensions in fiction; and to be sure, her subject matter (Protestant, 'fundamentalist') could hardly appeal either to literary critics today or even feminist apologists (Alcock's piety would no doubt cancel her sex except as an object lesson); she is a problem for criticism, and it is no wonder a clerical friend warned her on one occasion in a letter that 'the honesty and outspoken Protestantism of the MS. would effectually debar it from gaining access to the pages of the periodical we spoke of to-day'.[36] Alcock belonged to, and wrote during, that period of Irish and English religious history when Evangelicals were vigorously prosecuting a campaign against popish elements of the Anglican Church and, therefore, she was by implication (when not expressly) against Roman Catholicism. (Alexander seems neutral by comparison to Alcock.)

Clearly many Irish critics, too, would be put off, perhaps even offended, by her overt Protestantism. Her father John Alcock was involved both in the Home Mission (for the revival of spiritual life among Protestants, especially in outlying areas of Ireland) and the Irish Society, bringing 'Papists' to the Evangelical Christ by teaching the New Testament in Irish. The scholars of the Irish Society were always Catholic, the teachers generally Catholic, but the inspectors were always Protestant. When conversions began to occur, Irish Catholics began to object, sometimes violently and when she saw the faithful converts suffer, 'there sank into Debbie's heart undying horror of the awful tyranny of the Romish Church'.[37] These were early examples of the Protestant martyrdom with which she became obsessed with that special, pure sense of outrage with which Evangelicals are equipped. But what of Catholic martyrs? Well, alas, 'they generally have about them', as she wrote in a letter of 1886, 'a most provoking want of commonsense, highly irritating to a practical Protestant mind!' The exclamation mark suggests her tongue was part-way in her cheek, but it seems as if the practicality of Protestant martyrs was turned in her fiction into their capacity for heroic *action* as well as passive suffering when their end came; her use of the adventure narrative gave her Christianity its crusading quality.

Alcock's father was insistent in his Evangelical way that he was trying to bring souls to Christ and not Catholics to Protestantism, and sternly discouraged Catholics from changing religion in order to secure a position or legacy. His daughter thought the same way, though the distinction between proselytizing and evangelizing would be a blurred one for most people.[38] The Alcock attitude required a muscular innocence of mind that often fails to convey itself to others as such. Similarly, although Alcock senior was opposed to disestablishment he took it philosophically and thought that loss of its temporalities would put the Church of Ireland on its mettle.[39] In any event, despite the impediment of his daughter's certainty, and the foregone conclusion of her storylines, Alcock's fiction has a distinctive sinewy toughness and she an almost alarming fearlessness. She is a figure who pre-emptively destroys all male condescension towards the 'fairer sex' and 'weaker vessel' despite the outward piety of her life.

Only one thing gave Deborah Alcock prolonged pause: the 'horrible details of cruelty—often of ingenious, diabolical cruelty—that meet us continually in the records of persecution and of martyrdom'. She squared up to accounts of suffering that were personal holocausts. 'There are things which the eye can rest on—*must* rest on sometimes—if we are to read history at all—but the ear cannot bear to hear or the lip to utter them. The only comfort is, that they are past.'[40] She shared with her father the flinchless gaze into hell and if she shrank from despairing detail, that was why: it would cause despair; but she was fearless enough in her descriptions of the martyrdoms which provide climaxes and cruxes that few novels can match. It is arguable, indeed, that Alcock was doing with Christian material what Standish James O'Grady and other early Irish Revivalists were doing with pre-Christian material: recovering heroes from the past to 'resume' in their case ('continue' in hers) the story of Irish heroism and magnificent suffering; both kinds of narrative have an immediacy as though the past were alive now. Alcock went deeper into her cradle Protestantism to find her heroes, while the Protestant Revivalists abandoned their cradle faith and exchanged pre-Christian heroes (Cuchulain, Finn, Ossian, and the others) for the heroes she and they had inherited, and by doing so oddly drawing silent attention to their flight from the Church of Ireland.[41]

Alcock's father was a Church of Ireland curate in Kilkenny (where Deborah was born), Tralee, Cork, and Isle of Man and became Archdeacon of Waterford; he was a noted sermonizer.[42] Alcock herself became a Sunday School teacher, learned Hebrew, and read widely. She was a true believer from an early age ('I cannot remember a time when I was not thinking about religion') and at age 10, having devoured *The Pilgrim's Progress* and the oft-reprinted *Stories from Church History* (1828) by the Irish religious historical writer and storyteller Selina Bunbury, the Christian champions of the past became her heroes and she became a devotee especially of Protestant history.[43] The telling of biblical and historical Church episodes for children was a popular prose genre in Protestant Ireland and Britain, and Alcock seemed to regard children as her natural readership. Wilde mischievously borrowed the well-known name of the prolific Co. Louth-born Bunbury (1802–82)—fifty of whose titles and editions are listed in the British Library Public Catalogue, and who published into the 1870s—for Algernon's invented invalid friend in *The Importance of Being Earnest* who behaves in a selfish, irreligious, and most unphilanthropic way.

Alcock overheard her father reading aloud from Emile de Bonnechose's *The Reformers before the Reformation* about the burning of John Huss, and the account instigated what became her consuming passion for martyrs who were either Protestants or, like Huss, could be thought of as proto-Protestants.[44] Indeed, she was to insist that 'the Protestant Faith existed many ages before the Protestant name. When did the Protestant Faith begin? To answer that we must go back to the beginning of the Christian Faith itself.' To protest, she reminds her readers, 'means literally and derivatively to witness for'.[45] Her work in fiction, then, was a project to help rescue Christianity from the usurpation of Roman Catholicism and from the lethal threats of Islam, a quest as quixotic as those undertaken by her religious heroes. Her novels are, in that potent Protestant phrase, martyr's memorials cast in the mould of the adventure novel.

Alcock is essentially an historical novelist and adventure writer occupying a distinctive if peculiar niche, subjecting the genre of Church history for children to the blow-torch of her adult fervour. She is that unusual creature, a relentless Protestant hagiographer. But when she was approached to intervene by novel in the massacres of the Armenian Gregorian Christians by Turkish Muslims then proceeding gruesomely, and to write in the manner she had written of martyrdoms that took place half a millennium ago, she reluctantly agreed and thought out, studied for, and wrote her novel in five weeks, with the benefit of some documentary help from Armenian friends in London. This was indeed a novel with a purpose, an extended urgent tract and invitation to Christendom to intervene. No sermon we have referred to has quite the indirect power of the last chapter of *By Far Euphrates: A Tale on*

Armenia in the 19th Century (1897), when the hero, Jack Grayson, newly returned to England from Armenia where he witnessed the Muslim massacres of the Christians, listens to his cousin preaching on the subject of the suppression and murders that went on from summer 1894 and culminated in the massacre at Ourfa Cathedral in December 1896. Young Grayson has witnessed the martyrdoms, has borne witness, Alcock would say, and, having married a Muslim (who is killed during the pogroms), has survived only by dint of being a foreigner who, with others, reached the sanctuary of the American Mission. The witness of Grayson is the more important in the story because according to the Gregorian pastor, 'All special outrages upon the Christians are cleverly timed for some moment when the eyes of Christian Europe are turned elsewhere.'[46]

Alcock fictionalized the martyrdom of the Bohemian Church reformer John Huss on 6 July 1415 at the Council of Constance (1414–18) in 'A Story of Constance' which was published with 'A Story of Bohemia' (an account of German papist crusades against the Bohemian Hussites) as *Crushed Yet Conquering* (1894).[47] A 1940 edition of this novel bore the title *A Torch to Bohemia* with the 1894 title as subtitle. Alcock in her novels often speaks from and to the present, clearly because she regards the historical episodes of Christianity as, in their demonstrable and abstractable truth, timeless. Or to put it another way: the tale is told as an extended tract, a kind of allegory as well as historical event, and the framer of the allegory is simply using the time-honoured tactic of the tract-writer in drawing parallels as well as continuities between the past and present. The Christian story is of course unfinished so that the completedness or closure suggested by novels is not justified here; the story is still unfolding at her novel's end. This is an interesting aspect of the tension between Alcock's living faith and her obligations as a novelist, between the tactics of a Christian seeking to convert and a novelist seeking to create a shapely story with a beginning, middle, and end.

The combined novel covers the years 1401 to 1429 and then, in brief, roughly another forty-five years to around 1472. What holds the two parts together is a Christian version of the *Bildungsroman*: the growth of the half-English, half-French Hubert Bohun from orphan and clerical student to squire (earning his silver spurs) to knight (winning his gold spurs), from anti-heretic to muscular Christian (a Christian soldier going onward). And like Huss he is a proto-Protestant. From the Hussites developed the Taborites whose teachings largely informed the Church of the United Brethren of Bohemia and Moravia, which Bohun helped found.[48] The story of the Great Schism (with three papal pretenders), the Council of Constance convened to end it, the political machinations, and the conviction and burning of Huss and Jerome, is told with gusto and authority. Conspiracies, urgent embassies, battles, and eloquent debates propel the narrative and disguise the foregone nature of the chief events, yet Alcock uses footnotes to remind us of the strictly historical nature of her story and the researched elements of the tale.

FICTION AND FAITH

The perceived conflict between, on the one hand, the authority of the Pope and even the Church (when it contradicts conscience), and, on the other hand, private judgement is one that provides the plot and theme of Alcock's Protestant narrative. But another conflict is a difficulty that Alcock's novels share with other historical novels: how to make fiction out of the unchangeable matter of the past; what happened would seem to be in conflict with what is imaginable, the past demanding a captive fidelity, imagination demanding freedom and license. We know of course that imagination is not as free as we used to think, in part because of the independent properties of language, as well as the inherited stock of generic types and motifs that seem to function in literature as they do in oral tradition, if not as insistently. Nor is history as stably interpretable as we once thought it, and to think of the past, to see it, certainly to tell it, is always to an extent to 're-vision' it, to revise it, to see it again or anew. This general problem for historical fiction is for another occasion, but Alcock was faced with a special version of it since private judgement did not in her system of belief allow for tampering with the *religious* past, to see it radically afresh: the Old Stories had to be retold faithfully in both senses of the word. And so, of course, in Alcock's novels there is little ambiguity of event or character as befits mainstream novels. There can be development, of course, as the character of Bohun demonstrates. Belief, faith, rectitude propel the narrative, and yet *Crushed Yet Conquering* succeeds in being substantial, intelligent, and readable; it is hindsight with a sufficient illusion of freedom of incident.

Fiction's apparent contradiction of fact is the more important and troubling to an author whose belief in the fact is an aspect of her faith. Evangelicals and Puritans are suspicious of fiction, and Alcock's father was as hostile to fiction as Edmund Gosse's father, a Plymouth Brother (remembered vividly in *Father and Son*, 1907). Philip Gosse's son could not resolve the dilemma but John Alcock's daughter did by turning her early heroes into figures of piety without loss of heroism of the kind that maintains a fictional story—King David, Jonathan, King Alfred, Gustavus Adolphus, Archbishop Cranmer, John Huss, Czar Alexander, George Wishart. In her imagination, Kingsley's *Westward Ho!* (1855) and Foxe's *Book of Martyrs* (1563), fiction and martyrology, meet.[49] In her Preface to

Crushed Yet Conquering, she addressed the question of fact and fiction in her novel and maintained that she neither added nor altered, but only reproduced. When she claims that the figure of Huss and the instances of martyrdoms are 'strictly true' and 'strictly historical' she is fact giving herself some leeway ('strictly' is ironically an ambiguous word), explained away by the 'love' with which she has laboured. She has had to resist the temptation to wander into bypaths and linger over details (i.e. fictionalize) because the historical material is 'so abundant and so full of romantic interest'. In some letters she framed the dilemma as one of honouring the life of the imagination while remaining aware of 'its separations and its temptations', and came to the conclusion that God intended her to use her imagination but only if it were in balance with her soul; her stories, she felt sure, came from God but had to be shaped in such a way as not to imperil their divinity. The preoccupation with her heroes she described as her 'fever', clearly akin to spiritual possession but avoiding its wilder form by being an 'historical fever', as she amends the term when writing to a friend.[50]

Alcock's vision of the story of Protestantism as inherently romantic dictated her 1908 non-fiction book, *The Romance of Protestantism*, in which the story of Huss is reprised as 'The Romance of Failure (The Story of Bohemia)'. She saw herself bringing to light tragedies and epics hitherto recorded only in His Book of Remembrance ('God Himself is the best poet'). Hers was a small-scale version of Milton's choice of Paradise lost as the original and ultimate subject for epic.

Alcock's treatment of Christian martyrdoms as romance had a distant Irish precedent in *Love and Religion Demonstrated in the Martyrdom of Theodora, and of Didymus* (1687) by the chemist and physicist, theologian and writer Robert Boyle, born in Co. Waterford in 1627, and Boyle too squared up to the possible contradiction between fiction and faith, imagination and Christian fact. Boyle's romance recounts the fate of his heroine Theodora at the hands of the Roman authorities for whom her Christian faith and celibacy are criminal rebellion against the civil government. She is given by the judge a choice: to marry (thereby sacrificing her Christian chastity) or 'to be prostituted in the publick *Stews*'. She chooses the latter but is rescued by Didymus before she can be defiled; however, they are later captured and she and her chaste lover are put to death. In a lengthy preface, Boyle claims he is rewriting the genre of heroic romance by making his heroine a pious Christian virgin and his hero a lover strictly bound by his religion; he wishes 'to transform a piece of Martyrology into a Romance' even if it were regarded as 'a kind of Profaneness'. He is consciously combining the sermon or book of devotion (which provided models for his martyrs' speeches) and martyrologies with pagan romance to create something new. Boyle wished to show, in what we might call his Christian romance, that chivalry and heroic valour could be accompanied by 'eminent' piety. For the 'young

Persons of Quality' who were his desired readers, he wanted unfashionably to substitute 'Patterns of Vertue' for mere 'Models of Skill or Eloquence', and serious themes for romance's customary lower aim 'to Delight the Delicate [i.e. female] Readers'. Boyle defends the unfashionable intelligence of his heroine, who has to discourse learnedly on theology, and of women in general. The incongruity between hard matter and the pleasures of narrative, and the connection between romance and female readership, survived as both problem and opportunity (as Alcock shows) when the novel proper retained some of the elements of romance. Boyle was aware of the 'Liberties' he was taking by inventing speeches for his historical martyrs and supplying circumstances missing from the martyrological record, and admits that 'a youthful and heated fancy transported my Pen somewhat beyond the narrow bounds of History', but consoles himself that he was borrowing the device of invented speech from the heroic romances that in turn he called 'disguised Histories' and was supplying circumstances such 'as were not improbable'.[51] Boyle's *Love and Religion* has been called a precursor of the historical novel.

A similar challenge to take Christian episodes and turn them into story clad in the circumstantial detail and animated by the complex human thought and feeling that modern secular narrative demands was met by L. T. (Lillie) Meade (1854–1915) in her *Stories from the Old Old Bible* (1903). A substantial book of 400 pages with the heft of a novel, it is engrossing from start to finish. Actually, the repetition of *Old* signifies the Old Testament, so it is Judaic stories from the Bible that Meade turns into the semblance of linked short stories, and powerfully, the power deriving both from original biblical force and the profitable and necessary harnessing of her own prose to that original force (she might have called it divinity) in order to achieve an emotive urgency. They are not romances, since deliverance from persecution and slavery, though often requiring the courage of defiance and conversion against the odds, also requires obedience to an omnipotent external divinity intervening at crucial moments, precluding the free will that constitutes, say, Hamlet's tragedy, as he contends against fate. Yet Meade manages to lend the best of her stories an emotional logic, which is the assertion of her imagination. The stories seem in their own modest way to register in their retrieval of humanity from their remote biblical majesty our modern world with its decline from a greater Victorian conviction and acceptance of authority. (For when you humanize you at least dig the soil in which doubt can be sown. Unlike Alcock, Meade writes at times as though a humanist.) *Stories from the Old Old Bible* in the reading has dated less than have her other innumerable novels and stories. Certainly, although they may belong at first glance to the Protestant literary tradition of retelling biblical stories, saints' lives, and Church history for children, they escape that tradition in their tension and poise.

Meade has chosen sixteen major characters from the Old Testament, including Abraham, Jacob, Moses, Naomi, Esther, and David, and allowed them to tell their own stories. This was a risky permission but the use of the first-person pays off in the resulting sense of immediacy. The figures are humanized and their stories dramatized as if fiction. Eve, the first to tell her story, is a very real woman from the start. She will tell us in her own good time about the terrible death of Abel: 'But I must not talk of my son Cain now or I shall break down.'[52] She will tell us at first of the golden days in Eden, though naturally memory is filtered through the events that lost Eden; indeed, the Fall must have created memory itself, which is inextricable, for Eve and all humanity, from nostalgia. 'I have but to shut my eyes to witness the old scenes and to be present in the old places. The birds sing again in the branches of the trees and the flowers spring in the grass. Adam is like a god in his strength, and I am beautiful with the beauty of the morning. Is it a *dream* that I believed in a lie, and that I sinned?' (p. 3). She is perhaps more human already than Adam, he being obedient and unquestioning where she is perplexed about God's forbidding of the tree's fruit. Yet when she eats and tells her husband, he too disobeys and his fallen humanity is registered an instant before his transgression: 'How I tempted him I know not. Perhaps because I was a woman and he loved me; but as I held the fruit to his lips the likeness of God faded from his face; he took and he ate. Just at that moment a streak of forked lightning tore the centre of the cloud' (p. 7).

In Eve's second story, they have left Eden and have two sons, and her husband is 'the Adam of old and yet with a difference...the memory of his sin was present with him day and night' (p. 8). The tragic killing of Abel by Cain is poignantly told. Cain it seems has inherited his mother's perplexity while Abel has Adam's certainty though he is more cheerful and boyish than Adam ever was; Cain is courageous but defiant, cross-grained. Cain and Abel go to make their evening offering and the elder returns when God rejects his offering, only to disappear in anger and hatred of his brother who returns shortly. Waiting for Cain in the darkness, Eve remembers again the 'old happy time in the Garden' and feels the separation of her first-born from her. Come morning, she goes to the Valley of Desolation to find him, having sent Abel ahead of her. She comes on them and witnesses Cain murdering his brother. 'What was it that stayed my feet—what was it that held my voice, that kept me rooted to the spot so that I could go neither backwards nor forwards? I know not, I shall never know. I had gone through agonies of fear all day, but now I felt neither fear nor pain' (p. 18). Movingly, she thinks Abel's wide-open eyes signify sleep, she never having encountered human death, but she learns the truth from Adam's living eyes. Her story ends with sentiments and a tone that might make us think of T. S. Eliot's magus also looking back, though without

Eve's apparent but not untinged assurance. 'These things happened long, long years ago, and I, the mother of the lads, stand now on the brink of life. I have known the perfection of all joy, and also, I think, the depth of all sorrow, but as I wait now for the moment when I shall join my son Abel again, I am not without hope' (p. 20). It is the qualification 'I think' that is only one of the touches by which Meade gives Eve human flesh and blood and a woman's heart.

At the other end of the book, Daniel's stories of the deliverance from the furnace of Meshach, Shadrach, and Abednego, of his translation of the writing on the wall for the Babylonians, and of his survival among the lions are told in a richer, more sensuous prose that nonetheless, Daniel being a prophet, has a fitting stateliness of diction. The Babylonian kings are not entirely wicked and Daniel himself seems human; at times the stories accrue the portentous whimsy of folktale (with, in this extract, an echo of mad Sweeney): 'It was from my lips that the king heard of that which should befall him did he fail to give God the glory, for the Watcher and the High One from Heaven would come down in His wrath, and the kingdom would depart from Nebuchadnezzar, and he would eat grass as oxen and live as one of the beasts of the field. Now Nebuchadnezzar believed not this awful doom, yet it came to pass as the Lord had said. For his reason departed from him, and he was driven from the dwellings of men, and he ate grass as oxen, and his body was wet with the dew of heaven; and his hair grew like eagle's [*sic*] feathers and his nails like birds' claws' (p. 399).

ALTRUISM AND FEMININITY

Deborah Alcock despised self-pity and undue subjectivity, and this chimes with the externalism of her fictional dramas, the spiritual contests being easily and early won by the principals; it is *repercussions* of belief, the supreme testing of an achieved faith, that animate her stories rather than dark nights of the soul. Indeed, she promoted self-sacrifice and praised Buddha as a heathen who made his religion centre upon a life of self-sacrifice. Moral beauty for Alcock was compounded of 'the deeds of heroes, courage, generosity, self-sacrifice' (a rather Revivalist compound), and self-sacrifice took the form for her of teaching, home mission work, and caring for her father who spent a life of ministering to others, one way or another.

Alcock claimed, justifiably or not, that 'the early Evangelicals were the pioneers of all the great philanthropic movements of the nineteenth century, and we in Ireland were not behind them, as far as our abilities and opportunities extended'.[53] The Victorian period, late and soon, was indeed characterized by a plethora of charitable projects in Britain and Ireland, carried out at home and abroad. Little wonder that Lady Halliday in MacMahon's *A Pitiless Passion* (1895) remarks impatiently, 'The world has gone crazy over this altruism, or whatever you call it ... this mad, mawkish sentimentality over the happiness of *others*.' She finds tiresome 'sensible persons' (she is thinking of Magdalen) 'who seem to feel it their duty to place their own good sense at the service of others' foolishness'.[54] In Meade's *A Princess of the Gutter* (1896), a wealthy rackrenting landlord in London's East End tells Joan Prinseps, a new graduate of Girton College, Cambridge who has inherited the housing he is leasing, that 'The craze for colleges for women, and all that sort of nonsense, is just as objectionable as the philanthropic craze of the age.'[55] A lawyer in Crommelin's *A Woman-Derelict* uses the same phrase when he claims that 'the philanthropic craze shows a mind slightly off its balance'.[56] So does a social worker in Annie M. P. Smithson's *Her Irish Heritage* who remarks to an English visitor who has been taken to the slums by her cousin, also a social worker: 'Well! Are *you* suffering from the slumming craze too? ... it's becoming so fashionable just now amongst "the quality" that really we poor workers may soon take a back seat.'[57] But Smithson and Crommelin, unlike MacMahon and Riddell, in no way impugn the sincerity or necessity of slumming. In *A New Note* (1894), the narrator has a few sharp remarks on the 'requisitioning' of young Victoria the violinist by London promoters of charity concerts and she is soon in demand by 'the fashionable charities'. 'Everybody, who is anybody, nowadays has come to the relief of the Distressed Irish Ladies; and one of the readiest avenues for the soul which seeks to mount on high—in Society—may be found, if judiciously sought, by means of Ireland's distressful daughters.'[58]

The range of charitable societies and institutions was immense and testified to the absence of systematic government welfare programmes of the kinds begun in the United Kingdom shortly before the mid-twentieth century.[59] This is reflected in many Irish novels of the time which include missionary and charitable work of one kind or another, reminding us both of the social importance of these activities in late nineteenth-century Ireland and Britain and the way such work and vocation were thought to involve genuine drama and even heroism. *A Rich Man's Daughter* (1895) by Riddell begins with Dr Claud Dagley rescuing a poor woman fainting from hunger in a fashionable London street; she is brought into the Osberton house to recover by the girl of the title. Amabel Osberton is stung by the good doctor's verbal attack on the wealthy and recalls that her 'rich father gave much more than a bare tenth of his income in charity, and the daughter was searching for words in which to say how generously he subscribed to hospitals, missions, restoration funds, relief societies, refuges, reformatories, and all the long list of charities the existence of which a wealthy man is never permitted to forget'.

The experience of the fainting woman is 'thrilling' for Amabel: 'She had gone "slumming" with that renowned if mistaken philanthropist Miss Arabella Kirconnell, and been greeted everywhere with the enthusiasm a certain class of poverty gladly extends to youth and beauty, and to age and ugliness when it thinks money is to be given away; but this was better by far.' If Amabel is shallow, Dagley is a hypocrite and is a 'shilling doctor', ministering to the lower middle class (a kind of charity), when he craves instead a high-class clientele and a first-class address. He eventually becomes involved with Amabel with an eye on his prospects, gets her pregnant, marries her secretly, is disappointed in his hopes because his new wife has not the courage to tell her rich father of her marriage, leaves for India and dies of cholera after writing a letter to her ending the marriage, the apparent philanthropist a scoundrel. His young and foolish widow will in time be redeemed into humility and a second marriage.

The novel includes a portrait of poverty, drunkenness, and wife-beating in London's East End but without real sympathy or solution, Riddell drawing upon a reservoir of scepticism whose spring was perhaps her own financial insecurity that she faced up to with hard work. Amabel had turned down the suit of young Saughton (her eventual redeemer), telling him she wished 'to be a Sister of Charity'. The worldly Baron Questo replies: 'she is in love with somebody else. That is always the meaning of the Sister of Charity business'.[60] Certainly the novels suggest an emotional dimension to female religious retreat instead of a purely theological calling; there is a pattern of recourse to the seclusion of Anglican or Catholic orders by heroines who have been jilted, scorned, separated, widowed, or whose love is otherwise unrequited; these young women rebound into religion and good works. In Katharine Tynan's *Dick Pentreath* (1906), Dorothea Semple jilts Pentreath and comes to regret it, suffering deep pangs of remorse when she realises that she in fact loves him; she becomes a probationer of the Anglican Sisters of St Luke, an unenclosed society of women bonded together to nurse the sick of London's East End and of India. Nanno Troy in E. Temple Thurston's *Traffic* (1906) is developing an attraction to a visiting Englishman and dreads being married off to a local farmer so in desperation asks her parish priest if she can enter a nunnery (he tells her that religious vocations don't come in a moment, after work in the fields all day and an argument with one's mother in the evening). Stephanie in Grimshaw's *When the Red Gods Call* (1911), though a Protestant, seeks to become a nun after the arrest for murder of the husband she loved deeply. (The Catholic priest in London tartly reminds her that a convent isn't a moral casualty ward.) Lady Moira McWilliam in Elizabeth Hart's *Irreconcilables* (1916) wonders if her Catholic friend Kate Ryan knows of any Anglican sisterhoods she can join and do good, now that her lover is dead.

The cultural picture is of women restricted by their emotional integrity to one true love underpinned by their religious faith, a faith in which they seek exclusive solace, when the love becomes impossible or is taken from them. (Male characters emigrate, as do the title hero of Stephen Gwynn's *John Maxwell's Marriage*, 1903, and Harold an Wolf in Bram Stoker's *The Man*, 1905, or go hunting as does Pentreath, retreating for a time to the Rockies to shoot big game.) When the novels belong to the genre of romance, however, the novels' plots require the heroine to reclaim or rediscover love, thereby cheating religion and the poor, at least temporarily, of their sole fidelity and solicitude. Moore's *Héloïse and Abélard* and Waddell's *Peter Abelard* break this pattern when Heloise enters the cloisters for good, but these are not finally romances and are constrained by historical fact. In the romances, nevertheless, the exigency of the plots is not intended cynically to slight religion or the poor, but to illustrate the triumph of a different kind of love. The refusal of that triumph turns a modest novel, *A Woman-Derelict* by May Crommelin (1850–1930) from a secular into a religious romance.[61]

Crommelin's novel, which chooses lunacy as its secondary theme, takes the theme of female altruism about as far as it could go by interpreting the idea of selflessness literally. The amnesiac derelict who finds herself in a strange street in Brighton (a derelict is a vagrant or street-person) scratches through memory and the alphabet and names herself Elinor Grey, which turns out to have been her maiden name. Taken in by a local doctor, she almost immediately embarks on a new life of service to others, having heard a preacher's call to 'a life of renunciation and unselfishness'.[62] Having literally lost herself, Grey considers later that she had 'truly forgotten Self for the sake of others' (p. 187). Since no one can find her friends or relations, she must start again, and that she does so as a humble servant of others (she undertakes to care for the mad wife of Dr Strong who rescued her) means inevitably that she will eventually discover that she is a distinguished person. By her wedding ring she knows she is married or widowed but has no memory of her husband or family; her life is suddenly a clean slate, an awakening, and a distillation. Although Strong declares his love for her, she is, after a brief faltering, untempted by sexual or romantic love; she is an attractive woman in her thirties whose sexual life is suppressed, or transposed into selfless Christian goodness and since these are in Elinor Grey's view mutually exclusive, the relationship between desire and religious faith can be said to remain, though here ironic. Also, while staying with Strong's friend Lady Cotswold in the Manor Farm in Gloucestershire, Grey is untempted by the elderly and wise Lady's disbelief in the rewarding (or punishing) afterlife (though, oddly, her Ladyship is a spiritualist). Elinor Grey will simply serve, care for, and attend to the needs of the helpless, sick, or mad.

Then Grey meets her husband by chance and her memory instantly returns. She is the wife of a knight-hero of the Egyptian and Boer wars who has just inherited a viscountcy on the death of his lunatic father (whom Elinor befriended in Strong's asylum), making Elinor Grey (or Nurse Grey or Sister Grey, as beneficiaries of her goodness call her), Viscountess Erpingham. Erpingham, now bigamously married, wishes to resume his marriage to Elinor, despite having a child by his second wife whom he married in sorrow and on the rebound. In the novel, then, there is a choice necessary between two ideals of these popular novels: perfection of marriage and perfection of altruism. In this novel, true love and true marriage are trumped by the spiritual love of one's neighbour. Elinor Grey's is a pure, unchurched Protestantism that grows in the absence of self: 'She was aware that the roots of her faith had spread wider, waxing stronger, this past year; that the outward spiritual growth had shown itself in the green leaf of works and the blossom of thanksgiving' (p. 215). Strong's mad wife, Retta, is a 'religious maniac' forever singing hymns, attending church, praying, driving herself mad through wrong religion. (Though Elinor Grey discovers that whereas it is chiefly money anxieties or obsessions that drive men mad, it is failure or betrayal in love that scatters women's wits.) Her life leans indeflectibly into the future, towards her certain existence after death. Her old self, her loving self that found its apotheosis in marriage and motherhood (her two children died), is briefly in battle with her new self, the altruistic self that finds its apotheosis in distributing love to others and leaving none for oneself. She declines to resume her marriage and returns to her obscure life of goodness. She finds her apotheosis prematurely when Retta's religious mania proves fatal not only to herself but to Elinor whose glorious future existence arrives by dreadful accident, her self-sacrifice complete.

If it is arguable that religious attachment can be a reaction to displaced emotional desire, then it is also arguable that charitable work among the destitute was itself displaced emotional desire, but an active one, a search for ways of satisfying that desire but in a disguised form, perhaps disguised even from the philanthropist herself (or himself)—or from the novelist of philanthropy. May Crommelin may have referred to 'the indwelling charity of most British bosoms',[63] but the necessary and evident virtues of altruism, generosity, and compassion might have had their unacknowledged counterparts: prurience, vicarious gratification, self-indulgence, self-reassurance of one's own solvency and respectability. Of the vices of the disadvantaged on whom one English matron bestows her charity in The First Claim (1906) by M. Hamilton (Mary Churchill Luck), the narrator remarks: 'these proxy peccancies lent a spice to her blameless wifehood and motherhood.'[64] Indeed, in a fascinating study, Seth Koven has gone further and makes the case for slumming in

Victorian London as sexual politics. One of his exhibits in making his case is *A Princess of the Gutter* by L. T. Meade (1854–1914), a story (told by herself) of an orphaned heiress and university graduate whose uncle's will obliges her in inheriting his wealth and property in London's East End to be the good steward of his poor tenants that he was not, having leased out his property and taken no interest in the welfare of the tenants who are living in slum conditions. Soon after, Joan Prinseps, like Crommelin's Elinor Grey, is converted by something close to a religious experience to belief in this cause; she becomes fascinated by London poverty, leaves her mother's sister's house in Bayswater and goes to live in a notorious slum, the better to alleviate the slum-dwellers' suffering. Her cousin Anne believes Joan's plan to be an 'experiment' to find 'happiness in self-denial' and 'self-sacrifice' (p. 110) but it soon develops beyond such tentativeness, though Koven's reading requires Prinseps soon to be engaged primarily in sexual slumming. He draws attention to the absence of men in the heroine's life and her deep friendship with Martha Mace, a girl of the gutter, that spills in a prison cell scene into what Koven reads as a candidly erotic piece of lovemaking: 'I put my arms around her neck...and then she kissed my lips again and again, as if she were starving, and I had given her a full and satisfying meal.'[65] Koven quotes Edward Carpenter's belief that many male and female philanthropists were inspired by same-sex love that was camouflaged by the cross-class scene in which it expressed itself virtually or actually.[66]

The romance–sensationalism of Meade's title detracts preemptively from what is on the whole a sustained depiction of London slum life as experienced by a kind of New Woman who sacrifices an immediate career advance of some kind for the altruism of philanthropic activism: 'Eastward Ho!' she cries as she sets out briskly to live and work among 'the unclassed...the submerged tenth'.[67] There are two plot-strands rooted in contemporary slum-life. One is the resignation (at best), hostility (at worst) Prinseps encounters from lawyers, landlords, and middle-class citizens in her campaign to better the lives of those who inhabit the two slum complexes (or 'courts') she has inherited. In her progress amidst the crime, squalor, violence, and disease (all thickly and atmospherically painted in), her only real help comes from Ranald ('Father') Moore, a hands-on priest, like Mulholland's Father Tim or the real-life Alexander Irvine (both of whom we will meet later), who works among the poor but who faces the suspicion, even animus directed by the poor at 'the religious dodge' (p. 121).[68] His precise denomination is unclear but Father Moore appears to be an Anglo-Catholic. Close to his vicarage and men's club in Shoreditch are the men from Oxford who live in Balliol House in Bethnal Green, a University Settlement among the poor. (Meade as usual has done her homework thoroughly in preparing to write her problem-novel.)[69] Alongside the Church and university, Joan Prinseps represents philanthropy as private enterprise, a third and auxiliary way. (Elinor Grey's way is private but hardly an enterprise.) She starts a girls' club and builds model housing but combines kindness and personal charity with the teaching of self-help and the work-ethic, taking to heart Father Moore's insistence that she not 'pauperise' the poor by merely providing them with what they need (p. 233). From this we can infer Meade's own philosophy of social alleviation, which clearly did not envisage any long-term socio-economic solution.

Prinseps's work survives difficulties, including an attempt on her life, and distractions, one of which provides the second plot-strand. Prinseps be-friends, or rather, is befriended by, two brazen young slum-women, Lucy Ash and Martha Mace, who are inseparable 'mates' until Lucy's boyfriend, Michael Lee, becomes her husband while Martha, who is the brutish Lee's real sexual interest, is ill and out of the picture. Meade paints the working and workless lives of these East Enders with a detail that reminds us of the eloquent pages of Henry Mayhew; for example, Martha becomes for a time a watercress-seller, one of the lowest-ranking jobs, getting her supply of cress at Farringdon Market which as a source for cress-sellers Mayhew describes at some length in *London Labour & the London Poor* (1851–65),[70] a reminder that the Victorian and Edwardian problem-novelists shared with social in-vestigators such as Mayhew and W. T. Stead some motivation and methods of field-work. Mayhew remarks on the 'most imperfect idea of the sanctity of marriage' entertained by the London costermongers and the casually brutal way in which the costerlads treat the costergirls,[71] but Meade as a novelist goes beyond Mayhew, though not Stead, in depicting love and marriage among the poor. Lee marries Lucy and impregnates her but is cruelly oblivious to her and stalks Mace until his insanely jealous wife stabs him to death. In an act of self-sacrifice that outdoes even Joan's, Martha takes the blame because she loves Lucy and at the Old Bailey is sentenced to hang; but there is a happyish ending for Martha and Lucy's baby if not for Lucy, and for Joan's philanthropic enterprise there is the prospect of continuing modest success in cushioning the lives of some of the impoverished.

The difficulty in generalising about Meade (and other prolific novelists), for example on the question of sexuality, is the sheer diversity of her work; if a sexual subtext is discovered, it is unlikely to signal an authorial preoccupation or sexual proclivity unless it resurfaces in other Meade novels and Koven has no time to show that it does. Koven contrasts Meade's sexual outspokenness on the lesbian theme with E. M. Forster's caution in deferring publication of *Maurice*; but this comparison implies that *A Princess of the Gutter* is Meade's *Maurice* whereas, although Forster wrote a very few novels, all highly pon-dered as a result, Meade wrote hundreds, not one of which could claim the kind of weight and *oeuvre*-altering significance for itself that *Maurice* could. Also, there is the possibility that in such a novel as *A Princess of the Gutter*, Meade is herself 'slumming' as an author, in the sense that she was, as a professional writer working to a deadline, hastily hybridizing the genres of romance, schoolgirl fiction, and slum-novel and occasionally slipping gears while doing so; in such a hybrid, Victorian emotional overplus, even sentimentality, could appear to us on those occasions like barely disguised lesbian expression. But to some extent the novel even on its own terms might explain the scenes of apparent sexuality slightly differently from Koven though without denying some truth to his interpretation.

Certainly there is a larger catalogue than even Koven suggests of peculiar intimacies in *A Princess of the Gutter*, with Joan, Martha, and Lucy forming a triangle more intimate than, if not as tense and dangerous as, the triangle formed by Lucy, Lee, and Martha. Although the two have just met, Lucy 'without the least warning' lays her head on Joan's shoulder (p. 134) and this establishes the physical demonstrativeness of the women characters, whereas the men are stiff and reserved (the lawyer and landlord), disqualified (Father Moore), or sexually aggressive but unfeeling (Michael Lee). The relationship of Joan and Martha is rather more charged; Joan has made Martha a blouse and praises her beauty lavishly ('God gave you a beautiful face, and a grand figure' p. 143); for her part, Martha can't explain 'wot I feels when I'm with yer' (p. 153), though here the feeling seems to border on religious worship, Martha having already likened Joan to an angel on the stained-glass window of Moore's church, a recurring motif in the novel; in any case, Martha's is an intense feeling: 'I love you, Jo-an (*sic*); I think o' you day and night' (p. 185); Joan finds Martha's compliments heady—'like draughts of champagne—strong, fresh, invigorating, direct. I prized them more than I could say. No girl with her lover could enjoy sweet praise more than I did from the lips of this strong maiden of the East End' (pp. 194–5). At the same time, Martha's feeling for Lucy is just as intense: although Lucy has shrunk from her in jealousy and although Martha is having trouble rebuffing the man with whom she had been involved and still, beneath her hatred, loves, Martha maintains that 'I love 'er—I'm true to 'er to the 'eart's core' (p. 195). When they are reunited, Joan overhears Martha speaking to Lucy in a voice 'with a wonderfully passionate thrill in it' (p. 279); leaving the two alone to make up, Joan leaves and returns to see Lucy's arms around Martha's neck, then Lucy sinking and clasping Martha around the knees kissing her dress, and at last sinking far enough to kiss Martha's 'roughly shod feet' (p. 280). The triangle becomes a rectangle when Joan's cousin, Anne Bannerman, won over from her scepticism and loathing of poor people and dirt (p. 113), arrives to join forces with Joan, exclaiming, somewhat out of character, 'you never guessed that I could have such a feeling towards you, hungering for you' (p. 208).

It is the very festival of apparently lesbian desires that ought to give us pause. If Meade is in fact at some level of her writerly consciousness indulging those desires, as novelists expressly and routinely indulge heterosexual desires, that need not detract from my own reading of *A Princess of the Gutter*—that Meade has decided to interpret literally the idea of philanthropy, and has made her heroine a lover of the poor in a quite physical and emotional fashion, imbuing that love with an evangelical (though non-denominational) fervour. The scenes of intimacy are connected, thus, with the running motif of 'Martha's angel' (who is both Martha and Joan, the angels of the slum); expressed in the heated registers of Victorian sentiment, this is love of one's neighbour in so unabashed a form as to resemble romantic and sexual union.

Moreover, although Mayhew has nothing to say on the subject, it is possible that slum girls, like factory and mill girls of not so long ago, had 'mates' whose close and confidential company was emotionally necessary but whose support in the endless scrapes and trials of life, at work, at home, and with men friends, was also a practical survival device as they boxed each other's corner. Martha claims that 'All on us 'ave our mates' and that 'it's much more'n friend—we're mates, that's wot we calls each other. It's as good as bein' married in some ways, an' with none of the troubles' (Lucy's marriage to Lee proves the truth of this.); 'we sticks to each other through thick an' thin, an' fights for each other, and shares each other's bite and sup. There ain't a gel in our factory wot 'aven't 'er mate' (p. 127). Much later, Prinseps returns to this odd phenomenon: ' "You girls in East London think a great deal of being mates." "It's as close as marriage," said Martha, in a husky whisper; "it's till death do us part" ' (p. 187), and so it proves with Lucy and Martha.

If the bond between Lucy and Martha is not importantly sexual, that leaves the stranger bond between Martha and Joan. Just after her uncle's death and reflecting on the deathbed promise he seemed to have exacted from her on the strength of his wealth, Joan recalls for us that 'I did not want money, and I did not want marriage. I had an aspiration for a perfect friendship, either with a man or a woman—I did not much care which' (pp. 26–7). Her Uncle Ralph had already said to her: 'I greatly fear you have got too much of the masculine element in you' (p. 14), but I assume this is not to establish her bisexuality, rather to prepare the reader for her dispassionate approach to life and a practicality that will take the form of a good business head. Her uncle regards her as 'young and strong and modern. You have been educated up to date' (p. 20), and of course men told themselves to cover their anxiety that such young women were not wholly feminine. Prinseps also recalls for us: 'I had a vague uneasy wish to rise to a height where I could breathe a sort of spiritual air, but I did not want goodness in the abstract' (pp. 26–7). Like Elinor Grey, Joan Prinseps needs to clear the decks of conventional love, marriage, and wealth in order to achieve herself in altruism. In each novel, romantic love is meant to be tranposed and transmuted, but whereas in *A Woman-Derelict* Grey turns her back on romantic, sexual, and marital intimacy, Joan Prinseps has still to find intimacy and a friendship which is goodness, not in the abstract but in the concrete, in the flesh, the perfect friendship being with Martha, perhaps, and possibly Anne. But the rhetoric of that perfect friendship is not distinguishable to the casual reader from the rhetoric of heterosexual romance applied to female friendship. Indeed, in the prison cell scene that caused Koven's eyebrows to rise, one might detect both an unfortunate vampirish metaphor (though Meade's novel was published before *Dracula*) and a hunger allusion that fits literally the novel elsewhere but in this scene is meant to signify hunger for human company and emotional support. Mayhew observes of the costergirls that 'everything is sacrificed...in the struggle to live—aye! And to live *merely*. Mind, heart, soul, are all absorbed in the belly. The rudest form of animal life, physiologists tell us, is simply a locomotive stomach. Verily, it would appear as if our social state had a tendency to make the highest animal sink to the lowest'.[72]

All this said, the 'all-female arcadia', as Koven calls it, the 'small community of loving women'[73] that the heroine constructs for herself at the end of the novel bears resemblance to the female sanctuary that Dagmar Olloffson establishes in Meade's *The Cleverest Woman in England* (1898), and does at least suggest an agenda of sorority that is gender-specific even if it may not be sexually motivated, implying in turn that philanthropy certainly had for Meade a gender dimension.

Many did not question this dimension, but in fact promoted the connection between gender and philanthropy. The other side of Baron Questo's (and perhaps Riddell's) cynicism is the prevalent and sincere notion in several of these novels that altruism and femininity are intimately connected. MacMahon can be hard on contemporary woman and in *A Pitiless Passion* Georgie foxes Grain with 'a weapon of irresistible force' in the 'armoury' that Nature has given her: 'coquetry'. Later, the narrator observes that 'for one woman who will lie openly, straightly, honestly—so to speak—there are ten thousand women who will only lie by prevarication, by evasion, by a half. To lie by evasion is a woman's readiest resource'. Moreover, 'it is not always the woman who is the injured party in the relationship between the sexes, as we like to call it now. Fortunately, so far as women are concerned, certainly it is more difficult, as a rule, to corrupt a man's entire nature, than a woman's'.[74] Yet the novel could bear the subtitle given to *Tess of the d'Urbervilles* by Hardy: *A Pure Woman*. Magdalen receives what she considers to be a visit from Christ when she lifts the 4-year-old child of a groom in her arms and becomes, as it were, a Madonna: her self-sacrifice is an essential portion of her womanhood.

This cross-grained presentation of women and the novel's hesitation about the virtues of self-abnegating charity is part of what makes MacMahon an interesting writer.

Self-sacrifice is the lesson, too, of Letts's *The Rough Way*. At the end of the novel Julie Vibert is unsure what to do with herself, Antony having entered the Order. He tells her God has invented two of the finest vocations: gentleman and lady: 'to be a lady implies every virtue and self-sacrifice; renunciation is but a preliminary stage, in all life construction is the main work. Construct a lady'. She decides to try it. Earlier Antony has thought there are two kinds of women, one characterized by utility and an obvious womanliness, the other by poetry and romance which leads to a kind of feminism. (His sister believes the choice is between mistress and mother.) In any case, Hesketh's terminal ideal is of the first kind and sounds like his own mother whose life gives the novel one meaning of its title. She is of yeoman stock and as a minister's wife she has performed, we might say, 'yeoman service': being the drudge of a large family, bringing seven children into the world, devising means of feeding, clothing, and educating them, accepting 'her wifehood in a spirit essential to later happiness, as a hard vocation for which she had been trained'. She 'never repined when she found her lot rough, bare and hard ... Very wisely she looked upon marriage as the end of personal freedom, the close of youth's holiday'. She has enjoyed the struggle and romance settled in the form of love for her son Antony.[75] No wonder it is Julie Vibert who is reading Synge's *The Shadow of the Glen* or that Antony is repulsed by the character of Hedda Gabler when he sees her on the stage. The fact that women's self-sacrifice does not in the novel include the almost romantic *activism* of Hesketh's slum work makes it harder to accept today Letts's religious vision of true womanhood.

Charity required self-sacrifice of some sort and it was thought, especially from a Christian perspective such as MacMahon's, Crommelin's, Meade's, and Letts's, that self-sacrifice was part of woman's nature whereas it had to be achieved by men. Even in the late Victorian period there was an attitude to human beings, and therefore to society, that informed the value systems of those who were at the same time conscious of the need for women's freedom. Letts, for example, is aware of the necessary attraction of female self-fulfilment, and the woman in the title of her novel *Christina's Son* (1915), set in Southport in the 1880s, is an unmarried 25-year-old 'late Victorian' (daughter of a retired Manchester cotton broker) in whose being 'stirred that passion for freedom that long ago sent Daphne flying after Apollo'. She wants passion and romance but something else that she can't define; she seems 'muddled': 'The real me is asleep, or it's dead, or something,' she complains. But the fate of this proto-New Woman will be decided inside the context of religion. She marries an evangelical Church of England rector, is widowed, and is later converted to Catholicism by Ingleby, the new man in her life.[76]

NOTES

1. I discuss the former in *Recoveries: Neglected Episodes in Irish Cultural History* (2002); to Protestant sermons we can add such a Roman Catholic text as the *Pastoral Address* of the Irish Catholic Hierarchy issued in reaction to Tyndall's Address. I discuss the sermons preached in response to the famous shipwreck in *The Age of Titanic: Cross-Currents in Anglo-American Culture* (2002); one Belfast newspaper painstakingly reproduced the texts of the *Titanic* sermons.
2. I have reinstated in this quotation the preacher's original direct speech (the *Belfast News-Letter* reporter having turned the sermon into indirect speech): see J. W. Foster, *The Age of Titanic* (Dublin: Merlin Press, 2002), pp. 91, 93, 214.
3. The Catholic hierarchy refused to accept the University of Dublin (Trinity College) because of its Protestantism and the 'godless' Queen's Colleges (in Cork, Galway, and Belfast) and wanted a National University with a Catholic ethos.
4. Richard D. Altick, *Victorian People and Ideas* (New York: Norton, 1973), p. 203.
5. James Douglas, *The Unpardonable Sin* (London: Grant Richards, 1907), pp. 161–3.
6. L. T. Meade, *A Princess of the Gutter* (New York: Putnam's, 1896), pp. 118–19.
7. Toynbee Hall, named after a young Balliol tutor, was the first such programme begun in 1884 and others followed through 1913; they were also started in the slums of the United States. The idea was that students would live, temporarily or during vacations, in slums while carrying out charitable, educational, and advisory activities. Meade's novel is roughly based on these programmes of alleviation. See J. F. C. Harrison, *Late Victorian Britain 1875–1901* (London: Fontana, 1990), pp. 194–5.
8. F. E. Crichton, *The Soundless Tide* (London: Edward Arnold, 1911), p. 66.
9. Alexander, *The Rambling Rector* (London: Edward Arnold, 1904), pp. 3, 122.
10. Alfred Barry, 'What is Ritualism?' *The Contemporary Review* 74 (1898): 643. See also H. C. Corrance, 'The Development of Ritualism', *The Contemporary Review* 74 (1898): 91–106. A brief account of the so-called Revision Controversy in Ireland can be found in Donald Harman Akenson, *The Church of Ireland: Ecclesiastical Reform and Revolution, 1800–1885* (New Haven: Yale University Press, 1971), pp. 302–9. The longevity of the issue in Anglicanism is demonstrated by George Orwell's novel, *A Clergyman's Daughter* (1935) in which the title character has been brought up in 'the peculiar, frigid *via media* of Anglicanism', a road bounded on one side by the liberties of modernism and on the other by the 'Roman fever' and ritualism of Anglo-Catholicism. This 'continuous pull devil, pull baker' between the three branches of Anglicanism is happening after 1908 and apparently as late as the 1920s: *A Clergyman's Daughter* in the George Orwell novel omnibus (London: Secker & Warburg, 1976), pp. 265–6, 292–3.
11. Altick, *Victorian People and Ideas*, p. 216.

12. Alexander, *The Rambling Rector*, pp. 252, 102, 266, 278. Alexander's father, William, Archbishop of Armagh, had warm memories of the evangelicalism of before 1870 and its fondness for positive, often extemporaneous sermons: see Alan Acheson, *A History of the Church of Ireland 1691–2001* (1997; Dublin: The Columba Press and APCK, 2002), p. 182.

13. I take the phrase about the respective powers of pulpit and altar from A. O. J. Cockshut, whose essay, 'Faith and Doubt in the Victorian Age', includes an overview of the Oxford Movement and its later followers, called Ritualists: in *The Penguin History of Literature*, vol. 6: *The Victorians*, ed. Arthur Pollard (1969; London: Penguin Books, 1993); see pp. 36–7.

14. See Vergilius Ferm, ed., *The Encyclopedia of Religion* (Secaucus, N.J.: Poplar Books, 1945), pp. 665, 263. For an overview of the issue in England, see Altick, *Victorian People and Ideas*, pp. 208–19.

15. Alexander, *The Rambling Rector*, pp. 184, 13, 158, 155. Akenson discusses the financial difficulties of the Church after disestablishment in *The Church of Ireland*, pp. 309–21.

16. Winifred M. Letts was born in Wexford in 1882 and died in Kent in 1972. She wrote novels, plays, poems, memoirs, children's stories, and hagiography, the last two combined in the beautifully illustrated and produced *Helmet & Cowl: Stories of Monastic and Military Orders* (1913), with M. F. S. Letts. The book gives accounts of the lives of St Anthony, St Jerome, St Benedict, St Bernard, and St Catherine of Siena at key moments of their religious significance. The internal storyteller, the Bishop of Silchester, tells his nephews and nieces that 'these legends of saints are quite as good as fairy stories'. Letts is offering the religious counterpart to the rejuvenated fairy lore of the Revival but her book belongs to the Protestant tradition of illustrated Church history for children cast in story form.

17. W. M. Letts, *The Rough Way* (Milwaukee: The Young Churchman Co., 1912), pp. 58, 224, 17, 140, 24.

18. The young Dublin scholar Mary Hayden, a Catholic, recorded in her journal the spiritual effect on her of *John Inglesant* when she read it in 1883: see *The Diaries of Mary Hayden 1878–1903*, ed. Conan Kennedy (Killala, Mayo: Morrigan, 2005), vol. 1 (*1878–83*), pp. 421–2.

19. Letts, *The Rough Way*, pp. 26, 140. For the Molinists, see Alfred J. Freddoso, 'Molinism', http://www3.nd.edu/~afreddos/papers/molinism/htm

20. A. O. J. Cockshut, 'Faith and Doubt in the Victorian Age', *Penguin History of Literature*: vol. 6, *The Victorians*, p. 36; Altick, *Victorian People and Ideas*, p. 217. In 1907 Stephen Lucius Gwynn observed that a vaguely socialistic humanitarian-ism with which the High Church party allies itself is a movement that 'sends so many brilliant young Englishmen into work (temporary or permanent) in the East End of London': *Irish Books and Irish People* (1920; Freeport, New York: Books for Libraries, 1969), pp. 67–8.

21. Altick, *Victorian People and Ideas*, p. 212.

22. Harry Furniss has a recollection of Hobbes and instances her as the type of 'authoress' whose effort and success were predicated on an unhappy marriage; he seemed to disapprove of her tough business sense: *Some Victorian Women* (London: John Lane The Bodley Head, 1923), pp. 23–8.

23. *Edwardian Fiction: An Oxford Companion*, eds. Sandra Kemp, Charlotte Mitchell and David Trotter (Oxford: Oxford University Press, 1997), s.v. 'MacMahon, Ella'.

24. MacMahon, *A Pitiless Passion* (New York: Macmillan, 1895), pp. 96–9.

25. But the alcohol problem was seen as severe in England, too. See, for example, 'The Present Phase of the Temperance Question' and 'Practical Temperance Legislation', both in *Contemporary Review* 76 (1899). Also, G. M. Trevelyan, *English Social History* (1942; Harmondsworth: Pelican Books, 1964), pp. 582–3.

26. MacMahon, *A Pitiless Passion*, pp. 127, 119–20, 277, 285.

27. MacMahon, *A Pitiless Passion*, pp. 223, 159–60, 212, 300, 345. *Daughters of Men* is a novel by Hannah Lynch (b. Dublin 1862, d. Paris 1904) published only three years before *A Pitiless Passion* and which MacMahon might have known. The title phrase of this novel set in Greece comes from the modern Greek reference to girl babies as 'daughters of men' (boy babies being called 'sons of God') who are also described as 'these explosive engines, known as daughters, born to poor harassed man').

28. Mrs Erminda Rentoul Esler was herself the daughter of a Manor Cunningham, Co. Donegal manse. Her maiden name was Rentoul and she married Dr Robert Esler.

29. E. Rentoul Esler, *A Maid of the Manse* (London: Sampson Low, Marston & Co., 1895), pp. 35, 33, 34.

30. Father Mathew (1790–1856) of the Capuchin order began a total abstinence movement and 'hoisted the banner', as he put it, throughout Ireland.

31. One character in Mrs Humphry Ward's once-famous *Robert Elsmere* (1888) undergoes a change that is profound and said to be symptomatic of a broader cultural transformation: 'that dissociation of the moral judgment from a special series of religious formulae which is the crucial, the epoch-making fact of our day'. Quoted by J. F. C. Harrison, *Late Victorian Britain, 1875–1901* (London; Fontana Press, 1990), p. 125. John Kucich echoes and broadens this when he observes that 'One cause of Victorian doubt was a growing sense that moral sensibility was no longer served by the religious and social institutions that were supposed to represent it': 'Intellectual Debate in the Victorian Novel: Religion, Science, and the Professional', in *The Cambridge Companion to the Victorian Novel*, ed. Deirdre David (Cambridge: Cambridge University Press, 2001), p. 214. Margaret Maison provides a survey of the Victorian religious novel in *Search Your Soul, Eustace* (1961) which includes novels of conversion and apostasy. Six of her chapters are devoted to Anglican novels, two to Catholic novels, one to Nonconformist novels. I am indebted for this citation to Lisbet Kickham, *Protestant Women Novelists and Irish Society 1879–1922* (2004). Kickham offers brief discussion of three Esler novels, including *A Maid of the Manse*.

32. Ingersoll's lecture provoked outcries. One reply to it was Allan Magruder's *The Bible Defended and Atheism Rebuked* (New York, 1881) and *The Mistakes of Moses and Other Sermons* by William Patterson, pastor of Cooke's Presbyterian Church, Toronto (1899) and no doubt an Ulsterman.

33. Esler, *A Maid of the Manse*, pp. 275, 276, 302, 315.
34. Autobiographical notes quoted by Elisabeth Boyd Bayly, *The Author of 'The Spanish Brothers' (Deborah Alcock): Her Life and Works* (London: Marshall Brothers, n.d. [1914]), p. 41.
35. Ibid., p. 158.
36. Ibid., p. 116.
37. Ibid., p. 34.
38. Ibid., p. 248.
39. Ibid., pp. 141–2.
40. Alcock, *The Romance of Protestantism: Tales of Trials and Victory* (1908; Neerlandia, Alberta; Pella, Iowa: Inheritance Publications, 1999), p. 9.
41. See Vivian Mercier on the Church of Ireland background of many of the Revivalists and on evangelicalism as a root-strand of the Revival project: 'Victorian Evangelicalism and the Anglo-Irish Literary Revival', *Literature and the Changing Ireland*, ed. Peter Connolly (Gerrards Cross: Colin Smythe, 1982), pp. 59–101.
42. Before Waterford, Revd John Alcock (whose wife died soon after the birth of Deborah in 1835) was in charge of Bethesda church and orphanage in Dublin, where one of his staunchest supporters was Arthur Guinness, doing his part for temperance by inventing the recipe for porter (Black Protestant Stout, now known as Guinness) that was considerably weaker than whiskey. At Bethesda, according to a correspondent who contacted Bayly after Deborah Alcock's death, her father was a literally awe-inspiring preacher who stressed the hellbound consequences of leaving this world unsaved; the paraphrases of his sermons might remind one of the sermon on hell in Joyce's *Portrait of the Artist*. See Bayly, *The Author of 'The Spanish Brothers'*, pp. 67–8, 74–9. In Dublin (1852–66) the Alcock father and daughter lived at the Joycean address of 39 Eccles Street.
43. Bayly, *The Author of 'The Spanish Brothers' (Deborah Alcock)*, pp. 19, 21.
44. Alcock would no doubt have read Bonnechose's book in the 1844 translation made by Campbell MacKenzie of Trinity College Dublin.
45. Deborah Alcock, *The Romance of Protestantism*, p. 32, 56.
46. Deborah Alcock, *By Far Euphrates: A Tale on Armenia in the 19th Century* (1897; Neerlandia: Alberta; Pella: Iowa: Inheritance Publications, 2002), p. 116.
47. Because of the persistence of a Christian readership, Alcock's novels cannot be said to have competed in the marketplace in the usual way. Nevertheless, the reprinting history of some of her novels is impressive. *Crushed Yet Conquering* was reprinted in 1940 and 2002; *Under the Southern Cross* (1873) was republished in 1874, 1878, 1884, 1894, 1897 and 1900. Her most famous novel in her own day was *The Spanish Brothers* (1870) which was republished in 1871, 1888, 1891, 1950–6, 1966, and 2001. Her books after 1890 include *Doctor Adrian: A Story of Old Holland* (1897), *Under Calvin's Spell* (1900), and *Robert Musgrave's Adventure: A Story of Old Geneva* (1909).
48. Alcock, *Crushed Yet Conquering: A Story of Constance and Bohemia* (Neerlandia, Alberta: Inheritance Publications, 2002), pp. 427–9.
49. She has a sophisticated spiritual response to Kingsley (whom she loved but whose influence she feared) in an 1877 letter: Bayly, *The Author of 'The Spanish Brothers' (Deborah Alcock)*, pp. 168–9.

50. Bayly, *The Author of 'The Spanish Brothers' (Deborah Alcock)*, pp. 201–2.
51. Boyle's *Love and Religion* can be read at Eighteenth Century Collections Online.
52. L. T. Meade, *Stories from the Old Old Bible* (London: George Newnes, 1903), p. 1.
53. Bayly, *The Author of 'The Spanish Brothers' (Deborah Alcock)*, p. 41.
54. MacMahon, *A Pitiless Passion*, pp. 316, 317, 212. Since Wilde's *The Importance of Being Earnest* was first performed the same year that MacMahon's novel appeared, Lady Halliday cannot be echoing Miss Prism who says: 'I am not in favour of this modern mania for turning bad people into good people at a moment's notice. As a man sows so let him reap': *The Portable Oscar Wilde*, ed. Richard Aldington and Stanley Weintraub (New York: Penguin Books, 1981), p. 459.
55. Meade, *A Princess of the Gutter*, p. 162. Some observations on girls' colleges are contained in a brief discussion of Meade by Mary Cadogan and Patricia Craig, *You're A Brick, Angela! A New Look at Girls' Fiction from 1839 to 1975* (London: Gollancz, 1976), pp. 50–4.
56. May Crommelin, *A Woman-Derelict* (London: John Long, [1901]), p. 43. For brief descriptions of real-life slumming, see *The Diaries of Mary Hayden*: vol. IV *(1893–1898)*, p. 2045, vol. V *(1899–1903)*, pp. 2116, 2120, 2150, 2151, 2155, 2197. Hayden 'slummed' in the Coombe district of the city; she mentions the societies that participated in this philanthropic activity. Hayden maintained a critical distance from the unfortunate poor.
57. Annie M. P. Smithson, *Her Irish Heritage* (1917; Cork: Mercier, 1988), p. 63.
58. MacMahon, *A New Note* (1894; New York: R.F. Fenno, 1895), pp. 135–6.
59. Stephen Lucius Gwynn refers in 1907 to a recently organised 'Social Service Society' which attempts to do for the Dublin slum poor what educated young Englishmen are doing for the East End poor, but this Society would appear to have been voluntary rather than state funded: *Irish Books and Irish People* (1920; Freeport, New York: Books for Libraries Press, 1969), p. 68.
60. Riddell, *A Rich Man's Daughter* (New York: The International News Company, 1895), pp. 29, 33, 161.
61. Maria Henrietta de la Cherois (May) Crommelin was of the Huguenot family that settled in Donaghadee and Lisburn, Co. Down and began the linen industry in the north of Ireland. She published at least forty-eight books, most of them popular novels. Among her books is *Over the Andes: From the Argentine to Chili and Peru* (1896) which intends 'to give a woman's bird's eye view of life out there' and is a readable survey knowledgeable on the plantlife, agriculture, food, homes, commerce, and ethnic diversity of these countries. She makes several comparative observations about Ireland and appears to have known the wife of Her Majesty's envoy and plenipotentiary to Paraguay and Argentina, Francis Pakenham, back in Ulster. As a travel book, *Over the Andes* puts Crommelin, barely, in the company of Hannah Lynch and Beatrice Grimshaw.
62. May Crommelin, *A Woman-Derelict*, p. 251.
63. May Crommelin, *Over the Andes from The Argentine to Chili and Peru* (London: Richard Bentley, 1896), p. 204.
64. M. Hamilton, *The First Claim* (1906; New York: Doubleday, Page & Co., 1907), p. 210.

65. Seth Koven, *Slumming: Sexual and Social Politics in Victorian London* (Princeton: Princeton University Press, 2004), p. 219. The passage occurs in *A Princess of the Gutter*, p. 295.

66. Koven, *Slumming*, p. 219.

67. Meade, *A Princess of the Gutter*, pp. 83, 160, 166, 306.

68. According to Koven, Father Moore was modelled on Father Jay, the celebrated Anglican slum priest who worked in the district of the Old Nichol, the original for Meade's Jasper Court: Koven, p. 217.

69. However, on the strength of Koven's research, we know that the tireless Meade already knew a good deal, actively involved as she was in evangelical philanthropy in London, especially engaged with the SPCC: Koven, p. 216.

70. See Peter Quennell's abridged version of Mayhew: *Mayhew's London* (London: Bracken Books, 1984), pp. 112–16. See also p. 91.

71. See Mayhew, pp. 90, 93–4.

72. Mayhew, p. 91. (That the economically comfortable Anne Bannerman 'hungered' for Joan might weaken the force of this point a little.)

73. Koven, *Slumming*, pp. 219–20.

74. MacMahon, *A Pitiless Passion*, pp. 197, 199, 244, 285.

75. Letts, *The Rough Way*, pp. 340, 5, 35, 36.

76. Letts, *Christina's Son* (London: Wells Gardner, Darton & Co, [1915]), pp. 28, 13, 24.

4

'Their Patience Folly?': Catholicism and Irish Fiction

FICTION AND CATHOLICISM

If the sermon, such as that which ends *By Far Euphrates* or is preached near the start of May Crommelin's *A Woman-Derelict*, was not a Protestant preserve (as we are reminded by one of the most famous sermons in literature, that in Joyce's *A Portrait of the Artist*),[1] no more was philanthropy in nineteenth-century Ireland, which preoccupied many religious Irish, particularly Irish women, of both main Churches. The range of involvement by women in organized charity, from the 'benevolent ladies' represented by Aunt Jane in *The Rambling Rector* through nuns and charitable sisters to girls resolving sexual and social crises by way of philanthropic labour and what we would now call outreach work, was very broad. A novel that depicts the most dedicated kind of philanthropy—not money given but selfless works performed—is *Father Tim* (1910). The author, Rosa Mulholland from Belfast (1841–1921) who became Lady Gilbert when her husband was knighted in 1897, moved in exalted social circles and she may have qualified as one of the Belfast counterparts of the *grandes dames* among Dublin Catholics to whom Tynan refers. Certainly her connection and circle make nonsense of the widespread idea that there was no real Catholic middle class, much less Catholic upper class in Ireland, with the associated implication that the British prevented these classes from coming into existence (not that the contemporary literary critic would cherish such classes in any case!).[2] And if one wishes to read literature written from a point of view almost as decidedly Catholic as Alcock's was Protestant, Mulholland is a fair candidate.

Of course, there were other readable and educated women fiction writers of the time who were Catholic and they included Katharine Tynan, Julia M. Crottie, Clara Mulholland, Mary Maher, Katherine Cecil Thurston, M. E. Francis, George Egerton, Hannah Lynch, Alice Dease, Charlotte Dease, Helena Walsh (Mrs Concannon), Ellen Mary Clerke, Gertrude M. O'Reilly, Elizabeth Hart,[3] and, to add three converts from Protestantism, Ella MacMahon, Annie M. P. Smithson, and Beatrice Grimshaw. Most of these were educated at convent schools and often in Europe or England. (George Moore opens his 1886 anti-clerical and anti-Society novel, *A Drama in Muslin,* in an English convent school.)

These Catholic novelists on the face of it might challenge George Moore's conviction that Catholicism was the enemy of literature and George Orwell's similar belief that prose literature is an individual thing, demanding mental honesty and a minimum of censorship. Catholicism, Orwell was sure, is inimical to the novel ('the most anarchical of all forms of literature'): 'How many Roman Catholics have been good novelists? Even the handful one could name have usually been bad Catholics. The novel is practically a Protestant form of art; it is a product of the free mind, of the autonomous individual.'[4] One possibility here is that these Irish novelists (to which we can add Canon Sheehan and other Catholic novelists, before and after) simply refute Moore and Orwell. Another is that these educated Catholic novelists were culturally Protestant while being theologically Catholic or, to put it another way, they bracketed off their Catholicism (if in fact they were worshipping Catholics) when writing their fiction. (One or two could not divide themselves in this way, for example Maher and Smithson and, as a result, one would have to say, wrote inferior novels.) Another is that the novels these novelists wrote were not fully expressive of the autonomous individual, any more than was Alcock's: that these writers managed inside the novel form to endorse collective will and social value and did so by writing unadventurously and formulaically. Or perhaps Orwell meant only to show the rarity of *first-rate* Catholic novelists. My own view is that there is some truth in all of these responses to these Irish novelists in the light of Orwell and Moore.

In any case, a version of the same issue arises with some of the Protestant counterparts of the female Catholic novelists, who, as well as Alcock, included W. M. Letts, L. T. Meade, Mrs J. H. Riddell, Eleanor Alexander, Helen Duffin, M. Hamilton (Mary Churchill Luck, née Ash), B. M. Croker, Dorothea Conyers, Jane Barlow, Emily Lawless, Ethel Mayne, Edith Somerville and Martin Ross, May Crommelin, Erminda Rentoul Esler, F. E. Crichton, and Eleanor Hull. Many Protestant women fiction writers were daughters of clergy: Eleanor Alexander, Barlow, Croker, Esler, Catherine J. Hamilton, Frances Craig Houston, Maggie J. Houston, Mrs Hungerford, Rosamond Langbridge, Mabel S. Madden, Meade, Ella MacMahon, Lydia M. Foster. An impressive number of Protestant women authors were educated at Alexandra College, founded 1866: they include Miriam Alexander, Mary E. Butler, Hull, Letts, Edith Somerville, Violet Martin (Martin Ross),[5] Katherine Frances Purdon, and Margaret Barrington. When the college moved into new premises in 1888, the Irish Clergy Daughters' School (founded 1843 to educate the daughters of Anglican clergymen in straitened circumstances) joined forces with the newly situated college. Deborah Alcock was offered the post of Headmistress in the Clergy Daughters' School in 1890 but declined. This is a pity, since had she accepted she might have personally hired (or declined to hire) Patrick Pearse who taught at Alexandra College in 1899. Perhaps the fact that from the start there were small numbers of Catholics, Nonconformists, and Jews at Alexandra College made it attractive to Pearse, or it may be that only in the early twentieth century was an otherwise reasonably homogeneous society, especially at the middle-class level and above, deeply and irrevocably fissured by religion and nationalism. In any case, the cultural importance of the Clergy Daughters' School and Alexandra College is not to be underestimated.[6]

It was the Catholic women writers who were prepared to identify themselves publicly as such. *A Round Table of the Representative Irish and English Catholic Novelists* (1897) includes short stories by four Irish novelists out of twelve, all women: M. E. Francis, Clara Mulholland, Rosa Mulholland, and Katharine Tynan (Hinkson). The story by the Co. Dublin writer M. E. Francis (Mrs Francis Blundell: this alternative name appeared below her pseudonym on her novels' title pages), 'In St. Patrick's Ward', is set, fittingly for our context, in a Union infirmary run by the Sisters of Charity. Only the piety and care of the Sisters allay the horror of the poorhouse. A new patient in the infirmary pathetically awaits the return of her son from America to rescue her from the Union. Whereas 'as a rule the Irish poor die calmly and peacefully, happy in their faith and resignation', Mrs Brady is not going gentle into that good night, chatters incessantly about her son, and begins to despair of his return. As she is dying, she treats the statue of St Patrick in the ward as the real man who tells her to accept the will of God. She dies resigned, even happy, and this is the message she leaves for her son who turns up to hear her story and take the beads and medal she has left him, and who is overcome with emotion. The piety, sentimentality, and pathos of the story are repeated in the other Irish stories, as is the figure of the mother, the theme of charity, and in one other (Rosa Mulholland's) the motif of the returned American. The poorhouse beckons too in Mulholland's 'Granny Grogan' which takes place in a small-town slum: 'Isn't purgatory itself a crowned king to the Union?' declares the title character threatened by the poorhouse when the neighbourhood decides it has supported her on charity long enough. Mother and daughter, who believe themselves strangers, are reunited, in a more real sense than the spiritual sense in which mother and son are reunited in Francis's tale. The daughter is a kindly returned American (she was carried to America by mistake when she went on board ship to buy bread for her starving family), caring for Granny Grogan and taking her in rather than letting her go to the Union even before she discovers the old woman to be her long-lost mother.[7]

Only the story by Tynan ruffles the piety and pathos of the collection (Clara Mulholland's story is also about the reuniting of a mother with her son and he with his fiancée), though the editor takes care to remind us that Tynan's first prose book was *The Life of Mother M. Xaviera Fallon* and that she writes occasionally for the religious magazine *Ave Maria* in the United States. 'The Wardrobe' is the sad story of a 50-year-old country bachelor, until lately under the sway of his mother (in a way familiar to readers of Irish fiction and Patrick Kavanagh's *The Great Hunger*) of whom he had been 'dutifully fond' and for whom he remained a 'boy'. In his new freedom John Marnane imagines—and is induced to imagine by bantering neighbours—that he is ripe for marriage and has the pick of the country girls if only he can buy the necessary furniture, especially the immense wardrobe, 'a wardrobe as big as the *Great Aistern*'), at the auction with which the story opens. He spots a rosy-faced girl in the crowd, suffers a shock of attraction, and tells himself he is buying the wardrobe for her and has to outbid her to do so. He follows her to see where she lives and returns to renovate his house for his prospective young wife, though he catches sight of himself in a cracked mirror and is shocked a second time. 'He had a sense of his own weakness in desiring that strange foreign commodity known as love.' The work is finished; the workmen leave. A neighbour casts doubt on the wisdom of buying the still uninstalled monster of a wardrobe and thinks he should have let the girl buy it as 'she was called the third time last Sunday'. Marnane is stopped in his tracks: 'A cold sweat gathered upon his forehead, and a mist before his eyes.' When the neighbours leave, he breaks down in self-pity and disappointment, in the kind of negative epiphany that ends several stories in *Dubliners*. The conclusion strikes a modern note. Coming to, 'he spoke out his latest thought in words. "I'm thinkin'", he said that I might as well break up the ould wardrobe wid a hammer"'.[8] The story has pathos but is without sentimentality and is a grim little portrait of Irish familism and rural loneliness.

In 1917 *On Tiptoe: A Collection of Stories and Sketches by Irish Women* was published in Dublin by M. H. Gill.[9] These seventeen pieces are even more pious and sentimental than those in the above collection but add the ingredient of nationalist faith which is mixed with their Catholic faith to produce a dish palatable then (one assumes) to Americans and Irish-Americans, though America is seen as an undesirable alternative to Catholic Ireland. Religious faith, patriotism, exile, self-sacrifice, family: these are the repeating ideas. In 'The Message of the Shamrock', for example, by Nora Ni Arrachtain, the deserted boyfriend who sends his sweetheart in America a shamrock each St Patrick's Day, is seen at last by the foolish girl as someone who 'would always be Catholic and Irishman first, ready like his forebears, to sacrifice self in the Cause of his religion and his country'. She had fallen away from her Catholicism in the United

States and become engaged to an American. One year the shamrock does not come. But it has! Only it is concealed inside a copy of the *Catholic Bulletin* that Phil rather than her sister has sent this year. She resolves to break off her engagement and return to Phil the faithful (in both senses). This might have been the ending of 'Eveline' had Joyce not been Joyce; these pieces have the slightness of many of the early stories in *Dubliners* (in the latter's cases, the *apparent* slightness) and Joyce in his collection may have been wilfully rewriting such pious, patriotic stuff. In 'The Bogwood Rosary' by C. M. Lynch, the narrator laments: 'Oh, for the brush of an artist to paint the wonderful light in that Gaelic face.' In 'Fanny's Folly' by Mary Prendergast the title anti-heroine apes English ladies in manners and accent and has contempt for her home and family. She emigrates to Australia but there becomes lonely for Ireland. But in those days exile was a kind of life sentence with no remission, and the story ends: 'Bitterly she realises at last that she has bartered her birthright, and has not got in exchange even the mess of pottage.' The mess of pottage recurs literally in 'On the Bog Road' by Maire Ni Chillin that might almost have been written by Rosa Mulholland. It is set during the Great War and a grandmother tells at Christmas time to her grandchildren, clamouring for presents, a story set in Famine times about the souper schools and how a young girl is tempted to change her religion for food but resists and keeps the faith. She was that young girl! The children are ashamed of their Christmas wish-list and are grateful for their Catholicism and, one assumes, their poverty. The Great War setting seems incidental and as an event is dwarfed by the Famine.

The primacy of faith over social life and self-fulfilment, the necessity of gratitude for being Catholic in the midst of poverty, are themes embraced by Rosa Mulholland though she is a readable writer cuts above the contributors to *On Tiptoe*. Her touches of descriptive power are beyond them: of the countryside: 'Behind the house the dun mountain raised a great shoulder against the sky, and in the lowest stoop of the landscape a streak of sea was visible, blue, or grey, or black at the will of the season, and the weather.' Of the city slum: 'Dirt and stench outpour from the open door and windows where squalor and hunger gaze on the world unabashed and unashamed, so accustomed to themselves and their condition that they will expect a bird or a geranium to live with them on a hook in the broken brick-work, or in a corner of the sooty lintel.' Besides, she looks unflinchingly at what ails her native island. *Father Tim* (1910) is the story of the making of a holy man, Father Tim Melody, who early has a vision, like Letts's Antony Hesketh. It is a vision of service and in Mulholland's Ireland badly needed, when government intervention is never contemplated and even the hoped-for Home Rule promises to bring little material comfort. 'He saw distinctly the silhouette presentment of a bowed figure cut out of the rock, and an angel made of the cloud-rack standing by—the Lord's cup-bearer!'[10] Young Tim wants to become a saint and more or less succeeds; Mulholland's Catholicism is frank and unembarrassed but she is careful to include Melody's awareness of his own inadequacy, a necessary saintly virtue of humility. He becomes a priest and like Meade's Ranald (Father) Moore in *A Princess of the Gutter*, ministers to the poor and afflicted, in Father Tim's case in the Wicklow Hills and then in the Dublin slums.

The number of prevalent social ills in Ireland that Mulholland diagnoses stretches to capacity the term problem-novel. There is the problem of illegitimacy, and in the slums the unmarried mother will often willingly hand over her baby to anyone who will take it; Mulholland makes reference to a 'baby-farming establishment' which sounds like a hideous kind of orphanage or mart for bastard children. There is the problem of emigration, from which Tim sees only two goods: carriage of the Faith to new worlds, and the reluctance of future expatriates to fight for Britain against the Yellow Peril, the undeserving step-mother country having driven Irish emigrants from her shores (p. 271). (Between the 1890s and the Great War there was much talk of the Yellow Peril, the danger posed to the Empire by China. M. P. Shiel, a popular writer of Irish extraction, published an apocalyptic novel in 1898 entitled *The Yellow Danger*.) Mulholland knowledgeably uses the ill-treatment of Irish workers in Brazilian coffee plantations as her case study. There is the problem of fewer marriages owing, one character believes, to increasing post-Famine material desires among the peasantry who refuse consent to marriages that do not bring a secure settlement, while the young who do not emigrate live under 'an unwritten law of compulsory celibacy'. There is the problem of suicide, and several women in the novel destroy themselves; suicide is a problem also touched on by Riddell in *A Rich Man's Daughter*. There is the problem of wife-beating; 'painting' it's called in the impoverished East End of London in Riddell's novel, because of the coloured bruises that betray it. There is the problem of the decline of the rural gentry, exemplified by the Shines' country house, 'The Monastery', according to the returned and widowed Brazilian who speaks (with Mulholland's assent, one suspects) of 'the great place they used to live in long ago, when they were far grander than they're now, by raison of some o' them murtherin' failures that does pull down the genthry' (pp. 81, 228, 284). There is the problem of financial speculation which partly accounts for the Shines' reduced circumstances and which caused the mental collapse of a woman whom Margaret Killester (Mulholland's Magdalen Ponsonby) takes care of after her father's speculations come to nothing in a financial crash. Finally, there are the problems of poverty and unhealthy living conditions.

THE DRINK PLAGUE

'The temperance question is simply the question whether an impertinent minority shall prevent a long-suffering majority from enjoying what they are willing to pay for.'

Herbert M. Pim, *The Pessimist* (1914)

Above all, there is the 'drink question' or the 'drink plague' as it is also called in *Father Tim* and which endangers the career of Edmund Shine. Ella MacMahon might not agree with the racial claim of Mulholland's judge that the alcohol which merely stupefies British brains 'excites the Irishman to the point of madness', but she would agree with Mulholland's choice of a wealthy man as victim of drink. Sarah, Edmund's sister, sees less repentance and anxiety among the afflicted moneyed than among the poor, making the rich man's condition more perilous. She sees affluent Dubliners muddle their brains in restaurants at lunchtime, 'preparatory to the excess of dinner-time'. Mulholland is enlightened on the drink question. Edmund's father loves his wine and encourages his son to praise alcohol, but Mrs Shine tells Father Tim that whereas her husband's family could drink comfortably, hers could not and thus Edmund cannot help his inability to master his liquor: he has inherited it. Father Tim embraces the idea of heredity (one of the big ideas that track through these novels and often alluded to as 'blood', good or bad) and tells Edmund: 'You are stricken with disease as surely as is the victim of tuberculosis.' After Edmund's reform he resumes contact with the hard-drinking Rorke, a returned American, and the temptation to drink looms; he has 'a hereditary taint', Dr Darcy remarks to Edmund's wife, Janet, 'The disease lies dormant when not provoked.' Edmund's fall and recovery convert his father to temperance and he tells his son that 'the best medical authorities of the day deny the benefit to health of any kind of alcohol. The world has been under a delusion with regard to it'.[11] And there is the collateral damage of alcohol: the suffering of the wives or husbands who cannot cope with those in the horrors of drink.

The notion of inherited predisposition and the pathological nature of alcoholism are now current wisdom but this was not the case in Mulholland's day. MacMahon too is relatively enlightened. In *A Pitiless Passion*, Magdalen sees Georgie's alcoholism as possibly the result of remote heredity but more likely the result of 'an inherent strain of weakness' of character, a generalized debility; but MacMahon refrains from accepting wholly a pathological explanation and seems, moreover, irritated that we have now reversed the natural evolutionary process of the strong prevailing over the weak and require the strong, such as Magdalen, to offer themselves up on behalf of the weak, such as the alcoholic Georgie.[12] It is as if MacMahon admires her creation Magdalen while despising a little the recipients of her goodness, and this lends the narrative texture an interesting nap; she seems equally torn in sympathy between her male and female characters.

In several novels of the time, it is simply the effects of drink that are exploited by authors with no intrinsic interest in the causes of serious drunkenness. Still, *Where the Shamrock Grows: The Fortunes and Misfortunes of an Irish Family* (1911), a mediocre novel by George H. Jessop, is aware of drink's social role. The novel is in part an attack on Irish drunkenness; Mat O'Hara is the drunk and he is a jumped-up imitation of the real gentry, a squireen who is the beneficiary of inherited money and is outside Society which he attempts to gate-crash by pursuing the widow Delaney. He destroys his chances during the Cushion Dance, a customary part of the Tenants' Ball (the most interesting scene in a low-intensity country-house tale) by making an appearance dead drunk. The novel's title is a pun, since Kate Fetherstone's country house, the Priory, owes its existence to her grandfather's distillery and his Shamrock Blend Irish Whiskey. She has money but no love and envies those who do, and so has to expiate as it were the tainted source of her wealth before she can find happiness.[13] O'Hara is a throwback to the thriftlessness that caused the decline of the Irish country house but since he is new money, it isn't clear if the genuine gentry before him who lived the good life were as reprehensible or as dissipated as he is, or if love and a salary are the preferable ways of life.[14]

Mulholland by contrast has a serious interest in the phenomenon of Irish drinking.[15] In a chapter of *Father Tim* called 'Janet's Dinner Party', the drink question is thrashed out as a social problem in a kind of spontaneous symposium. The judge drinks a little but would abstain if he thought it would help lift the curse of drink from Ireland; the doctor wants him to do so, to set an example. The judge inveighs against the magistrates who grant licenses promiscuously to houses in country towns to sell wine and spirits; the magistrates are also the landlords and the rents are larger from licensed premises. Father Tim agrees, only to have a wealthy distiller call priests allies of the publicans and the best patrons of the distillery. So serious was this issue of wanton licensing that Captain Shawe-Taylor—whom Yeats so admired as the type of the hawklike decisive man—identified the 'licensing question' as one of three obstructive Goliaths lying across the path of late-Victorian Ireland, the others being the Land Question and the University Question; Shawe-Taylor helped answer the Land Question and thought he might be able to help answer the other two likewise.[16]

Mulholland's bishop insists that his Church is not subsidized mainly by the publican's gains or the rich man's cheques but by the poor who withhold money from the drink-shop in order to give it to the Church. The bishop himself likes his glass of claret and remembers a time when he was revived at midnight in a fainting condition by a wayfarer who gave him 'a timely dose of what he called good John Jameson' and so he allows his priests their drink 'as a restorative to nerves and aid to the nourishment derived from food' but decides at the dinner party that henceforth he and the priests of his diocese will be total abstainers.[17] Father Tim returns to his church in the slums off St Stephen's Green (the boundary of the 'City of Pleasantness') and thinks of the difference between the rich drinkers and the poor: the former drinking out of animal indulgence, the latter out of despair. And from drink springs all manner of vices. In the slums, Jacob's factory which offers employment to women when their husbands are out of work or drunken 'does more good than a charitable institution'.[18] Mulholland's portrait of the slums off Cuffe Street (her 'Dismal City') is strong meat—even Dantesque: 'the circles of squalor, like unto the circles of Dante's Inferno'—and this 1910 novel proves that Augustine Martin was in error when he wrote that James Stephens's *The Charwoman's Daughter* (1912) 'is the first novel to deal with life in Dublin's slums'.[19]

Mulholland's depiction of the almost surrealistic Dublin slums associates her novel with the portraits of the 'sinking classes' in late-Victorian and Edwardian documentary revelations such as General William Booth's *In Darkest England and the Way Out* (1890), Revd Osborne Jay's *Life in Darkest London* (1891), and Charles Masterman's *From the Abyss* (1902), and fictional explorations of the urban deeps, such as George Gissing's *The Nether World* (1889), L. T. Meade's *A Princess of the Gutter* (1896), and Jack London's *The People of the Abyss* (1903). It is the world E. M. Forster declined to descend into in his novel published the same year as Mulholland's, *Howards End*: 'We are not concerned with the very poor. They are unthinkable.'[20] Forster aside, theirs is a British, more narrowly London and Dublin context in which are mingled a documentary realism and a social concern that can in some cases assume an interventionist, even evangelical fervour, the latter consorting at times with romance plots and even fairy-tale-like resolutions.

There is one curious and troubling subculture depicted in *Father Tim*. In the first part of the novel, in the Wicklow Hills, young Dinny has his own secular vision to match young Tim's religious one; it is of a young flower and fern seller who works a beat on Dinny's hills. She appears like the vision of beauty in an Aisling poem (appropriately she has no name in the novel) but before he can capture her she marries another and they go to Dublin where they have a child and where her husband batters her. Three years later she returns to Dinny's hills with her child, an Aisling 'sky-woman' now with clay feet, but goes away again; her later probable suicide leaves her daughter Maelie who is fostered out. According to the foster-mother, 'the fern-woman has broken out' in Maelie who follows the tramp flower sellers down to Dublin 'prompted by the instinct of her vagrant blood'. These flower dealers are a wandering tribe, like gypsies, 'the lowest dregs of the race, if indeed they are of our race', comments Sarah Shine who attends an evening sodality which the dealers attend also and where Sarah hopes to find Maelie for Father Tim. The flower dealers sit in the slums, attend early morning mass, are unmarried mothers, spring up around docks and barracks: they have a touch of all nations about them and have curiously lovely hair. They demand their freedom: the 'greed of absolute liberty is the passion of their lives' and are uncivilizable.[21] The Sisters of Charity look for Maelie, attempting to catch and tame her. They succeed and Maelie eventually marries a respectable man and is content with a small 'dealing' on a Wicklow hillside. What became of Mulholland's flower dealers and were they now those we call Travellers?

PROBLEMS AND PIETY

Mulholland's Ireland presents the poor with a terrible dilemma: to starve on a hillside, or try to earn good wages in the city but perhaps lose religion and endanger soul, *or* to emigrate and give their Irish-born talents to a foreign nation. Yes, there is a famed beauty of countryside—'the purple hills . . . the splendours of moor and bogland, the cries and whispers of moor-fowl and sea-birds'—but also ruin amidst the countryside—'But oh, the broken cabins and sloppy causeways, the tumble-down villages, the vice of cities, the squalor, the drink-shops!' (pp. 151–3). Through it all, Father Tim with no time for theology grows a saintly heart and becomes a predatory St Francis among the poor, 'on the war-path, bent on the healing of wounds and the capture of souls'. Indeed, Mulholland's only solutions to these terrible problems she has taken pains to recite are charity and ministration. And a recognition of the spiritual superiority of the destitute over the comfortable. The poor are rich, thinks Father Tim, because they have nothing, the rich poor because they have riches. Father Tim's sermon on a Wicklow hill (on the mount, one is tempted to say) takes as its text, indeed, verses from the Sermon on the Mount—those beatitudes assuring the poor, the meek, and the bereaved of their spiritual security—and St Paul (1 Timothy) on the evil of money, the temptations of the rich, and the nakedness of our coming and going. Mulholland lauds the poor Irish congregation 'whose souls they know to be their only great possession' and declares: 'Who will dare to tell them that their faith is a delusion, their patience folly . . . ?' On a visit home from Dublin, Father Tim preaches a sermon again on the text 'Blessed are the poor in spirit' during which he tells his listeners 'that it might be God's special loving intention to keep Ireland always poor. Riches might rob us of our inheritance!'[22]

The same idea impels Annie M. P. Smithson's portrait of the Dublin slums of the Coombe neighbourhood in *Her Irish Heritage* (1917) in which a visiting English cousin is initiated into Irish culture, including the urban destitute. Her cousin Bride Blake is 'secretary to an influential philanthropic society, and a great social worker. She lived for her work amongst the poor and existed in a whirl of district visiting, free breakfasts, social clubs and committee meetings'.[23] In the chapter entitled 'In the Slums', the Dublin poor are cheerful but that is because of their Catholic faith which spiritualizes all aspects of life and makes it almost worthwhile, it seems, to be indigent. All they need are occasional visits from 'the quality' and a few handouts and they are happy enough.

Smithson is certain that the answer to all of Ireland's problems lies in what became after 1922 an orthodox chain of beliefs, positions, and values created by Catholicism, Gaelicism, and republicanism. She implies that Irish Irelandism with its economic self-sufficiency and boycott of English products will serve the day, though there is no suggestion that it would be good to eradicate the slums which in her world seem to exist as spiritual exemplars and opportunities. Nothing even as vaguely concrete as Smithson's sentiments is entertained in *Father Tim*. There is nothing on trades unions, medical breakthroughs (in the novel tuberculosis and appendicitis are caused by drink), cooperative schemes of distribution, congested districts boards, Irish Ireland enterprises, the Fabian Society or British and Irish socialism. The position of the gentry is not seen as part of the Irish problem; even in a novel that depicts eviction, Mulholland's *Norah of Waterford* (1915), Miss Lilla from the Big House is philanthropic and well-intentioned; the real villain is the gombeen man, Rogan. Change instead comes as conversion, repentance, self-reform in a kind of Catholic Dickensianism. In *Father Tim* Edmund reforms, his father reforms, the Bishop reforms, Rorke reforms, Maelie reforms. Spiritually, Mulholland positively celebrates the poverty of the Irish as testament to their innate goodness, which is rich coming from a woman of Mulholland's social stature and connections. And Irish spirituality is in the hands of the priests among whom Father Tim is a shining saintly light—at the end indeed 'He is Saint Francis'—and of a legion of lay women like Margaret Killester who has 'become a sort of free-lance guardian angel in the slums'. The work that women like her perform in the 'terrible places' that are cities, 'is angels' work'.[24] She is in part answering the summons for more women to work in the slums and 'who are not bound by convent rules', women who would be Florence Nightingales of the soul. These strong and remarkable women are like inversions of feminists, intensely pious and in their own way patriotic, and examples of them people many of these Irish popular novels.[25] On the topic of strong women outside the feminist fold, I am reminded of William O'Brien's aphorism when remembering warmly an elderly housekeeper of the London Law Courts during the time of the Parnell Commission: 'She was a Tory of the quaintest old pattern, but, whatever the New Woman will thinks of her, hers was one of those minds in which politics has no chance against human nature.'[26]

In her reference to convent rules, Mulholland is alluding to a tension in Catholic charitable effort: the tendency during the nineteenth century for nuns to displace lay Catholic women in charitable institutions, for convents to predominate as such institutions, and for constraints to be placed on lay Catholic women when they did perform charitable work.[27] As to Irish convent schools, Michael J. F. McCarthy in 1901 launched a vigorous attack on them, believing that they supplanted immeasurably superior Catholic lay schools: 'the many really good girls schools, kept by Catholic ladies in Ireland, have been all crushed out of existence' because the Catholic Church wishes 'to crush the Catholic lay element under the surface'. He favourably compares the usurped Catholic lay teachers to 'Miss Mulvany, head mistress of the Alexandra School, Dublin, on the Protestant side today'.[28]

We can send packing Mulholland's largely spiritual and band-aid solutions to Ireland's socio-economic problems without impugning the courage and self-sacrifice of the women who are her heroines. There is a glimpse of how many they were in real life and how strong and remarkable they were, in Rosa Mulholland's fascinating memoir which prefaces the *Essays* (1896) of the formidable Sarah Atkinson (1823–93): Catholic philanthropist, critic, historian, and translator whose work should certainly be revived for proper critical assessment. (Mulholland may have named the wise and charitable Sarah Shine after her heroine.) Sarah Gaynor, born in Athlone, grew up in Dublin and married George Atkinson MD, who was joint-proprietor of the *Freeman's Journal* while practising as a physician. The Atkinson home became the venue for gatherings of the learned and witty. The Atkinsons travelled often to Italy, France, Germany, and Belgium, studying art and architecture. She worked with two collaborators, Ellen Woodlock and Bessie Raynor Parkes (an Englishwoman who came to the Social Science Congress in Dublin in 1861, met Atkinson, and converted to Catholicism), important figures in nineteenth-century Irish philanthropy.[29] She was not just a passive philanthropist but an active one: a 'royal giver', Mulholland calls her. She supervised the Children's Hospital in Upper Temple Street (initiated by Woodlock), managed the Sodality of the Children of Mary in Gardiner Street, and patronized the Hospice for the Dying of which her sister was, at Mulholland's time of writing, Mother Rectoress. Tynan seems not easily to have been taken in, but saw Atkinson on a visit to a Dublin hospital and as she looked after the beautiful woman who stopped by every bed with cheerful words and a gift

'I thought her indeed a ministering angel', of the type, one might add, we find in *Father Tim* and *A Princess of the Gutter*.[30] Atkinson was only one woman among many engaged in charitable work in nineteenth-century Ireland and, combined, they constitute a generous subculture that is the social historical background to what might otherwise appear in *Father Tim* as pious tosh. Piety there was aplenty, and Maria Luddy emphasizes the essential religious dimension of the subculture.[31]

Atkinson herself might have been a champion of the Catholic Truth Society, but she confounds any prejudgements.[32] Her religious fervour did not prevent Atkinson's being a versatile essayist and researcher: reading a paper to the 1861 Social Science Congress, writing brief biographies of Eugene O'Curry, John Hogan, and John Henry Foley (the latter two sculptors), besides lives of the Irish saints. She published her essays mainly in the *Irish Quarterly Review* and *Irish Monthly*. She kept a *Workhouse Journal* which no doubt it would be an educating pleasure to read. She wrote a biography of the foundress of the Irish Sisters of Charity: *The Life of Mary Aikenhead* (1879, the historical portions of which were praised by the historian Lecky), and Mul-holland thought it showed a great undeveloped fictional talent: 'one cannot but wish that her genius for sympathy might have found another outlet, and we had seen in her the great novelist of Ireland.' In compensation we have Atkinson's lively and informed essays written with the authoritative prose style we see in a writer of the following generation, Hannah Lynch. Each was one of the most brilliant Irish women of her generation.[33]

But I mention Atkinson here because she inhabited and helped to create an important cultural context. The popular Irish novel before and even after the period 1890 to1922 is in many cases informed—in the very real sense of that word—by the religious culture of Victorian feminine philanthropy and 'the genius for sympathy', which often lapses into bare talent, but often results in a great readability and the creation of characters fully engaged without solip-sism in the troubles of the society they inhabit.

For a brief conspectus of that culture it is only necessary to read *Woman's Mission: A Series of Congress Papers on the Philanthropic Work of Women by Eminent Writers*, edited by Baroness (Angela Georgina) Burdett-Coutts (1893). Woman's mission might seem to be suggested by the epigraph from Chaucer: 'So womanlie, so benigne, and so meeke'. There is a verse epigraph by Mrs Cecil Alexander, wife of the Archbishop of Armagh and mother of Eleanor Alexander, in which readers are reminded that charitable women, if they have to seek 'the haunts of sin' to carry out their work, do not dispense their charity indiscrim-inately or embrace socialism in order to pit class against class, but instead teach self-help and 'free dependence each on each'. The verse is written out of the Christian conservatism of the female philanthropic movement. In her Preface,

Burdett-Coutts claims that the 'beautiful word "Philanthropy"' combines piety and charity and that 'women have always had a full, perhaps an unrecognized, share in maintaining and continuing works of mercy'.[34] But Alexander also reminds her readers that these are women who have escaped 'the chain that fettered woman's life', that they are historically emancipated figures.

The papers that follow demonstrate that the natural altruism of women is the philosophical basis of what nevertheless is impressive self-determination. The image of women that emerges from this compilation (in the shape of reports from all the major churches, the charitable or social bodies, and individual philanthropists, all intended to compose the department of 'Women's Work' for the Chicago World's Fair of 1893) suggests strength and determination rather than meekness or delicate womanliness. It is surely true that having been discouraged from direct political involvement (or disinclined that way), institutionally-minded and action-minded Victorian and post-Victorian women engaged instead in well-organized philanthropic work.[35] Organized charity provided an outlet for intelligent, active, and stalwart women who, debarred legally or customarily from the professions, created what we might call the profession of philanthropy. To read Burdett-Coutts's book is akin to reading the reports of a contemporary meeting of the British Association for the Advancement of Science, a coming together of professional and amateur scientists, almost all men: there is a comparable energy and pioneering spirit and process of cooperation. Interestingly, Josephine Butler announced in 1869 that 'the feminine form of philanthropy' (individual ministering) had failed and that 'We are now about to try the masculine form of philanthropy' by which she meant 'large and comprehensive measures, organizations and systems' but that it too will fail unless the feminine powers generated in home life are allowed to be brought to bear, lest 'the magnificently-ordered Institution' becomes as pauperizing an influence as the Lady Bountiful (Butler, pp. xxxvii–xxxviii).

The contribution 'On Philanthropic Work of Women in Ireland' is provided by Rosa Mulholland (here also using her philanthropic name, Mrs John T. Gilbert, her husband not having yet been knighted) and it is a survey of female charitable and missionary work in Ireland in the year 1893. (Amusingly, Lady Gregory of Coole is identified solely as an improver of the red flannel made by the local country people in her part of Galway.) It is a large and busy canvas of good works, classes, courses, and cottage industries.[36] There is reference to a home for Irish gentlewomen down on their luck, a reminder that in Jane Barlow's *Flaws* (1911), the heroine founds 'a small colony of homeless gentlewomen'. (In keeping with the confusingly multiple plot-strand in this novel, the gentlewomen's home soon after drops from readerly view.) Only with Mulholland's references to the Magdalen Asylums, set up to care for 'poor fallen girls and women', teaching them laundry work, does an amber light switch on in one's head, as one remembers the alleged cruelty and hardship sometimes visited on those same girls and women: the dark side of institutional charity, its exercise of power and sadism during which charity was a kind of captivity and even death.[37] (We get a faint whiff of it in Joyce's semi-allegorical story 'Clay' in *Dubliners*.) But the sunnier side is the culture out of which a great many novels by women seemed to emerge in terms of their social content and philosophical basis, their characters, plots, and resolutions. One longs for at least one novel set by contrast in the shadows of philanthropy from the perspective of the institutionalized inno- cent, victimized by religious prejudice and community cruelty.

CATHOLICISM AND FICTION

The philanthropic culture was a British one, and Burdett-Coutts's reference in her Preface to the 'Anglo-Saxon' nature of this efficient philanthropy is one to which one can't imagine Mulholland taking exception, though she was a Catholic. (E. J. Hobsbawm makes the point that one third of the prominent British women in 1895—as listed in a contemporary reference book—came under the heading 'Reformers, Philanthropists etc.'; another large category was 'Authors'.)[38] The culture gradually receded in the twentieth century with the Land Acts that solved the Land Question, the broader distribution of wealth, the demise of the great landowners (such as Gregory herself) from whose town and country houses the philanthropy had often radiated, the rise of labour parties and the idea of the welfare state. It remained alive longer in the South than in the North of Ireland because of the greater poverty of the South, the entrenched power of the Catholic Church that was reluctant to relinquish control of social and welfare matters, and the busyness of the various religious orders and lay associations of that Church that wielded a greater proportionate power in the greater part of the island where Protest- ants were not numerous. In any case, the social problem-novel that emerged from the culture dwindled and changed, while the new literature of the Revival steered clear of social concerns (if not political concerns) and the new literature of modernism did likewise.

On one side of the religious divide, the religious culture can itself be traced back to what has been called 'the devotional revolution' in mid- and late nineteenth-century Catholic Ireland (Protestantism as we have seen had its own evangelical revolution). The revolution accomplished 'the wholesale building of new churches... the introduction of Roman practices, such as sodalities, benediction, and novenas, to replace the now frowned on wakes and patterns', and the 'spectacular growth in full-time religious personnel'.[39] Yet Roman Catholicism was to produce its gifted questioners and apostates, and readers of Irish literature from the time of the Revival think mainly of lapsed Catholic authors, including Moore and Joyce, rather than church apologists. But Catholic apologetics in fiction were written before Joyce and while Moore was getting properly into stride, and before the philosophy of the Irish Revival (the pagan and mystical elements of which tried to function below the radar of the Catholic Church) was, it seemed, firmly rooting itself. Through such novels as *Scenes and Sketches in an Irish Parish, or Priest and People in Doon* (1903) and *The Soggarth Aroon* (1905), Canon Joseph Guinan (1863–1932), for example, is read as an almost fulsome defender of Catholic Ireland against its detractors. (And a successful one, if success is measured by copies sold: *The Soggarth Aroon* saw four editions in 1905—selling 9,000 copies—and successive editions in 1906, 1907, 1908 and 1912).[40] Whereas Mulholland writes from a Catholic upper-middle-class point of view, repos-ing the spiritual centre of her world among well-born charitable women and priests with a philanthropic mission, the centre of Guinan's spiritual world is the essential workaday bond between the Irish priest and his peasant flock; the relationship is indeed the centre of Irish life, as Guinan sees it.[41]

A different kind of apologist is Patrick Augustine, Canon Sheehan (1852–1913). Murphy reminds us that Irish Catholic society around the turn of the twentieth century was no simple homogeneous affair (which in some critical accounts is very simple indeed: a vast raftwork of peasantry with aboard it a sparser and exploitative set of gaugers, agents, gombeen men, Dublin Castle lackeys, and Royal Irish constables) and identifies a Catholic gentry, upper middle class, lower middle class, intelligentsia, urban working class and, of course, peasantry.[42] One might be tempted to describe the priests as a class, though of course individually they ranged from lower-middle-class status (even barely glorified peasantry)—though always educated to a sufficiency for ordin-ation—through to well-read and thinking sophisticates wherever their place was on the hierarchy. Some of them we would wish to describe as belonging to the intelligentsia, and Sheehan and Gerald O'Donovan are two such.

Sheehan published his novels between 1895 and 1915 (his last, *The Graves at Kilmorna: A Story of '67*, was written in 1911 and published posthu-mously). 'Catholic apologetics' is a phrase we might be tempted to use to describe these novels but it would do them an injustice. *Geoffrey Austin, Student* (1895) and its sequel, *The Triumph of Failure* (1899), follow a young man spiritually astray who must acquaint himself with degradation before finding God and donning the habits of the Carmelite brotherhood. If this sounds like an orthodox version of Yeats's apocalyptic stories, with Austin a Catholic Owen Aherne, that is because Yeats and Sheehan both inherited the *fin-de-siècle* theme of spiritual brinkmanship and were similarly fascinated by debauchery, dreams, and dark nights of the soul as necessary preludes to salvation. Sheehan in *The Triumph of Failure* quotes Francis Thompson's 'The Hound of Heaven' and places Austin among the apparently irredeemable souls of a decade that represented the fag end of romanticism with its subjectivist resistance to a materialistic century. (Joyce's *A Portrait of the Artist* also burns that fag end of the Romantic nineteenth century.)

The Triumph of Failure is a strenuous, eloquent, and outright attack on the nineteenth-century cultural forces that have seduced Austin: paganism, realism, materialism, German metaphysics, liberalism, and humanism. Sheehan gives these forces a fair shake, particularly German philosophy, since the author himself was attracted to German civilization.[43] The necessity of the attack might recall for us the larger British and European cultural context that the thoughtful and educated Irish inhabited, a useful reminder lest we think that Irish thought consisted of anti-British, anti-colonial, pre-revolutionary sentiments. (Several of the Catholic women authors I've mentioned were educated in English or European convents and one or two, most notably Hannah Lynch, demonstrate a European perspective, whereas Rosa Mulholland does not.)[44] Chief among the philosophers Austin follows before repudiating them are Kant and Fichte, and as Ben Knights has shown, both philosophers were important resources for the clerisy of the nineteenth century.[45] Austin also comes to repudiate Carlyle, another key figure among the nineteenth-century clerisy. So despite the end-of-the-century parallels between Sheehan and the mystics of the Irish Revival, Sheehan's novel by implication repudiates an Irish Revival of Yeats's sort, opposed as it is to the idea of a clerisy and devoutly wishing as it does an exclusively Irish Catholic revival—the revival that did indeed take place, despite the success in the shorter run of Yeats's Revival. In any case, *The Triumph of Failure* is set in the Dublin of the 1870s, and one character can say, without argument: 'I know, for example, that there is no literary instinct just now in Ireland. I know we lack imagination. I know we never shall, for example, produce a great poet. We cannot. Our enthusiasm is not imagination ... We ought to be the greatest dramatists or critics of the world. We never can be great poets.'[46] Sheehan muses (prophetically) on the desirability of a Catholic theocracy in Ireland and proclaims the superiority of Catholic art and Catholic philosophy over their fashionable rivals, a pre-emptive strike, as it were, against the opposing view espoused by George Moore in *Hail and Farewell* (1911–14). Moore's attitude to Catholicism and the priesthood, however, varied not only during his lifetime but according to which historical period of Catholicism was in question and in his novels, *The Lake* (1905), *The Apostle* (1911), *The*

Brook Kerith (1916), and *Héloïse and Abélard* (1921) he employed a variety of approaches. He retained a deep if sceptical interest in the subject but in the event that interest has not attracted as much Irish critical attention as his attitude to Yeats and the Irish Revival.

NOTES

1. In his memoirs, Bodkin remembers some of the most famous preachers he heard, outstanding among them being Fr Tom Burke who would fill a church in Rome to capacity and whom the Pope himself thought the greatest of Catholic preachers: *Recollections of an Irish Judge* (London: Hurst and Blackett, 1914), p. 75.
2. Mulholland's father was a Belfast MD; her brother became a QC of Lincoln's Inn; her elder sister became Lady Russell, wife of the Lord Chief Justice of England; a younger sister, Clara, became a novelist; her husband wrote a history of Dublin and became Sir John T. Gilbert. This all might blunt somewhat the remark by one character in *Father Tim* (London: Sands and Company, 1910), p. 124, that the English 'had not arrived yet at the point of liberality that would allow of a Roman Catholic Lord Chancellor'. For the *grandes dames* of Dublin Catholics, see Tynan, *The Middle Years* (London: Constable, 1916), pp. 1–2.
3. Brown places Hart's name in inverted commas, suggesting a pseudonym. He tells us she was educated by the Ursulines in Ireland and France.
4. 'Inside the Whale,' in George Orwell, *A Collection of Essays* (New York: Doubleday & Co., 1957), p. 246. I discuss Moore and Catholicism in *Fictions of the Irish Literary Revival* (Dublin: Gill & Macmillan; Syracuse: Syracuse University Press, 1987), pp. 119–38 passim.
5. Violet Martin's family had originally been Catholic, being Old English, i.e. arriving in Ireland before the Reformation. Her great-grandfather turned Protestant in order to marry a Protestant but reverted to his old faith on his deathbed; his eldest son married a Catholic and the rites of both Churches were celebrated in Ross House: see Gifford Lewis, *Edith Somerville: A Biography* (Dublin: Four Courts Press, 2005), pp. 17, 25–6.
6. I thank the Secretary of Alexandra College, Susan Harman, for sending me some material concerning the school.
7. *A Round Table of the Representative Irish and English Catholic Novelists* (New York: Benziger Brothers, 3rd edn., 1897), pp. 41, 252.
8. *A Round Table*, pp. 325, 334, 337, 338.
9. The writers, entirely unknown to me, are—I list the names exactly as they occur— 'Mary Prendergast' (two pieces), Nora Ni Arrachtain (three pieces), Stephanie de Maistre, Mary O'Sullivan, Mary Cross, 'Mary O'Dea', G. F. C., Maire Ni Chillin (two pieces), Marie Conroyville, S. M. E., Mary (*sic*), C. M. Lynch, Maire J. Blake.
10. Rosa Mulholland, *Father Tim*, pp. 32, 173, 23.
11. Mulholland, *Father Tim*, pp. 229, 284, 223, 246, 97, 147, 136, 266, 146.

12. MacMahon, *A Pitiless Passion*, p. 302.

13. Jessop (?1850–?1915) was educated at Trinity College Dublin and went to the United States in 1873. He died in London. He wrote six volumes of fiction and a romantic opera. He apparently converted to Catholicism on his deathbed. We associate drink in nineteenth-century Irish fiction with the rollicking gentry or the peasantry, but in *A Maid of the Manse* (1895) by E. Rentoul Esler, we find a drunken Co. Donegal Presbyterian whose dissipation is threatening the family farm and who causes the suicide of his despairing brother.

14. In 1940 Elizabeth Bowen, who grew up in one, discussed the country house (or Big House) in terms of chronic shortage, as though for most country houses decline had been a steady state: 'The Big House' in *The Mulberry Tree: Writings of Elizabeth Bowen*, ed. Hermione Lee (London: Virago, 1986), pp. 25–30.

15. According to one historian, alcohol abuse was endemic in Ireland at the end of the nineteenth century. He quotes 100,528 as the number of arrests for drunkenness in 1891–2. He remarks that some nationalist politicians blamed excessive drinking on British rule. Diarmaid Ferriter, *The Transformation of Ireland, 1900–2000* (London: Profile Books, 2005), pp. 13, 56–7.

16. M. McDonnell Bodkin in *Recollections of an Irish Judge*, p. 255; Bodkin, who refers to 'Shaw Taylor' (*sic*), is quoting the reminiscences of Judge Dick Adams. Yeats has a 1911 portrait of Shawe-Taylor in *The Cutting of an Agate* in *Essays and Introductions* (1961). The English, too, were concerned about the excessive number of points of sale for alcohol, which was addressed in Balfour's Licensing Act of 1904: see Trevelyan, *English Social History* (1942; Harmondsworth: Pelican Books, 1964), p. 583. Brown in *Ireland in Fiction* groups together in his Appendix B what he calls 'Temperance Stories'; there are nine volumes, novels or stories, and a tenth, *Temperance Stories* by M. A. C., can be found under the heading 'Messenger Office' (office of *The Irish Messenger of the Sacred Heart*). In her novel, *The Big House of Inver* (1925), Edith Somerville creates a town of 2000 in which there are sixty public houses! On over-liberal licensing in Ireland, see also Ferriter, p. 57.

17. In which case the bishop was reflecting a sentiment, even a movement, inside the Irish Catholic Church. In an article published in 1915, Very Revd John T. Murphy, addressing students in Maynooth, called for a 'crusade' against drink that he felt sure the people themselves were calling for. He denied that any physical goodness could be derived from alcohol, citing contemporary medical authority. He believed that 'there is in our race a certain temperament which incites to the use of alcohol and, in a corresponding manner, renders the use of intoxicating drink very attractive to us'. He compared the relation between total abstinence and temperance to that between virginity and chastity, and called for the exercise of the former 'until the face of things, in this respect, is changed all over the land'. He went on to emphasize the necessity of Irish abstinence in the light of the imminence of Home Rule when independence would require the utmost sobriety to succeed. In the defeat of alcohol, as in the defeat of 'the robber' (i.e. the Englishman) in their midst, the priest would be in the vanguard: 'Total Abstinence', *Irish Ecclesiastical Record* 5 (1915): 281–94. Stephen Lucius Gwynn told his

readers in 1907 that the Gaelic League promoted temperance (and Irish industry) as vigorously as it promoted the Irish language: *Irish Books and Irish People* (1920; Freeport, NY: Books for Libraries, 1969), p. 80.

18. Mulholland, *Father Tim*, pp. 222–35, 175, 182.

19. Mulholland, *Father Tim*, p. 234. Augustine Martin, Introduction to *The Charwoman's Daughter* (Dublin: Gill and Macmillan, 1972), p.4. This is a judgement I accepted in *Fictions of the Irish Literary Revival* (1987) because I had not read Mulholland's work.

20. E. M. Forster, *Howards End* (1910; Harmondsworth: Penguin Books, 1973), p. 44. I discuss the Victorian and Edwardian fiction in *The Age of* Titanic (2002), pp. 103–12. The slums of Dublin and other cities may have been unthinkable and almost surrealistic but they were real. Ferriter tells us that despite a Mansion House (Dublin) conference in 1903 on urban poverty and the Irish Housing Act (1908) that focused more attention on urban housing problems, the slums continued. In 1911, 66 per cent of the Dublin working class (128,000 strong) were judged to be living in substandard accommodation; 118,000 of the poor were packed into a mere 5,000 tenements (over twenty persons per house); almost 23 per cent of Dublin's population lived in one-room tenements: *The Transformation of Ireland*, pp. 51–3.

21. Mulholland, *Father Tim*, pp. 175, 185, 188, 247–8, 266. In her 'Memoir' of Sarah Atkinson in Sarah Atkinson, *Essays* (Dublin: M. H. Gill, 1896), pp. x, xx–xxi, Mulholland describes some of the young female paupers of the south Dublin workhouse who were moved for attempted rehabilitation to 'The School' begun by Atkinson and her friend Ellen Woodlock, as in an 'almost savage state, looked on as untamable'. These 'almost savage maidens', born in the workhouse and known as 'the gipsy band', would swagger through the workhouse, attack the officers, seize and consume provisions, dance and shout, strike each other, and even set fire to the buildings. Only Atkinson was able to bring them over time gratefully to heel.

22. Mulholland, *Father Tim*, pp. 314, 92, 103–6, 160.

23. Annie M. P. Smithson, *Her Irish Heritage* (1917; Cork: Mercier Press, 1988), p. 15.

24. We have seen the importance of the angel idea in Meade's *A Princess of the Gutter*, while in *A Woman-Derelict* (1901), Elinor Grey is called by Dr Strong 'an angel from Heaven' (London: John Long, 1901), p. 177.

25. Mulholland, *Father Tim*, pp. 312, 219, 164. When the Irish cultural revival got under way, some of the female energy was diverted from philanthropic social work to cultural patriotism. There were strong women among the language revivalists, including Eileen Nicholson (who drowned off the Blasket islands while on field work) and Kathleen Sheehy (said to be the model for Joyce's Molly Ivors), but women were often welcomed in auxiliary positions. Joyce in *A Portrait of the Artist* (1916) has Father Moran refer patronizingly to 'the ladies' as 'the best helpers the language has': *A Portrait of the Artist as a Young Man* (1916; New York: Penguin Books, 1976), p. 239.

26. William O'Brien, 'London Revisited', *The Contemporary Review* 69 (1896): 805. I realize, of course, that it might have been easier for O'Brien to praise a strong woman who does not pose a political challenge.

27. See Maria Luddy, 'Women and Philanthropy in Nineteenth-Century Ireland', p. 10: http://www.indiana.edu/iupress/books (this is an extended version of a paper that appeared in *Voluntas* 7.4, n.d.).
28. *Five Years in Ireland, 1895–1900*, 3rd edn. (London: Simpkin, Marshall, Hamilton, Kent & Co.; Dublin: Hodges, Figgis & Co., 1901), p. 289. Miss Mulvany makes several appearances in *The Diaries of Mary Hayden 1878–1903* (2005), the diarist having known her in her own capacities as student and teacher at Alexandra College.
29. See Mulholland, 'Memoir.' For other biographical details on Atkinson, see the online *Catholic Encyclopedia*. According to the latter, Atkinson resolved to spend the rest of her life in charitable work after the death of her only child, a 4-year-old son.
30. Mulholland, 'Memoir', p. xv.
31. Luddy, 'Women and Philanthropy in Nineteenth-Century Ireland.' See also Maria Luddy, *Women and Philanthropy in Nineteenth-Century Ireland* (Cambridge: Cambridge University Press, 1995).
32. The Catholic Truth Society of Ireland was begun in 1899; the CTS Atkinson supported was therefore the society founded in London in 1868 and mobilized in the 1880s to publish Catholic literature; it was publisher to the Holy See and therefore in this regard was the cisatlantic equivalent of Benziger in the U.S.A.
33. For example, her essay on the Dantesque fourteenth-century poem *Il Dittamondo* by the Florentine poet Fazio degli Uberti appears to this non-Italian speaker (and without a knowledge of Italian literature) as a tour de force. Atkinson from an 1865 sale catalogue for the Charlemont Library learned that Fazio had mentioned Ireland in the poem, specifically her exports of wool to Florence. She decided to track the reference to its source, guessing from a brief quoted passage that he may have visited Lough Derg. She reminds us of the early European references to St Patrick's Purgatory, avails herself of the account in *History of the Viceroys of Ireland* (1865) by Sir John T. Gilbert (Mulholland's husband) of fourteenth-century Italian pilgrimages to Lough Derg, and from there assembles the Celtic sources of the *Divine Comedy*. But she lacks the text of the poem and has a friend travelling to Milan search the bookshops; he succeeds in bringing back to her an 1826 Milanese edition. The passages on lakes 'of various natures' are worth waiting for and she offers us the Italian original and her prose rendition. There is an allusion to Lough Neagh and its weird chemical properties as well as to Lough Derg and a lake isle on which no one dies since as death nears they simply hurl themselves from the island into the life-giving waters; and there are caverns where no flesh corrupts so tempered is the air.
34. *Woman's Mission: A Series of Congress Papers on the Philanthropic Work of Women by Eminent Writers*, ed. Baroness (Angela Georgina) Burdett-Coutts (London: Sampson, Low, Marston & Co.,1893), p. xx.
35. In the previous generation, though, Josephine Butler entertained hope that philanthropy and politics would eventually unite in one stream, 'when philanthropists become conscious of power to reach the *sources* of crime and misery' and politicians realize that their end is philanthropy: Introduction to *Woman's Work and Woman's Culture*, ed. Josephine Butler (London: Macmillan, 1869),

p. xvii. Her Introduction also illuminates the Christian and conservative dimensions of woman's work and mission as Butler sees them. She also discusses love and marriage: all of these being favourite topics of the popular novel, particularly by women.

36. The Sisters of Charity and Sisters of Mercy loom large in Mulholland's survey. To offset the depressing picture of Irish sectarianism we might note her report of the Sisters of Mercy opening a factory for linen weaving in their convent, assisted by the great Belfast linen merchant, Sir William Ewart, who advised them, donated two looms, and opened up a market for them: *Woman's Mission*, pp. 229–30.

37. The young Mary Hayden (a future historian) has a poignant and indignant paragraph on the Drumcondra Magdalen Asylum which she visited in 1882, during which she writes: 'a sin is committed and man condemns the weaker and (generally) the more ignorant of the two sharers in it to shame and to a bitter (and for this world, vain) expiation while he applauds it in the other world under the euphemistic name of gallantry or at most condemns it as a "peccadillo"; it is well there is another world to amend the judgements of this': *The Diaries of Mary Hayden 1878–1903*, ed. Conan Kennedy (Killala, Mayo: Morrigan, 2005), vol. 1 (*1878–83*), p. 343.

38. E. J. Hobsbawm, *The Age of Empire, 1875–1914* (New York: Pantheon Books, 1987), p. 211. When the British retreated from most of Ireland in 1922, they left behind 'Royal' bodies of this and that good work, which honorific was not removed in many cases. I discuss the British race-consciousness of the period 1890–1914, including the concern with Anglo-Saxonism, in *The Age of* Titanic: *Cross-Currents in Anglo-American Culture*, pp. 120–33.

39. James H. Murphy, *Catholic Fiction and Social Reality in Ireland, 1873–1922* (Westport CT: Greenwood Press, 1997), pp. 3–4. Murphy credits Emmet Larkin with the phrase 'devotional revolution'. Murphy discusses the effects of this revolution in rural Ireland among the Catholic farming society, and discusses the dowry system in marriage, and the relationship between farming, marriage, and celibacy that recurs in Irish novels in our period, 1890–1922. Larkin's devotional revolution can be found analysed in his book, *The Historical Dimensions of Irish Catholicism* (1984). Unfortunately, Larkin is concerned here only with the political power of the Church and not with its social history, which would include accounts of the development of sodalities and charitable institutions, and the role of women and philanthropic labour in Catholic Ireland.

40. Catherine Candy in *Priestly Fictions* discusses Guinan, Canon Sheehan, and Gerald O'Donovan. She tells us that Guinan's novel was first serialized in the *Ave Maria* (the American Catholic magazine in which Tynan also published): *Priestly Fictions: Popular Irish Novelists of the Early 20th Century* (Dublin: Wolfhound Press, 1995), p. 51.

41. Murphy, *Catholic Fiction*, pp. 115–17.

42. Murphy, *Catholic Fiction*, pp. 6–7.

43. Terence Brown, 'Canon Sheehan and the Catholic Intellectual', in *Ireland's Literature: Selected Essays* (Mullingar: Lilliput Press, 1988), pp. 65–76.

44. The continental convent schools presumably did not deserve the strictures Michael McCarthy levelled at the Irish schools in *Five Years in Ireland, 1895–1900*.
45. Ben Knights, *The Idea of the Clerisy in the Nineteenth Century* (Cambridge: Cambridge University Press, 1978), pp. 18–21.
46. Canon Sheehan, *The Triumph of Failure* (London: Burns Oates & Washbourne, 1935), p. 143.

5

Bad Blood: Sectarianism in the Irish Novel

DARK ROSALEEN

In the North of Ireland, the rival to Catholicism was, and is, not paganism or art, but another Christianity. To whatever religious problems existed in the rest of Ireland during the twenty-five years before the Great War that would excite the novelist, the north-east corner (as John Heron Lepper calls it in his busy historical novel of that name)[1] of the island could add an especially heated version of the relationship between the two major faiths in Ireland, Catholicism and Protestantism.[2] It is simple; what was true for all of Ireland is still true for Ulster: where there is religion there is sectarianism; between the sects there is a grim history of bad blood.

There have been a few laudable fictional attempts to laugh sectarianism away: the stories of Lynn C. Doyle (1873–1961, the pseudonym for Leslie A. Montgomery and itself a joke: linseed oil) are examples once well known inside Ulster, but never well known outside though Doyle's first book, *Bally-gullion* (1908), was published by Maunsel in Dublin. Such attempts are rarely satisfactory since they evade by definition the seriousness, intractability, and frequent violence of sectarianism. Alexander Irvine (1863–1941) accomplished something against the odds in the much reissued *My Lady of the Chimney Corner* (1913): a moving little autobiographical tract against sectarianism written by the son of a mixed Protestant–Catholic marriage in Ulster. It succeeds because it treats sectarianism on the story's own muted and personal grounds, being a memoir of an impoverished boyhood in Antrim town in the 1860s and 1870s cast in narrative form; it hardly mentions the organized churches of Ireland and no priests or ministers stalk its pages. Chiefly, however, it is a modest, charming, and loving reminiscence of the author's mother, Anna, the theme of which is identified in the epitaph Irvine proposes for his parents' headstone: 'Love is Enough.' The sentiment is less banal when set in the context of Ulster life, especially in hard and faction-ridden Antrim, for his mother when a pious Catholic girl had to choose between love for her sweetheart, a young Protestant shoemaker, and her church. His father does not seem to have had the same awful choice to make though he must have had to pay a different price: social ostracism from some coreligionists; but he is never centre stage so we are in the dark about that, this being a mother–son story.

That the Famine was in its terrible progress at the time adds to the poignancy of Anna's choice. In reaction to the price of choosing her suitor, she maintained a simple and churchless belief in God, dispensing her wise and unchurched Christianity from the chimney corner to which she gradually retreated. Her son Alexander, her ninth child, eventually became religious himself, receiving the calling during one night's intense awakening. When he left home, Irvine was half-literate, yet remarkably went on to become a religious slum-worker in the New York Bowery, a successful doctoral candidate in theology at Yale University, an Episcopal minister to a Fifth Avenue church, and during the Great War a YMCA padre in the trenches. While turning religious as a boy, he became filled with denominational certainty and regarded his mother's belief in the paramountcy of love as a sort of heresy; he drew apart from her, though one imagines he had in fact received the baton of belief from her. But he later came to repent of his snobbish folly and to see that her expression of religion was unimpeachable; his remorse is affecting. In several ways *My Lady of the Chimney Corner* is the inverse of Edmund Gosse's well-known *Father and Son* (1907): it is Mother and Son, and it is the son who is possessed of certainty; it represents the triumph of feeling over intellect, sensibility over dogma. The last outing of Irvine and his mother—she girlish and simple, he self-conscious and loving—has the quality of some of the scenes between Paul Morel and Mrs Morel in Lawrence's *Sons and Lovers* (published in the same year of 1913), for like that novel, *My Lady of the Chimney Corner* is a love story.

My Lady of the Chimney Corner is dedicated 'To Lady Gregory and the Players of the Abbey Theatre Dublin'. One might indeed have expected that a tale quietly celebrating simple peasant ways (using local dialect in doing so) and life without boundaries—be they denominational boundaries or social class boundaries—would be welcomed into the canon of the Revival, but it may be that the story too obviously courted sentimentality; its Ulster-Scots accents were the wrong kind of Hiberno-English; sectarian Antrim was the wrong setting; and evangelical Protestantism the wrong kind of faith, neither Catholic nor pagan. In any case, for decades the book was much read by the people but rarely mentioned in commentaries on Irish literature.

As for Anna's mixed marriage, it was a victory over sectarianism, an undiluted success with umpteen children and a great deal of laughter, and the author of the memoir was one of the trophies of its success—from the narrator's perspective, the story implies a rags-to-riches, Famine-to-feast trajectory that must have appealed to American readers (it was published in New York in 1913). But perhaps the Irvine family's victory was too lonely to mean much in Irish terms beyond the touching and folklike quality of the story. A few other Irish writers were willing to risk putting flesh on the sectarian bones and to approach the cultural and even political threats of sectarianism. For example, the industrious southern Catholic novelist M. E. Francis tackled sectarianism in an almost embarrassingly four-square manner in *Dark Rosaleen* (1915): four-square because she did not flinch from the notion of the essential outlandishness of the Ulster-Scots Protestants and the unfortunate maintenance of their foreignness in Ireland through heredity. It can be said straightaway that the idea of the essential otherness of the Scots Irish—who had not been culturally incorporated into the national life of Ireland—was current in some quarters before and after Francis was writing. Douglas Hyde, for example, expressed it in his famous manifesto, 'The Necessity for De-Anglicising Ireland' (1892), and Yeats in a letter to Maud Gonne in 1938.[3] Their animus against the Ulster Scots must have been increased by the northerners' refusal to turn their gaze southwards (Irvine's epigraph strikes an incongruous note), to participate in any national movement of unity or even revival, by what was perceived as their obduracy and disobligingness (known to their sympathizers as staunchness).

The far more volatile and dangerous settings of *Dark Rosaleen* switch between Connemara and Londonderry and are very different from the largely reassuring setting of Francis's *In a North Country Village* (1893). The likely end of Victorianism suspected in the earlier book is in contrast to the perseverance of pre-Victorian sectarianism and racial enmities depicted in *Dark Rosaleen*, though the author sees light at the end of the tunnel for one Irish population, darkness for the other. The action takes place roughly between the second and third Home Rule bills. *Dark Rosaleen* is both a convincingly realistic novel in its portraits of a mixed marriage trying to prosper in the impossible circumstances of the Ireland of 1890–1914, and a rather embarrassing allegory of an Ireland that might just be in the process of being born. To tell the plot is both to sketch out the allegory and suggest the embryo science of Francis's narrative, since it starts with what might be described as a kind of 'twins' experiment before the heyday of eugenics (a device employed by Sarah Grand in the earlier *The Heavenly Twins*, 1893). The plot is entertaining enough and culturally rich enough in implication to sustain its own summary.

Honor Burke is 'a magnificent specimen of Irish womanhood'—dark Rosaleen, indeed—who has a child called Patsy but also cares for red-headed Hector, six months old (three months younger than Patsy), son of the Church of Ireland minister's gardener, Alexander McTavish from the North and about the only Protestant in Cloon-na-hinch. The novel opens in around 1890 in

Connemara with Honor's bringing Hector to Dr Bodkin for vaccination, since Hector's mother Rose (read: a *false* Rosaleen) is sickly (read: Protestant Ulster cannot mother a nation). Bodkin calls the two boys Honor's twins and so in the story they are, and when Bodkin visits Honor to check on the babies, he finds Honor suckling Hector (read: Honor, Mother Ireland, is Hector's true mother). Honor's husband is a small farmer but being an only son he has not had to spend any of his wife's marriage portion to compensate younger siblings on his inheriting the farm and is therefore comfortable (read: Ireland is well enough off to look after the Ulster Scots in the event of Home Rule). Bodkin marvels at the ability of Mother Ireland to nourish both her own flesh and 'the stranger within her gates'.[4] This proves literally true in the novel when the scene shifts to Derry and the Protestants, recalling the siege, are indeed Honor's strangers within her gates.

Hector loves Patsy and thinks of himself as Patsy's brother but his stiff-necked father discourages his friendship for fear the Burkes ('a set o' traitors') will make a Papist of him. And Alexander resists the local customs (read: resists Irishness). Yet Alexander is a Presbyterian who has come from Belfast in broken health and changed into an Episcopalian to get his job and expects his wife to follow suit, though she bridles: 'Be true to your releegion', her father had told her. (Read: Protestants for all their bluff and bigotry are not reliable in their religion and are renegades at heart.) When young Hector is missing in a boat at sea, his father promises God to take his son back to Belfast to recover for them both the true religion of the Covenanters. Hector is washed ashore on the Aran Islands and given succour in a cottage but is mistaken for a malevolent changeling when he refuses to cross himself, and is banished. ('In those days' [around 1900] 'the Gaelic League had not penetrated to Inishmaan, and the inhabitants had not become familiarised with any people who, though kindred to them in race, and often in degree, were aliens in religion.') A kindly younger woman of the house, Sheila, takes pity on him and leaves him food and finds him shelter. (Read: the true Irishwoman is no believer in superstition but a sensible Catholic.)[5] Hiding in the room of a cottage, Hector hears the trample of feet and the sound of a bell: 'The bell sounded again, and there was a movement in the next room, a sudden rustle and stir, something like that which might be produced by a field of corn in bending before a rushing wind.' It is an episode in the conduct of the Mass and Hector flees in horror. When Father Casey of the rescuing party from the mainland hears of it, he tells young Father Murphy: 'The prejudice has been handed down for generations. It's in his blood.' Nurture to the contrary, nature will out, blood will tell, especially bad blood such as Hector's.

Heredity in the novel is a regrettable bio-cultural process but works only in the case of the Protestants; Catholics do not *inherit* as such; they simply *are*.

One suspects that for Francis the scientific outlook was as reprehensible as unionism and Protestantism. Father Casey deplores the superstitions of the Aran islanders but tells Father Murphy that the prejudices of the Orangemen are, after all, 'nothing but bogies too'.[6] But it's back to the Orangemen that Alexander decides to take his son and wife to rekindle the faith of his fathers. For years after they leave, Hector in his mind's eye 'could see the noble figure of the woman, who was to him the embodiment of all motherhood, standing with her arms outstretched' and he would hear 'the echo of Honor's voice, keening for the loss of her foster-son' (p. 104).

Part II of the novel opens with Hector's return to Connemara on a visit thirteen years later (about 1912 or 1913). He is now an engineer (very much the Northerner), wears a tweed suit and rides a motorcycle (the mechanical Northerner from industrial Ulster) though feels something of the 'wild rapture' he once felt in Connemara. (Read: rural Ireland is freedom, northern industrialism a kind of captivity.) His father has succumbed to the hardships of mill work in Belfast. (Read: industrial Belfast is unhealthy as well as un-Irish.) Patsy is now becoming a priest. Young Norah Burke, Hector's foster-sister, is there and he falls in love with her. He thinks had he stayed in Connemara they might have married and lived the life of fisherman and wife in a house by the sea. For a time his love for Norah contends with his memory of his father's counsel: 'Always be true to your releegion, laddie' but he accepts Father Pat's blessing out of courtesy and attends the latter's first Mass where he hears again the wind in the corn as the congregation bends forward on its knees. (Read: this beauty— and Francis's image is a fine one—is what Protestants are missing by resisting the poetry of the elder faith.) Hector lures Norah to Inishmaan and there virtually coerces her into giving him her hand in marriage. His desire to possess is 'some distant strain of the freebooter in Hector's Covenanter blood'. On being told, Honor fears he is like his father: 'I'm afeard you're just as bigoted.' He promises not to interfere with Norah's practice of her religion; ' "Aye", said Honor, "an' if there's childer?" ' Father O'Flaherty and Father O'Casey remind him that the Catholic Church 'discountenances mixed marriages'. But if Hector and Norah marry, the children must be baptized and brought up in the Catholic religion: Father Casey justifies the rule with point-blank candour and sweet reasonableness. Hector assents and signs the pledge with cold reservation which merely reveals how through the mechanism of heredity he is becoming in looks and attitude his father, 'the fanatical bigot'. The return to Connemara was Hector's last chance.

In Part III, Hector takes his new wife to Derry. The novel becomes a poignant and brutally realistic picture of a mixed marriage in Ulster. In *Protestant* Ulster, of course, the implication being that this is the least likely place for a mixed marriage to work, which was probably true. The allegory fortunately falters and the emotional foreground of the picture discourages us from making condescending parenthetical interpretations. This portion of the novel could stand alone as a moving novella. The growing isolation of Norah in a Protestant quarter of Derry, the blatant sectarianism ('No Home Rule. To Hell with the Pope' she sees on the walls and naively starts to wipe the words off before being dragged away by an alarmed companion), the friend-ships aborted in the disclosure of religious identity, the deterioration of the marriage under the pressure of growing neighbourhood hostility, the rapid triumph of the communal and tribal over the personal and emotional, hate over love—all this is well done to the point of the reader's discomfiture. Francis is alive to Protestant grievances; a Catholic family outside Derry has bought two more farms under the Land Purchase Act (1888) but Hector is sure they feel no gratitude and will express no loyalty as a result of their England-subsidized prosperity. He genuinely believes the priests are behind Home Rule and that they seek Catholic dominance in Ireland, that Ulster Protestant industriousness will be set at naught by Home Rule, and in these beliefs Francis gives him a fair hearing. But when a child is born, Hector reneges on his pledge and wants the child to remain unbaptized in any religion until he is old enough to choose for himself and threatens to foster his son out if Norah objects. (This for his creator is Hector McTavish showing his true colours.) The novel climaxes with the Twelfth of July processions and associated expressions of sectarian fervour and disturbances. Norah takes her baby, wearing its orange ribbon, and flees to Connemara.

Hector follows with a band of armed Orangemen to retrieve his abducted son (though Francis does not see Norah's action as abduction). This stretches credulity and the novel collapses into sentimentality, undoing the good work of the Derry scenes. Violence ensues; Hector is wounded and Father Pat absolves him ('*Ego te absolvo*'); Father Pat himself is already wounded but manages to baptize young Alexander junior; then he dies, side by side with his foster-brother who will recover but, it is to be hoped, says Dr Bodkin, repentant as well as remorseful. The allegory reasserts itself and Norah amidst the carnage holds her baby, who is Ireland in prospect, 'the new Ireland', the child of blood and tears, but embodying the promise of accomplishment.

Dark Rosaleen is no rant but its implication is that no solution is possible that compromises the spiritual hegemony of Catholicism. The child of Hector and Norah will be no religious or cultural hybrid but a Catholic. Whereas Protestants are bigots, Catholics are simply firm in their religion, and firm because their religion is true, whereas Protestantism, like pre-Christian pa-ganism, is false. Catholicism is the natural default religion of Ireland, just as nationalism is the default political position, and native Irishness the default racial identity. This view was clearly as easy to hold from the privileged vantage-point of Crosby Hall in Lancashire as in Connemara, perhaps easier. And elsewhere; for the idea that Catholicism and Irishness are inseparable was a common one in our period. It receives rhapsodic expression in *When We Were Boys* (1890), a novel by William O'Brien (M. McDonnell Bodkin's boss at *United Ireland* and like Bodkin a Nationalist MP); it was the belief of Edward Martyn; James Stephens attributed it to James Joyce in his memoir, 'The James Joyce I Knew';[7] it was the view also of Daniel Corkery. How far the idea was a defensive one and basically a social and political one, rather than a religio-racial one, is hard to gauge. Emmet Larkin is of the opinion that 'By 1914 Irish and Catholic had not only become interchangeable terms [in Ireland], but Catholic had come to be the inclusive term.'[8]

The idea that firmness of faith in Catholics is mere bigotry when exhibited by Protestants animates an earlier novel, *Fidelity* (1898) by Mary Maher. In this novel and her later novel, *Her Father's Trust* (1901), Maher employs the same subtitle, *A Catholic Story*, by way, presumably, of warning some readers and inducing others. The fidelity of the title refers to Catholic faith and also to the lifelong loyalty of the old servant class to a single family. One major character, Agnes, is enjoined to practise 'fidelity to God, fidelity in small things, fidelity under all circumstances'.[9] The novel is set among the Catholic upper middle class and nobility in London (during the Season with its balls and debutantes), St Louis, and Ottawa and these settings depict an international Catholic society. The chief Catholic apologist is Gertrude who is strenuously exercised by the heresy of Jansenism (which flourished between the sixteenth and eighteenth centuries) with its Calvinistic tendencies, including belief in human depravity, and predestination. She is also exercised by the earlier French heresy of Albigenses (twelfth to thirteenth centuries) that was ruthlessly crushed by the Inquisition under Pope Innocent III. These heresies Gertrude calls 'a cold poison'(pp. 75, 78). Since among the circumstances favourable to the spread of the heresy was 'the wealth, leisure, and imaginative mind of the inhabitants of Languedoc',[10] it appears that Maher through Gertrude is attacking the contemporary Catholic upper classes, among which a selfish materialism had recently appeared among the master and mistress classes, damaging the fidelity of the servant classes.

Gertrude also explains Catholic devotion to the Virgin Mary and defends it against the Protestant charge of Mariolatry, a species of idolatry. She defends Ireland as an oppressed Catholic country and lends Sir Henry Ellingham a new book entitled 'The Persecutions of Irish Catholics by an Irish prelate'.[11] Given the theological tide of the novel, dilemmas only notionally impede its progress. After hearing a sermon in Ottawa, Agnes turns away from a young man she has come to love; she becomes 'a professed nun' in a convent. Gertrude falls for Sir Henry, a Protestant, thereby potentially violating a deathbed assurance to her father (a convert to Catholicism) that she would never marry outside her faith. She turns Sir Henry down, faith being above happiness, religion above the heart. The greatest virtues are seen in the novel as unselfish devotion and heroic patience and these virtues (Catholic in coloration if not exclusively in substance) combine with a male perception in the novel of ideal womanhood. If Gertrude is a heroine, her father is a hero and martyr, not a zealot, despite his reference to one character as a Northern Irish Protestant 'and consequently very bigoted' (p. 134).

THE TWELFTH OF JULY

As we know from *Dark Rosaleen*, the Twelfth of July Orange parade is a boon to the novelist, laden as it is with colour and menace, celebration and enmity. It occupies a chapter of a sombre novel by M. Hamilton, *Across an Ulster Bog* (1896). Before likening the author's method to Crabbe's, a *Manchester Guardian* review of E. Rentoul Esler's *A Maid of the Manse* (1895), appended to Esler's '*Mid Green Pastures* (also 1895) by Sampson Low, Marston & Company, welcomes the novel because 'Ulster has hitherto been a region which has found little favour in the eyes of the novelist, and it is indubitably not one which lends itself readily to the illusions of romance'. In 1895 the first half of this observation was a fair comment (the second half is true to this day): Shan F. Bullock had just begun to publish while Forrest Reid and St John Ervine were still in the offing. By 1914 it was no longer fair, and the gap between Carleton and Bullock that inexcusably yawns in my own study of 1974, *Forces and Themes in Ulster Fiction*, I would now fill with the names of John Heron Lepper, Robert Cromie, Mrs J. H. Riddell, Filson Young, F. E. Crichton, Rosa Mulholland, J. J. Abraham, Beatrice Grimshaw, James Douglas, Sarah Grand, Arthur Mason, Alexander Irvine, Andrew James (J. A. Strahan), E. Rentoul Esler and M. Hamilton (Mrs Mary Churchill Luck).[12]

Hamilton's short novel inhabits the category of local or rural naturalism I discussed in *Forces and Themes in Ulster Fiction*. It is a small thesaurus of Ulster-Scots dialect words unselfconsciously and accurately used; there is a kind of genre painting in the book, with descriptive glimpses of lint-pulling and life by the bog, an unswerving picture of the intimacies of sectarian relationships in a village (here Ballyturbet, perhaps in Co. Derry), and a reader's sense that the communal forces of life in Ballyturbet will issue in violence and tragedy. Over all is the louring sky of north-western Ireland: 'It had been a long, dreary day—a regular October day, with the sky hidden in thick grey clouds, and an oppression in the air which meant rain in the future.

The lake lay dull and leaden behind the poplars, and there were no bright colours in the bog.' The grim seasons revolve. The Orange parade is life in miniature for the Ulster Scots and Catholics. 'The field was gay with flags and bright dresses and orange scarves . . . A gorgeous arch of orange lilies, with an effigy in coloured shavings of King William on a prancing steed hanging from the middle, marked the entrance to the festive scene and the skill and taste of the Ballymagra Lodges.' By day's end and the return of the procession, there is a general disorder with brethren hitting the pubs and Willy and Eccles Lindsay, major characters in the story, fighting drunk and wanting to bait Catholics. By novel's end the Lindsays have killed a man (though not a Catholic) and lower his body into the bog, in anticipation of the end of Frank O'Connor's great story, 'Guests of the Nation': 'In the light of the lantern the circles in the water grew gradually less distinct; while they stood silently it closed, dark and quiet as ever. "He's there till the Judgment Day," said Willy. "God forgive him." "And God forgive us!" said Archie Kennedy under his breath.'[13]

The foreground of this drab rural Ulster setting, depressingly familiar to anyone from Ulster, is the desperate attempt by the Revd Samuel Duffin, the Church of Ireland rector and son of a South of Ireland farmer, to penetrate Society (the Barings and Lawsons) in Ballyturbet. Though handsome, he is a man with an unfortunate personality, a man ill-at-ease, ambitious, self-doubt-ing, egocentric: rather like Riddell's Claud Dagley. Wishing to turn himself into a gentleman, he cannot do so. 'He was in many ways fitted to please a Northern congregation. He believed devoutly in hell and the devil, and preached about them, and he hated Roman Catholics and Presbyterians with great heartiness. He was also absolutely clear from any ritualistic tendencies, and had no desire to progress in any way.' Yet 'to be outside seemed his place always—out of all cheerfulness and companionship—solitary always' (pp. 29, 43).

Duffin's hatred of Presbyterians is unassuaged by the class difference that until recently kept the two sects properly apart; now the threat of Home Rule and the need for unionist solidarity has thrown these two sects together: Mr McCune of the Manse and the Revd Duffin of the Rectory 'were con-strained to meet frequently at the Unionist Club, and at Orange and other political meetings' and detest each other cordially (p. 30). The novel is set in the years somewhere between 1891 and 1896. Nelly Baring is anti-Home Rule—she throws cold water on the Home Rule argument that there is gold in Ireland awaiting native exploitation (an idea floated by O'Connell Shine in Mulholland's *Father Tim*); the McFaddens, Catholics, are for Home Rule; Mrs Mawhinney, surrounded by Catholic neighbours, is fiercely anti-Catholic and anti-Parnell ('that black divil Parnell') though the Chief is dead by the time the novel opens. The Orangemen are on the march with a vengeance

(Loyal Orange Lodges of the Independent Heroes and McCance's True-Blues). The voltage of sectarianism is abnormally high. Eccles and Willy Lindsay are virulent with sectarian hatred; 'Black Wully', a furious Orangeman, especially: he 'was an excellent Churchman as far as hating all other denominations went, though he seldom or never went to church'. Some are of the opinion there's a 'bad drop' (i.e. bad blood) in the Lindsays.

It is Duffin's misdemeanour and misfortune to seduce 16-year-old Ellen Lindsay, Willy's sister, a restless girl who wants to go into service elsewhere and flee Ballyturbet, and who stops attending church. She and Duffin are stealthily involved at the outset of the novel, despite her prophetic warning that 'There'd be murder done if my father or the boys—' (pp. 75, 45, 55). Pregnant, she now feels the weight of their dangerous intimacy and 'she felt in a strange way outside herself, as if it was another person she pitied'; like Duffin she is an outsider in a society in which it is dangerous to be such. She is oppressed already by life in a community where the only pleasure is 'the Twelfth' and Methodist or Plymouth Brethren meetings. Hamilton captures well the almost surreal claustrophobia of lower-class rural Protestant life in the nineteenth century. Duffin wears her down and now she is ashamed and adrift. It is a double calamity. Added to all its other distortions of life is the sexism of the community: 'In her class no question of equal morality for men and women had ever been raised. A girl who did not know how to take care of herself was a fool, and worse. Men were—as God made them' (pp. 56, 57, 58–9). Then Duffin, knowing her to be pregnant, suggests marriage and they arrange to meet in a distant registry office. The novel here resembles Hardy's *Tess of the d'Urbervilles*; Ellen makes her lonely but hopeful way to the office, but he never arrives and she returns disconsolate in steady rain and collapses by the bog. Her condition is revealed. Duffin has argued himself out of the arrangement while suffering guilt; he uses the transparent excuses of a cold and a lame horse not to rendezvous with Ellen; in truth he prefers to accept an invitation that might secure his entry into Society. Ellen is delivered of a premature baby ('The baby was a poor, puny thing, with great eyes full of sorrow and hands and feet like claws... a misfortunate wee crowl') and is disgraced: 'When a girl had once lost her character nothing she could do was of any use. There was no hope for her...' (pp. 118, 144, 129). She plays with the idea of drowning herself in the bog and nearly does so. The unforgiving gossip rises when she doesn't stay at home out of sight and even attends the Twelfth and it expands to include Duffin after the registrar's son sees Ellen at the field and remembers the name Ellen asked for. The community gets wind of Duffin's guilt; the Bishop gives him a slap on the wrist but the Lindsays take matters lethally into their own hands.

Hamilton, without blinking, connects in *Across an Ulster Bog* the personal and public, communal and political at a dangerous Irish crossroads. The novel belongs beside Shan Bullock's Ulster novels and is a precursor of *December Bride* (1951) by Sam Hanna Bell, the novels of Olga Fielden in the 1930s, and of Maurice Leitch in the 1960s and 1970s as an insider's view of her own rural Protestant community in all its grimness. And beside all of these, Hamilton's novel can stand on equal footing.

In most of his Irish novels, Bullock (1865–1935) deals exclusively with Protestants in the Erne country of Co. Fermanagh, but in *Dan the Dollar* (1906) he explores what he sees as the opposing psychologies of planter Scots and native Irish. The novel has two interwoven plot-strands. One concerns the return from America of the natural son of Sarah and Felix Ruddy who, with their adopted children, Phelim and Mary, are trying to subsist on twenty-six acres of 'bad to middling' land. Dan has made his fortune in Chicago but he finds the stay-at-homes perversely reluctant to accept his bounty, especially since he has disdain for their Irish ways which he finds wanting in comparison to American ways. The changes he introduces—up-to-date business methods, industry, and social reform—are alien to the loughsiders. (The refusal of modernity is a thematic motif in Irish fiction of the period.) He prevails on the family to move to a big house and the family is unhappy and broken (Phelim refuses to move). As though in retribution, Dan hears from Chicago that he is financially ruined and returns to start fresh; he asks Mary to go with him but she refuses; he sets sail and the family return to the original homestead where Phelim awaits them. Bullock records a terrible conservatism in his people: they see success beyond as hubris and hug their little destiny to themselves, to borrow a potent phrase from Seamus Heaney.

The other plot-strand is the sectarian one. Like Hamilton, Bullock knows his cast too well to bring allegory to the fore like Francis, but there is a pattern of impersonal cultural meaning in his tale with which anyone from Ulster is familiar. There is a clear difference between Sarah and the other three members of the family, Felix, Phelim, and Mary. In the family's attempt to stave off destitution before Dan's return, only Sarah is of worth, a hardworking Protestant married to a feckless product of a mixed marriage and burdened with two equally unworldly Catholic children. Phelim plays his fiddle and tells his stories, Mary has her piety, Felix his rambling idleness. Sarah alone has kept the family's heads above water. Once the family had rented a good farm of thirty-five acres in 'fruitful Gorteen', then another in Garvagh, and now the present small and barren one that thwarts Felix's indifferent efforts to make it productive. When Dan returns he is in sympathy only with his mother, whose 'Protestant' qualities he has inherited with a vengeance. At the end of the novel the forces of unworldliness win out in a kind of cultural reversion or retrogression that is symbolized in the land's return to unfruitful wildness. 'The hedges grew wild over ditches choked with brambles. Gaps were deep in mud. Gates hung twisted or broken. Once in old ancient times some fields had been in cultivation; now they lay barren, the rounded lands showing like ribs in a skeleton.'[14]

Bullock's interest in sectarianism is in racial and cultural differences rather than religious strife but the alleged differences bespeak an original and recurring strife. The belief that Catholics were inadequate custodians of their land, that the land was made fruitful, redeemed, and therefore *earned* by the Scots planters, was a sustaining one for Protestants who might have had qualms about their original 'sin' of dispossession of Catholics from the Ulster Plantation onwards. (A similar belief reassured settlers in the future United States in their hostile and usurpatory relations with native Americans.) The differences run through Bullock's Irish novels. *The Squireen* (1903) begins: 'Now Bilboa, Armoy and Drumhill are big and bare, and these regions are Catholic; but Gorteen is small and fruitful, and this is Protestant.'[15] But fruitfulness, like fortune, is precarious, and both the land and its original owners, must be fought; the useless fertility of wildness threatens reversion as Catholics threaten reversion of ownership: this is an idea that has retained its force to this very day. For a Protestant to 'turn', to marry out, is to lose purchase and grip, to revert in some sense. Vigilance and forcefulness: these are the constant Protestant necessities turned into virtues. Needless to say, there is an answering folk myth entertained by Northern Catholic writers from William Carleton to Michael McLaverty. And like the Protestant myth, it is rooted in history and with justification.[16] In Ireland the myths too often are true. The myth of a Celtic aboriginal possession supported by 'proof' in saga, song, and story was being elaborated by the Irish Revivalists as Bullock and Hamilton were writing and beside it the Planter myth seemed miserly, reducing itself to its essence of siege and negation.

The Twelfth of July and its aftermath are the circumstances of resolution in *The Soundless Tide* (1911) by F. E. Crichton (1877–1918).[17] Stephen J. Brown believed that the author pictured religious strife 'with perhaps undue insistence', but what is an author to do in Ulster when bad blood between Catholics and Protestants is as primary a fact of life there as race relations are in the southern United States?[18] Actually, *The Soundless Tide* is a familiar country-house novel with the frequent two-tier representation of society: the gentry and the peasantry (servants, estate workers, tenant farmers) without the complication of a noisy, thinking middle class. There is, as in Eleanor Alexander, the Church of Ireland minister with a dubious theology. At one point, there is a stand-in for the Revd Hamilton, as William Dugan, a stout Orangeman, reports:

'It was some sthranger that tuk an' altered the service, if ye please! He done a quare presumptious thing, to my way o' thinkin'.'

'Annythin' wi' crosses?' inquired Mrs. Logan, deeply stirred.

'Wait to A tell ye now! We had a hymn as usual, an' he up into the pulpit like anny other body. But then, instead o' prayin', "The Lord be with you" he says, an' begins his sermon. "The Lord be with you!"...'

'Well, well,' said Mrs. Logan, 'he'll have been some soort o' Ritualist. A thought ye were goin' till tell us o' carryin's on wi' crosses, or generrections'....

'Generrections' [genuflections] appeared to be an interesting and mysterious assault on Protestantism, and he was much intrigued.[19]

Since the setting is the Co. Down shore, instead of peasants we have feisty, vigilant inhabitants of a lowly seaside village called Cockle Row. (The character of Sarah McKillop is a fount of that sharp one-line pessimistic wisdom familiar to anyone who grew up in lower-class Ulster.) And, of course, we also have sectarian clashes.

The country-house formula is hard to maintain under these circumstances, though Crichton tries. She establishes the gentry–Unionist Party–Orange Order alliance (some might say conspiracy) that controls matters and opposes Home Rule. The main plot, however, is personal and to do with love. Gillian Ward of the big house, Connswater, has a childless marriage to an older colonel whom she has never really loved. 'There had always been a curious contrast between the spacious, ordered calm of the old house, and the baffled strivings of her own restless spirit.' Still hopeful in her restiveness, she subsides into bitterness once her young niece Patty arrives and through her vitality ('the spring-tide note in her voice') puts paid to Gillian's optimism and hopes for the future. However, the Colonel dies and Gillian, now 50, sets her cap at Randal, her younger cousin who lives with them. 'The love, whose roots must have been slowly spreading in the dark through long unconscious years, had pushed its way into the light at last. Now it was blossoming before her wondering eyes, making a very spring-time of the heart.' She declares her love, but it is Patty whom young Randal desires and Gillian is mortified and further embittered. (As often with such novels, the plot requires characters to withhold from each other essential feelings on the state of affairs.) She forgot 'that bitter law which decrees that by the time a woman is worth taking to, she isn't worth looking at any more'. She thinks in anguish back to 'the great central flaw of all' (greater than her childlessness): 'a marriage without love'.[20] In the end, Randal and Patty (who thought Gillian stood between her and Randal and who suffered accordingly) come together, and Gillian finds surprising peace of mind through the agency of Andrew Gilchrist whose wisdom and goodness save her soul.

Meanwhile, the approach of the Twelfth during July is a deceptive count-down from happiness to unhappiness; things begin as happily as they do in *Across an Ulster Bog*—'It was a hot evening in July. The orange lilies rose in gay battalions in the garden, and the beat of drums practising in the distance sounded like throbbing pulses in the still summer air.... The July days crept on towards the historic "Twelfth", always brilliantly, steadily hot.... The morning of the "Twelfth" was calm and brilliant.... the air was athrill with that nameless sense of festivity' (pp. 111, 121, 148). The celebration is the crisis for the subplot: the love between young Mary Ellen Logan, a Protestant, and Michael Dempsey, a Catholic, for whom she has refused the suit of Robert Dunwoody. Mary Ellen, the poor girl, experiences the love denied to wealthy Gillian but her love too is thwarted and just as cruelly. Nationalists, feeling under the yearly provocation, attack the procession and a riot ensues. Mary Ellen watches 'women, blind with passion and inherited hatred, trying to tear the Orange scarves and banners from the men ... The crash of broken windows and cries of the wounded seemed to fan the flames of excitement and rebellion, as the smouldering animosity of years found an outlet' (pp. 165–6). She sees her lover Michael Dempsey, 'with the red fire of hatred in his eyes' (p. 166) leap on Dunwoody and assault him, causing him to fall and strike his head. Once again sectarianism determines personal relationships and overpowers love. Dempsey is sent to jail where—rather conveniently for Crichton and Dunwoody—he dies. At the end of the novel, it is likely Mary Ellen will accept Dunwoody. The novel endorses the true love that comes through fire and is no unrealistic thing, as was the love of Gillian for the younger Randal, and of Mary Ellen for the Catholic Dempsey.

BELFAST AND SECTARIANISM

The opening salvo of a radically different kind of novel, *The Unpardonable Sin* (1907) by James Douglas (1867–1940), is the birth of Gabriel Gordon in Protestant Belfast on the now familiar Twelfth of July and the novel accelerates from that slow beginning. For all its instabilities and absurdities, and though it is most likely set in the 1870s and 1880s, *The Unpardonable Sin* is in part a work of Edwardian realism (a little earlier than some of the work of Bullock and Ervine), but in its totality it is a novel that anticipates the peculiar, busy, and spacious modernism of, say, Eimar O'Duffy's Cuanduine trilogy, that is both backward and futuristic, of the eighteenth and twentieth centuries equally. It is a rambunctious multi-style work that has too many targets and story-forms but has the pace and ambition of the new technology of its time. It joins the homely comic absurdity of sectarianism we find in Lynn C. Doyle and 'humorous' Irish tales to the darker energies of James Stephens—the first part of the novel has something in common with *The Charwoman's Daughter* (1912), the second with the apocalypse of *The Crock of Gold* (1912).[21]

Douglas's scene-setting analysis of Belfast ('Bigotsborough') is ruthlessly accurate and one imagines Francis would agree: the Gordons 'had drunk fear and hatred of the Roman Catholic religion with their mother's milk'... Belfast 'is the loneliest city in the world. It would be happy if it were on the Clyde, for its blood is Scottish. But it lives in exile amid an alien race... It is a mistake to attribute the lawlessness of Bigotsborough to religious animosities. Its roots strike down through the strata of religious hate into economic degradation.' Equally lively and accurate is his depiction of the lawless and impoverished corridor between the Falls Road ('the Roman Catholic Alsatia') and Shankill Road ('the Orange quarter') where the Orange parade is ritually ambushed. The spirited account (though feverishly weary with what we sense is the author's familiarity with it all) of the nationalist assault might be modelled on the events in Belfast of 1886 or almost any year back then,[22] and though Douglas visits the pox broadly on both houses, his special venom is reserved for loyalism. He has a bilious profile of 'the Ulsterman' (Protestant): 'He is an arrested growth who retains the unlovely elements in his ancestral character. In him Scottish frugality becomes stinginess, and Scottish prudence turns into sour suspicion... The religion of the Scot... calls upon human nature to choose between damnation here or damnation hereafter.' The Roman Catholic quarter of Belfast is called a 'Ghetto', an early application of the term to Belfast. Gabriel Gordon grows up here and learns to regard 'Tagues as vermin.' There are scenes in a National school in which Douglas's dislike of an absurd system and a bully of a schoolmaster are conveyed in a vinegary prose.[23] The novel's subject-matter is a high-octane blend of poverty, surplus energy, unemployment, sectarianism, evangelism, and industrialism that is true and perceptive in its fundamentals. Brown is right to quote the *Irish Book Lover's* opinion in 1907 that *The Unpardonable Sin* was 'the finest delineation of Belfast boyhood ever penned'.[24] Forrest Reid's later delineations were, of course, middle class (Gabriel's father is a riveter in a shipyard and Gabriel himself is apprenticed to a linen merchant) and the contributor to the *IBL* would have had to wait for St John Ervine to read comparable (and stabler) delineations.

Gabriel Gordon's boyhood ends when he awakes to a knowledge of himself. He attends an evangelical mission conducted by Moody and Sankey and forthwith becomes an evangelist himself and, soon after, a popular preacher appointed by the Methodist Conference to a chapel in a slum. From there the novel heads into open water, its justification being that 'Human character is rarely monopolised by one idea or passion'; for Douglas 'The drama of life is based upon the conflict of the characters which are imprisoned in the living prison of personality.' Hitherto, we read, 'we have seen the development of Gabriel in his relation to external forces' and he has seemed a unity, but 'he was in reality the theatre of many conflicting ideas and many heterogeneous passions' since 'At a very early stage of life character throws off living organisms which in their turn generate others, and the process which we call growth is simply the evolution of the mind from the simple to the complex' (pp. 83, 84–5). Gabriel, already born again, must now, he thinks, be born a third time, since the questionings he feels may be divine in origin, not infernal and therefore he may by ignoring them be committing 'the unpardonable sin', the sin against the Holy Ghost, whereas the saintly Mr Kelso to whom he goes for religious guidance believes he may be guilty of intellectual pride. Besides, his path will grieve his mother yet he cannot betray the truth. Douglas gives us a depiction of a Protestant spiritual crisis which is uncommon in Irish fiction.

Chapter XV of the novel opens on the eve of St Patrick's Day, with the city's nationalists planning a march from Smithfield market along the Falls Road to Milltown; meanwhile rumours have spread that Catholics have attacked Shankill Road 'Islandmen' coming home from the shipyard. Gabriel has become an enemy of sectarianism and tries to stop the next day's ambush of nationalists by loyalists. Of the loyalist riot, Douglas remarks acidly: 'It was thus, and not for the first time, that Bigotsborough displayed its loyalty to the British Crown and its love of God' (p. 122). His brother is killed and he accuses Dr Ryan (and the Orange Institution) of his murder through his sermons and speeches. But by this time the novel has developed a fever. Fionula, a nationalist Maud Gonne figure, is introduced ('The Queen of the World') along with her henchman, Cormac Achill (a young Yeats), who has 'grafted Maeterlinck and Mallarmé, Verlaine and Baudelaire, Leconte de Lisle and Barbey d'Aurevilly, upon the mystical mythology of the Celtic renascence' (p. 176). Gabriel himself becomes something of a Symbolist poet and like the Yeatsian heroes of his 'apocalyptic stories' 'there was in him a pale yearning for the occult and the unknown' (p. 177). Swinburne exerts an influence on him. He sleeps with the Gonne figure and suffers tortures of guilt immediately afterwards. He may dislike the Church of Ireland, 'the iron formality of the Kirk, and the hysterical vacuity of Methodism' (p. 188), but he yet feels in his bones the steely resolve of the Covenanters and the inherited dread of Rome and distrust of religious beauty. He is a feverish representative of the ambitious and cultivated Ulster Protestant. His life is 'pleached and interlaced with contradictions of taste and temper . . . he knew himself to be a living maze of imaginative complexities. His mind was a mart of dreams and a caravanserai of ghosts' (pp. 177, 188, 144).

The nature of the unpardonable sin changes: it is now 'the sin against love' (Gabriel loves Aideen). He goes to London, becomes famous as an Edwardian Oral Roberts evangelist and builds a New St Peter's (like American evangelist Robert Schuller's Crystal Cathedral in our own day) which is rumoured to be subsidized variously by the Pope, American millionaires, a secret society of Socialists, and Anglican Ultramontanists. By now the reader sees the justification of the description of the second part of *The Unpardonable Sin*, quoted by Brown, as 'the dream of an opium-eater'.[25] But that judgement was made by someone who had not read the future *Ulysses*. For portions of Douglas's novel read like inferior versions of portions of Joyce's epic, for example the apocalyptic opening ceremony of the new cathedral (pp. 241–51), pages of crescendo that employ catalogues, verse, the descriptions of a 'symphony of religious beliefs' from a hidden orchestra, music greater than Richter and Strauss, soaring and snarling: 'it turned sick with the carnage of war and the carnage of industry. The shrieks of women and children crawled under the roar of machinery, the melancholy hum of elevators, the moan of motor-cars, the whistle of locomotives, and the wail of steam syrens and factory hooters.' It is Douglas's version of a global religion and global culture: Calvinistic, Gregorian, Bacchanalian, Evangelical. It culminates in Gabriel's sermon when he appears from behind a cloth of gold and enacts the Day of Judgement. His sermon is a new set of commandments and Beatitudes, a vision that proclaims the dissolution of all barriers in this Church of Man and commands joy, justice, equality: everything that is absent in bitter Bigotsborough and the world. The delirium would not be as bizarre to a reader of the Nighttown episode of *Ulysses* as it must have been to the Edwardian reader. This is not to compare stylistic merit, since there is far too much rodomontade and sub-Swinburnian prolixity in Douglas's novel; and there is some tosh—'Speech is but the relapse of the soul after it has soared to the Gates of Death.' And Douglas offers mere description where Joyce can verbally *represent* his subject.

The novel is a farrago of contemporary concerns. Gabriel advocates 'with unflinching courage...the emancipation of womanhood from its political and economic disabilities': a wife, he urges, is a worker without wages and union and her services should be financially evaluated; a husband should have to pay his wife and the longer she stayed married to him the less dependent she would be upon him; 'Wages for Wives' became his rallying call; 'he pleaded for an imaginative revolution in the imaginative conscience of society' and attracts the support of 'feminist leaders'. He founds a League of Humanity, a kind of United Nations of social justice. Douglas means Gabriel to be a self-revolutionizing human being; Aideen, he believes, has allowed him to see that the soul is a state of living thought, that we can reconceive ourselves. He has grown disillusioned with London and Fame and finds his final form in his love for Aideen. As in so many of these novels of the period (a period, we might see in hindsight as teetering on the brink of post-Christianity), Love is seen as the ultimate virtue and destination: the unpardonable sin is the sin against Love, which *is* the Holy Ghost. No, Aideen says, the unpardonable sin is despair, but they aren't in disagreement.[26]

The delirious second half of the novel, with its tenuous connections to the transfiguration theme of Irish Revival fiction,[27] might distract us from interesting resemblances between the first half and *A Portrait of the Artist*. Both are *Bildungsromane* and *Künstlerromane*, one set in a unionist community, the other in a nationalist. Both boys attend coercive schools (Douglas and his pals mitch off to the docks, as do the boys in 'An Encounter' in *Dubliners*). Both Gabriel and Stephen exhibit intellectual pride, and both develop beliefs that pain their mother. Both sleep sinfully with women and suffer pangs of guilt afterwards. Both question their faith in interview with a spiritual elder and fall from grace. Both have visions of redemptive girls. Joyce names his hero after the first Christian martyr, and Douglas has Gabriel (whose name is shared by Joyce's dubious hero in 'The Dead') cry to the loyalist mob who begin to hurl stones at him: 'stone me, if you please! Stone me as they stoned Stephen! I care nought for your stones'. Both are failed Symbolist poets. But whereas Joyce leaves Dedalus lonely in his apostasy and pride, Douglas brings Gabriel into the community of Love. One is faintly tempted to ask if Joyce read *The Unpardonable Sin* and borrowed a little as he borrowed from Bret Harte, Anatole France, George Moore, Ibsen, Defoe, and others.

Growing up in Ballymacarrrett in the 1880s and 1890s, St John Ervine (1883–1971) knew his Belfast as well as Douglas and he lingers with the Edwardian realism of his representation where Douglas flies into bizarre regions of the overheated imagination. And like many Ulster writers, Ervine makes use of the motif of bad blood, particularly in *Mrs Martin's Man* (1914) which Harold Orel reports as having been a notable seller in Britain in 1914.[28] In it, family quarrels play a big part and are a metaphor for the sectarian feuds in Belfast at the beginning of the anti-Home Rule agitation in the decades of Ervine's childhood and youth before he left for London in the early years of the twentieth century.

The fictional image of Belfast depends upon the eyes through which it is viewed. Rural Catholics and rural Protestants tend to see it in the fiction as dark, damp, and menacing, which is how it appears in local naturalism and in stories by outsiders. Belfast Catholics may love their city but it is a love that especially after Home Rule agitation (and until recently) seemed to be tempered by their sense of alienation from the city's official and aggressive Protestantism, witness the views of the Catholic stranger in *Mrs Martin's Man*. The love which Belfast Protestants have for their city, a love which informs Ervine's novels, is mingled with pride in the industrial achievements of Belfast with which, especially after partition in 1921–2, Catholics found it harder to identity.[29] Yet many Protestants live with a suffocating sense of the city's provincialism when compared to Dublin and London; Ervine's love for Belfast, for instance, has in it an element of contempt (as did young Joyce's for Dublin).

Both themes of industrialism and provincialism sit well with the tradition of lower-middle-class fiction into which Ervine settled himself, that (as John Boyd rightly said in 1951) was cocreated by Wells, Galsworthy, and Bennett.[30] This tradition has hardly been charted on the Irish critical map, in part because of a reluctance on the part of many critics to read Ulster fiction closely if at all; in part (a related reason) because the tradition could apparently play no part in the grand narrative being told by the Irish Literary Revival; in part (also a related reason) because the depiction of the lower middle class, particularly the urban lower middle class, the world of industrial and other clerks, shop assistants, and minor officials, was anomalous in Southern Irish fiction of our period, and even thereafter. The social world of *Dubliners* and *Ulysses* is preponderantly lower middle class but to describe them as works of Edwardian realism would be laughably reductive; besides, Joyce's lower middle class is so idle and put-upon that it barely floats above the working class. Joyce's attention is elsewhere and so, too, one feels, is Daniel Corkery's whose cast of characters in *The Threshold of Quiet* (1917), commercial travellers, small businessmen, is on the lower fringes of the middle class.[31] It is to Northern writers we have to turn, and we catch glimpses of the employed lower middle class in Forrest Reid whose young heroes, deriving from a descending middle class, shrink from it in fear and horror.[32] Shan Bullock is almost exclusively associated with rural Ulster but his *Robert Thorne: The Story of a London Clerk* (1907) is an interesting sortie into Edwardian realism replete with documentary details of the lives, at desk and hearth, of 'pen-drivers', emasculated drudges beset by poverty, duty, and routine. Ignored by English and Irish critics since, it was warmly received in its day and according to Waller, social historians nowadays think of it as a remarkable work and human document of the times.[33] It is worth remarking, however, that Thorne's deliverance at the end of the novel is by emigration to New Zealand, whereas the real answer lies in the 'manliness' he might have achieved, not in the city but in his native Devon. Bullock thus returns to the countryside for his core values, but to the benign west-country English countryside, not the sectarian landscape of his native Ulster. Incidentally, it is Waller who reminds us that Bullock essayed 'another adventure in the City clerk genre', *Mr. Ruby Jumps the Traces* (1917), modelled on Wells's *History of Mr. Polly* (1910).

Ervine's is more characteristically a world of small shopkeepers, often vain and ambitious. But among these figures of small lives, a few black sheep come down with wandering fever and sail the seven seas in clippers and schooners during the time of Ervine's own boyhood in the 1890s. In *Mrs Martin's Man*, *The Foolish Lovers* (1920), and *The Wayward Man* (1927), wanderlust propels the narrative and offers a lifestyle that threatens the stay-at-home shopkeepers. This aspect of his fiction is romantic, in the senses of involving adventures in London and America and involving women in the life decisions of the heroes.

The life choices facing his young heroes as they approach manhood are a staple of his fiction; the choices seem pre-Joycean in so far as they involve lifestyles rather than truth or vision; in that sense Douglas was ahead of Ervine and closer to the Joyce who was about to break into print. But it is Ervine's late Victorian Belfast that I mean merely to mention here since I have discussed it more fully in *Forces and Themes in Ulster Fiction*. Ervine depicts the exoticism for Ulster Protestants of Catholicism (for example, the adventure of young Robert Dunwoody—we have met the same name in *The Soundless Tide*—in the Catholic chapel in *The Wayward Man*), an exoticism that turns dangerous, as when Dunwoody after an abortive running away to sea makes his way home to Ballymacarrett through the Catholic neighbourhood of the Short Strand where he is set upon and beaten up. Ervine incorporates such episodes of sectarian experience into the general pattern of his heroes' adventures where they have the truthful ring of intimate familiarity.

NOTES

1. John Heron Lepper, *The North East Corner: A Novel* (London: Grant Richards, 1917).
2. Dissenters in Ulster would be content with the word 'Catholics' to describe their enemies, though Anglicans—in some contexts called 'Protestants' to dissociate them from Dissenters—would insist on the term 'Roman Catholics', since they regard themselves also as Catholics.
3. See Joseph Hone, *W. B. Yeats 1865–1939* (1943; London: Macmillan & Co., 1965), p. 469.
4. M. E. Francis, *Dark Rosaleen* (London: Cassell and Company, 1915), p. 11.
5. A young priest on the island laments the superstitions and reminds the older priest, Father Casey that 'it is practically only the other day that you were able to stop that business of sending a naked man on a white horse riding into the sea during the spring tides. That must have come from some heathen rite of propitiation' (p. 91). This custom might be one on which Synge drew in *Riders to the Sea* (1904).
6. Francis, *Dark Rosaleen*, pp. 65, 91, 79, 90.
7. *When We Were Boys* (London: Longmans Green,1890), pp. 136–7. For Edward Martyn, see George Moore, *Hail and Farewell: Ave, Salve, Vale* (1911, 1912, 1914, ed. Richard Cave; Gerrards Cross. Colin Smythe, 1976), pp. 123, 235. For Joyce, see 'The James Joyce I Knew', in *James, Seumas & Jacques: Unpublished Writings of James Stephens*, ed. Lloyd Frankenberg (New York: Macmillan, 1964), p. 149.
8. Emmet Larkin, *The Historical Dimensions of Irish Catholicism* (1976; Washington, DC: Catholic University of America Press, 1984), p. 91.
9. Mary Maher, *Fidelity: A Catholic Story* (London: Burns & Oates, 1898), p. 58.
10. 'Albigenses', *Catholic Encyclopedia*, http://www.newadvent.org/cathen/01267e.htm

11. Almost certainly she gave Sir Henry a copy of *Historical Sketch of the Persecutions Suffered by the Catholics of Ireland* (1865; 3rd edn. 1884) by Cardinal Francis Patrick Moran.

12. Mrs Mary Churchill Luck was born around 1860 in Co. Derry. The British Library Public catalogue lists eighteen of her novels, the latest published in 1928.

13. M. Hamilton, *Across an Ulster Bog* (London: William Heinemann, 1896), pp. 151, 183. The novel was published in 'The Pioneer Series' (which included Stephen Crane's *The Red Badge of Courage* and Robert S. Hichens's *The Green Carnation*). Its ironically unsuitable but beautiful title page shows a coloured illustration of an Oriental procession with banners and musicians, like an Asian translation of the Orange parades into courtesy and cultivation. This handsome title page is missing from the copy of the novel in the Henry Collection, Queen's University, Belfast.

14. Shan F. Bullock, *Dan the Dollar* (Dublin: Maunsel, 1906), p. 53.

15. Bullock, *The Squireen* (London: Methuen, 1903), p. 3.

16. I discuss these competing myths and beliefs in *Forces and Themes in Ulster Fiction* (1974).

17. Mrs F. E. (Frances Elizabeth) Crichton was born in Belfast, educated in England, and travelled widely in Europe. She wrote novels for children (e.g. *The Little Wizard of White Cloud Hill* and *Peep-in-the-World*) as well as adult novels.

18. Brown, *Ireland in Fiction*, p. 72.

19. Crichton, *The Soundless Tide* (London: Edward Arnold, 1911), p. 231.

20. Crichton, *The Soundless Tide*, pp. 207, 81, 206, 240–1.

21. Born in Belfast, Douglas became literary critic for the *London Star* and editor of the *Sunday Express*, 1920–31. His novel reveals his metropolitan ties. Douglas was the author of *Theodore Watts-Dunton: Poet, Novelist, Critic* (1904). I discuss Eimar O'Duffy and James Stephens in *Fictions of the Irish Literary Revival* (1987).

22. The historical background to Douglas's riot can be found in Henry Patterson, *Class Conflict and Sectarianism* (1981).

23. Douglas, *The Unpardonable Sin* (London: Grant Richards, 1907), pp. 5, 6–11, 18–25, 27–9, 31.

24. Brown, *Ireland in Fiction*, p. 90.

25. Ibid.

26. Douglas, *The Unpardonable Sin*, pp. 340–3, 412, 417.

27. See my discussion of the ideas of enchantment, the changeling, transfiguration, etc. in *Fictions of the Irish Literary Revival* (1987).

28. Harold Orel, *Popular Fiction in England, 1914–1918* (Hemel Hempstead: Harvester Wheatsheaf, 1992), p. 22. Orel says that Katharine (Hinkson) Tynan's *When First I Saw Your Face* was also a big seller that year, but he must mean 1915 when this novel was published by Hutchinson.

29. Despite my use of the present tense, things have changed drastically in the past twenty years or so. Belfast's heavy industry has almost entirely vanished and the city is much more Catholic and nationalist than it was three decades ago. The legendary loyalist Shankill Road and Sandy Row areas have shrunk in extent and importance; the working-class and lower-middle-class Catholic-nationalist neighbourhoods

have multiplied and grown; the equally legendary Malone Road Protestant affluent enclave is mixed now; many comfortable Protestants have moved elsewhere (often to north Co. Down) to create a rival to the old middle-class Protestant Belfast. The geography of sectarian confrontation has been reduced to one or two dividing lines where clashes erupt, including the borderline Ervine knew well, between loyalist east Belfast and the Catholic Short Strand enclave, both of which have been in the sectarianism business for at least 150 years.

30. John Boyd, 'Ulster Prose', in *The Arts in Ulster*, ed. Sam Hanna Bell, Nesca A. Robb and John Hewitt (London: George Harrap, 1951), p. 118. The sense of suffocation that ambitious and educated Protestants once felt about Belfast has much diminished. There is a much greater sense for such people now of intimacy with Britain as a whole, with Ireland as a whole, even with Europe as a whole (in the era of the European Union, accessible plane travel, and proliferating tourist destinations); internet communication too has done much to lessen the effects of provincialism, even when the raw factors of provincialism are still in place.

31. I discuss Corkery's novel in *Fictions of the Irish Literary Revival* (1987).

32. I discuss the role of social class in Forrest Reid in *Forces and Themes in Ulster Fiction* (1974).

33. Philip Waller has several fascinating pages on Bullock's star-crossed career: *Writers, Readers, and Reputations: Literary Life in Britain 1870–1918* (Oxford: Oxford University Press, 2006), pp. 138–40.

6

Studies in Green: The Condition of Ireland I

THE SOCIAL-PROBLEM NOVEL

Writing of English fiction between 1895 and 1920, Trotter observes that 'a number of writers sought to emulate their heavyweight Victorian predecessors by combining a didactic intention with healthy sales figures. For them the novel was diagnostic. They set out to analyse the "condition of England". The criterion of relevance which enables us to sift the information they provide is partly the plot, as in popular fiction, and partly the diagnostic intention.'[1] The condition of England had been a concern of thinkers as early as Carlyle ('The Condition-of-England Question') and of novelists as early as Disraeli, Mrs Gaskell, and Charles Kingsley. Arnold Kettle identified the political, social, and religious aspects of the Question broached by Disraeli.[2] As Trotter remarks, the social-problem novel combined commercial aspirations with social concerns, and this is the case with many of the Irish novels I have so far discussed that have been concerned both with religion in Ireland and the emotional lives of their main characters; the ratio of indirect social analysis to romance formula varies between novels.

Actually, many of the novels have been as much concerned with the Condition-of-England Question as with the Condition-of-Ireland Question. This is not to be wondered at, nor to be ignored as somehow un-Irish, and for two reasons. First, many Irish—especially the wealthy and the poor (seasonal labourers, impoverished emigrants)—knew England well and several popular Irish novelists lived there and naturally wrote about their adopted country (and some of them would have said, their mother country). A large if specialized group, Irish members of the Westminster parliament, travelled to and fro and were at home in the House of Commons and London where they lived part of the year; Bodkin the fervent nationalist was sorry when the time came to leave the House of Commons ('the best club in the world'), was a tremendous admirer of Gladstone, and an avid London theatregoer, especially when Shakespeare was staged. He set his detective stories in England no doubt because he knew England well and thought England the home of the genre. Second, the Irish Question was inseparable from the Condition-of-England Question, more so, naturally, from an English point of view but also from an Irish point of view, because of the very familiarity I've mentioned. It seems absurd, then, to divide the novels of an Irish novelist into those that are 'really Irish' and those which are not.

David Thomson has listed some of the problems inherent in the England Question between 1875 and 1914, including of course the problem of Ireland, 'the greatest single source of violence and political upheaval in English politics'.[3] The problem was acute because it involved a clash between two nationalisms, one developed enough to be a form of imperialism, the other quickly making up lost ground, of necessity inward-looking yet with an important American dimension. We have already seen reflected in Irish popular novels the agitation caused by the Home Rule campaign particularly between 1886 and 1914, both in Ulster and in the rest of Ireland. The interlocking religious questions—the doctrinal disputes within the Church of Ireland, the evangelical movement, the Catholic education question, the relationship between Roman Catholicism and Irish nationalism—are also reflected in the popular fiction and are to some extent versions of the religious component of the England Question that English novelists were addressing.

The problems arising from industrialism in Britain and Ireland, including the labour disputes that afflicted industrial England and industrial Ireland (chiefly Belfast and parts of Dublin), are less represented in the Irish popular novel, in part because most of the novelists by background and upbringing were unsuited to the theme. I can only assume, too, that the absorption of so much energy by the constitutional question (seen as a life-or-death issue by both Irish unionists and Irish nationalists) meant that other elements of the Condition-of-England Question were not reflected in the Irish problem-novel, even though much of it was in effect a Condition-of-the British Isles Question that related to Ireland as well as England, including the developing concept of social welfare. In Ireland, as we have seen, the organized religions were in on the social welfare act and dominated the foreground, so that if we look for the depiction of charity in the fiction, we find an abundance.

There is, however, a fitful address of industrialism in Ulster fiction. Ervine is useful on the white-collar side of factory life, and he knew the unique sectarian dimension of Belfast industrialism. For his part, the highly popular Donegal writer Patrick MacGill (1889–1960) in *Children of the Dead End: The Autobiography of a Navvy* (1914) and *The Rat-Pit* (1915) offers grim portraits, bordering on caricature, of the under-class struggling to survive on the fringes of both British industrial society and Irish agricultural society on its least fertile margins (chiefly the windswept periphery of the north-west): navvies, seasonal farm workers, down-and-outs, tramps: desperate members of the sinking classes.[4]

His Irish town is dominated by the police barracks, the Catholic chapel, and the workhouse—images of bondage and oppression in MacGill's fiction, which in its socialist sympathies lives entirely outside the culture of philanthropy. Gombeen merchants and gombeen priests drive MacGill's poor to Scotland for seasonal work, movements that compose loose narratives that are picaresque and bristle with ructions: despite their shortcomings they are mysteriously engaging, full of memorable characters and incident. Their world straddles the famine-racked countryside of nineteenth-century Ireland and the urban industrial squalor of twentieth-century Britain. MacGill rightly calls his cast of characters and the places they inhabit—from Donegal to Glasgow—'the underworld' and his novels can be set beside the English fictional and nonfictional portraits of the 'sinking classes' by Gissing, Booth, London, Jay, and Masterman to which I've already referred.

A novelistic study by an Irish writer of the underside of industrialism and capitalism, carried through with an economic and effective realism, came from an unlikely pen. *The Bomb* (1908) by Frank Harris (1855–1931) is a plausible fictional autobiography of an historical figure, Rudolph Schnaubelt, the German anarchist said to have thrown the bomb that killed and wounded policemen during a police break-up of an anarchist and socialist-labour meeting in Haymarket Square, Chicago on 4 May 1886. This event is said to have provoked the first 'Red Scare' in American history. James Thomas Harris (nicknamed by his family 'Joe' but later renamed by himself 'Frank') was born in Galway, spent his infancy in Kerry and Kingstown (Dun Laoghaire) and his boyhood in Galway, Belfast, and Carrickfergus, Co. Antrim. He was educated at Royal School, Armagh before going to a public school in Wales.[5] In 1869 when he was still a youth he emigrated alone to the United States and returned to Britain in 1882 where he began his controversial literary career. His Irishness surely contributed to his sympathy and friendship for Wilde, of whom he wrote a splendid biography, whatever its factual defects and episodes of self-promotion, and to his portraits of the Irish in New York and Chicago that appear in *The Bomb* as well as in the once scandalous *My Life and Loves* (privately printed 1922, published in 1964).

The primary theme of *The Bomb* is the making of terrorists, and so has a dim collateral relevance to Ireland. One of these terrorists is Schnaubelt who on arrival in New York from Germany becomes socially and politically disaffected and in Chicago becomes radicalized when he joins the ranks of the socialists, then the anarchists, almost all of whom are European immigrants. The novel opens with Schnaubelt's account of his boyhood near Munich where he becomes a freethinker and republican, before his story moves swiftly to New York where through failure to get steady employment he joins the social underworld and 'sank to utter destitution'. 'How had I fallen so low?', he asks himself. 'I have been down in the depths', he tells us, and explains that only the poor help the poor in the half-life of the wretched he calls 'purgatory'.[6] He discovers that European immigrants are detested by Americans and discriminated against, even when the immigrants are educated and cultivated, while Americans protect their own simple, ruthlessly individualistic, self-serving, and materialistic culture that offers only riches as reward for effort, and then only if the race criteria are met. When Schnaubelt gets a hazardous job digging foundations for the Brooklyn Bridge, working in a compressed air capsule on the river bottom (requiring the navvies to be compressed and painfully decompressed at the start and finish of each shift), the novel makes more literal the metaphors both of purgatory and of the sunken proletariat.

Harris shares MacGill's penchant for the episodic (derived from the necessary shifts of their chief figures in search of livelihood and reflecting the restlessness of the authors themselves), and Schnaubelt removes to Chicago where his American radicalization begins, but Schnaubelt's voice, grimly serious for the most part since after all he is telling his story of suffering while dying of tuberculosis back in Bavaria, gives the novel an intense singlemindedness that avoids any hint of caricature. He meets Louis Lingg, the brilliant and handsome labour organizer and radical thinker, whom he comes to idolize; he becomes Lingg's apostle and spreader of his gospel, in the end bearing testament to Lingg's martyrdom. Lingg's is the chief portrait in Schnaubelt's gallery, a charismatic figure who finally embraces force and who said when faced with police fire: 'If they use cannons against us, we shall use dynamite against them.' Harris makes Lingg a genius, not of word, though he is a formidable thinker and speaker, but of deed and gives him this memorable sentiment: ' "The writer", he said, "tries to find a characteristic word; the painter some scene that will enable him to express himself. I always wanted a characteristic deed, something that no one else would do, or could do. One should be strong enough to bend and constrain deeds to one's service, and they are more stubborn than words, more recalcitrant than bronze..." ' (pp. 208–9).

This sentiment lends a sense of inevitability to the novel's proceedings, which sits comfortably with the conclusion Lingg and others arrive at—that retaliation by the working class is made necessary by the practice of capitalism and the brutal behaviour of its running dogs. It sits well, too, with the importance in the story of the material world, of *things*—especially tools and weapons—culminating in Lingg's ingenious bomb (dwelt on in detail) as well as of ideas and theories. It also sits well with the plain prose style Harris gives to Schnaubelt (who must learn 'American' in order to survive) and which his narrator comments on. 'This English language is figurative; it has all been made by poets and romance writers, by people with imagination, and not by people with open eyes and clear judgment; but new experiences demand a new telling, and the language of plain fact is sufficiently impressive' (p. 286). Harris anticipates Orwell in the plainness of his narratve and in his connection between plain prose, clear thinking, and political disabuse. In his story Schnaubelt recalls starting his autobiography but tearing up the first hundred pages because it indulgently concerned his boyhood and was not sufficently germane to the story of his radicalization and role in Chicago socialism and anarchism. But he continues with his autobiography and sends two handwritten copies off to two women friends, Lingg's partner and his own girlfriend, leaving only one chapter to complete, the chapter in which we read of this. By this device, Harris achieves a sense both of immediacy and of reflexiveness in the text. There is also an 'editor' who contributes the odd footnote and who is not identified but is clearly Harris, though in an ambiguous role.

Schnaubelt also meets the others who in time would with Lingg compose the Chicago Eight, arrested for their part in the Haymarket affair. Schnaubelt quickly becomes convinced that the conditions of manual labour in the United States are producing a proto-revolutionary proletariat. Not only are the workers underpaid but the conditions are inhuman and often dangerous and in the case of the pork-packing establishments, of which Harris paints a lurid picture, filthy and unsanitary. Reasonable if strenuous demands for an eight-hour work day are met with capitalist fury, police brutality, and with the complicity of the pro-capitalist and pro-law enforcement press, the law courts, the churches, and the professions. Moreover, hiring and firing practices are xenophobic, corrupt, and arbitary. The two decades before the Great War saw a flood of European immigrants into the cities of the United States causing great social unrest. Although 'Anglo-Saxon' resistance to the assimilation of the Latin races is well known, the Germans, if Harris's Schnaubelt is to be believed, were also resisted and disliked.[7] Through his experiences as a radical journalist in Chicago, as a worker and as a striker, Schnaubelt comes to believe that American competitiveness is an organized swindle. Later, when after the Haymarket atrocity the police ride roughshod over the rules of evidence, arresting the innocent and fabricating charges, he is confirmed in his belief in 'the hollow mockery of American justice' (p. 250); it too is a swindle, conducted and controlled by big business. *The Bomb* is an unflinching indictment of the unjust gap between American democratic principles and democratic practice at the time.

Through the speeches, debates, and discussions of Schnaubelt, Lingg, and their fellow socialists or anarchists, Harris broaches the bigger issues of the day.[8] One issue is the effect of the Machine Age on labour and equality. The historical Albert Parsons, an American and editor of the left-wing paper, *The Alarm*, was one of the Chicago Eight who walked into court on the first day of the trial and gave himself up. (He was one of the four hanged, though he had left the Haymarket rally before the bomb was thrown.) In *The Bomb* he explains how machinery has increased productivity many fold and how this has simply meant a grotesquely disproportionate increase in profits, creating a plutocracy, while the worker has been left behind in earnings, an idea Lingg adopts and later expounds.[9] A bigger but related issue in the novel is the concept and practice of individualism and the degree to which it is a virtue and vice. Michael Schwab (Harris makes him a professor) tells the Anarchist Club that individualism has been pushed too far in England and America where it has 'run mad' (p. 101; the historical Schwab was sentenced to life in prison but after seven years his sentence was commuted). Lingg, addressing the militant group *Lehr and Wehr Verein*, tracks individualism back to the invention of the spinning jenny and the use of steam and the publication of Smith's *The Wealth of Nations*, after which the principle of individual greed took hold. Agreeing with Schwab that individualism has got out of control, he nonetheless recalls it as the vital force behind scientific discovery and proposes not to extirpate it but limit it through what later became known as nationalization (pp. 153, 110–11, 158) and he believes that an inborn sense of justice is beginning to make itself felt. Later, having escaped to Europe, Schnaubelt finds Lingg's proposal to embrace a competitive individualism, albeit limited by certain state socialist mechanisms, unacceptable to socialists there (p. 293–4).

Schnaubelt's championing of Lingg's individualist-competitive socialism is an aspect of the fiction of *The Bomb*. Here, as elsewhere, Harris is imbuing these historical figures with his own belief in individualism, since Harris, like his friend Wilde, felt a genuine attraction for socialism yet could not entertain the thought of individuality (i.e. his own chromatic and forceful personality) submitting to the herd instinct.[10] Recalling debates in Philadelphia with his friend, (Professor) Byron Caldwell Smith in the 1870s, Harris tells us: 'I wanted to see both principles realized in life, individualism and socialism, the centrifugal as well as the centripetal force, and was convinced that the problem was how to bring these opposites to a balance which would ensure an approximation of justice and make for the happiness of all' (*My Life and Loves*, p. 165).

Despite the exotic settings of his novel for English readers, Harris believed it relevant to the lives of those readers. In his Foreword to the American edition of 1909, Harris reminded English readers that they had no grounds for complacency since justice in the United States is as fair as, and more human than, in England. Moreover, he has Schnaubelt find competitive, possessive individualism more malignantly advanced in England of the late 1880s than the United States. His sympathy is clearly with the virile and violent reaction of men who are suffering, whose leaders manage to combine action with their own unselfishness (particularly Parsons and Spies), indeed their willingness to undergo martyrdom. Lingg has 'an absolute genius for self-sacrifice' (p. 109) yet he is cool, calculating, self-concentrated. Harris's fiction, then, occupies a moral habitat very different from the (largely but not exclusively) female habitat of suffering and martyrdom relieved by individual charity and organised philanthropy: there are incidents of individual charity in Harris's American cities but they are most likely to involve the poor helping the poor and are entirely unequal to the task of allaying, much less remedying, an unjust system.

Indeed, *The Bomb* constitutes, in part through the attractive character of Lingg, an explanation of terrorism that comes close to being an apology for it, something that reads uncomfortably after 11 September 2001, though it would not have read so uncomfortably before then when many in the United States and even Britain were willing to see terrorist bombers of the Irish Republican Army (from the 1970s through the 1990s) as sympathetic (certainly *understandable*) actors in a drama. At times, Harris's sympathy for Schnaubelt and Lingg can come close to seeming like irony, as though Harris were a novelistic *agent provocateur*; interestingly, Schnaubelt himself, who was arrested but released, and then vanished, was suspected by some of being just that, an *agent provocateur* in the pay of the authorities.[11] Yet it is difficult for the reader to distance Harris from Schnaubelt when the latter remembers what Lingg told him, that 'the bomb thrown in the Haymarket put an end to the bludgeoning and pistolling of unarmed men and women by the police; it helped, too, to win the Children's Charter, and to establish "Labour Day" as a popular festival' (p. 326).

Schnaubelt sees Lingg as a quixotic figure, willing to stand alone against society and draw fire to himself to save others if necessary, a figure not unlike his younger Irish contemporary Patrick Pearse who a handful of years later would lead a quixotic revolution in Dublin and when captured request to take sole responsibility for it. After the bombing, Lingg relays to Schnaubelt from jail his assertion about what happened: 'it was necessary to prove that if we held the lives of others cheap, we held our own cheaper. Men do not kill themselves for greed or hate; but for love, and for an ideal' (p. 322). Schnaubelt recalls Lingg as a great man in whom was 'the blood of the martyrs; he had the martyr's sympathy with suffering and destitution, the martyr's burning contempt for greed and meanness, the martyr's hope in the future, the martyr's belief in the ultimate perfectibility of men' (p. 328). If Lingg's suicide in jail echoes that of the 'father' of Irish republicanism, Theobald Wolfe Tone, in custody in 1798 more than it anticipates the suicides of contemporary Islamist bombers, it yet might set off uncomfortable vibrations in the reader. Similarly, Schnaubelt's claim that by the time the trial started, thousands were still in prison—from twelve to fifteen thousand, he claims, every foreigner the police could lay their hands on (p. 265)—having been rounded up and 'held there in defiance of law' (p. 274), might prompt readers today to think of Guantanamo Bay. Certainly there was panic and overreaction to the atrocity, particularly in Chicago, fuelled by amazing rumours of imminent revolution that helped activate witch-hunts. Avrich refers to police response as a 'reign of terror' but writes that hundreds (not thousands) were rounded up.[12] Historically, however, despite the contemporary claim that some suspects were beaten and subjected to indignities, a better analogy than Guantanamo Bay would be the internment of hundreds of suspected IRA activists or sympathisers by the Northern Ireland police and British authorities in 1972.[13] (Historically, however, the proximate context for the Chicago Eight was late nineteenth-century events in Russia and even earlier events in Paris, and Schnaubelt when telling us that a monument to the police dead in Haymarket Square was later removed finds echo in this of Marat's interment in the Pantheon in Paris and his later indignant removal, p. 327.)

Lingg confides to Schnaubelt the fundamental principles of terrorism. Whereas one bomb can be construed by the authorities as an accident, two show sequence and purpose; it is the third and fourth bombs that are 'terrifying' (p. 171), a proposition Schnaubelt finds itself terrifying yet dreamlike, making him feel like an automaton (the ideal state for a terrorist, one assumes). Moreover, Lingg deemed it crucial for the first bomb-thrower to escape scot-free: 'Nothing spreads terror like sequence and success' (p. 227). Schnaubelt is convinced that Lingg's method of suicide—using one of his own tiny bombs—had had the secondary purpose of terrifying Chicagoans, 'to get the terrorizing effect he wanted without hurting anyone else' (p. 318). The extraordinary thing is that Harris manages throughout to make Lingg an attractive figure and Schnaubelt an almost honourable figure.

Almost every character in *The Bomb* is historical, a daring strategy on Harris's part, not only because he could be accused of tampering with history but he could (and no doubt did) provoke the anger of American readers for whom the anarchists were anathema. Tamper with history he did, a necessary thing in order to make fiction out of fact. But he does so chiefly in his recreation of Schnaubelt and it was history that gave him license to do this, since his narrator was in history a shadowy figure. True, Harris withholds the fact that Schnaubelt was Michael Schwab's brother-in-law and was an anarchist already by the time he reached Chicago, presumably so that the novelist can provide the more gradual structure of a *Bildungsroman* in the first person. He also withholds the fact that the entire Schnaubelt clan, as Paul Avrich puts it, played a conspicuous role in the International Working People's Association, a loose federation of radical groups.[14] As a result, Harris has to omit the fact that the day after the explosion Schnaubelt went to police headquarters to go bail for his brother-in-law and was refused; speaking German (Harris has him as a fluent American speaker by then) to a socialist attorney, he voiced incendiary stuff, and now having drawn police attention to himself and having been seen on the speaker's wagon on 4 May, he was arrested two days later, on 7 May.[15]

Harris has him get away scot-free, going to earth in accordance with Lingg's advice. Schnaubelt was released soon after his arrest, the police believing his story that he had left the meeting before the bomb was thrown. Nevertheless, the real Schnaubelt was one of ten indicted by a grand jury on 27 May but by then had been at large since his release on 7 May.[16] According to Avrich, Schnaubelt stayed on a farm outside Chicago before heading for the Canadian border, crossing it on foot and working on a Quebec farm. Earning enough for his passage he shipped to England where he met London-based radicals who helped him pay for a ticket to Buenos Aires under an assumed name and spent the rest of his life in anonymity.[17] In *The Bomb*, Schnaubelt gets to New York where under the assumed name of Willie Roberts he takes ship on the Cunarder *Scotia* for England and hides out in Soho, London. There he writes 'The Reign of Terror in Chicago', an account the title of which refers to state terrorism not that of the anarchists, and attends meetings of the Social Democratic Federation where he meets William Morris. Ill and troubled, Harris's Schnaubelt is driven from London by the fogs of November and December, sojourns in Bordeaux then travels via Paris to Cologne where he resumes his radical journalism. When the US Supreme Court renders its judgement, affirming the guilty verdicts, Schnaubelt returns to London to stir up the radical clubs but it is all hopeless and Schnaubelt is confirmed in his opinion that there is little justice in the world. It is back in Cologne that Schnaubelt receives word of Lingg's horrific suicide, and he continues work on his book about Lingg with all the passion of the gospel writers recalling the ministry of Jesus. (In the novel there is a Judas, one Raben, a journalist whom Schnaubelt had met on the steamer to New York.) The book he is finishing as we come to the close of *The Bomb* is mistakable for the novel itself and he is now writing in Reichholz to where he has travelled from Munich in order to avail himself, but too late, of the health-giving air of his native Alps.

Although Harris's Lingg is both a romantic and serious figure, the novelist tampered less with him than with Schnaubelt. Even to his police interrogator, Lingg was 'scrupulously honest and conscientious in his dealings with his fellow-men'.[18] To one acquaintance, Lingg was one of the handsomest men he had ever met and resembled a Greek god. Young anarchists of the next generation imitated Lingg's athletic walk.[19] It is a moot point, though, whether Harris was true to history in presenting Lingg's belief in the power of the individual to shape events not only as a component of an ideal socialism but also as a romantic justification of his own lone martyrdom by suicide. In recreating Schnaubelt, Harris accepts without qualification the German's guilt. *The Bomb* begins with a bang: 'My name is Rudolph Schnaubelt. I threw the bomb which killed eight policemen and wounded sixty in Chicago in 1886.' Yet Avrich maintains that there is not a shred of evidence that Schnaubelt threw the bomb or committed any other violent act.[20] In any case, to round Schnaubelt out, Harris drew on more of his own experience than a belief in the contribution of individualism to an ideal socialism or anarchism. Schnaubelt's experience in the caisson or iron capsule digging the foundations of the Brooklyn Bridge was in fact Harris's own, as he tells us in *My Life and Loves* (pp. 67–8). But more important for anyone interested in Harris is the deployment as thematic motif in both books of the concept of self-restraint as a form of self-mastery. Schnaubelt celebrates Lingg's 'iron self-control' and Lingg's restraint is simply a more graphic version of the general self-discipline with which Harris credits Chicago's radicals.

One of the ways in which Harris infuses Schnaubelt with elements of his own personality is by giving him a sex life that is a paler version of Harris's own as recounted in *My Life and Loves*. Schnaubelt meets a girl called Elsie Lehman who befriends the stranger to Chicago. Although Elsie has aristocratic pretensions and was invariably 'on the side of the prosperous and the powerful, against the dispossessed and the poor' (pp. 76–7), Schnaubelt courts her, loving and wanting her, and though she loves him back, she keeps him at bay in several episodes, his desire almost but not quite uncontrollable, her self-control 'immutable' (p. 130), though she maintains it is because to yield would require her to marry him and to do so would be to endanger him should he be out of work. Eventually Schnaubelt in an onset of self-mastery resolutely puts the 'bridle' on himself and refuses to yield to tormenting desire (p. 182), though in fact political events supervene before his campaign of the flesh has come to its own conclusion. *My Life and Loves*, of course, is composed of a series of such campaigns to lay successful siege to women and to enter their temple; the series is in the end tedious and is certainly formulaic, Harris's repertoire of seduction techniques being curiously limited. However, it is made fractionally more interesting through the periodic attempts by Harris to discipline and master himself by exercise of the will, thereby attempting to satisfy the excessive demands both of his bodily and intellectual ambition.[21] Clearly he thought Schnaubelt would have been one-dimensional were sexuality not consonant with his thrusting political activism.

IRELAND AT THE CROSSROADS

In some important respects, the 'Condition of Ireland'—at least in significant parts of the island—was more grievous than England's or America's. Industrialization may have spawned massive social problems associated with too rapid development in a few urban areas, especially Belfast which shared those problems with Glasgow, Liverpool, and other manufacturing cities—including Harris's Chicago. But in the rural Irish peripheries it was often the absence of work, industry, and productivity that was the problem. There may have been an agricultural depression in England in the late nineteenth century,[22] but Ireland had rural poverty unmatched elsewhere in the British Isles. Depictions of rural difficulty were plentiful. George Moore showed a moribund countryside in *A Drama in Muslin* (1886) and thought it bad enough to suggest a countrywide revival must be at hand; he painted it presciently as 'the inevitable decay which must precede an outburst of national energy'.[23] Eight years after the publication of this attack on the Irish gentry (from which he sprang), Moore dreamed of writing a novel entitled *Ruin and Weed*.[24] It remained unwritten but in 1901, after a revelation in 1899—the famous telegram from Edward Martyn in Dublin to Moore in London: 'the sceptre of intelligence has passed from London to Dublin', the famous dinner at the Shelbourne with Yeats and other luminaries of the developing Revival—Moore moved to Dublin and stayed until 1911. When he lambasted England for its materialism and cosmopolitanism and saw Ireland's spirituality and nationality as far superior, he sounded not unlike Rosa Mulholland or M. E. Francis.

But the end of his affair with Revival Ireland can be dated as early as 1902 when a rift opened with Yeats; in any case, the very depth of the need for revival seemed to put Moore at odds with the Revivalists because Ireland itself seemed irredeemable (largely because of Catholicism). Soon after he arrived he conceived a volume of stories about peasant life after the manner of Turgenev's *A Sportsman's Sketches*. The stories were to be translated into Gaelic in order to plough and seed the 'untilled field' of Gaelic literature. (The first six stories appeared in Gaelic but apparently made no impression on readers of the Irish language; these and the rest were published in English in 1903 as *The Untilled Field*.) And because he thought then that the revival of Gaelic should take precedence over the necessary anti-clericalism, he would publish them in the *New Ireland Review* edited by a Jesuit. But as composition progressed, Moore found his stories straining the alliance with Father Tom Finlay, and in *Hail and Farewell* his recollection of composition slides effortlessly into detailed memories of his growing preoccupation with the incompatibility of literature and Catholic dogma.

It is sufficient here to register the picture of western rural Ireland in the volume that justifies the title and leave aside the major themes of anti-clericalism and bafflement of self-realization.[25] The picture is of rural Ireland's 'slattern life': choked drains, empty cabins, fallen bridges—the untilled fields of Ireland. In one story the feebleness of the west is contrasted by a returned Yank, James Bryden, with 'the modern restlessness and cold energy' of Americans, much as Dan the Dollar noted the same instructive contrast in

Bullock's novel of that name three years later. And the incoming human traffic of America, a vast dynamo of energy and fresh starts, was only too readily contrastable to the ongoing haemorrhaging of the Irish countryside through emigration that Moore portrays. This volume, a rural precursor of Joyce's stories of untilled urban lives in *Dubliners*, is recognized as establishing a realism uncomfortable for Revivalists who sang the praises of the west and identified it as the spiritual centre of the coming Ireland, the site of inspiration for a new national beginning.

In 1909 Charles Masterman, a Liberal MP, published a highly readable book entitled *The Condition of England* (revised and republished in 1912). The Irish equivalent, an attempt at an overview but inevitably with a political agenda (though a practical one) and just as readable, is Filson Young's *Ireland at the Cross Roads: An Essay in Explanation*, published six years before Masterman's diagnosis of the neighbouring island and the same year that saw Moore's *The Untilled Field*. Young spent two months back in Ireland in 1903 and thus his book joins the populous genre and lengthy tradition of books by English visitors to Ireland reconnoitring and diagnosing the island's condition and offering remedies—a tradition that includes Arthur Young's famous report in the eighteenth century and Thomas Carlyle's in the nineteenth century; the latter's *Reminiscences of My Irish Journey in 1849* (1882), is the closest in style and address to Young's survey that I can think of. In this non-fiction genre, travel and reconnaissance take the place of temporary (or, as may happen, permanent) sedentary sojourns of the kind we find in many of the novels. However, since Young had been born in Co. Antrim and spent his boyhood summers in Co. Down after his family moved to London, he hit the Irish ground in 1903 running. His book belongs in fact to a subgenre, that of the native returning to take the temperature of the country he once left; the return of the native (or first visit of the English resident of Irish extraction) is a plot-feature of many Irish novels of this period.

Young identifies the Irish symptoms and effects of illness and they are surprisingly similar to those George Moore was identifying and, to the extent that description in non-fiction is comparable to that in fiction, they are just as eloquent. At times Young seems to be writing a kind of documentary fiction as he was to do in *Titanic* (1912). He invites the reader to follow him into the lush 'Arcadies' of Meath, Westmeath, Kildare or Dublin, there to sense 'something wrong, jarring, out of tune': beauty without human result; 'a kind of dusk of humanity seems to brood over the scene...Where are the people?' The countryside 'sleeps ruinous and deserted in the sunshine' around boarded-up cottages, 'while the green army of the nettles stealthily closes in upon its final and melancholy destiny'. Along these deserted ways you see 'a small group of dirty cabins, inhabited by silent, purposeless, helpless, and thriftless people, whose personality seems to consist of a mass of vestiges: powers disused, capacities rusted, ambitions dead, propensities frustrated. Only the religious emotion flourishes; and upon minds weakened and sapped of the power of seeing things as they are, the Church spreads its narcotic and comfortable cloud of symbolism.' The mind of the inhabitant stagnates; we are asked to note that 'the increase of lunacy is greatest in the pastoral districts, and that the ratio of lunatics per hundred of the population is greater in Meath than in any other county'. To this scene the west coast adds a difficult climate: 'the endless struggle, and the blighted life, and the illness, and the poverty, and the lunacy. You can walk for miles in Donegal and not see a sign of Nature's clemency or kindness . . . along the whole western Irish coast is to be found one great natural influence, unchanging, paralysing, daunting.' The western ports, so naturally well endowed for shipping 'just exist, derelict and half ruinous', unvisited except by the punctual tides.[26] Here indeed are Moore's contemporaneous untilled fields of Edwardian Ireland.

Emigration both causes and symptomizes the malady of peasant Irish landscape. 'The drain of emigration has reached a point at which, if it is not arrested, it will speedily wipe out the nation; for even now the raw human material of reformation is dangerously scarce . . . The population diminishes because the people emigrate; they emigrate because there is not work for them to do in their own country' (pp. 15, 107). So, providing work—that is the first great task and a practical one. Broadly, Young's was one of three fundamental approaches to Ireland's ills. We have seen evidence of the first: the top-down programmes of alleviation through charity and lightly interventionist social work that did not try to shake the foundations or even the superstructure of Irish or British society and did not on the whole involve the middle and lower middle classes; the constitutional position of Ireland was hardly a factor in the operation of these programmes. Social work could of course shade into plans for, and practices of, reform in various spheres (the second fundamental approach): changes in marriage laws, for example, or inheritance laws, or schemes of industrialization, all of which could have been termed forms of modernization and which would have had economic and cultural implications, and even, if carried far enough, political implications, for example in land redistribution; reform might or might not have ultimately involved Home Rule, a kind of constitutional reform that awarded Ireland a good deal of autonomy while leaving the Empire and ultimate English control intact. The third approach was reform radical enough to be a virtual or actual revolution, and these, as it turned out, included forms of separatism or self-sufficiency, be they Irish Ireland economics, Gaelic or pseudo-Gaelic revival, or republicanism. (Actual revolution was attempted in 1916, substituting national liberation for the class-revenge contemplated by Harris's socialist-anarchists.) The Irish literature of the period that is celebrated and assumed to constitute the national canon is not that which is philanthropic or reformist in impulse, but that which is thought to have furthered the cultural and, by extension, the complete political independence of Ireland. Young, however, was a reformer.

But should reform be the choice of action, there are Goliaths other than the provision of work lying across its path. Succinctly, Young diagnoses 'three great tumorous growths' that are 'triumphant and alive'—the lunatic asylum, the public house, and the Catholic chapel; a trio of Irish illnesses: madness, drink, and the Irish version of Roman Catholicism. (MacGill substitutes the police barracks and workhouse for Young's public house and lunatic asylum.) Young pulls no punches in seeing these as enemies of Irish peace and prosperity, though drink and madness, like emigration, are clearly effects or symptoms, and only Catholicism a cause. 'It is my profound conviction', Young writes, 'that a large proportion of the present misery of Ireland is not only bound up with, but is actually a result of, the country's religion.' This conviction does not prevent Young from offering a very fine account of his stay at Mount Melleray, that monastic institution in Co. Waterford that enlivens the pages of *Norah of Waterford* and *Father Tim* by Rosa Mulholland and plays a small but character-istically telling part in Joyce's great story, 'The Dead'.[27] It is a warm and sympa-thetic episode (pp. 88–106) and has the unity and momentum of a short story.

But of course the monastery cannot harbour the answer to Ireland's woeful condition. That condition is worsened by the antics of the waning gentry. Young evokes an 'old lord, doting in his library of memoirs . . . he and his house are a bit of old Ireland; fast fading and being exterminated before the invasion of events; but clinging still upon the very skirts of change'. All over Ireland are these 'minute and aristocratic settlements. The landlords, where they are resident, are often anchored to their estates by no better chain than that of poverty.' Often they aren't resident. Their interests are outside Ireland and Young believes that the Land Act of 1903 will weed out the discontented landlords and leave the country to get on with it. His explanation of the decline of the gentry is one later proffered by George H. Jessop in *Where the Shamrock Grows* (1911). According to Young, it was different when London was a week's journey from Dublin and so the landowners had their town-houses in Dublin where they met in season and formed a metropolitan society (Moore in *A Drama in Muslin* shows them in this theatre just as the waves of threatening change were about to crest); but then the railways and steamships brought Dublin within a day's journey from London, English ideas were increasingly introduced, and the landowners could buy town houses in London, did so, and Dublin was abandoned. The Viceregal system declined accordingly and in any case 'It is an alien, and in some hands may be an unsympathetic establishment in the heart of the country.' He refers to 'the mummery of a mimic court', echoing Moore's phrase, 'the awful mummery in muslin'.[28] 'So stands Ireland, weak and emaciated, at the cross roads; ready now, as I believe she has never been ready before, to be guided and directed in a more prosperous way.' She can either maintain the status quo under the domination of the Church, or heed the voices of the reformers. But if she takes the road of reform she comes immediately to a fork in the road, since the reformers are of two kinds: those promoting a Gaelic cultural revival (of which the literary revival is for him in 1903 a minor part), and those promoting economic reform. Young's conviction that the second road is the right one, his enthusiasm for economic reform, places him alongside the late Victorian and Edwardian 'Efficiency men' such as Rudyard Kipling, Joseph Conrad, H. G. Wells, Bram Stoker, and Erskine Childers who all denounced the kind of liberal muddle that E. M. Forster tried to champion in *Howards End*.[29] As befits someone with strong North of Ireland ties, Young espoused the philosophy of self-help which included, following Samuel Smiles, *national* self-help which Smiles advocated for Ireland in his chapter on Irish manufacture in the book he edited, *Men of Invention and Industry* (1897). One of the chapters in the book was contributed by the great shipbuilder Edward Harland ('Shipbuilding in Belfast—Its Origin and Progress') and Belfast's industrial success was one of the models Smiles adopted for Ireland as a whole.[30] The doctrine of self-help embraced both individual self-reliance (with its inevitable Victorian and Christian, indeed Protestant, religious and moral basis) and national self-reliance, and Smiles's chapter on Irish manufacture in his book fairly bristles with practical advice for the Irish to this end. The philosophy of Sinn Fein was, of course, a promotion of Irish self help, and there was also the Irish Ireland movement, but always it seemed that the constitutional question and sectarianism took primacy over economic renewal. In any case, the bottom-up doctrine of self-help stands in clear contrast to the top-down philosophy of philanthropy (one should no doubt resist the temptation to see one as more masculine than feminine, the other more feminine than masculine), and we can find both responses to Ireland's plight generously depicted in the fiction of the period.

Economic reforms normally, we would think, derive from enlightenment projects of rational reform driven by science, especially when they advocated industrialization in the towns and agricultural improvement (including mechanization) on the land. But in Ireland at this time, one wide-ranging proposal, agricultural co-operation, was put into practice by Horace Plunkett and the Department of Agricultural and Technical Instruction (DATI) and was supported by AE, the arch-mystic of the Revival (as if the two men who inhabited his body—AE the Dublin mystic and George Russell the Ulsterman from no-nonsense Lurgan, Co. Armagh—both found expression in the proposal). Young tells us that detractors of the co-op scheme, with AE chiefly in their sights, called it a case of 'creameries and dreameries', combining as it did hard-headed practical reform with Revival rural idealism. Young throws his weight behind the economic reforms alongside education. He praises the 'Irish movement' but believes that it will soon be halted or its continued good health will eventually bring it into 'violent and active opposition to the Church.' This as we know did not happen except in isolated skirmishes; Revival and Church ran on parallel tracks until 1922 when the Church slid into a more clear-cut, indeed constitutional, dominance. Young's expectations of a showdown were not realized but the 1903 Wyndham Land Act did at least hammer another nail in the coffin of an uncaring and doting 'Society, spelt big'.

BARREN NOSTRUMS

In the last decade of the nineteenth century and first decade of the twentieth, Anglo-Saxonism and xenophobia appear to have reached a high pitch in Britain and North America.[31] *The Hate Flame* (1908) by Percy Barron reflects these phenomena while purporting to be a novel about Irish Anglophobia, a phobia that sets at naught all the well-intentioned English proposals to remedy the island's ills. In this disturbing work of fictive propaganda, the author links and exaggerates familiar themes—love, marriage, English-Irish relations, the decline of the Irish country house, indeed the dereliction of Irish society, and ill-fated economic initiatives. It is the hero's opinion and experience that the dire condition of Ireland is made well-nigh irremediable by the Irish themselves. Engaging in a generous critical discrimination hardly available to us nowadays, it seems, the Irish literary historian, Stephen J. Brown SJ found that whereas bitter anti-Irishness and anti-Catholicism shipwreck the novel, the 'scene-painting and the handling of situation and of narrative are very clever' and, moreover, 'there is nothing objectionable from a moral point of view'.[32]

The 'hate flame' of the title is the toxic, outmoded, counterproductive hatred of England that Barron's English hero Jack Bullen (a slimmed-down, physically fit John Bull) thinks characterizes the Irish: 'they are dispirited, they are poor and their fathers and grandfathers were poor, and they see no real hope of anything better'. If he sounds here like Filson Young, he then sounds like Joyce's Haines in *Ulysses* when he rallies some sympathy for the Irish as he lectures his Irish girlfriend about her people: 'They have got into the habit of blaming England for everything. To a large extent they are right. England did give the Irish a jolly bad time—once. I can't read Irish history myself without getting hot all over'. But the Irish have only themselves to blame nowadays and they oughtn't to listen to their priests who tell them that 'this is a world of sorrow anyhow, and the only thing to hope for is a better life in the next world where the poor will have it all their own way'. Young too thought this was the case, whereas Mulholland thought the priests were justified when they judged Irish poverty as a spiritually beautiful thing, to be relieved only by charity and not by economic measures, which for her own purposes in *Father Tim* she translated into corrupt capitalism.[33] Barron is identifying what a modern Irish cultural commentator has labelled the MOPE syndrome which he thought afflicted, until recently, the Irish and caused them to see themselves as The Most Oppressed People Ever. Indeed, Bullen uses the example of his ungrateful pet squirrel that moped in his cage and that he could not prod into life and so left to its own devices whereupon it promptly died of starvation. The choice for both squirrel and Irish is between welcoming external help, however imperiously it is extended, and accepting out of contrariness the lethal status quo. It would seem that in 1908 Barron did not consider feasible a third option, a serious and popular nativist Irish revival, much less a popular front or armed rebellion.

Barron's idea of the English is a race-idea that far exceeds a nation of helpful doers and do-gooders. The novel opens in Heidelberg where Bullen is a student who takes part in the sword-play of the rival 'colour' groups. There is a rabidly anti-English Irish fellow student to whom Bullen loses in a duel. Later the Irish student insults Bullen who challenges him to another duel and kills him.[34] The German part of the novel is a hymn to youth, vigour, fitness, the open air, and more especially youth in love. The ambience of sunburnt youth is curiously predictive of both English left-wing Thirties outdoorism and the cult of Nazi Youth, both still a quarter century in the future. And as we later realize, Heidelberg is everything Ireland is not. After killing the Irish student, Bullen goes to Marne where his Irish girlfriend is in a convent school (the very opposite of Bullen's open air existence). Kathleen has to return to Ireland where an uncle is ill and his son, as she discovers, is dead; unknown to her and Bullen, her cousin is the Irish student her lover has killed. This uncle is virulently anti-English and on his deathbed swears Kathleen to seek vengeance against the English culprit. Barron uses as epigraphs bloodthirsty lines about revenge for Saxon guilt from Moore's *Irish Melodies* and other sources; Kathleen also plays these beautiful airs with their sentiments of hatred and violence. Whereas the English are manly and forthright, and live in the present, the Irish whine and conspire, mired in the past. Kathleen inherits the Waterford estate but it is impoverished because her uncle had spent his money on anti-English causes: the Boers, a 'secret league in Cork', and Irish agitators in the United States. The peasants suffer; there are evictions; but it is the fault of the Irish: the thriftless tenants hadn't paid their rent; the Irish landlord was negligent and distracted by hatred of the English.

While in Ireland Bullen tries to help the peasants before he sails home to England and takes Kathleen with him: he is a kind of yeoman, great-hearted, hard-working, utterly practical yet romantic. Jack's mother has lost two sons in India and Khartoum but unlike the keening of Irish women, she expresses only 'the quiet sorrow that the Mothers of the Empire bear without a murmur'! Still, Barron praises the endurance of Irish peasant women and reserves his contempt for Irish men who are unable to enjoy life to the full, to appreciate beauty, or to give over lamenting.

Nevertheless, Bullen tries to prod the Irish through a scheme to provide electricity and he persuades the English company he works for, the Electroforce Company, to open a branch plant on the run-down estate with Bullen in charge. A secondary plot allows Barron to castigate the Celtic Twilight brigade. Kathleen, bored back in Sussex, goes to visit Lady Glencullen, an Irish expatriate living in England, whose son Kevin is an anti-English Celt, Aesthete, Gaelic Leaguer, Irish Irelander, and something of an agitator. Bullen, while professing to be for ordinary Irishmen, who he says thrive and are industrious in young countries abroad, despises agitators of all descriptions. Bullen intends to build a model town on the Irish estate, of 20,000 people, a company town of industrious Irish, a kind of Port Sunlight or Bournville for Ireland. Barron's is a fevered and patronizing version of what was advocated by Filson Young in a lower temperature. Varieties of work and industry were also advocated for Ireland, with much less haughtiness, by Samuel Smiles and the industrial captains whom Bullen hymns in Carlylean fashion. It was a serious and practical attitude that might have allayed Ireland's poverty and abjection if implemented the right way. Bullen equates work with self-esteem, with patriotism, and even with freedom, as he tells the workers in the climax to the novel, though his speech falls on deaf ears (pp. 352–4). But in any case, the opening Heidelberg scenes unavoidably echo here to give a proto-fascist tinge to Bullen's equations.

Bullen's past haunts him, and Kevin travels to Ireland for confirmation, having begun to suspect that Bullen was the Englishman who killed Kathleen's cousin. Kevin tries to end the love affair between Bullen and Kathleen (clearly seen allegorically by Barron as the solution to Ireland's poverty) by playing the Catholic card: Kathleen is a Catholic, the union is impossible. Bullen confesses to Kathleen he killed her cousin; she tries to leave, misses the train, and goes to the graveyard where her uncle is buried and where Jack finds her. The priest, Father O'Darrell, vehemently opposes the union. And there is trouble at mill. The workers are agitated by the emerging religious coloration of the plant, Bullen and the company doctor being Protestants. The workers fire the works and turn on Bullen. Kevin and Father O'Darrell conspire to 'save' Jack if Kathleen disavows him. The priest becomes master of the situation and

Bullen leaves, defeated. In the novel's coda, Bullen returns after five years in Australia. The town works are now called 'Bullen's Folly' and most of the workers have emigrated. Kathleen married Kevin, believing that Jack was dead, and Kevin became 'a good Catholic'. Father O'Darrell tells Bullen how Kathleen died giving birth to her first son; she could have been saved but it is Catholic doctrine that the baby be saved in the event of a choice. The novel ends with Bullen's revulsion at this doctrine and at the inability of well-intentioned Englishmen to help a people kept in the dark by their Church. This rather unpleasant work nonetheless strikes an attitude that takes its place along the spectrum of contemporary opinion and analysis about the cause and remedy of Ireland's unhappiness.

Rosa Mulholland could never have seen her way to blaming the priests for Ireland's woes. After all, as we know, she interpreted Irish destitution as evidence of spiritual superiority and unlike Moore and Young was not about to blame the priests or Church, nor the gentry for that matter. But in *Norah of Waterford* (1915) she does make Land League nationalists co-authors of the ruinous countryside depicted by Carleton and Moore before her. She herself was both Catholic and gentry and unlike Moore of Moore Hall could not creatively change her colours. Yet within bounds, and no doubt through her philanthropic encounters with indigence, Mulholland is aware of the intimacies of poverty beyond a formulaic scrabbling on unproductive soil. In this novel she does for rural blight what in *Father Tim* she did for urban squalor.

Norah of Waterford opens with the eviction of the Fitzgerald family in Co. Cork because they cannot meet their debts and they seek shelter in the 'Huts', temporary accommodation for that purpose arranged by 'the Organisation', the Land League, which would date the events of the novel to between 1879 and 1882, unless Mulholland is eliding the Land League with the National League, founded in 1882, with the events taking place after that date. Meanwhile, Joe Aherne has his own difficulties, even though he is 'a good specimen of the better-off of the discontented classes'. He is in possession of the family farm but it is making less money each year; he has his mother and two children of a dead brother to support, and he needs soon to repay his brother Garrett for his share in the labour of the land. Joe needs capital and the only way he sees is marriage, which he is reluctant to undertake for that purpose. Besides, Joe has borrowed money from Rogan, the gombeen man, and is in the moneylender's grip. Meanwhile, Norah Fitzgerald arrives at the Ahernes as a servant and soon after Mrs Aherne sends her to the Cistercian monastery of Mount Melleray, in the shadow of which the Fitzgeralds had lived, there to seek advice from Brother Francis about the troubles of the Ahernes. Norah herself ponders emigration aloud and Brother Francis counsels strongly against it: 'an Irish girl like you is better half starved at home than earning good wages in New York. Emigration might do if you had a farmer husband—one like Joe Aherne'.[35] Joe, as it happens, has begun to fall for her but when he confesses his love to his mother she blames Norah and sends her packing: she is of no use as a wife to Joe and in her eyes is probably an opportunist.

It seems now that Joe's only hope is to marry Sabina Doolan, an elderly spinster back from America and dressed as a young girl in the marriage market and hence grotesque of appearance and demeanour: 'hard-featured, and wea-ther-tanned, dressed studiously in girl-fashion, and assuming the manners of seventeen' (p. 62). She is a fine fictional creation. Joe understandably resists her charms though it is said she has the money that would solve the Ahernes's problems. The gombeen man turns the screw, proving gombeenism to be the other co-author of Irish country sickness and the very opposite of the philan-thropic principle. Joe asks Norah to marry him and his mother swoons and falls ill when she hears of it. Sabina turns out to be the good fairy. She has been led astray by her friend Judy Neary as to Joe's intentions, and when she realizes that soon enough to turn him down, Mulholland has Sabina bar her door, go to the mirror, confront herself in all her grotesquerie, and divest herself in self-disgust of all her ludicrous fineries, go to bed, and arise the next morning reborn as an elderly woman with dignity. She gives Norah £1,000 so that she and Joe can marry and improve the Aherne farm they will live on. Rogan's hand is stayed, Norah and Joe reign on the farm, the Fitzgeralds are back into a small holding, and Sabina becomes the most popular woman in Youghal. Even emigration to America is okay (if not for single girls): Garrett goes out there, marries an Irish girl, and becomes prosperous.

Mulholland's solutions to Irish rural poverty are true love, marriage con-tracted out of love and not economic reasons, thrift and industriousness (not to be confused with industry), and charitable intervention. The gentry have no apparent part to pay except perhaps charging moderate rents. Mulholland knew about the Land League but declined engagement with its ideas; in fact, in its guise of 'the Organisation', it is in the novel a somewhat menacing outfit. Norah's young and disabled brother Declan is an aspiring poet whose muse is Miss Lilla from the Big House. She is kindly and attentive but leaves; he swoons after her and, mercifully for the reader, dies. The most interesting parts of the novel beyond the character of Sabina, are the four in-tales and ballads: Biddy Flanagan's 'Ballad of Emun's Ghost', Jimmy's story of Princess Farola, Connor's song purportedly sung by a boy who went to the North to work instead of 'Amerikay'—' "They were singin' it in the lanes of Belfast the last time I was there", said Connor'—and Terry Donnelly's story of Kaysar, granddaughter of Noah. Two of these are of the sort that Yeats plucked from novels that he otherwise discarded in order to compile his two Irish folk tale anthologies in 1888 and 1892.

SLUM STORIES

We have already come across fictional depictions of urban destitution, by Letts (1912), Smithson (1917), and by Mulholland herself (1910). Dublin and Belfast shared with towns and cities in the rest of the British Isles the cultural phenomenon of the slum, the urban abyss: the condition of both islands included it and so too did the fiction, as we have noted. 'Your cities are terrible places', says Father Tim. Forrest Reid was in the main a novelist of Belfast's affluent, leafy suburbs, but he could also send his young heroes into the philistine world of the lower middle class (for example, in *At the Door of the Gate*, 1915), but in his first novel, *The Kingdom of Twilight* (1904) he sends his young hero into the abyss of a Belfast slum:

Long, narrowly-paved, ill-lit streets of dirty little shops and dwelling-houses succeeded one another with a depressing continuity. An iron urinal, painted green, but
looking black in the dull-yellow light of the gas-lamp above it, stood close to the
footpath, and formed a centre of attraction for a swarm of ragged children as lending
an additional excitement to games of tig. Here and there the gloomy, grimy back of a
warehouse, or factory, broke the monotony of the smaller houses ... At corners, and in
doorways, groups of men and boys stood smoking, and spitting, and gazing at the
passers-by. From one of the many black, narrow alleys there issued the oaths and
obscenity of some drunken quarrel, and now and then the shrill, harsh laugh of a
woman, mirthless, horrible, would rise above the gruffer undertone of her companion. Slouching, staggering figures zigzagged along, clawing at the walls, and coming
every few yards to a standstill. At the door of a public-house the slow, silent invitation
of a prostitute was stared into their eyes from a puffed, bloated face.[36]

But this fine vignette is less for its own sake than to establish an artistic attitude, the way Wilde's descriptions of the London dock taverns and opium dens do in *The Picture of Dorian Gray* (in which Reid's description would not be out of place); that is, part of an artistic agenda centred on the hero rather than a social agenda centred on society itself.

The earliest fictional depiction of Dublin slums might be *Studies in Blue*, sketches published in Dublin in 1900 by Sealy, Bryers & Company. (The date is supplied by Stephen J. Brown, the novel carrying no date of publication; the British Library public catalogue lists a 1903 edition by the same publishers and Brown lists a 1905 edition as well.) The author was 'Heblon,' that is, Joseph K. O'Connor. *Studies in Blue* is a scramble of forty-one sketches that appeared in the Dublin *Evening Herald* and that began as humorous accounts of the Dublin police courts and developed, according to O'Connor's short preface, into 'pictures of Dublin slum life', often involving members of the blue-clad DMP (Dublin Metropolitan Police). Some of the boisterous sketches involve Dublin Jews (Schulskewski in one story, Nathan Lupinski-bovki in another), all Yiddish-speaking, hook-nosed specimens, packmen (or pedlars, see Edelstein below) or moneylenders, frequenting Camden Street, Henry Street and other poor neighbourhoods. If their poor Gentile customers are described as 'unfortunate', the Jews are not outright villains but merely, it seems, wily survivors. In 'The Jewman's Pony', the packman reverts cleverly to German to avoid the policeman's interrogation after his overworked pony collapses in the street. The packman's greed is exceeded by the tongue-twisting exoticness of his name, the sketch's chief source of humour. The pedlar in 'A Monday Morning Incident' summons Christy Flannery for arrears in payment for goods but the Christian and his wife are rogues and the pedlar is vindicated. And in 'Gentile and Jew', the two Jews who take the day off to play billiards, it being a Christian holiday with consequently no hope of trade that day, are the victims of a Christian onlooker in the pub—'a typical bourgeois, prominent of abdomen, double of chin, and with a face as impassive as the most stupid of respectabilities'.[37] The respectability is deceiving and the middle-class Christian steals money off the Jews who are engrossed in their hard-fought game. (The Christian immediately drinks the money in the same public house.) The routine way in which the publican rounds on the quarrelling Jews conveys the casual endemic racism, including anti-Semitism, of O'Connor's lower-class Dublin. And the casual racism is part of a larger social maelstrom of Dublin slum life with its drinking, hunger, greed, violence, and marital strife.

Despite the fairly unflattering vignettes of Jews in the stories, Leopold Bloom in *Ulysses* thinks of Heblon's *Studies in Blue* as a possible precedent for the budding writer Stephen Dedalus to follow: contribution of pieces 'to a publication of certified circulation'.[38] Joseph K. O'Connor (b.1878) attended Clongowes Wood College like Joyce (b.1882) where they may have over-lapped, and clearly Joyce knew *Studies in Blue*. Indeed, it is difficult not to think of Bloom and his creator's interest in Vico and recursions when at the end of 'The Jewman's Pony', the pedlar Schulskewski trudges behind the procession of former bystanders pulling the horse and four-wheeled buggy, 'like his wandering namesake, across the South Circular Road, until they were finally swallowed up in the Red Settlement'.[39]

A little later than *Studies in Blue* and earlier than *Father Tim* and *The Charwoman's Daughter* is an arresting short novel that is unusual both in its authorship and in its tone and point of view. *The Moneylender: A Novel* was published in Dublin in 1908. This uncommon work, published by Dollard, is listed in Brown but does not appear in the British Library public catalogue though it can be found in the library of Trinity College Dublin. The National

Library, Dublin holds only the fifth 'unrevised' edition (printed in Dublin for an unnamed publisher by Cahill & Co., 1931) and I have not come across any intervening editions.[40] I have seen the novel's title in no work of Irish literary criticism, nor is its author, Joseph Edelstein, mentioned in Richard Ellmann's *James Joyce* (1982) even though the novel (really a novella) depicts Jewish life in Dublin fourteen years before the appearance of *Ulysses*. About the author Brown gives no details and no catalogue entry furnishes his dates.

The stridency of *The Moneylender* might at times suggest it is the work of an anti-Semitic *agent provocateur* but this is perhaps explained by the peculiar pressures of Jewish life in Ireland at that time. Indeed, the novel is prefaced by the author's caveat: 'The author confidently commends his work to the impartial judgment of the public, his object being rather to expose the causes of usury for eradication than the effects for vituperation. J.E.' In other words, while he is aware that the work could give the appearance of being anti-Semitic because it shows so intimately the Jew at his baneful usurious business, Edelstein is really trying to uncover the reasons the Jew engages in usury and by so doing exculpating him by putting him into social and historical context while isolating the practice of usury and condemning *it*. The work is therefore an extreme form of the social-problem novel that Edelstein knows is not without difficulty in this case because it seeks to separate man from occupation, race from a racial association of long standing, i.e. Jewish love of money at any cost to others. Because he is a Jewish moneylender, the novella's hero–villain, Moses Levenstein, ran the risk of appearing to be at best a foreign gombeen man, which is the term by which the moneylender was portrayed in 1893 in an anti-Semitic editorial in the *Lyceum,* a magazine associated with University College Dublin and edited by Father Thomas Finlay, presumably the same priest who later edited the *New Ireland Review* and published stories by Moore that would become *The Untilled Field.*[41] Finlay in 'The Jew in Ireland' referred to the Jews' 'gombeen-ing propensities' which he saw as a threat to Irish social and economic life. Arthur Griffith launched an attack on the Jews in January 1904 in the pages of *United Irishman* and again in April of that year, fuelled by his belief that the Jew was an economic evil.[42] Irish anti-Semitism is the foreground context for *The Moneylender,* anti-Semitism in Europe the background context.

The rarity and oddity of the novel justifies, I think, an extended plot summary and annotations. The novel opens in a Russian village in 1900 where Moses Levenstein, 31, married with children, decides because of poverty and anti-Semitism to emigrate. He leaves his family behind (like a pioneer) and fetches up in Dublin to establish a beachhead with the princely sum on him of 1s 4d. He becomes a pedlar (or packman) for Chaim Greenblatt.[43] Greenblatt is running a 'wickleh' (perhaps from 'weekly'), a hire-purchase system in poor districts whereby he buys goods on consignment and sells them to housewives who pay by weekly instalment. This system for the housewives, which involved the packman ticking off payments as they were made, was known in Belfast as 'tick' and the Jewish pedlar was accordingly called a 'tickman' as Finlay observes; later the tickman could be a Gentile, one of themselves. Greenblatt's customers are referred to in Yiddish as 'laptzies', presumably a derogatory term.[44]

Moses feels contempt for the poor Dubliners who are his prey. He has arrived in Dublin smouldering with resentment at anti-Semitism which seems to him to be everywhere. It was especially active in Russia. A contemporary English writer thought there were nine million Jews in the world and five million of them living in Russia. The Russian persecution of Jews in 1881–2 resulted, he alleged, in the expulsion of about a million of them; 50,000 poor Jews arrived in Britain alone.[45] The columnist 'The Looker-on' in *Blackwood's Edinburgh Magazine* for March 1898 reported 'a general madness against the Jews over the whole of continental Europe, or nearly all'. He denies it is a religious revulsion, as the Jews insist, and sees it instead as a reaction against Jewish success and against the Jews' foreignness, a misfortune at a time in Europe of aggravated nationalism.[46]

At any rate, Moses is no peacemaking Leopold Bloom; the narrative is punctuated by Moses's angry and vengeful mental excursions on the theme of the *Judenhetz* and they are his self-justifications for the revenge he is exacting on Gentiles. His victims are the poor who inhabit the slums of south Dublin, the same slums in which Mulholland's Father Tim ministers. (Edelstein is precise in his slum-geography. Moses works 'the Coombe', a slum west of Mulholland's Cuffe Street and south of the Liffey. The Jews themselves live not too far away from their livelihood but in more respectable quarters off and around the South Circular Road, south of the Coombe, in Lennox, Lombard, Bride, Kevin, Richmond and Peter Streets, and Leinster Road; but it is still not affluent Dublin. Finlay identifies this area as the Jewish quarter.) Small wonder Moses breathes the oxygen of revenge: in the streets of Dublin he is despised and has skins (vegetable peelings), marbles, and stones flung at him. The novel is a tale of cruelty and casual beatings; it is a violent city anyway in its slums, but worse for a Jew. 'Wherever the Jew is, hatred and contempt meet him', Moses thinks.[47] When he considers that the Jew is 'for patriots, a man without a country; for all classes a hated rival. Since the Jew is nowhere at home, nowhere regarded as a native, he remains everywhere an alien' (p. 18), it is impossible not to recall Joyce's use of these sentiments in the making of Bloom.

Moses seeks revenge on Greenblatt too, in this case the revenge of success. He is introduced to the practice of moneylending and strikes out on his own. Edelstein explains the system with relished disdain. You lend money to the poor woman but take five shillings off the pound upfront. For example, the customer

wishes to borrow two pounds. You give her £1 10s 0d. Then she must immediately give you four shillings back from that sum so that in fact you go away
having given her £1 6s 0d while in your book she owes you £1 16s 0d and pays
you a hefty per cent as interest. The moneylender is a 'percentnic'. The rabbi
himself defends usury but only when practised by Jews on Christians. Moses
prospers by the system; he becomes a travelling 'financier' (moneylender)
among those we would recognize as O'Casey's tenement dwellers. He is full
of contempt and spits on one drunken client, Mrs Mulvany. The Dublin slum-
lice (an O'Casey character's term) spend what money they have on drink. We
meet young Bridget O'Brien and Michael Redmond who marry and get
furniture through Moses. At first they, like Moses, are happy; this novel is a
sorrowful tale for the main characters at the beginning and at the end but in the
interim they enjoy happy dreams of prosperity.

Moses revenges himself on Greenblatt's family after Greenblatt dies; he
buys houses, sues debtors, moves to Rathmines, and gains respectability by
Gentile standards. He is appointed president of a synagogue. In June 1904
(a Joycean month!) his wife Leah and children Abrom, Rachel, and Rosie
arrive from Russia. (The same year there was an anti-Jewish pogrom in
Limerick, which is adverted to in the novel; by June 1904 the Jews in Limerick
were being boycotted, Gentile hostility being provoked by sermons from the
Catholic pulpit. It was during the Limerick troubles that Griffith verbally
attacked the Jews.)[48] But there is a narrative undertow of disapproval, and
Abrom rebels against his father's way of life. In the novel's third excursion on
anti-Semitism, Edelstein expresses the 'true' Jew's detestation of usury. 'The
true Jewish heart's emotion, the true Jewish feelings arise in Abrom's breast,
and he feels a terrible hatred for those of his people who adopt this means of
obtaining a living' (p. 63). In displeasing irony, Rachel is courted by a poor
musician Marcus Himburg, a Russian Jew, but the virulently ambitious and
snobbish Moses prevents his daughter from getting engaged; as though in
retribution, Rachel falls ill like her brother Abrom and becomes delirious; she
dies of inflammation of the lungs and Abrom dies of a brain fever.

Meanwhile, Bridget and Mike are on the skids, hounded by debt to the
moneylender Levenstein, sucked into alcoholism. In the extreme temperance-
story strand of the tale, Edelstein seems to know whom to blame.

Mike pawned the little he had, and spent what he got in a place called a publichouse,
hundreds of which may be seen in Dublin, with thousands of those who go there and live
there, and do their best to die as quickly as possible. Mike thenceforth became an habitual
drunkard, and the publichouses, with nice large clocks on the walls ticking away the time
and the lives of the customers, and with gorgeously painted and wondrously decorated
and charming exteriors, received the few coppers, and thanked the welcome guest, and

administered the product of the firm of a great lord, who dines with the king and queen of Great Britain and Ireland and the dominions across the seas. (p. 95)

This was Lord Iveagh, apex of the Guinness family. Bridget is driven to the workhouse. Mike wanders Dublin, 'a reproach to the social conditions prevailing unchecked in the slums of the capital of Ireland' (p. 96), and takes a suicidal header into the Liffey. Beside Edelstein's Dubliners, Joyce's appear lower-middle class rather than working class, still less under-class; and it is Joyce's Dublin, moreover, without a shred of humour, the humour that prevents Joyce's Dublin from being a city of despair, however unfulfilled its citizens' lives. ('Unfulfilled' seems a preposterous adjective to attach to Mike and Bridget or the other 'laptzies' of Edelstein's novel.) Levenstein is unrepentant and declares to Father Murphy: 'Here we are, a handful of Jews in this country, Ireland, and still we are not allowed to earn our living honestly, while you point gleefully to our depravation when you, yes, you yourselves have done it.' There is, though, a Bloomian note. Levenstein insists that the way things are, there is no humanity, only nations and races for which every individual cares (and presumably as a result of which the Jew will always lose out). Father Murphy thinks this attitude betrays 'the peculiar patriotism of the Jewish moneylender' (p. 99).

And it is true that Levenstein's sole interest in Irish politics can appear a self-serving one. He asks his would-be son in-law 'to explain to him the meaning of the Devolution Bill then before Parliament, and if he thought that the passing of such a bill would be injurious to the Jews who lived in Ireland'.[49] This must refer to the Devolution scheme hatched by the Irish Reform Association in 1904, supported by George Wyndham the Secretary for Ireland, William O'Brien, MP and novelist, Lord Dunraven, and others but which was defeated by Irish nationalists and British Conservatives driving Wyndham from office.[50] Edelstein himself was honorary secretary of the Judaeo-Irish Home Rule Association, established in Dublin in 1908, the year *The Moneylender* was published. Edelstein proposed the motion pledging the Association's support for Home Rule, and it was seconded by Stephen Gywnn. The constitutional Home Ruler John Redmond was sympathetic to the Association.[51] The name of the society suggests that Home Rule was supported because it was, or was encouraged to be, compatible with Jewish security and advancement. Edelstein deftly here establishes the strange relationship the European Jew had (or was compelled to have at this period) with the nation of which he was and was not a part, a relationship Joyce examined at much greater length in *Ulysses*.

This strangeness extends to the narrative itself. The controlling vision is, unlike most of the problem-novels I have looked at (*The Unpardonable Sin* is an exception), an unstable one and *The Moneylender* veers between anti-anti-Semitism and a severe condemnation of the Jewish reaction to anti-Semitism, i.e. of the monomaniacal pursuit of vengeance and anti-Gentile usury; explanation and value judgement are in uneasy ratio. Brought low, Moses has a deathbed change of heart. 'He had done great wrong; he did very little good' (p. 103) is the narrator's verdict. When he leaves most of his money to Dublin charities, he is acting in keeping with British Victorian and Edwardian popular novels and setting the story, of which he is the dislikeable hero, in the context of the Irish philanthropic culture. That the charities are mostly Gentile suggests something akin to a religious conversion (this too would place the story inside the British and Irish novel context), but this sits oddly with the contention that it is not Moses's Jewishness that is at issue. However, it could be argued that the repentance is reparation and not religious conversion as such; he himself does not become a Gentile but a good Jew, true to his faith.

The Moneylender is a fevered crash course in the Dublin Jewish community. In the guest list of those attending the arranged marriage of Moses's surviving daughter Rosie to Schmerrele Bombom, Edelstein gives us a fictional directory of that community, however made-up the surnames might be, to accompany his earlier non-fictional gazetteer. We read of the names Darkovitz, Yuddock, Zulis, Cohen, Himburg, Horwitz, Kupperman, Whitningstone, Rubinstein, Schorstein, and others. Keogh tells us that in 1901 there were 3000 Jews in Dublin and Edelstein's novel suggests, rightly or wrongly, that a disproportion of them were packmen or moneylenders.[52] The perspective is a hothouse one and this fits with Moses's presentation. Edelstein's hero, like most of the Jewish characters, is emotionally theatrical and mercurial:

Moses walked on, looked back, wept, laughed, prayed, grinned, wiped his nose, examined his pocket wherein he had placed the roubles, counted them, examined both sides of them, kissed the bag containing his Talith, said, 'Sh'ma Yisroel' a dozen times, looked up to heaven, thought of his wife, his children, his aged mother, his friend Ginsburg, his cousin, his Talmud, his meeting with Rubinovitz, his past life, his ambitions, said to himself what he could do to earn money, laughed again at his fears, wept again, prayed again, and looked back again. (p. 6)

The realism is curious in so far as what is being realistically described reads itself as hyperbole. Abrom, for example, has a delirious vision of his father's end and passage to hell and even after he dies the night retains its nightmarishness with ghoulish forms seeming to flit to and fro through the darkened building while a storm rages outside. The quotation above exemplifies the compositional symmetry Edelstein uses and which gives his story the feel of a folktale or fable. Many chapters are ended with the topographical and genealogical formula— 'son of Channa Levenstein, of Wexney, Kouno-Guberneh, Russia' as though

Edelstein were a collector or transcriber rather than a writer. Edelstein is partial to lists and syntactical repetition like traditional storytellers. The narration is conducted at a compassionate height above the characters it approves of and is indifferent to those it doesn't, and in this has something of the impersonality of oral tradition. The tripartite sequence of fate—sorrow, imagined happiness, sorrow once more—also gives the story a folk feel and structure. Moreover, the text has a translated feel ('He walked very fastly down Lombard-street') but this of course would suit the notion that it ought to be told in Yiddish and English is a necessary compromise. Edelstein uses Yiddish terms generously and provides a glossary at the back; his Yiddish, like the Ulster Scots dialect in, say, *The Nabob* by Andrew James, is a reminder that the linguistic diversity of Ireland extends beyond generalized pre-Revival literary renditions of the 'brogue'—such as we read in Mulholland—and the western peasant Hiberno-English of Synge and others. In the light of *The Moneylender* and *Father Tim*, James Stephens's *The Charwoman's Daughter* (1912) is not quite as pioneering as previously thought as a display in prose of Dublin slum-life, but Stephens has a deftness of touch Mulholland simply did not have, while *The Moneylender*, albeit sharing with Stephens's first novel a fable-like quality, has a different axe to grind and an exceedingly sharper one.[53]

POSTSCRIPT

The Moneylender is a peculiar and powerful little tale and has more in common with the stories of Isaac Bashevis Singer than any Irish fiction writers. Its peculiarity is matched by the fact of its total neglect, given the celebrity of Joyce's Dublin Jew a few years later. One episode from Edelstein's largely anonymous story might incidentally suggest Joyce's daring in making a Dublin Jew his hero, and involves Timothy Healy who had provoked the boy Joyce's ire by deserting Parnell (expressed in his childhood poem, 'Et Tu, Healy').

At the Royal Commission of Inquiry into the circumstances of the shooting of the well-known pacifist Francis Sheehy-Skeffington in August 1916, T. M. Healy KC (counsel for the family of Sheehy-Skeffington) asked Sergeant John Maxwell, 3rd Royal Irish Rifles when he first saw a man named Edelstein in Portobello Barracks. Maxwell could not remember but said he knew the man well. Maxwell could not confirm that Edelstein was a 'spotter' for the military. (A spotter was presumably someone who fingered their enemies to the authorities.) The next day Edelstein rose at the back of the court, identified himself, and said he had been the victim of 'terrible insinuations' and asked to give evidence since the insinuations imperilled his life. He was told to stick around and he might be called. (I say 'stick around' to convey the apparent casualness with which his request was treated by the chairman of the Inquiry.) Healy asked Lieutenant Morgan, 6th Royal Irish Rifles, when he first saw 'this man Edelstein'. On the Sunday following Easter Sunday, was the answer. Morgan had heard of Edelstein that morning. Was he supposed to be in custody? Answer—he was not in custody. Was he ever in Morgan's custody? Yes. When? That Sunday night. It seems that Edelstein had been in Alderman Kelly's tobacconist shop on the night that Thomas Dickson (a Scots editor) and Patrick MacIntyre (an Irish editor), who were summarily shot alongside Skeffington, were arrested in the shop. Edelstein was arrested for giving out cigars wholesale to the public and after Morgan had contacted Kelly in prison and been told that Edelstein had no right to be there. He was ordered to be released but wasn't and instead was sent to Richmond Barracks. Healy wondered: 'Were the arrangements connected with the barracks so loose that in the middle of a rebellion *a man like this* [*sic*] could get inside your gates without your knowledge?' Edelstein, Morgan said, told him that he (Edelstein) had come to see Major Sir Francis Vane. Morgan confirmed that Edelstein had made a statement to the prejudice of Alderman Kelly justifying Kelly's arrest. As to its content: 'He had so much to say that it is very hard to remember what he did say.' (Laughter.) 'He had too much to say.'

One senses a general dislike of Edelstein over and above the assumption that he was a tout working for the British. Healy then asked if his client Dickson had been arrested on the information 'of this man Edelstein.' Edelstein at this point interrupts—'That is an awful lie.' Edelstein thought the reason for his victimization was obvious. 'I will be called as a witness', he demanded, 'and Mr. Healy can make as much as he likes out of me, and, being a Jew, he has his bait.' That is, Edelstein assumed Healy would be hostile simply by virtue of Edelstein's Jewishness. (A Moses Levenstein position.) Despite Edelstein's position in the Judæo-Irish Home Rule Association, most Lithuanian (or Litvak) Dublin Jews, according to Ó Gráda, were 'emphatically loyalist' and if Healy's dislike was not an instantly personal one, perhaps it was racially-inspired political dislike (the JIHRA was short-lived, Ó Gráda tell us).[54] The Chairman reproves Edelstein and threatens to have him removed. The Chairman then wonders aloud how the arrest could have been on Edelstein's information if the conversation between the witness and Edelstein had taken place the week after Dickson's arrest. But Healy counters by getting the witness to confirm that Alderman Kelly had told him that Edelstein had been in his shop the night of the arrest. Healy asks Morgan if he knew that Edelstein was a 'spotter'. 'I did not', replies Morgan. 'I heard about him being a great linguist.'[55] The proceedings of the Commission as reported by the *Irish Independent* were republished verbatim in 1933 as *Echo of Irish Rebellion 1916* and subtitled *Vindication of Mr Joseph Edelstein*. In it Healy is transcribed as at the close of proceedings apologizing profusely to Edelstein—'I am sorry, extremely sorry'—on discovering that his instructions regarding Edelstein were 'absolutely and entirely wrong'.[56] Still, it is hard not to see anti-Semitism at work in the Commission's attitude to Edelstein, a milder state of those affairs that provoked Edelstein to publish *The Moneylender* eight years before.

NOTES

1. Trotter, *The English Novel in History, 1895–1920* (London: Routledge, 1993), p. 83. A case could be made for the idea that just as a large and loose group of Irish writers (the literary and cultural Revivalists) responded between, say, 1890 and the 1920s to what they conceived to be the parlous cultural condition of Ireland, so a group of English writers, even more loosely aligned, responded during the same decades to the worrying condition of England with a literature that seen from a distance could look like an attempt at a cultural revival, or at least a concerted diagnosis of the condition. The Irish solution—the resuscitation of a national mythology—seemed unavailable to the English, though W. T. Stead, W. W. Skeat and others tried to revive medieval pageants and promoted the celebration of St George's Day and Shakespeare Day: see John Wilson Foster, *The Age of* Titanic: *Cross-Currents in Anglo-American Culture*, p. 131. Indeed, the lack of an English mythology is expressly lamented in Forster's *Howards End*. But the diagnosis was ampler in England and was conducted in both realistic and experimental fiction; the major writers were Galsworthy, Gissing, Wells, Conrad, Forster, Woolf, and Lawrence. (The last attempted to resuscitate or develop regenerative mythologies of several sorts.)

2. Arnold Kettle, 'The Early Victorian Social-Problem Novel', *From Dickens to Hardy*. The Pelican Guide to English Literature 6, ed. Boris Ford (Harmondsworth: Penguin Books, 1963), pp. 170, 174.

3. David Thomson, *England in the Nineteenth Century, 1815–1914* (Harmondsworth: Penguin Books, 1978), p. 182.

4. I have discussed these two novels in *Forces and Themes in Ulster Fiction* (1974).

5. I take these bare facts from Harris, *My Life and Loves. Volume One* (1922; London: Colporteur Press, 1994) and there seems no reason to doubt them, since nothing was to be gained for Harris by his Irishness. The biographer of Lord Alfred Douglas quotes Frank Harris's biographer, Vincent Brome: 'he was almost certainly born on February 14th, 1856, in Galway. . . .' Rupert Croft-Cooke, *Bosie: The Story of Lord Alfred Douglas, His Friends and Enemies* (London: W. H. Allen, 1963), p. 320.

6. Frank Harris, *The Bomb* (1908; New York: Mitchell Kennerley, 1909), pp. 31, 28, 29, 30.

7. I discuss these years of immigration and consequent racism in *The Age of* Titanic: *Cross-Currents in Anglo-American Culture* (2002). It may be that Germans were feared

as well as disliked, since German was once a contender for the dominant language in the United States, and Germany a contender for the role of cofounding nation alongside Britain.

8. *My Life and Loves* is a portrait of the artist, a semi-fictional *Künstlerroman*, and in it Harris recalls that it was under the unlikely circumstances of being a cowboy on the Great Plains in the 1870s that the big issues began to make impact on him: 'These constant evening discussions, this perpetual arguing, had an unimaginable effect on me. I had no books with me and I was often called on to deal with two or three different theories in a night; I had to think out the problems for myself and usually I thought them out when hunting by myself in the daytime. It was as a cow-puncher that I taught myself how to think—a rare art among men and seldom practiced. Whatever originality I possess comes from the fact that in youth, while my mind was in process of growth, I was confronted with important modern problems and forced to think them out for myself and find some reasonable answer to the questionings of half a dozen different minds', *My Life and Loves*, p. 89.

9. I discuss the Machine Age in *The Age of* Titanic: *Cross-Currents in Anglo-American Culture* (2002). There were more obviously material results of early mechaniza-tion. In her Preface to *Woman's Mission: A Series of Congress Papers on the Philanthropic Work of Women by Eminent Writers* (London: Sampson Low, Mar-ston & Co., 1893), which she edited, Baroness (Angela Georgina) Burdett-Coutts wrote of Britain: 'The invention of steam machinery filled a little town with factories, soon making of them crowded cities, and cities where home life was sacrificed to the factory by the common employment of husband, wife, and child at the machine, and also by the multiplication of close and crowded tenements' (p. xviii).

10. See the problem posed and solved in Wilde's *The Soul of Man Under Socialism* (1891). Individualism is also a prominent virtue in Harris's more familiarly historical novel, *Great Days* (1914), set in the aftermath of the French Revolution. It narrates the exploits of a young English smuggler, Jack Morgan, who demon-strates such seamanship around the French coast that he is offered an admiralty by Napoleon Bonaparte who is planning an invasion of England and who believes that one such individual is worth a thousand ordinary sailors. This novel, part adventure story, part love story, part historical romance, employs several histor-ical figures as characters, including Charles James Fox. The publication date of 1914 seems fortuitous or opportunist though it might seem to have a more distant connection to the contemporary war scare than Erskine Childers's *The Riddle of the Sands* (1903).

11. See The National Archives Learning Curve, 'Haymarket Bombing', http://www. spartacus.schoolnet.co.uk/USAhaymarket.htm p. 2.

12. Paul Avrich, *The Haymarket Tragedy* (Princeton: Princeton University Press, 1984), p. 221.

13. In the very year of the Haymarket atrocity, there was fierce rioting in Belfast to accompany the first Home Rule Bill. Sectarian and political unrest in Belfast

invariably involved the shipyards because of the large bodies of working men concentrated there, and this maintained an intersection between sectarian politics and industrialism.

14. Avrich, *The Haymarket Tragedy*, pp. 235, 76.

15. Ibid., p. 236.

16. For a timeline of the Haymarket affair, see 'The Haymarket Riot and Trial: A Chronology,' www.law.umkc.edu/faculty/projects/ftrials/haymarket/haymarket chrono.html

17. Avrich, *The Haymarket Tragedy*, p. 238–9.

18. Avrich is quoting police captain Schaack, whom Avrich calls 'the leading spirit of the inquisition' in the aftermath of the bombing: ibid., pp. 158, 223.

19. Ibid., pp. 158, 159.

20. Ibid., p. 439.

21. This strange drive to master, to order and discipline, to *prevent*, stretches to Harris's curious notion of how to forestall conception (with syringe, sponge, and water) and to his practice of restoring his friend and mentor Professor Smith to health by helping him constrict his penis nightly with whipcord.

22. There was agricultural collapse in England in 1875–84 and 1891–9 when corn acreage shrank alarmingly (by eight million acres between 1871 and 1899) and tens of thousands of farm labourers were forced off the land. See G. M. Trevelyan, *English Social History* (1942; Harmondsworth: Pelican Books, 1964), pp. 565–9. I think it is fair to say that Irish cultural and literary commentators tend to operate under the auspices of the exceptionalist theory of Ireland and turn a blind eye to any social and economic difficulties England may have been suffering.

23. George Moore, *A Drama in Muslin: A Realistic Novel* (1886; London: Walter Scott, 1918), p. 325.

24. Moore, *Hail and Farewell* (1911, 1912, 1914; ed. Richard Cave. Gerrards Cross: Colin Smythe, 1976), pp. 58–74.

25. I discuss these themes in this and other Irish volumes by Moore in *Fictions of the Irish Literary Revival* (1987).

26. Filson Young, *Ireland at the Cross Roads: An Essay in Explanation* (London: Grant Richards, 1903), pp. 38–40, 53, 57.

27. Young, and also Tynan in *The Middle Years* (1916), identifies it as a Trappist monastery, Mulholland as a Cistercian.

28. Young, *Ireland at the Cross Roads*, pp. 136–40. Young's suggestion that regular visits from monarchs, such as King Edward's visit to Ireland in the summer of 1903, would cement relations between the two islands is from our perspective naive; it may not have seemed so at the time, and Joyce's treatment of the same idea in 'Ivy Day in the Committee Room' can support either conclusion.

29. Jonathan Rose has shown that Efficiency was a dominant motif in Edwardian socio-literary culture in Britain. See 'The Efficiency Men' in *The Edwardian Temperament, 1895–1919* (Athens: Ohio University Press, 1986), pp. 117–62.

30. I discuss Smiles, Harland, and Belfast industrialism, with the building of *Titanic* as a focus, in *Recoveries: Neglected Episodes in Irish Cultural History 1860–1912*,

ch. 2. Smiles had earlier written *History of Ireland and the Irish People* (1844) in which he praised Daniel O'Connell's Catholic Association, seeing it as an example of what he would later term Self-Help.

31. This became apparent to me when I set the *Titanic* disaster inside its cultural context and found the racial dimensions of the calamity: see *The Age of* Titanic: *Cross-Currents in Anglo-American Culture* (2002).

32. Brown, *Ireland in Fiction*, p. 29. Brown furnishes no dates or biographical details for Barron, presumably an Englishman.

33. Percy Barron, *The Hate Flame* (London: Hodder and Stoughton, 1908), pp. 146–7.

34. I thought this sword play was of Barron's imagining until I came across Katharine Tynan's recollection of the summer of 1892: 'My share of the visitors was a Heidelberg student with two or three sword slashes across his face': *The Middle Years* (London: Constable, 1916), p. 7.

35. Rosa Mulholland, *Norah of Waterford* (London: Sands & Company, 1915), pp. 27–8, 54.

36. This novel is rarely encountered; Russell Burlingham quotes this passage in *Forrest Reid: A Portrait and a Study* (London: Faber and Faber, 1953), p. 67.

37. 'Heblon', *Studies in Blue* (Dublin: Sealy, Bryers and Walker, [1900]), p. 151.

38. *Ulysses* (1922; Harmondsworth: Penguin, 1969), p. 606.

39. *Studies in Blue*, p. 6. I have been unable to find the meaning and location of the 'Red Settlement'. However, Henry Mayhew in *London Labour & the London Poor* (1851–65) refers to an East End area where the poorer Jews live as a 'settlement', and if this is pertinent, it leaves only the meaning of 'Red' as a puzzle. See Peter Quennell's abridged version of Mayhew: *Mayhew's London* (London: Bracken Books, 1984), p. 286.

40. It is possible that the 1931 edition was self-published, like *Echo of Irish Rebellion* (see n. 56 below). The 1931 edition is dedicated to 'Reason and Israel's Friends' and carries laudatory comments by one J. Emerson Scott.

41. The speculation that they were the same man is mine. Finlay's editorial is discussed at length by Dermot Keogh in *Jews in Twentieth-Century Ireland* (Cork: Cork University Press, 1998), pp. 20–1. Neither Edelstein nor his novel is mentioned in Keogh's well-researched book.

42. Quoted by Ira Nadel, *Joyce and the Jews* (Iowa City: University of Iowa Press, 1989), p. 60.

43. James Douglas in *The Unpardonable Sin* has a parenthetical paragraph on the related 'pickyman' in working-class Belfast: '(A pickyman is a Jew pedlar who sells, among other things, gorgeously coloured German oleographs in florid gilt frames at prices ranging from five to ten shillings. The picture is paid for by small instalments of threepence or sixpence, which are collected every week. If the purchaser of the picture is unable to pay the instalment, the Jew will say in broken English, "Me take the picky off your wall!" This is the origin of the term "picky-man")': *The Unpardonable Sin* (London: Grant Richards, 1907), p. 153. Finlay referred to 'the "Jewman" of Dublin' and this too had a specific meaning. Rosa Mulholland in *Father Tim* mentions 'a travelling "Jewman" who tramped the

country regularly with such tempting merchandise for Christians', *Father Tim*, p. 154. Henry Mayhew has passages on the 'tally packman' or 'tallyman' in his account of London's poor districts in the mid-Victorian period, though the latter is in his account typically a 'Scotchman'; he has separate passages on Jewish street traders: *Mayhew's London*, ed. Peter Quennell (London: Bracken Books, 1984), pp. 175–6, 284–98.

44. Cormac Ó Gráda also believes it too to be derogatory and offers *schlemiel* as a comparable Yiddish term: 'Lost in Little Jerusalem: Leopold Bloom and Irish Jewry', *Journal of Modern Literature* 27: 4 (2004): 20. Ó Gráda's essay is essential reading for those who wish to know who Dublin's Jews were in Edelstein's (and Joyce's) time (in the main they were originally from Lithuania).

45. C. R. Conder, 'The Zionists', *Blackwood's Edinburgh Magazine* 163 (May 1898): 600, 602.

46. 'The Looker-on', *Blackwood's Edinburgh Magazine* 163 (March 1898): 424–7. 'The Looker-on' thinks the English, because of their economic success during a time of nationalism, excite something of the same envy into which he translates anti-Semitism, 'in our own case enhanced by certain British peculiarities, such as an exasperating unconscious swagger of earth-and-sea lordliness when we move amongst foreigners'; one suspects a little Scots anti-Englishness here politely pretending to be anti-Britishness.

47. Joseph Edelstein, *The Moneylender* (Dublin: Dollard, 1908), p. 15.

48. Dermot Keogh, *Jews in Twentieth-Century Ireland*, pp. 26–53.

49. Edelstein, *The Moneylender*, p. 73.

50. Edmund Curtis, *A History of Ireland* (London: Methuen, 1952), p. 392.

51. Louis Hyman, *The Jews of Ireland: From Earliest Times to the Year 1910* (Shannon: Irish University Press, 1972), pp. 200–1. See also Ray Rivlin, *Shalom Ireland: A Social History of Jews in Modern Ireland* (Dublin: Gill & Macmillan, 2003), p. 190. Rivlin devotes two paragraphs to Edelstein in her book.

52. Keogh, *Jews in Twentieth-Century Ireland*, p. 9.

53. I discuss Stephens's novel in *Fictions of the Irish Literary Revival*, pp. 252–4.

54. Ó Gráda, 'Lost in Little Jerusalem', p. 23.

55. See *Sinn Fein Rebellion Handbook. Easter 1916.* Compiled by the 'Weekly Irish Times', Dublin, 1916: 216–18.

56. *Echo of Irish Rebellion, 1916* (Dublin, 1933), p. 64. Rivlin is probably correct in suggesting that the book was self-published. The book is printed for unnamed publishers. Moreover, the Edelstein affair was incidental to the Sheehy-Skeffington atrocity, let alone the Easter Rebellion, but in this republication it takes on inflated public importance. That said, Edelstein's reputation was at stake and the imputation had been aired that he was somehow responsible for the arrest of Dickson, and thus indirectly his execution, and perhaps by extension the execution of McIntyre, perhaps even the well-known Sheehy-Skeffington himself. It might be fair to add that the kind of irregular behaviour that, according to Rivlin, Edelstein indulged in may have made him known in a jaundiced fashion to the court of Commission. Rivlin says Edelstein would dress immaculately and had a

propensity for breaking the glass of public fire alarms and waiting to be arrested; Grangegorman mental hospital certified him sane and he would brandish his certificate, claiming to be the only man in Ireland who could prove his sanity (Rivlin, p. 190). One must remember, of course, that in those days innumerable entertaining eccentrics roamed the streets of Dublin without provoking ire.

7

'Society—Spelt Big': The Condition
of Ireland II

THE COUNTRY-HOUSE NOVEL

One possible reason for the failure of Irish critics to 'recuperate' the popular
or mainstream novel as an object of study (individual merit or demerit aside)
is the status of many of the novels as what we might call Society fiction; they
concern what Alexander in *The Rambling Rector* calls 'Society (in the limited
sense)', MacMahon's 'society—spelt big'. The gender of the authors has not yet
rescued them from the obloquy of their settings and characters. Society novels
are set in elegant town houses in London or Dublin and in country houses in
England or Ireland. The Irish novels often have a simple dual cast of characters: the gentry and their servants and stablehands (as well as jarveys and local
peasants), and dual settings: the country house and either tenant cottages or
servant quarters (lodges, stables, sculleries). A few professional figures (solicitors, doctors, men of the cloth) mildly complicate this semi-feudal picture
and visitors have the lonely duty of personifying the world beyond. In their
bipartite cast, the novels are heirs to the 'Two Nations' division Disraeli
bequeathed in fiction and philosophy: gentry and peasantry are Irish versions
of Egremont's 'The Rich and the Poor' in *Sybil* (1845). At the same time—and
this may have been a uniquely Irish situation—there was, according to
Gifford Lewis 'an almost bizarre intimacy between gentry and servants in
families that had been isolated for generations together',[1] an intimacy that was
in contrast to the coolness, even hostility shown by the gentry to the middle
classes. This intimacy throws up the recurring fictional characters of the
absurdly loyal servant and the betraying servant (the intimacy came under
peculiar pressure from the days of the Land League through the rise of Sinn
Fein and the Troubles) and can, of course, provide the plot device of the
servant girl seduced by the son of the family, or perhaps genuinely loved, in
either case transgressing expected class demarcations; on occasion the intimacy
can transmogrify in novels into the stuff of Gothic narrative.

The social class divide qualified the familiar religious divide, since Irish gentry of our period were Catholic as well as Protestant, though more often the latter than the former. Catholic gentry were the immediate target of George Moore in *A Drama in Muslin* (1886) and he subjected their way of life and attitudes to a scathing if undisciplined realism. He attacked 'the social and political power of the Castle in Modern Ireland'[2] but indirectly by making the cruelty and frivolity of débutante life suggest the gaudy insolence of English power in Ireland and by concentrating on the inhabitants of a Big House in Galway. These gentlefolk are increasingly besieged by a restive peasantry incited by the Land League, yet they foolishly cast their eyes beyond the intervening reality to the marriage prospects offered by the Dublin season. Here and in his later fiction, Moore registered the ensuing decline of the country house. Brookfield in *A Drama in Muslin* is already a shadow of its cultivated eighteenth-century self; it reappears in *The Untilled Field*, further sunk in a narrow Catholic nationalism. A declining country house, Wood-view, even closes *Esther Waters* (1894), though the novel is set in England.

More popular novels using the same settings were usually less hostile while depicting the symptoms of malady. Perhaps Moore's influence did not stretch to the popular novelists; perhaps the popular novelists had the kind of deep reservation Katharine Tynan exhibited towards Moore when she came to revise Charles A. Reade's 1879 *Cabinet of Irish Literature* for 1902 publication; she thought Moore one of the writers 'unsuited to the Irish households which would purchase the monumental work. . . . I said I could not really find a suitable passage. The publishers offered me "Esther Waters" [1894] and "Sister Teresa" [1901]. I was obdurate.'[3] Moore's reputation was not of the highest among women who thought themselves respectable, including, one assumes, women writers. In any case, the novel that set significant parts in a country house continued to flourish after Moore's onslaught in *A Drama in Muslin*, usually but not exclusively written by women. One reason for women writers' partiality to the subgenre was possibly the knowledge of the house possessed by the intelligent woman who lived there—its rooms, furniture, social life, entertainment and work customs, status hierarchy, servant lifestyle, activity in the stables. Country-house novels published between *A Drama in Muslin* and the end of the Great War include Mrs Hungerford's *Mrs Geoffrey* (1886); Somerville and Ross's *An Irish Cousin* (1889); Ella MacMahon's *A New Note* (1894) and *A Pitiless Passion* (1895); Katharine Tynan's *A Girl of Galway* (1901); Catherine Mary MacSorley's *An Irish Cousin* (1901); Stephen Gwynn's *The Old Knowledge* (1901); Eleanor Alexander's *The Rambling Rector* (1904); Filson Young's *The Sands of Pleasure* (1905) and *When the Tide Turns* (1908); George Jessop's *Where the Shamrock Grows* (1911); Jane Barlow's *Flaws* (1911); F. E. Crichton's *The Soundless Tide* (1911);

B. M. Croker's *Lismoyle: An Experiment in Ireland* (1914); Ella MacMahon's *The Job* (1914); Dorothea Conyers's *The Financing of Fiona* (1916); Elizabeth Hart's *Irreconcilables* (1916); Douglas Goldring's *The Fortune* (1917); Helen Duffin's *Over Here* (1918). This is a mere sampling. Some country-house novels by Irish novelists are set in England: Mrs Hungerford's *The Hoyden* (1894); Bram Stoker's *The Man* (1906, a rather anachronistic one); Katharine Tynan's *Dick Pentreath* (1906); E. Temple Thurston's *The Evolution of Katherine* (1907); M. Hamilton's *The First Claim* (1907); some are set in Ulster (for example, *Over Here*); there are social differences between the Ulster and Irish country-house novels; some are not exclusively country-house novels, for example those by Filson Young, who always has more fish to fry than country-house life. And if we were to add novels that importantly show the privileges (and dramas) of rectory or manse life, my list would be longer.

Given the disproportionate importance of the country house in Irish life in our period—a disproportion that was exciting the very enmity that finally brought the country house to heel—it is hardly a wonder that until the end of the nineteenth century, country-house fiction dominated the novel and short story scene. Education, cultivation, and leisure, combining as they could in the country houses, particularly among the female inhabitants, more than they were likely to combine among the busy middle classes with their less cultivated, more materialist values, produced a large number of fiction writers. (This dominance lasted until Revival fiction, sympathetic to the Irish peasantry and with designs on an Irish readership, got into stride.) After all, the country-house novel brought with it membership of a long tradition in the English novel to which many Irish and English readers alike were partial.[4] A recent study of the 'silver fork' English novel, 1826–41, prompted a reviewer to observe that literary critics who dismiss the genre as part of a last-ditch effort to shore up aristocratic privilege and cultural hegemony in the closing days of the Regency 'have missed the opportunity to consider a fascinating body of fiction actively engaged with a tumultuous period in Britain's history'. Reading such novels will 'register the extent to which an ostensibly ephemeral literature may permanently alter the landscape of nineteenth-century fiction'.[5] One might say the same about Irish country-house novels set in the closing days of the Ascendancy. That there was an Edwardian silver-fork novel in England would as a bonus give these Irish novels collateral kin, though the display of wealth in the Irish novels is, as we shall see, ambiguous and peculiar.[6]

However, if we think of the genre of the country-house novel as merely a cadet branch of the Irish Big House novel, we can derive it in orthodox Irish critical memory from Edgeworth's *Castle Rackrent* (1800). The subgenre was also suitable for adaptation for young readers and several of the women novelists (most prolifically, L. T. Meade) had more than one constituency of readers. Of course, large sales and real popularity were possible only if a novel were available and successful in Britain; it had to be attractive to British readers, therefore, and in Britain there was a ready-made audience for Big House or 'great house' or 'stately home' novels with their built-in 'romance' of the lives of the rich and socially elevated. Upper-class novelists were at once more inclined and more qualified to dash off such novels. The wonder is that many of the novels fitted the bill commercially while reflecting the condition of Ireland in a way that makes them of interest to the social and literary historian a century or so later.

The disproportionate importance of the country house in Irish life was a function of the structure of Irish society that appeared stable if not sound until the Land Acts and the Great War. The 'Great War' Burdett-Coutts refers to in her Preface to *Woman's Mission* is in fact the Napoleonic wars and according to her the origins of organized philanthropy are to be found in the 'manor-house' or 'great house' in England after those wars.[7] The great house was a hub with spokes of concern (as well as self-interest) radiating outwards and that active concern was orchestrated by women. It might be possible to add the country house in Ireland to Burdett-Coutts's survey, though with the appropriate register of political and religious constraints. Certainly the Irish novel depicts the women of the country houses occupied in charitable work; and the Irish 'big house' and Dublin town house, despite the profound reservations at best, hostility at worst, shown by the surrounding native Irish, at least bred women who often engaged in what we would now call outreach work. The question of whether the work they did should have been necessary is beside my point; the answer is social as well as political, as the applicability of observations about rural England to rural Ireland would go to show.

Still, one suspects that minor country-house novels, even if they impinged on the contemporary critical consciousness, would offend political sentiments prevailing in that consciousness. Much criticism of Irish literature is conducted under the auspices of a liberationist ideology and while the reasons are obvious, it does create critical blind spots. Nonetheless, it is the case that the picture of the country house as a hub of philanthropic energy is what we might call a 'feminine' picture. The 'masculine' picture is very different. A recent study of literary representations of the Irish country house states its purpose to be an inquiry into how far the country house was crucial to the effort or project to 'impose or recreate civilisation in Ireland' and it takes it as material fact that the country houses were 'instruments of government'; they were locations of ideas and values but these (like organized philanthropy itself, one could argue) were implicated in the imperial mission to civilize.[8] This perspective has been the orthodox one since the organization of Irish Studies over the past thirty years or so and it seems pointless to belabour it. But the orthodoxy oughtn't to blind us to the modest merits of country-house novels. The chief reason for reading these novels, provided they are entertaining and competently written (the word 'professional' comes to mind for many of them), is because they are, at least in part, problem-novels, the chief problem being the decline of the Irish country house during the years of the disturbances, outrages, and structural alterations on the land. I prefer not always to use the loaded and overused term 'Big House', suggesting as it does the tyranny of a few isolated mansions on the hill, though very large country houses on immense estates and with hundreds of tenants do deserve the name.

The condition of Ireland was hugely bound up with the condition of the country houses and demesnes. There is often a time lag in the novel, and novels published between 1890 and 1922 might well depict events of twenty or twenty-five years before without being historical novels in the usual sense. Deep structural changes, such as land redistribution (or, say, a Government of Ireland Act, or a civil war, or an Anglo-Irish treaty), create quakes that produce tremors that continue for decades, and the novel records those seismic shifts. The background to the decline of the country estate can be given in shorthand as a series of events, an astonishing chain really and with huge social repercussions: Gladstone's Land Act (I, 1870); the Ballot Act (1872);[9] the founding of the Irish National Land League (1879); evictions and agrarian counter-outrages (1877–80); Coercion Bills (I, 1881, II, 1882); Gladstone's Land Act (II, 1881); agrarian outrages (1881–2); the Coercion Act (III, 1882); the Ashbourne Land Act (III, 1885); the Coercion Bill (IV, 1885); the Balfour Coercion Act (V, 1887); the Land Act (IV, 1887); the founding of the Tenants' Defence Association (1888); the Land (Purchase) Act (V, 1888); the Local Government (Ireland) Act (1898); the United Irish League founded (William O'Brien,1898); mild coercion (1898–1902); the Land Conference (1902); the Wyndham Land Act (VI, 1903); the Amending Act (VII, 1909); the Government of Ireland Act (1920).[10] By the time the chain was paid out, Ireland was sea-changed (or land-changed) and the loser was the country estate. Burnings up until the 1920s (Moore Hall was a famous casualty during the Irish civil war) completed the process of transfiguration of the literal and metaphoric landscape. Writing in 1917, Edith Somerville, having recalled the dereliction of Ross House in 1888 which Martin Ross was attempting to restore, brought the melancholy picture up to date: 'Ireland, now, is full of such places as Ross was then. "Gentry-houses", places that were once disseminators of light, of the humanities; centres of civilisation; places to which the poor people rushed, in any trouble, as to Cities of Refuge. They are now destroyed, become desolate, derelict.'[11] In early 1920, a commentator with a subtler class-sense could lament the fate of the gentry which he regarded as sealed: 'Their once hospitable mansions know them no more: they are now occupied by resident magistrates, petty sessions clerks, and profiteers. The demesne is broken up; the trees are cut down; the lawns, on which many generations of happy children played, are now potato-fields. The stables and kennels are in ruins. There is no longer any cheery rural life in the countryside.'[12]

It is useful to remember that not all of the decline suffered by the large country houses was unique to Ireland. In one interpretation, the decline of the English country house began during the agricultural depression of the 1870s and accelerated with the Great War when many of the staff dispersed for armed service and other duties. The land depression notwithstanding, G. M. Trevelyan contrasts the picture of rural England in 1901 with that a generation later. The 'feudal' society was still intact at Queen Victoria's death: country houses flourished socially, the squire still supplied 'friendly leadership', and the estate system still dominated agriculture. But even by that time, the estates were supported less by rural rents than by industry and investment. The Local Government Act of 1888 (Ireland's was a decade later) replaced a patriarchal system with county councils, and the power of the squire diminished.[13] Of course, the relative inability of the Irish estates to draw on industrial income (industry operated both more democratically and more plutocratically in the Irish North), added to the increasing rejection of the 'friendly leadership' of the gentry, signalled large differences between England and Ireland.

With varying degrees of seriousness, merit, and political engagement, the Irish country-house novel registers the immediate effects of the changes from inside the demesne walls, a privileged and necessary perspective and often from the point of view of a woman, both author and character. This point of view appears to refract most of the political lightbeam into the lateral business of love and marriage, legacies and inheritance, into family matters away from the political arena, but the family, because the country house interacts with native Ireland outside and even inside the walls, is to an extent a weather station for the political climate of the country. There was indeed a dangerous time lag between the deep changes taking place outside the walls (in field, cottage, town, and parliament) and the awareness and appreciation of those changes inside; the foreground concern of these novels with romance and marriage appears, oddly, a fictive correlative of the time lag. But we should remember that marriage (and the mechanism of inheritance it involved) was a dimension of the economic life of the country house, and also that love and marriage were significant social relations undergoing changes as radical as those taking place on the land.

The folly of the time lag was Moore's point in *A Drama in Muslin*. But other Irish novelists too were not unaware of the absurdity or frivolity, the air of unreality this time lag could produce. One of the marring, and jarring, effects of many of these novels is a prevalent archness of tone, a search after whimsy, a ponderous humour. In part it is due to an imperfect imitation of superior English models; it was Oscar Wilde who finally beat the English at their own game of drawing-room brilliance and mannerism and a deceptively limp-handed grasp of life (in which were disguised the iron fists of unforgiving English class structure and unforgiving English imperial hegemony). But it is not always easy to differentiate this tone from the possibility that it is a chronic criticism, that language, dialogue, even genre itself, are an ongoing critique, as Wilde's are (though sometimes one isn't sure if Wilde isn't in love with what he is satirizing, the English and English life). In *A Pitiless Passion*, MacMahon has young Sir Anthony Chenevix—who, *fin-de-siècle* style, is writing *The Autobiography of a Failure*—satirize the marriage market at the top echelons of society, particularly between rich Americans and titled Britons whose estates were sometimes 'heavily embarrassed', as Chenevix has it. (The 1890–Great War period was a great one for marriages between American heiresses and English nobles in reduced circumstances.) Chenevix playfully wants to set up 'The New Marriage Mart for the Convenience of American Capitalists and English Vendors'. (Lot 3 in his imaginary auction is 'The Honourable Adolphus John Charles Readmeup, M.P. for North Top-pington . . . has written *Philosophic Philanderings; A Note on the Condition of Ireland, or How to Make the Irish Clean*, in 72 pages, crown octavo, paper covers.')[14] MacMahon is more critical than most of the Irish country-house novelists but in many of them there is the sense of an ending, projected beyond their frivolous scenes of balls and parties, beyond whatever recovery takes place at the close of the novels.

COUSINS AND VISITORS

The marriage and romance mart is a large part of the plot of *The Financing of Fiona* (1916) by the indefatigable Dorothea Conyers.[15] The novel opens in Paris and then shifts to the south-west of Ireland, to Cahervane and the country house of Kinvarragh, the interior of which is fondly described in accordance with the subgenre. The story is of a thriftless rich girl (a 'spoilt child of fortune' and an orphan), Fiona Beresford, whose mother's brother, Colonel Beresford, owns Kinvarragh. The Colonel dies and due to a mix-up with the will leaves the house to Fiona but the estate to Challoner, the Colonel's younger brother's son. The 'open-eyed, slyly-moving, high-nosed, handsome Challoner' has already 'cultivated' a passion for Fiona because he knows that since Kinvarragh was not entailed, Fiona will inherit it; but he is much too shallow, grasping, and stupid to have appeal for her.[16] Two

Englishmen whom the Beresfords meet in Paris, Major Cecil Bohun and his ward, young Sir Henry Bohun, come to Kinvarragh to hunt, buying horses along the way, making elaborate preparation, setting great store by this expensive vacation, only to find to their dismay that the house is run by a woman and that the hunting, at the outset, is unpromising. The plot concerns the relationship of the Englishmen to Ireland and their gradual warming to a country about which they have deep reservations.

Here is the 'Visitor to Ireland' plot device that recurs in the country-house novel of the time: Somerville and Ross use it in *An Irish Cousin*, for example; Ella MacMahon uses it in *The Job*; E. Temple Thurston in *Traffic*; Helen Duffin in *Over Here*; Crichton in *The Soundless Tide*; Croker in *Lismoyle*. The plot-device sponsors the fictional theme of England–Ireland relations, a critically serious matter in the world outside the novel in the 1890–1922 period. Let me pause my discussion of *Financing Fiona* to say more about the Visitor to Ireland, a device which assumes a small number of formulaic guises as old as the early nineteenth-century Irish novel.

First of all, there is the absentee Anglo-Irish landlord (or more often landlord's young heir, who is not quite set in his social and economic prejudices) returning or, more promisingly (in the case of the heir), coming to Ireland for the first time, as in Lady Morgan's *The Wild Irish Girl* (1806) or Maria Edgeworth's *The Absentee* (1812). Although Irish land had been owned (granted, stolen, confiscated or otherwise appropriated) for centuries by Englishmen, many landowners had made their home in Ireland and until the Act of Union had bought or built their townhouses in Dublin. Thereafter, those of them involved in the government or civil service of Ireland trans-planted their town life to England, becoming more seriously absent and, increasingly, themselves visitors to Ireland when they returned to their estates and country houses. Second, there is the English relative or friend of an absentee landlord or the English relative of a residing Anglo-Irish landowning family, as in *An Irish Cousin* (by MacSorley) and *Lismoyle*. Third, there is the returning Irish expatriate. The earliest fictional example is probably Meriton Latroon, eponymous 'hero' of the picaresque novel, *The English Rogue* (1665) by Richard Head, born in Carrickfergus in the north of Ireland. Latroon, who (like his creator, apparently) left Ireland with his mother during the 1641 rebellion, returns to Ireland as an adult to evade creditors and finds there a country full of duplicity and poverty.[17] With the emergence of the national tale during the Romantic period (Lady Morgan's *The Wild Irish Girl* is regarded as pioneering), the visitor is a more benign and less incorrigible figure and in the popular novel the returnee is often an Irish girl or youth who has been brought up in England or, in the case of Somerville and Ross's *An Irish Cousin*, who has spent the last two years in Canada (her relatives having emigrated there). Edgeworth herself was 15 before she touched Irish shores and so enacted in life the device she helped popularize in fiction. Fourth, there is the holidaymaker or accidental tourist, as in *The Financing of Fiona* and *Traffic*. In all its fictive guises, the device implements the idea that England and Ireland are inextricably connected, by real or figurative kinship. Both device and idea characterized the national tale of the early nineteenth century which Ferris sees as a fictional response to the English genre of the Irish tour and a fictional way of completing the Union by reconciling Irish claims and English rule through a romance story.[18] Often in the later novels, too, the constitutional Union is tacitly being defended or accepted, *despite* the exoticness of Ireland, by which the visitor is captivated before he or she 'domesticates' it in a personal experience that is meant at some level to represent the pulling of Ireland into the civilizational orbit of the British Isles (or United Kingdom).[19]

There is one repeat visitor of the second type. In the popular novel, a recurring form of kinship between visitors and residents is that of *cousinage*, one made explicit in the title, *An Irish Cousin*, used by both Somerville and Ross (1889) and Catherine Mary MacSorley (1901). Cousinage implies close kinship but greater distance than that between, say, brothers or sisters, and besides, cousins usually live apart which is convenient for the novelist's plot, allowing stays of variable length, reunions and departures, entrances and exits. Large families meant that cousins were a salient feature of the Irish familial landscape. These included the typically large Anglo-Irish families and, beyond size, Anglo-Irish concern for property and inheritance meant that there was a high consciousness of relations and kin; there were a great many marriages between Anglo-Irish or English-Irish cousins. Martin Ross's mother and Edith Somerville's mother were first cousins, making the writers second cousins, and Edith Somerville remembered her mother saying that she had seventy first cousins, all grandchildren of Charles Kendal Bushe and his wife.[20]

It was appropriate, therefore, that the first collaboration in fiction between Somerville and Ross should be entitled *An Irish Cousin*.[21] It has several of the country house novel devices and themes that Conyers and numerous other novelists were to employ. The Visitor to Ireland (in this case, the young woman, Theo Sarsfield) arrives from Canada via New York on a transatlantic liner. Although she presumably knows Ireland—how well is not clear, since her Irish background is sketchy—she has preconceptions which, as she admits (it is a first-person narrative), are stylized and condescending.[22] The undercutting of these preconceptions makes her feel quite literally disillusioned and downcast and at the end of a very long journey from Canada to New York, New York to Queenstown, Queenstown to Cork, Cork to Durrus, her uncle's country house, she experiences an early onset of the curious spell of Ireland:

'a strange feeling of remoteness and unreality came upon me'; at Durrus for some time, she still feels like 'a stranger in a strange land'.[23] Here and in other novels, the spell of Ireland originates in a mingling of the exotically different and the ancestrally or mystically familiar. Later, the spell intensifies into epiphany, as Theo feels the landscape prophesy for her a new life.

That landscape, irregularly beautiful, is reflected in Durrus, a run-down, mysterious, dishevelled country house like many others in these Irish novels, a condition perhaps related—though the novelist may not always be aware of this—to the 'widowed' and irregular nature of the family within: Theo's aunt is dead, leaving behind Uncle Dominick and cousin Willy who form a dysfunctional family of mutual dislike—one example among many, one can't help inferring, of an increasingly dysfunctional caste. Theo, too, is an orphan and has been living in Canada with her aunt and uncle. Still, the dinners, hunts, and balls are not dysfunctional (if irregular in one way or another) and compose the set-pieces common in the country-house novel. The spell of Ireland begins by casting a glow over the irregular love triangle of the plot: cousin Willy falls in love with Theo who begins to fall for Nugent O'Neill, son of The O'Neill of the neighbouring Big House, Clash-more, but it transpires that Willy has been seeing a Catholic tenant's daughter, making the triangle a rectangle. When Nugent takes himself off, believing Willy and Theo are about to be married, Theo proposes to Willy, having rejected him earlier, offering herself, against the run of emotional play, what we might call a merely safe marriage, in place of the true love she might have found with Nugent, and offering Willy what seems to be his heart's desire. But Willy under some duress has just married the tenant's daughter at the priest's house: it is a 'mad' marriage that will do him no good socially, and Willy intends to flee with his new wife to Australia. Nugent returns and a marriage resting on true love will be the happy result. (More on safe, mad, and true marriages later.)

The narrative is psychologically insightful but in any case, psychology and romance alike are overtaken by another kind of story entirely; the spell of Ireland becomes a dark thing that falls on the characters and plot like a Gothic cloak. There is something rotten in Durrus. There is a will; there is a battle for inheritance; a fratricide involving Theo's father; possible incest; alcoholic fantasies of coaches that can drive through locked lodge gates.[24] It is hard to imagine Theo's romantic life flourishing after all of this. Oddly enough, the strange generic passage of the novel was anticipated in the circumstances of its composition. Early in their collaboration on it, (Violet) Martin and Somerville paid a visit to an elderly unmarried relative in a lonely country house on the rugged coast of west Cork. They both agreed later that the visit changed their outlook on life and their point of view in their work in progress; it was one of Somerville's more graphic Irish memories:

The sunset was red in the west when our horses were brought round to the door, and it was at that precise moment that into the Irish Cousin some thrill of genuineness was breathed. In the darkened façade of the long grey house, a window, just over the hall-door, caught our attention. In it, for an instant, was a white face. Trails of ivy hung over the panes, but we saw the face glimmer there for a minute and vanish.

As we rode home along the side of the hills, and watched the fires of the sunset sink into the sea, and met the crescent moon coming with faint light to lead us home, we could talk and think only of that presence at the window. We had been warned of certain subjects not to be approached, and knew enough of the history of that old house to realize what we had seen. An old stock, isolated from the world at large, wearing itself out in those excesses that are a protest of human nature against unnatural conditions, dies at last with its victims round its death-bed. Half-acknowledged, half-witted, wholly horrifying; living ghosts, haunting the house that gave them but half their share of life, yet withheld from them, with half-hearted guardianship, the boon of death.[25]

Here was the condition of Ireland imagined at its outermost edge of Anglo-Irish Society and suggesting Gothic as the most appropriate mode for its depiction. (The mad woman in the 'attic' becomes mad Moll Hourihane in *An Irish Cousin*, a demented key to the dark secrets of the past.) Theo believes that through her treatment of Willy and through her paternity she has brought ruin to Durrus. She hasn't, but as a visiting cousin she has been the agent by which the past has been exposed, and the larger declension in the Anglo-Irishry cannot be prevented by this revelation, or by her own imminent happiness in marriage, with its union of an O'Neill and a Sarsfield.

The visiting cousin is often English and is the means by which is revealed what binds as well as distances the English and the Irish; cousinage is often a relationship fully to be revealed by actual phsyical presence and turns out to be a kind of a priori resolution through reconciliation. Cousinage suggested a more realistic version than the commoner and rather condescending 'sister isle' epithet of the England–Ireland connection. Although many Irish coun-try-house families straddled the Irish Sea, branches of those families had developed quite differently in the two countries and cultures. The novels often tallied the mistaken English preconceptions about Ireland or registered the real differences in wealth and energy that allowed the English cousin to propose means by which the Irish could improve themselves or to proffer material help as well as advice. Before returning to *The Financing of Fiona* and other novels of primarily social concern, we might glance at a slight novel published twelve years after Somerville and Ross's fiction of the same name, in which the English cousin's aid is of a more religious and personal kind. Clearly, Ireland's malaise was variously diagnosable.

MacSorley's *An Irish Cousin* was published by the Society for Promoting Christian Knowledge (SPCK) and was meant, it would seem, for young readers to whom is directed the Christian message that we must all endure our sufferings willingly because they echo the sufferings of Christ, who willingly endured His for our sake; and that to endure the unique yet human pains of our existence we must conduct ourselves like soldiers. This message is brought to her unwell Irish cousin by a precociously wise English girl.[26] The military simile, of course, would at the time have suggested the familiar Victorian exhortation: 'Onward, Christian Soldiers!', that is, go out into the world to do good, to bear Christian witness, to defeat Christ's enemies by converting them to Christianity—an evangelical message that Deborah Alcock took very much to heart. But although one of the two English cousins in MacSorley's novel wishes to become a real British soldier, in *An Irish Cousin* to be a good soldier is to suffer one's ailments and pains courageously and the young and ill Gerald O'Donnell is enjoined to be a good soldier by his young English cousin; he is to accept his physical disability, buck up, venture into the open air, taking life on instead of recoiling from it, a physical and almost secular version of Milton's notion of the wayfaring pilgrim who is not content with a cloistered virtue. But the story barely disguises, as well, a social and political allegory. This is not to say that MacSorley is consciously constructing an allegory, but rather that her 'take' on Irish–English relations can hardly escape allegorical meaning and lends this slight affair its only real if still minor interest.

From her own prosperous English country house (Haybridge) comes young Nancy (the Visitor to Ireland, type two) to see her bedridden and orphaned cousin, Gerald, in the dilapidated Irish country house, Creevemore, owned by his grandfather who is distracted and preoccupied by some grand literary and scholarly venture. In the words of Bridget, the housekeeper in this melancholy pile in the west of Ireland, the O'Donnells are 'the reel ould ginthry, an' they as poor as ye plase' and far superior to the gentry growing up around them: 'people that has got up in the world, an' has made their money thimselves' (p. 97), a sentiment which Katharine Tynan for one, Yeats for another, would have endorsed but expressed without the dialect.

The poverty of the almost landless O'Donnells is mirrored in the sickness of young Gerald, pampered by Bridget who thereby keeps Gerald a premature valetudinarian, as though preferring her gentry ailing and dependent rather than healthy and independent. Nancy Warrington, followed by her no-nonsense brother Maurice, arrives like a breath of fresh air: almost literally, since she is an advocate of the healing properties of the open air, especially of the salubrious air in this land of bog and heather.[27] Gerald's disability is not as great as Bridget maintains and he can get on his two feet with the proper help and encouragement. Young Maurice is bluff and hearty, sporting and sportsmanlike, a team-player, the kind of English youth that was admired by Hannah Lynch, and, one can add, the ideal fellow for making, expanding, and holding the Empire. He inspires Gerald with tales of the playing fields of school and war. Young Gerald is not at first a good soldier, but rather fretful and petulant, self-pitying and reluctant to help himself. An allegorical reading begins to press its claims. Gerald is of an old Irish yet Protestant family; one of the recurring features of these novels is the blurring of the distinction between native and settler (or invader); Protestant families will often have native names. Gerald is Ireland, at first ungrateful for the cousinly help proffered by the well-meaning, pragmatic yet philanthropic and Christian (i.e. Protestant) English. Taken to Haybridge when his grandfather dies and the latter's will disappears and Creevemore (it might be Grievemore, such is the melancholy that has pervaded its dark and dank rooms) is sold to a local strong farmer, Gerald (now the Irish cousin) prospers in England and the company of his cousins. When he returns to Creevemore for a last stay before the farmer takes possession, he does so a stronger fellow, discovering his own strengths and virtues, though they are different from Maurice's. The lost will, stolen by an aggrieved peasant neighbour (despite the grandfather having been, as Gerald will be, a kindly landlord beloved of the tenants and neighbours), is ferreted out by Bridget and returned, thus nullifying the sale and restoring Creevemore to young Gerald. Young Gerald, promising now to be an upstanding fellow, receives from his neighbours and tenants their 'love and loyalty' as 'a great and precious thing' (p. 153). But he will return to England to be brought up and educated there and will return to take possession of Creevemore when he gains his majority, someone by then close, we assume, to the ideal of the Anglo-Irish gentry. Once more, the flourishing country house is envisaged as occupying the centre of a renewed and prosperous Ireland that will be bound closer to its cousin isle.

FINANCING FIONA

As well as the marriage and romance mart and the Visitor to Ireland premiss, the plot of Conyers's *The Financing of Fiona* involves the machinations of the heart (the sincere heart or the deceiving heart) and is the affable nonsense that sold such novels to a hungry clientele. Challoner pursues Fiona to get his hands on the house as well as the land; Major Cecil wants to fix Marian Codington up with his ward, Sir Henry; Major Cecil is attracted to Fiona but thinks she is drawn to Sir Henry (she rejects his suit); Juliette

McGeary wants Challoner; Lady Cortra wants Challoner for her daughter, Lady Julia. . . . But the main plot is the response of the spoilt child of fortune to being left poor by her uncle, with a house that costs the earth to maintain, a few horses that luckily were in the stables before Challoner claimed the estate, and her cousin pacing the boundaries of Kinvarragh House and becoming increasingly desperate and dangerous in his own blustery way. Fiona rises to the occasion; she is that recurring figure in the Irish novel by women: the strong and unconventional young woman who is a kind of New Woman but no feminist. Often this figure is a horsewoman, as though illustrating how the woman riding abroad is woman at large, free of male control and condescension (later, the bicycle performed this function, according to Beatrice Grimshaw), and appropriating to herself the strength of the horse itself (later, the speed of the bicycle: Grimshaw was a champion cyclist).[28] Fiona proves she does not need men to subsist but does need them in order to flourish, and in the end needs love and collaboration with another's heart.

Meanwhile it is she who decides to manage Kinvarragh alone (with the help of her small staff) by taking in paying hunting guests from England and it is a struggle, with Challoner waiting for her to fail and the Englishmen bemused by it all. She seems unequal to the struggle and the decline she sees around her might be written large as the decline of the entire unfair social system of which she is a part:

Fiona went out into the yards. Grass was springing up at the sides, a slate had crashed down and had not been replaced. The canker of poverty was spreading, slowly, but spreading. The big gates had not had their coat of paint, the walls had not been distempered. Brown required a new oat-crusher, a larger one than he had . . . Fiona felt afraid. She was so small in the vastness of the place which she meant to hold to, to keep, even if she starved there in two rooms . . . she could not wander off into the high field behind the cattle-yards where she had exercised for so long; it was Challoner's now. (pp. 212–13)

But gradually she impresses the sceptical men and Sir Cecil, who almost absent-mindedly comes to her aid, discovers that he is falling for her. His is quite a fine portrait of a man whose exasperation with Ireland, with Fiona, with everything and everyone around him, gradually resolves into a dew of loneliness, or rather the realization of his previously disguised loneliness and what he has so far missed in life. He and Fiona come together and he discovers from Fiona's papers that she is rich through her uncle's shares, that Challoner tore a page out of the will, and that Kinvarragh, house and grounds, are hers and which he will help manage. The financing of Fiona begins as her uncle's subsidizing her frivolous purchases in Paris, becomes her own struggles to make ends meet in landless and impoverished Kinvarragh, and ends as the riches of the estate and her uncle's Canadian Pacific moneys.

Underneath the exasperation with Ireland runs in descant Bohun's almost unconscious surrender to the spell of the Irish landscape. 'Forgetting the hills, Cecil Bohun felt the grip of the country, its grey stillness, the clear, soft air which blew in through his window with a whiff of bog and salt in its breath.' A little later: 'He got up to look out at the wonderful purple-grey of Ireland, with the silver of mother-of-pearl iridescent behind it, soft clouds gathering and massing, then lifting for the sunlit pearl to come through.' Later still: 'He strayed aimlessly about the big place, trying to fight against the charm of the grey lakes, the wild toss of little hills, the sombre beauty of the hall.' And again: 'And through it all the grey, lonely beauty of the old place fascinated him against his will', just as, later, 'The wild beauty of it struck him against his will.'[29] The appeal of Ireland is irrational, against the odds, below good sense, a matter of experience and feeling. It is a venerable notion in fiction, that the visitor's prejudice against Ireland is dissolved in first-hand experience, and we find it in Lady Morgan's *The Wild Irish Girl*. The implication is that if only the English and the Irish got to know each other, personally and intimately, then the resolution of political, even constitutional differences would follow.

Fiona learns the value of money (she becomes a pragmatist), two Englishmen learn the value of Ireland, all learn the value of collaboration and compromise. It is like a disguised political prescription, though one wonders how far Conyers was aware of this. Whether Conyers thought the decline of the Irish country house was reversible I am not aware. In this novel it is reversible, unrealistically as history has proven, though Fiona's notion of taking in paying guests who wish to enjoy the rural amenities was one that Edith Somerville put into practice.[30] (The notion, organized and commercialized later, became an element in the success of Irish tourism.) In such wise certain members of the gentry declined into what we might call the *haute bourgeoisie*, despite the gentry's traditional distaste for the bourgeoisie and those in trade. The lesson of *The Financing of Fiona* is that Ireland may be exasperating and different, but it has its unique charms and with a bit of help, and custom, from an England more commercially canny and experienced than its cousin isle, the two countries can prosper. It is an idea that some thinking people entertained with many practical schemes afoot; but others thought that perhaps things had gone too far to be remedied by such plans, while Home Rule supporters attracted to independence decided the idea was long past its sell-by date.

Conyers herself, coming from a country-house background, sold well as a writer of horsey stories, thereby prviding her own solution to any decline of inherited land-based wealth. (Taking our cue from Harry Furniss, it would be possible to write a socio-economic history of the Irish popular novel, relating many of its authors, particularly inhabitants or former inhabitants of country houses, to their changing domestic circumstances.) In *The Financing of Fiona*, too, there are riding and hunting passages, knowledgeable and even exciting. One passage in which Major Cecil imagines the hunt before it happens, a passage (pp. 175–6) in which Conyers switches to the present tense to signal an excited reverie, is a good one and attempts to justify the 'greatest sport on earth'. The hunting improves as the novel proceeds and therefore works its passage both in the writing of the novel and—on the allegorical level—in the saleable charms of Ireland. The later success of Bord Failte in an Ireland without English aid in selling to tourists the imagery of a romantic, ancient, and picturesque countryside (and with good fox-hunting, fishing, shooting, and horse-riding) has justified to some extent Conyers's wily, practical, adaptable romanticism. But meanwhile, of course, the condition of the country house was too far advanced to be solved by the recovered page of a will and overlooked Canadian Pacific shares, or by a discovered original and valuable painting, as in Croker's *Lismoyle*.

SAVING SOCIETY (SPELT BIG)

In her country-house novel, *A Girl of Galway* (1901), Katharine Tynan (1859–1931) essentially shrinks the Irish crossroads to the crisis of economic and social reduction faced by the gentry in their country houses, but at least registers, if unenthusiastically, the potential contribution of trade and industry to a solution that would also achieve prosperity and admit a limited modernization.

However, it is not really reform Tynan seems to advocate: it is more like reconciliation of existing oppositions, and the changes she countenances are not bottom-up; rather they are top-down as of old, but with business sharing Ireland with the gentry, a social class (or high caste) reduced certainly but still viable and influential and, importantly, still landed. Tynan's impulse is philanthropic rather than reformist. The heroine, young Bertha Grace, embodies the principle of reconciliation from the start. Her father is Irish, her mother English or, as it is put in the novel, her training is English but her blood is Irish. Already in her own self reconciling Saxon and Celt, Bertha is sent from England to Corofin House in Co. Galway (the real village of Corofin is in neighbouring Co. Clare) for a projected five-year spell while her mother joins her father in imperial India, in this manner helping her parents reunite by staying with her paternal grandfather, the landowning Sir Delvin Grace. Bertha is also given by her mother the task of reconciling Sir Delvin with his son Everard, whom Sir Delvin banished because he married a poor governess (Bertha's mother, Camilla) instead of a wealthy heiress picked out for him by Sir Delvin and whose dowry would have helped him regain some of his lost land. Her mother's explanation, uncontested by either daughter or narrator, is that 'It is the place of women to make peace.'[31] There will soon be a third task of reconciliation: promoting peace between the Corofin Graces and their neighbours the Ropers, a feud that started over the head of a woman. And beyond these, even greater, ultimately economic and cultural tasks of peacemaking await her, tasks that if successful would aid in the regeneration of Corofin House and environs.

Bertha Grace is the Visitor to Ireland of the second type identified above, soon falling under the spell of Corofin, particularly the spell of the woods that stretch five miles in every direction, and discovering an English ancestress. But Corofin is a house 'mouldering to its fall' (p. 70), which condition, while directly caused by the eccentric Sir Delvin, distantly enacts a wider decline, though at the novel's outset, one character—performing the role of spokes-woman for outmoded Victorian nostalgia—claims the decline began as far back as the Act of Union and loss of the Irish parliament: 'The glories of the Anglo-Irish departed with Lord Carlisle's viceroyalty [1780–2]. He was an elegant man. Dublin's a sad place today. Stale English ideals and a desperate cocksure-ness' (p. 38). Tynan, in fact, modernizes this kind of historical Anglo-Irish patriotism, politically and economically, and in her novel attempts to revivify it. The 'Quality', as Corofin's housekeeper, Mrs Butler, calls the gentry, are fash-ionably and charitably seeking to 'improve' the people (teaching them butter-making, weaving, dyeing, embroidering, etc.), but though the housekeeper complains about their meddling, the narrator clearly approves. But Sir Delvin is no 'improver' and indeed has been raising rents and evicting tenants and is now chasing squatters, all violations of the historical beneficence of the Graces. Clearly, the text early implies, Bertha as an additional task will need to reconcile tenants and landlord; at one point, Mrs Butler reminds Bertha that the Graces are Tories whereas she, young Bertha, utters the sentiments of a Gladstonian liberal in the matter of Ireland (p. 153)! Like Miss Lilla's in Mulholland's *Norah of Waterford*, her immediate reaction to the poverty of the peasants is a charitable dispensing of pennies and a nobler wish to sell treasures to redeem the poor, like a small, secular, and commoner version of Yeats's Countess Cathleen; indeed, she soon does so, charitably paying the tenants' arrears with money advanced by Archibald Roper against jewels in her possession.

The current custodian of tenant–landlord relations is Bulger, the coarse land agent who is the true spring of malice and malaise in the story. (The following year, Bulger raises the rents yet again, precipitating an identical crisis among the impoverished tenants.) According to Mrs Butler, Bulger rose from the peasant class which he now hates (p. 153), and in what we might now call self-loathing takes protracted revenge against the class from which he escaped. Sir Delvin, we are asked to believe for many pages, is ignorant of the true state of affairs among the impoverished and harassed tenantry, and one starving tenant is of the opinion that 'Sure Quality does their best', unlike the agents and middlemen (pp. 167–8). And since Tynan allows Bulger to stand for the land-agent profession (a veritable social class unto itself), she is exculpating the landlords and inculpating their employees. 'Bertha had yet to learn that land-agencies are the appanage [necessary accessories] of gentlefolk in Ireland, when the agent is often a more considerable person than his employer' (p. 58).[32] Bertha's job, it transpires, is to recall the Graces to their historic and noble calling of relieving the lot of their poor dependants; this induces her to see the peasants (ambiguously) as 'her own people', the title of a chapter in which gentry and peasantry are ideally connected. A class usurper, Bulger lives at Corofin, free to influence Sir Delvin for the worse in the absence of Marcella Lloyd, a family friend (the woman Sir Delvin wished his son to marry and 'an angel to the poor', p. 170) whose feminine goodness until recently had kept Bulger at bay. Instantly, Bertha becomes Bulger's enemy and rival for Sir Delvin's mind and heart, and if she is up to the job, that is because she is a 'modern girl' (p. 43), educated, athletic, strong, and self-reliant, a New Woman in all but name. Surprising Mrs Butler by doing her own housework, Bertha explains to the housekeeper—in an early occurrence of the later famous phrase—that 'the great joy of having a room of one's own was to do everything it required one's self' (p. 133). The New Woman takes on the old-style land agent in a new gender inflection of the Irish class war.

Bertha begins the task of reviving the house by rescuing its valuable treasures that have been locked away by Sir Delvin who resists Bulger's encouragement to sell them; Bertha's rescue is not just like the redeeming of family heirlooms from a pawnbroker: she is attempting to redeem the house's glorious past, the heyday of which was before the Act of Union. Her love of the trees is equally ancestral, as we learn from an extended in-tale told by Mrs Butler who is the custodian of the past, the figurative as well as literal 'housekeeper', a figure of continuity through her memory. Her tale is an eco-romance about the curse of a forebear settled upon anyone who would cut down the woods. The novel itself is an eco-romance punctuated by hymns to the woodland that is seen as the very spirit of a benign gentry.[33] However, threat materializes when Bulger discovers coal underneath Corofin woods and exhorts Sir Delvin to exploit it commercially, who does so by selling some of the Corofin estate to 'the coal syndicate' (p. 372), making the Graces rich again (the chief use, one feels, of industry). Bertha rebels against this violation of the woods and is expelled from Corofin, creating one more rift to be healed by novel's end. Bertha takes shelter in Bawn Rose, the country house of Marcella Lloyd, who returns to the area and who is of a Quaker family; it is the spirit of Quakerism that seems to hover above the story.

The ink is no sooner dry on the financial agreement than lightning ignites the woods and Corofin House itself catches fire and burns to the ground, apparently killing Sir Delvin and Bulger, who is seen trying to save his master, thereby partially redeeming himself, though Mary Butler is of the opinion that Bulger 'would have destroyed the woods' and that the trees took their revenge upon him in the spirit of her eco-tale. But in actuality all is well and the novel ends in a frothy surge of reconciliation. Bulger in fact succeeded in saving Sir Delvin and though fatally injured lives long enough to hear Bertha's apology and request for his forgiveness and then is conveniently out of the picture. Sir Delvin's trauma causes him to suffer memory loss and to return to his previous generous self, the real Sir Delvin. He recovers his memory but not of the recent past when 'he had been alienated and unforgiving' (p. 375), a turn of events constituting a Dickensian change of heart but by which even Dickens might have been embarrassed. In this way, tenants and landlord are reunited in affection and common purpose. The foundations for a new Corofin House are soon laid: it is a new post-Land Acts start, as it were, for the gentry—and for the peasants. In her salvage work among the threatened or deteriorated country houses, what is more important for Tynan than the role of new industry is the role of old philanthropy: 'The poor have so much done for them that they would be in danger of spoiling if it were not that it is done so wisely; and every day, the sphere of the Graces' beneficence widens' (p. 383). Meanwhile, Bertha had already fallen in love with Hugh Roper, son of Sir Delvin's erstwhile enemy, and Everard and Camilla return from India less than three years later for the wedding, thereby reuniting son and father as well as the two feuding families. Some differences require no reconciliation and it comes as no surprise to be told that 'As is often the case in Ireland, [the rector] was on brotherly terms with the parish priest' (p. 253).

Happily, too, the woods that burned down were those sold to the coal syndicate which would have cut them down anyway. The local doctor gazes at the surviving woods and reminds everyone that 'there is yet enough woodland to satisfy anyone except the man who planted those trees'. Everard can build the new Corofin enclosed by trees to keep out 'the grimy world of the coal-fields' (p. 373)...'the woods of Corofin are yet something of a marvel. Though they are reduced to about half the old dimensions they suffice to make an enchanted world between Corofin and the reek of the coal-mines' (p. 384). One can imagine Tynan holding her nose during her admission of industry to a revived west of Ireland. The upshot of the unavoidable alliance between industry and the gentry is that 'there is not now a more prosperous corner of the world than that of which Corofin is the centre' (p. 383). The alliance is less a partnership than a coexistence that is suffered by the gentry— and the novelist.[34] Parallel worlds divide the new Ireland Tynan envisages.

From the centre that will be the new Corofin Bertha will continue to be a ministering angel to the sick and needy, philanthropy in no way rendered redundant by the proximity of industry, indeed the parallelism of the two is an ideal solution to Ireland's problems under the circumstances.

We don't associate Ireland with coal (save for Swift's exhortation to the Irish to burn everything English but coal) but there have in fact been active mines, including significant ones in Arigna, Roscommon, and Castlecomer, Kilkenny.[35] For economic and geological reasons, they never grew large or productive enough to influence economic policy in the south of Ireland. In any case, Tynan is uninterested in coal-mining in her novel save as an undeveloped plot-function and clearly her attention was fastened on revival of the gentry, their country houses and demesnes, in part through modernization (including industrialization) and chiefly in order to imagine the philanthropy and beneficence of the landed classes as still viable and effective, a moral activity motivated by the practice of peace, moderation, and reconciliation. 'L'envoi' that ends *A Girl of Galway* is a soup of wish fulfilment, a bathetic end to a novel that began promisingly.

Perhaps, then, and ironically, it was easier for Tynan to imagine a preindustrial and happy society in England, even five years later, when she published *Dick Pentreath* (1906), a novel set in a suggestively immemorial Surrey village in which, we are approvingly told on the very first page, there is absolutely no middle class and that the *nouveaux riches* are actively discouraged, lest they disturb the ideal balance of life between a benevolent and popular aristocracy and squirearchy on the one hand, and a dignified, contented yeomanry on the other. The villagers are sure that there is 'enough there of diversity and delight for human happiness'. Tynan knows that Ireland is a 'sadder country' than 'golden and prosperous' England,[36] and by the time of the land agitation in the late nineteenth century, it was getting harder to imagine, let alone find in real Irish life, pockets of such undisturbed and serene feudalism, though clearly Tynan as well as Yeats, Lady Gregory, and others harboured fond images of it.

In *The Job* (1914), MacMahon, like the Tynan of *A Girl of Galway*, admitted (and almost as awkwardly) trade and industry as factors in a reversal of declining fortune faced by Sir Thaddeus (Thady) Muntfort's 'fine old Georgian mansion', Mount Pleasant, most of the ancestral land of which has been sold to the tenants. 'Ancestral' in this case means back to the time of Cromwell when a Thaddeus Muntfort received his land as reward for leading a regiment of dragoons at Naseby and accompanying Cromwell to Ireland; the remnant of the dispossessed O'Mores' land now composes the estate of nearby More Castle (deserving the name of Big House), seat of the Duke of Castlemore. While *The Job* is a country-house romance, moving between London and Ireland where

Muntfort's love life unfolds and he attempts to become a successful playwright, there is another plot strand. On the outskirts of the nearest town, Muntfort, having crossed from gentry to trade, while keeping his friends among the former, has built a successful carpet factory by which he hopes to maintain Mount Pleasant but also to establish and spread the renown of Irish craftsmen as they weave intricate carpets based on eastern designs. Thady's half-brother persuades him to invest the factory's reserve fund in a safe-as-houses stock-market option, but he loses disastrously and is heavily in debt, having built an expensive extension to the factory and, moreover, has to face his codirectors, several of them Catholic businessmen. As in *A Girl of Galway*, the novelist's interest in industry and commerce is perfunctory although it provides a climax in the novel. When the factory burns down and Muntfort faces ruin and Mount Pleasant its end as the seat of the Muntfort family, it is the Duke who comes to the financial rescue. (Fires are certainly handy devices for many of these novelists, but then, to be fair, there were a lot of fires in Ireland in the first two decades of the twentieth century.) The old gentry bales out the new Ireland. His Grace admits he is not at home in this new Ireland of rising Catholic businessmen (any more than was Yeats and many others), and he wishes his benevolence to be anonymous, since 'the safest way for a peer at present is to let himself be overlooked'.[37] Despite His Grace's tactical modesty, this is, like Tynan's, a top-down solution that reads like a rearguard action on the part of the gentry, be it minor gentry like the Muntforts or major Ascendancy figures such as the Duke of Castlemore. It is clear that MacMahon, like Tynan and others, thought that it might be possible to modernize Ireland in such a way as to leave intact, however diminished their land-holdings, a landed gentry; in this way, by a species of distraction through prosperity, English–Irish relations might be kept constitutional as well as social.

The major characters in *The Job* shuttle between London town houses and clubs and Irish country houses and in addition to its other concerns, the novel strives to make English preconceptions about Ireland look foolish. The depiction of industry in the Irish countryside is one way of doing it. Lady Hexham is MacMahon's chief device by which to tackle harmful English misconceptions; if Ria is the visitor to Ireland who becomes the romance heroine, Lady Hexham is the visitor who is to be socially enlightened. When told of the carpet factory, she expresses astonishment that the Irish busy themselves with anything useful instead of engaging exclusively in Home Rule agitation. She is amazed to find that Irish country houses resemble English country houses, though she finds the countryside around rather different and is disturbed by the number of idle men in the nearby town. On the whole, she finds Ireland delightful but cannot quite shed her condescension: Ireland is 'so unexpected and curious; it reminds one of those odd places where everything is on the verge of civilization and just has been skipped over' (p. 125).

Emily Eaton, whose family occupies a smaller country house near Mount Pleasant, is infuriated by English misconceptions. 'What I *hate*', she tells the visiting Ria, 'is the way Ireland is always held up to English people as a country of clodhopping peasants and barefooted children and nothing else'. '"I suppose", said Ria, smiling, "that is because all the stories and plays seem to be about those sort of people". "And I'd like to *burn* them every one," returned Emily, fiercely.' Emily believes that such plays and stories are popular because the English like to condescend and don't want to know that there are '*ladies* and *gentlemen* in Ireland'. Ria, perhaps with popular and even famous works of the Irish Revival in mind, thinks the writers must shoulder some of the blame, and Emily agrees. Others are at fault as well. '"You see," continued Ria, reflectively, "the sort of people in Ireland who are like ourselves don't seem to make themselves known and so the others attract all the attention". "Indeed, perhaps you're right," remarked Emily, more quietly… "There's Thady writing plays, and he goes and gives accounts of people outside Ireland, the Army and India, and things like that. I asked him once why he didn't write about his own country and he said there were plenty doing that, and why should he?"' (p. 194). Certainly the rather dispersed literary talents of the 1890–1922 period lacked the image power of the nationalistic Revival writers, though the literature by Irish writers that was set outside Ireland ('the Army and India, and things like that') was still Irish even if unregarded as such. Behind Emily's literary concern lies a greater social and eventually political concern: that the Anglo-Irish and well-heeled unionists were being outmanoeuvred by the peasant, lower-middle-class, and middle-class nationalists and were failing to speak up and speak out in a way that would reach and influence England.[38] The Duke of Castlemore is a good example right at hand.

MacMahon's implied narrator is full of ambivalence: whereas she knows the Anglo-Irish intimately and sympathetically, she keeps her distance from unionism, and in an early 'establishment' shot that dates it to what we now know was the run-up to the Great War, she remarks that on a mountain side near Mount Pleasant 'an alien government has carved a rifle range, or, to be more accurate, the mountain's precipitous granite caverns form a fitting target for big guns' (p. 26). The same narrator is equidistant from a certain kind of nationalist, one whom we will meet later in Somerville's *An Enthusiast* (1921): the Catholic nationalist (often a businessman) who is trying to have his cake and eat it too, advancing by indirections the cause of his country's independence while advancing in a more direct fashion his own upward motion into the company of the Anglo-Irish powers that be. The character of Magrath in *The Job* is a less likeable, urban version of Jimmy Doyle's father in Joyce's *Dubliners* story, 'After the Race'. One of the board members of Thady Muntfort's carpet factory, Magrath like Doyle's father started off as a nationalist but modified his views as he ascended the social ladder through business success. Magrath accepted the voluntary positions of Justice of the Peace and Poor Law Guardian and has been known to sign addresses of welcome to the monarch. If his nationalism is buried it is not dead; he gives lavishly to the Roman Catholic Church and surreptitiously to various republican societies and movements (p. 233). Unlike Mr Casey in Joyce's *A Portrait of the Artist*, he is a hypocrite who does not mean it when he tells Thady Muntfort in ingratiation: 'It's my opinion that there's too much religion altogether in Ireland. It's bad to have too little right enough, but I'm not sure if it is worse to have too much. And there's far too much here, anyway' (p. 237). One detects beneath Magrath's ingratiation the long memory of the Cromwellian outrages.

If Thady can see through and handle (pro tem) the Magraths of the neighbourhood, that is because Thady as a convert to business himself regards the position of the Anglo-Irish in a surprisingly pragmatic fashion, one which I have rarely encountered outside MacMahon's novel (we will meet it later in George Birmingham's *Gossamer*). When Thady is at a particularly low ebb, he is found weeping by a London bobby who confesses to his own troubles, telling Thady 'it's all in the job'; here the novel's title refers to the stern task of living (to borrow a phrase from *Dubliners*). But earlier, in conversation with Sir Arthur Champneys, the new ambassador to Turkey, Thady employs the novel's title in a different, richer, almost coded though perhaps not entirely unrelated fashion, since beyond the existence of the factory there is the merest hint of the white man's—or at least Anglo-Saxon man's—burden, a stern task to be performed in Ireland and its difficulty endured. There is a sense of shared professional fatigue and, in the case of Thady, a barely discernible vestige of a Cromwellian cause.

The eyes of the two men met.

'Ireland,' said the elder in duty bound, 'is an immensely interesting country.'

'It's my job,' said Thady with a smile.

'Does it never bore you' asked Edith, looking at him with a little spurt of genuine and unaffected wonder.

'Oh yes, often. One's job does, you see,' his eyes sought Champneys again, and the latter nodded comprehendingly.

'Then why not choose another job?' asked Lady Champneys, 'why be bored?' her voice sounded prettily plaintive.

'Any other job would bore too if it was the job,' he rejoined. She looked mystified but her husband's heavy face flashed into sympathy.

'That's it,' he said, 'the job is bound to bore, because it *is* the job, yet one can't leave it.'

'It won't leave us,' amended Thady.

'No,' said the Ambassador quickly, 'you are perfectly right, it won't leave us. It's odd, but it's a fact.'

'Specially if you're bred to it,' continued Thady. He found it easy to talk to this man who was Edith's husband.

Again Champneys nodded. 'And besides,' he said with another keen look at Thady, 'it's been the job for you and yours for rather a good while.'

'Since England put us there,' returned the younger man catching the meaning instantly. (pp. 81–2)

IRRECONCILABLES

So saving Society—which was much the same thing as saving the country house—was possible through economic reform, including the welcoming of trade and industry if absolutely necessary, but Somerville and Ross, MacSorley, Conyers, Tynan, and MacMahon were more at ease in the old dispensation of benefaction and with the old task of reconciliation, by which methods the severer political difficulties could be diverted and evaded.

So too was Stephen Gwynn (1864–1950), judging by his combined issue-novel and romance, *The Old Knowledge* (1901), in which friendships and mutuality represent the best hope of saving lower-case Irish society—indeed, southern Ireland itself—if not Society spelt big, which in any case cannot be saved in its present form. The novel is that of a Revivalist and nationalist (as James Joyce called him in a review of one of Gwynn's books of Irish essays)[39] and sets great store by the untapped pagan wisdom of the Irish peasant and his vigorous political desire for justice on the land. At the same time, the representative of the gentry, Colonel Lisle, though yesterday's man, is an engaging fellow who, one feels, must be welcomed somehow into the coming Ireland. Moreover, there is an alternative offered to these two competing dispensations (one past, one future) and that is individual freedom and fulfilment which take the female form of the New Woman philosophy. To complicate things still further, there can be, it seems, an irrational and darker side to the compounding of the peasants' 'old knowledge' and the Revivalists' 'modern mysticism.' The tall order is harmony between these Irish oppositions which Gwynn in his person and public life seemed to embody. Born in Rathfarnham (now a suburb of Dublin), his father was a Protestant minister who became Professor of Divinity at Trinity College Dublin, and his mother the daughter of William Smith O'Brien, a Protestant landowner and Young Irelander. Gwynn was educated at Oxford and became a journalist in London, a prolific travel writer, a member of the Irish Parliamentary Party, nationalist MP for Galway, and a Redmondite who later and appropriately fought in the Great War as a Connaught Ranger.[40] Yet on reading Gwynn's very fine essays, one feels (perhaps unfairly) that harmony was won—or at least attested—by dint more of will, intellect, and a sense of justice than of natural feeling, and the difficult simultaneous pursuit of all of these is what his novel is about.

Gwynn maintains in the novel, as he does in his essays, a critical distance from the country-house milieu, but his sympathy for the country-house idea—later elaborated by Elizabeth Bowen—is considerable. Colonel Lisle belongs to a passing era yet he is 'indigenous to the soil in his big house' (Ballinderry House); unlike the English country houses, his house supports life 'so perfectly centred in one atmosphere'.[41] Like MacMahon's Thady, Lisle knows that his continued prosperity and status depend on English policy and is aware that new and detrimental orders, as it were, are coming through from the metropolis. Not surprisingly, then, *The Old Knowledge* avails itself of several of the fictive motifs of the country-house genre. Millicent Carteret is a young Englishwoman living in London, a Slade School graduate who wishes to earn her living by her art. Seeking a painting holiday, she takes it into her head to go to Ireland where she knows no one, preferably a part of Ireland 'where no one had ever read a book or painted a picture' (p. 4), and so fetches up in the wilds of Co. Donegal, a Visitor to Ireland (type four). She is 'the modern young lady—the young lady with a taste for adventure', a budding New Woman who fishes, rides a bicycle, and is unafraid to travel alone. In Ireland—'decidedly Ireland was very unlike Bayswater'—she quickly comes under the spell of the charming peasants who are instantly friendly and natural: 'There was no constraint accompanying the perfect deference with which these peasants treated their guest' (p. 12). She is initiated into the 'old knowledge', what Wood-Martin called 'the elder faiths' of Ireland: visions, lore, and beliefs of the kind that became stock properties of the Revival.[42] One in particular becomes important in the novel, the peasant belief that if harm came to a likeness (or portrait) the harm would transfer itself to the subject; thus the peasants avoid having their likeness taken. (A kind of Irish voodoo that Wilde inverts in *The Picture of Dorian Gray* when harm by the subject is transferred to the likeness while the subject remains outwardly unscathed.) Carteret also becomes entangled in a love triangle formed by her simultaneous attachment: first to Frank Norman, Colonel Lisle's nephew and a nationalist of sorts, a companionable and sympathetic man whom she meets at first strictly on the level of intellect and class identity; then to Owen Conroy, a Catholic who was once a schoolteacher but is now an apiarist teaching bee-keeping as a cottage industry (Irish rural self-help), a mystic who works on the Lisle demesne but who 'stands for the new order' (p. 69) opposed to such estates.

Carteret is a kind of 'sensitive' and is drawn to Conroy's combination of peasant lore and his AE-like mysticism: like AE, Conroy has an 'uncanny' talent as a painter of the mystical entities he sees and he commends Millicent to canvas as an intense flame, representing what he believes to be her hidden and essential womanhood, passionate but unfulfilled. Carteret embodies at first both English ignorance of the real Ireland into the grievances of which she must be initiated, and by implication the shortcomings of English culture: reason and class-consciousness, notwithstanding her unfocused feminism and artistic temperament. But she has an 'instinct of sympathy' for Conroy's visionary intensity and for Ireland, though she has no time for politics. Frank Norman is jealous of the growing intimacy between Millicent and his friend Conroy, yet is sure that a relationship between them is impossible because of their differences of class and worldview: Conroy is a peasant and 'other'. She does not thank him for this observation and she recoils from Frank's touch: 'Instincts in her older than the sympathy born of intellectual admiration woke and stirred' (p. 232). The romantic attraction of Irish mystique is a cultural phenomenon Gwynn is both distant enough from and close enough to for it to be a component of his novel. By erecting such a barrier between peasant and middle class, Norman is violating what appears to be the thematic dynamic of the novel's own ideal: the growth of bonds between characters that should surmount or dissolve the barriers of nationality, social class, sex, temperament, religion, and politics (and along the way solve the Irish Question). 'Likeness beyond the differences' would appear to be the novel's thematic motto (p. 127), creating a pun when 'likeness' here means similarity and elsewhere 'image'.

Yet tension and triangle remain, for Norman's naturalness (congeniality and ease with the here and now), so unlike Conroy's straining visions of the other-world, will pay off. Indeed, Conroy, it seems, is discovering his own natural manhood; this lonely man is falling in love with Millicent, and thus threatens his own *raison d'être*, hindering his visions of invisible beings, she being a desire on *this* side of the veil. After speaking at an 'agrarian league' meeting in order to impress her (crying up Irish grievances, evictions, and forced emigration), he decides to become politically involved in order to surmount the worldly barrier between them, to become important enough to propose to her without its seeming a peasant's hopeless fantasy. She discourages him, and when she is forced in her straightforward English way to disabuse him of any romantic interest between them, he takes her to task and she contrasts this with Frank's 'ease of equal companionship' (p. 242). Her realization that he seeks to enslave her is vindicated for the reader when Conroy retreats to her painted likeness, sure that even were she to marry Norman, she would come back to Conroy, his ownership of the painting giving him possession of its subject. Not only does Conroy prove in his strange thoughts to be 'beyond sympathy', but his belief that Millicent embodies 'the woman's faculty to give rather than to take' (pp. 133–4) sadly misreads his emancipated beloved.

It is with Frank Norman that Millicent can be a New Woman, whereas commitment to Conroy would be a reversion to some older peasant femininity she rejects. Even before she leaves for London she knows she will say 'yes' to Norman's proposal but she insists on returning to Ballinderry House to accept him. Yet Gwynn is still pursuing reconciliation and the surmounting of barriers. When she sees Conroy again, Millicent persuades him to try to realize himself, to abandon predatory mystical ideas; he agrees and together they consign her likeness to the flames, thereby freeing him, since, as she told him, the painting was really his self-portrait: Millicent Carteret as Visitor to Ireland is an agent at least of symbolic resolution, certainly bringing England closer to Ireland in general, to the Anglo-Irish in particular. Then back to Ballinderry House where she and Frank are described as resembling an 'early Victorian' engaged couple, a curious reversion to the country-house genre and shelving of the New Woman way forward. Their love and vision of happiness are said to be a kind of knowledge as old as Conroy's.

In the light of Gwynn's cultural revivalism and interest in a New Ireland, it might be necessary for two reasons to see this as a merely novelistic denoument rather than a figurative agenda. First, as late as 1918, Gwynn thought that the Anglo-Irish could be reconciled to Ireland only by acknowledging that through their acquaintance with peasant Ireland 'we gained also our real knowledge, in so far as we ever had it, of the countryside, the traditional wisdom, the inherited way of life'. In this essay, chiefly devoted to Somerville and Ross ('Yesterday in Ireland'), he was convinced that even they must have known all along that the real worth of their fiction lay in their instinct for the poetry which in Gaelic-speaking Ireland 'sits in rags by roadside and chimney corner'.[43] Second, he had already decided by 1913 that the position of the gentry had been false from top to bottom and decided on reflection that the turning point in their fortunes had been when they failed to rebel during the Famine when the government failed to implement measures to prevent starvation among the people. (He thought that this failure drove his grandfather Smith O'Brien to desperate insurrection.) But in any case, Gwynn thought that with the Act of Union 'the whole body of the Irish gentry found themselves inevitably estranged from the heart of Ireland',[44] which is to posit a deep systemic alienation and an explanation for the nostalgia for pre-Act of Union Ireland we find pervading many country-house novels. He writes in his 1918 essay: 'Leadership resting on ownership is gone now, dead as the dodo' (p. 113). But apart from emulating the hearty and productive Ulstermen, those admired by Martin Ross who journeyed to Belfast to sign the Ulster Covenant in 1912 pledging opposition to Irish Home Rule, Gwynn here offers only what he had already offered in The Old Knowledge. (He might be thinking of his own Colonel Lisle; in the novel, Frank Norman tries to explain to Millicent the apparent discrepancy between the Colonel's abstract bigotry and anti-Irishness and his actual patriotism and toleration.) That is, recognition of the need 'to restore the old ways, the old friendships— the need to bring back the gentry to their old uses in Ireland, and to so much of leadership as should be theirs by right of fitness' (p. 110). It doesn't quite add up, or blueprint a genuine reconciliation, and meanwhile one wonders how the New Woman philosophy is to square with traditional Irish wisdom and old Irish knowledge.

Gwynn tried again to depict convincingly reconciliation between gentry and peasantry, landowners and tenantry, this time removing the action to 1761 and 1779. Irish nature, though (and Donegal nature in especial), is above and beyond political division at any time and as in *The Old Knowledge*, *John Maxwell's Marriage* (1903) obliquely shows in fine descriptions of landscape and fishing the kind of available Irish riches political discord is both violating and squandering. Here, though perhaps in too close focus, is the landscape reproaching Maxwell, as it were, as he prepares to go into exile:

As he trotted out of the gate, flinging coins in profusion to the people of the lodge, and pushed on along the road by the base of Slievemor, and then, turning to the left, took the bend towards Carrig and Lanan bridge, the eyes of all dumb things were bright to woo him. Bell heather stood up in clumps, the smaller, prouder, stronger kind glowing purple, the larger and less rigid blooming pink. They sprang in bright patches among straying bramble blossom, or through trails of honeysuckle; they contrasted with the soft gold of furze, with the clearer, more golden glory of broom; they set off, and were set off by, the young olive-green of bog myrtle. And where there were hedgerows there were roses; some white and small flowered—some the faint, pale, delicate trailing stars that all Britain knows; but many, too, were of a kind peculiar to northern Ireland, strong and vivid pink, vivid as the purple heather, lovely at the full spread of their petals, exquisite in the bud that reddened deeper and darker to the tip.... [45]

The first Book of *John Maxwell's Marriage* portrays the very bad old days, with two villainous Donegal landlords: a tyrannous Protestant, James Nesbit, and a renegade Catholic, Sir Garrett Lambert, who came into his father's estate when he turned Protestant, his conversion, in agreement with the Penal Laws (which were passed between 1695 and 1728 and which legalized and enforced sectarianism), one of which stipulated that a Catholic estate must be divided among the sons unless the eldest son 'turned' in which case he inherited the entirety. In the midst of, and somehow under the malign umbrella of, the whole rotten system, two brutal and mercenary marriages are contracted in the Protestant family, one drunkenly and forcibly effected when John Maxwell is jilted at the altar by Mary Nesbit in favour of a local and expatriate rebel Catholic whose father Nesbit had hunted from the region. These marriages demonstrate the distortion of patriarchalism and capitalism that Gwynn apparently thinks the system depended on. Maxwell is immediately remorseful for accepting Nesbit's offer of Mary's sister in lieu, and the following day he makes to his horrified bride the astonishing amendatory gesture of giving his entire estate to her (which includes ownership of the mortgage on her father's estate) and leaving the country. The selfishness and possessiveness of the Anglo-Irish landlord are inverted in Maxwell's case to become altruism and atonement. But Isabella is scarred by her abuse, becomes an absentee landlord, forecloses on her own father, rejects the baby she conceived when raped on her wedding night, and treats her tenants abominably; she both embodies and is the spawn of the inquity of the landlord system at the time. (Stephen J. Brown was of the opinion that the book's realism was not suitable for every kind of reader.)

Book II takes place at the time the Penal Laws are starting to be relaxed and when the American revolution is both advancing democracy and offering the occasion for revenge to evicted tenants who fled to America to escape poverty and injustice. Maxwell, like many Protestant Ulstermen (some of whom were evicted from Lord Donegall's estates in the 1770s), enlists in the cause of anti-British colonialism and returns to Ireland as an agent charged with discovering the ripeness of Ireland for revolution and helping French invasion and American conspiracy (it is entirely unripe in that regard, as the formation of the Volunteers is showing).[46] Revolution and disproportionate individual gestures such as Maxwell's clearly are not the answer, and Gwynn settles once again for personal reconciliation, of which there are several examples in the novel's plot. There is Mary Nesbit's elopement with a 'Papist' rebel, Hugh MacSwiney; she has learned some Irish herself, but it is love that trumps cultural difference. If romance fuels the elopement, it also suggests, against the run of realistic play, that Mary and her jilted lover should come together in some guise, and they do since she has returned from France with her son, Hugh, after her husband dies as a soldier of fortune in India. Mary is the guardian of Maxwell's daughter, her niece Grace, of whose existence he learns only after landing in Ireland. Hugh and Grace fall in love, Catholic with Protestant. Grace is reconciled (briefly) with her mother, Isabella, and with the father she blamed for her unhappiness. This historical romance with the 'strong colours' of realism, as Brown calls them, ends with the departure of Mary, her son, and Maxwell's daughter to join Maxwell in the United States, his daughter having chosen to live with him rather than with the unforgiving and sectarian Isabella. American-style democracy, removal of the gross injustices of the landlord system, inter-personal relations in aid of a new reconciliatory nationalism: these seem to be Gwynn's hopes and prescriptions for Ireland and the plots of romances, contemporary or historical, were a favourable medium for their expression.

Elizabeth Hart faced the stern task of reconciliation four-square in her novel, *Irreconcilables* (1916). The oppositions to be reconciled in the novel echo those in *A Girl of Galway*: two families, a landlord and his tenants, and a father and son. But for good measure, Hart adds Protestants and Catholics, nationalists and unionists (often implicit in the other novels), natives and settlers, Old Catholic patriots and Gaelic Leaguers, rich and poor, and (without the industry) the aristocracy and the middle class, the middle-class family in this case being the Catholic family.

Like Tynan's novel, *Irreconcilables* is chiefly set in Co. Galway (called 'Galwayshire'!) where the Duke of Galwayshire has his seat, Tirullem. We meet him as an affable man yet he is hated as a largely absentee landlord and leader of the unionists. His nationalist and Catholic counterpart is Dr John Ryan, brother of a member of the Irish Parliamentary Party. The novel depicts forms of reconciliation that are promising only at the outset but prove failures. Kate Ryan, the surgeon's daughter, may like a Thurston character rail against the narrowness of Irish middle-class life and be entirely indifferent to the Gaelic League (whose meetings we attend as readers), and exhibit the restlessness of an Irish New Woman, but she is steely in her resolve to remain Catholic and takes the side of Cardinal Byrne who forbids her marriage to a Protestant, Sisgismund Hastings, Chief Secretary in the Westminster administration. Another mixed relationship, between the Duke's daughter and an affable Catholic nationalist, is cut short when Tom Hackett dies prematurely. Although romantic and sexual relations imply in their significance the wider and troublingly divided society, Hart frustrates the easy notion of the mixed marriage as a symbolic resolution of Irish differences, a symbolism that was always going to appeal to Protestant more than to Catholic writers. The Duke's third son, Lord Gerald McWilliam, transgresses his heritage more than does Kate. He asks his father not to give him money derived from tenants' rents; he becomes a determined democrat, and earns his living as a 'grinder' (tutor) of 'middle-class boobies' (as his father sees them). Like his sister, he learns Irish from the servants, joins the Gaelic League (she does, too), and changes his name to Garret Williamson the better to advance his transgression of inherited boundaries. The Duke diagnoses in his son 'inflammation of the conscience' and indeed the novel seeks to show that mere volition cannot enable the well-intentioned individual to leap the social and political chasms in Ireland.[47] When the true identity of the McWilliam cultural converts comes out there is a tragic price to pay, giving renewed and urgent substance to the novel's title, and the story ends on a new and now merely exploratory note of reconciliation. This was apparently Hart's only novel and it is dense enough in its social and political permutations to escape a charge of superficiality. It is probable that the author's own religious conviction produced a feedback, insisting on a limit of tolerance and reacting against the wish-fulfilment contained in all those good intentions that were as numerous in Ireland as ill-deeds and evil thoughts.

POUNDS AND RUPEES

In Conyers's *The Financing of Fiona*, the title character's paying guests are strangers but Kathleen Conroy in *Lismoyle: An Experiment in Ireland* (1914) by B. M. Croker (1849–1920) has no compunction, times being what they are, in charging her niece a nominal fee when Rhoda Kyle, half Irish, comes from England for a six-month visit.[48] After all, Lismoyle, in the west of Ireland, once a fortified castle, 'is a ruin now', her aunt ('Madame' Conroy—'there has never been a Mrs. at Lismoyle') tells orphaned Rhoda by letter, and if Rhoda 'can put a few pounds a week into the family purse, we shall all be on the pig's back'. Rhoda's English aunt finds the letter 'vague and impulsive' and adds: 'Oh, by all accounts the Irish are different to other people; you'll soon discover that', just as Lady Codington in *The Financing of Fiona* was sure that funny things happened in Ireland (the novel proves that they do but they are good— a tacit proposition that flew in the face of contemporary happenings on the very land her characters are splendidly hunting over). Rhoda's aunt is going on a grand tour of the far east, necessitating the farming out of her niece to her Irish relations. She fears Rhoda will be besieged by every fortune-hunter in 'Ireland, where men are notoriously good-looking, fascinating, and adven-turous'.[49] So Rhoda the 24-year-old fashionable Society heiress—she comes into her money the next year—will pretend to be poor while in Ireland; she will play the poor relation and in that role get to know the Irish who might otherwise be frightened of her; for her own part, her Aunt Kathleen is not the 'Madame' of Lismoyle at all, but the widow and second wife of the previous landowner, whose heir and present landowner is Kathleen's stepson, Niel Conroy; she is a good-looking flibbertigibbet and is often absent, seeking good times in Dublin and elsewhere. English–Irish relations get off to a mutually deceiving start.

So does the journey. Rhoda is accompanied by her maid Parker, who has an idea 'that Ireland was a country where it rained a good deal, and the natives were given to quarrelling'. On 'the long Irish mail from Euston' Rhoda feels already the queer pull of Ireland. 'Was it the call of her Irish blood? Was it heredity stretching out its long arms?' This is the magic-spell-of-Ireland idea that we've already encountered. In any event, it promises to be a fuller experi-ence than Rhoda expects. An acquaintance had drawn for her 'a disheartening

picture of a most distressful country'. At Kingstown she and Parker board the
wrong train, an 'emigrant train' going to Queenstown and they travel with a
rambunctious group of emigrant girls led by a returned American on her way
back to the US; they watch scenes of 'harrowing farewells' at stations along the
line before alighting to catch the train back to Kingstown and thence to the west
(pp. 24, 27, 28). Niel Conroy later generalizes from such scenes when he tells
Rhoda: 'Steady emigration drains Ireland year after year. There's not enough
employment to go round. Down in the south, we have few manufactures, and
there's little or no amusement for the young people. I remember when there
was dancing at the Cross on Sundays. They have done away with that now, as
well as wakes.' The devotional revolution exacted its puritanical price. On their
way from the station to Lismoyle, Rhoda remarks on the emptiness of the
landscape. It is harvest time and the inhabitants are getting in the hay, but in
any case 'Crowds have gone away in thousands, and hundreds of thousands.
Fine upstanding boys and girls' (p. 48).

The jarvey recalls his grandfather's picture of the hunting, racing, and
dancing at Lismoyle in days past and even Kathleen when her husband was
alive entertained royally in the house. But now most of the estate 'had been
sold under the Land Act, and Lismoyle was now shrunken to nine hundred
acres, indifferently enclosed by the dilapidated walls of the demesne'. This is
what Niel Conroy found on return from the army and unlike his stepmother
he spends all his energy and time trying to save the house from ruin and weed.
(Like Mulholland, Croker clearly believes in the essential virtue of industriousness and thrift in Ireland.) When the Land Act broke up the estate, more
than half of the receipts went to pay off debts; and he is too chivalrous to tell
Rhoda that her aunt receives money—for nothing—from the estate. Lismoyle
is not alone in its decay; Kilbeggan House too is now a 'great dilapidated
mansion' and Mrs Donovan explains that 'what used to be called the landed
gentry, are now gentry without land. They can't afford to occupy great
barracks that soak up a lot of servants, and so the big places fall to pieces'.[50]
Showing Rhoda the countryside around involves taking her to see the picturesque ruins of a local Big House.

Nevertheless, this novel like others that chart the decline of the country
house depicts the life of Society, however restricted in theory. Money is at the
centre of a chain that includes the links of property, legacy, matchmaking,
marriage, and family hierarchy. Love is usually presented as it is here (Niel's
growing love for Rhoda, hers for him) as outside or beyond or hostile to this
chain of relations but in fact is another link in the chain, linking romance to
marriage and marriage to property.[51] And where there is poverty there are
charity and patronage. Rhoda's decision to reveal her imminent wealth and
devote money to the saving of Lismoyle makes of her a recurring figure in the

popular novel: the *deus ex machina* (arriving from England across the water rather than from the wings or stage-drop) who rescues the country house from ruin.[52] Her gesture is a kind of charity and one, moreover, that originates in England though Ireland deserves it by contradicting the inclusive stereotypes; yes, the Irish are mystical and lazy, as Rhoda decides after twelve hours' observation, and yes, they are disorganized, good-hearted (mostly), talkative if not garrulous, but there are industrious, honest Irish like Niel Conroy who deserve the help (allegorically speaking) England can give Ireland. As it turns out, a genuine Romney painting is discovered in Lismoyle as articles for auction are being assembled and so the grand old past of the flourishing country house redeems the penurious present. Croker fictionally enacts Filson Young's idea that a bit of British help and some Irish self-help will turn the situation around. To better balance the equation, Ireland offers fresh air, a salubrious climate, and great riding and hunting, which Croker knows, though not quite as intimately as Conyers or Edith Somerville, and depicts spiritedly.

On politics Croker is resolutely silent; the genre discourages all but the most anodyne political observations; it is assumed that however 'other' Ireland may be, it is still part of the United Kingdom and the Empire (Conroy soldiered in India, as did Croker's husband.) On religion (and race) Croker is likewise virtually silent. We might generously take these absences, these abstentions, as evidence of the obliviousness Young saw in the ailing gentry in 1903. So pervasive is the social theme in this novel (and others) that the physical description of characters is often implicitly furnished through the eyes of a rivalrous or judgemental, ultimately class-based scrutiny. Only the economic woes of Ireland permit the novel to spill out beyond Society romance. The Irish middle class is absent (in these novels it is often present only as Dublin family solicitors, executors of wills and legacies). The improvident Kathleen Conroy thinks the Kyles inferior because they were rumoured to have made their money 'in trade' and though her perspective is otherwise implied to be wrongheaded, there is no even reluctant Tynanesque suggestion that trade could indeed help save Ireland from poverty: instead, charity, donation, and English money must do the job.[53] On the evidence of this novel, Croker would likely not have agreed with Tynan that the society at the centre of which sat the country house could retain its identity while reforming itself to accommodate business and industry; one wonders how far Tynan really believed it herself. In either case, the solution was imagined through the medium of romance and not, as a genuine belief in trade and industry might have required or encouraged, through the medium of fictional realism.

In a novel by Croker published the year before *Lismoyle*, and a work much superior to it, *In Old Madras* (1913), the difference between Ireland and India is assumed by means of the presence of a few Irish characters. Ireland, after all, is one of the home countries. But there is also an implicit and contrary assumption of similarity (both are countries of the Empire) that is expressed by the reappearance of thematic motifs even when Croker changes setting, including a sense of an ending that afflicts the Anglo-Indians as it did the Anglo-Irish. These motifs are rather more specific than those belonging generally to the English as well as Irish country-house novel or Society-romance, both of which *In Old Madras* is.

This hugely readable novel follows a young ex-soldier who travels from England to India to find his uncle, who disappeared in India years before but left instructions for his nephew's income (which he still receives), though his nephew suspects that in fact he will find his uncle's murderer masquerading as the dead man and enjoying his wealth. The way in which this novel transposes to India many of the stage effects, props, and furniture (sometimes the literal furniture) of the country-house novel and Society-romance demonstrates both the formulaicness and adaptability of these genres. Just as Niel Conroy returned from service in India to find a dilapidated Lismoyle (of which he is caretaker by default), so Captain Geoffrey Mallender finds himself caretaker though not owner of Mallender Court in England, a house and estate which his recently dead father let fall into virtual dereliction and which young Mallender does not have the money to restore on behalf of his vanished uncle, the legal owner. Now by voyaging to India on a quest to find his uncle or uncle's impersonator, Mallender violates a condition of his income, which is to stop the instant he makes inquiries as to his uncle's whereabouts, which he does when, reversing Conroy's direction of travel, he presents himself at the offices of Brown, Brown and Co., Madras, his uncle's solicitors. The plight of Mallender Court simmers in the British background to the young captain's Indian adventures and exploits.

Mallender's manhunt—a detective story that becomes a quasi-romantic quest—is begun against the wishes of his relations in Madras, who try to stall him or deflect him from a 'wild-goose chase' from which he stands to lose all his income and which will rattle old bones of the past that would be best left undisturbed. He has already served for a short time in north-west India (with the 'Warlock Hussars') but it is on this private expedition to southern India that he comes to know, and love, the exotic land. His uncle's solicitors proving uncooperative and refractory, Mallender engages through another firm of smart lawyers a private detective agency, Jaffer & Co. of Hyderabad, but does not set out on his mission for some time, having been promised balls and gymkhanas and lured into polo and engaging society at the home of his dead mother's cousin, Freddy Tallboys; Hooper's Gardens is a suburban Indian version of our familiar country houses: 'these houses', Mallender is told, '—sort of nabobs' palaces—built by merchants in the Fort, were where they took refuge during the long-shore winds, such as we have today'.[54] At Hooper's Gardens he falls for the charms of the very beautiful if shallow and self-seeking widow, Lena Villars, and it is some time before he begins his manhunt in earnest. He has even joined the Tallboys in their seasonal trans-humance, removal to the hills for the hot season, the family and their friends lingering at a hill station in the Blue Mountains while Woodford, the Tallboy's 'country house', is made ready for them.[55] Croker's description of the trek that Mallender elects to make on horseback in order to escort Nancy Brander, is atmospheric and has, of course, its temperate Irish equivalents.

The heat, in the narrow gorge at the foot of the mountains, was stifling; the very bananas and bamboos looked wilted, and faint. As the pair rode between dense masses of acacia, babul trees, Palmyra palms, and thickets of heavy jungle, their horses were bathed in sweat, there seemed scarcely a breath of air; but by gradual degrees, as they mounted the rocky old road with its endless twists, and sudden steep ascents, the dank hot-house atmosphere fell away, and mile by mile they ascended into another, and cooler, climate. The narrow bridle-path lay through a primeval forest, carpeted in places with moss and maiden-hair; here and there, the tree-trunks were hidden by gigantic ferns, the sound of running water was never absent, crystal clear streams splashed and tumbled and made tinkling music in the dim light, as they hurried down the hill-side, through a tangle of rock, twisted roots, and creepers. Meanwhile, the riders breasted a precipitous road, that carried them from the tropics to an English summer; heavily laden coolies, donkeys carrying wood, and now and then a portly native on a pony, were all they encountered as they proceeded and fitfully discussed the recent season, and its most interesting, or remarkable events. (pp. 132–3)

But when a message from Jaffer & Co. tells him his uncle has been found (one of several false leads he is to endure), Mallender determines to return to the plains, to Madras, and begin his mission in earnest, which requires his resistance to the pleasures of Madras Society and the pre-nuptial advances of the lovely Mrs Villars in order to do so.

Mallender's introduction to Madras Society is also the reader's introduc-tion. The Visitor to Ireland has become the Visitor to India and the author takes the opportunity the device offers to enlighten her chiefly English readers about an unfamiliar land. Early on, Croker uses a dinner party cleverly to display for us a cross-section of Anglo-Indians. The reader's initial impression is of a society that is unreal (there is a gallery of eccentric and colourful characters) and the final impression is of a society living on borrowed time, like the Anglo-Irish. Throughout the novel Croker registers, sometimes poignantly, the passage of years. Fanny Tallboys collects Georgian furniture that was imported from England by Anglo-Indians but became 'rubbish' when the 'palmy days' passed 'and the Victorian Age dawned' (p. 50), as though Georgian taste and pre-Victorian furniture expressed the heyday of the Raj. Freddy is 'an infatuated Madrassi', speaking fondly of Clive and Hastings and 'so jealous, for the old, old original [Madras] Presidency' (p. 61). Colonel Harris ('20th Carnatic Rifles')[56] laments the passing of the hard-drinking soldiery of yesteryear and disdains the current young fellows who are 'all for tea and Pérrier water' (p. 116), his heroic ghosts an echo of yesteryear's roistering Anglo-Irishry. In one episode, Mallender and friends on horseback 'pass through that deplorable spectacle, an abandoned [coffee] estate. Here, the land was overrun with a climbing prickly plant, the desolate bungalow was dismantled, and the pulping-house a ruin' (p. 302). Following yet another false lead, Mallender travels to Wellunga, 150 miles from Madras, twice decimated by cholera and long abandoned. When he surveys the dead cantonment, he finds it remarkable that once again his search 'had brought him amidst ruins, and solitude' (p. 211). As he gazes around the tombs and gravestones, he asks himself 'Is anything in the world more forsaken and forgotten, than an up-country burial-place in India, where rest unremembered and unknown, the unconscious builders of Empire?' (p. 213). He reads on the headstones the identifying inscriptions dating back to the late eighteenth century, a roll-call of British soldiers long dead and regiments long disbanded. It is a moving scene.

The contender for being his lost uncle is immediately disqualifiable, turning out to be the remarkable nonagenarian, General Richard Beamish, living with his second family at the cantonment and with whom Mallender lingers, enjoying his learned company and the company of his beautiful daughter Tara. Born in 1818, the General when he arrived in India met an officer who had known Clive; he served at the siege of Delhi (1857), witnessed the siege of Cawnpore (1857), and served in Afghanistan. No doubt in order to make him a composite historical British soldier, the narrator also calls him a veteran of the siege of Lucknow (1857), Aliwal, the rebellion at Jhansi (1857), and the subsequent battle of Gwalior (p. 279). Beamish talks with spirit about distant events in Portuguese and British history in the subcontinent: the siege of Bednur, the town demolished in 1784 by Tippu Sultan ('Tippoo'), the son of Hyder Ali ('Haidir Ali'), and (Thomas Arthur) Lally, of the Galway Lallys, who fought for the French in India against the British.[57] But now he deplores war and is cognizant of what we might call the 'Ozymandias' truth of history. When Mallender remarks that there are few signs now in India of Alexander, the Moghul Empire, and the Cholas (a Tamil dynasty of southern India), the old General replies: 'I dare say there won't be much sign of *us* after a couple of thousand years. We shall leave no great monuments, temples and fortresses, such as still recall ancient Hindostan' (p. 244). Croker is rattling a few bones herself. And one can't help but think that the historical melancholy that colours *In Old Madras* derives in part from Croker's Edwardian Anglo-Irish consciousness, coming as she did from a class and caste itself under siege, in a reversal of those military engagements common in imperial history.

Before it concludes with a horrifying denouement, Mallender's hunt is interrupted by irresistible diversion or halted by dead ends which allows Croker to prospect as a narrator among fascinating and often remote Anglo-Indian characters, Mrs Villars, General Beamish, Major Rochfort, Miss Sim, Mota, Anthony (Mallender's 'boy') among them. It also allows her to fascinate her reader by Anglo-Indian history,[58] and not surprisingly her mostly but not entirely offstage Indian characters are not seen with the same vividness or inwardness as her British characters. Her novel's storyline cleverly plots a transect through Anglo-Indian culture, with a small atlas of place names (Panjeverram, Bonaghherry, the Neilgherries, Ootacamund, Vellore, Banga-lore, Mysore, Mercara, Conoor, Mettapollium, Trichinopoly, Seegoor Ghat, Coorg, Travancore), references to the choir of languages spoken in southern India, including Canarese, English, Tamil, and Telagu, and a generous but careful deployment of Anglo-Indian words (without their seeming like mere currants in a fruitcake), among them *shikar, punkah, gharry, huka, chuprassy, chunam, cooltie, gram, pilaws, dhoby* (or *dhobi*), *ayah, shabash, chota-hazri* (or *chotah-hazri*), *puckaroed, sholah, budmash, dirzee, sola topee, gosha, ghat, charpoy, dâk, tonga, Dâl, chokra, shako, mohur, maidan, ragi, cholum, khol, nullah, Begum.* Other words were then, or became afterwards, familiar words in the English vocabulary at home: *gymkhana, divan, mulligatawny, bungalow, sahib, pucca* (pukka), *wallah, zitar* (sitar).[59] However short a time Croker lived in India, she was no mere tourist and seems to have had the novelist's gift for quick and penetrating insight into foreign sensations and experiences.

At the same time, her brave descriptions of southern Indian landscape are at key moments consciously undermined by an admission of the failure of words to capture what is being contemplated, a failure due—as it is in Irish narrations from the non-native perspective—to what is indigenously ineffable, exotic, and spellbinding. The spell of Ireland becomes the spell of India and beggars language and metaphor. 'As [Mallender] gazed, he began faintly to realise the fascination of this old mysterious land, with its subtle appeal, that baffles all attempts at description' (p. 251). Later, as Mallender seeks respite, 'that curious smell, beyond analysis, that belongs to the East hung in the air' (p. 334). This, as it is in equivalent admissions by Beatrice Grimshaw in the South Seas, is a sincere tribute to a landscape incomparably more diverse, opulent, and spiritual than English landscape for which the English language and mind have been shaped. In the light of this attested linguistic helplessness, it is not surprising that in Croker's India, as in the Ireland of many of our writers, the supernatural flourishes, chiefly in the guise of spirits and ghosts from the past.

Of course, just as the use of Anglo-Indian dialect words could be regarded as a facile appropriation of native language, a kind of insinuation into what is culturally other, the implicitly self-justifying language of the colonizers and colons,[60] so the claim of the supernatural could be regarded as a tactic by which the occupied land is deprived of an exclusively material reality and an acknowledgement that this material reality is being exploited if not plundered. Even the admission of language's descriptive failure could be sniffed at as an aesthetic tactic by which to justify imperialism and an alien presence. In an echo of Grimshaw's use of Kipling's image of the red gods calling, Croker's epigraph for *In Old Madras* is from the same writer: 'When you've 'eard the East a-calling/You never' heed nought else.' But we recall that E. M. Forster, no friend or advocate of Empire, likewise in his novel *A Passage to India* (1924) found spiritual India and its landscape beyond the reach of language and in a crucial and famous scene fell back upon an ineffable sound from the Marabar Caves. Moreover, although it is possible to oppose colonialism on all kinds of cogent grounds, literary opponents of colonialism often base their opposition in part on the essential exoticness of the colonized places. But if the presence of explorers, travellers, settlers, colonizers, and imperialists is deplored on the grounds of the untranslatable otherness of the land where they illegitimately place themselves and which ought to be inviolable, it would be illogical to condemn, as well, their recognition and expression of that otherness. (We could use Said's Orientalism as a convenient hostile shorthand for this recognition and expression.) Actually, as in the Irish novels, *In Old Madras* displays the narrator's love of India which even the shocking cruelty of the novel's denoument does nothing to diminish.[61]

Love for the colonized country, a succumbing to its mystery and charm, can be a mixed blessing; General Beamish thinks that India refused to release him from its hold when his soldiering days were over. Love can take the form of the visitor's or settler's going native, the most disturbing example of which in English literature might be Conrad's Kurtz, though lesser examples are there in Grimshaw. The way in which Mallender's uncle has had to go native is likewise disturbing. In Croker's novel a sub-theme is that India can absorb and ruin a man—even though that man will not be Croker's hero, young Geoffrey Mallender—and the fate of his uncle might for the moment make the reader remember Kurtz's cry, 'the horror, the horror'. In Croker's novel, there are soldiers and widows who go to earth in India, refusing to return to England. Going native also takes the less threatening but still morally dubious form of the double life, a variation on the figure of the Double which we will meet later and which was popular in late-Victorian and Edwardian fiction. Just as the exotic in imperial experience sponsored the notions of the mysterious, captivating, and supernatural, so its domestic logistics—the husband for long periods separated from his wife and children, the widow electing to stay in the colonies—could tempt the colonizer into a culturally and even legally double life—bigamy in the case of Major Rochfort, with a wife at home and a wife and family in India, and two generations of family, in England and India, in the case of General Beamish. If India could function as a kind of alter ego for England, so could Ireland, and the binary cultural and even psychological fission that is fundamental to colonialism is there in Croker's novel, though she contains and frames it by the pleasing spirality of the action, Mallender arriving in India from England and at the end of the novel returning to England but with the promise of return to the East, this time married and rich, he having been gifted heirdom to Mallender Court and so the means to restore it. Fine though *In Old Madras* is, it is the romance termini of love, marriage, and cultural restoration that tame Croker's vision and place it far beneath Conrad's.

NOTES

1. Introduction to *The Selected Letters of Somerville and Ross*, ed. Gifford Lewis (London: Faber, 1989), p. xxv. The oddity of the intimacy may have been the product of the isolation of the Irish country house in parts of the island. One imagines that the relationship between the large landowner and the tenantry in England may have been more 'normal', in part through the mediacy of the squirearchy and the greater number of social gradations between both ends of the spectrum; and perhaps the intimacy of landowner and tenantry was not as pronounced in more populous areas of rural Ireland.
2. Moore in a letter, quoted by Joseph Hone, *The Life of George Moore* (London: Gollancz, 1936), p. 107.
3. Tynan, *The Middle Years* (London: Constable, 1916), p. 211.
4. Jefferson Hunter considers the Edwardian English country-house novel in *Edwardian Fiction* (Cambridge, MA: Harvard University Press, 1982), pp.189–214.
5. Lauren Gillingham, 'Quality fish guides', *Times Literary Supplement*, 23 & 30 December 2005. Gillingham is reviewing *Silver Fork Novels, 1826–1841* (2005), ed. Harriet Devine.
6. On the Edwardian silver-fork novel, see Jefferson Hunter, *Edwardian Fiction*, pp. 49–50.
7. Baroness Burdett-Coutts (ed.), *Woman's Mission: A Series of Congress Papers on the Philanthropic Work of Women by Eminent Writers* (London: Sampson Lowe, Marston & Co., 1893), p. xv.
8. Malcolm Kelsall, *Literary Representations of the Irish Country House: Civilisation and Savagery Under the Union* (London: Palgrave, 2003), pp. 1–6.

9. The prevailing view of historians is that Gladstone's Ballot Act of 1872 helped liberate Irish voters from the intimidation of their social superiors (particularly tenants of country estates) by making balloting for parliamentary representation a secret affair, allowed them fearlessly to vote for parties other than the two main English parties, and greatly aided in the accumulation of nationalist electoral and suasive power. For a critical view of this orthodoxy, see Michael Hurst, 'Ireland and the Ballot Act of 1872', *The Historical Journal*, 8.3 (1965): 326–52. Available online at Journal Storage (Jstor), the scholarly journal archive.

10. See F. S. L. Lyons, *Ireland since the Famine* (1971; London: Fontana/Collins, 1973), pp. 160–223.

11. E. Œ. Somerville and Martin Ross, *Irish Memories* (London: Longmans, Green, 1918), pp. 154–5. Somerville usefully relates the land troubles from a personal perspective: pp. 28–40.

12. Anonymous ('Ignotus'), 'Irish Realities', *Blackwood's Edinburgh Magazine* 207 (March 1920): 347.

13. G. M. Trevelyan, *English Social History* (1942; Harmondsworth: Pelican Books, 1964), pp. 588–90.

14. MacMahon, *A Pitiless Passion* (New York: Macmillan, 1895), p. 136.

15. Conyers's dates are 1871–1943. However, although Brown in *Ireland in Fiction* dates her birth to 1871, her dates given in the *Fiction Mags Index* are 1863–1943. In the Princess Grace Library eirdata bibliography her maiden name is given as Spaight whereas Brown identifies her as the daughter of Colonel J. Blood Smyth. She married into the Castletown Conyers of Co. Limerick. According to PGL eirdata her husband went down on the *Lusitania*. Beside her fifty-five plus novels, she published stories in *Windsor Magazine*, *Saturday Evening Post*, and *Strand Magazine*.

16. Dorothea Conyers, *The Financing of Fiona* (London: George Allen & Unwin, 1916), pp. 9–10.

17. I discuss *The English Rogue* in my Introduction to *The Cambridge Companion to the Irish Novel*, ed. John Wilson Foster (Cambridge: Cambridge University Press, 2006), pp. 5–7.

18. Ina Ferris, *The Romantic National Tale and the Question of Ireland* (Cambridge: Cambridge University Press, 2002), pp. 11–13, 48.

19. In her novel for teenage girls, *A Wild Irish Girl* (1910), the prolific L. T. Meade reverses the motif. Young Patricia Redgold is sent to London from her tumble-down country house in Ireland, Carrigraun, where she lives with her impoverished grandfather (her father having been killed in the Boer War, her mother already dead) because the house is now for sale. She goes to live with her father's rich second-cousin whose husband is an MP and she herself a Society woman engaged in philanthropy. Patsy is a wild Irish girl: natural, free, frank, lover of the open air and of the poverty she's used to; to her new family (and their daughters and the other wealthy girls she meets) she simply appears rude, disobedient, headstrong, impossible. But they are secretly in love with her. There are lots of schoolgirl crushes in the story. Patsy really is Ireland in all its trying insolubility

and at the end she has to be 'good' and become a young lady and does so, voluntarily and without loss of face. She has to be broken in, which is the horsey metaphor Meade uses several times. Meade may or may not be aware of her subtext: that patience and charity on the part of England will eventually 'civilize' lovable but anarchic Ireland. The Lovels's astonishment that Patricia is willing to defy the entire family makes one think that at the back of Meade's mind is Ireland's incorrigible but admirable willingness to defy the entire Empire (that putative family of nations), all the more astonishing in 1910.

20. Somerville and Ross, *Irish Memories*, p. 42. Gifford Lewis entitles the first chapter of her book on Somerville and Ross 'Somervilles and Martins—Cousins Innumerable': see *Somerville and Ross: The World of the Irish R.M.* (New York: Viking, 1985), p. 17. See also Lewis, *Edith Somerville: A Biography* (Dublin: Four Courts Press, 2005), p. 96.

21. *An Irish Cousin* was first published in 1889 under the names of Martin Ross and 'Geilles Herring', Edith Somerville's early pseudonym; the novel was reissued in 1903, 1915, and 1925 under the names of Somerville and Ross.

22. Theo's background was inspired by Violet Martin's mother's friendship with her Canadian cousin, Archer Martin, who belonged to that Ballynahinch (Galway) branch of the Martin family that scattered after the Famine.

23. E. Œ. Somerville and Martin Ross, *An Irish Cousin* (1889; London: Longmans Green, 1905), pp. 11–12, 163.

24. See Violet Powell's discussion of the novel in *The Irish Cousins: The Books and Background of Somerville and Ross* (London: Heinemann, 1970), pp. 22–5.

25. Somerville and Ross, *Irish Memories*, pp. 130–1.

26. Catherine Mary MacSorley, *An Irish Cousin* (London: SPCK, 1901), pp. 73, 100, 109, 151–2.

27. I briefly discuss the medical, cultural, and religious late-Victorian doctrine of the open air in *Recoveries: Neglected Episodes of Irish Cultural History* (Dublin: University College Dublin Press, 2002), pp. 128–33, 143–4 n. 12.

28. In her Introduction to *The Selected Letters of Somerville and Ross* (London: Faber, 1989), which she edited, Gifford Lewis remarks that 'Somerville and Ross wrote of a time when the Anglo-Irish gentleman had gone away [presumably she means the soldiers and parliamentarians and deceased among them], or at least was only home on vacation, and the fort was being held by his mother and his sisters and his cousins and aunts. During this period powerful women came into their own, and in their fictional portraits of this type Edith and Martin excelled' (p. xxvi).

29. Conyers, *The Financing of Fiona*, pp. 108, 148, 150, 173, 195.

30. See Lewis, Introduction to *The Selected Letters of Somerville and Ross*, p. xxv.

31. Katharine Tynan, *A Girl of Galway* (London: Blackie and Son, 1901), p. 14.

32. According to W. E. Vaughan, writing of an Ireland a few decades earlier than the Ireland in Tynan's 1901 novel, 'it was widely believed that agents were often the cause of trouble between landlords and tenants' and this belief was expressed in fiction, Vaughan citing William Carleton's *Valentine M'Clutchy* (1845). But Vaughan adds: 'On the other hand, estate records show that landlords often

pressed agents to act more firmly' and this evenhandedness is how the issue shakes down in Vaughan's study, *Landlords and Tenants in Mid-Victorian Ireland* (Oxford: Clarendon Press, 1994), pp. 112–13. Tynan also sees both sides of the question when she has Sir Delvin admit to Bertha that he is in fact aware of the ongoing evictions of tenants in arrears (p. 175).

33. As often with Tynan's places and characters, there is a sectarian ambiguity about Corofin. The family appears to be Protestant but in the house are chairs made by the wife of Bertha's great-great-grandfather who was killed at Aughrim, presumably while in the service of King James who sat upon the chairs (p. 134). In Tynan, social class often blurs religious affiliation.

34. By the end of the novel, Bertha has become 'a writer of beautiful poetry and delicate poetic prose' (p. 384), as though becoming Tynan herself and lending the story the suggestion of spiritual and literary autobiography.

35. In the 1880s Capt. R. H. Prior-Wandesforde succeeded to the Kilkenny mine that had been a family business on the estate since 1637. (It closed down in 1969.) He has been described as 'a paternal autocrat who looked on the miners not so much as his employees but as his people'. By what is perhaps not coincidence, a commissioner who visited the mine in 1842 as part of an investigation into child labour was called Roper. See http://www.sip.ie/sip019B/history/history.htm

36. Katharine Tynan, *Dick Pentreath* (Chicago: A. C. McClurg; London: Smith, Elder, 1906), pp. 252, 140. In this novel there are glimpses of London's impoverished East End where Revd Semple ministers to the poor; this is the world of Meade's *A Princess of the Gutter* and Letts's *The Rough Way*.

37. Ella MacMahon, *The Job* (London: James Nisbet & Co., 1914), p. 336.

38. We will encounter later versions of the complaint that the educated and affluent were failing to reach England and were being outmanoeuvred by nationalists during the 1919–22 period.

39. See James Joyce, *The Critical Writings*, ed. Ellsworth Mason and Richard Ellmann (New York: Viking Press, 1964), pp. 90–2.

40. Patrick Maume has useful information on Gwynn's political activities in *The Long Gestation: Irish Nationalist Life 1891–1918* (1999).

41. Stephen Gwynn, *The Old Knowledge* (London: Macmillan, 1901), p. 56.

42. W. G. Wood-Martin, *Traces of the Elder Faiths of Ireland: A Handbook of Irish Pre-Christian Traditions* (1902).

43. Stephen Lucius Gwynn, 'Yesterday in Ireland', *Irish Books and Irish People* (1920; Freeport, New York: Books for Libraries Press, 1969), pp. 115–16.

44. 'The Irish Gentry', *Irish Books and Irish People*, pp. 87, 93.

45. Stephen Gwynn, *John Maxwell's Marriage* (London: Macmillan and Co., 1903), pp. 137–8.

46. This period in Ulster history, a period of complicated ideological cross-currents, is well recaptured in Andrew James's *The Nabob* (*Ninety-Eight and Sixty Years After*, 1911).

47. Elizabeth Hart, *Irreconcilables* (London: Andrew Melrose, 1916), pp. 471, 24. Like Ella MacMahon in *Vignettes* and the author of *Tales of the R.I.C.* (for both, see

below, Chapter 14), Hart seems to suggest the appearance during the rise of the Gaelic League and Sinn Fein of a new Irish type: the longhaired, blackhaired, sallow, and fanatical young man. They also throw a spotlight on the shop-boys and shop-girls who flocked to both of these organizations. In their maturity, their class eventually came to prop up the lower middle class that dominated the Irish Free State.

48. The Somervilles rented out Drishane House in the summer, as a result of which Edith Somerville asked her sister on one occasion if she and Violet Martin could come 'as p.g.s [paying guests] for a week': see Gifford Lewis, *Edith Somerville: A Biography* (Dublin: Four Courts Press, 2005), p. 250.

49. B. M. Croker, *Lismoyle: An Experiment in Ireland* (London: Hutchinson, 1914), pp. 12, 15.

50. Croker, *Lismoyle*, pp. 70, 149. Cf. the observation of the narrator of *An Enthusiast* (London: Longman's Green, 1921) by Edith Somerville: 'The position of landless landlord is now a familiar one' (p. 3). I discuss this novel in a later chapter.

51. Elizabeth Bowen succinctly places love in the economic situation of the country house, remarking that the house's financial needs took precedence over love-marriages: 'The Big House' in *The Mulberry Tree: Writings of Elizabeth Bowen*, ed. Hermoine Lee (London: Virago, 1986), p. 27.

52. In Mrs Hungerford's *Mrs Geoffrey* (1886), there is a reversal of the device when the Irishwoman Mona Scully is the saviour of an English country house.

53. In Meade's *A Wild Irish Girl*, the decaying country house Carrigraun is bought by Patricia Redgold's English relation, her father's second cousin's husband, the MP, so that it can be saved for Patsy. Incidentally, like Croker, Meade makes no inconvenient distinction between the Anglo-Irish and the native Irish. Patsy is intensely patriotic, though presumably Protestant. In one sense this is evasion on the part of these upper-class Protestant writers; in another sense the genres of schoolgirl fiction/country house–town house fiction require the ignoring of the distinction; in yet another sense, the evasion may be a harking back to the old Anglo-Irish patriotism that patriotically saw one nation, Ireland (for whom they, of course, were sole spokesmen).

54. B. M. Croker, *In Old Madras* (1913; New Delhi: Rupa & Co., 2002), p. 29. This republication is littered with typographical errors, due no doubt to the text having been imperfectly scanned from the original Hutchinson or Tauchnitz editions (both 1913) or the 1919 British reprint.

55. Evocative photographs of the Blue Mountains and some of the places Croker mentions, are available on the Internet, assembled as a private album which shows vestiges of the British presence: http://members7.clubphoto.com/vijayaraghhavan541321/1087214/guest.phtml Further photographs are available at http://community.webshots.com/album/73405027DhLGjy See also 'All India Tourist Information', http://www.trainenuiry.com/StaticContent/Tourist_Info/blue.html The Blue Mountains (the Nilgiris) came under British rule when Tippu Sultan fell in 1799. See also online 'To the Blue Mountains', an article (with historical information) in the *Magazine* of *The Hindu*, 17 March 2002.

56. There was in the British army in India a number of Carnatic infantries but not Carnatic Rifles: 'Carnatic' means 'of Southern India'. See 'List of Regiments of the British Indian Army (1903)', Wikipedia, a major entry.
57. I have discussed the soldiers from the north of Ireland who fought with distinction in India on the other side, i.e. for the British (being themselves British) in my Afterword to Andrew James (James Andrew Strahan), *The Nabob: A Tale of Ninety-Eight* (Dublin: Four Courts Press, 2002).
58. Croker sets Mallender to read 'Orme's "History of India" ' (p. 207) which might be Robert Orme's *History of the Military Transactions of the British Nation in Indostan* (1763–78) or the same author's *Historical Fragments of the Mogul Empire* (1782).
59. For a glossary of Anglo-Indian dialect words, see http://alphadictionary.com/directory/Specialty_Dictionaries/Dialects/
60. Perhaps it is odd that this objection or ideological reservation has not been more commonly levelled against J. M. Synge, Lady Gregory, and other Irish Revivalists who wrote a literary Hiberno-English, a part-real, part literary dialect outside their own class and language. Their dialect has tended, on the contrary, to be regarded as one of the ornaments and successes of the Revival. Such a linguistic reservation did, however, lie behind the nativist author and critic Daniel Corkery's once controversial critique of the Revival, *Synge and Anglo-Irish Literature* (1931).
61. Depending on the perspective of the critic, this love can be regarded as a virtue or a vice, a reaffirmation or a denial of the imperialist impulse and condition. I offer one novel in which it is clearly offered as a virtue. In her novel, *The Golden Rose* (1924), the Catholic Irish novelist (and friend of Yeats) Katharine Tynan introduces an English character in Dublin during the Great War, like this: 'The officer, a Major Constable, had a face, a personality, in which gentleness and strength were subtly mingled. It was a charming face; and its owner was highly intellectual, and in love with all things Irish, as the imaginative English had a way of being in those days'. *The Golden Rose* (London: Eveleigh Nash & Grayson, 1924), p. 147. The character's name suggests the character's almost representative Englishness while the heroine's meeting with him is at the Abbey Theatre (the urban centre of the Irish Literary Revival) at a performance of Yeats's *Cathleen Ni Houlihan.*

8

Tiercel and Lure: Love and Marriage

> This is an important book, the critic assumes, because it deals with war.
> This is an insignificant book because it deals with the feelings of women
> in a drawing-room.
>
> Virginia Woolf, *A Room of One's Own* (1928)

ENDURING LOVE

Love inspires for readers the daydream element of the romance novel, but in its
association with marriage it is a component of the sociology of the country-
house genre. Love frequently in the fiction succeeds to marriage, and marriage
is both a literal device whereby oppositions are resolved and multiplicities are
unified, and a figurative device whereby apparently unrelated problems, e.g. the
relations between the English and the Irish, are solved, at least for the nonce,
but sometimes, by symbolic projection, it is hoped for good.[1] We can speak in
such a context of the Marriage Answer as well as simply the Marriage Question.
Love and marriage are in many Irish novels from the early nineteenth-century
national tale onwards a social and even political good.

In several cases, however, love comes to the foreground of the novel and is
examined with a steadiness of gaze, not in its social or figurative guise, not as a
fashionable subject, but as an enduring subject, endlessly fascinating in its
own right and as a challenge to other drives and aspirations. Eleanor Alexander's *The Lady of the Well* (1906) bears comparison with Helen Waddell's
later and far better known *Peter Abelard* (1933) and covers similar historical
terrain. Alexander's novel is set in the thirteenth century, a century after the
setting of Waddell's, but both explore the sublime necessity and inconveni-
ence of the love we would call romantic. Both are historical novels but not of
the kind that Stephen J. Brown is interested in: i.e. novels set in an Irish past
which most of them use to justify or explain some sectional interest or
political philosophy still relevant at the time the novels are written.

The Lady of the Well is set during the campaign of the thrice ex-communicated Emperor Frederick II (1194–1250) against the papacy of Innocent IV who ascended the papal throne in 1243); the action begins near Pellegrino and shifts to Borgo St Domnino where Frederick has stationed himself. The Emperor is a character in the novel and ends it a broken-hearted and generous leader (in the real world he was to die soon after, on the eve of a battle he intended to be decisive). The hero is Bernart, a would-be troubadour, the inhabitants of whose village, including his mother, have been slaughtered as heretics (Albigensians) by the White Company, the army of the Crusade led by King Louis of France. His family in fact are not Albigensians but suffer alongside them; his father Romeus, servant of the Count of Provence, escaped the massacre, and Bernart becomes a wanderer.

But amidst this Alcockian world are entwined with a brightness of literary touch the themes of love and song. Bernart is an apprentice troubadour whose songs leave audiences cold because, he decides, he is not a master of love. He wanders in search of that mastery, resembling Chaucer's bachelor knight sent on his quest in 'The Wife of Bath's Tale' to find out what women want most, the answer to which will promote him to squire, a true knight; it is what love should mean to the troubadour that composes the novel's second theme and quest. A hermit, who turns out to be the troubadour Peter Vidal, thought to have been driven to the Holy Land by the unresponsiveness of the Lady Louve, tells Bernart that love is for the poet a science not a sentiment, whereas Bernart believes he needs a 'peerless lady' to love and to serve and of 'whom to sing', before he can earn his spurs, as it were, as a troubadour.[2] The hermit's words haunt Bernart throughout his quest which properly begins when he stops at a well to drink, sees his reflection, and suddenly the reflection of a beautiful woman who speaks to him of love while he is put under embargo not to turn to see her. He swears allegiance to her, and calls her My Lady of the Well for whom he will compose his songs. Lady and poet, reflection and youth, discourse on love and agree greatly on its nature: it has no part in treaties and agreement, policy and interest; 'all the symbols of petty adventure, and slavery, and captivity but degrade the dignity of love.' But Bernart goes farther and thinks that there is a love higher than that of the troubadours, the everlasting embrace of spirits; the visionary lady has taught him instantly the importance to love of the soul.

It is a scene as fine as anything in the folk-like work of Yeats and Stephens. There is a pause in the vision: 'A horrible profanity was in progress. An irreligious green frog had taken it into his head to paddle across the pond from underneath the near bank as he had done a hundred times before its consecration.' The frog collides with the poet's mouth; the poet strikes with his sword and its point goes to the heart of the reflected vision and he hears a faint cry. The reflected picture is shattered 'like the squares of mosaic on a workman's tray. It seemed as if there were the fragments of two poets, as if two ladies strove together in the broken ripples.' When the water recomposes itself the lady speaks differently of love, of her ownership of Bernart as her troubadour, of his homage; he will now be the troubadour of Countess Gemma and must go to Borgo St Domnino and present himself as such (pp. 31, 33, 34).

The married Countess (Gemma Pallavicini, soon to be widowed) will later elaborate on her notion of love as an arena in which the woman exhibits her ascendancy and accepts her lover's fealty. It is neatly demonstrated by Alexander in a scene in which Gemma flies her male peregrine and is 'roused to most enchanting excitement by the exhilaration of rapid movement, and by the display of power that women love, even if it be only in the subjugation of a horse, or the obedience of a bird'. The falcon's flight is masterfully caught:

The tiercel, at full pitch, was a dark spot in the brilliant blue that one could scarce look into and not close the eyes; his ringing flight seemed to have left a thin track which remained in spiral curves on the retina when the lids fell over the dazzled sight. Gemma whistled; the spot grew bigger; presently it spread to the perfect lines of graceful wings. The bird swooped to the lure dangling below him, and finally settled on the wrist of his mistress, with his wise eyes fixed on things man knoweth not, and fool's bells tinkling from leather bewits at his feet.[3]

The handsome lover in his eloquent illusion of freedom always returns to this mistress who is at the dominant hub of his world, the only alternative being the war of the sexes. Love (and by implication marriage), rather than being a positive and unalloyed good, is divisive for the sexes and, as in the early stages of Chaucer's Wife's Prologue to the 'Wife of Bath's Tale', a promoter of inequality of sexual power. The opposing idea is that of the first reflection: 'two hearts should be equal, two kings upon two thrones' (pp. 110, 112). For the vision had been twofold, Gemma elbowing away the young maiden, Adelaide.

Bernart will later be tried at the court of love, convoked by Countess Gemma, but earlier he is arraigned by the Emperor to stand trial as a troubadour (is he one?) because a soldier has accused him of being no poet but a spy from rebel Genoa. Either accuser or accused is wrong and he will die. Bernart is given twenty-four hours to compose a new song for the Emperor. The prescribed theme of the challenge song is 'the longing of a lover who sees his lady's face reflected in a deep well, and who may speak only to the reflection, for she herself is so far above him'; the poem is to be in the Limousin tongue and its structure is prescribed. Alexander has read her troubadours and gives us their argot: *jongleur, gigue, tornada, serena, alba, tenso, chanson redonda, volta, sestina*. The scene in which the soldier in the same cell attempts to obstruct Bernart in his composition is a good one and Bernart struggles to recapture his love to inspire his composition; luckily a whisper from the first visionary lady reinspires him and during the ordeal of his performance before the Emperor she manages to appear again in vision to him. At the court of love (is he a true lover?) the judge is the hermit who reveals himself as Peter Vidal, but the Emperor happens by and discovering Bernart to be the son of Romeus (whom he regards as a faithful servant) he sentences Bernart to 'the perpetual society of the religious lady' (Adelaide), a sentence the Emperor is sure, with his tongue in his cheek, will end his career as a poet, since prosperity will follow his marriage; he will be 'a minor poet ruined by lawful love'. Bernart and Adelaide end the novel in the equality that is the preferred resolution also in Chaucer. Moreover, they have achieved the highest love that overshadows even the romantic love of the troubadour. Alexander herself has balanced well the theme of love and song against the background of ferocious warfare between orthodoxy and heresy.

ENEMIES OF PROMISE: SEX, LOVE, AND MARRIAGE

In *The Lady of the Well*, love and marriage compete with the obligations of the troubadour, with art, and with vocation; love can compel and consume and have its own imperatives and obligations. By impeding creativity and competing with career, love and marriage can, then, be divisive and threatening as well as, or instead of, being unifying.

This is the case in *The Night Nurse* (1913) by 'The Author of "The Surgeon's Log"'. *The Surgeon's Log* was also published anonymously, because the author was a medical doctor and it was considered unwise then for a doctor under the circumstance of authorship to use his real name, which in this case was J. Johnston Abraham (1876–1963), born in Coleraine and educated there and in Trinity College Dublin. Even Abraham's medical textbooks were written under a pseudonym, James Harpole. He was taught classics at grammar school, and at Trinity was torn between medicine and English literature. The Shakespearian scholar Edward Dowden persuaded him to qualify in the former in order to guarantee a living; he did so but enjoyed a Dublin 'seething with ideas' and the visible presence of George Moore, AE, Synge, and Lady Gregory.[4] As Abraham tells us in *Surgeon's Journey: The Autobiography of J. Johnston Abraham* (1957), *The Surgeon's Log: Being Impressions of the Far East* (1911) was a transatlantic best-seller which went through six editions by 1912 and twenty-one by 1936. *The Night Nurse*, a rewriting of a discarded earlier novel, was itself a huge success, going through six impressions; indeed, it was a *succès de scandale*, as it was banned reading in all the London hospitals save Guy's, presumably because it implied that student nurses and doctors spent a great deal of time in either sexual deprivation or sexual excitement.[5] It was in London that Abraham worked, including a spell as a 'shilling doctor', like Riddell's Claud Dagley. He was the son of a tea merchant and the grandson of a linen merchant, so his pedigree (his forebears were Abrahams, Johnstons, Morrisons, and Hunters) was classic Ulster Scot, and he claimed in 1957 that he was still influenced by thoughts of Lundy and the Siege of Derry. His mother's father, born in 1797, grew up on the knowledge of the '98 rebellion passed on to him from *his* father and Abraham inherited this sense of the past. This might translate, it seems to me, into the odd kind of biological predestinarianism offered in his best-known novel, *The Night Nurse.*

Yet *The Night Nurse*, like Young's *The Sands of Pleasure* and *When the Tide Turns*, Douglas Goldring's *The Fortune*, and Letts' *The Rough Way*, strikes a modern note, in part because of the scientific nature of the hero's vocation (he is a Northerner who becomes a doctor in a Dublin hospital), and seems, like these novels, to have decisively escaped the late Victorianism that still informs the works of Mulholland, Alexander, Francis, and most of the other women novelists. Abraham's attitude to love is certainly post-Victorian because it is uncoupled from sex, which receives its own unabashed attention. One character's eyes on seeing an attractive nurse soften 'with that strange, unquiet yearning which is the expression of the deepest primitive instinct—"biological continuity", the physical basis of all love'. Abraham's cast of student nurses and doctors are all young and nubile, at an age of sexual excitement linked to love and relationship, a crossroads of a kind. Moreover, they are advanced post-victorians: though unmarried, 'All of them had a knowledge of the hidden things in life unknown even to their mothers, a knowledge that made the ordinary barriers of convention futile, a knowledge absolutely undreamt of by the sheltered unmarried woman of their outside acquaintance.'[6] It was Abraham's experience as a student doctor in the eroticized environment of the hospital that allowed him to acknowledge with advanced thinkers of the day the strength of female sexual desire.[7] It may be, of course, that this desire was 'sublimated' or 'coded' even in the productions of the romance novelists we have looked at, purified as 'love' even when sex was intended; this may account for what looks like an acceleration of novels about love in the 1890–1914 period (love between 1914 and 1918 would have the unique poignant dimension of the Great War, as we shall see).

Love, sex, and marriage are the subject of *The Night Nurse* though the book is also something of a scientific equivalent of a *Künstlerroman*. One theme is the contest between the temptations of sexual love and the necessary self-abnegation and rule-bound life of a surgeon in training. Dermot Fitzgerald battles the primitive emotions of the 'natural man' and, moreover, is torn between his instinctively true love for Nurse Nora Townsend and his ethical obligation to marry Nurse Moira Otway. A second theme is the conflict between the scientific and humane attitudes to life. Despite being a doctor in training, the scientist in Dermot is opposed to philanthropy which rests on the exploded (Lamarckian) idea that acquired characteristics can be transmitted, that if you treat the unfit well they and their offspring will survive and prosper as good citizens, whereas he believes that heredity sets at naught philanthropy, that the unfit beget the unfit. There is a naturalism at work in *The Night Nurse* which combines with Abraham's realism of life in an early twentieth-century hospital. The artist La Touche has painted Nora as a stooping princess whose heart has been awakened by the first passionate kiss from her 'predestined mate' but this seems far from her reality when the novel opens. For his part, Dermot is certain that he has met Nora in the past, which he has not; indeed he feels he has loved her many times in the past, as though the experience of the species were repeating itself through him (pp. 7, 96, 100). Yet Abraham makes room in this baggy novel for the complexity of the individual, which he thinks is biologically rooted; this puts him closer to the scientific-artistic vision of Wilde (about which more later), whom his hero quotes in his fever late in the novel.

But his behaviour with Nurse Otway compromises him and he must commit to her. Anyway, he does not wish to fall in love. Nor does he truly believe in marriage, an institution in deepening crisis. If the 'best women' have begun to look on marriage as a career that is beneath them, men find marriage expensive and are marrying later; the resulting slump in the marriage market forces more unmarried women into the business world, thereby taking jobs from men, enlarging the vicious circle. Marriage is an even greater problem for the student doctor who is poor until he is in practice. Marriage is an immense sacrifice for the race, Dermot concludes. Nora is introduced in the novel as a 23-year-old New Woman of the 1890s: she insists she will not marry, and talk about love leaves her cold. 'Getting married has no attractions for me. Most women seem to marry for a home. I used to think that degrading till I came to see it was largely due to their economic dependence.'[8]

It is as though doctors and nurses were at the cutting edge of the insistent Marriage Question between the 1880s and the Great War. An even sharper cutting edge was provided by Frank Harris in his novel, *The Bomb* (1908), in which marriage is for its politicized hero, Louis Lingg, a bourgeois institution. Lingg's open cohabitation with Ida Miller somehow validates his extreme political views and, curiously, his views both of marriage and society are puritanical even though they invert what we will see later as Sarah Grand's inference concerning marriage and social purity. Ida tells Schnaubelt: 'we do not believe in marriage. Louis thinks moral laws are simply laws of health; he regards marriage as a silly institution, without meaning for men and women who wish to deal honestly with each other.'⁹ Schnaubelt is shocked and his girl Elsie's desire to be married and to withhold herself until then, is in marked contrast to Ida's attitude; since Lingg is the more authentic anarchist and rebel, Lingg's view of marriage is in turn validated by his politics. But just as love overtakes Schnaubelt, who has to fight its emotional autonomy, so it overtakes Abraham's Nora and Dermot, whose reluctance, reserve, and objection melt mutually. La Touche's painting of Nora as 'The Stooping Princess'—'the beautiful queenly girl sacrificing all for love, the chivalrous young knight [shades of Bernart and Adelaide] accepting the gift'—starts to materialize. But their love cannot become marriage because he is poor.

A familiar country-house motif is introduced. Dermot Fitzgerald is minor Protestant gentry and has a 'rotten old place down in the Co. Waterford' that he can't keep in repair. 'The land brings in almost nothing now.' His father wouldn't evict tenants and would turn in his grave if Dermot did. He hopes to sell 'under the Wyndham Act' and so solve his problem; but he has been caught in a compromising position with another nurse and Nora and he are driven apart. Nora grows cold; Dermot Fitzgerald is broken and goes off to Connemara to help with a typhus outbreak, his career disrupted. Fitzgerald's nurse contracts typhus and Nora volunteers self-sacrificially. (There is a grim scene of the leaving of Nurse Marr's coffin propped against the door of Fitzgerald's makeshift hospital by the fearful undertaker—'the whole episode struck him like a page from the Journal of Defoe.')¹⁰ It appears there is no hope for the thwarted love between Fitzgerald and Nora since Nurse Otway, also ministering to the typhoid patients, broke off her engagement with another to clear the way for marriage with him. But eventually Otway accepts that her engagement to Fitzgerald is the outcome of his chivalry rather than their love: when Fitzgerald falls ill with the fever and lapses into a coma (but not before he has deliriously revealed his love for Nora), Otway releases him in an act of self-sacrifice and stands aside to let Nora try to restore him. Her self-sacrifice is in itself compensation enough for Moira; but Nora too had been self-sacrificial in coming to Connemara and in denying her love for Fitzgerald in the teeth of its apparent failure. The reward for Fitzgerald's chivalry is material; Nora, it turns out, is a wealthy woman and will solve both of his problems: the run-down estate and the incompatibility of marriage with the impecunious condition of an intern. Abraham's 'New Woman' can have it all—male chivalry, love, marriage, the country house, and her own power.

MARRIAGE AGAINST LOVE

Scrutinizing marriage meant placing the institution in its fuller contexts—economic, social, psychological, sexual—and pondering the ways in which it could be regarded as the natural terminus for love, or as a sensible counterweight to a reckless, romantic love that threatened the family, which was society writ small. The latter was the subject of *The Fly on the Wheel* (1908) a finely paced novel by Katherine Cecil Thurston (1875–1911).[11] It is set in Waterford, a town that illustrates what Thurston calls the 'invasion of the middle classes', in this case the Catholic middle classes. Stephen Carey, 38, son of a builder, has quashed his earlier desire to flee the stagnation of Waterford and has accepted his slavery to a 'big machine called expediency' which doesn't stop even if you refuse to oil and polish it; as though to demonstrate his own metaphor he buys a large motor car, a rarity in Waterford at the time. The local priest, Father James, later offers his own metaphor for the same idea: Aesop's fable of the fly that cannot control the speed of the chariot by threatening to bite the mule, because the mule is controlled solely by the driver, just as some big power controls our own lives.

In his accommodation to life, Carey resembles that other middle-class Catholic, James Joyce's Gabriel Conroy in 'The Dead': no more than Conroy is Carey, a lawyer after all, a stupid or unimposing man. He listens to the new Gaelic movement's promise to rejuvenate Ireland (about which Daisy's brother Tom sounds like Miss Ivors in 'The Dead') but his own ideas for reform are just as radical and include, beyond economic progress, sousing the country 'with modern thought—Spencer and Huxley, Haeckel and Kant—and be hanged to sentimentality'. Thurston presumably does not agree with him, though the idea of a reformation alternative to the Cultural Revival is a recurring one in the Irish novel of the period, and the Revival does not play a large part in Thurston's novel which is primarily about a different alternative to bourgeois British-style respectability.[12]

What count for Carey are the conventional running of his family and the supervision of his orphaned younger brothers; in conformity with their class he regards his wife Daisy, 25, as 'a chattel, a being to be clothed and fed and housed to the best of man's ability, but beyond that hardly to be considered' (p. 12). The well-oiled machine grinds to a halt when he meets the orphaned Isabel Costello, 20, back from her convent schooling in Paris, headstrong and independent. She is the fly in the ointment, a Thurstonian heroine: her own woman in battle with convention, and that means family, love, marriage, and social expectations. Her youth, unusualness, and sexual attractiveness open doors, including those to a local country house, Fair Hill, home of the Burke family, as well as to Carey's country retreat. But whereas Daisy's sister shows a familiar unconventionality by looking coldly on the prospect of marriage, Isabel is far more threatening by falling in love with a married man. Marriage would be a snare to a woman like Isabel and compromise her individuality, but her plunge into love answers her southern European blood, so that heredity and individuality are at odds in her. But in any case, people of Carey's class cannot indulge romantic love, and he explains to her the incompatibility of impulsiveness of the heart with the economic welfare of the family (i.e. the Irish middle-class marriage). All the more ironic that Carey then falls for Isabel; both are weakened by the mutual passion, the development of which Thurston charts impressively, culminating in a dramatic 'flight' scene when Carey and Isabel steal away for a night ride in his fast car, followed by the 'recrimination' scene when he admits the affair to Daisy and is unrepentant. Father James, wise overseer of the family, dissuades Carey from wrecking his marriage, who then rejects Isabel. He returns to his naive wife to recant: 'No tragedy, no dramatic effect; and Daisy, the eternal type— the wife, the mother—accepted the words without question' (p. 310).

As an attractive, engaging, single but poor girl, Isabel's position had always been precarious: 'upon the stage of middle-class Irish life the godmother's wand has lost its cunning, the rags remain merely rags, and the lean mice gnaw the pumpkin. To girls such as Isabel, the future is cruelly stereotyped... in no country in the world does the feminine mind shrink more sensitively from the stigma of old maid than in Ireland, where the woman-worker—the woman of broad interests—exists only as a rare type.' The convent looms for those who fail to find matrimony but Isabel is not of the compliant or resigned type but rather the type who either marries or does not marry, 'and in that simple statement is comprised the tragedy of existence' (pp. 223–4). The other side of a failed love affair is either marriage or spinsterhood, both a kind of death in middle-class Ireland, as Thurston sees it. But Isabel has only a glimmering awareness of the culture that produces her own tragedy. Intending to kill Carey she is persuaded by Father James to see how Carey has suffered by his decision to sacrifice his love for Isabel (and his own last chance at rebellion and self-fulfilment) and instead drinks the poisoned wine herself. Is this self-annihilation an expression of her undefeated love for Carey? (Presumably Thurston does not intend us to see that the act will be a kind of revenge since it will create a scandal and violate the conventions.) Or is it an indirect acknowledgement of the impossibility of passionate love in a country so very different from the passionate one she carries, as it were, in her veins? Either way, romantic love is, in the ordinary way, defeated.

There is a curious biographical addendum to this novel. The shocking event on the eve of marriage, and a sudden, possibly suicidal death, combined in the real fate of Thurston herself. She died unexpectedly in a Cork hotel the same month in which she planned to remarry, having been separated from the prolific Cork-born novelist, E. Temple Thurston (1879–1933) since 1907 and divorced in 1910.[13] Rumour and speculation attended news of her death and, as Stephen J. Brown notes of *The Fly on the Wheel*, 'The manner of the Author's own death gives this [novel] a poignant interest', the implication surely being possible suicide, and suicide, moreover, connected with a troubled love life.[14] Janet Madden-Simpson in her Afterword to the 1987 Virago edition of the novel tells us that the coroner's inquest found instead evidence of suffocation during an epileptic fit.

To what extent the marriage informed E. Temple Thurston's *Traffic: The Story of a Faithful Woman* (1906) is probably irretrievable at this stage. If the union of Temple Thurston and Katherine Thurston (née Madden) was a mixed marriage, then it was contracted without the blessings of the Catholic Church and in *Traffic* it is the withholding of the Church's permission, let alone blessings, that is the chief issue. Because the Church disallows divorce, making remarriage (unless a spouse dies) impossible, a Catholic marriage from the author's point of view is in the sad case of Nanno Troy the enemy of the love she comes to bear for an otherwise eligible visiting Englishman, Philip Jerningham, a love that ought to translate itself into a true and blessed marriage. But her fidelity to a Church that contrives to keep a wife in a loveless and abusive marriage to a violent and unfaithful small farmer (the subtitle alludes to her faithfulness to her religion not to her husband) is only one of her disabilities. Thurston seems unsure if he is writing a problem-novel, the problem being the Catholic Church's stand against divorce irre-spective of the circumstances, and in theory soluble. (Clearly there is little to be done about another problem, what Thurston sees as the cruelty and idiocy of rural Ireland, here Co. Waterford.) Or if he is writing a tragedy along the lines of Hardy's *Tess of the d'Urbervilles*, the subtitle of which, *A Pure Woman, Faithfully Presented*, Thurston might be thought to echo; like Tess, Nanno Troy is a simple farmgirl who suffers from outrageous fortune. She is illegit-imate (her father a visiting English artist who abandoned her mother), raised by a man whose true relation is brutally revealed to her by her mother to compel her through gratitude to accept the hand of a man she despises; she is abused as a child; like Tess her beauty is betraying, 'the dangerous humanity of her mouth' being especially attractive to men; early on, as though a natural, intuitive New Woman, she insists that 'I don't want to marry', but she is forced into an arranged marriage ('Marriage is a mercenary matter in Ireland, and the solicitor is the most important factor concerned'), thus quickening a destiny common in peasant Ireland ('Once a woman marries in Ireland, she deteriorates'). It all adds up to a kind of fate ('hanging in her steps across the chequered-board of Life') and in face of the downwards trajectory that it inevitability guarantees, Nanno shares with Tess a kind of dignified resignation that can by turns infuriate and attract men.[15]

After being beaten by her husband, Nanno leaves home ('It was almost an unheard-of thing in those parts for a woman to leave her husband, however he ill-treated or was unfaithful to her', p. 120) and makes her way to London where Jerningham, whom she met before her marriage, chances upon her working as a waitress. She grows to love him, but when he proposes that she divorce her husband and marry him, she repeats impassively, knowing they are beaten before they begin: 'There is no divorce in our Church' (p. 212). She parrots back what the priest in Ireland warned her: ' "If I were to be divorced and to marry again", she said expressionlessly, "the Church would close its doors against me—I should be excommunicated" ' (p. 220). It is futile for her would-be rescuer to point out that it was men, not women, who fashioned this dogma, that excommunication would not endanger her relation to God and Christ. Her impassivity is a symptom of the Church's hold upon her: 'I must believe it', she repeats when Jerningham questions the grotesque results of excommunication in the events of divorce and remarriage: no absolution, no burial service, no prayers for her soul in Purgatory, straight passage into Hell for eternity.[16] Later, when again Jerningham attempts to reason her into divorce and marriage to him, she replies: ' "It's what I believe," she said fearfully, "It's what I'm told to believe" ' (p. 305). As a Protestant and Englishman, Jerningham is exasperated by 'the childish arrogance of her faith' (p. 305) which he watches destroying her. An English priest tells her she must return to her husband and suggests she invite him to London. She does but Jamesy Ryan is unchanged in his unfaithfulness and brutality and she leaves him a second time. But her path is downward and, losing touch with Jerningham, she is sacked when her pregnancy (by Ryan) shows; to survive with her baby she becomes a kept woman and finally, which Jerningham discovers when he chances upon her again, a prostitute, albeit an inept one, not cut out for the game, impassive, detached. When her baby dies and when after a last and hopeless encounter with Jerningham she decides to take her own life, there is a guardedly optimistic intervention by Jerningham and the reader is permitted to hope that Nanno may have hit rock bottom and can with help and luck begin an ascent.

Yet the philosophy of the novel would seem to set such hope at naught. When he happens upon her, Jerningham muses: 'She had shut the gates of a man's love in order to keep open the doors of the Church' (p. 309), and here he surely expresses Thurston's bitter recrimination against the Catholic Church; any victory against the social repercussions of its doctrine and morality would seem to be merely individual and local. And formidable as the power of the Church is over its less educated and poorer adherents, especially in rural Ireland, it is—in the tragic dimension of the novel—the unimportance of the individual that Nanno seems to embody, for in a rather Edwardian metaphor deriving from the machine age and which gives the novel its title, life is seen as a flow of traffic that cannot and does not stop when accidents occur and that consigns some vehicles and drivers to damnation in order that the flow be unchecked. (One might think of Katherine Cecil Thurston's image of the fly on the wheel in her novel published two years later.)

There is in *Traffic* some dubious wisdom about women: 'The desires of love are mostly created in a woman; they do not fully develop in the ordinary course of evolution' (p. 154); 'Religion was made for young girls, disappointed women, and the moral benefit of the state' (p. 37); 'In the mind of a woman, when life ceases to be a miracle it becomes a degradation' (p. 238).[17] Nonetheless, *Traffic* is a novel that at least aspires to rival both Hardy's *Tess of the d'Urbervilles* (1891) and Moore's *Esther Waters* (1894) and shares affinities with other realist novels of Edwardian London, with their close observations of daily lives in home, office, and city restaurants, lives hampered by chores and bills, errands and debt. Jerningham himself is a realist, defeated for most of the novel by Nanno's rote and perverted idealism that is its own defeated, pessimistic sense of reality. The novel therefore threatens to be an example of the lesser realism that Thurston repudiated elsewhere. In an essay, he maintained that 'Realism, which now means an expression of things as they happen without any relation to things as they immortally are, is robbed of its true significance.' He then tells an anecdote that would, he claims, furnish the raw data for fashionable pessimistic realism whereas he believes it illustrates 'an immortal truth' (and a comforting one) that can easily square with its reality.[18] It may be, then, that Thurston intended the close of *Traffic* to be more optimistic than it reads, even though any 'immortal truth' in it seems to be Hardyesque in its reduction of the individual human to negligibility amidst the impersonal traffic of being.

To what extent his own marriage also informed Thurston's uneasily titled novel, *The Evolution of Katherine* (1907: the year of the separation) is probably also irretrievable. Until near its close, this novel appears to depict a terminally and romantically unsatisfactory marriage (from the wife's perspective) between a beautiful and self-assured young woman and a socialist thinker, John Spurrier, who knows nothing of women. Spurrier inherits a Liberal seat in Middlesex and accepts it, exchanging his socialism for a liberal optimism based on the notion of evolutionary progress. In the eyes of her friend Barbara Katherine has contradicted their earlier duets on the necessity of romanticism and has even renounced love itself by marrying him. Barbara tells an offended Katherine that she is marrying Spurrier 'because there's a side of every woman that knows marriage to be a duty; and the more advantageous it is, the greater the duty it becomes'.[19] But Katherine is a strong-willed woman and the narrator reminds us that the foundation of marriage has undergone change in the past fifty years (i.e. between the mid-Victorian and Edwardian periods) and that women are now beginning to think for themselves. Yet having discountenanced romance, Katherine finds herself emotionally hungry after marriage to a busy and distracted man and she grows discontent with her husband's protestations of love, his worship of her, and his 'look of a faithful dog from the eyes' (p. 43). When a Captain Seyd, a veteran of the Boer War, visits their country house, she is stirred and gradually yields to his suit. Here at last is the 'truancy of Romance' (p. 118). She has become the 'disappointed woman' and rationalizes marriage as a war—'The ascendency of the man against the ascendency of the woman; dogs at each other's throats.' It is a mistake for a woman to love her husband blindly, she tells Barbara, who in turn is being drawn to John, his work and ideas, and is therefore abandoning her own romantic ideal.

Seyd is recalled to his regiment and will be gone for months; but he and Katherine grow closer in correspondence. On the eve of a trip to Ireland on which at the last moment Barbara and Katherine will be joined by John who will study the condition of Ireland in three weeks (In three weeks! Katherine scoffs: 'England's been studying Ireland in three weeks for the last three centuries'), Katherine learns she has breast cancer and has but two years to live. When Seyd returns, he escorts her while she is in London receiving treatment and resumes his courtship. Unlike the heroes and heroines of most country-house novels, the Captain suffers from 'boredom of the country' (p. 94), and it is in London where he will seduce Katherine to his side. For her part, Katherine has decided Seyd's romantic attentions will ornament her last two years. Ironically, her husband is meanwhile full of social Darwinism and believes that morality and immorality are merely terms and that there is no such thing as a moral or immoral deed save one that hinders evolution. Katherine is throughout a rather cold and assured woman but she yields to Seyd's overtures while listening to Mimi's farewell song to Rodolfo in *La Bohème*—'Serbarla a ricordo d'amor' ('Keep it in memory of our love')—an opera premièred in Covent Garden in 1897 but first sung there in Italian in 1899, four years before the action of the novel. (Katherine has seen *La Bohème* several times, it seems, before the night with Seyd.) Invited back to his rooms for what turns out to be champagne and a veritable feast, she realizes that he had presumed she would accept his invitation. It is a tense and fateful moment.

'Then you counted on me to-night?'
He stood by the table mute, with the wire-cutter half gripped in his hand. Here was her point. He saw it now. Never admit to a woman that you count on her human

nature—in the next breath add—never let a woman see where you wish to lead her. The one is tantamount to the other. He was in the trap; as he stood there he looked it.

'...I can see you when you ordered them, with a grin on your lips, as you might smile watching a bird-trap covered with bread-crumbs. You counted on me!' Her look withered him as she rose again to her feet. 'Oh, I can't tell you the keen pleasure it gives me now to go and leave you to the feast alone.' (p. 271)

Yet having verbally refused his invitation to visit Italy, she rethinks the matter and writes him a letter accepting. Then she learns that her cancer has been misdiagnosed and that she is in good health. Under these new circumstances she sees Seyd as a poorer marriage prospect than her husband and sends John to retrieve her letter to the Captain who returns it unopened to him when Spurrier threatens to investigate his wife's affair unless he does so. Katherine lets her husband read the letter accepting Seyd's invitation which, like all of Katherine's communications, lacks real intimacy and is perhaps even a self-serving desire, in her imagined sickness, for the warm south. She returns to the marriage and is forgiven by Spurrier. Marriage may be an enemy of romance but it is not an enemy of love, the wife asks us to believe. The 'school of Reality' has outlasted 'the truancy of Romance'. However, the novel ends when Spurrier entreats Katherine to see Barbara, who has been feeling that Katherine no longer wants her and who is the other party in what one senses is the only fully alive—but not in any sense the most fully realized—relationship in the book.

The Evolution of Katherine has itself the implausibility of plot of a nineteenth-century opera, and there is a good deal of recitative, when the implied narrator engages the reader in dialogue (at one point reproducing earlier narrative for perusal) or addresses the reader on love, marriage, and women. The operatic quality is something shared in greater or lesser degree by these late Victorian or Edwardian novels of social romance which at their best register contemporary concern about the sexes while at rare moments attaining the quality of modest arias. Indeed, the contemporary concern in *Katherine* goes beyond the war of the sexes. Seyd we are told is of a family that had served as soldiers as far back as Cromwellian and Elizabethan times. 'No one can deny the romance of it' (p. 62), but the narrator himself seems to accept a social evolutionary principle and sees Christianity, aristocracy, and then the soldiery as scheduled to disappear when 'men of intellect' turn upon them all and Englishmen generally grow more effete (something Sarah Grand, too, thought was happening—a sentiment that could not have had much currency when the distant rumbles of the Great War began to be felt). Romance itself, it seems, will be a casualty and the novel's title heroine has done her part to further this eventuality: her portrait is not a flattering one.

The heroine of Gerald O'Donovan's *The Holy Tree* (1922), something of a country version of Katherine Thurston's Isabel, and a very different woman from Temple Thurston's Katherine Spurrier, finds that her passionate love is attempting to bloom in a world inimical to such intensity, more especially, in an endemically puritan society, if the passion is adulterous. O'Donovan reverses Katherine Thurston's scenario by having an impressionable married woman fall in love with an available man. Adultery was a particularly risky sin in the largest part of Ireland dominated by the Roman Catholic Church and a risky plot element for an Irish Catholic novelist. O'Donovan had already run afoul of the Church by resigning from the priesthood (in which he was known as Father Jeremiah O'Donovan) on grounds of conscience. As Father Jeremiah O'Donovan, a priest of reformist and philanthropic impulse,[20] he has been identified as the original for George Moore's rebellious Father Gogarty in *The Lake* (1905) who stages his own drowning in order to effect his escape from the Church which he can no longer square with his emotional, sexual, and intellectual inclinations. Father O'Donovan left the priesthood in 1904, went to Dublin, then England, changed his name, and resurfaced as the novelist and editor, Gerald O'Donovan (1871–1942).

The fictionalized circumstances of his desertion can be found in his first novel, *Father Ralph* (1913), a novel in which the Church and its most faithful priests are grimly portrayed. The title character (the son of western Irish Catholic gentry) is enthusiastic about the emerging new Ireland of the cultural and economic Revival and the apparent loosening of Catholic doctrine through modernism, but comes up against the immovable object (and objection) of Rome where both movements are concerned, after which Father Ralph determines to pursue self-realization at whatever cost, spiritual or social.[21] In his second and very popular novel, *Waiting* (1914), O'Donovan focused on the Church's implacable opposition to another adjunct of the Irish Revival, secular and lay participation in education for Catholics.[22] To this O'Donovan added the Church's abhorrence of mixed marriages (i.e. marriages between Catholics and Protestants), aroused when a young Catholic teacher, Maurice Blake, falls in love with, and marries, a young visiting agricultural consultant who is a Protestant. Just as a papal encylical sounds the death-knell for Father Ralph's hopes (*Pascendi Dominici Gregis*, 1907, which crushed modernism), so a papal decree (*Ne Temere*, 1907, which rejected mixed marriage) invalidates Blake's marriage (as well as killing his chances for election as a west of Ireland Home Rule MP) and overnight makes him an adulterer and his wife a whore. Love might survive but probably only in exile, since the marriage could not survive the special circumstances of Catholic Ireland, the land of boycott and ostracism.[23]

O'Donovan in *The Holy Tree* depicts the likely fate in rural Ireland of the more familiar kind of adulterers. Whereas *The Fly on the Wheel* portrays the uncommonly depicted substantial Catholic middle class, *The Holy Tree* crosses territory more familiar to critics of the Irish novel—land-hunger and squabbles among kin in a country parish of Catholic small farmers. Young Ann Logan escapes the destiny of the loveless rural marriage contracted on purely economic grounds, but only because the proposed match is, like Nanno Troy's, so shamelessly financial in motive. She accepts a less odious proposal from a decent man who loves her, but to a degree she has still been bought and has accepted the proposal partly out of a sense of family duty, and her husband clearly cannot measure up to the standard she set herself in her daydreams: 'her man must shake her to the soul, like the beech woods in the autumn did; and set her blood on fire like breasting the wind on the uplands at Knockbrack with her face to the sun. . . . The look of him, and the touch of his hand, must take her breath away, like the song of a bird often did, or a blue flower in a ditch, or a star in a pool.'[24] After four years of marriage and the birth of a daughter, she grows increasingly frigid, then meets the man of her daydreams: Brian Hogan, a young visitor from outside the county, a collector of native Irish folksongs, a Gaelic speaker, an active Revivalist, and socialist organizer (follower of AE), a tolerant, non-sectarian young fellow. Soon she has joined him in his fieldwork and is daydreaming of being his wife. In a haymaking scene reminiscent of Hardy, they approach intimacy and in another scene in which he carries her across a stream they declare their love.

She grows more blatant and defiant in her love, despite the shadow of priestly disapproval always on her. If he sees their love as beyond the jurisdiction of right and wrong, she sees it as divine and thinks thoughts and feels feelings that her religion would condemn as blasphemous. 'And it's to feel a great holiness on her she did from it, like she used to feel at her monthly Communion, and Father John putting the body and blood of Christ Himself on her trembling tongue' (p. 160). When they kiss, 'It wasn't on earth at all they stood, but before the throne of God. . . . It's as small and weak as a wren she felt, and as full of power and virtue as the great God Himself . . . Nothing ever brought her closer to God; not His pardon of her first sin, nor her first communion' (p. 161). Challenged later by her angry and violent husband about her passion, she declares: 'My love is God in me.' Her assumed adultery is compounded by her apparent solipsism and pantheism as well as blasphemy and defiance. There is a naivety here as Ann tries in her own way to honour her religion and only unwittingly blasphemes against it. But when her lover speaks of the 'holy tree of love', deriving his metaphor from Yeats's poem, 'The Two Trees', which he then quotes ('Beloved, gaze in thine own heart, | The holy tree is growing there'), it is clear that O'Donovan is complicit with the lovers. Although Father John is depicted without rancour, the Church is the enemy of love which for O'Donovan transcends both the piety and the materialism that characterizes these rural communities. 'She was Brian's by all the laws of her own nature and of his', Ann thinks, 'and what were they but the firmest laws of God', commanding greater loyalty than the marriage laws of the Church or State.[25] O'Donovan clearly believes with one of the characters sympathetic to Ann Logan that 'Most of the wrong of the world came from thwarted love ... All the failure of the world was the failure to follow the truth of love' (pp. 302, 304).

Ann might sound at times like Pegeen Mike in actressy throes of romance (and Ann does see herself as Dido and Deirdre) or like Christy Mahon in naively blasphemous rhapsody, both of them subverted by the incongruous lowliness of their surroundings, but where O'Donovan's lovers are concerned, it is not a case of a merely 'gallous story'. Hogan is a serious Revivalist (as was O'Donovan) who finds that love is more important and consuming even than the movement. Ann's Uncle Maurice, disappointed in love and life, tells his niece that she has 'found the only thing in life worth a thraneen' (p. 147), the novel's chief lesson. Certainly the Hiberno-English of the narrative threatens to work against the story's realism—'It's to wash up you would after you, if you had any piety in you' (p. 147); 'It's to love Brian Hogan to the crack of doom I will' (p. 198)—but the threat derives only from our associations with the Revival romanticism of Synge, Yeats, and Lady Gregory. O'Donovan's sense of Gaelic-derived syntax is less colourful and more subdued but surer than Synge's and supports the story's peculiar realism rather than Syngean romance.

Ann's love is besieged by harsh disapproval from friends and neighbours, and of course from her priest who wages a campaign of de-programming—all the stuff of a realist novel rather than a tragicomic play. Hogan is sure she has refused to gaze in the bitter glass, with its image of Yeats's second tree of broken boughs and blackened leaves, and he is right, and yet O'Donovan needed to find a resolution equal to his own stern realism. The adulterous lovers clearly couldn't win in rural Ireland—this was his realism: Hogan is sacrificed and his lover returns to the living death of her marriage; love is crushed, piety and materialism close again over the disturbance of the love affair; the bartering and buying of men's souls deplored in Yeats's poem triumph. But neither, O'Donovan must have felt, should he show such a passion betrayed by its opponents or by the lovers themselves: this was his didacticism. O'Donovan's unsatisfactory but understandable solution is an accident that avoids both denouements, and leaves open the possibility of triumphant love in a future Ireland when Ann transmits her impossible passion to her daughter, having herself returned to her husband with outward wifely obedience: 'maybe, twined round about her own heart, there was still some withered root of the holy tree she had destroyed. ... One day, maybe, the child might quicken it into some sort of ghost life.'[26]

O'Donovan's frontal approach to the sanctity of romantic love and sexual desire even under adulterous circumstances declines to take the path of secret and masturbatory longings that Joyce has his main characters take in his vastly superior novel published in the same year of 1922, *Ulysses*, a path that invited charges of pornography. But there *is* something that connects the two novelists. Like Joyce, O'Donovan transposes his Catholic faith with its liturgy and language; Joyce transposes it into aesthetic theory, a religion of art (Stephen Dedalus in *Ulysses* and *A Portrait of the Artist* is to become a priest of the imagination), O'Donovan into a theory of love, a religion of love we might call 'erotheism'. In each case, a language, a perception, even a vision, are borrowed and reapplied, in the process demonstrating the lasting power of a Catholic upbringing over even the apostate Irish novelist.

DEGREES OF MARRIAGE

The loveless, contracted, rural Irish marriage that almost destroys Nanno Troy and that Ann Logan narrowly escapes (only to endure marital unhappiness of another kind) is the initial fate of Katharine Tynan's Rose Donoghue in *A Mad Marriage*, a novel published in the same year as *The Holy Tree*. Rose finds the holy tree growing, too, in her heart but Tynan, mistress of the country-house romance (albeit with elements here of tragic realism), and an unlapsed Catholic, no doubt felt constrained to widow Rose before making her available for true love and remarriage.

The same constraint had operated on Tynan in her earlier novel, *Dick Pentreath* (1906), an emotional page-turner once the scene is set in the English village and Pentreath's extraordinary popularity is established. The hero is a much loved and trusting fellow who finds true romance with the lovely Dorothea Semple, but when he drunkenly gate-crashes her night at the opera, she priggishly jilts him on the eve of their wedding, outraging his countless admirers. On the rebound, the devastated Pentreath marries Susan Sykes, a farmgirl with whom he had an earlier flirtation and who is, though only he does not realize it, a coarse and unpopular creature. Once she is installed in his country house, she shows her true colours; morale among the servants at Oakhurst plummets and what had seemed like a marriage of attraction fast becomes a loveless rural marriage (English this time). If Pentreath suffers the agony of loss after losing Dorothea, he suffers the agony of regret and humiliation after marrying Susan. It is a mixed marriage of the classes with dire results. When he meets Dorothea again, Pentreath tells her he has been in purgatory; she expresses her remorse, he forgives her, and they kiss. But they cannot reunite while his wife is alive and Dorothea, who has lived in her own purgatory, prepares to enter a religious order. The chief characters are Anglican (the locals disparage the Dissenters from the neighbouring village), but Tynan treats them as though they are Roman Catholic, and the Sisters of St Luke could pass as such.

On the eve of her departure for India to nurse the sick and impoverished, Dorothea learns that Pentreath wishes his former fiancée back, now that his wife is safely dead after years of dissipation and madness. The parched holy tree is revived. The novel ends with the prospect of three marriages, though that between Pentreath and Dorothea is the one that will not only heal the suffering of the affianced, but also restore Oakhurst itself to happiness and health. The reconciliation between Dorothea and Pentreath does not, of course, have the cultural or political significance it might have in an Irish setting. Their marriage and the other two marriages are given only a social significance and one inapplicable to Ireland: they reaffirm the integrity of life, happiness, and a kind of democratized hierarchy in this English garden village. Tynan's Catholicism was, of course, moveable between the islands. Tynan's Epilogue refers to those times when the world has a 'chrism and benediction' on it, and fittingly the Epilogue itself acts like a chrism on the novel's previous and highly readable narrative, adding unction to the familiar fictional resolution. Tynan's religious sensibility is in the end paramount, and the true marriages of romance must be blessed before becoming triumphant.

Pentreath's marriage to Susan is a bad one that we might also call 'mad', because it involves a mad spouse,[27] but in Tynan's later novel, the mad marriage of the title between Harry and Rose is in fact true marriage and bad only in the eyes of their friends. The truly bad marriage is contracted at the outset. The 16-year-old Rose had been loved from a distance by a 35-year-old neighbour who had not, however, disturbed 'the child's placid youth', unlike the elderly gombeen man, Teague Donoghue, who had watched the girl for years coming from convent school (stalking her, we would say nowadays), mentally grooming her before pouncing on her for a wife when she turned 17. When her admirer, Jim O'Donnell, an army medic, returns from war he finds Rose married off to Donoghue to save her family's farm that is in hock to the gombeen man, and his frustrated love unhinges him while he is family doctor to the Donoghues who are suffering what one character calls one of the many rural Irish 'marriages of repulsion'.[28] The wealthy Donoghue is a skinflint and a violent wife-abuser. Some but not all of this comes out in the novel's opening chapter, set in the west of Ireland at the trial of Rose for poisoning her husband. Though there have been love letters to her from her husband's nephew, an affair is denied by both nephew and accused wife, and the jury is directed to acquit Rose by a judge known for his prejudice towards women, Sir John Somers, a wise, congenial presence in the novel and perhaps Tynan's mouthpiece.

The scene changes in the next chapter to a London town house twenty years later during the brilliant season that followed the coronation of King Edward

(August 1902)—later scenes will take place in Scottish and English country houses with a brief return to Galway—and the sudden switch from rural naturalism to country-house romance (with later and well-done scenes from ghost fiction) is perhaps made less abrupt by the murder mystery the first chapter appears to initiate (who did administer the arsenic to Teague Donoghue?).[29] The generic juxtaposition does not prevent some finely detailed writing, including the description of a moorland fire. But love remains the heart of the matter. If her first marriage can only be seen in a bitter glass, Rose finds true love and the holy tree blooms when after her acquittal she marries Harry Lambert of Castle Lambert, High Sheriff for Galway. This is ruinous for Lambert because marriage to a peasant girl suspected of being a husband-killer is socially unacceptable to his equals and they go into exile, moving around aimlessly (like Wallis Simpson and another Edward) while Castle Lambert grows derelict (a variation on a familiar motif from the Irish country-house novel) but they remain in love for the rest of their lives because of, not despite, their 'mad marriage' (as others see it), a phrase which changes its meaning in the novel (pp. 232, 241, 245) from disapproval to accolade; in the end, the mad marriage is the marriage of true love.

There is an alternative in Tynan to both the loveless marriage and the 'mad marriage' of loving attraction (the passionate *mésalliance* that dares its social consequences). The alternative is the safe marriage Mary O'Donnell contracts with Ponsonby the banker (later elevated to a baronetcy) after Harry Lambert chooses Rose from all the contenders for his heart, including Mary. The relation of social station to love and attraction remains unclear in *A Mad Marriage*. Sir John recalls a visit to Lady Ponsonby and there seeing portraits of her grandfather and grandmother on the wall: 'Strong farmers', the Judge had pronounced upon the portraits. 'A class that hardly exists now in Ireland. Thoroughly honourable and high-minded. I expect he was a henchman of O'Connell's, and she was the friend of all the neighbourhood. They explain Lady Ponsonby.'[30] This marriage of female altruism and philanthropy ('friend of all the neighbourhood') with male Catholic highmindedness strikes me as Tynan's ideal but one declining in possibility in Ireland. The Judge would seem to discountenance social inequality when, predicting that Lord Malvern will marry Rose and Lambert's daughter, Hester, despite the revelation of her mother's background, he twice sings the verse of an old song: 'Has the lily less whiteness | Because of its birth? | Has the violet less brightness | For growing in earth?' But it is the paramountcy of female beauty over social station that the woman-loving Sir John intends the song to celebrate, and this is a quite restricted idea even of O'Connellite democracy.

Tynan flows with the country-house genre in admiring chivalrous, heroic, honourable specimens of the nobility, with Sir John's short hymn to the strong farmer class being a minor Irish variation. As they were in Tynan's *A Girl of Galway* (1901), the gombeen men, traders, and moneylenders (probably she felt similarly about the whole lower middle class) are the villains who are usurping their betters in Ireland. (Tynan's friend Yeats felt the same way.) This has its denominational dimension. Sir Edward Villiers is vilified by the narrator for his low-church ways, he being a puritan (either dissenter or evangelical Anglican) engaged indiscriminately in prayer-meetings, temperance-meetings, anti-smoking campaigns, and prosyletism whereas his daughter Mary shines in the story and has become High Anglican but practises her religion discreetly and courteously, as one suspects Tynan had to do when living in England. In this novel, love, no more than marriage as a social event, can be uncoupled from station in life.

We have met other safe marriages—marriages of social and economic convenience but with insufficient emotional and sexual fulfilment—such as that between Ann Logan and her husband; that between Gillian and the Colonel in Crichton's *The Soundless Tide*; and those between Major Rochfort and Sophy and between Fanny and Freddy Tallboys in Croker's *In Old Madras*. The marriage between Katherine and John in Temple Thurston's *Katherine* begins as a safe marriage teetering on the brink of becoming a loveless one, but is apparently refreshed at the end of the novel to become a true and loving marriage. That between Lady and Lord Hexham in MacMahon's *The Job* is and remains a safe one. The marriage between Lord Muntfort and his second wife is another safe marriage in MacMahon's novel: 'It was a very suitable arrangement. He wanted a wife and she wanted a husband.'[31]

The marriage between Gillian and the Colonel is also in terms of age lopsided, like that between Rose and Teague Donoghue. *The Job* has a dangerously lopsided marriage between Edith (Lady) Champneys and her older husband, newly appointed British ambassador to Turkey. Edith had once welcomed and then rejected the passionate advances of the young Thady Muntfort; fifteen years and four children later, she meets him again and this time views him as a possible lover and even husband, and sets out to rekindle him, and almost succeeds in a quite powerful seduction scene in a garden grotto.[32] Edith, it seems, is willing to risk the negatively 'mad' union, that is, the merely scandalous liaison. But the beautiful and highly sexed Edith proves to be merely a baffle on Thady's road to his true love, Ria Devereux, whom he wins at novel's end. *In Old Madras* has a trio of lopsided matches—Colonel Harris and Barbie Miller, Lena Villars and Geoffery Mallender, Lena Villars and Sir William Bream—in part a function of the abnormal imperial society. Barbie has a narrow escape and survives to marry Croker's hero, young Mallender, who himself has a narrow escape from Mrs Villars (41, it turns out to his amazement, but looking far younger), but Mrs Villars, who fails to entrap Mallender, is resigned to marriage with the far older Bream.

Croker like many of these romance writers deploys the four kinds of marriage—safe, lopsided, loveless, and 'mad'—for Mallender marries Barbie out of love, while his uncle has forfeited much of himself (literally, as readers will find out) for his love for the Indian princess (of the royal house of Coorg), renamed Alida and the love of his endangered life. Mrs Hungerford (1855–97) in *The Hoyden: A Novel* (1894) clearly delighted in these marital deployments in a country-house romance that frothily reduces itself precisely to them. The novel consists chiefly of dialogue of a weightless, sub-Wildean kind that we associate with drawing-room comedies (in addition, the opening echoes that of *Dorian Gray*), and its cleverest speakers are cheerful, selfish, and unphilanthropic. It is the story of a marriage contrived for candidly fiscal reasons between a wealthy heiress, Tita Bolton, and an impoverished young aristocrat, Sir Maurice Rylton. The matchmaker is the groom's beautiful but tyrannical mother, herself the surviving spouse of an arranged marriage, who insists that 'a marriage based on friendship, even between two young people, is often successful'.[33] The union is meant to be safe even if lopsided (one of 'these unequal marriages', p. 261), and even if it unites Trade and Society, a teenage wife with a maturer husband (Tita, however, is higher-spirited and more wilful than Tynan's Rose Donoghue). It is in fact as a marriage sheer folly or 'madness' as Lady Rylton's niece contends (pp. 17, 174). Soon, despite the attempt at an open marriage without emotional commitment or obligation on either side, there is trouble caused by their respective suitors already on the scene, a beautiful cousin and a handsome cousin. Another distraction is the warmth between Tita and Lady Rylton's niece, Margaret Knollys, which at times resembles a lesbian passion: 'I never loved anyone as I love you', the tomboyish Tita tells Margaret (p. 265) who has 'contracted . . . quite a romantic affection' for Tita (p. 73) and who gives the hoyden a pearl ring; 'You are mine now, my own cousin!' whispers Tita to Margaret (p. 80) as they take the fictional theme of cousinage to a passionate depth. Yet the novel's dilute plot is merely a deferment of what the reader early guesses—that the safe, even loveless marriage will turn out, as in Temple Thurston's *Katherine*, to be a 'mad' marriage in the Tynanesque sense after all, when the undercurrent of mutually denied true love breaks surface.

In fact, however, the social dynamics of this otherwise trivial novel ensures it is not at all a passionate *mésalliance* like that of Rose Donoghue and Harry Lambert or Ann Logan and Brian Hogan. In *The Hoyden*, Society (in the guise of Sir Maurice, newly come into his own aristocratic fortune) turns the tables on Trade (in the guise of Tita whose family fortune is foolishly squandered by her uncle who then commits suicide) and Tita herself is recruited through her refreshed marriage into Society which she had mocked, regarding herself as someone whose function it was to administer electric shocks to it (p. 92). Tita's country house, sold when her fortune is lost, is secretly bought by

Sir Maurice who installs his young wife as chatelaine, a Trade heiress no longer. After its mild social satire of a *Rape of the Lock* variety, *The Hoyden* reverts to the essential conservatism of the country-house novel.

Although the young married heroine of *The First Claim* (1906) bears a passing resemblance to feisty but put-upon Tita Bolton, M. Hamilton's novel is far more daring in several respects. It soon deserts English country-house society, delving deeply and seriously into marital difficulties in a way that avoids slumming, exceeds the problem-novel, and develops a convincing domestic tragedy. Even the country-house Prologue is uncommon in showing a 20-year-old wife, caged in a lopsided and, from her side, loveless two-year-old marriage to 50-year-old Sir James Palmer (she has come to shrink from his touch), deserting husband and home in favour of life in a terrace house with a young soldier of modest means, Charley Osborne. But the problems attending a bad marriage, infidelity, separation, and divorce are quickly compounded when the story proper begins five years after the bad marriage is left behind for a 'mad' marriage, a liaison whose scandal is muffled and off-stage.

For Valerie Palmer (née Damien, from a half-French family 'not "county"') abandoned her beloved baby when she went off with Osborne and now she conceives an ineradicable longing to see her child. Her decision to seek her daughter out unleashes or uncovers a fraught series of anguishing dilemmas few other popular novelists tackled: the competition between emotional claims and legal claims, between kinds of affection, between kinds of need, and between duty and love. It seemed easy for Valerie to resolve her early dilemmas—a wife's need for freedom clashing with her marriage vows, and clashing too with a mother's love for her child, a love qualified by her general dislike of children. Easy, too, to resolve a later difficulty—remarriage while the first spouse remains alive, though Valerie acknowledges to herself how because of the existence of a child her bond with her ex-husband is stronger than her marriage vow.[34] But even these pale beside the resurrected dilemma: the clash between her guilty love for (or, more accurately, her duty to love) her daughter and her deep love for her second husband. This dilemma is sharpened by the insufferable nature of Valerie's daughter Gwenny, ruined by her stepmother's alternating flattery and cruelty amounting to child abuse. (Valerie herself had been abused as a child, causing in her case a damaging shyness the very opposite of her daughter's precocious and articulate wilfulness.) When Valerie returns to her marital home to ask for young Gwenny, the wicked stepmother reminds her she has no legal or moral claim to her daughter, and so when Valerie steals her daughter, she commits the crime that today would be called parental child abduction. She inserts her daughter into a marriage that had seemed to solve the difficulties of remarriage, only to create an instant stepfamily as troubled in its own way as the one from which she had abstracted her daughter.

The First Claim is a level-headed and unrelenting analysis of a subject as intractable as the sectarianism Hamilton took on in *Across an Ulster Bog.* Facing manfully, as he tries to do, the mounting pressures exerted on his wife's second marriage by problems his wife has imported into it, Charley Osborne is in fact the most sympathetic character in this tragedy. He is a decent man and his relationship with Valerie lies in terms of passion midway between those of Rose Donoghue and Harry Lambert on the one hand, and the rejuvenated Tita Bolton and Sir Maurice Rylton on the other. Charley is a conventional and law-abiding man, and on the face of it is less blameworthy than Valerie, the wife who left her husband and child. Moreover, Valerie, having decided to resolve the dilemma posed when her duty to Gwenny clashes with her love for Charley by 'stealing' Gwenny again, takes her this time to France, putting the onus of decision on Charley whether or not to follow her. And en route to France, and even after arrival there, Valerie tacitly encourages the attentions of a young Frenchman and allows him to believe that she is still in her lopsided marriage. Yet we never lose sympathy for Valerie, and the success of *The First Claim* lies in the extent to which its hero and heroine are irreducible to ciphers in a problem-novel. The emotionally complex heart of the story is Charley's jealousy of Valerie's devotion to Gwenny, which is also his jealousy of his wife's past, and the shame he feels in hosting his jealous feelings. Chapter 20 finely depicts husband and wife facing with growing embarrassment the unwelcome issue of a disruptive stepchild. Valerie believes that Charley, in favour of respectability and the law, has 'percepts' where she has 'feelings' but the reader, privy to Charley's recurring shame and self-dislike, knows better.[35] When the tragedy strikes and Charley becomes her mainstay, he knows that he and the marriage are frail enough craft, since deception, albeit maintained out of love, is whence cometh his strength.

B. M. Croker's *The Serpent's Tooth* (1912) shares so much of the plotline of *The First Claim* as to seem derivative. A 17-year-old half-English, half-Irish orphan, Lettice (Letty) Glyn, cages herself in a lopsided and loveless marriage with 36- or 37-year-old Hugo Blagdon, rich owner of a Yorkshire country house. Each is on the rebound (she from a love-match made impossible by a tyrannical aunt, Doodie Fenchurch, acting *in loco parentis*; he from Monte Carlo high life of which he is temporarily weary) and soon regrets the arranged marriage. He infantilizes, beats, and despises her, and then envies Americans for their laxer divorce laws. There is a daughter, Cara, but Letty decides to abandon her when she flees to London with her young soldier-lover, Lancelot Lumley. Unlike Hamilton's Valerie Palmer, she returns the next day, her need for freedom and love quickly succumbing to her maternalism. But her husband denies her entry; there is a scandalous divorce; though she loves Lumley she refuses to marry him, and he returns to his regiment in India while Mrs Maude Hesketh, an elderly widow, takes Letty under her wing. The daughter, like Hamilton's Gwenny, is unprepossessing, in part through being abused by her father and his sister, in part through heredity on her father's side. Yet Letty abducts her, when two years later she discovers her with a nurse in Folkestone, and takes her to Switzerland. Some years later she runs into Major Lumley on a ferry-boat who again invites her to marry him and to return to India with him, and again she refuses to abandon Cara for him, though not before he succeeds in removing her wedding ring and flinging it overboard.

Like Valerie Palmer, Letty lives a life of self-sacrifice, always imposed upon by another, in the end by her daughter, and failing to follow the example of Doodie Fenchurch ('a notable example of the strong-willed active woman' whose philosophy is that 'marriage without money is misery'), the advice of Maude Hesketh ('marriage is a blessing to few, a curse to many, and a great uncertainty to all'), and the counselling of Lancelot's young sister, Frances ('Your husband has old-fashioned ideas about his partner's duties ... The wife creed is in his blood, and belongs to to the prehistoric race that treated women as beasts of burden, and beat them with clubs; later on, women were domestic slaves, and more recently—say a hundred years ago—mere nurses and upper servants, kept at home all the year round making samplers and pickles, and shirts, and jam—and having babies').[36]

The Serpent's Tooth cannot divest itself of its baggy country-house costume—it is set in the days before motor cars, perhaps the 1880s—and the range of settings (Yorkshire, London, the Riviera, Folkestone) and country-house motifs (hunts, balls, and house parties; the young visitor, this time to England; the dilapidation of the house and the dissoluteness of its master; the force of heredity) diffuse its force and prevent the novel from having the single-minded attention of *The First Claim* to unhappy marriage, wifely desertion, divorce, child abduction, the competing claims generated by broken marriages with children—which are the real themes of both novels. Yet although the long-deferred and loving marriage between the patient Lumley and the still beautiful Letty (now 35) is a handy resolving device that we associate with the country-house novel, it is employed at last only when Letty jettisons the ungrateful daughter who abandons her mother's love for her father's gold and who gives the novel its title ('"How sharper than the serpent's tooth it is to have a thankless child," so said old King Lear', p. 364). Letty, an undeveloped pianist, singer, and composer, is an embryo New Woman (perhaps before her time) who in the end wins a measure of self-respect and independence even if she needs the intervention of a lover to do so. (On his new wife's behalf, it is Colonel Lumley who writes the farewell note to Cara after her bankrupt father dies and she seeks refuge with her mother.)

At last, Letty embodies the woman whom the candid Maude Hesketh has encouraged her all along to be. Hesketh is in Proppian terms Letty's helper, donor, and even dispatcher, and she herself is very nearly the novel's co-heroine. (Blagdon is the villain, Lumley the helper-cum-hero, Letty the victim-cum-heroine.) Maude is the woman who settled for a safe marriage when she should have followed her heart and who has lived long enough to see both changed times and the error of her ways and who wishes to prevent her young friend Letty from living a similar life of self-sacrifice. Using a bridge metaphor, she tells her:

> it is unnatural for a girl of twenty-one to cut herself adrift from the world, and devote her life absolutely to a baby of four. As I said to Blagdon, I have no doubt these things were done in years gone by,—when a wife's whole existence was concentrated on her kitchen, and her nursery; but now we live in more advanced times; every woman has her place in the world, her individual life—and, so to speak, her hand to play, and you are sitting down to take the part of Dummy! (pp. 254–5)

Whereas Hamilton relied on tragic accident to resolve her heroine's dilemma, Croker for all her country-house windiness declines to remove it so entirely from the world of hard choice.

THE SWORD AND THE SCYTHE

Gifford Lewis, who has read everything written by Somerville and Ross, observes that their heroines 'settle for the unexciting but steady suitor [the safe marriage] and discard the dangeous but sexually exciting alternative [the 'mad' marriage]'.[37] Although Edith Somerville (1858–1949) was consciously depicting a variety of contemporary political viewpoints across a span of social classes (but chiefly gentry and small farmers), attempting, as she claimed in a prefatory note, 'the cold virtue of Impartiality' (a virtue she acknowledges as rare in Ireland), the marriage she chose to subject to scrutiny in *An Enthusiast* (1921) was that between a 55-year-old baronet, an ex-colonial governor, and his 28-year-old bride.

Violet Martin ('Martin Ross') was six years dead when this novel was published, but Somerville listed her on the title page as a collaborator and dedicated it to her in that capacity. This was because Somerville believed that Martin from beyond the grave was still an active partner, for she had told Somerville in a séance that their work was unfinished.[38] In *An Enthusiast* the young wife asks her shy suitor to try to contact her should she 'go over first', perhaps an echo of a pact between Martin and Somerville.[39] But collaboration was also a fact, since in the novel Somerville drew on Ross's work, for example on the latter's September 1913 article on the Irish horse and its prowess over tall banks, one of which brings defeat to young Lady Ducarrig as she competes against a man succumbing to her charms, Daniel Palliser; in an 1889 letter to Somerville, Martin was convinced that 'a large bank with a tired horse is much more terrible than a shaky ceiling'. So exalted a regard did Ross think the horse was held in Ireland that she thought it could help, in the dangerous year of 1913—when Ulster was flexing its muscles against the prospect of Home Rule—especially through the Dublin Horse Show, to hold North and South together and guarantee a future 'pure of politics'; indeed, referring to the horse, Ross entitled her article, 'An Incorrigible Unionist'.[40] The year in which *An Enthusiast* is set, 1920, was even more dangerous, with Sinn Fein/IRA not just flexing but using its muscles in night-time raids for arms in isolated farmhouses and country houses and attacks on the RIC, and the newly arrived Black and Tans (a special soldiery mainly recruited from Great War veterans) already earning their fearsome reputation with their violent reprisals. 'Look at this country!' Somerville's hero exclaims. 'The police gone, our arms taken from us, either by raiders or by the Government—it comes to the same thing! Our houses absolutely defenceless...' (p. 74).

But agrarian changes of longer duration and that were a staple of country-house novels are still occurring in *An Enthusiast,* causing it to hang unstably between the anachronistic and the contemporary, not just in theme and plot (the decline of the gentry and the threat to their estates) but also in style, with Somerville's brave attempt at a prose realism that is adequate to the serious-ness of Irish affairs being sabotaged by her familiar, reflex (and popular) archness and levity of narration. On the death of his father, Colonel Palliser, Daniel faces a choice between renting out Monalour, his country house, and absorbing crippling death duties, opting for the former and retreating to a lodge on the demesne. There are two plotlines in the novel. One (attempting to serve social and political realism) is Palliser's attempt to hold the middle ground between a defensive unionism and a nationalism on the offensive. His strategy is to develop an agenda of agricultural reform and an immersion in strictly local politics, despite his outburst (quoted above) about the vulner-ability of the country houses. The second plotline (serving what ends as tragic romance) is the one that interests me here: Palliser's slowly deepening attrac-tion to the young wife of his new tenant of Monalour, Lord Ducarrig.

As Palliser's attraction grows, the Ducarrig marriage coincidentally declines from the adequacy of some of Tynan's fictional marriages to lovelessness, with Ducarrig increasingly neglectful of his wife (Car) and increasingly attentive to Palliser's cousin Eileen, unsuccessfully chosen by Palliser's mother as her son's future wife. Palliser's fall into love is gradual because his northern breeding (his mother is an Ulsterwoman) has encouraged him to strangle sentiment: 'He had always banked down his fires, and no one suspected their intensity'; there has been emotional diversion, perhaps sublimation—'his romance, his passion, was Ireland' (p. 56); his cousin thinks of Palliser as a romantic utilitarian (p. 100), a man passionate about practical things. Yet in a moment that resembles in significance Brian Hogan's carrying of Ann Logan across the stream, Dan and Car make intimate contact: 'He was standing beside her; as she rose from her seat on the rock, she stumbled and caught at his arm, steadying herself; her hand, a lovely hand, white, sensitive, flashing with rings, rested there for an instant' (p. 74).

Palliser is a man who is unsure and unmoored but the music that Car plays and sings bewitches him and begins to focus his life. One evening, in a scene that exploits the romantic potential of the country house and the symbolic potential of its landscape (the confused darkness of shrubbery, the lure of decorative bridges and moonlit extensive lawns: small rubicons to be crossed), and the sexual figurativeness of music, Palliser steals through his demesne to Monalour.

The house that had been his father's—he could not even yet feel that it was his—was a denser grey shadow at the farther end of the lawn. It was but little past ten o'clock and some lights pierced the shadow. He went nearer, and the delicate sound of a piano came to him through the quiet night. His wandering steps lost their indefiniteness. This was luck coming to him. The night wanted but music. He went in long strides to the bridge across the sunk fence, while the sound deepened and gained body, and that strange conviction of romance that can sometimes be born of music made by one unseen, coming out of the hidden secret of a house to a listener in the open air, came upon him. He crossed the bridge, and keeping in the gloom of the shrubs, crept nearer. The music ceased. Dan waited; he thought that the intensity of his desire to hear her voice again must have effect. Perhaps that was in truth the reason that gradually, almost as a perfume makes itself felt, her voice stole to his ear. (pp. 81–2)

For her part, Car is, like Thurston's Isabel, a beautiful and self-assured young woman; like Palliser she is a Great War veteran, she a nurse, he a soldier. Her feelings are more measured than those of O'Donovan's and Tynan's heroines, used to suitors and admirers and condescending to the awkward Palliser in her thoughts. Yet she too succumbs to the prospect of true love and at last contemplates leaving her husband for Palliser and what would be, in Tynan's term, a second and 'mad' marriage and in O'Donovan's, the fruit of the holy tree. (For his part, Palliser thinks that the imminent necessary sale of part of the Monalour estate, agrarian times being what they are in Ireland, would make flight with Lady Ducarrig feasible.) Towards the end of the novel, Father Hugh MacNamara, a priest sympathetic to Palliser's attempts at reform, sees Palliser and Lady Ducarrig in an afternoon lakeside rendezvous and thinks of them as Dante's star-crossed Paolo and Francesca.

That evening, Dan Palliser dines at Monalour House and Car sings a song that accurately and poignantly expresses his desire: 'Come o'er the sea, Maiden, with me' ('Let Fortune frown, so we love and part not—| 'Tis life where thou art, 'tis death where thou art not!').[41] The evening builds in romantic suspense, and a guest requests another song that again expresses Palliser's feelings, just at the moment Lord Ducarrig confronts Palliser with an anonymous letter that exposes the affair. The song is Salaman's 1836 setting of Shelley's 'I Arise from Dreams of Thee' with its lines that echo Palliser's earlier approaches to Monalour: 'I arise from dreams of thee, | And a spirit in my feet | Has led me— who knows how?—| To thy chamber-window, sweet!', and presages the imminent tragedy: 'The nightingale's complaint, | It dies upon her heart, | As I must die on thine, | O, beloved as thou art!' It is from her chamber-window that Lady Ducarrig sees the tragedy unfold in a trice as both plotlines fatally cross after Dan has weighed with his 'responsible tristia' (to borrow from Seamus Heaney) the conflict between his love for Car (and his duty to it) and his vow to help Ireland (but knowing Ireland's history of betrayal of its helpers).

Palliser dies with his father's Crimean sword in his hand and when Somerville provides as his epitaph the last stanza of Rossetti's narrative poem, 'The Staff and the Scrip', we might recall that Rossetti's pilgrim was equipped with a sword by the besieged Queen Blanchelys before going out to do battle against Duke Luke on her behalf. The pilgrim succeeds but at the cost of his own life, and Palliser's achievement is equally ambiguous; just as the Queen eventually dies and joins her lover in heaven, so Lady Ducarrig's eventual death will (we can surmise) permit her to join Palliser, who has merely 'gone over first'. But as my later discussion of the other plotline in *An Enthusiast* will suggest, Palliser does not taste victory in the military lists, save perhaps in the case of this one IRA raid on a country house, and then for a mere moment before his death, though Somerville (who was a constitutional or perhaps only a sentimental nationalist) might have believed that the IRA would be eventually defeated in arms.

However, Somerville's use of song and poem suggests that the terms of romance in which she was writing were more importunate than those of realism. There is an undoubted power of romance in the last scenes of *An Enthusiast*. Yet Somerville cannot, any more than the other novelists, carry through on the themes of adultery and true love and depict a Lawrentian smashing of convention, in this case the convention that forbade a man from alienating the affections of a woman even when she was trapped in a marriage 'that was no marriage' (p. 259). In K. C. Thurston, Hamilton, O'Donovan, and Somerville, tragic accident may validate the forbidden or unfulfilled love but it is also a resolution by which the novelist can evade the implications of true love successfully pursued amidst social disapproval. True, an emotional realism could be argued. In an 1890 essay, Ross, having noted the rarity of romantic feeling in peasant marriages, saw love as twofold. 'It is romance that holds the two-edged sword, the sharp ecstasy and the severing scythe stroke, the expectancy and the disillusioning, the trance and the clear vision.'[42] Somerville may have agreed, for in *An Enthusiast* love, like politics, is seen bifocally as naively idealistic and then as ruinously real. Lewis suggests that both women may have been disappointed in love. Ross's death may have emboldened Somerville (to whom in their joint composition, according to Lewis, Ross left the romantic and sexual portions of their novels) to take the possibility of true love farther than Ross might have felt comfortable with. Moreover, the failure of Thurston, Tynan, and Somerville to carry through may be a literary hesitation due to the conventions of the romance genre (which allows tragedy but not a final realism), not to mention the expectations of their customary readers; or it may be a social hesitation due to the authors' grasp of Irish reality with its hostility to adultery or even second marriages contracted out of true love. Yet failure is what it seems like from our perspective, despite the considerable alternative achievements of these novels.[43]

FAITH, LOVE, AND MARRIAGE

Beatrice Grimshaw's notion of social station would in her early life have been as firmly conditioned as Tynan's or Somerville's but as a young woman she rebelled against Victorian social hierarchy and formal relationships and later encountered varieties of liaisons, cohabitations, and marriages in her travels and sojourns in the South Seas. This rebellion may have been made easier because she hailed from a majority Protestant population in the north-east of Ireland (led by merchants and industrialists) and did not grow up with the same degree of entitlement, minority, and endangerment as the southern Protestant inhabitants of the country house. In her novel, *Nobody's Island* (1917), her hero expresses an intense dislike, as withering as Tynan's, for idlers and middlemen, and for mere capitalists, yet her admiration, here and elsewhere, is not for the titled and blueblooded English or Anglo-Irish, or for the higher orders generally, but rather for the energetic: the restless traders, prospectors, adventurers, and go-getters of the South Pacific islands. Her self-imposed task as a novelist is to show true love flourishing among these incorrigibles with their seemingly material drives. Ben Slade, the Australian 'rough-rider, company-promoter, mine-exploiter, discoverer, pioneer, and a score of things beside'—voices contempt for 'the landholding, non-producing classes' and tells Edith, his true love, 'Now you're seeing that money may be the cleanest thing on earth, and the getting of money much more dignified than the taking of it, as the kept classes do.' Edith herself in turn admits to him: 'When I was unhappy, I used to be something of a suffragette; wanted votes and independence, and couldn't stand being paid for by... by... But your money is another thing... It seems to be mine, as much as the sky and the air—and you.'[44] For Grimshaw, money at its best is a just reward for hard work, enterprise, and good luck; though it can be shared, the best money is not inherited nor should it support profligacy and idleness or shore up social stature.

The true love between Ben and Edith surmounts 'social differences' (p. 75) and this because Ben is 'naturally' well-bred. One of the themes of *Nobody's Island* is in fact the superiority of natural man or woman to the 'over-civilised people' (p. 34) whom Slade, and presumably Grimshaw, dislikes. Although it is tempting at first to see Grimshaw as an exploiter of exotic colonial spaces, playing with ethnic stereotypes against a backdrop of entrenched prejudice and imperialist snobbery (Australia and New Zealand are the proxy imperial powers in the novels), her narration is in fact often slanted towards a sympathy for the native South Pacific islanders. In the adventure story, *Vaiti of the Islands* (1906), for example, she mocks a yacht's complement of upper-class English visitors to a New Hebridean island where they stumble on a party of cannibals helping themselves at Vaiti's invitation to the visitors' picnic consisting of 'gold-necked champagne bottles lying coolly embedded in ice-baskets; of topaz-colored jellies, trembling on silver dishes; of flaky, savory pies, and delicate cold meats, and crisp green salads' (p. 274), and the narrator enjoys their discomfiture as much as do the laughing cannibals. Grimshaw is mocking European race-snobbery and class-snobbery as well as luxury unearned by work, and during the scene mocks also the visitors' European romantic primitivism (which is not a thousand miles away from the primitivist enthusiasm of the more romantic Irish Revivalists). Moreover, although this too could be regarded with a jaundiced eye as exploitation, Grimshaw often enthusiastically incorporates native superstition and lore (real or made-up) into her plots, using them to exact revenge on superior or unscrupulous whites or, as in the episode of the horrific monstrous centipede (the 'black viri') in *Vaiti of the Islands*, showing them to be true in order to generate excitement; this novel is primarily an exotic romance and a colonial adventure novel, much thinner and more episodic than *When the Red Gods Call* (1911) and *Nobody's Island*, though there are still interesting things we can say about it.[45]

At the same time, Grimshaw is unsentimentally aware that there are limits to European identification with natives (whether by author or by characters) and in *Vaiti* the unscrupulous adventurer Donahue demonstrates the proposition that 'a white man cannot "live native" without going downhill very fast' (p. 212), and Donahue is nearly at the bottom, a downward trajectory which Conrad gave apocalyptic force when he followed Kurtz in *Heart of Darkness*. Vaiti's father, Saxon, a former gentleman and London clubman who was disgraced and lit out for the South Seas, is on the same trajectory, being a trader sailing close to the wind, dabbling in grave-robbing (selling native bones to a German scientist), engaging in blackbirding (kidnapping native labour, in this case for the Queensland sugar plantations), drinking like a fish. But he is kept off the bottom by his daughter. Saxon not only changed his name after his disgrace but also faked his death, and we are assured that 'Many such substantial ghosts roam the South Seas unexorcised' (p. 15) and that typically they try 'not to run the risk of meeting other ghosts (with university accents, tea-colored families, and a preference for modest retirement on steamer days) who may possibly have been alive together with you, before...' (p. 126).

At worst, Grimshaw's is a hybrid perspective and Grimshaw has an almost didactic interest in the half-caste. Vaiti is the product of an English gentleman and a Maori princess; she has been schooled in a Tahitian convent but also in the South Seas school of hard knocks, and though she possesses 'The double soul that is the curse of the half-caste', derived from the 'soldier of fortune, and the sensuous island princess' (p. 287), on balance Vaiti's ability to move between cultures, as between islands (which in Grimshaw can seem like metaphors of separate identities), is a gift rather than a curse. At the end she marries a native island king rather than the English naval officer who courts her, but it is not suggested that by this marriage she has compromised her profitable hybridity, her cultural mobility. In some sense Vaiti is surely reflecting a more graphic version of Grimshaw's own biculturalism into which, time and again in her novels, she reads freedom and increase rather than dilution or reduction.

However, Vaiti's marriage is not inspired by love and is a spurious reversion to her Maori identity, and the novel ends with the implication that rocky times lie ahead for husband and wife, for king and princess (now queen), because of Vaiti's reckless independence, her boyish ardour and aggressiveness, her insubordination and refusal to kowtow. Mating and marriage secured by true love can work, though, between those who are, in terms of social class, radically different, and *Vaiti of the Islands* includes the story of the elopement of a Russian princess, promised to the Czarewitch, and a Polish lieutenant in the Hussars who vanish and whose whereabouts are unknown until Vaiti finds the princess's grave and that of their day-old son, and the skeleton of the lieutenant lying beside a rusted revolver. The lovers had found their own paradise on a South Seas island. Marriage launched on love can surmount the differences even between heathen and Christian. Vaiti is the progeny of such a union while in *Nobody's Island* Captain Campbell marries the 15-year-old half-caste Murua and intends to take her to England, though he regards her as a purely natural woman beside whom even Edith is 'shut up within the fence of a plain gold ring ("By Jove, more than one ring", he thought', pp. 319–20).

But these are lesser unions in Grimshaw, for whom there is only one ideal marriage: a marriage of love between two Roman Catholics. The marriage of Stephanie and Lynch in *When the Red Gods Call* just qualifies because it is sanctified by the Protestant Stephanie's adherence to the Catholic proscription of divorce, making her a kind of honorary Catholic. Marriage and Catholicism is one of Grimshaw's chief themes. If the plot of *Nobody's Island* is tortuous, it is because in it Grimshaw tries to play enough variations to satisfy as many current ideas of love and marriage as possible before reaching her grand and perfect finale.

The opening chapter is set in Portrush, Co. Antrim where a small boy sees a woman crying alone on the strand before she boards a train with a man. The boy and his fishwife mother are 'Scoto-Irish' but though they are vividly sketched in, they play no further role when the scene shifts to London (in chapter 2) and to the southern hemisphere thereafter; perhaps Grimshaw here is merely representing her own migration from Co. Antrim, one that followed the same direction. The woman is an Englishwoman, Edith Campbell, and we conclude later that she has been accompanying her husband on a golfing holiday ('Every golfer in the United Kingdom knows the station of Portrush, that wide gusty hall above the green Atlantic,' p. 2) and been expressing in solitude the unhappiness of her marriage. In ensuing chapters we learn why.

Edith Cardillion had married Slade but when he tells her on their one-way honeymoon voyage to Ceylon that he had been married unhappily for ten years, she as a Catholic is appalled, knowing that, as a priest on board confirms, any Catholic who marries a divorcé is without exception excommunicated. To his sorrow, they shake hands and go their ways: she to London where in time she marries Godfrey Campbell, the wealthy 'Cocoa King', he to New Guinea where he learns, too late, that his first wife has died. Nevertheless, Slade cannot forget Edith and travels to London to tell her, guessing that her second marriage has been a form of 'suicide'. Here the plot creaks noisily. Slade arrives by coincidence as Edith is leaving her house, having just found her husband dead; she is afraid that because he was drunk and insulted her she will be suspected of having poisoned him. Slade and she decide to flee to the South Pacific by taking ship, though they remember with anxiety the recent case of Crippen, the murderer caught at his destination port by telegraphy. She travels as Mrs Godfrey Campbell but feigns her suicide and continues the voyage as 'Mary Phelps', having disguised herself and flung her engagement ring and 'plain gold band' overboard. They marry, this time as Catholics, in New York, cross America to San Francisco and from there reach the South Sea islands with which she falls in love, and eventually the sanctuary of Nobody's Island, an uninhabited island paradise that Slade owns. Campbell's brother tracks them down but he too succumbs to the lure of island life and falls in love with young Murua; besides, it turns out that the authorities concluded that Godfrey had in fact committed suicide.

But if Edith can escape the past, she cannot escape 'her inflexible Catholic ideas about divorce' (p. 308), nor clearly does Grimshaw believe she should. For Edith discovers that Slade had been married to yet another still-living woman, Mabel, and as a result leaves Slade, taking their child with her, and returns to London. She comes back to Eden and to Slade only when she learns that since Mabel was Catholic while Slade was not, theirs was no genuine Catholic marriage (any more than her own first marriage to Slade), unlike her own second marriage to Slade, which she now happily resumes.

There are loveless marriages in Grimshaw, as in Tynan, and safe marriages, as in Tynan, but the ideal marriages are not the 'mad' marriages we find in Tynan, marriages thought by Society to be foolish but in reality love-inspired. Rather, they are marriages just as Catholic as those in Tynan, but thought by Catholic society back home in otherwise decadent and unvirile Britain (the only society for Grimshaw finally to count where marriage is concerned) to be right, not mad. 'Madness' in Grimshaw takes other forms much more colourful than the love-matches in Tynan and O'Donovan but in the end it is kept in check by what we might presume to be the obligatory religious strictness of the convert.

NOTES

1. For the function of marriage in earlier Irish fiction, see Miranda Burgess, 'The National Tale and Allied Genres', in John Wilson Foster (ed.), *The Cambridge Companion to the Irish Novel* (Cambridge: Cambridge University Press, 2006), pp. 54–6.
2. Eleanor Alexander, *The Lady of the Well* (London: Edward Arnold, 1906), pp. 2–3.
3. Alexander's use of falconry is apt, as Frederick II himself wrote a famous treatise on falconry to which the novelist refers (p. 113).
4. James Harpole (J. Johnston Abraham), *A Surgeon's Heritage* (London: Cassell, 1953), pp. 18–19, 24.
5. *Surgeon's Journey: The Autobiography of J. Johnston Abraham* (London: Heinemann, 1957), pp. 121–2. *The Night Nurse* was adapted into a film in the United States, entitled *Nora O'Neale* (in Europe, *Irish Hearts*); 'Nora Townsend', as the name appears in the novel, wouldn't have been a sufficiently Irish name for Hollywood.

6. Abraham, *The Night Nurse* (London: Chapman and Hall, 1913), pp. 50, 101.

7. On this topic, see E. J. Hobsbawm, *The Age of Empire, 1875–1914* (New York: Pantheon Books, 1987), pp. 206–7. It was fitting that later Abraham should from his Harley Street surgery write an Introduction to a translation of *Het Volkomen Huwelijk* (1926) by the Dutch scientist, Theodor Hendrik van de Velde, a wide-ranging work of sexual physiology and technique (as a component of marriage) that nevertheless has sections on love-play, love as an abstract concept, and love as a personal emotion. The epigraph on the title page is from Balzac: 'Marriage is a science.' See *Ideal Marriage: Its Physiology and Technique,* trans. Stella Brown. Introduction by J. Johnston Abraham (London: Heinemann, 1928; New York: Civici Friede, 1938).

8. Abraham, *The Night Nurse,* pp. 116, 94–5, 6. Hobsbawm tells us that many British middle-class women who sought a career solved the domestic problem through childlessness or spinsterhood; in any case, the excess of women (1.3 million in Britain in 1911) made marriage impossible for many: *The Age of Empire,* p. 216. There are other nubile women in novels of the period set in Ireland who initially do not wish to marry; they are strong women who are not self-consciously New Women yet who in the end (or secretly from the start wish to) submit themselves to marriage or love; they include Mona Scully in *Mrs Geoffrey* (1886) by Mrs Hungerford and Nanno Troy in *Traffic* (1914 and set partly in Waterford) by E. Temple Thurston.

9. Frank Harris, *The Bomb* (1908; New York: Mitchell Kennerley, 1909), p. 106.

10. Abraham, *The Night Nurse,* pp. 113, 116, 162, 247. This typhus outbreak apparently occurred, for Abraham (as 'James Harpole') remarks that typhus at the time of his writing (1930s) was unknown in Europe save for Russia, the Balkans, and the west of Ireland: *Leaves from a Surgeon's Case-Book* (1937; London: Cassell for the British Publishers Guild, 1941), p. 149.

11. *The Fly on the Wheel* was first serialized in *Blackwood's Edinburgh Magazine* (1907–8) before publication as a book by Blackwood & Sons.

12. Katherine Cecil Thurston, *The Fly on the Wheel* (1908; London: Virago, 1987), pp. 3, 82, 105–6.

13. According to a contemporary profile of Thurston, it was her husband who encouraged her to try her hand at fiction: 'The Making of a Novelist', *The Lady's Realm,* April 1905: 655.

14. Stephen J. Brown, *Ireland in Fiction,* p. 293.

15. E. Temple Thurston, *Traffic: The Story of a Faithful Woman* (1906; London: Chapman and Hall, 1914), pp. 141, 53, 49, 94, 265.

16. Stephen J. Brown remarks that the novel 'contains strange misconceptions of Catholic doctrine and morality' (*Ireland in Fiction,* p. 292) and this is the kind of passage he may be alluding to. But what is at issue is what a simple Irish country woman like Nanno Troy *believes* the doctrine and morality to be, having, surely, been fed a cut-and-dried version of them.

17. We find the same condescension elsewhere in Thurston; e.g.: 'I often wonder why God evolved a creature so antagonistic to all His laws as woman'; 'If I could

approach mathematics with the same spirit as do ninety-eight women out of a hundred, I might be rather good at them.' These and other remarks occur in essays collected as *The Patchwork Papers*. But we must remember that the differences between women and men were on many commentators' and writers' minds at the time. Also, the majority of Thurston's readers would have been women and I often feel he is trying to entertain them with mildly provocative humour.

18. E. Temple Thurston, 'Realism' in *The Patchwork Papers* (London: Chapman and Hall, 1910), pp. 43–51.

19. E. Temple Thurston, *Katherine: A Novel* (New York: Harper & Bros., 1907), p. 31. The American edition abbreviated the British title.

20. For Fr O'Donovan's social work in Loughrea, Co. Galway, and for his later work at Toynbee Hall, a University Settlement house for those engaged in social work in the impoverished East End, see Jane Emery, *Rose Macaulay: A Writer's Life* (London: John Murray, 1991), pp. 164–8.

21. I discuss *Father Ralph* more fully in *Fictions of the Irish Literary Revival* (1987).

22. Harold Orel refers to the popularity of this novel in *Popular Fiction in England, 1914–1918* (New York: Harvester Wheatsheaf, 1992), p. 21.

23. I discuss *Waiting* in *The Cambridge History of Irish Literature*, ed. Margaret Kelleher and Philip O'Leary (Cambridge: Cambridge University Press, 2006), vol. 2, pp. 144–5.

24. Gerald O'Donovan, *The Holy Tree* London: William Heinemann, 1922), p. 30.

25. Curiously, what Ann says is very similar to what the married Englishwoman Edith Thompson wrote to her young lover in September 1922 (the year *The Holy Tree* was published): '[my husband] has the right by law to all that you have the right to by nature and love,' *Trial of Frederick Bywaters and Edith Thompson*, ed. Filson Young (1923; Edinburgh: William Hodge and Co., 1951), p. 212. She and Bywaters were hanged in January 1923 for the murder of her husband. Living in England by then, O'Donovan would have known this well-publicized and well-documented case though whether or not he read Thompson's words before completing his novel I do not know.

26. Like *Father Ralph* and *Waiting*, *The Holy Tree* had some basis in autobiography. Having left the Church, O'Donovan married an Anglo-Irish Protestant in 1910. A daughter later called the marriage a 'misalliance' (Emery, p. 170), though the couple stayed together. After being invalided out of the army (RASC), O'Donovan became an editor at Collins, then during the Great War he worked for the Government in London. (Emery remarks that with his upper-class British accent, O'Donovan seemed to have transformed himself into someone 'courtly' and 'Anglo-Irish', pp. 163, 168. His daughters were sent to Oxford and Cambridge.) While at the Ministry of Information, he met the unmarried Rose Macaulay, the English writer, and they fell in love (reversing the gender of the spouse in *The Holy Tree*). Apparently Macaulay and O'Donovan kept their affair secret from most of their friends for the twenty years it lasted. See Miranda Seymour's review of Sarah Lefanu's *Rose Macaulay* (2003), 'A Lilo for Cleopatra', *Times Literary Supplement*, 27 June 2003: 11. In 1939 Macaulay was at the wheel when her car, carrying

O'Donovan, crashed. O'Donovan suffering concussion, then a stroke, and finally the cancer that killed him in 1942. After he died, Macaulay told Rosamond Lehmann that *The Holy Tree* was about them, and that Ann Logan's hymn to love was O'Donovan's coded contribution to their debate about whether to become secret lovers: Emery, pp. 186–8.

27. The marriage in which a wife or husband (more often the wife) goes mad recurs in Victorian fiction. In Crommelin's *A Woman-Derelict* (1901), one character tells Elinor Grey that Dr Strong's young wife Retta went mad shortly after their apparently loving marriage (she became a religious lunatic) and reminds Grey that madness is not a ground for divorce in Britain though she has heard tell that it is in Victoria (she must mean Australia). (This is just as well, since Elinor does not love Strong, which love would in any case have impeded her charitable impulses.) This mad marriage is brought to an end when Retta in her lunacy takes her own life, but since she takes Elinor with her, Dr Strong's problem (he has fallen in love with Elinor) is not solved. Crommelin tackles another marriage problem in this novel, the one caused when a spouse disappears and is assumed dead and the surviving spouse remarries, only to have the first spouse reappear, rendering the second marriage bigamous. This marriage problem is solved when Elinor dies, leaving her husband (with whom she had a true and loving marriage) in a 'safe' marriage with a woman who is kept in the dark about Elinor's return. The recurrence of these marriage problems in the fiction reflects the extent to which marriage, its discontents and legal complexities, and grounds for divorce, were being debated in Britain at the time.

28. Katharine Tynan, *A Mad Marriage* (London: Collins, [1922]), p. 3.

29. There is a serious problem with the date of events in the novel. Chapter II opens in the coronation year of 1902; Judge John Somers has not seen Hilary St Austell, the novelist who accompanied him to Rose Donoghue's trial, for twenty years (p. 15). This would date the trial some time in the 1880s. When Sir John drives Hester from the train station to see her mother and father he does so in a 'station fly' (pp. 211, 216) which would square with 1902 or thereabouts. However, when later in the novel the judge recalls the trial, he begins: 'It was in 1901, I think, that I was Judge of Assize on the Western Circuit. I remember that St Austell went down with me...' (p. 202). This would date later events, and the solving of the murder, at around 1920 or 1921 (the novel came out in 1922), implying that the war Jim O'Donnell came back from was the Great War. (But in 1921 surely Sir John and Hester would have taken a taxi from the station?) I cannot find sufficient dating in the text to solve these discrepancies.

30. That Lady Ponsonby's grandfather could have been a henchman of the Liberator, Daniel O'Connell, the architect of Catholic Emancipation and who flourished in the 1830s and 1840s, would square with the novel's being set in the main in the months after 1902 rather than 1920 or 1921.

31. Ella MacMahon, *The Job* (London: James Nisbet & Co., 1914), p. 191.

32. The *Times Literary Supplement* reviewer clearly didn't agree, since he or she thought that *The Job* from cover to cover is 'nice' and could be given to 'young

persons of the schoolroom age': quoted by Harold Orel, *Popular Fiction in England, 1914–1918* (Hemel Hempstead: Harvester Wheatsheaf, 1992), p. 39.

33. Mrs Hungerford, *The Hoyden: A Novel* (London, 1894), originally published in three volumes by Heinemann. I have quoted from the Project Gutenberg online version, p. 191.

34. M. Hamilton, *The First Claim* (1906; New York: Doubleday, Page & Co., 1907), p. 96.

35. Ibid., p. 212. Two slight subplots connect *The First Claim* with other popular novels by Irish women: young Vera Carruthers's passionate attachment to Valerie (shades of L. T. Meade and Mrs Hungerford), and young Gwenny's cross-dressing disguise as a boy (shades of Katherine Cecil Thurston and Sarah Grand).

36. B. M. Croker, *The Serpent's Tooth* (London: Hutchinson, 1912), pp. 2, 83, 132, 184.

37. Gifford Lewis, *Edith Somerville: A Biography* (Dublin: Four Courts Press, 2005), p. 447.

38. Gifford Lewis, *Somerville and Ross: The World of the Irish R.M.* (New York: Viking Penguin, 1985), p. 193; Lewis, *Edith Somerville: A Biography*, pp. 289–90, 306.

39. O. Œ. Somerville ('in collaboration with Martin Ross'), *An Enthusiast* (London: Longmans, Green & Co., 1921), p. 169.

40. *The Selected Letters of Somerville and Ross*, ed. Gifford Lewis (London: Faber and Faber, 1989), p. 128. Martin Ross, 'An Incorrigible Unionist', in Somerville and Ross, *Stray-Aways* (London: Longmans, Green & Co., 1920), p. 196.

41. *An Enthusiast*, p. 252. 'Come O'er the Sea Maiden with Me' is attributed both to Jane Sloman (1857) and Gustave Geary (1881): see the 'Music for the Nation: American Sheet Music' website.

42. Lewis, *Edith Somerville*, p. 447. Either Violet Martin was deeply ambivalent about marriage or Lewis is inconsistent. In her biography of Somerville, Lewis suggests that that both Somerville and Martin had considered marriage to others as a possibility but that they had 'concealed this' (p. 447) and writing had provided an alternative way of life. But in an annotation to a letter from Martin to Somerville, Lewis remarks that for Martin 'marriage was a thing to be avoided if possible', perhaps because of the unpromising models of her half-sisters' arranged marriages: *The Selected Letters of Somerville and Ross*, p. 82.

43. This plotline of *An Enthusiast* is full of the longing in forbidden or unconsummated love, and one is tempted to see in the relationship of Dan and Car a transposition by Somerville of her relationship with Martin, a retrospective reading by Somerville of their partnership as a thwarted romance. Their practical relationship was a marriage of minds and perhaps a kind of unacknowledgeable marriage in a more literal sense.

44. Beatrice Grimshaw, *Nobody's Island* (London: Hurst & Blackett, 1917), pp. 5, 71–2, 51–2. Perhaps less convincingly, Grimshaw's eponymous adventuress in *Vaiti of the Islands* (1906) tries likewise to sanitize money but admits that money equals power, importance, and freedom—as well as the means to buy pretty Paris dresses: *Vaiti of the Islands* (New York: A. Wessels, 1908), pp. 42, 48.

45. The exotic romance has a lengthy pedigree: see Miranda Burgess, 'The National Tale and Allied Genres,' in *The Cambridge Companion to the Irish Novel*, pp. 40–1.

9

Métier de Femme: New Woman Fiction

PORTRAIT OF THE ARTIST AS A YOUNG GIRL

If Grimshaw was a rebel from an early age, her rebellion was perhaps made more possible for her as a Protestant. The irony is that a short while into her revolt she became a Catholic and as such accepted beliefs that set strict limits to the very freedom in marital relations that she adopted as one of her major fictional themes. To understand how difficult it would have been to become a Revolting Daughter in an Irish Catholic household and community, and having already read Katherine Cecil Thurston's *The Fly on the Wheel*, we might turn to Hannah Lynch's *Autobiography of a Child*.

One particular woe in Croker's Ireland depicted in *Lismoyle* is the plight of young Catholic country girls. Mrs Donovan expresses sorrow for these girls: 'The boys are always started out in life; their sisters left at home, with never a glimpse of a lover, or a chance to see the world. Look at those seven Miss Parsons—I call it downright pathetic—and the three Moores.' And another character later remarks that 'bad as it is, the men, as usual, have the best of it...I asked a young woman lately, what they did with themselves on a holiday? And she replied: "we go to Mass, and after that we just sit at home, and chat." Now the men crowd to football matches, and play cards, and poach, but the poor girls must find it deadly. No wonder, they go off to Australia, and America.'[1] A more impassioned protest than Croker's against the treatment of girls in Ireland, poor or rich, is made by Hannah Lynch, another unjustly neglected Irish writer of the Victorian period.[2] *Autobiography of a Child* was published in *Blackwood's Edinburgh Magazine* 1898–9 and in book form in 1899 and is an alarming testimony of girlhood suffering and martyrdom beside which Stephen Dedalus's upbringing was a Sunday excursion. Lynch's implication is that 'Society—spelt big' means, where the Irish girl is concerned, a Catholic society unjust from top to bottom. If *Autobiography of a Child* is fiction, it reads with the unflagging honesty of autobiography. The narrator, the grown-up Angela, regards herself as now 'resting in the equable tones of middle life', as having achieved a 'drab-robed content', but her story is one of nearly surrealistic suffering at the hands of her mother, sisters, uncle, and, later, nuns in a convent school. Her life has charted three phases: the passive and suffering phase; the rebellious phase; and the present phase of contentedness.[3] The settings for these phases are, respectively, Kildare (in what seems to be a biggish house or even country house), an English convent school, and Ireland again in her maturity.

Growing up in Ireland, Angela would 'warble my strange symphonies' and a friend would recall her stepfather's prediction that 'She'll be a Catherine Hayes yet... or maybe she'll compose illigant operas.' (Catherine Hayes was the nineteenth-century Limerick-born diva.) The grown-up Angela remarks sadly: 'Alas! I neither sing nor compose, and listen to the singing and music of others with unemotional quietude. So many different achievements have been fondly expected of me, that I have preferred the alternative of achieving nothing. Better demolish a multitude of expectations than build one's house of the perishable bricks of a single one.' The *Autobiography* is a reverse *Portrait of the Artist as a Young Man*: the artistic ambition has been killed not roused by adversity, for Angela is a girl and thus already labours under disability; it is a *Portrait of the Artist Manquéé as a Young Girl*. In convent school, Angela hears the dancing master Parker play the air *Nora Creina* on the violin (to which Thomas Moore set 'Lesbia Hath a Beaming Eye') while performing the *chassé-croisé* and back in Ireland she gives her impersonation of him, chanting the song. She adds: 'On the stage, whether actress or dancer, my fortune would long ago have been made, and as an acrobat I should have won glory in my teens. But old-fashioned parents never think of these things. If you are a girl, and fortune forsakes the domestic hearth, they tell you to go and be a governess, and bless your stars that, thanks to their good sense, you are enabled to earn a miserable crust in the path of respectability' (pp. 96, 162, 224).

Artistic ability and ambition aside, the Irish girl is still disadvantaged. This too is part of the Condition of Ireland that caught the attention of the fiction writers. Angela recalls being told of the arrival of a new baby in the house and remarks (with a curious demographic spin):

another lamentable little girl born into this improvident dolorous vale of Irish misery. Elsewhere boys are born in plenty. In Ireland,—the very wretchedest land on earth for woman, the one spot on the globe where no provision is made for her, and where parents consider themselves as exempt of all duty, of tenderness, of justice in her regard, where her lot as daughter, wife, and old maid bears no resemblance to the ideal of civilisation,—a dozen girls are born for one boy. The parents moan, and being fatalists as well as Catholics, reflect that it is the will of God, as if they were not in the least responsible; and while they assure you that they have not wherewith to fill an extra mouth, which is inevitably true, they continue to produce their twelve, fifteen, or twenty infants with alarming, and incredible indifference. This is Irish virtue. The army of inefficient Irish governesses and starving illiterate Irish teachers cast upon the Continent, forces one to lament a virtue whose results are so heartless and so deplorable. (pp. 196–7)

The governess, of course, was a familiar figure in the life and literature of Britain as well,[4] where the position of governess allowed a young woman to be a teacher without leaving the domestic sphere and without submitting herself to the pressures of the educational system; moreover it could result in social class advancement, even if only by association, and broaden her horizons if the position were away from her home town and even home country. But Lynch implies that a different and harsher set of circumstances obtained among Irish middle-class Catholic families, and which constituted a dark crevice of Irish life she felt constrained, as a traveller and self-taught cultural observer, to expose to the light; I know no modern dedicated study of Irish Catholic middle-class life in the Victorian and Edwardian periods.

Whereas Lynch's membership of the Ladies' Land League and her publishing of *United Ireland* from Paris on its suppression[5] would suggest a familiar Irish nationalism of the distaff auxiliary variety, the Europeanized Lynch's field of view was far wider than Irish nationalism's. Fifteen years or so before Joyce, she travelled in Europe, lectured in Paris on English literature, published a book on George Meredith, and had influence at *Le Figaro*. She was that figure who is by now familiar to the reader: the strong, independent woman who was neither dogmatic feminist nor mere subscriber to any male doctrine. She was much concerned with the education of girls and devotes a great deal of space to the subject in her study, *French Life in Town and Country* (1901) during which she examines (clearly with deep personal interest) convent education.[6]

In case we are tempted to dismiss the narrator's remarks in *Autobiography* on grounds that she is after all a fictional persona, we need only read a passage of Lynch's in an essay published in *Blackwood's* the month before the first instalment of *Autobiography*. In 'The Spaniard at Home', which includes among other observations a marvellous passage on her reaction to two bullfights, she is of course particularly interested in the upbringing of girls and decides that only were she content with 'the wadded atmosphere of a pussy cat or the pet canary, not free to live or think for myself, but smothered in satin cushions and caresses, fed upon the sweets of life' would she 'choose to be an over-loved Spanish girl, the captive of home and parents, the spoiled idiot of humanity' But Ireland has taught her that this is not the worst fate for a girl. The swelling period of the next sentence is the majestic indignation of Lynch, thinking of her own country.

When one studies the problem elsewhere, and sees the unmerited misery of the daughters in Ireland, the coldness, inhumanity, and selfishness of the Irish mother to her girls of every class, the monstrous way in which the girls are sacrificed to their brothers, left without education that these may play the gentleman, deprived of the enjoyments and pretty fripperies of girlhood, the money that might have helped to establish them squandered by the most heartless and least sacrificing of parents on the face of the earth, and nothing left the unfortunate girls but penury and struggle and the dull old maidenhood of dull and narrow Irish towns and villages, one is forced by sympathy to greet the excessive devotion of the Spanish mothers and lamentable spoiling of the Spanish daughters with indulgence.[7]

It is hard not to sense the personal experience recorded in *Autobiography* and attributed to Angela (as Joyce attributed it to Stephen) as colouring, or discolouring, Lynch's views of certain matters, but the details of her observations, her role as travel-writer cum social anthropologist, lend her work a conviction that encourages our willingness to accept their truth.

This refreshingly unusual perspective is repeated in Lynch's attitude to other aspects of Irish society which have not as far as I know ever been registered in the work of literary critics. In *French Life in Town and Country* she observes contempt for Paris fashion among Dublin women, 'it being alleged here that the women of Dublin dress with far greater taste than their sisters of Paris. Those who are inclined to make light of these pretensions should go to Dublin in the Horse Show week, where I am assured that the dresses of the girls and women of Dublin leave Paris nowhere'. She assures us that 'Silver appointments and splendid napery, which you will find nowadays in the commonest Irish homes, are here [in Paris] unknown.' When she returned to Ireland to write this book, she was surprised to find the female Irish tradespeople, even in small towns, 'dressed daily as Solomon never was in all his glory, with tailor-made gowns of ten and twelve guineas, with high and haughty manners to bewilder a princess of the blood, the one cutting the other, Heaven only knows on what assumption of superiority, and all hastening from their counters in smart turns-outs, duly to subscribe their names to the list of the Queen's visitors. I felt like Rip Van Winkle, as if I had waked in my native land, and found everyone gone mad with pride and pretension.' She was glad, she writes, to pack up her papers and go back to Paris, 'to a race more simple and less pretentious'.[8] This is a wonderful inversion of Yeats's advice to Synge in Paris, tendered five years before the publication of Lynch's book! I don't recognize Lynch's Ireland (or portions of Tynan's Ireland) from the pages either of the Revival or of later literary commentators, but it is the Ireland that makes an appearance in the Irish novel of our period.

Lynch sees the Spanish, like the Irish, as a race in decay, and in a race in decay 'the question of blood runs down among the lowest. In Ireland every grocer and bootblack imagines himself descended from a king....' This fancy, though Lynch was not to know it yet, was encouraged among the country people by the Revivalists who relished the notion of a hidden aristocracy among the peasantry. The race in decay is in need, Lynch thinks, of deep resuscitation. She prescribes for Spaniards 'an austere wave of puritanism and religious intellectuality, the exercise of the untrained conscience, the blighted will'. This prescription is for nothing less than a cultural revival. But she clearly would not recommend a wholly backward look; she finds herself exasperated by the absence of what we would now call efficient infrastructure; she finds herself 'wandering among a race of gentlemen, devitalised by regret'. For an indication of the other values she thought might help Ireland we can turn to *French Life in Town and Country*. She commends the 'fine domestic qualities' of Frenchwomen, and their capacity to make the home happy; she praises commonsense in women and deplores the religious superstition of educated Parisian women; she values taste and efficiency; She also finds admirable the British method of educating boys ('to make men of boys, to teach them to think and act for themselves, to be self-sufficing, self-supporting'); the British moral training is superior to the French and she judges it to be 'a fine thing to be a British lad, with his cricket, his football, his occasional black eyes' and not such a fine thing to be a French lad, taught to be a prig and a humbug. I was about to write that nothing could be farther from the values of the Irish Revival (and certainly this is true for the first few values in this list) until I remembered Pearse's idea of how an Irish boy should be educated: rather as a Victorian British schoolboy, actually, but with strictly Irish content poured into the British mould. And as for Lynch's women (and in France, she writes, 'no one plays a more and [*sic*] important *rôle* in the ranks of humanity than the French woman') why, 'Give French women the freedom, the liberal education of England, a dash of Protestantism—that is, mental and moral independence—and you will have womanhood in its perfection.'[9]

NEW WOMAN AS WIFE

Katherine Cecil Thurston's next novel after *The Fly on the Wheel* was at once more ambitious and cumbersome. *Max* (1909) has a subject fascinating and rather daring for the day. Maxine, a Russian princess and artist who has disappeared on the eve of her marriage, arrives in Paris as a boy, Max, and strikes up a friendship with Edward Blake, a castle-owning Clare man with whom she tastes bohemian life. Isabel Costello in the earlier novel was clearly a fledgling bohemian but unidentifiable as such in bourgeois Waterford. As though recalling Isabel's experience, Maxine disavows love as well as marriage in favour of a measure of personal independence and independence of convention and 'male' bonding with Blake. (Though the phrase does not occur in her vocabulary, Maxine is a

New Woman by experience but also by temperament and principle.) Eventually her resolution weakens and she is apparently undone by her deepening
love for Blake, to whom she reveals herself as Max's sister; the scene in which
she becomes a woman once more is a good one. The change back allows
Blake's friendship to reveal itself as love for a woman and not just a male
friend. However, Max and Maxine alternate as the conflict inside Maxine
continues and it is a conflict larger than one between love and marriage on
one side, independence on the other. It is a question of our twofold nature.
She exclaims to Jacqueline, the Parisian wife who has guessed her secret: 'We
have all of us the two natures—the brother and the sister! Not one of us is
quite woman—not one of us is all man!...It is war,...a relentless, eternal
war; for one nature must conquer, and one must fail. There cannot be two
rulers in the same city.' Maxine wills the man in her to triumph because as
a man it is easier to escape the snares of love and marriage, because 'the world
has made man the independent creature—and I desired independence. Sex is
only an accident'. Her femininity is her weakness. She therefore repudiates
love (and thus marriage, both of which Blake offers her) as the enemy of
a woman's identity: 'I know love—I know all the specious things that love can
say; the talk of independence, the talk of equality! But I know the reality, too.
The reality is the absolute annihilation of the woman—the absolute merging
of her identity.'[10]

What she seeks as an artist makes sex irrelevant: individuality, in praise of
which Thurston is insistent. In Notre Dame cathedral, though an unbeliever,
she prays for the strength to possess herself. This higher theme keeps in check
what might otherwise appear to be Thurston's flirtation with Blake's homo-
erotic friendship with Max and with the transvestism involved in Maxine's
regular impersonations. The modernity of the novel lies not in that but in
Thurston's notion of self-fashioning as an expression of individualism. The
theme of impersonation is big in Thurston and we could argue that even
Carey has subdued his real nature and is impersonating a member of the
Waterford bourgeoisie. But if nature tragically loses in *The Fly on the Wheel*, it
wins out in *Max* and self-fashioning as an expression of will fails in the end,
while love succeeds, and this is Thurston's conservatism behind her daring.
Max realizes in a kind of vision the wisdom as well as depth of Blake's love and
returns finally to him as the beautiful Maxine and delivers herself into his
hands. However, it is while listening to a neighbour playing on the violin
excerpts from Gustave Charpentier's *Louise* (1900) that Maxine has her vision.
This opera, which is the background music of the novel, is about a young
Frenchwoman's choice of her love for Julien and his bohemian way of life over
loyalty to her devoted but narrow-minded working-class parents; she chooses
love and bohemia and at the end her father, whom she visits because he is ill,

curses Paris and its allurements when she leaves her parents again and returns to her life of freedom and love. Blake calls *Louise* Charpentier's 'hymn to Montmartre'.[11] Thurston seems drawn to the combination of love (even marriage) and bohemianism that the opera champions, however unhappy or even tragic its consequences.

The major themes from both of these novels had already appeared in Thurston's *John Chilcote M.P.* (1904), commercially a hugely successful earlier novel set in London.[12] Once the implausibility of the idea that a man could replace himself with a lookalike stranger whom his friends and even his wife would fail to detect is accepted, the novel reads as a surefooted piece of storytelling.[13] Chilcote is a successful Westminster MP who has become a morphia addict and is in fast decline; to escape the pressure, he arranges for a stranger to change places with him. Love in the ordinary way is under defeat, but it triumphs in an extraordinary fashion (again, Thurston's deferred traditionalism) when Chilcote's substitute, John Loder, falls in love with Chilcote's neglected and beautiful wife Eve who reciprocates it even after discovering the deception. Even as Chilcote flees from himself, John Loder, something of a failure, discovers during his impersonation his 'fundamental egotism' and grand ambition which presents him with tremendous scope since the background to the drama of duplicity is the Grand Game played by Russia and Britain in Persia and in which crisis Loder as an opposition MP makes a magnificent speech. Impersonation releases the real self rather than concealing it as in *Max*. It becomes a form of self-fashioning which successfully releases his individuality; he sings 'the great song of Self'.

As well, impersonation steadily becomes usurpation. Loder's transformation into a 'triumphant egotist' coincides with Chilcote's decline in self-esteem, suggesting that together they form the two natures eternally at war on which Max/Maxine discoursed. The novel exhibits the contemporary interest in the Doppelganger and the Other that we find in Stevenson's *Dr Jeykll and Mr Hyde* (1885), Wilde's *Dorian Gray* (1890), Stoker's *Dracula* (1898) and Conrad's 'The Secret Sharer' (1912). (Loder is the 'sharer of the secret' of Chilcote's situation.) Loder wishes to 'trample out Chilcote's footmarks with his own' in fidelity to the principle of the survival of the fittest and does so by becoming a candidate for Undersecretary for Foreign Affairs and by winning the love of Chilcote's wife.[14] It is when he sees a dramatic adaptation of a novel about two men's exchanging identities, *Other Men's Shoes*—the novel that gave Chilcote his idea—that Loder realizes the likely end of the deception, the divorce court, and sees the emptiness of his victory. Even when he discovers that Chilcote has overdosed on morphia, he is only prevented from leaving by Eve who succeeds where Isabel failed and binds her chosen man to herself, offering to Loder the bonus virtue of patriotism, Britain needing his talents during the international crisis. Loder delivers himself into Eve's hands as Maxine delivers herself into Blake's; Loder at the end of the novel literally holds out his hands to Eve and announces that his acceptance or refusal of the imminent offer of the undersecretaryship 'lies with—my wife'.

THE SEVENTH WAVE

Sarah Grand took a sterner line on the Marriage Question than most other novelists, as befitted the coiner of the term New Woman.[15] Female self-sacrifice of Abraham's Nurse Otway's sort was not something that Sarah Grand could easily accept, nor was love likely to triumph in the lives of her heroines as it did in Maxine's life. For Grand the Marriage Answer was rather the Marriage Question, the Marriage Problem. Once it became absorbed into the legal, moral, and even political Woman Question, marriage became something rather more serious than what the romances and country-house novels suggested. The heroine of Grand's novel, *The Heavenly Twins* (1893), an independent-minded young woman who wishes to get married, who does so, and who then expels her new husband from the marriage bed when she discovers he has led a dissolute life, resolves the matter like this: 'I see that the world is not a bit the better for centuries of self-sacrifice on the woman's part and therefore I think it is time we tried a more effectual plan. And I propose now to sacrifice the man instead of the woman.'[16] There is little evidence, though, that Grand changed her mind after having her heroine, Ideala, in her first novel of that name, express belief in marriage, indeed the sanctity of marriage. Ideala believes that marriage has corrupted itself through divorce, the consequent casualness of entering into marriage, and the consequent selfishness of husband or wife—particularly of husband. The frequent failure of husbands, as women saw it, the inequality of marriage, and the double standard of behaviour expected of, and tolerated in, men was a large part of the Marriage Question posed in our period. The lack of female electoral representation and the economic disparities of married men and married women also loomed large and were reflected in fiercely contested parliamentary debates and bills. So all in all, it was easy for Bridget Bennett to assemble thirty short stories by women (chiefly British and American) under the title of *Ripples of Dissent: Women's Stories of Marriage in the 1890s* (1996). Only three of her writers are Irish—Jane Barlow, George Egerton, and Lady Gregory (four if we include Ella D'Arcy, who was born in London of Co. Dublin people)—but Bennett could have recruited many more, especially had she excerpted novels, though they would have been preponderantly Protestant.

Grand's absence from Bennett's anthology is puzzling since she published volumes of stories, including *Our Manifold Nature* (1894, stories that had been rejected before the success of *The Heavenly Twins* changed her fortune with publishers and readers) and *Emotional Moments* (1908). From the latter, 'When the Door Opened—?' would have been an excellent choice, subjecting marriage as it does to trial by experiment as does the equally lightweight but intriguing enough novel, *A Domestic Experiment* (1891), both works using costume and mask by which, in *fin-de-siècle* style, to conduct the experiment of testing the institution, questioning essence, trying out roles. Her absence is puzzling also because Grand was a formidable figure in the feminist landscape of the 1890s. In the United States, Conan Doyle, proving the vitality of contemporary English literature to a sceptical American interviewer, included her name in a list of young writers that also included Barrie, Kipling, Schreiner, Stevenson, Rider Haggard, and George Moore.[17] In an 1894 letter, Shaw bracketed her with Whistler, Ibsen, and Wagner—artists who had suffered attacks for their genius. It was W. T. Stead, the busiest bookman in Britain and its most famous journalist, who made the reputation of *The Heavenly Twins*, because he endorsed its view of the Woman Question.[18]

This journalistic interest reveals something about Grand's fiction, which is highly didactic and polemical and threatens the form of the novel, even the bagginess of the Victorian three-decker, which she later abandoned.[19] In any case, the novel was reprinted six times by Heinemann in 1893 and again in 1895, 1901, 1912, and 1923. *Ideala* (1888), that was self-published at first, was republished the same year by Heinemann and reprinted at least six times by 1894. A third novel, *The Beth Book* (1897), completed her trilogy on the Woman Question. By 1916 she seems to have written herself out, though she lived on until 1943. Although when she lived in London she was a member of an advanced crowd, and knew Hardy, Meredith, Gosse, and Meynell, when she died her obituarists, her biographer noted sadly, 'could scarcely remember her'.[20] This was in part because the cause she furthered through her fiction had in fact been largely won.

The recovery of Grand's reputation appears to have begun with Elaine Showalter's *A Literature of Their Own: British Women Novelists from Brontë to Lessing* (1977); the following year Grand was briefly treated in Gail Cunningham's *The New Woman in the Victorian Novel.* Such criticism has no need to claim Grand for Irish literature but it is in my remit to do so. She was born Frances Elizabeth Bellenden Clarke in Donaghadee, Co. Down in 1854, the daughter of a naval lieutenant in the Coast Guard who was posted from Donaghadee to Co. Mayo when young Frances was aged 2. Her father died in 1861 and her Yorkshire mother returned there with her children. Frances was to recall her Irish upbringing in the first ninety pages of *The Beth Book*: the spiritedness of young Beth (the embryo New Woman) seems at one with the political disturbance of the country (that included agrarian unrest in Mayo). Ireland was the setting and stimulus of all the border crossings to come in the life of a wilful girl. Frances was removed from a Twickenham school for bad behaviour and proto-feminist activity, sent to another in Kensington, then went home to keep her mother company, having had a total of two years' formal education. An autodidacticism pervades her work and gives it its bristling manner, frequent clumsiness, and its quirky changes of narrative focus and direction. Grand became a strenuous advocate of the proper education of women, and the scandalous deprivation of it became a feminist theme in her fiction, placing her alongside Hannah Lynch in this regard.

Marriage too was to become a huge theme in her work in a more determined manner than we find in the country-house novels and Society romances. She was married at 16 to a 39-year-old army surgeon, Lieutenant Colonel David McFall. He had been serving in India, then retired, but on the voyage home lost his wife and one child; he became Medical Officer of Depots in England. He had been born in Magherafelt, Co. Londonderry and with his remaining children returned to Ireland, to Bangor, Co. Down, and somewhere met Frances Clarke who married him 'in cold blood', as Kersley remarks, adding that she thinks Grand didn't really like men very much.[21] The new family moved around—Kent, Singapore, Hong Kong, Norwich, and then Warrington, Lancashire. In Warrington—which is sketched in *A Domestic Experiment*—rejection slips and marital dissatisfaction accumulated and in 1890 Frances McFall abandoned her husband and stepson and went to London. There she renamed herself and began to write in earnest, often about marriage, forcefully but without rancour. Her feminism seems to have been in default. Much of it is explained in her first novel, *Ideala*. The title heroine, like the heroine of *The Beth Book*, is an inconsistent character, acknowledged as such ('She was full of inconsistencies') but while this, like the monologues that often dominate character and action, can seem to damage the novels qua novels, it is in line with Grand's notion that advanced women in her day were in transition and disorientated. For they had lost their faith in men; marriage was not working. Beyond the damage caused by divorce and the double standard, there was the more important moral issue.

Whether Grand gained from her husband more than some of his medical knowledge is unknown (he worked at the Orford Barracks with infected prostitutes), but she became preoccupied in life and her fiction with sexually transmitted disease, then much debated because of the Contagious Diseases Acts of 1864, 1866, and 1869 that in effect blamed loose women for infecting men who were in turn untainted by moral condemnation—another double standard. The Acts 'provided for the compulsory examination by a naval or military surgeon of a woman believed by a special police superintendent sworn before a magistrate to be a "common prostitute" in what became by 1869 eighteen "protected districts", covering up to ten miles beyond the limits of the major garrison stations in southern England and Ireland' (including The Curragh, Cork, and Queenstown). Women diagnosed as venereally diseased became liable to detention and fortnightly inspections.[22] Impurity is a theme in all three novels of Grand's New Woman trilogy in which young women recoil from men on grounds that combine moral and physical revulsion. Grand in no way invented this theme. In late-Victorian Britain there was a social purity campaign waged by the Social Purity Alliance, National Association for the Promotion of Social Purity, Moral Reform Union, and White Cross League Church of England Society. Josephine Butler gave a famous address in Cambridge in 1879 entitled 'Social Purity', published as a book that year and again in 1881 and 1882, and became a leading campaigner. Butler was convinced that the 'unequal standard [in morality] has more or less coloured and shaped the whole of our social life'.[23] The air was thick with sermons, addresses, and pledges on the subject, with girls, women, boys, and men as their respective target audiences: the campaign meant to purify womanhood and cleanse manhood and recapture both from any infecting or degrading passion.[24]

Grand's nonfictional writings on social purity have been recently collected.[25] Yet her own repetition of the theme of purity and danger in both her fiction and nonfiction surely implies some deep fear or experience on the part of the author and gives her feminism a psychological basis that might itself mask a simpler explanation, such as a lesbianism that could not express itself verbally or bodily in the 1890s but must seek an elaborate diversion and sublimation. In any event, it was necessary for women to step into the breach and save not only themselves, but their nation, and even their race, the morality and health of both of which were in decay. 'It all rests with us women', insists Ideala. But women would not work through direct political action, but rather through subterranean influence. 'Our influence is most felt when it is quietly persistent and unobtrusive', she says. 'A woman's best work is done beneath the surface.' The struggle for political power can unsex a woman and this is bad. This might make Grand's feminist resemble Forster's seemingly reactionary Mrs Plynlimmon in *Howards End* rather than the more activist Schlegel sisters in that novel, but Ideala wishes women to use their influence *simultaneously* and *steadily* which is its own form of action.[26] The nature of conditions and influences and how they might be exploited are explained by Grand in her Preface to *Emotional Moments*. Still, Grand herself was not opposed to political membership and when she moved to Tunbridge Wells she became a non-militant suffragist, a member of the Women Writers' Suffrage League (begun 1908), an auxiliary formation of the National Union of Women's Suffrage Societies, founded in 1897. In late Victorian Britain and Ireland, female philanthropic organizers, Social Purity campaigners, New Women, female Aesthetes, and female suffragists composed a turbulent and overlapping constellation of cultural figures.

Katharine Tynan had met Grand earlier in London but they crossed paths again in Tunbridge Wells where Tynan went to live in 1910. Tynan had thought there was too little in common for there to be friendship, Grand being an active, Tynan a passive feminist; but Tynan too joined the NUWSS and found Grand to be 'soft-voiced, gentle, delicately feminine, and most lovable. The only masculine quality was a certain simplicity'! Grand became for Tynan 'a green oasis in the arid waste of Tunbridge Wells'.[27] Tynan would probably not have been the mild suffragist she was had she not lived in England. For back in Ireland, the political dimension of women's rights was enthusiastically embraced chiefly by Protestant women.[28] Indeed, a disgruntled (male) nationalist wrote from Dublin to the *Irish News and Belfast Morning Post* (letter published 20 April 1912 under the heading 'Suffragettes and the Convention') complaining that the suffragists who planned to demonstrate at the forthcoming National Convention (at which the independent constitutional future of Ireland was to be comprehensively discussed) were 'Unionists', wives and daughters of 'prominent Tories and Orangemen' who like the 'aboriginal suffragists have declared "war" on Irish Nationality'.[29]

I do not know about the wives and daughters but the indignant letter-writer was probably right in saying that most Irish feminists were Protestants (and therefore unionists even if Irish patriots of the since discredited unionist sort). Indeed, Mary Kenny recently claimed that the female suffrage movement 'was an exclusively Protestant movement in Ireland'. It would be interesting to know how many members of the Munster Women's Franchise League, founded in 1910, were Catholic. Edith Somerville was first president of this League and Violet Martin one of its vice presidents, though Lewis calls her the more thoroughgoing feminist.[30] The League opened branches in Waterford and Skibbereen and held public meetings at which Somerville became an accomplished speaker.[31] If Kenny is correct, her explanation for the asymmetrical religious representation seems weak: 'Catholic Irishwomen being more concerned to wring survival out of their five-acre farms'.[32] This hardly explains the lack of involvement of those numerous middle-class and upper middle-class *urban* Catholic Irish women who have appeared in the pages of this book.[33] It might instead be the case that the Irish Catholic family developed alongside and inside the Irish Catholic Church and that the woman—even the middle-class woman, wife, or daughter—was discouraged by her husband or father and the parish priest from holding independent political views, especially on a subject as fraught—because 'British' and 'Protestant'—as electoral representation at Westminster. Educated, middle-class Catholic Irish women of our period remain an enigma: some of them were active and involved not just in Church sodalities and other religious societies and in organized philanthropy but in the new Revival nationalism. But they seem unrepresented in those issues we might loosely call 'feminist', and remained so throughout much of the twentieth century.[34]

It is her missionary zeal that constitutes the New Woman, but it is also her transitional being.[35] We have already met in Irish fiction women who resemble the New Woman, in the pages of *The Financing of Fiona, Lismoyle, Over Here, The Night Nurse, Christina's Son, When the Red Gods Call, A New Note, A Pitiless Passion, A Modern Man, The Fortune,* and other novels. But few of these novels approximate the focused attention that Grand gives such women, though *A New Note* comes close. Ella MacMahon's heroine is also in transition and one meaning of the title is the new note struck by Grand's New Woman. MacMahon, though, eschews the relentless didacticism of Grand. Ideala sees women struggling to arrive, not quite sure what they want (which perhaps makes less reprehensible Freud's notorious question, 'What do women want?') and Ideala's mind itself is offered us in Grand's Preface as in 'a transitional state'.[36] In *The Heavenly Twins,* Lady Adeline—something of a New Woman herself—writes to Elizabeth Frayling about the unwisdom of their keeping young Evadne before her marriage in the dark about the dangerous aspects of life since she will find out anyway but in an unprepared and unsuitable manner: 'We are in a state of transition, we women, and the air is so full of ideas that it would be strange if an active mind did not catch some of them...'(p. 41). Later in the novel, the sympathetic Dr Galbraith explains to Mrs Orton Beg (Evadne's aunt) his theory of the 'seventh wave' in a small sermon that might, at the edge of our attention, cause us to think that Grand's extended expression of her feminism might on one level be a transposition of the religious expression (Ideala has broken away from the Church of England) that we have noted in the Irish novel of our period.

'Women have been cramped into a small space so long that they cannot expand all at once when they *are* let out; there must be a great deal of stretching and growing, and when they are not on their guard, they will often find themselves falling into the old attitude, as newborn babes are apt to resume the ante-natal position. [Evadne] will have the perception, the inclination; but the power—unless she is exceptional, the power will only be for her daughter's daughter.'

'Then she must suffer and do no good?'

'She must suffer, yes; but I don't know about the rest. She may be a seventh wave, you know!'

'What is a seventh wave?'

'It is a superstition of the fisher-folks. They say that when the tide is coming in it pauses always, and remains stationary between every seventh wave, waiting for the next, and unable to rise any higher till it comes to carry it on; and it has always seemed to me that the tide of human progress is raised at intervals to higher levels at a bound in some such way. The seventh waves of humanity are men and women who, by the impulse of some one action which comes naturally to them but is new to the race, gather strength to come up to the last halting place of the tide, and to carry it on with them ever so far beyond.' (pp. 98–9)

Grand almost certainly thought of herself as a seventh wave, and it is interesting that the passage implies feminism will not succeed until around the middle or late twentieth century. Interesting, too, the idea that women's rights is an evolutionary matter (women had the potential for evolving farther than men), indeed a matter of what in biological terms is called 'punctuated equilibrium'. Grand of course, as well as being exposed to notions of transmission of characteristics and diseases from her husband's work, shared the interest of the day in heredity and temperament.

Now Dr Galbraith might believe that women have been cramped by men into a small space, but it is also the case that one motif in this second phase of feminism that subsided with the achievement of full female enfranchisement in 1928 (the first phase being the activity between Mary Wollstonecraft and John Stuart Mill, the third being that between Betty Friedan and the present) is the idea that a woman needs a room of her own. Grand (like Ella MacMahon) anticipates Woolf by more than half a generation on this topic. Evadne in *The Heavenly Twins* dozes over lessons by day and comes awake at night: 'Having a room of my own always has been a great advantage', she says. At night in her own room in her aunt's, she reads and thinks—becomes a feminist, indeed—in the privacy of self-growth. Her aunt replies: 'The room to yourself has been a doubtful advantage, I fancy... It has made you theoretical. But you will lose all that by and by'(pp. 36–7). But she won't. In *The Beth Book*, the heroine seeks sanctuary from her tyrannical husband in a secluded corner of the large house he had bought with furniture from the previous occupant still there. She finds a hidden door to a room off the attic with fireplace and window; she fills it with her books and becomes the feminist in the attic. She feels that she has been there before and that it is utterly familiar (the implication being that it is her Platonic home awaiting her); 'On the other hand, she could hardly believe in the reality of what she saw, she thought she must be dreaming, for here was exactly what she had been pining for most in the whole wide world of late, a secret spot, sacred to herself, where she would be safe from intrusion.'[37] The private space is the private self emancipated from pressure and expectation; and the room of one's own is the very opposite of the more public and social reception rooms, drawing rooms, dining rooms, kitchens (where orders were given), and bedrooms where the woman of the house was meant to spend her time and share herself almost endlessly. The contrast between the need for a private space for creativity and the ability of Tynan and Annie S. Swan to compose in the most public of rooms might be a kind of shorthand for two kinds of strong female attitude to the world and to men.

For all her feminism, Grand on balance seems in favour of marriage, though one revealing remark, attributable both to Evadne and the narrator of *The Heavenly Twins*, suggests that Grand felt that sexual passion merely postponed the truth of marriage: 'She would have been happiest when passion ended and love began, as it does in the happiest marriages' (p. 96). It is not the 'flesh' of the man that attracts Ideala more than initially, and then only shallowly, as the colour of a flower attracts; it is his mind, and if the mind is corrupt she must abandon him. (Grand was drawn in the manner of more obviously *fin-de-siècle* writers to the idea of degeneration and the phenomena of the corruption of mind and body.) Moreover, marriage ought to be a union of equals (a more radical idea in the 1890s than today). 'When the Door Opened—?', a story in *Emotional Moments*, depicts the danger when, in the absence of mutuality of interest between husband and wife, the differences are not respected. The equality Grand has in mind is a curious echo of Chaucer's Wife of Bath's. The New Woman will lead the renovation of relations between the sexes and among Ideala's armoury will be 'love, constancy, self-sacrifice'. But there will be times when the husband will be weak and the woman needs to 'take the reins of government into her own hands'. But this is not a victory, since such a woman will 'face life, a disappointed and lonely woman'. For 'the prayer of every woman worth the name is not "Make me superior to my husband", but "Lord, make my husband superior to me!"... There is in every educated and refined woman an inborn desire to submit, and she must do violence to what is best in herself when she cannot.'[38] Of course this is submission as a kind of higher self-sacrifice, and may not contradict what Evadne writes in a letter to her mother: 'The mistake from the beginning has been that women have practised self-sacrifice, when they should have been teaching men self-control' (p. 92). It could be the Wife of Bath talking when Ideala asserts that 'however much she may clamour for equality with men in general, the man she herself loves in particular will always be her master' (p. 17). I'm not certain that the future Lady Mayoress (or honorary 'Wife') of Bath changed her mind entirely. Despite her feminism (or, rather, *because* of her feminism—if we interpret that feminism in certain ways), Grand inhabited the same world as several of the other women novelists we have looked at: concerned about education of girls, involved in charity of one form or another, exercised about love and marriage in the pages of extreme problem-novels, though far less concerned with the 'fleshly' attractions of story and colour and character, devoid of that familiar common archness and whimsicality (which were meant, I think, to convey the incipiently comic social superiority of their characters), more sternly focused on social issues, deaf to the siren calls of romance.

NEW WOMAN AL FRESCO

Despite what I have just said, there is in Grand a strain of female moral triumphalism to do with the degeneracy of the man. Moira O'Neill, for one, would have none of it. O'Neill (1864–1955) is remembered if at all as a lyrical but lightweight Celtic poet from Cushendun, Co. Antrim (she was born Agnes Shakespeare Higginson—called Nesta—who married and became Nesta Higginson Skrine, later Keane), but in another vein entirely she published in *Blackwood's Edinburgh Magazine* a forceful and eloquent account of her life in Alberta, Canada entitled 'A Lady's Life on a Ranche' (1898). It is an essay of the 'Letter from' variety. O'Neill is at pains to dispel the idea that life in the colonies is a species of failure and that it is a doomed quixotic gesture. She admits that social life is different: there are no dinner parties, no exchange of cards, no unannounced calls. But there is the comfortable, if not luxurious, life in a log house, and the changing charms of the outdoor life. She registers the revolving attractions of the seasons within sight of the Rockies, including riding, shooting, and fishing, and sings knowledgeably and feelingly the yearly sequence of spring and summer flowers.

O'Neill's implication is that the open air is one true habitat of the strong and independent woman, a recurring idea among some women's rights advocates of the day. In 1901, Mary E. Ponsonby, for example, sketched her ideal woman: 'I dream of a possible woman having something of the frank fearless grace, the self-reliant daring, the open-air freedom of the Englishwoman of the past. Give her also charm and sympathy and capability of deep passion.'[39] O'Neill must have found Grand's preoccupation with disease morbid.

Moreover, O'Neill wishes to deny that a woman's life on the ranch 'consists necessarily and entirely of self-sacrifice and manual labour'. She agrees to address 'the household question,—that question which is with us all, and always with us' and which we might call in terms of the fiction we have looked at 'the Domestic Question'. True, the wife works at domestic chores and with the help of just one servant, but two hours' household work a day will do the job, she crisply insists, leaving time not for the idleness of her peers at home but for her outdoor pursuits. And for what she regards as real and rewarding domesticity. The home on the range is another true habitat of the strong woman. Even the most domestic creature alive, impervious to the lure of the open air, would find in Alberta 'the finest field she could desire for the exercise of her special gifts. Nowhere else, I venture to say, do the domestic virtues shine with such peculiar lustre as on a ranche.' Once the newcomer has adapted to initially upsetting incidents, then 'the notable woman begins her reign, and it is a glorious one. Praise and submission surround her; soap and water scour her path. Rich jams and many-coloured cakes own her hand, and the long-neglected socks her needle.' Alas, O'Neill is not such, she laments, loving too much the outdoors when she rides over the prairies just as she strode the 'springy heather of an Antrim grouse-moor', but to each her own, which is her point, and the great virtue of the democracy of her life in Canada. She is Grand without the chronic disapproval. 'Every woman seeks her vocation, and, consciously or not, desires a sphere in which to reign and serve, a place that no one else could fill, her own niche among "the polished corners of the Temple". Now the greatest attraction of the West is that it offers such scope to the woman who really knows her *métier de femme.*' She would like to transplant there one of those women who are 'firm believers in the natural depravity of man and the born superiority of woman'. Such a woman would arrive full of high sentence and the determination to civilize the natives, only to learn respect for the primitive virtues and the equality of men and women in such an environment. 'In time she might even come to revise some pretty theories about the nature and habits of men which she has taken on trust from Mrs Sarah Grand and her like, to compare them with living examples, and let experience teach her more wholesome views.'[40]

Theory and experience can, though, be combined as experiment. The controlled interaction between the two, and the subjection of relationships and marriage to experiment was, at least on paper, though often in reality, much in the air during our period. It would, for example, have been appropriate for the tireless L. T. Meade to have entitled the novel she published in 1898 (or perhaps it was only *one* of the novels she published in 1898!), *A Domestic Experiment*, except Grand had already taken the title seven years before. Meade's experiment is one that involves a woman equally at home on the Swiss mountains as an expert climber and in the committee rooms of suffragist organizations, a woman so 'aggressively healthy' that her bodily perfection suggests the social purity that Grand advocated but that is here achieved by means of which O'Neill would have approved.[41] In this feminist problem-novel, Meade has unpacked Grand's world and agenda and repacked them into a novel-by-formula that is interesting by dint, and only by dint, of the cleverness of the formula. Dagmar Olloffson, the heroine of *The Cleverest Woman in England*, is an identikit New Woman, the complete article engaged on woman's 'mission' (as she defines it): an egalitarian and socialist (hater of luxury and Society, propagandist for the cooperative movement), an organizer, writer, and speaker in the female suffragist movement, a temperance advocate, a charity worker, a charismatic figure who enthrals her feminist sisters, 'a woman of genius [echoing the description of Grand's Beth of the year before] and an angel to boot' (pp. 331–2), and a beauty into the bargain. She has been independent-minded since she was a girl, even directing her mother to write schoolgirl penny fiction to make money after the death of her father, offering her editorial help (and allowing Meade to mock herself or her legions of readers): 'if you write nonsense about little girls, and say the kind of things about them that don't happen, I shall be able to put matters right' (p. 36). She inherits £12,000 from an uncle on the very day her mother dies and is from that moment quite literally independent, free to become champion of women and the downtrodden.

The novel begins *in media res* with Dagmar's startling announcement at the Debates Committee of the Forward Club in London that she is marrying Geoffrey Hamlyn, a newspaper board member who is opposed to all she stands for and detests 'the shrieking sisterhood' (p. 191). She loves him but primarily she is intrigued by the idea of opposites meeting; she will conduct an experiment to find out if marriage can survive deep ideological difference, if it is compatible with her 'mission'. Her husband-to-be agrees to enter on this domestic experiment, loving her as much as he disagrees with her. When young she had forsworn marriage, as if a follower of Grand, but then sees marriage as having the capacity of enlarging women's power and perception. She rhetorically asks her erstwhile pupil Imogen, who is stricken by Dagmar's engagement, putting it in propaganda terms: 'What is an unmarried woman, after all, but a one-sided creature? Can she possibly review the whole position? No, it is the married woman, the one who sees life from every point of view, who alone is fully capable'(p. 76). She and Hamlyn marry and move into a mansion in Russell Square. Imogen's love for Dagmar is meant to be the worship women have for their more accomplished sisters though, despite Dagmar's proscription of emotional display (she calls the holding of hands between women 'effeminate'!), it hovers between girlish infatuation (appropriate to the schoolgirl novels Meade wrote) and an unrequited lesbian desire in a manner that recalls *A Princess of the Gutter*. She offers Imogen a room of her own in her mansion, which she intends anyway to turn into a kind of feminist community centre, but it is not enough. In the novel, the relationship of the two women rings far truer than the merely stated love between husband and wife. Of course, because she is juggling so many causes and problems, Meade hardly has time for real emotional substance in this novel, which is little more than a dry experiment though not without historical interest.

The experiment begins to unravel when it approaches three crises. There is the crisis of Dagmar's continuing to work after marriage, to which Geoffrey is opposed, partly on the grounds that working women take bread out of the mouths of men, though Imogen's interpretation of his opposition is more sweeping: 'The domestic woman, the woman of a hundred years ago, the woman of our grandmother's days alone suit him. The woman who exists now, Dagmar, the woman who has from necessity to exist at the end of the nineteenth century, the woman who has to struggle for her living, who has to falter and fail, who must provide bread in many cases for those who belong to her, he has no conception of' (p. 73). Dagmar has been offered paying work on Geoffrey's own paper, and the radical opinions she offers in her columns antagonize Geoffrey and readers and create a second crisis, provoking him to issue an ultimatum: either he relinquishes his post at the *Daily Despatch* or she relinquishes her public life, a life he regards as inappropriate to a woman, especially a young married woman. Dagmar's otherwise enlightened editor adds to the pressure on her by telling her that her duty to her husband and child trumps her feminist mission, that she must under the circumstances abandon the disenfranchised and suffering women.

Before the ultimatum deadline is reached, smallpox strikes London, which overtakes a third crisis: Dagmar employs, against her husband's wishes, a battered and sickly wife (who lost her own child) as a nurse for their baby daughter whom Dagmar has named, also against Geoffrey's wishes, Benedicta, a name he finds sentimental. But the name reflects the religiously philanthropic element in Dagmar's nature that underlies her feminism. Indeed, the relapse of late nineteenth-century New Woman thinking back into mid-Victorian philanthropic sentiment helps Meade solve the dilemma she has written herself into: how does the experiment work out? Is every marriage, as a friend of Geoffrey's claims, 'a dangerous experiment?' Dagmar becomes preoccupied with suffering as the story takes a Christian turn, and precise (and theoretically remediable) female grievances blur into a generalized portrait of female victim-hood and self-sacrifice. 'Suffering', a condition that comes to dominate the novel begins as political disability and ends as actual bodily and spiritual suffering. Dagmar becomes the champion not of healthy, aggrieved women but sick, suffering, helpless women of the kind with whom Atkinson and her followers were at ease. When the aggressively healthy Dagmar catches smallpox from one of her charity cases in Russell Square, O'Neill's open-air world collapses into the contagiously diseased world of Grand; the Swiss mountains shrink into urban sick-rooms. But since unlike Grand's, Dagmar's end is passive, it is rather the world of Mulholland into which O'Neill's world collapses.

Meade simply did not have Grand's ideological seriousness or singlemind-edness, being primarily a professional fiction writer with the necessary impulse of opportunism that professionalism requires. To the extent that women's nature is self-sacrificial, Dagmar's death from smallpox, having nursed a particularly malignant case in a woman, is a triumph for the female spirit, otherwise her life can read like a betrayal and a failure. When Meade tries after her heroine's death to editorialize Dagmar into success, as 'one of the pioneers in a great movement', she hardly convinces. But there is sufficient interest in the novel's debate about marriage and a wife's place in contemporary society, to make it readable and at times provocative.

FROM PAPA TO PAPUA

Earlier in Meade's novel before sentiment triumphs, when Dagmar wishes to put heart into Imogen for the women's struggle, she recalls her Scandinavian ancestry when reaching for a favourite metaphor: 'You and I, remember, go North; you must not be discouraged at the hardness of the road . . . The cold of the wind and the pressure of the icebergs ought not to discourage me. I long ago elected to go north' (pp. 162–3). No writer of the period took more literally the idea of the outdoor New Woman, or took the idea, and the New Woman herself, farther than did Beatrice Grimshaw who, instead of taking the figurative road North, took the very real sea-roads east and south. She left the cluttered Victorian interior of a Co. Antrim country house, went to Dublin, then London, and finally took ship for South Seas vastnesses, choosing a life of travel and exploration.[42] Looking back in an autobiographical piece written in 1939, Grimshaw wrote:

I am a Victorian. I was born in the 'Seventies, in a big lonely country House five miles— a whole hour's journey—from Belfast.

I was governessed and schooled and colleged. I was taught to ride and play games. I was taught to behave. To write notes for Mamma. To do the flowers. To be polite but not too polite to Young Gentlemen. To accept flowers, sweets and books from them, but no more. To rise swiftly with the rest of the six daughters and sons when Papa came into the breakfast-room, to kiss him ceremoniously, and rush to wait upon him. He liked it, and we liked it. . . .

But I was the Revolting Daughter—as they called them then. I bought a bicycle, with difficulty. I rode it unchaperoned, miles and miles beyond the limits possible to the soberly trotting horses. The world opened before me. And as soon as my twenty-first birthday dawned, I went away from home, to see what the world might give to daughters who revolted.[43]

In one of her nonfiction books best-known to her contemporaries, *Isles of Adventure* (1931), Grimshaw had recalled that in the 1890s one became a New

Woman (though she did not use the expression) by becoming a 'careerist'—most commonly a shorthand typist, lecturer in a ladies' college, or a fashion or gossip columnist—and that every careerist had a bicycle, the more daring riding it in bloomers disguised as a skirt.[44] She herself became something slightly more unusual, a subeditor on a sporting paper in Dublin, where the careerists were daring—'but within iron limits' (p. 4). Not content with merely riding a bicycle, Grimshaw made a successful attempt on the world's women's twenty-four hours road record, though having to ride through the Irish night by herself because the morality of the day would not permit her to be accompanied in darkness by a male cyclist.

Having moved to London but still gripped by a potentially expensive wanderlust, Grimshaw hit on the ingenious idea of offering to collect newspaper advertising abroad for shipping lines in exchange for travel tickets, an authentically peregrine Leopold Bloom. She travelled widely and adventurously until alighting for years in New Guinea (from Papa to Papua, one might say) and coming finally to rest in Australia. When Stephanie in *When the Red Gods Call* (1911) returns to New Guinea to find her estranged husband, she mentally celebrates a freedom the polar opposite of Grimshaw's prescribed (and circumscribed) life in a Victorian country house. 'I had an odd sense of freedom in roaming about like this, due, I suppose, to the re-waking of the old New Guinea feeling that "nobody cared." I suppose there never was a country in the world where everyone was, and is, so completely free to do what seems good in his or her own eyes, without remark.' And so this well-dressed woman 'with the manners of society, traveling unaccompanied', attracts none of the inquisitive stares she would have attracted even in 'early Victorian Britain'.[45]

In the South Seas Grimshaw found all the elbow room she needed. Whereas she hankered for such a life from an early age, her heroine Stephanie does not hear the red gods call until they speak through the person of Hugh Lynch whom she loves and whom she returns to New Guinea to find. Having changed already by deciding to return from England, the journey in search of her husband alters her radically and for good. To find Lynch, she must travel through a society that is still primitive despite the inroads of trading and even tourism until she reaches an unexplored region. Her penetration of the jungle recalls a much greater story. Her arduous journey into the heart of darkness with the colourful trader and old New Guinea lag, Mr Worboise, a journey beyond society, indeed beyond white men—into the Purari Delta with its fierce cannibals—is a journey beyond the edges of known civilization and therefore beyond the conventions of female behaviour. Unavoidably, her passage by boat into the interior, because Mr Worboise has heard rumours of Lynch's whereabouts, recalls Marlow's in search of Kurtz. Grimshaw's descriptive powers are impressive enough.

We were lying in the center of a huge plain of livid yellow water, with a livid yellow sky, hot as burning brass, above us. In front of us, a long way off, stretched a level-topped, unbroken rampart, black against the sky, and dropping sheer into the sea without a trace of shore-line. This colossal wall, apparently a hundred feet in height or more, wound in and out as far as the eye could reach, following every curve of the island, and hiding everything that lay behind....

'What is it, Mr. Worboise,' I asked nervously, 'That great wall—I don't understand it—and where is the river?'

'Lord bless you, Mrs. Hugh, that's nothin' but the mangroves,' answered Mr. Worboise, lifting his head from the engine-hole... 'All this coast is mangrove and swamp. Trees, you understand. They grows as close as 'airs in an 'air-brush....

A Papuan was driving the engine now, and my guide was at the wheel, keeping a cautious eye ahead for the floating tree-trunks, immense masses of timber as solid as steel, that came charging out into the bay on the current of the river, constantly threatening to ram the sides of our fragile little vessel. We were getting into the stream; the mangrove wall was parting right and left of us, as the sea parted before the Israelites, and almost as miraculously. A hundred feet on each side of us it stood up, close-massed trunks set in black gleaming water, without a sign of land. Beyond the wall, clumps of a strange water-palm sprang straight up out of the river, like bunches of ostrich plumes twenty and thirty feet high.... We crept steadily up the river.... Rank with an unwholesome luxuriance, green with a venomous brilliance of color, [the foliage] fairly flung itself at the water—a tangle of leaves sword-like, fan-like, snake-like, fern-like, finger-like, flag-like; an army of trunks scaled like alligators, or spined like porcupines, or splashed with gouts of unaccountable blood-like hues; a tangle of reptilian creepers, twisting and choking and coiling around every branch and no flowers, no colors, nothing but the poisonous green of the forest, and the liquid green of the river, and over all, the thunderous, low-hanging, threatening sky. (pp. 310–12)

However, although she is finding herself, Stephanie is doing so by searching for her lost marriage, which is where the story of Kurtz and his Intended diverges and veers away. Moreover, Stephanie Hammond is a portrait of the imperial woman who shared the courage and intrepidity of the kind of man the trader Mr Worboise is, 'the true Empire-maker and breaker in of new lands' (p. 309). Because imperial women existed before the 1890s, Stephanie is not necessarily a New Woman, but clearly, like her creator, she coincides with the New Woman movement. Stephanie becomes the woman Lynch suspected her to be when she answered his love-overtures, someone who has inherited the genes of the empire-makers and explorers. 'Why', he asked Mr Worboise, and might easily have been thinking of a woman like Lady Margaret Gilliland in Grimshaw's *Victorian Family Robinson* (1934), a woman on her way out to join her husband, a colonial governor in Australia,

what's there in her different from the women who helped to make Australia forty years ago, that she shouldn't care to take the chances they did? They were just her sort, many of them—and they came out from home with their men, and stuck to them through thick and thin—and I'd stake my life on it that if you could round up all that's left of that crowd, and all that's left of their sisters who stayed at home, and kept their nice complexions and their place in society—you'd find the Australian lot thought they'd made the best use of their lives.... And think of her people, who they were—Admiral Steve Hammond of Nelson's staff—Scott Hammond, who nearly did Speke out of the discovery of the sources of the Nile—Gilbert Hammond of the Crimea—and as for her father, he's the hardest case I ever met, but people do say the battle of Alexandria wouldn't have gone the way it did if he hadn't been there. Blood tells,—a girl with that ancestry wasn't meant to spend her life curling her hair for dinner-parties. (pp. 169–70)

And so it proves. Stephanie's journey back demonstrates both her empire-making, trail-blazing heredity and her makings of a New Woman, a combination that might not suit feminist tastes today but which is in Grimshaw's terms incontrovertible.[46] On that journey, Stephanie reflects with satisfaction and a little amazement: 'I, who after so many years of sheltered dependence, was learning at last, slowly and painfully, to stand alone' (p. 298). This new woman is a New Woman of a special sort, one who becomes new by embracing the old, indeed the ancient and primitive.

When we had been three days tracking and threading the mazes of this most wonderful place, I felt as if the Stephanie of London days, who used to be seen in and out of cabs, and met at suburban railway stations, never had existed, and as if this new Stephanie who periled her life so readily, went ashore with a loaded revolver stuck in the belt of her dress, and looked without emotion at garlands of human skulls and necklaces of human teeth, was the real woman after all. Something of what Carlyle would call 'husks and wrappages' had been stripped away in those few days; what was left was the real me, and I knew that, being thus found, it would never be lost again. (pp. 323–4)

Edith Campbell in Grimshaw's novel, *Nobody's Island* (1917) thinks comparable thoughts when she flees London with Slade and voyages to the South Pacific: 'English Edith, daughter of castle lawns and cathedral closes ... felt ... the lodestone pull of things unlike. These new, rude countries, with their men who were men, their life that was earth-touching, earth-fed life—was it such a hardship, after all, that she should have been swept away from her smug, sheltered luxury, and her grocer husband, into the windy, real world?'[47] Like Stephanie, Edith must be 'de-civilized' in order to reveal her real womanhood, to discover, in O'Neill's phrase, her *métier de femme*. This is a process of successive peeling back of identities, of becoming serially and pretty literally a new woman. Mary Edith Cardillion becomes Edith Slade who becomes Mary Edith Cardillion again who becomes Edith (Mrs Godfrey) Campbell who becomes 'Mary Phelps' who becomes Mary Slade (also known to Slade as 'Joan' after Joan of Arc) who becomes, finally, Edith Slade again (but not quite the same Edith Slade as she was, since she is now Edith Slade married to a Catholic Ben Slade). It all adds up to what we might call, in counterpoint to the domestic experiments in other novelists, experiments al fresco, conducted in the vast exteriors of her fiction— Samoa, Fiji, the Solomon Islands, Papua-New Guinea, Cook Islands, New Zealand, Australia. At times Grimshaw reminds us of the life experiment of Robert Louis Stevenson, whom in her mind's eye Vaiti pictures on Samoa (as Tusitala), and even at times of the experiments in sexual relations and identity carried out by D. H. Lawrence in Australia and Mexico, all three writers reflecting a contemporary restlessness, impatience with civilization, and attraction to the primitive and authentic.

Interestingly, as in the case of Stephanie, the truer female self approaches sympathy with, even identification with, rugged men whom they both resemble when they at last put on hardihood and strike into the rivers or jungles with revolvers and resolve. The suggestion of bisexuality (perhaps bi-gendering is the more accurate term, since they never lose their sexual attractiveness to men) is repeated in the characters of Murua in *Nobody's Island* and Vaiti in the novel named after her. These latter two are tough girls raised as boys and who face down and outwit all the hostile men they encounter. It is a variation on the politer bisexuality in Thurston's Max. The cigar-smoking Vaiti ('she smoked like most women, very hard and fast')[48] is full of salty talk, knows navigation as well as her father, and has the woodcraft that enables her to find the lost island on which the Vasilieffs are buried. Young Murua, carrying a pistol, cowboy hatted, in Papua bush costume, claims she gets tired of being a woman—women do, she says, 'only most women just have to stay that way. I haven't' (p. 317). As novelist, Grimshaw enacted and emulated her own 'fast' characters, showing a knowledge of schooners (not to speak of maritime geography) that compares with Conrad's, as in this passage in which her father recalls her exploits as a sailor:

He had seen her run the 'Sybil' in the trough of the very last swell alongside a barrier reef, for miles, sailing all the time so close to the wind that the shifting of a single point would have meant destruction. He had heard her raving about the deck in half-a-gale, as they swept up to the iron-bound coast of Niué, abusing Harris in the strongest of beach talk, because he had not another main topsail in the locker to replace the two that had just carried away one after the other, and battered themselves to ribbons . . . He had seen her perform tricks of steering, getting in and out of Avarua in Raratonga (a perfect death-trap of a port at times, as old islanders know). (pp. 151–2).

It is fair to say that Grimshaw's narratives read as both masculine and feminine, and I suspect she appealed as much to male readers as to female, perhaps more. In *Vaiti of the Islands*, this narrative bivalency—the assault on essentialism and unity that recurs in other novels as well—stretches to pidgin English, the hybrid lingo in which much of her dialogue is conducted.

All this is of a piece with Grimshaw's representation of admirable women. As half-castes as well as young women with bi-gendered attributes and expressions, Murua and Vaiti represent for Grimshaw one kind of ideal new woman: mobile, natural, self-reliant, adapted to life in the virile, pre-civilized or post-civilized South with its vacant oceans and scatters of islands.

But the ideal was itself adaptable, for Grimshaw had another kind of woman in mind more suited to the congested, 'civilized', indeed over-civilized, parts of the world and who had to fashion herself anew as tough, independent when need be, yet married to a fellow Catholic. Like Grimshaw herself, she could function in the North but was finally most at home in the South. The criterion of Catholicism remains odd in Grimshaw since her books show more interest in heathen beliefs and customs than in Catholic doctrine or dogma, which come into play only when marriage and divorce are at issue. It would appear that Grimshaw herself exhibited a bi-culturalism that is damaging to her fiction by sabotaging her storylines—however it affected her life—rather than enabling satisfactory complications and resolutions and a unified vision of early twentieth-century society and life.

CROSSING LINES

Like O'Neill and Grimshaw, George Egerton (b. Mary Chavelita Dunne, 1859) also rejected Grand's virtual exclusion of healthy and passionate sexuality from her ideal world, and her attribution of impurity to men and the innate pursuit and valorizing of purity to women.[49] In 'A Cross Line', a story from Egerton's landmark volume of stories, *Keynotes* (1893), it is the wife who suffers from thwarted sexual and romantic desire and who has sexual day-dreams and fantasies that Grand would no doubt have called impure.[50] The story is set in rural Ireland but without close attention to landscape and the woman who will almost cross the line before story's end is, when the story opens, reading a sketch of a fountain scene in Tanagra, Greece. Greece seems to have been one of the few countries in which Egerton did not live. She was born in Melbourne, Australia of an Irish soldier father (John J. Dunne) and a Welsh mother, and raised in New Zealand, Chile, Wales, Ireland, and Germany. In Ireland and Germany she was educated in convent schools. Hoping to study art, she had to settle for nursing, in New York, Dublin, and London. She eloped in 1887 to Norway with a married man, met Knut Hamsun, and read Ibsen. The following year she returned alone to London where in 1891 she married a minor Canadian writer, George Egerton Clair-monte, and they lived in Co. Cork. She divorced Clairmonte (retaining his forenames for publication purposes) and later married Reginald Bright, a theatrical agent.[51] She died in Sussex in 1945; Irish literature has some claim to her fiction.

In 'A Cross Line', a singing and grey-clad, grey-eyed fisherman, a tireless pursuer of women, happens upon the daydreaming wife with her 'gypsy ease of attitude' and discovers to his surprise that she herself fly fishes and can offer him advice. At the mention of her husband, he retorts 'Lucky fellow!' and the sexual undercurrent is set in motion; his questions have been a kind of fishing as he probes her availability. But he leaves feeling curiously diminished, she being the dominant player in the opening act of the little subdued drama.

The story is conducted as a series of scenes or movements—painterly or musical—and in the next we meet the husband (whistling out of tune unlike the musical fisherman) who is chummy with her but cannot seem to help her escape her bouts of 'qualmish feeling'. The scene ends with an averted quarrel over his love of young animals and his insistence that he would not have allowed her to ride the filly he once had, which by the time we finish the story we see as his suppression of restlessness and motion in his wife. Theirs is a prematurely old relationship, she calling him 'dear old man' and he calling her 'old woman', though sometimes with naive insight 'gypsy'. She regrets his inability to tell her he loves her, to compliment her eyes and her hands, of which she is proud: when she smokes she holds up her hand with a cigarette poised between first and second fingers and admires idly 'its beauty of form'; earlier, the fisherman had noted 'the thick wedding ring on her slim brown hand, and the flash of diamond in its keeper'.[52] She complains: 'A woman doesn't care a fig for a love as deep as the death-sea and as silent, she wants something that tells her it in little waves all the time. It isn't the love, you know, it's the being loved; it isn't really the man, it's his loving.' And adds: '*You* are an awfully good old chap; it's just men like you send women like me to the devil.'

It is unclear how far Egerton is aware of the curious detachment from the man the wife's attitude implies. Indeed, the wife's wish to *be* a man (and her whimsical suggestion that perhaps in a previous life she *was* a man) is an indirect expression both of the desire to have the man's freedom to be amoral (like the fisherman?) and the detachment from the other sex that men routinely exhibit. The wife is transferring responsibility for a wife's walking on the wild side from the wife to the husband. Of course, repression and fantasy are solipsistic in any case. In another 'movement' of the story, the wife lies 'on the short heather-mixed moss at the side of a bog-stream' and has two intense wish-fulfilling fantasies: of riding an Arab horse in Arabia (a day-dream of sexual motion) and of dancing in some ancient theatre in the open air (the 'open air' motif in women's emancipation): an accelerating dance (the sexual motion again) before an audience of men whose cheers rise to a crescendo as her fantasy of sexual exhibition climaxes in a daydream orgasm. Only when the fantasy subsides do her thoughts turn to other women, and she wonders if they too crave excitement and motion. In her mind she is a kind of focus for women who seem to seek her out (the seventh wave motif). Then she ponders the simple male image of woman that blinds them to her complexity and cross-currents; men fail to see how cunningly women promote that image while secretly undermining it; they cannot see the woman's wildness which is the keynote of her strength, and women help each other delude the man, who cannot see her witchery.

The fisherman again happens upon her but as he tries to lure her away with him, it is as if her spent passion has given her renewed strength. Some, she admits, have bridled against her self-sufficiency; she no longer appears to need people, especially men, though she confesses that the grey-eyed man is the only one who has never misunderstood her. But she is a creature of moments, she says (too fleeting and restless for the man who appears cumbersome by comparison) and she will give the fisherman his moment. He tries to seize it, to possess this 'sphinx'; he offers her a good life on a yacht, travel, passion; he paints a picture for her of his submission to her in their future life together; he prefigures the poetic wandering seducers in Synge's plays. (Her solo dance-fantasy resembles one Synge later described breathlessly in *The Aran Islands*.) She is cool and denies she is without affection; indeed, affection is 'the crowning disability' of her sex. Without it—and she is unwittingly echoing what the fisherman has said to his male friends—men would be no match for women. It is affection that binds her to her husband; affection tames the restlessness and passion in women, so it is really a necessary disability. In another Syngean scene, the fisherman says he will be leaving two days hence and should she decide not to go with him she should hang something white on the lilac bush that he will see as he passes.

Between now and then, her thoughts turn to the young ducklings her husband loves, and she sits bolt upright, suddenly certain she is pregnant. Her unwed maid happens to have baby clothes from a baby that died and the wife is given them, and she tells the maid to hang a nightgown on the lilac bush to air: 'mind, the lilac bush!' To the end, the lines of the wife's life and love cross; the baby solves the immediate dilemma of the fisherman, but it seems detached from the husband and her affection for him; the baby is a mere idea on the periphery of her vision (or at least, the story ends before it could be anything else); the self-sufficiency of the wife remains; the world, including poor Lizzie's past unhappiness, is subsumed into the distending moments of the wife's life. Despite Egerton's rejection of Grand's asexuality and misanthropy, she herself creates a woman no less self-reliant than Grand's heroines. Nelson makes the observation that Egerton generally casts a cold eye on marriage yet celebrates maternity, refusing to connect the two.[53] The uncoupling of sexuality and maternity from marriage seems to be the case with 'A Cross Line', though it is unclear in the story how sexuality and maternity are connected, even if she regards both as desirable, even necessary, experiences for women; the wife's pregnancy is the result not of a feral passion but of a marital affection; one strong emotional experience has simply been followed by another.

Egerton followed *Keynotes* with *Discords* (1894). The long first story, 'A Psychological Moment at Three Periods', tracks the development of a female as child, girl, and woman; her self-reliance could be that of the wife; she too is a creature seemingly formed by moments (cf. the story's title); yet the tragedy suggests a pattern above and beyond moments: a destiny or fate against which Isabel is powerless and which she yet meets with stoicism. 'The greatest tragedies I have ever read', says the wife in 'A Cross Line', 'are child's play to those I have seen acted in the inner life of outwardly common-place women.'[54] As in 'A Cross Line', 'A Psychological Moment' attempts to capture the contradictory nature of a woman, one of which is the ultimate and acknowledged virtue of self-sufficiency which is nevertheless conjoined to an involuntary outreaching sympathy with the suffering in the world and also to a threatening but ungainsayable sexual need for men.

We meet young Isabel at home in Ireland, mortifying herself into a precocious self-control. We next meet her (the story proceeds by music-like movements as in 'A Cross Line') in the playground of a school in Rathmines, Dublin telling a tall story and owning up the next day in a display of ruthless honesty. We are then with her in a convent school in Holland where she has an epiphanic experience of suffering and rails against God's injustice. She is a woman when we meet her next at the British Museum Reading Room and outside she is enjoined by a married acquaintance called St Leger to become his mistress. He has incriminating letters of hers and he brandishes them to secure her reluctant agreement to let herself be set up by him in Paris; he will return the letters to her when she ceases to be his woman. But like the wife, she keeps part of herself proof against the sordidness of her new life as a kept woman, and keeps him essentially at bay as the wife did the fisherman, though both women are clearly seducible and need a sexual relationship. In the British Museum before the head of Rameses in the Egyptian Room she has taught herself endurance, to accompany her honesty and self-control. But above all she senses an evil destiny to which she half accedes and of which St Leger is but a crude implement. She believes that 'There is no half way for a woman. There is one straight, clean road marked out for her, and every by-road is shame.' There is no great difference between this disguised puritanism and Grand's similar either/or representation of women; Egerton means this forthrightness to cohabit with the inner contradictions of her heroines; there is the faintest suggestion of martyrdom that might track this kind of feminism back to Catholicism and Protestantism of the Irish varieties.

We meet Isabel next in Paris, as an outwardly self-assured and fashionably dressed mistress who nonetheless accepts everything from St Leger 'with the same irritating indifference'. Inside she is suffering and is alienated from her family in Ireland. An Irish solicitor arrives to arrange the end of the relationship; she is proud and disdains his offer (really St Leger's offer) of a pay-off, being ready to leave without a scene. She remembers the Finnish gypsy legend of the girl-child's ability to outstare the sun but whose gaze falters once she loses her innocence. 'Well, she can no longer look fearlessly into the eyes of the day god; there will always be a shrinking fear of hurt.' While she is packing, a woman is shown in, who turns out to have been a fellow pupil. Isabel tells her of a letter from a Queen's Counsel's wife, offering her an introduction to a convent 'where they receive Magdalens of a better class'. The visitor tells her own story: about her Catholic father's physical intervention when she fell in love with a Protestant; her marriage in the Dublin Cathedral to a Catholic man she detested; her cleverness when her aunt left her money to acquaint herself with 'the marriage laws as to separate property for women in Ireland' that 'are as good as void, because few women care to insist on them', though she did. Her babies have died and her revenge will be to leave her money on her own death to her estranged sweetheart or his family: husband, family, Church: none will benefit from her wealth. 'My case [a case of priestly and family bullying and sectarianism and the treatment of unmarried grown women as errant children] is not an uncommon one in Ireland. Most of the women find their consolation in piety, and a few in drink, and neither stops a mortal heartache.' Like Grand, Egerton tries to depict female lives of quiet desperation.

But Isabel cannot help her; she has taught herself endurance from an early age, as though in tragic prevision of the future. 'We have all got to thole our assize of pain... *always you must come back to yourself.*' It is this element of passive suffering and tragic endurance that makes the New Woman a literary as well as social and historical figure: a propaganda writer or even problem-novelist would have had the two women band together in active solidarity like the militant suffragettes. Yet Isabel will not live a life of hypocrisy and play the penitent Magdalen. She will apologize to no one and take the other road, living on her wits, scorning 'the mangy idols of respectability, social distinctions, mediocre talent with its self-advertisement and cheap popularity'. (This is incisive but alas Egerton allows Isabel to prolong her indignation into a ranting sermon.) She sends the other on her way, perhaps emboldened or fortified in her suffering, while she herself takes 'the first step of her new life's journey'. One cannot help hearing Egerton's own voice in these stories, for her biography seems to suggest she was indulging in no futile daydream when she had her heroines utter their manifestos.

NOTES

1. B. M. Croker, *Lismoyle* (London: Hutchinson, 1914), pp. 158, 208.

2. Among Lynch's novels are *The Prince of Glades* (1891), *Rosni Harvey* (1892), *Daughters of Men* (1892), *Denys d'Auvrillac* (1896), *An Odd Experiment* (1897), *Jinny Blake* (1897), and *Clare Monro* (1900).

3. Hannah Lynch, *Autobiography of a Child* (New York: Dodd, Mead & Company, 1899), pp. 269, 270. The novel was first serialized in *Blackwood's Edinburgh Magazine*, 164 (October–December, 1898) and 165 (January–April, 1899). Conrad's *Heart of Darkness* was also serialized in vol. 165 (February–April, 1899).

4. For a brief survey, see M. Jeanne Peterson, 'The Victorian Governess', in Martha Vicinus (ed.), *Suffer and be Still: Women in the Victorian Age* (Bloomington: Indiana University Press, 1972), pp. 3–19.

5. According to the entry for Lynch in the Princess Grace Irish Library EIRData bibliography.

6. Lynch, *French Life in Town and Country* (London: George Newnes, 1901), pp. 116–23.

7. Lynch, 'The Spaniard at Home', *Blackwood's Edinburgh Magazine* 164 (September 1898): 353, 354.

8. Lynch, *French Life in Town and Country*, pp. 62, 157, 159. But Lynch's sight is not monocular. She acknowledges that the French peasant woman lacks 'the lovely complexion and beautiful eyes of the Irish'. And she praises (I *think*) Irish men when she remarks that they alone among the men in Catholic countries take their religion seriously (p. 177).

9. Lynch, *French Life in Town and Country*, pp. 13, 18–19, 100, 112, 171.

10. Katherine Cecil Thurston, *Max: A Novel* (1909; New York: Harper & Brothers, 1910), pp. 183, 303, 304.

11. Ibid., p. 72. The opera's plot summary can be found in *The Penguin Opera Guide* (New York: Viking Press, 1993), s.v. 'Gustave Charpentier'. The opera, we are told, was premiered in Paris on 2 February 1900 and Thurston may well have seen it there, or in London where it was first performed on 18 June 1909, though this may seem too close to the publication date of *Max* (some time that year).

12. *John Chilcote* was first serialized in *Blackwood's Edinburgh Magazine* in 1904 before appearing as a book published by William Blackwood. It was adapted for the Broadway stage and (four times) for the cinema.

13. However, the following paragraph appears in a book by J. J. Abraham ('James Harpole'): 'Some of you may remember the story of Adolf Beck, a Norwegian business man in London who was sentenced to seven years' penal servitude for

some alleged very despicable frauds on women. After he came out of prison he was again arrested on an exactly similar charge. His old record was gone into, he was identified by his victims, there seemed no doubt whatever about the matter, and he was awaiting sentence for the second time, when the real culprit, an ex-convict John Smith, was discovered. The two men were so alike it was difficult to tell them apart. Their handwritings even were similar; and Beck had the greatest difficulty in convincing the Crown that there had been a miscarriage of justice. Eventually, however, Smith confessed, Beck was completely exonerated, and the Government paid him £5,000 as compensation for the years of false imprisonment he had suffered,' *Leaves from a Surgeon's Case-Book* (1937; London: Cassell for the British Publishers Guild, 1941), p. 179.

14. Katherine Cecil Thurston, *John Chilcote M.P.* (Edinburgh: William Blackwood, 1904), pp. 271, 320, 331, 255.

15. Perhaps the coinage honours should be shared by Grand and 'Ouida'. The two writers appeared in the same volume of *North American Review* (158, 1894), authors respectively of articles entitled 'The New Aspect of the Woman Question' and 'The New Woman'. In her second paragraph, Grand uses the term 'the new woman'.

16. Madame Sarah Grand, *The Heavenly Twins* (New York: Cassell, 1893), p. 80.

17. *Sir Arthur Conan Doyle: Interviews and Recollections*, ed. Harold Orel (London: Macmillan, 1991), p. 111.

18. Later acknowledged in *The Bookman* 35 (1912): 348. The same section of *The Bookman*, 'Chronicle and Comment', recalls that *Dracula* (1898) was at first refused by American publishers, forcing Stoker to copyright it in the United States at his own considerable expense; then an American publisher took it on and it had enormous sales in the United States and Canada. The section writer also remarks that no modern realist had yet turned his attention to the tragedy of *Titanic* which could have stimulated the powers of Zola; he declines to mention that Stead lost his life in that tragedy.

19. Arnold Bennett was entertainingly insightful about Grand. He thought that if any recent novel had been saved instead of damned by its purpose, it was *The Heavenly Twins*, which he called 'the modern equivalent of *Uncle Tom's Cabin*', Philip Waller, *Writers, Readers, and Reputations* (Oxford: Oxford University Press, 2006), pp. 852–3.

20. Gillian Kersley, *Darling Madame: Sarah Grand & Devoted Friend* (London: Virago, 1983), p. 14.

21. Kersley, *Darling Madame*, p. 33.

22. I quote from a qualified defence of the Acts: F. B. Smith, 'The Contagious Diseases Acts Reconsidered', *Society for the Social History of Medicine* (1990): 197–215. The compulsory portions of the Acts were repealed in 1886.

23. Josephine Butler, *Social Purity* (London: Morgan and Scott, 1879), p. 5. Butler deplored the idea that a female sinner was worse than a male sinner, did not believe that marriage in itself improves or redeems a man, and deplored likewise the male categorization of women as either good or transgressive; as a result of these ideas, the sense of justice, love of freedom, and public spirit had all

weakened. She combined what we find in many of the popular novels: a liberal desire for, or expression of, sexual equality and female emancipation on the one hand, and a conservative impulse to censor and censure even while doing good.

24. Titles of addresses and sermons between 1880 and 1918 include *Our Duty in the Matter of Social Purity, An Address to Young Men; The Purity Pledge: A Talk to Girls; Women and Social Purity; The Vital Question: An Address on Social Purity to all English-speaking Women* (this from the Theosophical Society); *Manhood a Word for Men; Quit You like Men; Brotherly Honour versus Selfish Passion*.

25. *Sex, Social Purity, and Sarah Grand*, ed. Ann Heilmann and Stephanie Forward (London: Routledge, 2000), 4 vols.

26. Sarah Grand, *Ideala: A Study from Life* (1888; London: Heinemann, 1894), pp. 256, 14–15, 16, 266, 262.

27. Katharine Tynan, *The Middle Years* (London: Constable, 1916), p. 380.

28. The scene in the City Hall, Armagh on 17 April 1912 would have been rare, perhaps impossible in Catholic Ireland. This large meeting held to promote women's suffrage was addressed by Cicely D. Corbett, Revd Hugh Chapman (Chapel Royal, Savoy, London), and a local woman, a Mrs Cope of Drummilly. The meeting passed a resolution almost unanimously in favour of women's enfranchisement. A lengthy report of the meeting can be found in *The Belfast News-letter*, 18 April 1912 under the heading 'Women's Suffrage Movement'. The *Literary Digest* (New York) of 10 August 1912 has a photograph of 'An Irish Suffragette' being arrested for shouting 'I represent Tipperary' during a speech by Lloyd George in London on 13 July. She looks rather a *grande dame* and is, one assumes, Protestant.

29. Patrick Maume briefly describes Irish Party opposition to women's suffrage in early 1913 during the Home Rule debate, an opposition in part reflecting social and religious conservatism: *The Long Gestation: Irish Nationalist Life 1891*–1918 (Dublin: Gill & Macmillan, 1999), pp. 122–3.

30. Gifford Lewis, *Edith Somerville: A Biography* (Dublin: Four Courts Press, 2005), p. 5.

31. See Gifford Lewis, *Somerville and Ross: The World of the Irish R.M.* (New York: Viking, 1985), pp. 214–15. Lewis's previously cited book examines the suffragism and feminism of Martin and Somerville in greater detail.

32. Review of Carmel Quinlan, *Genteel Revolutionaries: Anna and Thomas Haslam and the Irish Women's Movement, Times Literary Supplement* 14 November 2003: 30.

33. If lack of involvement it was, rather than a case of historical erasure.

34. The religious dimension of these issues (and by 'religious' we unavoidably mean in Ireland cultural, ethnic, and political as well) is usually delicately stepped around by Women's Studies historians. An example would be Quinlan herself. In her well-researched account of the Irish women's suffrage movement, the terms *Catholic, Protestant, nationalism, England, Britain,* and *Belfast* are not indexed. The subject of her monograph and the pioneer, as she sees her, of the Irish women's suffrage movement, the Quaker Anna Haslam, was as Quinlan admits, 'a staunch unionist' while the organization she and her husband led, the Dublin Women's Suffrage Association, 'was largely unionist in sympathy': *Genteel Revolutionaries*

(Cork: Cork University Press, 2002), pp. 110–11. Quinlan warns us that she will not rehash the debate between unionist suffragists and separatist (i.e. pro-Home Rule or republican) women (many of whom Quinlan asserts were suffragists). One wonders why not, since it is not at all well known. The effect of the lacuna is to elide the deep political divisions in the activism of Irishwomen, many of those divisions originating in religious, ethnic, and geographic identity, which may be embarrassing to the nationalist or feminist historian but are unavoidable. There is one convenient example of the elision. Several times William Johnston MP is credited with being 'indefatigable' in support of the DWSA. Quinlan identifies him as Conservative MP for Belfast 1868–1902, educated at Trinity College Dublin (p. 223) but neglects to tell her readers the most salient fact about him. He was the famous (or notorious, depending on your politics) Johnston of Ballykilbeg (1829–1902), a legendary Orangeman and anti-Home Ruler. His dates of parliamentary representation were actually 1868–78, 1885–1902 because in 1878 he was dismissed for the violence of his anti-Land League and anti-Home Rule speeches. Clearly the same Irishman (or Irishwoman) could strenuously support women's suffrage while being anti-republican and anti-Home Rule. Most students of Irish Studies have been trained to see such a thing as an anomaly and so Quinlan might have hesitated to record its simple explanation: that such an Irishman or Irishwoman saw both causes inside the larger cause of the optimum operation of the Union. Roy Foster has a footnote on Johnston in *Modern Ireland: 1600–1972* (1988; London: Penguin, 1987), pp. 389–90, n. xvi.

35. The New Woman spanned a spectrum of attitudes and types, and convenient profiles can be found in Jenni Calder, 'New Women', in *Women and Marriage in Victorian Fiction* (1976); E. J. Hobsbawm, 'The New Woman', in *The Age of Empire 1875–1914* (1987), and *The New Woman*, ed. Juliet Gardiner (1993).

36. Grand, *Ideala*, p. 16.

37. Sarah Grand, *The Beth Book* (1897; Bristol: Thoemmes Press, 1994), pp. 346–7.

38. Grand, *Ideala*, pp. 260, 257, 259, 258.

39. 'The Rôle of Women in Society', *Nineteenth Century* 49 (January 1901): 76.

40. Moira O'Neill, 'A Lady's Life on a Ranche', *Blackwood's Edinburgh Magazine* 163 (January 1898):12, 3, 14–15, 16.

41. L. T. Meade, *The Cleverest Woman in England* (London: James Nisbet, 1898), p. 11.

42. The journey, largely literal, is recounted for us in typically no-nonsense yet eloquent fashion in Grimshaw's book, *From Fiji to the Cannibal Islands* (1907).

43. 'How I Found Adventure', *Blue Book* (April 1939), reproduced online http://pulprack.com/arch/2003/02/beatrice_grimsh.html It is unclear if the apparently well-known phrase 'Revolting Daughter' derived from Sarah Grand's discussion of daughters who revolt in 'The Modern Girl', *North American Review* 158 (1894): 706–14. Amy Cruse put the Revolting Daughter into historical context in *After the Victorians* (London: Allen & Unwin, 1938), p. 127.

44. Beatrice Grimshaw, *Isles of Adventure: From Java to New Caledonia but Principally Papua* (Boston and New York: Houghton Mifflin, 1931), pp. 2–4.

45. Beatrice Grimshaw, *When the Red Gods Call* (New York: Moffat, Yard & Co., 1911), p. 293.
46. I turned to LeeAnne M. Richardson's *New Woman and Colonial Adventure: Fiction in Victorian Britain* (2006) to find help in putting Grimshaw into a wider literary context, but whereas this study is long on theory, it is short on female texts; only three or four women novelists are discussed at any length and none of the discussions approach the space given to H. Rider Haggard. Grimshaw goes unmentioned.
47. Beatrice Grimshaw, *Nobody's Island* (London: Hurst and Blackett, 1917), pp. 33–4.
48. Beatrice Grimshaw, *Vaiti of the Islands* (New York: A. Wessels, 1908), p. 205.
49. See Carolyn Christensen Nelson, *British Women Writers of the 1890s* (New York: Twayne Publishers, 1996), p. 22.
50. I am using the text of the story in *Daughters of Decadence: Women Writers of the Fin de Siècle*, ed. Elaine Showalter (London: Virago Press, 1993).
51. The Princess Grace Library EIRData catalogue has Egerton divorcing Clairmonte in 1895 and marrying Bright in 1901; *Edwardian Fiction: An Oxford Companion* (ed. Sandra Kemp et al.,1997) has her divorcing Clairmonte and marrying Bright in the same year, 1901. In her 1902 revision of Read's *Cabinet of Irish Literature*, Egerton's contribution is primarily under the name of 'Mrs. Golding-Bright' which must have been Bright's full surname.
52. Elaine Showalter has discussed the importance of smoking in the subculture of the New Woman: 'Smoking Room', *Times Literary Supplement*, 16 June 1995: 12.
53. Nelson, *British Women Writers of the 1890s*, pp. 25–6.
54. I am using the text of this story from *Discords* in a combined *Keynotes* and *Discords* volume entitled *Keynotes*, Intro. Martha Vicinus (London: Virago Press, 1983).

10

Fin de Siècle: New Women, Art, and Decadence

'Nowadays all the married men live like bachelors, and all the bachelors like married men.'
'*Fin de siècle*', murmured Lord Henry.
'*Fin du globe*', answered his hostess.

Oscar Wilde, *The Picture of Dorian Gray*

ART AND THE NEW WOMAN

More than Sarah Grand, George Egerton was a conscious shaper of her fictions and the longish story fitted best her artistic inclinations. *Keynotes* appeared with a cover by Aubrey Beardsley (reproduced by Virago in their republication) which suited the musical and painterly analogies that play around Egerton's stories, including the titles of her two volumes. She introduces motifs, such as inflections of the 'cross' of the title, 'A Cross Line' (*across, crosses, cross, crossed*) which echo and supplement the meanings of the title of the story, or the hurdy-gurdy tune in 'A Psychological Moment'. The motifs have the effect of creating an agreeable tension between the social and psychological content of the stories and their accomplishment as analogously musical forms, with both vying for dominance. *Keynotes* itself struck a new note and inspired a series of that name put out by John Lane (with whom it is said Egerton had an affair) and she also published in the inaugural issue of the *Yellow Book*. Egerton is regarded as a New Woman writer but she was also a 'daughter of Decadence', to use Showalter's phrase.

Mangum shows the extent to which Grand was opposed to the aims and practices of Aestheticism, to the notion of art for art's sake.[1] Unlike female Aesthetes in whom Talia Schaffer sees a relative disengagement from women's political concerns and also some fear and ambivalence about their female characters' futures and the idea of their control over their sexual choices, Grand was fully engaged and showed little ambivalence and less fear.[2] But of course she considered herself a writer, an artist; it was just that art was to serve the spirit and the needs of the day. And Grand could create an ambience very similar to that created by Wilde and the other 'Decadents'. I would point to the strange 'Interlude' in *The Heavenly Twins* in which The Boy (actually a married woman, one of the Twins) masquerades as her brother to seduce The Tenor, a beautiful young man. The shock of his discovery of The Boy's true sex effectively kills The Tenor. This might even be a Wildean resolution, but un-Wildean is the woman's leaden explanation, that she merely wanted 'free intercourse with your masculine mind undiluted by your masculine preju-dices and proclivities with regard to my sex'[3]—i.e. she wants a gender-neutral equality rather than heterosexual play—but the experiment itself, like its counterpart in 'When the Door Opened—?' is rather *fin de siècle*. And there is the Lord Henry Wotton-like La Motte in Grand's novel, *A Domestic Experiment* (1891), who sets out to seduce Mrs Oldham then induce her husband to believe she is having an affair with Sir Alec Graham.

One intriguing story by Grand does explore the relationship between the New Woman and art. 'The Undefinable: A Fantasia' appeared in *Cosmopolitan* 17 (1894) and the *New Review* 11 (1894) before being collected in *Emotional Moments* (1908). A self-satisfied and highly successful Society painter, idly pondering his latest portrait and oddly finding no power in it to move him, is visited in his Kensington studio by a model looking for work. He will sell the work and it will defray the costs of his season's affair with Lady Catherine Claridge, but still, the painting moves him not. Against his will and better judgement, the artist engages the model who from the start addresses him as an equal. She has the 'mocking eyes of that creature most abhorrent to the soul of man, a woman who claims to rule and does not care to please; eyes out of which an imperious spirit shone independently'.[4] The more time they spend together, the more she loses her initial unattractiveness and the more she influences him; he finds her lure and influence unaccountable, indefinable yet irresistible. Indeed, the usual power relation of artist–model, man–woman (woman he thinks 'the whimsical sex') are quite quickly reversed and his smugness and self-satisfaction recede to be replaced by an eagerness to learn from her.

The wife in Egerton complained that man has 'fashioned a model on imaginary lines' and then set out to possess her; Grand's woman is both artist's model and man's model, and both artist and man must learn the flaw in their model, the error of their ways. Grand's model is dismissive of his art so far, lacking as it does a true soul and he a true rage for expression. 'Your work at present is purely Greek—form without character, passionless perfec-tion, imperfectly perfect, wanting the spirit part, which was not in Greece.'

Later we learn what it is 'a modern man must add of the enlightenment of to-day' to perfect himself and his art. He becomes her pupil and turns his back on Society. It is he who begins to pose to impress her and who towards the end is dressed for a celebration dinner by her in Greek raiment: *he* has become *her* model; 'she begged me to assume a classical attitude, and then proceeded to dispose herself in like manner on the other couch opposite.' The tableau begins as the elaborate staging for a painting but becomes an occasion for what Katherine Mullin describes in another context as 'The *fin-de-siècle* fashion for *tableaux vivants*, or "living pictures", posed tableaux of "classical" subjects usually accomplished by actors in flesh-tights.' Social purity campaigners protested against this practice, which lends an ironic context to a story written by a writer who was herself a social purity campaigner.[5]

'Who is the model?' the artist and the reader wonder. Grand hardly needed to have the artist at the end of the story—after the model has vanished, her work done—remark that 'there was a kind of allegory'. Grand's dignified model, coming into a house and altering its occupants for all time, plays a role rather similar to her contemporary, Yeats's Cathleen Ni Houlihan. She is the Muse, or rather, the Muse-in-waiting, the artist not having yet received his instructions. She is the soul of art, its passion. So far, the artist has indulged only the senses; the soul of art is its *je ne sais quoi*, its indefinable quality that will elude man until he come to terms with woman. She is the spirit of egalitarianism, who upsets the hierarchy of man–woman, master–servant (under her influence, the artist's manservant assumes equality with his master). She is the spirit of naturalness in art and life, disdainful of the artificiality of Society and society art. She is Sappho, Ceres, Venus, Diana: universal woman, woman of the ages. But she is also the spirit of Grand's day; she is 'the glorious womanhood of this age of enlightenment'; and it is this 'enlightenment of to-day' that even the Greeks wanted and that the new man and new artist must receive to perfect themselves.

In short, Grand's model is the New Woman. She has not lost her personal attractiveness (in the story it grows, and could be confused with old-fashioned womanly allure) nor as a New Woman should she. In her essay in the *North American Review* of 1894 (same year in which 'The Undefinable' was published) in which she coined the term, Grand wrote that the New Woman would retain her grace and feminine charm while sloughing off the silliness and hysterical feebleness of her sex. 'True womanliness is not in danger.'[6] Grand was a member of the Rational Dress Society yet still liked dressing well, and has her model claim that there have never been more delightful days than the present for woman, the creature of clothes. The New Woman, then, is a confusing creation, embodying insolence and ideality, gravity and levity; according to the model, she is 'an impossible mixture of incongruous qualities, which are all in a ferment at present, but will eventually resolve themselves, as chemical combinations do, into an altogether unexpected, and...admirable composition'.

This will have repercussions for art. For at present the model is not herself an artist: 'if I could paint myself I should not be here. I should be doing what I want for myself, instead of using my peculiar power to raise you to the necessary altitude', she tells the artist. He assures her that no woman has truly distinguished herself 'except in her own sphere' but she responds that this will change. The New Woman is an emergent creation. The model herself is a kind of 'Joan the Baptist': 'I *am* a woman with all the latest improvements. The creature the world wants. Nothing can now be done without me' (a seventh wave). If she is a catalyst, the women coming behind her will progressively emancipate themselves and become, some of them, artists. After all, up to now, during women's 'slavery', there have been more great women than great men who were also slaves. Full emancipation is imminent and art will be the beneficiary. Meantime, the man will be the beneficiary of the emergent New Woman. The artist feels a shock of awakening and she vanishes as he is about to attack his canvas with passion and rage. He searches for her but to no avail. He seems to hear her voice, telling him about a promised symbiosis: 'Give me my due; and when *you* help *me*, I will help *you*.'

Among other things, Grand's model has the poise and authority of the professional, but Grand was aware of the difficulties in the way of the woman who would enter the professions. Nelson quotes her essay of 1899, 'Should Married Women Follow Professions?' in which Grand answers in the affirmative but is conscious that in her own case financial independence and separation from her husband (i.e. from obligatory domesticity) cleared the way for her choice.[7] (On the non-allegorical level we learn only that Grand's model is well-to-do, with a suggestion that she is self-made, and there is no mention of husband or children.) All women should have that choice, but choice it is and clearly only available to the middle-class women with talent to whom Grand appeared to address herself. Both Hannah Lynch and Ella MacMahon choose to depict their female professionals as musicians, in *Daughters of Men* (1892) and *A New Note* (1894) respectively, thereby covering the themes of the woman professional and the woman artist, themes that arose out of the Woman Question and out of the Art Question that underlay 1890s Aestheticism. Set in Athens and the Greek islands, *Daughters of Men* covers some of the same thematic ground MacMahon was about to cover in *A New Note* and *A Pitiless Passion*: the woman artist and thinker and her internal conflicts, love, marriage, types of woman ('the variability of the feminine temper', 'these explosive engines, known as daughters, born to poor harassed man') and the feminine triumph. *Daughters of Men* is written with the same sophistication Lynch displays in her nonfiction.

It is as if MacMahon seized on Grand's artist's conviction that there has been no truly distinguished woman artist and decided to portray such a woman artist, generating the necessary frictions of her story out of the impediments that lie in her heroine's path. *A New Note* is a set of variations in the familiar subgenres of the problem-novel, country-house novel, and romance-novel and on the familiar themes of love, marriage, and England–Ireland relations. Here and in other popular novels, England–Ireland relations could be regarded as forms of engagement, unhappy marriage, and infidelity, between countries rather than between men and women, with England playing the male part. Moreover, in the country-house novel that involves these relations, the adjective takes on the double meaning of 'countryside' and 'nation'. England–Ireland relations are lightly established in *A New Note* through Victoria Leathley's visit to Castle Connaught owned by Fitzgerald (Jerry) Annesley who at the opening of the novel (in 1888) proposes to her at her English country house home (her father is a Liberal MP) and is turned down but who never gives up hopes and whose loyal persistence is rewarded at the end of her visit three years later when she becomes engaged to him; in 1891 it is a hot summer in London both literally and politically, with Irish affairs in turmoil.

But the novel is focused on the assaults on young Victoria's determination to resist all persuasion to marry and to resist any temptation to fall in love while establishing her career as a professional violinist which she sees would be impossible were she to marry. She firmly chooses art over love and marriage, reflecting that men are primitive in their delusion that women are made solely to be made love to. Her father supports her (in a kind of emotional liberal laissez-faire) but he and she know that her decision is risky in and of itself, and even were it to pay off, her fame would in fact be notoriety since she is a woman. At the start she like Grand's model is the self-reliant woman whom other women in New Woman fiction have to struggle to become; she even has that necessary room of her own filled with books, pictures, flowers, and music. She is leaving Jerry behind, indeed all men behind, 'going away from him, away into a great *terra incognita*, a land of which he and men like him are profoundly ignorant'.[8] She is the Victorian girl ('Victoria' recumbent) entering the new post-Victorian age and plans to be victorious in doing so ('Victoria' rampant).

MacMahon was timely in making her heroine a would-be professional violinist. Marie Hall was described in 1909 as 'the first woman violinist in England'. She was born in 1884 and so was only 10 when *A New Note* appeared; she received instruction from Elgar in that same year of 1894 and made her debut in Prague in 1902 and London in 1903[9]. Maud McCarthy, born in Tipperary, made her concert debut even earlier, at the Crystal Palace in 1891.[10] In an 1898 article entitled 'Violins and Girls', H. R. Haweis discussed the peculiar and natural affinity women have (or ought to have) with violins and after mentioning two women performers on the instrument, ended with the following: 'I prophesy that the name of Maud McCarthy, now a mere child, will stand out as the brightest violin genius of the last decade of the nineteenth century'.[11] However, neuritis ended McCarthy's career as a professional concert violinist in 1905.

During the three years that elapse between the first and second portions of the novel, Leathley has become a well-known but not supreme violinist; however, she writes a one-act opera, *Sappho*, that sweeps London, with everyone demanding to know the identity of the composer; an aria, 'Sappho's Song', has become a national hit, competing with 'Ta-ra-ra-boom-de-ay' (the popularity of which allows us to date the two parts of the action of the novel to 1888 and 1891). 'No woman has ever done anything to equal it in music', her partner says. Her name is revealed and she suffers the penalty of modern fame ('the constant presentation of flattery and congratulations, the inevitable whirl of publicity, the blaze of notoriety'), complete with what the novels claims is the new-fangled medium of the celebrity interview. But she begins to fall in love with her singing partner, Louis Loevio, and, bewildered and worn down, accepts Annesley's second proposal in Ireland; she hears in her head her aunt's words: 'Perhaps some day you will find, as many a woman has found, that safe, comfortable marriage cuts the black knot of a woman's difficulties in the only effectual and permanent way.' She returns to London alone where, suddenly vulnerable because falling more deeply in love, she is pursued by Loevio. Although she realizes the pioneering nature of her achievement as a composer and performer, she succumbs to her feelings and the novel declines into romance with a layer of unconvincing late Victorian class realism.[12]

The famous Loevio (love you + leave you?) wins her away from Annesley but turns out to be a cad, a lower-class bounder called Lewis Higgins; he is exposed when a woman appears in order to warn her off him, telling how Higgins left her after winning her heart and, after she married another (an apparently 'safe marriage' that turned out to be to a wife beater), returned and seduced her, then abandoned her when she left her husband for him. In a scene that anticipates the scene in *Howards End* when Margaret Schlegel confronts Henry Wilcox about Jackie Bast (though she unlike MacMahon's heroine forgives the man for holding a double standard) Leathley confronts Loevio and ends their relationship. The novel is a lengthy and bitter attack on marriage and those who promote it as a safe haven for women. It is jaundiced also on the subject of love; the narrator's refrain, 'Victoria was a woman—a woman in love', grows increasingly sardonic; Victoria's own customary expression of 'slightly sarcastic weariness' is, like her initial self-reliance and rejection of love and marriage, justified. The novel ends with her returning to her own room (living room, den, and studio combined), alone but self-sufficient: 'Everything was in order once more.' In having solitude as the ending of this phase of her heroine's quest, MacMahon ensures that *A New Note* is an anti-romance-novel that was written and read mainly by women, though until the exposure of Loevio it exploits the features of the romance subgenre.[13]

The Sapphic element in *A New Note* is not pursued and MacMahon invites us off the trail by having Leathley accept love (before Loevio's exposure) at the expense of her art as a kind of resigned sharing of Sappho's fate: Sappho's accomplishments have been overlooked and her fame reduced exclusively to her reputation for love. But the exchanges with Ada Barclay in the novel have an erotic overtone and one might wonder if female self-sufficiency is a way of *not* dealing with that second form of feminist transgression that unlike the first—genius in composition—could not be handled forthrightly in print in the 1890s.

A New Note, like *A Pitiless Passion*, is in part a study in what is called in the latter work, 'the artistic temperament.' Magdalen in the second novel is by temperament a happy woman : 'happiness is the result of temperament; there is no other recipe for it', we are told. It is Magdalen's temperament ('strong, reliant, sanguine') that prevents her from contemplating the misery of others with equanimity, for hers 'was a temperament singularly sensitive to outer influences'.[14] MacMahon subtitled a later book—*The Straits of Poverty* (1911)—*A Study of Temperament*. In the earlier novel, reference is made to Tony Chenevix's temperament: ' "Temperament!" he cried impressively, "oh, come now, that's too much! I never had a temperament in my life. I wouldn't have such a thing. I'm too old-fashioned. Your temperament and your temperature are the inventions of a modern devil".'[15] He seems to have a point. Kate Chopin published 'Athenaise: A Story of a Temperament' in 1896. The British Public Library Catalogue lists ten novels published between 1903 and 1923 subtitled *A Study of Temperament*. But many novels of the period might easily have borne the same subtitle. In 1914, when *The Job* was published, MacMahon was still exercised by temperament as a modern fixation. During their mutual effort to imagine Ria Devereux as a suitable mate for Thady Muntfort, Lady Hexham and Thady agree that Ria Devereux has temperament. ' "That's it", Lady Hexham seemed to wake up suddenly. "Temperament! I always forget what it is that all the young women have nowadays—but it's temperament. We didn't have it in my day. At least I can't remember ever hearing about it . . . I suppose it wasn't in us. One thing, I think was against it—the style of dress. It—didn't seem to lend itself to—to temperament somehow. But Ria has temperament, and *you* have temperament and that is why you young people nowadays seem to get on with each other so well".'[16]

The contemporary concern with temperament, which recurs in the Irish novels, was clearly related to interest in personality and also in environment and heredity, the tensions between which account for a great deal of fiction of the time. Riddell's *A Rich Man's Daughter* (1895) is partly the portrait of a man (Dr Claud Dagley) who can exhibit neither love nor optimism. 'Whether his pessimism were the natural outcome of a very unpleasant temper [his heredity], or his unpleasant temper the result of a too constant contemplation of a state of society in which everything needed remodeling [his environment], is a problem concerning which only an Ibsen dare hazard a conjecture... Old families mating in and out eventually decay, but old families mating incongruously often develop such a "sport", as Claud Dagley.'[17]

THE PICTURE OF DORIAN GRAY

Oscar Wilde was in fiction (*The Picture of Dorian Gray*) and 'fact' (*De Profundis*) deeply interested in social conditions (environment) and heredity and in the socio-biological fate of old families. In this regard he was very much of his time, and his celebrated novel, despite its unique Wildean qualities (the dandified tone of voice, the epigrammatic conversations, the opulent descriptions), occupies the world of the popular Irish novel. The most vivid figures in his fiction and drama are those whose temperaments—unlike Magdalen Ponsonby's—prevent them from contemplating the misery of others with other than equanimity (though we know that the author himself was a charitable human being) but this is an inversion that nonetheless proves my point. *The Picture of Dorian Gray* (1890) is above all 'A Study in Temperament'. In a moment of unusual self-candour when his moral descent is in mid-trajectory, Gray regrets he did not ask Basil for help is resisting Lord Henry's influence (such influence forming part of Gray's 'environment') 'and the still more poisonous influences that came from his own temperament'.[18] Poison courses through the narrative and is in one sense malign traits or what we might call today 'bad genes'.

Heredity, says Gilbert in 'The Critic as Artist', is a mechanism that science has begun to understand and because it *is* a mechanism over which we have no control, our behaviour is freed from the constraints of morality; in a characteristically Wildean double-edged way, Gilbert seems both encouraged and terrified by this. We are unfree in our actions; this too is a good since it emancipates us into the contemplative life of inaction if we so choose (think of the Wildean cultivation of idleness and languor); but the contemplative or imaginative life can also be of dubious hue in so far as heredity can come as a 'terrible shadow, with many gifts in its hands, gifts of strange temperaments and subtle susceptibilities'. We live the memories of the race; through imagination we escape the present but even in the apparent liberty of imagination we inherit the maladies of the past, the most colourful elements of which (for Wilde) are the bizarre, curious, and sinful. Although in other regards, the personal for Wilde is a decided virtue and goal, Gilbert sees imagination as the result of heredity, not the expression of the unfettered individual.[19]

The author's own aestheticism, his knowledge of science, particularly of evolutionary biology which he studied at Oxford, and his unique brilliance, set Wilde apart from the other novelists I have been considering. Yet he shared his fascination with heredity with those novelists. Dorian Gray is a specimen of flawed heredity, a blemished nature, as well as a specimen of Lord Henry's malign nurture. His parentage (the quarrelsome, mean grandfather, the beautiful, romantic mother, the socially insignificant father) is for Lord Henry a fascinating tragic background for the decorative portrait of the boy he intends to 'paint': all pattern and 'symbolical value' after 'the new manner in art'. (Basil Hallward's painting of Gray begins life as very different—skin deep where its subject is concerned and revealing only of Hallward's abject fascination with his model—but as Gray falls under Lord Henry's sinister supervision, the painting becomes the literal expression of the 'symbolical value' Wotton intends.) 'The men were a poor lot,' says Lord Fermor of Gray's family, 'but, egad! The women were wonderful.' Gray has inherited only his mother's wonderful beauty; otherwise he has inherited the character poverty of his male forebears. He acts out the consequences of Lord Henry's misguidance and (like Lord Alfred Douglas as Wilde came to see him) his own genotype. Gray has also inherited tendencies from decadents and tyrants, exponents of a meretricious indifference portrayed in dramatic procession in the pages of Huysmans's *À Rebours* (1884) whom Gray is reading—Tiberius, Caligula, Domitian, Elagabalus—as well as tendencies from writers, including Petronius and Gautier. 'Yet one had ancestors in literature, as well as in one's own race, nearer perhaps in type and temperament, many of them, and certainly with an influence of which one was more absolutely conscious' (pp. 177, 302). Either way, like Huysmans's Des Esseintes, Gray suffers from an inherited sickness, and both Huysmans's novel and Wilde's are studies in pathology, indeed of that pathological condition once called monstrosity and that so fascinated the Victorians in that age of moral and medical obsession, including the writers, as Stevenson's *The Strange Case of Dr Jekyll and Mr Hyde* (1886), Stoker's *Dracula* (1897), and even Conrad's *Heart of Darkness* (1902) testify.

A refrain in *De Profundis* (1897) is the flawed heredity of the Douglases; Lord Alfred, Wilde claimed, suffered from a hereditary condition. He wrote to Lord Alfred: '[Your mother] saw, of course, that heredity had burdened you with a terrible legacy, and frankly admitted it, admitted it with terror: he is "the one of my children who has inherited the fatal Douglas temperament," she wrote of you'; 'Through your father you come of a race, marriage with whom is horrible, friendship fatal, and that lays violent hands either on its own life or on the lives of others'; 'the fact that the man you hated was your own father, and that the feeling was thoroughly reciprocated, did not make your Hate noble or fine in any way. If it showed anything it was simply that it was a hereditary disease.'[20]

Certain sad ironies attach to Wilde's belief in the power of heredity. Self-realization, normally a virtue in Wilde, could be an incidental vice in the sense of the fulfilment of an individual's heredity, as in Douglas's and Gray's cases. Behind Wilde's allegation of Douglas's vicious mole of nature lay a contemporary idea, deriving from the theories of the Italian psychiatrist, Cesare Lombroso, author of *Delinquent Man* (1875): that of degeneration.[21] Lombroso also wrote *Insanity and Genius* (1861) and to him the Hungarian physician and critic Max Nordau dedicated *Degeneration* (1892; trans. 1895) in which Wilde himself is discussed as an example of 'a pathological aberration of a racial instinct...a malevolent mania for contradiction...the egomania of degeneration'.[22] It is as if by his own assessment and not just Nordau's, Wilde had become his own creation, Dorian Gray, or that he had inherited traits *from his own fictional character* in accordance with the process by which, Gilbert had said, one could have literary and historical ancestors more important than actual forebears.

Nordau's analysis is the more ironic given Wilde's social Darwinism which *Dorian Gray* instances. When in search of adventure Gray wanders eastward in London, 'soon losing my way in a labyrinth of grimy streets and black, grassless squares' (in which he discovers Sibyl Vane in an 'absurd little theatre'), he enters the territory of portions of Riddell's *A Rich Man's Daughter* and Meade's *A Princess of the Gutter*. Moreover, *The Picture of Dorian Gray* shares the binary setting of many of the popular novels, set as it is in fashionable town houses (situated in the Albany, Grosvenor Square, Mayfair) and country houses (Gray's Selby Royal in Nottinghamshire, its name echoing the German word for self); both of Gray's houses are described as 'great'. Wilde likes to score witty variations with the familiar town–country duet; in *The Importance of Being Earnest* he inverts the usual urban perceptions of the country while in *Dorian Gray* he also inverts the usual equation of (urban) culture with good living when Lord Henry invites Gray to see the connection between culture and corruption. Gray carries this corruption, it seems, into the countryside. The economic and social decline of the country house, so common a feature of the Irish popular novel, takes the form in *Dorian Gray* (since Wilde normally shows his aristocrats in robust economic health) of the alleged moral decline at Gray's country house about which Hallward has heard disturbing rumours (pp. 193, 310).

As in many of the other novels of the period, there is a yawning gulf between Society and the urban underclass or rural peasantry. (Riddell is one of the few novelists to portray centre stage the middle classes and in their business dealings.) Gray crosses the abyss that reappears in late-Victorian and Edwardian social fiction and of which Wilde's novel is a curious but recognizable representative.

His friends, Hallward charges, have under Gray's influence 'gone down into the depths'. Gray travels from his 'own delicately scented chamber' to 'the sordid room of the little ill-famed tavern near the Docks' and ends up in opium dens. Other swells have often crossed too, but for purposes of charity. Ironically, Lord Henry first hears Dorian's name at his own aunt, Lady Agatha's; she finds the young man 'earnest' and with 'a beautiful nature'. She wishes Dorian to help her in her charitable efforts in the East End. Earnestness seems certainly to have been a quality of many of the charitable of the period, and one looks in vain for humour in the work of the most thematically philanthropic, for example, Rosa Mulholland.[23]

Lord Henry naturally is cynical about philanthropy and he is relieved he has not gone to his aunt's where 'the whole conversation would have been about the feeding of the poor, and the necessity for model lodging-houses. Each class would have preached the importance of those virtues, for whose exercise there was no necessity in their own lives. The rich would have spoken on the value of thrift, and the idle grown eloquent over the dignity of labour'. He believes Dorian is far too charming to go in for philanthropy. He doesn't wish Gray to 'squander the gold' of his days, listening to the tedious 'trying to improve the hopeless failure'; no, he promotes instead a 'new Hedonism', which proves, of course, to be Gray's undoing. It is Lord Henry's opinion that the 'emotional sympathy' behind philanthropy limits knowledge and prevents the solving of any social problem; and whereas it is easy to have sympathy with suffering, it is difficult for the philanthropic to have sympathy with thought. When taxed by Lady Agatha for drawing Gray away from charitable work in the East End, Lord Henry responds by finding 'something terribly morbid in the modern sympathy with pain'. Moreover, the nineteenth century has gone bankrupt 'through an overexpenditure of sympathy' and he suggests that it is to science they should go to solve the problem of the East End. Besides, Lord Henry in one of his silver paradoxes believes that in their harassing of potential donors and helpers 'philanthropic people lose all sense of humanity. It is their distinguishing characteristic'.[24] Wilde's remarks about good works among the poor must have been shocking in that age of professional and amateur philanthropy, though some might have seen the underlying wisdom of his suggestion that science had more chance of saving destitute humanity than good works. Arnold White certainly did.[25] On the other hand, it is a different science, Darwinism, Lord Henry has in mind when he remarks that 'Good resolutions are useless attempts to interfere with scientific laws' (p. 251). Evolution was seen by some as a formidable challenge to the rationale for philanthropic intervention in the lives of the poor and disadvantaged.

Lord Henry assails the self-denial that the charitable were required to practice. The poor had no say in the matter, and the good lord thinks that 'the real tragedy of the poor is that they can afford nothing but self-denial'. For the rest of us, the aim of life is 'self-development. To realize one's nature perfectly—that is what each of us is here for'. And of course, self-development is held to be an Hellenic ideal. Anti-philanthropy in Wilde constitutes an attack on the practice of charity and the notion of self-sacrifice that surface in so many other contemporary novels. Little wonder that Gilbert in 'The Critic as Artist' and Cecily in *The Importance of Being Earnest* speak slightingly of the three-decker novel that in the 1880s and 1890s was dominated by women authors. The anti-philanthropy theme is not of course an isolated strand of thought; it connects with Wilde's deep scepticism about the freedom and efficacy of action. It connects also with Wilde's persistent dismissal of sincerity and lauding of insincerity; sincerity kills the multiplicity that Gilbert seeks in criticism; in art, says Gwendolen in *Earnest*, style not sincerity is the vital thing; while Gray thinks insincerity enables him to reflect the truth that 'man was a being with myriad lives and myriad sensations, a complex multiform creature that bore within itself strange legacies of thought and passion' (his multiple heredity), a fair description of Wilde himself.[26] Fittingly, Wilde's *oeuvre*, though not huge, displays a virtuosity that was beyond the novelists we have looked at.

It is individuality—a goal and condition opposed to self-denial and undue sympathy—that for Wilde is the motive power behind achievement in life and literature.[27] In *De Profundis*, Wilde returns again and again to the desirability of individuality and self-realization. 'The supreme vice is shallowness', he tells Douglas. 'Whatever is realized is right.' 'I am far more of an Individualist than I ever was... Nothing seems to me of the smallest value except what one gets out of oneself. My nature is seeking a fresh mode of self-realisation... People used to say of me that I was too individualistic. I must be far more of an individualist than I ever was.'[28] He had earlier observed that charity and its requisite self-denial impede the progress of the race whereas individuality advances the race and saves us from 'monotony of type'; and sin, which is an extreme expression of the individual, 'increases the experience of the race', a notion that would have been a shocking inversion of the belief system of the philanthropic in London's East End and Dublin's south city slums.[29] But in *De Profundis* Wilde appears to be deepening his sense of individuality. Whereas he had claimed there that 'Christ was not merely the supreme Individualist, but he was the first in History' (p. 479), he later in the letter calls self-realization inadequate (p. 488), with the wise acceptance of the enigma of man's soul being the ultimate virtue, a post-suffering position closer to some of the female philanthropic, empathetic novelists.

In Wilde, women seem to be disqualified candidates for self-development. *Dorian Gray* is strewn with witty misogynistic remarks which advertise women's materialism, their barrenness of genius, their impediment to male creativity, and their charming but inartistic artificiality. Such prejudices ought to have outraged contemporary feminists, though over against them can be set the New Woman, even Grandian, sentiments of the pretty Duchess of Mon-mouth (e.g. 'Courage has passed from men to women. It is a new experience for us') who keeps pace with Lord Henry's witticisms, returning him strong ripostes. He has the gall to find that her 'clever tongue gets on one's nerves', a remark that redounds to the discredit of either Lord Henry or Wilde, one is not sure which.[30] Yet Wilde's editorship of *Woman's World* hardly bespeaks misogyny; and of course one has to take into account in all readings of Wilde the essentially provocative, wilfully contrary and what we would call today politically incorrect energy of Wilde's humour. The degree to which he exag-gerates his own position on any topic for purposes of shock and humour is hard to assess; and since his ideas form a kind of moral and aesthetic system, it is possible that the whole system itself is deliberately overheated.

About marriage, that other theme beloved of the Irish novelists, Lord Henry is relentlessly cynical, and his cynicism is part of the Wildean mock-system: the charm of marriage is that it makes a life of deception necessary; the drawback to marriage is that it makes one unselfish; marriage is simply a habit, and a bad one at that (this after his wife has run away with a pianist)—and habit, of course, is the inverse of self-realization. With these observations the New Woman might have agreed, but the romance novelist and country-house novelist would have found them epigrammatically reductive and abhorrent in their flippancy. And whereas the artist Basil Hallward tells Gray that 'Love is a more wonderful thing than art', Lord Henry is predictably and wittily scathing on the subject; love he calls an illusion. Romance leaves one unromantic; the faithful know only the trivial side of love, the unfaithful its tragedies. 'When one is in love, one always begins by deceiving oneself, and one always ends by deceiving others. That is what the world calls a romance': in such a saw there is an uncomfortable grain of truth that prevents Lord Henry from being a mere phrase-monger.[31] It is love, of course, that destroys Sibyl Vane's acting, her engagement to Dorian, and her life. Love is inimical to life, art, and marriage, a proposition to which, again, the bosom of the New Woman might have returned an echo, though it makes ribbons of the romance and country-house novels.

If some of the Irish novelists interpreted Ireland for their English readers ('There *are* quiet silent Irishmen', MacMahon's narrator assures her English readers),[32] and if the point of view in many of the novels seemed actually or figuratively to originate in England, even when the novel was set in Ireland, Wilde *appeared* to reverse the relationship by criticizing England and not Ireland and by locating *his* point of view figuratively outside England, allowing him to see that country steadily and see it whole while professing to dislike what he saw. Gilbert in 'The Critic as Artist' airily alleges the philistinism, mediocrity, and coarse-mindedness of the English and *Dorian Gray* continues the witty onslaught.[33] The English among the peoples of the world have the least sense of literary beauty, according to Lord Henry; and it is Lord Henry or Wilde (it is unclear which) who refers to 'the inherited stupidity of the [English] race' but it is certainly the lord who lists beer, the Bible, and the 'seven deadly virtues' as the secrets of England's greatness.[34] Wilde had no real interest in Ireland's poverty or in England's economic capacity to extend charity to her impoverished sister isle; nor had he interest in those in Ireland who were wealthy enough to extend charity to the native poor. Instead, transposing the problem, he professed to see the Irish as rich and England poor, not in the spiritual terms of Rosa Mulholland but in the aesthetic terms by which everything was finally to be judged. Gilbert insists that it is the Celt who leads in art (p. 122). Wilde proudly regarded himself as a Celt (in England at any rate) and thought, surely not wholly seriously, that he and George Bernard Shaw spearheaded 'the great Celtic school'.[35] He wrote to Grant Allen in 1891 praising Allen's essay in the *Fortnightly Review* for its 'scientific demonstration' of the Celtic spirit of art that Arnold had merely divined.[36]

So it might be thought that Wilde inverted the point of view of the Irish novelists on the theme of the interrelations between England and Ireland, and to a degree he certainly did; in one of the innumerable examples of his use of reversal of expectations, he writes as though Ireland were the senior partner in the relationship. But Wilde himself had not outgrown the damaging stereotype of the Celt as lazy, imaginative, and unrealistic any more than had, say, B. M. Croker.[37] He, too, thought in the race terms that were prevalent in contemporary Britain and Ireland and that had received a popular cultural boost from Darwinism (about which Wilde was knowledgeable) and that had become particularly heated, for a variety of reasons, from Wilde's time until the Great War.[38] Moreover, Wilde's fictional, dramatic, and critical personae are essentially English. And not only did he himself move easily between the two islands as a citizen of both, but in his literary imagination it was to the English realms of gold he travelled, among which was Greece in its spiritual and artistic guise. His inversions and reversals of the values of the Irish novelists were not in the service of a Celtic revival or an Irish renaissance, as such inversions and reversals were in the writings and philosophy of Yeats. Rather, the brilliance was expended in the cause of art itself, and if beyond that he wished his ideas and his literature to convert anyone, it was the English he wished to convert, not Ireland; his rich and essential universe of discourse was England and that Anglo-Irish middle earth he inhabited.[39] But inside that pale, he generated much of his criticism, and *Dorian Gray* too, out of his opposition to the world and world-view of the popular novel, Irish and English alike.

BOSIE IN DUNMURRY

The strongest Irish echoes of Wilde, however distorted and unreliable in their transmission, are to be heard from the pages of Herbert Moore Pim (1883–1950), essayist, novelist, pamphleteer, and political activist. The unreliability of the Wildean echoes is matched by the curious instability of Pim's career. He was born in the Queen's University area of Belfast into a Protestant business family, was educated at Friends' School (a Quaker grammar school in Lisburn, Co. Down), married the daughter of a Presbyterian linen merchant, and was a member of the Junior Conservative Club, after which things began to go sideways. He converted to Roman Catholicism, became 'a violent Irish Nationalist', lost a position with an insurance company because of his new political allegiance, and in 1915 was briefly imprisoned in Crumlin Road gaol in Belfast, having involved himself in the Sinn Fein movement, edited the separatist magazine, *The Irishman*, and used his Belfast house as an armoury. His life was threatened when he reconverted to unionism and defected from republicanism and he fled to London. After his London interlude he became a naturalized Frenchman, chiefly in order to leave him free to marry his French mistress. He went to Italy in the 1930s where he became a Fascist and finally returned to England where he died in 1950, a confirmed British imperialist.[40]

 The Wildean echoes are less surprising when we learn that Pim became a friend of Bosie, Lord Alfred Douglas, whom he had met through a mutual friend. During the Great War Pim invited Douglas to his cottage in Dunmurry, then a village on the outskirts of Belfast, now incorporated into the city. They already shared conversion to Catholicism. Conversion to Catholicism had a *fin de siècle* association and, sincerity of belief aside, was for some writers a way of cocking a snook at the English establishment and bourgeoisie. Roman Catholic churches and liturgy could be readily recruited for the sensuous imagery of Aestheticism; one of Wilde's setpieces in *The Picture of Dorian Gray* is the description of what Gray is drawn to: the ritual and symbolic daily sacrifice, the vestments and aromatic ambience of it all, what Frank Harris called 'the perfume of belief' which he said Wilde liked.[41] But of course, in Ireland Catholicism had other associations and Pim introduced Douglas to Irish nationalism which Wilde's former intimate embraced with a convert's enthusiasm. In 1920 Douglas invited Pim to London to become assistant editor of his lay Catholic, Tory weekly, *Plain English*.[42] By then, as a result of Sinn Fein/IRA outrages during the 'Troubles', Pim was a unionist and Douglas followed him again in this cause, giving space in his weekly to the Ulster Defence Council. When Rupert Croft-Cooke met Douglas in 1922 the only friend of Douglas's he heard of was Pim. (Later, the highly litigious Douglas took offence—and legal steps—when Pim printed in a volume of his poems Douglas's praise for a single poem years before, an offence all the greater because Douglas thought the poems were mere doggerel.)[43]

Bossence tells us that Pim regarded his novel, *The Pessimist: A Confession* (1914) as his masterpiece. It was published under the name 'A. Newman', a pen name he used because, he told his son, he became a new man after he joined the Catholic Church (his young son winced when told this at the time). The novel is an attempt at literary fiction, not popular fiction, and it is a rather strangled version of *Dorian Gray*. It concerns a famous sage, originally from Donegal where his family seat is, who has left his Oxbridge post to become a kind of Carlylean prophet of pessimism and who at his friends' London houses or his own country house in Hampshire trades sub-Wildean paradoxes and aphorisms with other characters: 'Punctuality is the least excusable of the vices'; 'It is the duty of everyone to talk cleverly; but it is the duty of those who cannot say clever things, to create beautiful silences'; 'Women should never try to be paradoxical...Their life is a paradox; so their speech should be direct and obvious, or their subtlety will be suspected'; 'Women are the critics of pure reason! And the Militant Suffragette merely exists because men have begun to treat women as reasonable beings, and women quite naturally object.'[44] And so on.

This often tedious verbal sparring sits awkwardly with the serious pessimism about life into which the rather secretive John Grampier sinks deeper— life is all a tangle, expressive only of misery, incapable of improvement, impossible to square with a loving God (though believe in God he does) or indeed any ultimate spiritual meaning. Only art commands Grampier's admiration and, as it was for Wilde and the Aesthetes, art is immortal in its beauty, functions on a unique plane of being, and exists above life's miseries, and in the novel its praises are sung frequently. But the remedies for life's sickness grow less effectual as the novel goes on. Grampier briefly contemplates escaping the fret and fever of the world by living in the seclusion of Oxbridge and eventually being soothed to eternal slumber by Anglicanism's 'incomparable liturgy', but decides against it. He cannot accept socialism as a way of curing the fret and fever. And charity? His socialist friend Moberly thinks charity is immoral and his Lord Henry Wotton-like friend, Sir Archer Grafton, is cynical about it ('Charity covers a multitude of sins! That's what makes philanthropists so contented as a class', p. 212); Grampier, since he is weighed down as much by his endlessly required compassion as by compassion's provocations, thinks charity is an excellent lifeboat for those who will make use of it. But when he is invited to go 'slumming' and witnesses the death of a young girl, the idea occurs to him that sudden and painless death would be the world's greatest friend.

Here is Wilde's *fin du globe* made literal. The 'gentlemen's club' strand of the novel means that Grampier has a scientist friend, Avermal (averring evil?), who discovers that a single ray of radium can create a form of life that can in turn extirpate all known life.[45] He demonstrates the prototype of this omnipotence to Grampier who sees it as the solution to the problem of life. The ruthless experimenter and vivisectionist Avermal faintly suggests Dorian Gray's friend Alan Campbell, while this strand of the novel shares something with the 'mad scientist' fiction of Wells and others. Grampier, wanting to soothe the world to sleep, agrees that on Avermal's death, he, Grampier, will release the new death force on an unsuspecting world that will include even his own new wife, Marjory, Moberly's lovely daughter. She is unaware of his secret but knows that he is at war with God. Confronted with poverty and disease, here is action the polar opposite of charity; or it is philanthropy taken to the logical conclusion of global euthanasia. Grampier has a vision by Shelley's 'Ozymandias' out of Wells: 'He pictures to himself the calm repose which would creep over the world; how in the great cities the noise of commerce would be still; the tired and under-paid would no longer rise up to toil; the great steamers of the ocean would stop upon their way, and drift like funeral barges until they sank slowly through very age, or grounded upon some lifeless shore; how the Sun would rise and set upon a silent world; and how all the mighty works of miserable man would crumble, and rust, and totter to their inevitable grave' (p. 105).

But thereafter Grampier's steadfast pessimism is stirred to some extent by his marriage, though even after Avermal has died and he has in his hands in a railway carriage the death-dealing jar which need only be broken for universal death to ensue, Grampier's vision becomes personal yet he resists the urge to call off his mission:

His war with Heaven had commenced... He seemed to see Marjory sitting in the sunshine, as he had so often seen her. She was, perhaps, speaking of him to Edward, smiling at the thought of his return. And even as the smile lay upon her lips, death would sweep in a circle of unmeasured power, like a great wave of oblivion, carrying her life with it. As this force pressed forward, the birds would fall from the sky and from their perches in the trees; the flowers would grow pale with disease; the hum of insects would cease; and there would be silence such as had never been since the beginning of the world. (pp. 245, 259–60)

But Grampier has been tricked by Avermal out of revenge and the death-jar is a dud when he smashes it on the carriage floor. It is a turning point for Grampier who interprets it as a sign of God's victory; he recovers his soul and belief in the goodness of God, and—in an un-Wildean note—comes to see that the Bishop was right when he said that no man can have a say in the life or death of mankind; 'the sorrow of the world', Grampier comes to see, 'was a small thing compared with the all-reaching love of God' (p. 284). He returns to his wife a new man, careful now to limit his pride of intellect. A posthumous letter arrives from Avermal claiming to have avenged himself against Grampier, certain that God will not forgive his enemy, and sure that Grampier's pessimism will be left without solution or goal. But Grampier is secure in his renewed faith, certain now that the artist worships at the shrine of nature, not art, though he disavows pantheism.

An 'Author's Apology' defends the conception of the unlikely figure of Grampier (combining within himself the soul of an Isaiah and an iconoclast), partly on the grounds that he is a typical Irishman who inhabits the alien culture of Oxbridge! He also tells us that *The Pessimist* traces his own four-year intellectual history before his reception into the Catholic Church. The Bishop whose wisdom Grampier comes to approximate steers a course, we are told at he outset, between Exeter Hall and the Vatican, which might suggest Anglo-Catholicism. (Exeter Hall in London, completed in 1831 and used for large revival meetings and philanthropist gatherings, was demolished in 1907, three years before Pim was received into the Catholic Church.)

The Pessimist is simply one odd work among several Pim wrote.[46] It was followed by a set of strange philosophic essays entitled *Unknown Immortals in the Northern City of Success* (1917) and published under Pim's own name, each story or sketch devoted to a 'character' or species of 'character' on the streets of late 1880s, early 1890s Belfast. 'From childhood', Pim tells us in his Preface, 'I have had a special affection for certain queer people', and knowing that realism would not be a successful style by which to capture them, he chose another style which he cannot describe except by calling it something more than idealism. It is a peculiar combination of periphrasis, allusion, epigram, and the affected simplicity of the folktale; the result is of the eighteenth rather than nineteenth century and not without its irritating charm. Pim is here a distant affine of James Stephens. With characteristic pretentiousness he calls his book 'a species of "retrocessional progression": a return to the ample, classical age'. Among others, the characters include the willick woman (the periwinkle monger: 'willick' a Belfast dialect version of 'whelk'), the rent man, the rag and bone man, and the fish man. There is a potentially first-rate evocation of the once famous Smithfield market in Belfast, marred by Pim's use of circumlocution in order, one assumes, to gain rhetorical altitude by consigning identifiable details to his own footnotes. Thus 'Here, among the sombre outpourings of silent houses whose owners are asleep, there slumbers the music of this marvellous land, to be awakened only by a vision of royalty'[47] means, once footnoted, that among the contents of second-hand furniture stalls, there is an ancient automatic spinet that is silent until a penny (with its monarch's head) stirs it into action. It is a surprise to learn in this essay that sixty years before (i.e. the 1850s) there were three theatres in Smithfield and though they have gone, 'the actors, who should long since have died, remain like moths upon some ancient web, living while it lives' (p. 31). In his concern with the minutiae of Belfast and its buried lore, Pim at times reads like an ancestor of Ciaran Carson. 'The Soul of Smithfield' ends with what since 1974, when the market was bombed by the IRA and destroyed by fire, has been an ironic and prescient note: 'In Smithfield…we have a storehouse of splendours, for the loss of which nothing could compensate this city of success' (p. 31).

When he was a boy Pim was taken to a lunatic asylum and became fascinated: he later wrote 'The Madman' but later still took four years to write 'Monsieur Among the Mushrooms', a fantasy-memoir of one of Belfast's strangest characters, a kind of philosophical idiot savant for whom the mushroom incorporates all significant meaning and embodies all organic forms; meanwhile, as the Preface to *Unknown Immortals* tells us, he is an irresistible street logician, proof against allcomers. It is a study in mental pathology and appeared in the august pages of the *Irish Ecclesiastical Record* in 1915 under the name of A. Newman and is reproduced, shorn of numerous learned footnotes, in *Unknown Immortals*. With the original version, it is as if Pim has decanted us from the *outré* connoisseurship of Des Esseintes (in Huysmans's *À Rebours*) and Dorian Gray and deposited us, before the fact, in the disturbing surrealistic universe of Flann O'Brien's De Selby and his commentator, whose faux pedantry accretes around the action of *The Third Policeman* (1940) and of which Pim's footnotes are a precursor. Here, however, the author shares the part of De Selby with the autodidactic mycomaniac. The footnotes cite Descartes, Joseph Butler, Berkeley, Hobbes, Spencer, Hume, and others far less known, including mycologists, as well as numerous species of mushroom and toadstool, all correctly furnished with their Latin names.

Monsieur becomes an avid mushroom gatherer in disused industrial tunnels and soon acquires disciples, founds a philosophical school dedicated to the laws of harmony and reflection, and invites martyrdom. He is clapped into the local lunatic asylum, 'a Daniel dragged to Bedlam'.[48] His philosophy of the mushroom continues to grow. 'How poor a thing man appeared, after all, compared with the mushroom that could set its seal upon man's food, and say: "That is mine!"—grasp a tree in its embrace, make the forest its own, lay its fingers on the fields; encompass eternity indeed, and set bounds upon the dances of the dead' (p. 593; every clause comes with a footnoted reference to a particular species of fungus). The keepers and doctors study Monsieur, feed him mushrooms with his meals, lead him to a puffball colony on the asylum grounds where, in fact, he conceives his plan of escape. The governor surrounds himself with fungi and with depictions and the literature of fungi, the better 'to persuade

Monsieur to exhibit the peculiar symptoms of madness which made his case so attractive' (p. 596). He is denied freedom when by means of one of his familiar logical tiltings he belittles the chairman of the Asylum Committee during a sanity hearing. But he has been collecting the spore-dust of puffballs and when he communicates to his followers outside the asylum wall by means of a pitched cake of fungus, a scaling ladder is shot over the wall and Monsieur escapes, the pursuing keepers being covered in a cloud of puffball powder ('the sand of some celestial desert') which induces in them a 'stupor of sympathy' (p. 605). Pim's ghost must be gratified that the American Council on Spiritual Practices has read this character sketch as possible evidence that there was knowledge of psychoactive ('magic') mushrooms in early twentieth-century Ireland, and that an excerpt warrants inclusion in the CSP's ongoing 'entheogen chrestomathy', a phrase Pim would have relished: 'entheogen': the god within; 'chrestomathy': a collection of literary passages. The CSP shares with Pim a certain brinkmanship on the edge of religious self-parody.

The footnoted epilogue to Monsieur's escape records Monsieur's work in a plant nursery under the protection of a believer, his continued belief in the doctrine of the Mushroom (a belief so enthusiastic that he paints his glass-houses with a black light-excluding fluid), attacks on the nursery, and the purchase of a sailing ship by the nursery keeper. After that the trail is lost save for an entry in '*Merchgoldt's Diary*' referring to an island the diarist came upon with no vegetation save fungi, some immense, several bearing 'an absurd resemblance to human faces' (p. 605).

NOTES

1. Teresa Mangum, 'Style Wars of the 1890s: The New Woman and the Decadent', in Nikki Lee Manos and Maeri-Jane Rochelson (eds.), *Transforming Genres: New Approaches to British Fiction of the 1890s* (New York: St Martin's Press, 1994), pp. 47–66.
2. Talia Schaffer, *The Forgotten Female Aesthetes: Literary Culture in Late-Victorian England* (Charlottesville: University of Virginia Press, 2000), pp. 14, 71.
3. Sarah Grand, *The Heavenly Twins* (New York: Cassell, 1893), p. 459.
4. I am using the text of Sarah Grand, 'The Undefinable: A Fantasia', repr. in Elaine Showalter *Daughters of Decadence* (ed.), (London: Virago Press, 1993) pp. 262–87.
5. Katherine Mullin, *James Joyce, Sexuality and Social Purity* (Cambridge: Cambridge University Press, 2003), p. 25.
6. Sarah Grand, 'The New Aspect of the Woman Question', *North American Review* 158 (1894): 274. For Grand the true threat was not from women becoming more manly but from men becoming *less* manly: see 'The Man of the Moment', *North American Review* 158 (1894): 620–7, and 'The New Aspect of the Woman Question': 275.

7. Carolyn Christensen Nelson, *British Women Fiction Writers of the 1890s* (New York: Twayne, 1996), p. 31. 'Should Married Women Follow Professions?' appeared in *Young Woman* 7 (1899): 257–9. Other Grand articles included 'Is it Ever Justified to Break off an Engagement?'; 'At What Age should Girls Marry?'; 'Does Marriage Hinder a Woman's Self-Development?'; 'On the Choice of a Husband'.

8. Ella MacMahon, *A New Note* (1894; New York: R. F. Fenno, 1895), pp. 11, 101.

9. See *The Review of Reviews* 40 (1909): 162 and *Etude* music magazine, November 1909, available online.

10. When neuritis ended her career as a concert violinist in 1905, McCarthy (1882–1967) became a singer, composer, collector, mystic, and feminist. With her husband, the British composer John Foulds, she co-wrote incidental music for Yeats's *At the Hawk's Well*: Malcolm MacDonald, *John Foulds and his Music: An Introduction* (White Plains, N. Y.: Pro/Am Resources Inc., 1989), pp. 21–2. Neither MacMahon, Lynch, Meade, nor Temple Thurston (see below) appears in Phyllis Weliver's *Women Musicians in Victorian Fiction, 1860–1900* (2000) though there are some pages on women and the violin and women and the piano.

11. *Contemporary Review* 74 (1898): 111–12. One of the characters in 'Wayfarers', a 'sketch' in *A Cluster of Nuts* by Katharine Tynan is a young married Cork woman whom we meet on an emigrant train travelling to Queenstown (Cobh) via Cork; she is an expert violinist, first restringing and retuning an emigrant's fiddle, then dazzling her carriage mates with music 'from the great masters' and then with Irish airs '— "The Coolun" and "The Blackbird" and others—while the tears rolled down the faces of the two emigrants': *A Cluster of Nuts* (London: Lawrence & Bullen, 1894), p. 22. Anne Bannerman in L. T. Meade's *A Princess of the Gutter* (1896) is a violinist and composer who sacrifices the possibility of a musical career to work in the slums of London's East End with the novel's heroine. A significant character in E. Temple Thurston's *Traffic* (1906) is a Miss Shand who makes her living playing violin in a trio (with cello and piano) that performs in the restaurant of Maynard's store in London—an early department store, it seems. Her affinity with the instrument is of a kind that Haweis only hints at: 'She gave the impression that, as she fondled her violin, so she would cling in passive passion to the man whom she would love': *Traffic: The Story of a Faithful Woman* (1906; London: Chapman and Hall, 1914), p. 186.

12. Ella MacMahon in a later novel, *The Job* (1914) uses music as background rather than foreground. Thaddeus (Thady) Muntfort is a pianist and an ardent Wagnerian, but the music that resounds through the novel is Mendelssohn's *Rondo Cappriccioso*, played at key moments of emotional tension.

13. For these features, see Pamela Regis, *A Natural History of the Romance Novel* (Philadelphia: University of Pennsylvania Press, 2003), pp. 10–12.

14. Ella MacMahon, *A Pitiless Passion* (New York: Macmillan, 1895), pp. 103, 71–2, 298, 302.

15. Ella MacMahon, *A Pitiless Passion*, p. 119. Chenevix is right to couple temperament with temperature. Three definitions of temperature in the *OED* equate the concept with temperament: the character of a substance determined by the proportions of hot or cold, dry or moist; the combination of humours in the body;

constitutional bent of mind or disposition. The sense in which MacMahon seems to be using temperament—constitution or habit of mind, natural disposition—is recorded first in 1821, and an 1894 usage is probably what she had in mind: 'those qualities and dispositions which belong to [a man] from birth'.

16. Ella MacMahon, *The Job* (London: James Nisbet & Co., 1914), pp. 129–30.

17. J. H. Riddell, *A Rich Man's Daughter* (London: International News Company, 1895), p. 79.

18. Oscar Wilde, *The Picture of Dorian Gray* (1890), in Richard Aldington and Stanley Weintraub (eds.), *The Portable Oscar Wilde* (Harmondsworth: Penguin, 1981), p. 273.

19. Oscar Wilde, 'The Critic as Artist', in *The Portable Oscar Wilde*, pp. 105–6.

20. *The Letters of Oscar Wilde*, ed. Rupert Hart-Davis (New York: Harcourt, Brace, 1962), pp. 448, 433, 440, 451.

21. The career of the concept of degeneration in the nineteenth and early twentieth centuries is traced in a collection of essays, *Degeneration: The Dark Side of Progress*, ed. J. Edward Chamberlin and Sander L. Gilman (1985). The essay by Chamberlin, 'Images of Degeneration', is particularly relevant here.

22. Max Nordau, *Degeneration* (London: Heinemann, 1913), pp. 318–19. Seven months before he began *De Profundis*, Wilde petitioned the Home Secretary for release from Reading gaol, on the grounds that his misdeeds were due rather to a curable sexual pathology than to criminality, citing in evidence Nordau's assessment of the petitioner: *Letters*, pp. 401–2.

23. *The Portable Oscar Wilde*, pp. 310, 284, 154. Since 'earnest' was apparently contemporary slang for gay, Wilde might be mischievously having Lady Agatha describe Gray as he 'really' was, a meaning that presumably she would have found revolting. Gray's 'beautiful nature' is also a terrible irony, given the way in which it reveals itself.

24. *The Portable Oscar Wilde*, pp. 153, 156, 164, 109, 111, 184, 178.

25. In *Efficiency and Empire* (1901; Brighton: Harvester Press, 1973), White attacked the whole business of charity (and he *meant* 'business'). On the topics of the philanthropic harassing potential donors, and of the Darwinian folly of charity, he echoed Wilde: 'People who wanted baronetcies pestered people who wanted to be let alone, to cure destitute invalids so that they might propagate the unfit' (p. 112). White criticized the inefficiency of 'cheque charity' (instead of personal contact) and of the 'charity middlemen' that had sprung up. 'The struggle for life among professional philanthropists', he remarked with irony, 'tends to pauperise the masses by killing the wish for self-help' (p. 113). Wilde would hardly have accepted White's eugenically inclined strictures, but Wilde was at heart a self-help advocate and in his own way an efficiency man.

26. *The Portable Oscar Wilde*, pp. 227, 158, 73, 459, 118, 491, 300.

27. 'The Critic as Artist', *The Portable Oscar Wilde*, p. 71.

28. *The Letters of Oscar Wilde*, pp. 448, 467, 491.

29. 'The Critic as Artist', *The Portable Oscar Wilde*, pp. 110, 76.

30. *The Portable Oscar Wilde*, pp. 192, 228, 254, 362, 371, 385.

31. *The Portable Oscar Wilde*, pp. 143, 222, 378, 233, 360, 153, 197.
32. Ella MacMahon, *A New Note*, p. 7.
33. *The Portable Oscar Wilde*, pp. 108, 121, 51, 131.
34. Ibid., pp. 187, 343, 359.
35. *The Letters of Oscar Wilde*, p. 339.
36. Ibid., pp. 286–7.
37. See e.g. ibid., pp. 429, 666, 751.
38. I discuss race and racism in contemporary British (and American) culture in *The Age of* Titanic: *Cross-Currents in Anglo-American Culture* (2002) and elsewhere in this book.
39. Peter Ackroyd's identification of the English as Wilde's 'oppressors'—up to whom, Ackroyd claims, Wilde is putting a mirror in *The Picture of Dorian Gray*—is therefore ludicrous. Wilde could be regarded as oppressed only during and after his trial, and even then the factor his Irishness represented is moot. See Ackroyd, Introduction to *The Picture of Dorian Gray* (London: Penguin Books, 1985), p. 11.
40. For this biographical information I am grateful to have come upon 'The Quest for Herbert Moore Pim', by Ralph Bossence: *Belfast Newsletter* 21 November 1966. Bossence (whose phrase 'violent Irish Nationalist' I have quoted) was provided with biographical facts by Pim's son, Terence. See also the few lines provided by Brown, *Ireland in Fiction*, p. 254.
41. Wilde and Harris are quoted by Michael Wheeler, *The Old Enemies: Catholic and Protestant in Nineteenth-Century English Culture* (Cambridge: Cambridge University Press, 2006), p. 288.
42. There are references to Pim in a biography of his and Lord Alfred Douglas's pugnacious friend and coeditor: W. Sorley Brown, *The Life and Genius of T. W. H. Crosland* (London: Cecil Palmer, 1928), pp. 24, 324, 391, 424, 464. Pim was part of the frenetic and litigious Douglas–Crosland clique. From Brown's biography we learn that another Ulster-born fiction writer, Filson Young, was a friend of Douglas's wife Olive, who wrote to Crosland asking him for her sake not to make an enemy of Young through the journal he edited, *The Academy* (p. 246).
43. When he was gaoled for libel in 1923, Douglas met IRA men in Wormwood Scrubs and thought them Catholic gentlemen. For Pim and Douglas, see Rupert Croft-Cooke, *Bosie: The Story of Lord Alfred Douglas, His Friends and Enemies* (London: W. H. Allen, 1963), pp. 283–4, 292–3, 312, 365, 333. Until reaching the period when he met Douglas, Croft-Cooke seems rather dependent on William Freeman's *The Life of Lord Alfred Douglas: Spoilt Child of Genius* (1948) which has a few references to 'Moore Pim'.
44. A. Newman, *The Pessimist: A Confession* (London: David Nutt, 1914), pp. 110, 144–5, 272.
45. Pim acknowledges James Moore, MD, FRCS for the suggestion regarding radium. It is probable that this was the Belfast novelist Brian Moore's father, who was likewise James Moore, MD, FRCS.
46. His political pamphlets include *What Emmet Means in 1915* (1915), *Three Letters for Unionists Only* (n.d.), *Unconquerable Ulster* (1919), and *Sinn Fein* (1920).

There is an account of Pim's republican activities in Patrick Maume's *The Long Gestation: Irish Nationalist Life, 1891–1918* (Dublin: Gill & Macmillan, 1999), pp. 162, 187–8, 240. There is a small collection of Pim papers in Queen's University, Belfast, library. In 1924, Pim published (as A. Newman) *From a Lover's Garden*, a privately printed volume of love poems that had they been Wilde's would have done him no good in the dock, either legally or literarily. These slight, gawky, and often cloying lyrics are addressed to a boy-lover, Norman (whose name in one poem suggests the poet Norman Douglas) and seem to skirt danger: 'Now Norman goes a-fishing | A-fishing for a wife: | The only fish he'll ever catch—| Imprisonment for life!' The epigraph poem is called 'On a Departed Paidophil'. The other Douglas, Lord Alfred, contributed a sonnet, 'The Unspeakable Englishman'(a bitter denunciation of Crosland), to *The Irishman* under Pim's editorship: see W. Sorley Brown, *R. W. H. Crosland*, p. 391.

47. Herbert Moore Pim, *Unknown Immortals in the Northern City of Success* (Dublin: Talbot Press; London: T. Fisher Unwin, 1917), p. 24.

48. A. Newman, 'Monsieur Among the Mushrooms: A "Modern" Philosopher at Large,' *Irish Ecclesiastical Record vol.* 9 (May 1915): 591.

11

Science and the Supernatural:
Among Genres I

SCIENCE FICTION

As the curious career of Herbert Moore Pim demonstrates, other novelists shared with Wilde—though not so relentlesssly or triumphantly—the stylistic apparatus of Aestheticism, such as a superior tone of narrative voice (at once wise and cynical, scintillating and fatigued), wit, and an epigrammatic reduction of the world and humanity. Such writers after Wilde continued to exploit the movement by adding a bohemian dimension to their plots, such as Katherine Cecil Thurston in *Max* (1910), or by having their heroes engage in a youthful fling with Aestheticism as part of their development, such as Filson Young in *The Sands of Pleasure* (1905) and *When the Tide Turns* (1908), W. M. Letts in *The Rough Way* (1912), and Douglas Goldring in *The Fortune* (1917). Sometimes it is simply the Wildean device of clever repartee that is in evidence, and in Mrs Hungerford's frothy three-decker, *The Hoyden* (1894), there are countless scenes of drawing-room witticisms about matches and marriage, flirtation and infidelity, uttered by frivolous characters in which one might be listening to snatches of *The Importance of Being Earnest*. But Wilde's Aestheticism was of a different order from all of these, and there was another substantial side to him that could with a little effort be associated with it.

Elsewhere, for example, I have discussed Wilde's very real interest in science and his knowledge of it gained as a student at Oxford.[1] He was particularly interested in scientific method, especially experimentation, and he has Lord Henry fascinated by natural science and determined to practice its methods not on its usual subjects but on himself and others. Wilde's dandy could appear like Huysmans's Des Esseintes to be cultivating self-development on scientific principles. And as for those around him: Lord Henry's attitude he describes as 'vivisection', since his subjects are alive. Knives play a recurring role in *Dorian Gray*; they are literal but also metaphoric weapons of destructive surgery as when Gray accuses Lord Henry of cutting life to pieces with his epigrams. Gray blackmails Alan Campbell into performing the difficult task of annihilating with chemicals the body of Basil Hallward, an experiment from the pages of some scientific horror fiction, such as *Franken-stein, Dr Jekyll and Mr Hyde, Dracula,* or *The Island of Dr Moreau.* Campbell is asked to conduct himself with the cold curiosity of the scientist; he is to do so in secret, necessarily, and Lord Henry elsewhere praises secrecy; Gray lives a secret other life and does so with the dispassionate determination of a scientist; the sordid dens he frequents are like hidden laboratories (such as Frankenstein's, Dr Jekyll's, or Dr Moreau's) in which he, following his mentor but in the realm of fatal reality, experiments with and vivisects, his companions' lives and destroys them. Science is rarely absent from *Dorian Gray*; the pretty Duchess of Monmouth says Gray believes that her elderly husband, an insect collector, married her on 'purely scientific principles as the best specimen he could find of a modern butterfly'. Gray becomes a collector, in the manner less of the Duke than of Des Esseintes. In Huysmans's hero, Gray sees a strange blend of the romantic and scientific temperaments, like Wilde himself, one could say, and the Aesthetes he emulated.[2]

Lord Henry is a literary equivalent of the mad or hubristic scientist common in fiction of the nineteenth century. Supremely, he experiments with Dorian who then looses himself from his mentor (even creator) and goes his own dark way, like Frankenstein's monster, Stevenson's Mr Hyde, or Moreau's animal-men. Lord Henry would assent to Gilbert's claim in 'The Critic as Artist' that science like art stands out of the reach of morals; this coupling allowed Wilde to underpin his Aestheticism with his knowledge of science, and it brilliantly solved the problem of the Two Cultures (be they science and literature, or, in education, science and classics) that divided Matthew Arnold and T. H. Huxley.[3]

However, it may not be necessary to draw on Wilde's parallel between science and art to see certain scientific concerns as belonging to the 1890s. Whereas we might think of both science and its literary progeny, science fiction, as inimical to Aestheticism, Bernard Bergonzi has chosen to see the scientific romances of the young H. G. Wells as expressions of the *fin de siècle,* and it is very easy for us to extend the classification to other writers whose science fiction shares the end-of-the-century characteristics Bergonzi sees in Wells's stories of the 1890s. It might be said that Dorian Gray is a kind of Time Traveller; like Wells's Traveller, he stays still while time goes on around and past him. Also, Bergonzi identifies in Wells's science fiction the feeling of *fin du globe,* the very feeling the Duchess of Monmouth expresses in response to Lord Henry's murmur, '*Fin de siècle*'; 'I wish it were *fin du globe*', said Dorian, with a sigh. 'Life is a great disappointment' (p. 341). The terminal fatigue

Bergonzi sees in both Aestheticism and Wellsian science fiction was accompanied by the symptoms and themes of decadence and degeneration, by contempt for traditional views of custom and morality, by self-realization as a goal worthier of effort than altruism, by an embrace of the primacy of Darwinian struggle, and often by a fixation on the future. Surprisingly, Wells appeared in the *Yellow Book*, and there are other circumstantial Wells–Wilde connections. Wilde was apparently impressed by an early Wells story, 'The Rediscovery of the Unique', that Wells had sent the *Fortnightly Review*; when Wells was appointed drama critic for the *Pall Mall Gazette*, the first play he reviewed was *An Ideal Husband.*[4]

Wells's *The Time Machine* was published in 1895, and though versions of it appeared in the *Pall Mall Gazette* and *Pall Mall Budget* two years previously, it could not have influenced *A Plunge into Space* (1890) by the Co. Down novelist Robert Cromie (1856–1907).[5] As a journalist in Belfast, Cromie would have inherited knowledge of his native city's illustrious history in applied science. The likenesses between this novel and *The Time Machine* (as well as *The War of the Worlds*) might even suggest that Wells had read it, though in fictional method Cromie resembles Jules Verne (to whom the novel is dedicated and who wrote a Preface for the second, 1891 edition) rather more than he does Wells.[6] The opening dialogue between MacGregor, a good Scottish man of the Empire, and Henry Barnett the scientist and inventor (the 'mad' scientist for the novel's purposes) anticipates the opening of *The Time Machine* with its dialogue between the Narrator and the Time Traveller. The Traveller's voyage back through time is a sophisticated version of Cromie's voyage through space, though in this regard Cromie's novel more closely anticipates John Jacob Astor's *A Journey in Other Worlds* (1894).[7] Those who listen to Wells's Time Traveller's tale are representative professional men (the journalist, the medical man, etc.), just as those on board Barnett's Steel Globe on its voyage to Mars are representative: the literary man, the artist, the politician, the special correspondent, the capitalist, the imperial explorer. In both novels there is the sense of an 'old boys' club' that reflects the (loosely) political structure of English society of the time rather than that of Society as we have it depicted in the Irish novels we have discussed. The Mars these representative men (not women) travel to is more advanced than earth, as is the case with *The War of the Worlds*. The Martians, for example, travel in 'aerial cars' at a speed of 1,000 mph; writing before the invention of the aeroplane, Cromie describes Martian flying machines as yachts, galleons, ships. What begins as the logical extension of imperialism on the part of the earthlings receives a setback not only because the Martians are more advanced but because their society, as a result of their advance, is in the end boring and distasteful to the less developed Europeans.

For the Martians, it transpires, are perhaps *too* advanced and they resemble Wells's future earthlings in *The Time Machine*. Indeed, Cromie's Martians share with Wells's Eloi their triumph over material needs. (The Eloi have been read as Wells's attack on the Aesthetes.) They need to work only two hours a day and they have dispensed with nations, government, economics, money, linguistic differences. Women have the same privileges as the men. Martian science has eradicated disease. All the social problems that beset Cromie's Britain and Ireland have been solved on Mars—the Woman Question, the Race Question, the Nationalism Question, the Empire Question. Cromie paints a stark contrast between the early scenes in Alaska, when the space explorers readying their ship have to quell an uprising by Indians and half-breed (Métis) descendants of Louis Riel's rebels, and the later scenes on Mars. (In one exchange with the Irishman Blake, the Martian girl Mignonette claims Ireland must be a huge and important country because it takes up so much of the newspapers the travellers have brought with them. This is an allusion to the contemporary political unrest, presumably agrarian outrages and the Home Rule stirrings.) By the time the travellers arrive there is nothing left on Mars to invent. Martians have already gone through the stage of capitalism and internal colonialism, with the climatically and geographically favoured region of Lagrange (named after the Turin mathematician and astronomer) playing the role of England in Martian history. Post-imperial, post-capitalist Martian society brings no comfort to the dictator, capitalist, or socialist. Once a 'State Frankenstein' rose and ruled but passed away forgotten.[8]

Both the planet and its population are at the pinnacle of their perfection and face decay. Martian society exists at the end of history, a utopia apparently on the cusp of a downward slide into decadence, a condition into which Wells's Eloi are much further sunk. (For Wells, after decadence comes dystopia and finally the end of life and even the planet.) In their placid happiness, the Martians grow daily less curious about their visitors, like the Eloi or Swift's elevated Laputans. As among the Eloi, the sexes on Mars resemble each other. Wells's Weena is anticipated by Cromie's Mignonette; both are gamines and are corrupted by the attractions stirred by the newcomers. Action had given way to contemplation, as though in the realization of Wilde's recipe for the ideal society. Cromie clearly believes in the inevitability of progress by the enlightened nations, such as England. But he also believes that progress in order to be maintained requires an alliance in time between human nervous force and scientific insight; that nervous force the Martians have lost and with it physical courage.[9] Three stages of human social development are depicted in the novel: the underdevelopment of the Indians and half-breeds, the development of the Europeans, and the over-development of the Martians. The Europeans occupy the moment of colonial expansion and can look forward to progress of a Martian kind, but then will follow the inevitable decline. Humanity itself is at a kind of crossroads, a recurring theme in late Victorian fiction that outside science fiction assumes national or cultural forms. Here too are the themes of future decadence and degeneration that held fascination for Wells and other science fiction writers, as well as for E. Ray Lankester, Wells, and other biologists or science writers, for Wilde and the Aesthetes (who seemed to court these themes), for Conrad and other observers of the Empire, and for Lord Charles Beresford and other social commentators who feared the decline of the Anglo-Saxon race.[10] Wilde's own belief in evolution notwithstanding, biological, psychological, and racial anxiety—the dark side of evolutionary theory—all lay behind the fear and contempt shown to the Aesthetes by many in England.

We might regard the sudden destruction of the earth through the agency of science as an extreme mutation of degeneration; the literal *fin du globe* is the theme of Cromie's 1895 novel, *The Crack of Doom*. The novel is of the 'apocalyptic' subgenre of science fiction, like *The War of the Worlds*; Stableford calls the subgenre 'eschatological fantasy', the alternative to the other futurist subgenre, utopian fiction.[11] Pim's *The Pessimist* is an apocalyptic or eschatological fantasy. *The Crack of Doom* tells the story of a secret society (the *Cui Bono* Society) founded by a 'mad' scientist, Herbert Brande, who wishes to destroy the earth and if possible the solar system because he regards Nature as an absurd and disordered non-system of utter materialism maintained by the force described in the 'gospel' of evolution; the universe is a ceaseless, remorseless story of the reaggregation of atoms and without meaning, aspiration, or lesson. It is as if Cromie has taken on board the ruthless materialism that Wicklow-born John Tyndall outlined in his famous Presidential Address to the British Association for the Advancement of Science in Cromie's home city of Belfast (when Cromie was 18) and allied it to a destructive nihilism.[12] Brande has harnessed the same force Henry Barnett exploits in *A Plunge into Space* and has developed something akin to the atomic bomb with which he intends to destroy the globe. He has discovered an agent that will release 'the vast stores of etheric energy locked up in the huge atomic warehouse of this planet'.[13] Arthur Marcel who tells the story joins the Society in order to thwart Brande's design and travels to the Arafura Sea with him, manages to alter Brande's formula which results only in the destruction of an island, the escape from which, excitingly told, turns the novel like its predecessor into a scientific romance.

The Preface by Cromie, which (in a familiar narrative device) suggests that the novel has been constructed out of notes given to him by the man telling the story (Arthur Marcel), is datelined 'Belfast, May, 1895', and the novel opens on board the White Star liner *Majestic* on its way to Queenstown, which suggests the story's contemporaneity.[14] An important theme strand is the Woman Question: Brande's sister Natalie and her friend Edith Metford are advanced specimens of the New Woman, wearing masculine 'rational dress', smoking, dismissing 'the conventional New Woman' as 'a grandmotherly old fossil', and interpreting man's protection as 'enslavement'. But under the pressure of dangerous events, Edith allows her self-reliant nature to dissolve into Arthur's protection as the novel becomes a romantic thriller, and sheds her rational dress. (Natalie for her part has been mesmerized by her and her feminism is therefore unreal.) But oddly, despite the prefatory dateline, we are told that a secondary expedition for the same purpose has set out for Labrador in case Brande's expedition fails in its object of global destruction. The leader of the second expedition has orders to detonate 'before the 31st December, in the year 2000': 'And the end of the century will be the date of the end of the earth.' Brande destroys an island but is prevented from accomplishing the final destruction which is scheduled to be carried out in 'a few years', which would suggest that the novel is set in the future, around 1995, which is at odds with the prefatory note and the life depicted in the novel. Whichever *fin de siècle* is intended, it means in any case *fin du globe*, that peculiar fear exhibited in 1890s Irish and English fiction.[15]

TALES OF THE SUPERNATURAL

Cromie tried his hand at ghost stories, as did many writers of the 1890s, including Wilde, author of 'The Canterville Ghost'. Bergonzi reminds us that ghost stories were forms of fictional romance (or fantasy) and that science fiction and supernatural fiction sometimes overlapped, as they do in *Dr Jekyll and Mr Hyde*[16] and, we might add, *The Picture of Dorian Gray*. Moreover, there is a parallel. Science fiction frequently imagines other worlds besides earth whereas supernatural fiction imagines versions of the Otherworld, a disturbing, sometimes frightening realm superimposed on nature, revealing itself and impinging, sometimes fatally, in human affairs. The specific branch of supernaturalism we call spiritualism, which courted and investigated psychic phenomena, often in a scientific manner, began a long period of popularity in Britain after 1850, and George Bernard Shaw later remembered the decades before the Great War as those in which people were 'addicted to table-rapping, materialization, seances, clairvoyance, palmistry, crystal-gazing and the like to such an extent that it may be doubted whether ever before in the history of the world did sooth-sayers, astrologists, and unregis-tered therapeutic specialists of all sorts flourish as they did during this half century of the drift to the abyss.'[17] We can lengthen Shaw's list of Edwardian paranormalities to include telepathy or thought-reading, clairaudience (including 'phone-voyance'—'seeing through a telephone wire', as it was defined), mesmerism, hypnotism, levitation, automatic writing, and astral voyaging. There were also magic, theosophy, a belief in a fairy kingdom (important to some Irish Revivalists), and assorted mysticisms. By 1901 Wells was complaining in his short story, 'The New Accelerator', about 'these absurd days... when we are all trying to be as psychic, and silly, and superstitious as possible!'[18] He clearly felt that the literary entertainment of supernatural phenomena was different from a literal belief in them, since it might have been remarked that scientific possibility in Wells sometimes shaded into fantasy (the romance in 'scientific romance'), as in *The Time Machine* itself.

I have discussed elsewhere the vogue for a belief in ghosts and the communicating afterlife in the decades before the Great War, and we might remind ourselves that the eminent literary figures who at some point in their career interested themselves in spiritualism or the occult included Alfred Lord Tennyson, John Ruskin, 'Lewis Carroll', Rudyard Kipling, Andrew Lang, Cesare Lombroso, William Butler Yeats and his Irish literary cohorts, and Arthur Conan Doyle. Oppenheim, who has studied spiritualism in our period, believes that spiritualism and psychical research served as substitute religions for refugees from Christianity in the late nineteenth and early twentieth centuries.[19] But clearly they were also eccentric products of the vogue for science itself in the same period. The Society for Psychical Research was founded in 1882 and before long had eminent members, including Gladstone and Arthur Balfour (Prime Ministers both), Alfred Russel Wallace (co-formulator of the theory of organic evolution) and eight Fellows of the Royal Society. Scientifically-minded spiritualists distinguished spiritualism from superstition (*pace* Wells) and rejected the notion of the supernatural as a separate category of being and experience, instead viewing it as a researchable extension of the natural. Science fiction and supernatural fiction combine in stories of ghost hunters and exorcists who are convinced of survival after death.

Clearly it would be possible to put the activities and beliefs of Yeats, AE, and other Irish Revivalists into the context of contemporary British enthusiasm for spiritualism, theosophy, Rosicrucianism, magic, and mysticism—all involving belief in, and attempts at contact with, a world above and beyond nature, and representing measures to overthrow the tyranny of materialism and mechanism. It would also be possible for us to put into this context Yeats's and Lady Gregory's interest in folklore, and even in the old sagas recorded in the medieval manuscripts, since theirs was primarily an interest in belief in the supernatural; they were convinced that Irish peasants were carriers of the older, pre-Christian faiths rather than heirs to Christianity, far less the Enlightenment or materialism, cities, industry, and commerce. There was a streak of condescension here not a thousand miles from Rosa Mulholland's conviction that the poverty of Irish peasants kept them purer of faith. If the revival of Irish interest in folklore belonged also to the context of the British and European folklore revival of the 1880s onwards[20] (which veered between nationalist and internationalist understanding of tales, making it possible for tales to illustrate national culture but also international diffusion and structural transmission), Yeats, AE, Gregory, and others were yet chiefly interested in folktales, not as oral literature but as narrative reports of supernatural phenomena: fairies, changelings, revenants, visions, so-called sky-women, ghosts, mediums, and so on. Yeats's two early anthologies, *Fairy and Folk Tales of the Irish Peasantry* (1888) and *Irish Fairy Tales* (1892), were in fact compilations not of fairy tales in the European sense or even of fiction *per se* but rather of miscellaneous stories or excerpts of stories extracted—in a kind of asset-stripping—from novels that illustrated Irish belief in the Otherworld. In other words, supernatural belief was released from the fiction back into what Yeats regarded as the real Irish world.

Not surprisingly, Yeats's approach to the fairy world was almost scientific, so convinced was he of its existence, and in his anthologies he provided a taxonomy of Irish fairies almost Linnean in detail; he even lectured on fairies to the Belfast Naturalists' Field Club in 1893.[21] But the science was pseudo-science and began with the credulous premiss that the Otherworld was as real as this one; and in Yeats's case the 'science' was subordinate to the anti-Enlightenment movement Yeats thought the Irish Revival should constitute. Whereas spiritualists like Doyle were chiefly reactive in the matter of psychic phenomena, responding to reports and claims, Yeats and others who were engaged in magic were active promoters of the supernatural and participants in its ritual evocations and conjurings. Magic required careful planning, ritual preparation, and artful, indeed pseudo-scientific, execution but it was at base an arational, even anti-rational practice.

In any event, fictional narratives of the supernatural abound in Irish Revival writings, both in folktale collections and in adaptations by sophisticated writers such as James Stephens, Gregory, and Yeats himself in *The Celtic Twilight* (1893) and *Stories of Red Hanrahan* (1905). Some of these writings were popular in Ireland and England, but they have been acknowledged and celebrated by critics in a way that the popular novel has not, and so I will not linger here on the Irish folk genre.[22] A modest postscript, however, is the fact that although Lady Gregory was her cousin, Violet Martin ('Martin Ross') did not approve of the Celtic Revival, any more than did her collaborator, Edith Somerville. According to the editor of their letters, they thought the Revival 'a strange phenomenon' and disapproved 'of something that had been brought

back to life with so much artificial respiration'.[23] Molly Keane, who provided
the editor with a Foreword, confirms Gifford Lewis's opinion when she writes
that neither writer approved of Lady Gregory (p. xvii). It is thus no surprise to
find that Edith Somerville, though exposed to spiritualism and séances in
Castletownshend (the local big house belonging to Somerville's mother's
family), and something of a medium herself, had a no-nonsense (yet whimsical) and quasi-scientific attitude to spiritualism very different from the
credulous mysticism (or hyperdeveloped imaginations) of Yeats and AE.
However, after Violet Martin's death in 1915, Somerville took spiritualism
more seriously.[24] In her essay, 'Extra-Mundane Communications', published
in *Stray-Aways* (1920), she poignantly traces her new seriousness not to
Martin's death (at least not directly) but to the Great War when the death
of the young brought the next (or Other) world that much closer since one
could envisage the youthful dead shouldering past the old through St Peter's
Gate. Their premature death naturally prompted their loved ones to send
messages imploring them to send in return messages of reassurance from the
other side. Since Martin died during the War, it is probable that in Somerville's mind and memory, Martin was one of the premature wartime dead.[25]

GHOST STORIES: RIDDELL AND CROKER

Although she was Irish, Mrs J. H. (Charlotte) Riddell's ghost fiction inhabited
a different cultural environment than the Otherworld writings of Yeats and
the revivalists. Riddell (1832–1906) grew up as Charlotte Cowan, the daughter of the High Sheriff of Co. Antrim, left Carrickfergus with her widowed
mother, first for Dundonald, Co. Down (out of which came her novel, *Berna
Boyle*, 1884) then, when she was about 21, for London where she spent years
struggling to become a successful writer. (She edited *Home Magazine* and
St James's Magazine during her London years.) Bleiler, who has read widely in
her forty or so novels, has identified the three dominant subjects of her
fiction: London, business, and social rank. (Cowan married a businessman,
J. H. Riddell, lived in London and, of course, already enjoyed the memory of
high social rank in Co. Antrim.) Riddell's success was ensured with her novel,
George Geith of Fen Court (1864), 'the first important novel', Bleiler claims, 'to
point out the romance of commercial life in the City of London', though the
earlier *City and Suburb* (1862) had surely pointed the way. (Both novels were
published under the name 'F. G. Trafford'.) But aside from her 'realistic
romances', Riddell has been called 'the best distaff writer of ghost stories'
during a time when, as Bleiler tells us, many authors—and the majority of

them women—wrote ghost stories for a wide readership.[26] Four of Riddell's supernatural novels appeared before our period and at least one of them, *Fairy Water* (1873), reprinted by Bleiler under the title *The Haunted House at Latchford*, has a Jamesian density of syntax and insight and is a very fine piece of sustained work.[27] There is only apparent discrepancy between Riddell's realistic and supernatural fiction, for her ghost stories are businesslike, operating narratively as far from the supernatural as possible in order to render its intimation or manifestation more convincing.

In her ghost stories, Riddell combined the familiar role of large houses— venues for hauntings—with her intrinsic commercial interest in houses as property. 'Walnut-tree House' in *Weird Stories* (1882) is set in a house that makes the figurative journey from country house (a gentleman's seat) to town house, through Victorian London's spreading conurbation. 'The Open Door' in the same volume involves estate agents and auctioneers, while 'Old Mrs. Jones' requires leases and tenants. The latter story, set in a rambling, cellared London house in the days of fewer cabs and buses, has Riddell's slow-going prose by which mundane domesticity is inexorably subjected to the increasing pressures of the previous and now ghostly tenantry. In Riddell, the 'decency and restraint of respectable English society'[28] is under threat from the submerged scandal or crime that ghosts unlock or exhume. Like the slightly later M. R. James, Riddell is normally restrained in her effects; this, for example, is all that is thought necessary to conjure a ghost: 'Mrs. Tippens, returning to her house, felt a "waft of raw air" meet her the moment she opened the street door, and something "brush along the hall after her", as she passed into the sitting-room.'[29] Still, the story ends with a briefly described but spectacular blaze that combines the burning Irish big house with the purging power of fire familiar in tales of the supernatural.

'Conn Kilrea', which appeared in *Handsome Phil and Other Stories* (1899), is a slighter performance than the foregoing. It tells the story of Private Conway Kilray, the scion of an illustrious Irish family whose seat is Moyle Abbey. Kilrea has enlisted in England, having come to see he has led a wasteful life, and is discontent and melancholic; he has voluntarily 'thrown himself out of the rank in which he had been born' (see Bleiler's third theme), changing his name to Kilray to hide his tracks. While writing a long letter in barracks he sees a ghost, that of the ancestral family enemy who has vowed to appear in order to signal, or cause, the death of the head of the family. Kilray has seen Lord Yiewsley, dead for a century and a half (killed by an ancestor of Kilray's in 1640), and believes the imminent death is his own; he saw the dead lord before his own father died and thinks it is now his own turn. The family has already been decimated by revenge from beyond the grave and but three men and two women remain. Riddell, like Cromie after her, recruits the decline of the country house for supernatural service; here too is the idea of an oppressive heredity translated into inheritance; it is common for the two ideas to be intertwined in the fiction of the period. But it is his grandfather who is ill and to be with him Kilray speeds to Moyle Abbey. A rival for the affections of his family, his cousin, Major Kilrea, commits the Dr Dagley-like gaffe of not rushing like Conn to Ireland and offends the social sensibility of the mother of the girl he is wooing. The Major pays dearly for that, dying in an accident on his way home from the ball in England. Lord Yiewsley has claimed another Kilrea. The grandfather begins to recover on hearing of the Major's death (the Major being disliked, it seems), and Conn wins hearts by the humility with which he accepts his new position as heir. The plot bears out Bleiler's suggestion that for the hard-headed Riddell the ghost story was a means of carrying morality, that ghosts were for her chiefly literary devices.[30]

The decline of county families and the fate of country houses were tailor-made for ghost fiction and Croker, too, availed herself of them. Among her dozens of books are two volumes of ghost stories, *To Let* (1893) and *Odds and Ends* (1919). A selection of her stories appeared in 2000 in a 'Mistresses of the Macabre' series, and included two stories well known in their time: 'To Let' (*London Society*,1890) and 'Number Ninety' (*Chapman's Magazine of Fiction*, 1895). The first is set in India and has a female narrator, the second in London and with a male narrator; the other stories are set in Ireland, Scotland, Australia, France, and the United States, Croker being an itinerant of the imagination as well as in real life.

'Number Ninety' is the street number of a rambling empty town house and pits science and scepticism against the supernatural. At a bachelor's dinner party, one of the guests, a civil engineer, accepts a wager to sleep overnight in this haunted house, and when his 'second', the narrator, arrives the next morning to meet him, John Hollyoak, the engineer, has survived and tells the narrator what occurred. The house is indeed haunted and during the night he was summoned downstairs to dinner by an importunate liveried footman and found himself welcomed by a party in eighteenth-century dress. Are they actors? Members of some club? He concludes that they are in fact of a bygone upper class of society. Each face expresses 'reckless, hardened defiance'. The engineer has the presence of mind to ask to say grace before accepting their hospitality, and in the ensuing uproar the apparitions vanish. He tells the narrator he wishes to return that night to find out exactly whose these ghosts are or were. He returns with his bulldog to sleep over again. This time he is not so lucky. The narrator spends a disturbing night at home: 'More than once I was certain that I heard John Hollyoak distractedly calling me; and I sat up in bed and listened intently. Of course it was fancy, for the instant I did so, there was no sound.'[31] The presentiment proves justified. When the narrator goes back to the house the next morning he cannot gain entrance and when he peers through the keyhole he sees another eye—'a very strange, fiery eye'—returning his gaze. He applies his mouth instead and shouts John Hollyoak's name; when the echo dies away in the empty house he hears a mocking snigger from the other side of the door. When at last he gets in with the aid of a policeman he finds the answer to his question of what befell John Hollyoak. In Croker, as in Riddell, the past, the demonic, and the supernatural inhabit the otherwise prosaic world of the professional middle class.

'To Let' is a more substantial affair and in it Croker transposes the country-house ghost story, with its upper-class cast, to India and can do so convincingly because of the insulation of British life in the Empire; the story is written with first-hand knowledge of British India and peppered with Anglo-Indian words. There is a brief and informative sketch of British life in Lucknow and a fine description of a journey the Britons make to the hills during the hot season. The narrator, Susan Shandon, her brother Tom (an imperial civil servant), his wife Aggie (a competent and self-willed woman) and their two children, have rented near Kantia, the hill station, a splendid stone bungalow with an immense verandah on the edge of a thousand-foot precipice. The bungalow is fully furnished as though by a family, not agents, and even includes 'two sketches of an English country house', p. 75); it is full of passages, steep stairs, nooks, and dressing-rooms. They soon find out why the rent is so low. Like Number Ninety, Briarwood is haunted. Years ago some tragedy overtook the retired colonel, his wife, and niece at the bungalow and each monsoon season the tragedy is repeated *in sound only*, the long dead players in the tragedy being invisible but audible.

The first disturbing sign of trouble is the antics of the African grey parrot that has outlived its owners and now lives behind the bungalow with an old '*chowkidar*' (*chokidar*: watchman or caretaker). The Shandons return the bird to the main part of the bungalow and Croker sketches it with a deceptive humour. 'The ancient parrot talked incessantly now that he had been restored to society; he whistled for the dogs, and brought them flying to his summons, to his great satisfaction and their equally great indignation. He called "Qui Hye" so naturally, in a lady's shrill soprano, or a gruff male bellow, that I have no doubt our servants would have liked to have wrung his neck. He coughed and expectorated like an old gentleman, and whined like a puppy, and mewed like a cat, and I am sorry to add, sometimes swore like a trooper; but his most constant cry was, "Lucy, where are you, pretty Lucy—Lu—cy?"' (p. 78).

Susan attends a picnic that is ruined when the monsoon rains arrive and during her absence the tragedy is re-enacted, terrifying Aggie. The family takes to staying out as long as possible, hoping the ghostly drama will happen in their absence, but one day the atrocious weather precludes their venturing out and they decide to light the lamps at twilight and draw the curtains. Before they can do so, Susan wishes aloud for a visitor and when she hears hooves along the road she believes it is her admirer, Charlie Chalmers. 'He did not stop at the front door as usual, but rode straight into the verandah, which afforded ample room and shelter for half-a-dozen mounted men.' Her sister is in a state of terror. '"What is it, Aggie?" I said, "are you ill?" As I spoke the horse's hoofs made a loud clattering noise on the stone-paved verandah outside and a man's voice—a young man's eager voice—called, "Lucy"' (p. 80). They see a chair near the writing table being pushed back and hear a fumbling with the French doors.

Aggie and I were within the bright circle of the firelight, but the rest of the room was dim, and outside the streaming grey sky was spasmodically illuminated by occasional vivid flashes that lit up the surrounding hills as if it were daylight. The trampling of impatient hooves and the rattling of a door handle were the only sounds that were audible for a few breathless seconds; but during those seconds Pip [their terrier], bristling like a porcupine and trembling violently in every joint, had sprung off my lap and crawled abjectly under Aggie's chair, seemingly in a transport of fear. The door was opened audibly, and a cold, icy blast swept in, that seemed to freeze my very heart and made me shiver from head to foot. At this moment there came with a sinister blue glare the most vivid flash of lightning I ever saw. It lit up the whole room, which was empty save for ourselves, and was instantly followed by a clap of thunder that caused my knees to knock together and that terrified me and filled me with horror. It evidently terrified the horse too; there was a violent plunge, a clattering of hoofs on the stones, a sudden loud crash of smashing timber, a woman's long, loud, piercing shriek, which stopped the very beating of my heart, and then a frenzied struggle in the cruel, crumbling, treacherous shale, the rattle of loose stones and the hollow roar of something sliding down the precipice. (p. 81)

To convince Susan the terrible happening is unreal and that Charlie Chalmers has not gone over the precipice, Aggie shows her the intact verandah rail and predicts that when Susan looks down she will see the lights of would-be rescuers in the valley far below. This is the case and Susan watches the lights as they converge and then proceed back up the mountainside and hear the search party reach the verandah and the heavy footsteps of the bearers carrying their burden through the room and deposit it in Aggie's bedroom. They learn later that the niece Lucy destroyed herself with grief after the death of her suitor and her uncle and aunt did not long survive her.

The servants are deserting their posts in Briarwood, the Shandons retreat to a local hotel, and the bungalow falls empty again, save for the chowdikar and grey parrot. Aggie visits the bungalow the following season and sees the fading 'To Let' sign and hears the parrot crying, 'Lucy, where are you, pretty Lucy?' In Briarwood it is difficult not to see a version of the ruin and decline that attended the Irish country house with which Croker was so familiar. It might seem to be going too far to see also, in our own hindsight, the future of the Raj (in which the Irish played their role) and the translation of the incongruous British in India into ghosts from the past. But, on the other hand, Croker redeployed the ghostly rehearsal of invisible violent cacophonies in *In Old Madras* (1913), a novel highly conscious of the passing of orders and dispensations. Capt Mallender is told at Wellunga, the dead cantonment, that 'It is said, that in some directions, at sun-down, or by moonlight, you can see great big camps, with men, and horses, and elephants, and standards, and hear shouts and bugles, and drums.'[32] Later, Mallender is to witness the truth of the legend when, in a scene as effective as any hosting of the sidhe in Stephens's *The Crock of Gold* (1912) or Yeats's *The Celtic Twilight*, he is told to bend his ear close to the ground upon which he hears the call of an invisible bugle: 'Yes, he heard it distinctly; from the far distance came another immediately followed by a brisk roll of drums, the drums and fifes—accompanied by the tramp and thunder of an approaching host.' It is the gathering onset of battle. 'The ground seemed to tremble and vibrate under the tread of a large body of troops who were rapidly advancing,—and yet, amazing sensation, these troops were nowhere to be seen'. Mallender starts about in stupefied bewilderment and sees nothing. Gradually the noise of the tramping feet subsides; the feet 'become fainter, yet fainter, and finally died away; one far-distant bugle-call sounded a piercing, lingering, almost agonized challenge—then followed complete, absolute,and ghastly silence' (p. 267). Young Tara Beamish tells Mallender he has just heard a British column on the march and that she believes it is a portion of Lord Cornwallis's old army, 'who were led into an ambush, and butchered' (p. 268). Cornwallis, despite his achievements and complex opinions, is chiefly remembered as a member of the colonial forces that attempted to crush the American revolution but was forced to surrender at Yorktown in 1781, as the Governor-General of India (1786–92) who led military campaigns against native insurgents, and as Viceroy and Commander-in-Chief in Ireland (1798–1801) who crushed the 1798 rebellion and supported the Act of Union (1801). Cornwallis's chequered career serves to remind Croker's readers of the defeats and passages of history as well as the ghostly perseverance of violent events, something that occurs in a contemporary work of fiction by Andrew James.

GHOST STORIES: CROMIE AND JAMES

Supernatural and science fiction stories by Cromie were collected in *Told in Twilight* (*c.*1907) and the fifty-two-page opening story, 'The Great Mystery', bears some resemblance to *The Crack of Doom* with a 'mad scientist' figure, Charlie

Smith, who has developed a form of telepathy through 'electro-psychology', having invented 'a transmitter of etheric waves of extraordinary complexity'.[33] The story unfolds aboard a cruise ship in the Norwegian fjords and the mysterious Smith at length saves the passengers from death by avalanche through his telepathically transmitted thoughts. Cromie's prose style resembles the nononsense style of Wells's narrator in *The Time Machine* and like Wells he tends towards social or professional types in his fiction, the better to get on with the plot.

The name Smith recurs in 'The Spectral House' (first published in *Madame*) in which Smith is the 'motorman' (i.e. mechanic) travelling in Ireland with an Englishman named Robinson—the narrator—and two other Englishmen, Brown and Jones; their names suggest English hardheadedness. They are caught in their touring car in bad weather between Clifden and Galway; Brown and Jones go on to Athlone by train, Smith and Robinson drive on, now (they believe) finding themselves between Ballinasloe and Athlone. The English worldly narrator travelling by car whose machine falters and who as a result encounters the supernatural: this premiss reminds one of Kipling's great story, 'They'. 'Daylight and a motor car are surely not congenial environment for a ghost', remarks Cromie's narrator; both stories play on the incongruity set up between the new world of technology and the old world of the living dead. In a desolate region Smith and Robinson happen on a spectrally lit-up Big House. It is a Regency scene. They stop, question the footman or butler who tells them festivities are in progress, and drive on to Athlone after Robinson gives the servant half a crown. The Athlone hotelier, O'Malley, has a daughter, Norah, who is 'an exquisite type of the Celt, such rich black hair, and deep, tender, mournful blue eyes'. Here are the submerged idealized erotics of English and Protestant perceptions of the Celt, for underneath the ghost narrative, the story concerns the theme of English–Irish relations. Robinson tells O'Malley of the adventure and next day takes Norah back in search of the spectral house. But they cannot find it: 'But, shades of Haroun-Al-Raschid, where was the house that lay just below the hill?'[34] They discover only the ruin of Castle O'Malley. (Here pressed into familiar service of a supernatural story is the motif of the declining country house.) It had burned down nearly a century before, during the festivities Robinson had seen in progress the night before. They find the half-crown with which Robinson tipped the manservant: it has aged overnight to suggest an eighteenth-century coin. This episode is told as an independent ghost story by Eleanor Alexander in her exquisite imaginative biography, *Lady Anne's Walk* (1903); in her telling, the experience happens to 'a traveller in the county Donegal', so it may well be a mobile urban legend (that is, one that involves sophisticated or city dwellers who travel in lonely or twilit places).[35]

Twice before the O'Malley castle has been seen after its destruction and each time the sighting preceded bad luck for the family. The legend stipulates that the third sighting will bring good luck to the O'Malleys, which will welcome since Norah's father lost heavily with investments in the Mozar.. bique mines. As though in fulfilment of the legend, Robinson proposes marriage to Norah, though he is aware of 'the shocking difference in our social positions'. This is not what the reader expects: it is Norah who is the hidden and unacknowledged aristocrat (the idea of the hidden or natural aristocracy of the Irish peasantry was important to Yeats and other Revivalists[36]); the narrator admits the 'mesalliance' that Norah—'the descendant of a hundred Kings—was making in marrying a plain stockbroker.' The Saxon–Celtic distinction (with which Wilde played also) is a version of the English–Irish distinctions we have already met that is suitably graphic for a ghost story. The story also draws on the notion widespread among the English (from which perspective Cromie writes in this story and in his other fictions) that practical help from the English can reverse the imaginative excesses and impracticalities of the Irish. An O'Malley reappears in 'A Golden Butterfly' in which the impoverished incumbent of O'Malley Castle, preparing to emigrate to Manitoba in despair, meets two touring English girls, contrives to win one of them in order to secure the future of the castle and apparently succeeds. Cromie here exploits a familiar motif from the country house problem-novel. The storytelling narrator is cynically aware of the drawing power of his own Celticness among the English, particularly the female English, always suckers for a good romance. Given that the story first appeared in *Lady's Pictorial*, it may not be off-target to sense Cromie's own cynicism in this story.

A set of interconnecting tales by 'Andrew James' that also recruits for ghost fiction the decline of the big house, the family presentiment, and oppressive heredity and inheritance, but is altogether richer in genre and cultural interest and full of gritty historical details, is *Ninety-Eight and Sixty Years After* (1911), the first two stories of which were published in *Blackwood's Edinburgh Magazine* in 1907. For James, the supernatural is no mere device but a way of showing a fearful immanence of Irish reality created by religious division and political hatred. *Ninety-Eight* (the first set of tales) is historical fiction set in the immediate prelude to the 1798 uprising in Co. Antrim, which was crushed within a week, and the immediate aftermath of the rebellion. An elderly schoolmaster recounts in Lowland Scots to an unidentified listener the brutal events that preceded the rising when the yeomanry savagely cracked down on perceived sedition led by Ulster Scots Presbyterians whose disaffection stemmed from deteriorating relations between landlords and tenants and the radical influence of the French Revolution. This reign of terror, which made of Ulster 'a far waur place to live in than hell',[37] according to the old schoolmaster, is implemented among others by Galloper Starkie, alias the Nabob. Starkie is soon to be known also as Hangman Starkie, the ruthless and dissipated inhabitant of Nabob Castle (once Macdonnell Castle or Dundonnell), recently returned from India where he had accumulated a fortune by dubious means, hence his nickname, Nabob. Now Starkie is a colonel of yeomanry taking full advantage of the Insurrection Act of 1796 (making lawful sweeping powers of search) and exhibiting breathtaking cruelty in his dealings with the rebels, flogging and hanging them without compunction. The old schoolmaster's father was the Nabob's sergeant, and relaying the awful outrages and counter-outrages of the time that his father witnessed, Master Thompson laments the horror of 'what things men will do to ane anither' (p. 52). He is convinced that 'there's a dormant deevil in every man's breast and when the blude's het enough it warms to life' (p. 45).

Some of James's most striking events he adapted from historical fact, including the episode of the Moanin' Sands in which rebels, dead and dying were indifferently buried in sand after the Battle of Antrim, and the episode of the terrifying Red Man, a hooded figure who fingers rebels for the Nabob.[38] James required little or no highlighting or exaggerating in order to turn historical reality into an historical fiction of a darkly adventurous kind reminiscent at times of William Carleton's *Wildgoose Lodge* (1833) and with attention to the prevailing ideas of the time, as is the case with Carleton's equally brutal realism. The difference is that events are seen (unusually, as it must appear to contemporaries in Irish Studies) through the eyes of Dissenters rather than Catholics, for *The Nabob* is an uncommon addition to Ulster Scots literature.

After Sixty Years (the second set of tales) is rather different. The first is told about a century after the rebellion, with the narrator, Master Thompson, bearing an echo of Scott's schoolmaster Jedediah Cleisbotham in *The Tale of Old Mortality* (1816). The second set is told in standard English by 40-year-old Michael Macdonnell 'not many years after' 1858 when he arrived from the United States to become chief of the Macdonnells, thirty years after he vowed to his dying father in America to do so. His father was brother of the 'auld maister', Michael, who had re-purchased Nabob Castle but inherited, as it were, a dissolute life from its previous owner, the Nabob, whose spirit never left the Castle and who revels and rides nightly as a ghost with his living successor. However, though different in narrator, language, generation and genre—'Sixty Years After' is primarily a ghost story—the two sets of tales are counterparts, with doublings of character and event; what is ravelled in the first set is unravelled in the second. The sets are coupled, moreover, by the survival of the Nabob and his wife as ghosts; the mysterious death of their son Clive early in the old schoomaster's tale-telling which Michael must solve before the unquiet dead can return to their graves and rest forever; and the overarching theme of hatred, which Michael is tasked with dissolving and replacing with harmony.

Michael's story is a supernatural one we would call Gothic, complete as it is with a dilapidated and forbidding Castle, living portraits of dead ancestors (a device Wilde cleverly adapted as a living portrait of a living man who is *morally* dead), gravestones, walking and wailing ghosts, and mysterious occurrences. If these elements are married to the familiar, mundane, and historical decline of the Irish country house, a decline often brought about through the dissipation of a roistering and irresponsible gentry, the supernatural in *The Nabob* has its specifically Ulster coloration. The ghost of the Nabob admits that 'We carried our hatred beyond the grave' (p. 125), defying the centuries and the clay. Reprisal, a familiarly awful repetition of event in troubled Ireland, receives the suitable formalism in *The Nabob* of *reprise*: characters and motifs in part one reappear in part two, sometimes with the suggestion of reincarnation, as though the violent past of Ireland is literally lived over again. (James Joyce, writing *Dubliners* when James was writing *The Nabob*, was haunted by the idea of Irish life and time being circular, of history as a nightmare. The supernatural in Ireland can thus seem real and natural.) And so the ghost story (and Joyce's 'The Dead', which closes *Dubliners*, is in a sense a ghost story) is a very fitting genre by which James illustrates this dark theme which is that of life in sectarian Ireland.

If Gothic is what we might call an overheated genre, then it is no surprise that it flourished in a troubled island of overheated political passions, from the eighteenth century through to early twentieth-century Ulster; on occasion, Gothic could seem in Ireland like an allegorical species of realism. And Ulster was especially tense and troubled when James composed *The Nabob* roughly between 1907 and 1911, between the second and third Home Rule Bills which were regarded as particularly provocative in a region of the island where the majority of the inhabitants opposed Home Rule. It could look during those years as if it might be a case of 1798 come again. The fall of 'the house o' Dundonnell' under a curse could read like a miniature version of the threatened fall of the House of Ulster.

Michael Macdonnell is a kind of redeemer of the past in *The Nabob*, bringing the old schoolmaster's tales to completion and solving the book's central mystery of Clive's disappearance, and laying the unquiet ghosts to rest and bringing peace to Dundonnell, among other ways by destroying the portrait of the Nabob now that its living-dead model had returned to the grave. But the optimism James expressed through him is strictly a narrative function and required James to switch from realistic historical fiction in *Ninety-Eight* to less realistic genre fiction in *Sixty Years After*. Stephen J. Brown saw in *The Nabob* sympathy for the rebels even if the author avoided 'blind partisanship'.[39] But in real life, as we shall see later, the author a decade after the publication of *The Nabob* had lost sympathy for the contemporary versions of the rebels, perhaps in part because the erstwhile rebels of 1798 Antrim had become, as he was to see it, the lawful and besieged in 1919 in Antrim and elsewhere in Ulster.

NOTES

1. 'Against Nature? Science and Oscar Wilde', *University of Toronto Quarterly* 63. 2 (1993/4): 329–47.

2. *The Picture of Dorian Gray*, in Richard Aldington and Stanley Weintraub (eds.), *The Portable Oscar Wilde* (1890; Harmondsworth: Penguin, 1981), pp. 203, 248, 331, 360, 282.

3. *The Portable Oscar Wilde*, p. 119.

4. Bernard Bergonzi, *The Early H.G. Wells: A Study of the Scientific Romances* (Toronto: University of Toronto Press, 1961), pp. 3–5, 6, 9, 10, 35. On the Wells story and Wilde review, see Norman and Jeanne MacKenzie, *The Time Traveller: The Life of H.G. Wells* (London: Weidenfeld and Nicolson, 1973), pp. 85, 109.

5. Born in Clough, Co. Down, Cromie was on the staff of the *Northern Whig* newspaper in Belfast: see Princess Grace Library EIRData catalogue. According to Brian Stableford, Cromie gave up a career in banking to become a professional writer: *Scientific Romance in Britain 1890–1950* (London: Fourth Estate, 1985), p. 121.

6. Brian Stableford claims Cromie thought that Wells with *The First Men in the Moon* (1901), though it appeared eleven years after *A Plunge into Space*, had stolen his thunder with an anti-gravity technology Cromie had already employed. However, anti-gravity technology had been first imagined by 'Chrysostom Trueman' in *The History of a Voyage to the Moon* (1864); see Stableford, 'Science Fiction before the Genre' in Edward James and Farah Mendlesohn (eds.), *The Cambridge Companion to Science Fiction* (Cambridge: Cambridge University Press, 2003), pp. 20, 24, 27. See also Stableford, *Scientific Romance in Britain*, p. 121.

7. I discuss Astor's novel in *The Age of Titanic: Cross-Currents in Anglo-American Culture* (2002); the author was the richest man on board the liner and perished with it. Mars and the possibility of life on it were of tremendous interest when Cromie and Astor wrote their novels. Schiaparelli's identification in 1877 of 'canals' on the planet suggested life, and Cromie's Mars boasts seas, luxuriant plains, flowery hills, and cities.

8. Robert Cromie, *A Plunge into Space* (1890; Westport, CT: Hyperion Press, 1976; repr. of 1891 2nd edn.), pp. 179, 183–4, 174, 172, 180, 181. Cromie's novel was reprinted until 1910.

9. Robert Cromie, *A Plunge into Space*, pp. 104, 203.

10. Besides *The Time Machine*, see Wells, 'Zoological Retrogression', repr. in R. Philmus and D.Y. Hughes (eds.), *H. G. Wells: Early Writings in Science and Science Fiction* (Berkeley: University of California Press, 1975). See also E. Ray Lankester, *Degeneration: A Chapter in Darwinism* (1880); Joseph Conrad, *Heart of Darkness* (1902);

Lord Charles Beresford, 'The Future of the Anglo-Saxon Race', *North American Review* 171 (1900): 802–10.

11. Brian Stableford, *Scientific Romance in Britain*, p. 34.

12. I discuss Tyndall's notorious Address and the reaction to it by scientifically-minded Irish Protestant clerics in *Recoveries: Neglected Episodes in Irish Cultural History 1860–1912* (Dublin: University College Dublin, 2002), pp. 7–48.

13. Robert Cromie, *The Crack of Doom* (London: Digby, Long & Co., 1895), p. 121.

14. This Belfast-built ship had already appeared in fiction three years before Cromie's novel, when W. T. Stead (who was to perish on *Titanic*) published at Christmas 1892 in the annual of the *Reviews of Reviews* a spiritualist story on board the ship commanded by the real-life Captain E. J. Smith, who was himself to go down with *Titanic*. I discuss Stead's story in *The Age of* Titanic.

15. Cromie is more optimistic in the far inferior shipwreck-desert island fantasy, *The Lost Liner* (1899). Here the future is told rather than shown, chiefly by the hero who lectures his fellow-survivor on the ideal future society. As befitting a character created by a Belfast author, Drury believes in human progress and considers a first-class ocean steamship a grander wonder of the world than an Egyptian pyramid, one the product of slavery and brute force, the other a triumph of brains and free labour. Science fiction at the time owed something to the tremendous progress achieved during what we might call the Machine Age of the late nineteenth century.

16. Bergonzi, *The Early H. G. Wells*, p. 15. The Machine Age and the Spirit Age (the heyday of British spiritualism that straddled the nineteenth and twentieth centuries) overlapped easily in, say, Astor's *A Journey in Other Worlds*.

17. Shaw is quoted in Janet Oppenheim, *The Other World: Spiritualism and Psychical Research in England, 1850–1914* (Cambridge: Cambridge University Press, 1985), p. 28.

18. 'The New Accelerator', in H. G. Wells, *The Country of the Blind and Other Stories* (Oxford: Oxford University Press, 1996), p. 375.

19. Oppenheim, *The Other World*, pp. 1–2, 59–62.

20. See Richard Dorson, *The British Folklorists: A History* (1968).

21. The talk was given on 21 November; for reports on it see *Irish News and Belfast Morning News* 22 November 1893 and *Proceedings of the Belfast Naturalists' Field Club* (1893–94): 46–8.

22. In *Fictions of the Irish Literary Revival* (1987) I discuss Irish tales of the Otherworld written to advance the Revival.

23. *The Selected Letters of Somerville and Ross*, ed. Gifford Lewis (London: Faber and Faber, 1989), p. 238.

24. Gifford Lewis, *Somerville and Ross: The World of the Irish R.M.* (New York: Viking Penguin, 1985), pp. 182, 186. Lewis is confusing on Violet Martin's attitude to spiritualism. In the book just cited, Martin shares with Somerville an 'intense interest in premonitions, apparitions and the workings of Fate' (p. 186) and respects the 'strong spiritualist beliefs that she encountered in Castletownshend' (p. 189). Yet she is described as disliking ghosts and spirit manifestations' (p. 182),

while in Lewis's biography of Somerville, Martin is said to have 'bolted' from spiritualism in fear because it was irreconcilable with her Christian faith: *Edith Somerville: A Biography* (Dublin: Four Courts Press, 2005), p. 7.

25. E.Œ. Somerville and Martin Ross, *Stray-Aways* (Longmans, Green & Co., 1920), p. 277. Somerville appears to have written this essay especially for this miscellany of pieces by both authors. The next year, Somerville used the dialect word 'stray-aways' in its literal meaning to refer to cattle or horses that stray out of their fields into the roads or other farmers' fields: *An Enthusiast* 'by E.Œ. Somerville . . . in collaboration with Martin Ross' (London: Longmans, Green & Co., 1921), p. 27. In that novel, Car Ducarrig describes herself as a spiritualist, but only when she is with her friend, a more confirmed spiritualist. She has been told that we are reunited on the other side with those with whom we have an affinity (p. 169), perhaps a subtextual expression of Somerville's desire to be reunited with Violet Martin after death.

26. *The Collected Ghost Stories of Mrs. J.H. Riddell*, sel. and introd. E. F. Bleiler (New York: Dover, 1977), pp. xiii, ix, v.

27. *Three Supernatural Novels of the Victorian Period*, ed. E. F. Bleiler (1975).

28. Mrs J. H. Riddell, *Weird Stories* (1882; London: Home and Van Thal, 1946), p. 137.

29. *Weird Stories*, p. 146.

30. *The Collected Ghost Stories of Mrs. J. H. Riddell*, p. xxiii.

31. B. M. Croker, *'Number Ninety' and Other Ghost Stories*, ed. Richard Dalby (Mountain Ash, Wales: Sarob Press, 2000), p. 8.

32. B. M. Croker, *In Old Madras* (1913; New Delhi: Rupa & Co., 2002), p. 231.

33. Robert Cromie, *Told in Twilight* (Dublin: Sealy Bryers & Walker, [1907?]), p. 51. In *The Age of* Titanic (pp. 151–2), I discuss the analogy between telepathy and telegraphy, particularly in the thinking of W. T. Stead.

34. Robert Cromie, *Told in Twilight*, pp. 66, 64, 66.

35. Eleanor Alexander, *Lady Anne's Walk* (London: Edward Arnold, 1903), pp. 118–19. This book is a series of musings and imaginings stimulated by Alexander's thoughts of the sister of John George Beresford, Archbishop of Armagh and 106th successor of St Patrick. Alexander, who lived at the palace with her father, who was the 110th successor, and her mother, Cecil Frances Alexander, became aware of Lady Anne Beresford's neglected garden in the palace grounds and it provoked her quiet and eloquent flights of fancy about a young woman to whom she gives various experiences and personalities. Alexander's imagination ranges beyond Lady Anne's sparsely documented life into the history and legendry of the neighbourhood of the palace. In the preface to this beautiful book, Alexander acknowledges a dozen books and journals on which she has drawn, from Hyde's literary history of Ireland through saints' lives to historical biographies. The inquiring postcards she wrote a few years after publication (1907–1910) to Francis Joseph Bigger, the Ulster antiquarian, and now contained inside the Trinity College Dublin library copy of the book, suggest her antiquarian interests as well. But a special interest of *Lady Anne's Walk* is the trafficking between history and fiction.

36. We find the idea, for example, in Annie M. P. Smithson's novel, *Her Irish Heritage* (1917).

37. *The Nabob: A Tale of Ninety-Eight* (1911; Dublin: Four Courts Press, 2006), p. 47. I am using this edition of *Ninety-Eight and Sixty Years After* which I annotated and for which I provided an Afterword; I renamed the two sets of tales *The Nabob*.

38. I discuss the historical basis for these and other figures and events in my Afterword to *The Nabob*, pp. 146–9.

39. Brown, *Ireland in Fiction*, p. 146.

12

Dracula and Detection: Among Genres II

HORROR FICTION: *DRACULA*

In the popular classic by Bram Stoker (1847–1912), the title villain, in one of Stoker's many inversions, indeed perversions, of the popular country-house novels, is in fact his own heir to Castle Dracula, he being for all intents and purposes capable of immortality. Arthur Holmwood, who becomes Lord Godalming in the course of the novel, is the more familiar inheritor of the big house. In another bizarre twist to the familiar events and situations in these novels, Riddell's character Lord Yiewsley's ability to reach from beyond the grave to harm the living becomes in *Dracula* (1897) the Count's occupation of the grave by day and his literal reaching out to harm by night. Stoker's novel cranks the country-house ghost story up to the highest pitch of horror to become virtually a different subgenre. But we can still recognize the fictional elements of the period with which we are familiar. The decline of the country house has been trajected into utter moral degradation—Dracula inhabits a deeper moral abyss than even Dorian Gray—indeed into a 'steady state' degeneracy that mirrors like a subterranean existence the quotidian, normal daylight world (but not literally, of course, since the vampire casts no reflection). Young Wilde, who read a great deal of science at Oxford, was fascinated by early pathologists of the eighteenth century whose object 'was to show that there is a science of the abnormal'; and such a science was possible because 'even animal monstrosities are now known not to be capricious but essentially natural; a new science is thus produced, that of Teratology'.[1] Dracula's monstrosity is due in part to his being both descendant and ancestor: he relates to Jonathan Harker the feats of the Dracula Voivode and of a later Dracula who crossed the Danube time and again to battle the Turks, but Van Helsing is certain that Count Dracula and those two illustrious, bloodthirsty Szekelys are one and the same.[2] Again, past and present converge. Dracula, though, is not entirely timeless since he boasts that he carries in his veins the blood of Attila the Hun (p. 41), but Stoker's adoption of the theme of heredity in his horror novel is extraordinary and out-Wildes Wilde.

Like Dracula, and despite our awareness of genes, we too think of blood figuratively and even literally as the route and vehicle of hereditary transmission. When Dracula sucks your blood, or you his, you and he become kin; he is an agent of instant heredity; he is the heredity principle gone utterly to the bad. Throughout, Dracula is referred to by his enemies as a 'monster' and despite the Gothic revival furniture of the novel and the resemblances between Dracula and Milton's Satan,[3] Dracula is a strikingly late Victorian, *fin-de-siècle* monster.

Whereas Wilde in *Dorian Gray* allocates the agencies of heredity and influence to two sets of figures (to the Gray forebears and Lord Henry's direct influence), Stoker conjoins them in Count Dracula alone. (It is arguable, though, that since Lord Henry is acting as a vector for the poisonous inheritance of his own and Dorian's *literary-historical* ancestors, Lord Henry is Gray's forebear.) When Dracula punctures the throat of his victim and sucks blood he infects the victim, as Van Helsing tells Mina Harker, who later acknowledges that there is poison in her blood as a result of Dracula's nocturnal visitations (pp. 380–1, 392). Dracula infects by *extracting* blood but such extraction is also a kind of *infusion*, a procedure the more obvious when he causes Mina Harker to drink *his* blood. The fact that Wilde draws on the metaphor of poison in *Dorian Gray* and was fascinated by Wainewright the poisoner and forger suggests that perhaps infection, contagion, poison, malign influence, destructive inheritance, and hereditary bad blood formed a thematic syndrome in *fin-de-siècle* writing. Nor would it be bathetic to situate *Dracula* inside the context of the wider social preoccupation with contagious diseases and their threat to social purity in which we have placed the work of Grand and other popular novelists and in which we could likewise place *Dorian Gray* and even *De Profundis*.

'The blood is the life', the unhappy Renfield insists, adapting the scriptural phrase to degenerate purpose as the Count adapts the biblical 'children of light' (Ephesians 5: 8) to become 'children of the night' (pp. 171, 280). Dracula himself flouts the biblical taboo against blood-cannibalism (Genesis 9: 4, Deuteronomy 12: 23). Moreover, he is a perverse or reverse Christ, drinking the blood of others instead of shedding his blood *for* others. In the novel, the blood flows through the veins not only of the individual but of the family and of the race. *Dracula* is drenched in the intense race-consciousness of the time. The Count gives Jonathan Harker a lesson in east European race history, and from 'the whirlpool of European races' he identifies carefully the racial groupings, discriminating by quotient of bravery and success in conquest. Dracula is like a three-decades-early presentiment of Hitler, finding the present time 'days of dishonourable peace', a time when blood is absurdly thought precious, whereas he is prodigal in the flow of blood, doing his best to return Europe to the glory days of invasion, war, conquest, as Hitler was soon after to do (pp. 41–2). Above all, he seems to relish the memory of his ancestor's wars against Turkey. He is really reliving a medieval Christianity against Islam, though he cannot bring himself to identify or name Christendom. Instead, in his re-creation of Europe, Christendom becomes a feverish residue and spin-off of dark superstition; ironically, the faith is reduced to the magical power of its symbols, the wafer of transubstantiation and the crucifix which are deployed against *him* by his neighbours and by Van Helsing and his allies. Dracula's attempted invasion of England with a one-ship armada is his next crusade, but in another inversion Dracula becomes the embodiment of medieval darkness and superstition while Van Helsing and his band of resisters become their own Christian crusaders, as well as agents of Enlightenment reason.

Dracula, then, is an invasion story. If Jonathan Harker on his mission to Transylvania resembles the Visitor to Ireland of the popular novel, then Count Dracula turns the tables by returning the favour, malevolently. But of course, the Visitor to Ireland analogy works only if the reader sees some sustained resemblance between Transylvania and Ireland as host countries or between England and Ireland as host countries. Recent academic interpreters of *Dracula* have insisted on the novel's being a political allegory of English–Irish relations. After coming upon the following use of the vampire metaphor in 1920, we might at least entertain it, though the validity of the metaphor is being angrily denied by the writer: 'The underpaid National School teacher, in the bitterness of his soul, has brought [the young Irish Sinn Feiner] up to believe that the English are pirates and vampires and have always been sucking the life-blood out of Ireland.'[4] But the political reading is unstable since Dracula is understood both as a landowning Anglo-Irish Ascendancy gone to the bad (and gone away, absent) and as the 'embodiment' of the native Irish oppressed seeking revenge at the 'heart' of the Empire.[5] In contemporary criticism, Dracula as an Englishman or Anglo-Irishman would be a villain but Dracula as an Irish insurgent, a Fenian, for example, would be a sympathetic figure with Van Helsing and the others as crusading reactionaries.

A reading that places *Dracula* amidst contemporary British and Irish popular writings seems on firmer ground. If the novel is an invasion story, it is, more specifically, a 'coming war' story (see below) and as such takes its place beside science fiction works of the day, including Wells's *The War of the Worlds*, and even certain non-fictional warnings of imminent calamity (again, see below); in Stoker's novel, as in Wells's, England takes the role of the world, certainly the civilized world. Dracula seeks to conquer by a kind of biological warfare, infecting the actual bodies of his victim-recruits and also, he hopes, the body social of England. He brings not an army against England but only himself, planning to raise his army inside fortress England from those he turns into renegades and 'irregulars'; through vampirism, it will be an army that sleeps by day and conducts its guerilla warfare by night. He himself is a foreign body—utterly Other—that seeks like a parasite to lodge itself in the host of civilized England.

A case could be made for the idea that the invasion scare that simmered in Britain in the late nineteenth century and took the imagined forms both of space-invasion and German invasion was equally about the migration of dark races about the globe, graphically illustrated in American immigration; when coloured races, swarthy or yellow, moved around they were identified as 'hordes' (just as working-class assemblies were called 'mobs') and assumed to be hostile as well as alien. Dracula is 'a monster of the nether world', chief denizen of the Abyss that writers and early sociologists were fascinated by, and frightened of, in Stoker's day.[6] Dracula is the embodied contemporary threat to Anglo-Saxon society by those swarthy masses in Italy and east of Italy and the yellow masses in the Orient.[7] (The American Quincey Morris belongs to that Anglo-Saxon world, since in Stoker's time America and Britain made up the core Anglo-Saxon alliance.) Dracula himself when he takes the semblance of a normal human being, personifies the very English society he wishes to destroy. He caricatures the role of cultivated gentleman by what is in his case not merely imitation but also a form of shape-changing, that ability he shares with Milton's Satan. Impersonation by an alien became a stock idea in twentieth-century space invasion thrillers and shockers.[8] Familiar too is Stoker's idea that Dracula is to establish a beachhead in England from which an invasion can be launched through recruitment of the living into a conquering army of the 'undead'. The proliferation of aliens on our very doorstep from their modest and overlooked beginnings became a staple notion in modern science and horror fiction; Van Helsing believes Dracula intends to become 'the father' of 'a new order of beings' (p. 360).

The figure of Dracula is a variation on that of the ghost, the vampire being 'undead', or alive and dead at the same time, corpse and living being by turns. Against the power of the supernatural, Van Helsing pits science. In another irony, Dracula is himself a would-be or imitation scientist, experimenting with the zoophagous patient Renfield. If he is recapitulating the development of European science, having at present only the child-brain of medieval man, he was also in life (in a near contradiction) a student of alchemy ('the highest development of the science-knowledge of his time') who attended the Scholomance in Romania ('where the devil claims the tenth scholar as his due'); Dracula belonged, that is to say, to that medieval, alternative, underground network of magic and scholarship that Yeats was already championing seriously when *Dracula* was published.[9] The battle in *Dracula* is between two kinds of science; it is also between science and superstition. But in another irony, modern science can win, according to Van Helsing—and he returns to the idea time and again—only if it is open-minded enough to accept the validity of superstition as a useful precursor to modern understanding, at the very least a kind of index to the real state of affairs.[10] Science, then, can find itself colonizing the territory of the irrational, so that Van Helsing even begins to resemble the mad or hubristic scientist. Dr John Seward, too, threatens to do so; Seward longs to be able to pursue his experiments with Renfield so that he can advance the scientific understanding of encephalopathy far beyond the observations of Burdon-Sanderson and Ferrier. He would do so had he a good cause to serve in doing so, for he believes that he himself might be 'of an exceptional brain, congenitally'. Seward and Van Helsing can appear to be thwarted Victor Frankensteins. Stoker is rehearsing in his strange way the contemporary concerns about science, its inherent possibilities and moral limits, its rewards and dangers.[11] In one of several ironic parallels, Van Helsing reminds Seward how hypnotism (which he wishes to use to save Mina Harker and help defeat Dracula) can allow the hypnotist—in Van Helsing's ungainly English—to follow 'into the very soul of the patient that he influence', a description that could equally fit Dracula's own brand of hypnotism (p. 230).

And science was under anxious scrutiny in part because of the astonishing advances in both theoretical and applied science, especially in the two and a half decades preceding the Great War. Stoker was greatly interested in the advances of science and technology and it shows in *Dracula* when Stoker allows Van Helsing and the anti-Dracula posse to deploy shorthand, the telegram, the Underground, the typewriter (indeed, the state-of-the-art 'Traveller's', or portable, typewriter), the Winchester repeating rifle, field-glasses, and the phonograph (a dictation machine using wax cylinders). In short, *Dracula* depicts the war between late Victorian 'modernity' (Jonathan Harker's word) and the old nineteenth century and the time before, a war we have already encountered as cultural skirmish in the Irish novel. But, although Harker reminds himself that 'the old centuries had, and have, powers of their own which mere "modernity" cannot kill', nevertheless modernity does in the very end vanquish Dracula and the 'undead' Middle Ages (p. 49).

Part of the success lies in the efficiency of the business firms Stoker is careful to list through the novel. It is in this element of the campaign against the Count that the author of *Dracula* is recognizable as the author of 'The World's Greatest Ship-building Yard' in which Stoker wrote up the results of his visit to Harland & Wolff's shipyard in Belfast in May 1907; among other examples of efficiency, he included the dispensing of wages on Friday afternoons to 12,000 employees *in ten minutes*.[12] (Stoker's appreciation was no doubt the greater because he had been in his time a civil servant in Dublin Castle—like his father before him—and around the island as Inspector of Petty Sessions. Also, his occupation as Sir Henry Irving's manager required him in a small but essential way to exercise his own business acumen and efficiency.) In the novel it is Mina Harker who is the very embodiment of efficiency. The story is told by a sequence of diary entries, journal entries, letters, and telegrams, and Mrs Harker, the resistance group's unofficial secretary, undertakes to transcribe both handwritten letters and phonograph voice cylinders into type, 'knitting together in chronological order every scrap of evidence they have'. into 'a whole connected narrative', a prerequisite for the defeat of Dracula (p. 269). The Count himself is no slouch in the matter of logistics, and if the story is a battle between two kinds of science, it is also a battle between two kinds of business efficiency, and efficiency, as Jonathan Rose has shown, was a dominant motif in Edwardian culture in Britain and Ireland.[13] I am surprised to find Stoker absent from Rose's sizeable repertory of writers. Matching Dracula's supernatural versatility of resource and appearance is made easier by Van Helsing's ability as a linguist, in the older sense of someone who speaks several—or in his case, many—languages. The story itself employs in its telling various dialects as well as Van Helsing's broken English; this adds to a linguistic version of the diversity of evidence that Mina Harker must reduce to connectivity and coherence. Fighting Dracula is also made easier by 'the wonderful power of money' (p. 423), be it the old money of Lord Godalming or the new money of the American Morris, and a phrase that echoes Pip's discovery of 'the stupendous power of money' in *Great Expectations*. Dracula is beaten by the energetic virtues demonstrated in successful commercial enterprise: get-up-and-go, efficiency, initiative, communications, wise delegation of authority, up-to-date transport systems, and good business contacts.

Very much of its time, too, is *Dracula*'s exploration of the nature of, and differences between, manhood and womanhood, a theme (or themes) we have already seen much of in the popular novel. The men seeking Dracula are all 'brave', the recurring epithet, fine specimens of manhood, and Lucy Westenra and Mina love them for it; in their bravery and chivalry they are heroes of the country-house romance novels.[14] The women are rather more complicated, as are the relationships between the men and women. The women are motherly as well as attractive, self-sacrificial, emotionally open, man's helpmate, and weaker than men (which must be why Dracula like Milton's Satan goes after the women rather than the men as his chosen victims and weapons). Dracula is clearly a pressing sexual and social threat to the men's ability to protect and keep their women, which they fail to do in the case of Lucy and almost fail to do in the case of Mina ('Your girls that you all love are mine already', Dracula boasts); this male fear of course is not voiced explicitly by the men in the novel, nor the threat of impotence that Dracula poses. But the attractiveness of the women to Dracula is also their attractiveness to the other men, and both Lucy and Mina combine the familiar double contradiction of the mother–virgin and the whore–sweetheart. Passages of *Dracula* are troublingly erotic, the most erotic perhaps being the scene in which John Seward in his diary recounts the scene in Mina Harker's bedroom with Dracula at his horrific work, then quotes his own retelling of it to Jonathan (who was in the bedroom stupefied by Dracula like a husband drugged by his wife's lover but witnessing his own cuckolding), and finally quotes Mina Harker's own version of her ordeal, of how Dracula punctures her throat lovingly, drains her strength, declaims with macabre humour a kind of mock-marriage ceremony ('flesh of my flesh; blood of my blood; kin of my kin; my bountiful wine-press for a while') and then presses her mouth to his self-inflicted breast-wound, a scene which has all the appearance of transposed rape and forced fellatio. When Van Helsing presses the communion wafer on her forehead it burns her flesh, and the red scar suggests the scarlet stigma of adultery on Nathaniel Hawthorne's Hester Prynne.[15]

Stoker's dark variation on the themes of love and marriage is extended in the curious polyandrous situation in which Stoker places Lucy and Mina and in which they create and enjoy a kind of male harem. Lucy is proposed to by Quincey Morris, Arthur Holmwood, and John Seward and she wonders in a letter to Mina why a girl can't marry three men. The admiring trio becomes a quartet when Van Helsing swells the male group. All four men consecutively give Lucy a transfusion of their blood, and so intimate, even sexual is this, that the others do not reveal to Lucy's fiancé Arthur their blood-giving after he tells them that his donation of blood to her and her receipt of it was a sacred thing and tantamount to marriage. After Arthur leaves with Quincey, Van Helsing has a fit of hysterics, laughing and crying simultaneously ('just as a woman does', Seward remarks disapprovingly to his diary) and it turns out he is laughing at the proposition that blood transfusion is marriage, for if so, then 'this so sweet maid is a polyandrist' and he himself is a bigamist. Lucy is sexy and dependent, whereas Mina reverses the intimate ministrations of Lucy's 'polyandry' when it is she who comforts in a physical way and in turn Arthur, Quincey, and Jonathan; it is still a male harem but the woman is in charge and the men dependent; hers is a feminist harem. Mina, Van Helsing believes, has the heart of a woman but the brain of a man; she is also 'brave' like a man, which means fearless and unselfish.[16]

Yet Mina, she herself makes clear, is no New Woman; when she and Lucy have high tea in a sweet old-fashioned inn she is sure that the New Woman would have been shocked at their hearty appetites; 'Men are more tolerant, bless them!' she confides to her journal. When she looks at Lucy asleep, she observes how sweet she is in that condition and remarks that 'Some of the "New Woman" writers will some day start an idea that men and women should be allowed to see each other asleep before proposing', presumably because it is a condition of candour which offers the prospective spouse a chance to see their intended with their guard down. 'But I suppose', Mina goes on, 'the New Woman won't condescend in future to accept; she will do the proposing herself' (pp. 110–11). *Dracula* involves an attack on the New Woman and Stoker offers us the kind of woman we have already met: the strong, attractive, competent woman who does not need ideology or politics to emancipate her. Though in other respects, *Dracula* enacts an inversion of elements of the popular novel. It is Mina who has the 'business head' among the men and who is the logistical commander even while carrying the stigma of approaching vampirism.

It is to be expected in the light of the above that Stoker would embrace the selflessness that the New Woman rejected and that the popular non-New Woman female writers extolled, in men as well as women. And indeed, Mina, Quincey, and the 'allies' are praised in turn for their unselfishness. It is having a cause that promotes unselfishness.[17] But on the other hand, Dracula's selflessness is bad because it is precisely that: absence of a human self that can throw a shadow or a reflection in a mirror. In another sense, Dracula is pure self, being utterly single-minded, tyrannical, and self-centred, and his selfishness is an aspect of his criminality. He is the inverse of the charity principle. (In this and other ways Stoker turns the popular novel inside out.) Van Helsing believes Dracula embodies the egoism and selfishness of the age itself. The Count is of course a very sick man indeed, transcendently so, and Lucy commits to her diary the observation that sickness and weakness are selfish things and turn our sympathy and inner eyes on ourselves whereas 'Love' liberates the self; Dracula is without the sympathy that love requires and though he protests to his vampire chorus that he too can love, the three vampire women allege that he has never loved; if he is right it is a perversion of love that denies its own authenticity. Nevertheless, a sense of self can be good, as in the case of Mrs Westenra's stoic reaction to her daughter's illness; it is as if Nature generates an envelope of insensitive tissue to protect us in crises and promotes 'an ordered selfishness' that we might easily mistake for egoism.[18] It could even be said that the novel recounts the campaign each character wages to retain or return to his or her 'old self'. At moments of hope, Lucy, Arthur, Jonathan, Quincey, and Mina are like their old selves; their nearness to their old selves signals their health, happiness, and normality. Dracula's 'true self' is the paramount danger to their own true (or old) selves which they must recover or die (or become one of the undead).[19]

FROM NEW WOMAN TO REAL WOMAN

The theme of male and female selves Stoker took up with greater concentration in *The Man* (1905), a novel that ought strictly to have been discussed in those chapters above devoted to New Woman fiction, especially on those pages devoted to Sarah Grand, Katherine Cecil Thurston, and Ella MacMahon in which sexual identity, love, and marriage can be conducted as forms of experiment, reflecting the uncertainties and transitions of the age in which these matters were of deep concern. But *The Man* is a thematic sequel to *Dracula* once vampirism is subtracted from the equation, though even in *The Man* bad or wrong relations between the sexes are seen as a kind of unhealthy mutual parasitism. And a crypt plays a large role in the early pages, as though to reassure readers of *Dracula*, though when the heroine as a young girl faints in front of the coffin of her mother and is revived, we might later imagine it was meant to suggest the dead self she needs to leave behind, the Lucy Westenra in her. It is solely as a thematic sequel that *The Man* can be of much interest since, in its lumpishness and longwindedness, it is a sore disappointment after *Dracula*. Like the latter, it is a peculiar kind of English country-house romance, set in the days of the Boer War but with pronounced and anachronistic medieval, even Gothic appurtenances and atmosphere and having nothing to do with that war. And like *Dracula* and other fictions of the day, the novel is preoccupied with race, inheritance and succession, heredity and the limits of nurture.

It is as if in order to create his hero/heroine in *The Man* Stoker returned in his mind to his description of Mina Harker as having the heart of a woman and the mind of a man. The heroine is the child of a man of identical name, Stephen Norman, a wealthy country squire, whose wife bears him a daughter instead of the longed-for son and who names his daughter after himself and brings her up as a boy. He wishes her to become a woman but a 'resolute' woman with a man's knowledge, courage, and responsibility. Whereas Thurston's Maxine voluntarily puts on a man's identity, Stoker's Stephen (the daughter) has no choice. Since her mother has conveniently died soon after her birth, there is only one of our familiar elderly Victorian aunts to promote the conventional female interest in young Stephen's upbringing, that interest being chiefly one of womanly duty.[20] Stoker's self-imposed task is to modify and update the Victorian conception of a woman's place and nature but while doing so undermining the New Woman conception. Yet Stephen's success as a boy seems at first to prove, in today's distinction, that gender is a cultural matter and is more powerful than sex. When the time comes, she is equipped to become Squire Norman, her father's successor, and even to succeed eventually to an earldom (though her title of Countess is a reluctant acceptance of femininity). Indeed, not only is nurture used by Stephen's father to offset nature, but it appears as if nurture (like some form of Lamarckianism) can actually determine or modify individual nature, since Stephen grows up with a firm-set jaw and a squarer chin than is usual in a woman. She exhibits Mina Harker's good business head and takes an interest in courts of justice, an exclusively male preserve. And clearly remembering his prediction in *Dracula* about the New Woman of the future, Stoker has Stephen do an unheard-of thing and propose marriage to Leonard Everard, a haughty, selfish, and domineering young man who rejects her proposal, thereby triggering a crisis of identity in Stephen.

When told about her proposal, a strapping young man she has known since childhood, Harold an Wolf, wonders to himself if she is testing one of her theories. In part she is, since early she determines that if she were in fact a woman 'and had to abide by the exigencies of her own sex, she would at least not be ruled and limited by woman's weakness. She would plan and manage things for herself, in her own way. She had some good models of manhood within the circle of her own life, and she would take from them example [*sic*] and all the lessons of the nature of man which she could get' (p. 80). 'Some day', she tells her aunt, 'women must learn their own strength, as well as they have learned their own weakness... The time will come', she says, sounding like Grand's Ideala, 'when women will not be afraid to speak to men, as they should speak, as free and equal' (pp. 92–3). Stephen had from the start championed the idea of sexual equality. But unlike the Grand heroine whom she can otherwise sound like, she relapses into conventional femininity on occasions; thus, when her father dies, she reverts to a Victorian female altruism, her duties towards neighbours becoming a kind of passion. And despite her strength of will, she cannot compete with young men who in any case look at her as a girl not an equal (p. 78). Like Maxine's in Thurston's novel, Stephen's sexual exchanges are alternations and not an achieved androgyny.

What cannot be altered is what Stoker calls on the same page 'the sex-content'. And the narrator has warned us as early as chapter 2 that 'sex is sex all through' (p. 19). The relapses are into Stephen's true self. Her New Woman proposal of marriage to Everard is a ghastly error of mere will and the execution of an agenda for which she pays dearly. She arranges the tryst, which opens the chapter entitled 'The Meeting', and arrives there first, flouting the conventional idea that the woman should never precede the man. 'But real women, those in whom the heart beats strong, and whose blood can leap, know better. These are the commanders of men. In them sex calls to sex.' Even before Everard arrives, Stephen has learned that it is easy to yield to a dominant man. Crushed by Everard's disbelieving rejection, Stephen on the rebound rejects Harold's proposal of marriage, angrily mistaking it for pity and disrespect. It is the turning point; almost immediately she regrets her rejection since she has always loved Harold, whereas Everard was the object of her feminist experiment and has dented her pride.

But crushed himself, Harold has betaken himself to Alaska under a false name. As in Gwynn's *John Maxwell's Marriage* (1903), the hero exiles himself and returns, unrecognized at first, a new and better man; he becomes the real man for whom the real woman in Stephen will be waiting. But even when he returns, the hero of a shipwreck, and there is eventually mutual recognition, the inevitable must still be postponed. For he cannot propose marriage in case Stephen feels obliged to accept him because she had earlier rejected him; for her part, she cannot propose because she had once rejected him and because her proposal to Everard was a disaster. But through a go-between, the peculiar figure of the Silver Lady, who is the good fairy to Dracula's demon, it is arranged for Harold to come to claim Stephen, now Countess de Lannoy. At the end she resembles a cross between Chaucer's patient Griselda and contemporary American 'Real Women': 'She was all woman now; all-patient, and all-submissive. She waited the man; and the man was coming!' (p. 434) Unlike Everard's stealthy approach, she hears the sound of his 'sweeping gallop. It was thus that a man should come to a woman!' (p. 435) She has shed all thought of self, and her nature reigns alone; Harold an Wolf's love is, as a man's should be, 'dominant and self-believing' (p. 436). The novel might have been called *Waiting* except that the name given to Harold by a child he meets on the ship to San Francisco, 'The Man', echoes a girlish thought of Stephen's in an earlier chapter ('In the Spring') when as her 'vague desires of . . . womanhood' are merely 'budding . . . she became aware that her objective was man. Man—in the abstract. "Man," not "a man"'. Harold an Wolf is both, a man and All-man, ideal and material presence in one. Stephen, who ought to have been a Victorian woman, is brought up as a secluded version of the New Woman but is rescued from that fate by Harold and becomes at last a Real Woman.

The Man would be at base a kind of Harlequin Romance save not only for its verbosity—one reviewer called it a 'disheartening mass of unprofitable verbiage'[21]—but also for its lengthy subplot concerning a family Harold meets on board ship. As well, there is a persevering subtext relating reality in sexual identity to reality in racial identity and to reality in national identity, the novel gesturing towards a kind of Hardyesque English epic. When Stephen and Harold come together, her Saxon and Norman blood meets his 'Gothic' (German) blood—infused via the Netherlands—to create the ideal and un-beatable English–European blood-formula which Stoker's version of the New Woman philosophy, were it enacted and somehow to get into the blood-stream, would dilute and weaken—its own kind of vampirism.

SORCERY, NOT SOCIALISM

Its readers' suspension of disbelief is necessary to the success of *Dracula* though I suspect few imagine Stoker was himself a believer in vampires. However, another Irish writer of the time, Elliot O'Donnell (1872–1965), did write about vampires, werewolves, and ghosts as a believer, even when writing in his own voice. In *Werwolves* (1912), for example, he claims to be at one with Paracelsus in accepting the two spirits of humanity—the animal and the human—with the 'werwolf' being the embodiment and liberation of the animal spirit.[22] *Werwolves*, which was originally published by Methuen, is an historical survey cum casebook, though since the subject is (nowadays, at any rate) imaginary, the book is an exercise in fiction. O'Donnell furnishes us with a definition of the vampire which, like ghosts, werewolves, and other 'super-physical' forces, are 'Elementals': 'A vampire is an Elemental that under certain conditions inhabits a dead body whether human or otherwise; and, thus incarcerated, comes out of a grave at night to suck the blood of a living person. It never touches the dead ... Vampirism is infectious; every one who has been sucked by a vampire, on physical dissolution, becomes a vampire, and remains one until his corpse is destroyed in a certain prescribed manner' (pp. 133–4). There is little about Ireland in this book, but O'Donnell claims that there are many Irish legends of the werewolf (p. 109).

The obscure O'Donnell's forename sometimes occurs as 'Elliott' and I can find little about his life, even though he is a large figure in the landscape of popular horror and supernatural fiction. He is described on the Internet Book List as having been 'descended from one of the oldest and most honoured families in Ireland'. In another online booklist, his father is identified as The Revd Henry O'Donnell who was murdered on a safari in Ethiopia. Like Yeats, O'Donnell knew Aleister Crowley, the notorious black magician, and like Yeats he disapproved of him.[23] O'Donnell used his knowledge of black magic in his novel *The Sorcery Club* (1912) which starts promisingly when an educated down-and-out in San Francisco discovers a seventeenth-century book by one Thomas Maitland who was burned at the stake by the Inquisition in Madrid in 1693. Shipwrecked off Inishturk, Co. Mayo, Maitland had happened upon a chest on the island which proved to contain books written and published in the lost island city-state of Atlantis by its inhabitants, the oldest intelligent race in the world, contemporary with Stone Age humanity. The manuscripts in the chest had been transcribed, and the books assembled, by a survivor of the 'tremendous submarine earthquake' that destroyed and sank Atlantis.[24] The books and manuscripts are histories and accounts of Atlantean civilisation, the main feature of which was the total belief in Occult

Powers and the practice of sorcery (the daily use of occult powers) by the islanders. The Atlantean polytheistic belief system is very similar to O'Donnell's own implicit system outlined in *Werwolves*.

Maitland was rescued and carried to London; in Cheapside the chest of books was destroyed by fire but not before Maitland, having managed to decipher the Atlantean language, had sent his own account of Atlantean culture to Bettesworth and Batley. These London publishers overcame their fear of the authorities and published the book, which was immediately suppressed. The publishers found themselves in the stocks and fined, and Maitland was ordered to be flogged and imprisoned.[25] He took ship to Boston before he was arrested but the ship was blown off course and ran ashore on the Yucatan isthmus. There Maitland found material evidence of Atlantean culture brought by a colony of earthquake survivors and inscriptions that told of events on the eve of destruction. The writings allowed Maitland to study further the Atlantean language and see strong connections between Atlantis on the one hand and Ireland and Egypt on the other. Indeed, he came to believe that the earliest inhabitants of Ireland and Egypt had migrated from Atlantis, thereby explaining the reputation for mysticism and the highly developed 'psychic faculty' in both countries (on which for their own reasons the Irish Revivalists fastened when characterizing the native Irish culture they wished to resuscitate). He wonders if one of the great Atlantean rulers was an ancestor of Ireland's Niall of the Nine Hostages.[26] The Atlantean language, too, bears some resemblances to Gaelic. Maitland was rescued again and taken to Boston, Massachusetts where his own growing belief in sorcery and black magic found a contemporary context. Like Swift's Gulliver, though, Maitland had a roving instinct and he set off for Spain in 1692 where the next year he met his fate as a heretic at the Auto da Fé mounted by the Inquisition but whose body, according to the testimony of two Boston friends who travelled to Spain to be with him at the end, endured no pain whatsoever, he exerting his sorcerous powers over the material world.

This historical background to the novel's present is, in fact, reminiscent both of the kind of travel literature Swift satirizes in *Gulliver's Travels* (1726) and Swift's work itself; as historical fantasy it is, like *Gulliver's Travels*, a genre parallel to the science fiction of O'Donnell's day, with the exotic past taking the role of the science fiction's exotic future. But the Maitland affair is set inside an initially realistic narrative concerning three colleagues recently unemployed when their firm went bust and who are now down on their luck in San Francisco and desperate for food and money. Both the hungry and the opulent streets of San Francisco are knowledgeably mapped out in *The Sorcery Club* and O'Donnell's recreation of the depressed city (and later of the London underclass) bears resemblances to Frank Harris's recreation of the unemployed and the overworked of New York and Chicago in *The Bomb* before O'Donnell's novel veers off in another direction entirely. One of the trio is a womanizing anarchist, one an intelligent cynic, the third a short-sighted materialist, but together they resort to theft in order to survive until they peruse Maitland's book and realize that they can substitute sorcery for the obvious contemporary alternative to capitalism, i.e. socialism. They are at least modestly prepared, one of the characters having attended a lecture by the historical Mrs Annie Besant, one of the mentors, incidentally, of the mystical side of the Irish Revival.[27] They initiate themselves into the black arts, following Maitland's recipe for membership in the dark brotherhood. Possessed now of occult power, they profit themselves by blackmail and extortion through divination and second sight, conferring power on themselves over the plutocratic with secrets to maintain.

Hamar, Curtis, and Kelson become rich themselves and the scene suddenly shifts to London where they have incorporated themselves as the Modern Sorcery Company Ltd., offering the hardware and software (as it were: both the apparatus and the spells, charms, etc.) of conjuring and illusion: the world of Houdini so popular at the time of O'Donnell's novel. They seek profitably to spread sickness, failure, and unhappiness in accordance with their mandate. They set out to destroy their only competition in a one-sided battle, using the real powers of the occult against the merely human abilities of Martin and Davenport Ltd. (The character of Shiel Davenport is doubtless a nod to a popular writer as peculiar as O'Donnell, M. P. Shiel.) But their victory in this commercial contest is complicated by the love rectangle that develops as a result, and the ensuing occult romance vies with commercial romance to create an unsatisfactory hybrid novel. The conditions of the trio's Faustian grip on their powers of sorcery includes the prohibitions against marriage and disunity, but sexual love in the end will not be gainsaid and causes the disaffection that enables the 'luminous, striped figures' of the Occult Powers to return and exact their horrific price.

Its spiritualist and occult matter to the contrary, *The Sorcery Club* does not breathe the same air as the works of the Irish Revivalists, and its cynicism (which includes anti-'Suffragette' and anti-semitic sentiments we can attribute to the implied narrator) is not on behalf of any cause other than popular readability and a worldliness of the journalistic sort that expresses itself through revelation of arcane rites and recondite ceremonies. (Two elaborate illusionists' tricks are unmasked.) The morality of the novel, like that of *Dorian Gray*, is almost accidental but Wilde's salubrious wit is absent, leaving the Swiftian premise and the depiction of economic disparity in San Francisco as the novel's chief interests. Though published in 1912 there is no mention of the earthquake that levelled much of San Francisco in 1906 and the city seems to be in its pre-quake intact form. Whether the Atlantean earthquake—set in motion by the benign occult powers to destroy, Sodom and Gomorrah fashion, a civilization that had gone entirely to the bad—is meant to be a prefiguration of the 1906 quake seems doubtful since the bulk of the narrative is set in London and the narratorial cynicism doesn't suggest O'Donnell's ideological hatred of capitalism and luxury.

DETECTIVE FICTION: BODKIN AND FURNISS

Dracula's true self is an imperfectly formed one. According to Van Helsing, it resembles a child in so far as the Count will repeat actions; but whereas the child will through experience learn to adapt and alter behaviour, the Count has not yet done so and Van Helsing believes they must destroy him before he develops (or evolves) through adaptation, which would make him cornering much more difficult; meantime, what they have to advantage is their own empiricism. The criminal shares with the vampire this characteristic of mind. It is Mina Harker who succinctly puts Van Helsing's fumbling attempts at an explanation of the criminal mind into the context of contemporary thinking, and she cites Lombroso and Nordau on the criminal type, a type which exhibits relentless self-centredness and single-mindedness.[28] As the story of the pursuit and capture of a 'murderer', *Dracula* is a detective novel, and the Holmesian figure of Van Helsing has as partner Mina Harker, the lady detective.

Dora Myrl, The Lady Detective (1900) was one of a series of detective volumes written by M. McDonnell Bodkin, author of the entertaining *Recollections of an Irish Judge* (1914). As in the case of other writers' collections that feature one hero-detective linking various episodes, Bodkin's exist midway between novels and familiar assemblies of free-standing short stories. Although Bodkin was a Home Ruler and nationalist MP, and deputy editor of *United Ireland*, he cheerfully set his detective stories in England. McDonnell Bodkin was a citizen of the British archipelago, as much at home in London as in Dublin or Galway. Moreover, the plot complications in Bodkin's detective stories of wills and legacies (occasions for chicanery) and of love, engagements, and marriages (particularly in their financial implications) also align these stories with the country-house fiction we have already met. They frequently have a country-house setting and titled characters and fit perfectly the bill of what we regard as the classic English whodunit. The alternative settings of seaside hotels and golf links that Bodkin often chooses ally his tales not only with Conan Doyle's Sherlock Holmes stories but also with M. R. James's antiquarian ghost stories.

The two genres, ghost stories and detective stories, overlap, of course. They overlap in one way when a believer in the supernatural engages in psychical research to justify the belief. Elliot O'Donnell, for example, called himself a 'ghost hunter', by which he meant an investigator who through the methods of a detective reveals the presence or occurrence of supernatural phenomena.[29] They overlap in another way when ghosts and other apparent impossibilities turn out to be hoaxes or criminal deceptions. For example, John Bell, whose stories are told in *A Master of Mysteries* (1898) by the always readable L. T. Meade in collaboration with Robert Eustace, is a 'professional exposer of ghosts' who solves the mysteries of haunted houses. These stories are 'the histories of certain queer events' that are, when 'grappled with in the true spirit of science, capable of explanation'.[30] A ghost is likewise exposed as a hoax in 'The Horror of Studley Grange', a story in Meade's *Stories from the Diary of a Doctor* (1895). Meade in her 'ghost' fiction promotes science and reason as Riddell promotes morality, and Bell, like the anti-Dracula posse, has recourse to the new technology, the telegraph and kodak photography, though unlike them he is up against merely clever mortals rather than supernatural presences, as he already surmises. Meade's stories are set in England and are populated by the professional middle classes (especially lawyers and doctors) and inhabitants of country houses and are written in the steady tones of detective fiction without sentimentality or romance. All elements of the stories exist to justify the plots which are ingenious, with contraptions and sleights of hand that suggest the influence of Poe and Collins but without their power of atmosphere.

A very different, and markedly unsteady ghost story and detective novel— though the ghost, in whom the narrator has never believed, turns out to be a hoax—is *Poverty Bay: A Nondescript Novel* (1905) written and illustrated by Harry Furniss. Furniss (1854–1925) was born in Wexford and left for England when he was 19, where he became a cartoonist for *Punch* and a well-known illustrator of the works of Lewis Carroll and Charles Dickens on whom he famously lectured. Besides being a serious illustrator and graphic artist, Furniss was a political caricaturist fuelled by his firm pro-Union stance on the Irish Question. He was also a writer (novelist, biographer, and memoirist) and when he later left England for the United States he became an actor in black and white silent movies, a screen writer, and a pioneer of animated movie cartoons.

Poverty Bay is as multifarious and unstable as Furniss's curriculum vitae and it is close to a sleight of hand for me to introduce a brief discussion of this work in parenthesis at this point of my study. The narrator claims in his preface to be a mere living combination phonograph-and-typewriter (shades of the phonograph-using prolific best-selling novelists), uninterested in artistic hindsight, a mere mechanism of truth-recording (in an interesting anticipation of Christopher Isherwood). He then proceeds to write a novel that confects a ghost story, episodes of Edwardian realism, a romance, a satire (a kind of verbal caricature), and a detective story ('The Mystery of the Gull's Nest', he dubs it at one point). The novel is set in a former fishing port seventy miles from London and now far from the sea because of land reclamation, and in a seventeenth-century cottage (the Gull's Nest), once a sailor's abode now high and dry like the rest of the village, Redcliff Bay. Having listened, like the narrator, to the stories of various eccentric characters—most of whose stories involve their exploitation at the hands of assorted villains, especially unscupulous middle-men, including artists' agents and gallery owners—we realize that Poverty Bay (as one character christens it) is the repository of disappointment, disillusionment, and foundered dreams, a place we might think contrived by an author with a fair share of grievances, real or imagined. And indeed, at times Furniss resembles Swift in his animus against charlatans and exploiters. As well, in its dramatic surrealism, the work reads at times like a novelistic anticipation of Dylan Thomas's *Under Milk Wood*.

His stay in Poverty Bay transforms the narrator from an indifferent and cynical spectator of life (made so by a broken and warping homelife but with a hint of Wildean ennui) into a concerned, engaged, and enlivened participant chiefly through the agencies of romance with a lovely woman and encounters with the bitter and the resigned. The whole is melodramatically theatrical; there are disguises and dressings-up, and life as theatre runs as a metaphor through *Poverty Bay*. When after his return with his bride to London the narrator turns his back on the city and the privileged, empty club-life in which he spent his early manhood, choosing instead Poverty Bay, the narrator is turning his back on idle selfishness (and perhaps on a Wildean pose of cynical contemplation and rejection of action, certainly altruistic action) and choosing instead community and beneficence, family and friends. But it is too late to reverse the reader's heated feeling that he or she is entangled in a net of genres between two covers, including a passable ghost story (the apparitions are well described) and detective story (with hidden treasure and codes to be broken for its discovery). The novel's relationship to caricature is telling, for the story has the suggestion of delirium that Coleridge likened to fancy, instead of suggesting the focus of true imagination. To that extent, *Poverty Bay* is perhaps too close to being genuinely nightmarish.

The woman who attempts for her own reason to scare Furniss's narrator away from the Gull's Nest and then falls in love with him, is a clever woman who combines the strength of the New Woman with the philanthropic impulses of the Victorian angel (she is an expert nurse). This could serve as a reminder that Bodkin's very different and differently readable stories written to exhibit Dora Myrl's cleverness deserve a second pause mainly because of the presentation of her character. In her debut story, 'The False Heir and True,' Myrl is an orphaned young woman who is a Cambridge wrangler and doctor of medicine who, when a practice failed to materialize, became by turns a telegraph girl, a telephone girl, and a lady journalist. 'There was certainly nothing of the New Woman, or for that matter of the old, about the winsome figure' of Dora Myrl, yet she is a bicyclist, a bit of a tomboy ('My father grieved at first that I was not a boy') who can match at tennis, croquet, and billiards the master of the country house to whose wife Myrl has just been appointed companion. When she finds herself amidst a mystery and solves it (a case involving switched babies and a black-mailing woman), she decides she has found her vocation and drafts her future business card: 'MISS DORA MYRL, *Lady Detective*'.[31]

Dora Myrl is girlishly attractive—as indeed all of the chief women in Bodkin's stories are; the narrator, shall we say, has an 'eye' for the ladies—and she is not above using her attractiveness as a way of lulling her opponents into a false sense of security. Yet she is essentially a modern girl who inhabits and is alive to a new world in which Bodkin himself is therefore at home: the world of the telephone, the telegraph, the motor-cab, the train (reaching 60 mph), the electric car, electric lights, electric doorbells, the bicycle, and fingerprints.[32] In 'The Wings of a Bird', Ernest Fairleigh, Senior Cambridge Wrangler, tells Myrl (this is three years before the Wright brothers) that he has invented the power of flight, borrowing from the discoveries of the 'aero-plainist' but using human muscle-power. (Fairleigh has coined the odd word 'aeroplainist' though the word 'aeroplane' clearly pre-dated the power of mechanical flight.) Three nights before, he flew five miles in just over a quarter of an hour and with little fatigue. He seeks her help now because there have been attempts to burgle his blueprints, the more alarming because he has not patented his potentially epoch-making invention. Like many of the popular novelists we have looked at, Bodkin sets his stories at a time when Victorian England is metamorphosing into the twentieth century, when values and roles are changing, and when technology is fast becoming a dominant force. So fast, one might say, that Bodkin sets one of his stories on board RMS *Titanic* four years before that ship sank and three years before she was launched! I do not know if Bodkin happened coincidentally upon the name *Titanic* or somehow got wind of a name that had already been fixed upon by the shipbuilders who decided in the summer of 1907 to build four gigantic steamships, including what became *Titanic*. In 'The Ship's Run', a story in *The Quests of Paul Beck* (1908), *Titanic* of the Blue Star Line (a lightly fictionalized White Star Line) is 'the largest and fastest passenger boat afloat,' travelling at 20 mph (23 knots, just about the real *Titanic*'s speed).[33] This story turns upon the gambling over the distance of the ship's daily run that well-heeled passengers engaged in.[34]

Bodkin's stories would be on a par with, say, those of his American contemporary Jacques Futrelle, the detective writer who went down with *Titanic.* Futrelle and Bodkin belong to the readable second rank of detective writers, and Julian Symons pays tribute to Bodkin in his history of the genre.[35] Bodkin's primary detective was Paul Beck who made his first appearance in *Paul Beck, The Rule-of-Thumb Detective* (1898), followed by *The Quests of Paul Beck* (1908). The Beck stories resemble the Myrl stories in setting and cast, and 'The Murder on the Golf Links' in the later volume includes a sportier version of Dora Myrl, the character of Mag Hazel, 'undisputed queen of the links', and no women and only one or two of the women can even 'give her a game' (a slang phrase in Bodkin's day); 'her wrist was like a fine steel spring, as sensitive and as true.'[36] Bodkin's women seem to be crosses between New Women and high achieving head girls from English schoolgirl fiction. One or two Irish characters make their appearance in stories that are otherwise clearly written for an English readership, and since Bodkin is a Home Ruler and patriot, he does not show his Irish characters in a poor light, even if, as with Ned Ryan in 'The Murder on the Golf Links', they might display typically 'Irish' characteristics such as impetuosity and emotional volatility. The capture referred to in the title of a 1909 collection, *The Capture of Paul Beck* (1909), is a nuptial one and it lessens the New Woman dimension of Bodkin's lady detective: Dora Myrl secures Beck in marriage, and in *A Chip off the Old Block* (1911), Bodkin introduces their son, Paul junior, as a budding detective.[37]

DETECTIVE FICTION: MEADE, CONYERS, AND CROFTS

Dora Myrl was not the first woman detective in fiction. Mrs Paschal appeared in *The Lady Detective* (Anon.) in 1860 or 1861. Then came the anonymous heroine of *The Female Detective* (1864) by Andrew Forrester Jr. Then came *The Experiences of Loveday Brooke, Lady Detective* (1894) by Catherine L. Pirkis, and *Dorcas Dene, Detective: Her Life and Adventures* (1897–8) by George R. Sims. But if Bodkin was early in the gender stakes in the crime genre, Meade may have pipped him at the Irish post by collaborating with Eustace to create her detective Florence Cusack who appeared in magazine stories between 1899 and 1901.[38] Miss Cusack like Dora Myrl combines personal attractiveness with 'one of the most acute detective brains in the whole of London' (p. 54); she is a 'young and handsome woman' (p. 3) who lives alone in a large London house with a staff of servants, is superabundantly energetic, like Meade's Dagmar Olloffson (but subject to nervous attacks, no doubt due to her highly-strung intelligence), and is admired by London detectives and respected in the police courts. She solves crimes or mysteries (often in a variation of the closed-room formula) among the moneyed classes, involving theft, fraud, and gambling, together with the mechanisms of wills, legacies, and stocks and shares: a wholly capitalist environment. Dr Lonsdale who recalls her cases of the early 1890s is Dr Watson to Cusack's Holmes and like Holmes Cusack is an entirely private investigator, independent of, and superior to, the police. Meade's personal philosophy of the sexes aside, Miss Cusack is clearly a strong woman who could easily exemplify the New Woman of the 1890s.[39]

Soon after creating Miss Cusack, Meade and Eustace created Diana Marburg, in doing so combining the New Woman in detective mode with the New Woman in spiritualist mode, thereby at once reflecting contemporary fascination with the occult and overlapping the literary genres of crime fiction and supernatural fiction. Marburg is a clairvoyante who studied Reichenbach (presumably Dr Carl Ludwig von Reichenbach, 1788–1869, who propounded vitalism and the 'Odic' life force) and Mesmer (Franz Mesmer, 1734–1815, discoverer of animal magnetism or mesmerism) and was a pupil of the Scotsman James Braid (1795–1860, developer of hypnotism). She nows works in London as a fashionably patronized palmist. Her cases, however, take her to country houses as befits the crime investigation subgenre of Society-fiction and country-house fiction with its adaptation of the plot mechanisms of engagements and marriages, wills and legacies, debt and blackmail, and the white-collar crimes of fraud and jewellery theft, etc. 'Finger-tips' employs the familiar device of a crime which had to have been committed by one or more of the country-house party guests (or host). Marburg narrates cases she solved to one Edward Dering in three stories that lead off *The Oracle of Maddox Street* (1904). Reading palms allows her to identify future perpetrators and future victims but thereafter she has to use natural powers of detection to solve each crime. Indeed, in one story Marburg reads a palm print as contemporary detectives were learning to read finger prints, thanks to the researches of Galton whom Marburg credits for the discovery of the uniqueness of our hand and finger prints. In each case, the part identifies the whole, the print identifying the man or woman. Meade uses the device of palm-reading to short-circuit the normal, more descriptive establishment of character; Marburg can tell character and destiny instantly: interest in the story lies merely in the solution to how the crime was committed and identification of the perpetrator. If there is any interest in the character of Diana Marburg it is that the reader and her creator clearly take her as a detective entirely for granted and see no need to applaud her as a New Woman.

Meade played variations on the themes of detective fiction and in *Stories from the Diary of a Doctor* (1895) she, with her collaborator 'Clifford Halifax

MD', created a medical doctor as sleuth and in so doing created, Greene claims, the earliest medical detective.⁴⁰ The first story opens with Halifax— the narrator and doctor of the title—reading (Alfred Swaine) Taylor's 'Practice of Medical Jurisprudence' (actually *The Principles and Practice of Medical Jurisprudence*), but although this textbook appeared in 1865, a tenth edition appeared as late as 1948 and so Meade and Halifax are perhaps justified in claiming that the stories exploit the newest advances in medicine, for which reason the stories could be regarded as a kind of science fiction, a cross between the doctor's casebook and the private detective's casebook. For example, 'My First Patient' involves a stomach pump and electric batteries to effect artificial respiration; 'The Horror of Studley Grange' a laryngoscope and battery to fake a supernatural visitation. But the establishment scenes and plot premises of classic English detective fiction are here too: the sudden summons of the professional in his study or office, the railway schedules and urgent train journeys, the waiting servant with the brougham or cab at the station, the country house, the merry fire, the subdued library, the comfortable bedroom in contrast to the agitation astir and the crime afoot. The symptoms of the patient are the equivalent to evidence and clues in detective fition; the true diagnosis of the malady is the identification of a crime but only a step towards the solution: identification of the culprit and his or her motives. The motives are not criminal but psychological, and the ill-doing is the product of a deranged mind; 'My First Patient' involves a planned husband–wife suicide, 'The Horror of Studley Grange' the attempted murder of her husband by a terminally ill wife. The ethos that dominates the stories places them, like all detective fiction, in the context of a late Victorian and Edwardian fascination with professionalism and efficiency often placed at the service of, or commissioned by, the landowning, county or aristocatic sets. The stories themselves are more professionally written, with a firmer narrative grasp, than the Marburg and Cusack stories, suggesting that perhaps Halifax (Beaumont) had a larger, or more effective, say than Eustace (Barton).

With Eustace's collaboration, Meade pursued the association of medicine with crime in *The Sanctuary Club* (1900), the narrator of which, Dr Cato, is an ambitious and philanthropic doctor who founds a club in Hampstead that functions as a combination sanitorium, resort, hotel, laboratory, and hospital, though the template would seem to be the gentleman's club familiar to us from science fiction, detective fiction, ghost stories, and numerous novels and stories by late Victorian writers, including Oscar Wilde. Club members (well-off professionals) qualify only by suffering from a disease which the medical staff tries to cure or palliate; in the complex all medically prescribable climatic conditions (pine forest, mountain top, spa, desert) have been artificially duplicated (rather like today's giant indoor malls). This is the setting for a series of criminal events, chiefly orchestrated by a Dr Kort (vivisectionist, mesmerist, physician, murderer, and thief) who, among other deeds, mesmerized his wife to get her to agree to marry him, and later so that she cannot reveal the experiments he conducted on her in his attempt to track thoughts and feelings back to the cellular structure of the brain; after these experiments, his young wife could function mentally only at high atmospheric pressure. She is of course saved in the end and Kort foiled. Meade like other writers of the period worked with a baseline fear that science, which seemed inexorable in its advance at the time, possessed a power that could profit evil-doers as readily as benefactors, philanthropists, and patients.

Paul Gilchrist is the hero of 'Adventures of a Man of Science', a series of stories by Meade published in the *Strand* magazine in 1896 and 1897 and republished in book form as *A Race with the Sun* (1901). Gilchrist is a well-rounded student and practioner of science, knowledgeable in chemistry and physics and a formidable inventor and discoverer, someone comparable to the heroes of scientific romance by Wells, Cromie, and others. But instead of narrating events that are highly improbable or far-fetched but in advanced scientific theory feasible or at least conceivable, Gilchrist tells stories that are unusual and adventurous but scientifically explicable: they are not, in other words, the stuff of scientific romance and more resemble those in *Diary of a Doctor* and other detective fiction while still inhabiting the category of science fiction, science being the true hero (or villain, since 'Science', as 'Edward Dering' reminds us in his Introduction to *The Oracle of Maddox Street*, can destroy as well as save). The title 'A Race with the Sun' refers to Gilchrist's efforts to save himself from a chemical detonation, which the rays of the sun will set off at sunrise, by escaping from a hot-air balloon to which he has been lashed by villains who have stolen by deceit his notes for a revolutionary new means of explosion and propulsion, his scientific *magnum opus*. This story and the others are well-told adventures and little more.

Dorothea Conyers (1863–1949) wrote detective novels as well as popular romances, and published detective stories in such magazines as *Saturday Evening Post* and the *Strand* in which she was publishing in the teens of the century. Her detective, Mervyn Henderson, who appears in 'Justice Evaded', the story Peter Haining includes in his compilation, *Great Irish Detective Stories* (1993), is, as Haining remarks, reminiscent of Sherlock Holmes. Henderson is referred to as 'the human bloodhound', a metaphor that nicely connects Conyers's detective fiction to her legion of novels with heavy horse-and-hounds action. It is a clever enough piece, with Henderson himself recalling as a story the case in question, inside a first-person plot and during which Henderson switches to a third-person narrative. It is a thoroughly English example of the genre and set in familiar rural England off a railway branch line.[41] Conyers herself exploits the double entendre of fox-hunting/man-hunting when in a volume of stories collected in 1930 and entitled *Hunting and Hunted* she jostles vigorous hunting stories with detective stories. One of the former, 'Scarlet Fever', is a paean of praise for fox hunting and a lesson on how the rider should comport herself on the hunt. The expertise eloquently conveyed would probably be vitiated for most contemporary readers by the hearty anthropomorphism, here and in 'The Unforgivable Sin', by which the 'red fellow', the 'lad', the 'little red excited varmint' enjoys being hunted, and if he dies does so gloriously, 'in the interests of his own race'. Readers might also be put off by the flagrant toff economics of it all, the fox being 'a money spinner to thousands of people' and the hunt provoking costly lawsuits by irate farmers.[42] In 'The Poisoning of Hector Alhuson', Mervyn Henderson again relates a crime from his casebook, one that was ingeniously committed in a spacious town house in Grosvenor Square, London at a dinner party (the house party setting of detective fiction) and involving a troubled marriage and adultery but which, as in the genre, hinges not on human frailty or passion but on something as mundane as the cutlery. And in line with our expectations of the genre, the crispness of the dialogue and pace of narration finally stand or fall by the plausible ingenuity of the crime and solution.

No Irish writers were as dedicated to the genre or as accomplished practitioners of it as was Freeman Wills Crofts (1879–1957), who brought detective fiction into the modern era that we associate with the 1930s and after. Crofts was born in Dublin but moved north to Belfast where he spent his working life, becoming chief engineer of the Belfast & Northern Counties Railway. According to Haining, Crofts's first novel, *The Cask* (1920), sold 100,000 copies over the succeeding twenty years. In rapid succession he published *The Ponson Case* (1920), *The Pit-Prop Syndicate* (1922), and *The Groote Park Murder* (1923), all four novels republished in *The Freeman Wills Crofts Omnibus* (1932); the author's favourite detective, who made his creator famous, was introduced in *Inspector French's Greatest Case* (1924). Crofts's knowledge of trains came in handy in his detective stories, since examples of the genre frequently relied on that method of transport (along with fast cars), especially in the 1920s, 1930s, and 1940s. *The Cask*, distributing its settings, and its three detectives, among London, Paris, and Rouen, is punctuated by journeys by train but also by taxi, bus, metro, ferry, and even horse and cart: components of the complex logistics of the field detective for whom schedules and distances, time and space, are crucial. It is tempting to see Crofts's evident interest in engineering as originating in, or at least reinforced by, his time in Belfast since that city was one of impressive engineering accomplishment.

The Cask established at once Crofts's modus operandi of painstaking, even labyrinthine detail, density of prose, and dispassionate removal of crime from morality and even contentious social reality. The dense texture of his writing can be thick enough to suggest a curiously puritan opulence (I offer this oxymoron to describe the impassive single-mindedness of Crofts's narratives) and can in pursuing its goals of plausibility and conviction threaten to achieve their opposite through the reader's suspicion of excess, be it of words, details, or ideas.

Removal from morality and social problems is characteristic of the classic English whodunit, and it holds even in *Sir John Magill's Last Journey* (1930), a later case set in the recently founded Northern Ireland in which Inspector French solves the murder of a noted Orangeman, unionist, and linen manufacturer. The geography (placenames and journeys) are accurate and detailed (from Larne to Belfast to Whitehead) but Crofts is too engrossed in the extraordinary intricacies of evidence, red herrings, testimonies, hypotheses, and dead ends that can tax the reader to register the tense politics of a fledgling statelet feeling itself under siege from the Irish Free State. Still, French has crossed to assist the Royal Ulster Constabulary in their murder inquiries and behind his admiration of their commitment and prowess we might see Crofts's admiration of Northern Ireland itself.[43] Even so, this did not prevent either *The Pit-Prop Syndicate* or *Sir John Magill's Last Journey* being translated and published in Gaelic in the Irish Free State, in 1933 and 1935 respectively.

As in many English detective stories from Conan Doyle onwards, crime in Crofts, even in *Sir John Magill's Last Journey*, is committed in a context that generates in the reader an oddly reassuring and even nostalgic and escapist warmth; at story's end the fabric of a desirable England (and in *Sir John Magill*, a desirable Northern Ireland), briefly rent by crime, is invisibly mended. Many of the stories by these Irish writers are virtually by-products of British country-house fiction set in England. Haining's attempt to construct a native Irish detective genre founded on the Irish extraction of Edgar Allan Poe, Wilkie Collins, Arthur Conan Doyle, Sax Rohmer, Alfred Hitchcock, and Raymond Chandler is hardly convincing. I am happier to suggest that a few incontrovertibly Irish writers have easily and un-selfconsciously contributed to the British and international detective genre.

NOTES

1. Wilde is in part quoting H. T. Buckle into his notebook: see *Oscar Wilde's Oxford Notebooks: A Portrait of Mind in the Making*, ed. Philip E. Smith and Michael S. Helfand (New York: Oxford University Press, 1989), p. 159. See also John Wilson Foster, 'Against Nature? Science and Oscar Wilde', *University of Toronto Quarterly* 63.2 (1993/4): 339.

2. Bram Stoker, *Dracula* (1897; London: Penguin Books, 1979), pp. 41–2, 287–8, 405.

3. Renfield recounts how Dracula appeared at his window (through which he cannot pass without being invited) and offered him the lives of the countless rats he has conjured up if Renfield will fall down and worship him, a grotesque echo of Christ's Temptation by Satan: *Dracula*, p. 333.

4. Anonymous ('Ignotus'), 'Irish Realities', *Blackwood's Edinburgh Magazine* 207 (March 1920): 349.

5. Paul Murray in his recent biography of Stoker offers a convenient survey of the 'Irish' interpretations of *Dracula*. It is clear from his round-up of Irish and non-Irish inspirations for, influences on, and interpretations of *Dracula* that it is a novel for all seasons: *From the Shadow of* Dracula: *A Life of Bram Stoker* (London: Jonathan Cape, 2004), pp. 165–208.

6. Bram Stoker, *Dracula*, p. 303. See John Wilson Foster, *The Age of* Titanic: *Cross-Currents in Anglo-American Culture* (Dublin: Merlin, 2002), pp. 103–12.

7. This race anxiety surfaced during the *Titanic* tragedy and the ensuing inquiries: see my *The Age of* Titanic, pp. 120–33.

8. While registering the appropriate significant differences, we might note that Wilde the Irishman himself impersonated the thoroughly English toff and eccentric, clubman and country-house habitué, to the point of caricature and, his plays and writings would suggest, for subversive purposes; in the end he was 'unmasked' as an alien and diseased threat to English society, originating in Ireland and retreating in the end to France, the natural habitat of the dandy and decadent and, of course, traditional opponent of England during the Great War (as it was called) of 1793–1815 and after.

9. Bram Stoker, *Dracula*, pp. 360, 404, 359–60, 288.

10. Ibid., pp. 137, 223, 229, 231, 262, 283, 293, 390, 416.

11. Ibid., p. 90. J. S. Burdon Sanderson (1828–1905) was a famous pathologist who drew criticism because he championed vivisection. Stoker champions it also on the page from which I have just quoted. David Ferrier (1843–1928) was another famous student of the brain and wrote *The Functions of the Brain* (1876) as well as *Historical Notes on Poisoning* (1872). Van Helsing believes John Seward would be a better scientist were he to expand the boundaries of science's ignorance and welcome 'new beliefs', just as the great (Jean-Martin) Charcot (1825–1893), author of *Lectures on the Diseases of the Nervous System* (1871, 1880), learned the power of hypnotism (he also practised experiments on animals): *Dracula*, pp. 229–30.

12. Bram Stoker, 'The World's Greatest Ship-building Yard', *The World's Work* (UK) no. 54 (1907): 647–50. I discuss this article and its cultural context in *The Age of* Titanic, pp. 18, 166–7.

13. Jonathan Rose, 'The Efficiency Men', in *The Edwardian Temperament, 1895–1919* (Athens, Ohio: Ohio University Press, 1986), pp. 117–62.

14. Bram Stoker, *Dracula*, pp. 284, 289, 370, 389, 393, 423.

15. Ibid., pp. 365, 336, 339, 343.

16. Ibid., pp. 209, 210, 281, 404, 347, 366.

17. Ibid., pp. 205, 226, 277, 366, 408, 91.

18. Ibid., pp. 226, 154, 53.

19. Ibid., pp. 122, 185, 205, 227, 280, 391, 403, 410.

20. *The Man* (London: William Heinemann, 1905), p. 47. The versions of this novel available online (Project Gutenberg) and in print (Doylestown, PA: Wildside Press, n.d.) are abridged.

21. Quoted in Paul Murray, *From the Shadow of* Dracula, p. 232.

22. *Werewolves* (Royston, Herts.: Oracle, 1996), pp. 18–19. *Werwolves* was O'Donnell's 1912 title.

23. The online list in question is Zillion. For Yeats and Crowley, see *The Collected Letters of W. B. Yeats*, vol. I, ed. John Kelly and Eric Domville (Oxford: Clarendon Press, 1986), pp. 487, 498. For O'Donnell and Crowley, see 'Elliott O'Donnell: A Biographical Sketch of a Friend & Acquaintance of Aleister Crowley': http://www.redflame93.com/Odonnell.html

24. Several online copies of *The Sorcery Club* are accessible, including one (with the original illustrations) in Project Gutenberg. The book was originally published in London in 1912 by William Rider & Son.

25. A. Bettesworth and J. Batley were real London publishers. Among the books they published was *Admirable Curiosities, Rareties and Wonders in Great-Britain and Ireland* by Robert Burton (Nathaniel Crouch) (1728).

26. I discuss the mythology of islands off the west coast of Ireland, and Revival mythology of western islands, as well as the role of real western islands in the Irish Revival in 'Certain Set Apart: The Western Island in the Irish Renaissance', *Studies* 56 (1977): 261–74.

27. I quote Besant on Ireland and spirituality in *Fictions of the Irish Literary Revival*, p. 58. The Irish-born violinist and student of Indian music, Maud McCarthy was a disciple of Besant's.

28. Bram Stoker, *Dracula*, pp. 405–7.

29. See O'Donnell, *Confessions of a Ghost Hunter* (1928). A posthumous collection of O'Donnell, *Elliott O'Donnell's Casebook of Ghosts* (1969), called him in its subtitle *One of the World's Greatest Ghost Hunters*.

30. L. T. Meade and Robert Eustace, *A Master of Mysteries* (London: Ward, Lock & Co., 1898), pp. 7–8. Douglas G. Greene identifies Robert Eustace as Dr Robert Eustace Barton who later collaborated with Dorothy Sayers: see Introduction to L. T. Meade and Robert Eustace, *The Detections of Miss Cusack*, eds. Greene and Jack Adrian (Shelburne, Ontario and Sauk City, Wisconsin: Battered Silicon Dispatch Box, 1998), p. ix.

31. M. McD. Bodkin, Q.C., *Dora Myrl, The Lady Detective* (London: Chatto & Windus, 1900), pp. 1, 5, 19.

32. Since Francis Galton did not publish *Finger Prints* until 1892, Myrl (and Bodkin) were punctual in the idea of using finger prints for legal identification.

33. But if he had got wind of the real ship's name, it seems odd that he chose it for his imaginary ship of 23,000 tons, half of the announced tonnage of the proposed liners, *Olympic, Titanic, Britannic,* and *Gigantic.* See my article 'A New Anticipation of

Titanic,' *CQD Titanic* (Official Journal of the Belfast Titanic Society), 24 (Spring 2004). A less striking anticipation occurs in Robert Cromie's *The Lost Liner* (1899) in which the newest ship of the Line sails between San Francisco and Auckland, meets a hurricane and, though she is the best ship afloat, with the most 'modern' equipment and is 'unsinkable', sinks. During the sinking, there is an ugly rush for the too few lifeboats, there is a cry from the bridge of 'Women and children first!', a terrified foreigner attempts to flout this order and is shot dead by the Captain because 'this is a British ship!', all circumstances and episodes repeated during the *Titanic* disaster: *The Lost Liner* (London: George Newnes; Belfast: R. Aickin, 1899), pp. 30, 45.

34. *The Quests of Paul Beck* (London: T. Fisher Unwin, 1908), p. 164. Bodkin's interest in technology is further displayed in his fascinating account in his memoirs of the invention of the pneumatic tyre, assumed to be by John Boyd Dunlop, the Scots inventor who at the time was a veterinary surgeon in Belfast. (Bodkin himself was something of an inventor and sold a patent for combined lamp bracket and carrier for a bicycle.) The pneumatic tyre at first serviced the bicycle, then the motor car, and finally the aeroplane. It turned out that another Scotsman, one Thompson, had invented the pneumatic tyre before Dunlop who therefore could not patent his creation. Had his patent been deemed valid, said Dunlop, 'we would have earned enough money to pay the National Debt.' (Bodkin had an early financial interest in development and production of the pneumatic tyre.) As it was, the factory was driven out of Ireland by Dublin Corporation because of the smell of the naphtha required in the solution of rubber smeared on the tyre's tubing, and relocated in Coventry, to the dire economic detriment of Ireland. Dunlop was later visited by a mad and pistol-packing Dutchman who claimed he was a co-inventor of the tyre but was distracted by Dunlop's brave wife until the police arrived: *Recollections of an Irish Judge*, pp. 258–67.

35. Julian Symons, *Bloody Murder: From the Detective Story to the Crime Novel: A History* (London: Faber and Faber, 1972), p. 89.

36. M. McDonnell Bodkin, KC, *The Quests of Paul Beck*, p. 112. Bodkin himself was a keen golfer.

37. Patricia Craig and Mary Cadogan briefly discuss *The Capture of Paul Beck* in which Myrl and Beck meet, compete, and then become lovers: *The Lady Investigates: Woman Detectives and Spies in Fiction* (London: Gollancz, 1981), pp. 33–4.

38. I am indebted to Douglas G. Greene for this bibliographic chronology and for information on the publishing history of the Miss Cusack stories: Introduction to *The Detections of Miss Cusack*, p. xi. Greene claims that Meade also created the second female spy in fiction (the nasty Mlle Francesca Delacourt in *The Lost Square*, 1902), preceded only by *A Diplomatic Woman* (1900) by Huan Mee: Greene, p. x.

39. Craig and Madogan briefly discuss two Cusack stories in *The Lady Investigates*, pp. 30–1.

40. Greene, Introduction to *The Detections of Miss Cusack*, p. viii. Greene identifies Clifford Halifax as the pseudonym of Dr Edgar Beaumont.

41. See *Great Irish Detective Stories,* ed. Peter Haining (New York: Barnes & Noble, 1993), pp. 297–309.
42. Dorothea Conyers, *Hunting and Hunted* (London: Hutchinson, [1930?]), p. 272. The stories collected in this volume would have been written in the 1920s or perhaps earlier.
43. Crofts is catalogued as the author of a Northern Ireland government report published the same year as *Sir John Magill's Last Journey,* and entitled *Bann and Lough Neagh Drainage* (Belfast: Ministry of Finance, 1930).

13

'Years of the Shadow': Writings of the Great War

THE RIDDLE OF THE SANDS

In *The Riddle of the Sands: A Record of Secret Service* (1903), Erskine Childers (1870–1922)—decorated British soldier, Irish republican executed by the Irish Free State—wrote a subgenre of the detective novel we might call the spy novel, and because it combines detection with high adventure, we might call it also a thriller. (Symons tells us that the spy story took its rise with concern about national security, the impulse behind Childers's novel.)[1] To complete its generic richness: it is also an invasion story, and like that other invasion story, *Dracula*, it has rarely if ever been out of print, with at least thirty-five editions in English between 1903 and 2002. In order for the central character Carruthers—a bored Foreign Office official stuck unseasonably in London when Society has abandoned it—to have the experiences that form the story, to join his friend Davies in the Baltic and accompany him on his yacht, he had to forgo the promised pleasures of a September house party at Morven Lodge thrown by Lady Ashleigh. *The Riddle of the Sands*, then, opens on the threshold of being a country-house novel; it then seems as if it will become a semblance of Young's *Sands of Pleasure*, or for that matter, Wilde's *Dorian Gray*, for Carruthers, having politely refused Lady Ashleigh's invitation, then has a passing thirst for adventure that takes him into 'some shady haunts in Soho and farther eastwards; but was finally quenched one sultry Saturday night after an hour's immersion in the reeking atmosphere of a low music-hall in Ratcliffe Highway'.[2]

Carruthers turns his back on both real-life country-house romance and real-life lowlife romance, and the 'Romance' that beckons him, once he commits to joining Davies, is 'not that bastard concoction I had tasted in the pseudo-Bohemias of Soho; it was not the showy but insipid beverage I should have drunk my fill of at Morven Lodge; it was the purest of her pure vintages, instilling the ancient inspiration which, under many guises, quickens thousands of better brains than mine, but whose essence is always the same: the gay pursuit of a perilous quest' (p. 80). Carruthers comes to see in their adventures 'a strain of crazy chivalry more suited to knights-errant of the middle ages than to sober modern youths' (p. 180). But this purer romance, though the presence of young Clara Dollmann retains elements of it, will soon become the impurer romance of spy-and-detection narrative in which the knights-errant have a purpose that becomes almost puritanical in its single-mindedness, certainly practical to an extreme. That purpose is to discover by stealth if there are any grounds for Davies's suspicion that the rich German, Dollmann, is actually a renegade English lieutenant of the Royal Navy, a spy aiding Germany to concoct some plan to the detriment of England. There are such grounds and the plan in question is the invasion of England by barges of German soldiers from the obscurity of the Frisian Islands.

By the time of the action of the novel—1901 or 1902 perhaps—suspicion about German intentions was growing in Britain. Shane Leslie in *The End of a Chapter* (1918) thought that 'the German war scare, dating from 1900, fell flat in England because people remembered a similar French scare'. Because of this, 'With the exception of the Admiralty, the English social machine, politically, educationally and even morally, was unprepared and reluctant for war.'[3] It is this unpreparedness that was the stimulus of the novel; it is in one sense an extreme problem-novel, the problem to be solved being the threat posed to England and her Empire by German ambitions and exertions. *The Riddle of the Sands* was written by an English patriot exercised by what Carruthers calls 'the burning question of Germany' (p. 89).

The novel's Epilogue is written in the character of the 'editor', 'E. C.', and is the novel's 'non-fiction' version of itself, explicating the possible invasion of Britain by Germany, a nation with 'a peculiar genius for organization, not only in elaborating minute detail, but in the grasp of a coherent whole', and uncovering the many defects of the English defence system, including the lack of a North Sea naval base, North Sea fleet, and North Sea policy (pp. 281–2). It seems Childers disliked his book being promoted as a novel and thought of it more like an extended Foreign Office memorandum, cast in fictional form in order to draw attention to itself.[4]

The upbringing of the author as an English patriot was almost, but not quite, exemplary: he was educated at an English prep school and attended Haileybury public school, followed by Trinity College, Cambridge to which he went up as an exhibitioner, taking a First in the finals of the Law Tripos. He then sat the Civil Service examination and was appointed a clerk in the House of Commons. However, when his parents died early, young Childers went to live with his mother's brother in Glendalough House (a country house in Wicklow); only this sojourn blemished or qualified an otherwise English identity. The Pophams put it succinctly when they reflect on his youth: 'one begins to detect the emergence of the particular type of Englishman he was to become. Anglo-Irish he was, Irish he was later to claim to be; yet, in many ways, he was English to the bone', and they see in him the personal reticence, modesty, courage, and integrity displayed by many outstanding soldiers and imperial administrators in the years before the Great War that shattered 'all the moulds of greatness'.[5]

The singleness of purpose that unifies *The Riddle of the Sands* can be seen as early as Childers's record of his experiences as a soldier during the Boer War in which he served with the City of London Imperial Volunteers as a driver of field artillery. Those experiences he narrated in *In the Ranks of the C.I.V.* (1900)—though there is some disagreement about the extent of Childers's involvement in the book's publication[6]—and the narration reflects his Englishness. The book is a fine example of Childers's (somewhat deceptive) modesty, for it does not offer a panorama of the war but instead fastens on the daily practicalities and argot involved in being a soldier, from improvised recipes to toothache to inadequacies in the harness for horses. (As he was later to linger on the daily practicalities and argot involved in being a sailor in *The Riddle of the Sands*.) In any case, the ordinary soldier rarely grasps the nature of his contribution or the overall battle plan. The book is a good read, with the pace of a popular novel, and retails one amusing Kiplingesque story of how by sheer chutzpah twenty-one men and four officers of the Kimberley Light Horse convinced an entire Boer town to surrender on the grounds that a massive British force was approaching behind them; they held the town for six weeks on the strength of this deception and were treated like conquering heroes, until 'the ubiquitous De Wet' marched up and returned warfare to its own kind of sanity.

The Royal Irish Rifles and Munster Fusiliers make their appearance on the veldt but they are part of the imperial effort and when Childers's brother turns up unexpectedly from British Columbia, Canada, the author remarks: 'A fancy strikes me that it is symbolic of the way in which the whole empire has rallied together for a common end on African soil.' He has a 'jolly talk with some Paddies' of the Munsters, about Ireland and they are merry and dream of the beef, bacon, and stout ('but chiefly stout') they'll treat themselves to on their return to the old country, but there is in them no hint of dissatisfaction or nationalistic unrest. 'It was pleasant to hear the rich Cork brogue in the air. It seems impossible to believe that these are the men whom Irish patriots incite to mutiny. They are loyal, keen, and simple soldiers, as proud of the flag as any Britisher.'[7]

What impressed Childers was the efficacy that derives from unity of purpose; like Kipling, Wells, and Conrad, he was a late-Victorian and Edwardian 'efficiency man'; it was not the idea or policy of Empire that interested him (though he had read his Kipling, as the book shows); the Empire was a given and therefore at least ought to work properly.[8] For example, he was impressed by what an eccentric soldier told him of the difference between Boer and British cavalry methods, one difference being the more flexible, improvising attitude of the Boers (p. 120). This difference later provoked Childers to write two quite impersonal book-length advisories: *War and the Arme Blanche* (1910), in which he recommends substituting mounted riflemen for cavalrymen armed with steel, and *German Influence on British Cavalry* (1911), discouraging any dependence on foreign, especially German models, in favour of 'our own war experience and our own racial aptitudes'.[9] The two books are clearly meant to serve as warnings in the foreshadow of a coming conflict. They might be said with *In the Ranks of the C.I.V.* to constitute Childers's Imperial trilogy; separately and together they also register as surely as any of the Irish novels the end of Victorianism, certainly in the experience and conduct of war. Boer flexibility also founded Childers's later optimism in the capacity of irregulars, culminating in the republican irregulars that opposed the Irish Free State, to change the directions of whole countries.

But those irregulars are foreshadowed in Carruthers and Davies in *The Riddle of the Sands*. The sea is not Carruthers's element but he learns to adapt and flourish in it. The novel incidentally registers Carruthers's apprenticeship as a sailor and shows his growth in knowledge and confidence in negotiating the irregular shores and waterways and the eventualities of their adventure in pursuit of Dollmann. In some ways this improvisation is carried forward in the narrative form of the novel; the editor ('E.C.', the initials allowing Childers to become the fictional editor different from the real-life author) has been told Carruthers's story directly which he has then 'ghost-written', having required Carruthers to retell his story in greater detail, and drawing also on Carruthers's diary as well as Davies's own oral account and his maps and charts, and embedding also, where desirable, excerpts of Davies's log. There is a moment or two when Carruthers's story approaches the reflexiveness of Conrad's *The Heart of Darkness*, published as a book the year before, in 1902, though Childers might have read Conrad's novella in *Blackwood's Magazine* just before the turn of the century.

Davies of course is the seasoned yachtsman and yet he too has much to learn. 'I could not help missing this professional element', writes Carruthers: 'Davies, as he sat grasping his beloved tiller, looked strikingly efficient in his way, and supremely at home in his surroundings; but he looked the amateur through and through, as with one hand, and (it seemed) one eye, he wrestled with a spray-splashed chart half unrolled on the deck beside him' (p. 39). It is hard not to see an implied resemblance between the unpreparedness of Carruthers and Davies to carry out their dangerous self-imposed mission and the unpreparedness of England (or Britain, but like all patriotic English-men Childers prefers to speak of England) to resist German aggression or even perceive it as a danger. The transformation Carruthers and Davies have to undergo is a miniature of that which England will have to undergo. Germany was the professional, England the muddling amateur. Carruthers like many Englishmen of the time lauded Germany's achievement: 'her marvellous awakening in the last generation under the strength and wisdom of her rulers; her intense patriotic ardour; her seething industrial activity...'. Several times Davies expresses genuine admiration for the Kaiser who has rallied and inspirited his great nation, and also understanding of Germany's imperial ambitions which England, having 'collared a fine share of the world', is in no position to denounce in principle (p. 90). This (in its own way rather British) admiration for professionalism and efficiency requested admiration for Germany to the point where one could imagine English patriotism toppling by degrees into disloyal pro-Germanism. Childers's two heroes suggest to me that Childers himself entertained the kind of patriotism that could *under certain circumstances* slide almost imperceptibly into its opposite because in fact a third thing attracted it.[10]

Kipling, Conrad, and Wells all denounced muddle, perhaps the reason the liberal and pacifist Forster in *Howards End* claimed muddle and amateurism as virtues, professionalism and businesslike efficiency as vices. (Forster also championed the *personal* over against the professional; Childers introduces the personal element in Davies's infatuation with Clara Dollmann but this is the least convincing part of the story.) And yet what Childers championed—and this surely has a bearing on his later activities as an Irish republican—was a kind of inspired amateurism, freelance initiative generating its own kind of efficiency. 'The command of the sea is *the* thing nowadays, isn't it?' Davies asks Carruthers, but Carruthers/Childers clearly thought that command could take surreptitious, irregular form. It required of those involved 'pluck' and absence of 'funk' (both rather English contemporary virtues that Car-ruthers learns to acquire). Carruthers thinks of the Frisian Islands as an 'ideal hunting-ground for small free-lance marauders'. Carruthers even fashions a parallel between land and sea as regards the tactics he and Davies thought Germany might adopt in the ragged islands off their brief coastline. When he expands on the idea it begins to seem as if he imagines Davies and himself as just those marauders: the waterways through to the heart of commercial Germany 'are like highways piercing a mountainous district by defiles, where a handful of desperate men can arrest an army'. Surely Childers had the Boers freshly in mind when some race-consciousness came to the fore. 'People your mountains with a daring and resourceful race, who possess an intimate knowledge of every track and bridle-path, who operate in small bands, travel light and move rapidly. See what an immense advantage such guerillas possess over an enemy which clings to beaten tracks, moves in large bodies slowly, and does not "know the country".'[11] Although Carruthers admits the parallel must not be pressed too far, he is sure that naval guerilla warfare will come, just as he is certain that the probable war between Germany and England will be primarily a maritime war.

From this point of view, Dollmann the renegade is exercising both the initiative as well as the secrecy of his trade as spy, and he does not really impress as the villainous traitor the story requires him to be. Something in Childers admired simultaneously German prowess and anti-German efforts that exhibited energy, intelligence, and some cunning and stealth. And so it is perhaps not surprising that inside the larger coming (and then declared) war against Germany, he began to help wage a smaller war in which England this time was the efficient aggressor and the Irish the resourceful race that should, and could, fight back. Even in the imminence of England's war with Germany, the enemy was transformed in the crucible of Childers's imagination into England herself and Carruthers's daydream of English guerilla war on the water against Germany became a daydream of Irish guerilla war on land against England. What is more remarkable than any substitution of loyalty on the part of Childers was his *superimposition* of loyalties, his allegiance in the larger coming war being subverted by his allegiance in the smaller coming war. This was a dangerous and in the end fatal duality. He ran arms for the pro-Home Rule, pro-neutrality Irish Volunteers in his yacht in July 1914 (the land war must be initiated on the sea, so *The Riddle of the Sands* was not entirely outdated) and *then*, when war broke out between Germany and England, he was summoned to the Admiralty and with superb irony was set the task of planning for the occupation of the German Frisian Islands! He became a lieutenant in the Royal Naval Volunteer Reserve ('volunteer' smacks of the freelance irregular) and was observer in the leading plane in the first-ever naval air operation, according to the Pophams—the attack on Cuxhaven on Christmas Day.[12] He was awarded the DSO in 1916. Meanwhile the arms he landed were being distributed and readied for guerilla use against England. Childers became, in short, the renegade Lieutenant X in *The Riddle of the Sands*. When he was later executed by the Irish Free State for conducting war against the new state on behalf of die-hard Irish republicanism that rejected the Anglo-Irish Treaty, Churchill expressed grim satisfaction at the end of a 'mischief-making, murderous renegade'.[13]

Childers fought the Boers for England and the Empire and was prepared to fight the Germans in the same cause, but in the end became himself a kind of Boer, entertaining a guerilla war against England. At first, the idea was born out of the need for England to change traditional tactics in order to defend itself against German invasion. 'What you want is *boats*', Davies claims, '—mosquitoes with stings—swarms of them—patrol boats, scout-boats, torpedo-boats; intelligent irregulars manned by local men, with a pretty free hand to play their own game' (p. 113). (Childers had he lived might have enjoyed the spectacle of local and amateur involvement in the retreat from Dunkirk.) But then the idea transferred its location and allegiance. Childers belongs to a thin tradition of well-born Anglo-Irish who became Irish republicans after being pro-imperial British patriots: it begins in modern times with Theobald Wolfe Tone and carries through to Roger Casement and Childers; because of the first loyalty, the tradition entailed renegation.[14]

It is a tradition that could be subjected to psychological as well as social and political scrutiny; I would not be surprised to conclude that behind the renegation—even in the case of Childers who might be thought of as simply having followed his own love of freelance efficiency and irregular romance— lay some form of imperial disillusionment taken personally. Childers seems to have been part-Carruthers, part-Davies. Carruthers escapes from his quotidian Foreign Office desk job and becomes a venturesome field operative, as it were, while his creator has to make do with his clerkship of the House of Commons. As for Davies, his comrade describes him as 'a sun-burnt, brine-burnt zealot *smarting under a personal discontent* [my italics], athirst for a means, however tortuous, of contributing his effort to the great cause, the maritime supremacy of Britain'. (This sounds like Tone and, *mutatis mutandis*, Casement.) Davies was no 'arm-chair critic' but rather like a rush of fresh air through a gentleman's club (of the kind Carruthers grows bored in before receiving Davies's letter of invitation to join him on his yacht in the Baltic). What Davies proposes is what Carruthers calls Davies's golden opportunity, his 'chance' (p. 91). Gun-running for the Irish Volunteers was Childers's own 'chance' for freelance, irregular activism and like Davies he took it.

CROMIE AND SHIEL

The fear and expectation of a coming war for forty years before it happened created a minor tradition of fiction, and *The Riddle of the Sands* is a kind of flagship in the armada of novels and stories.[15] Future war fiction that did not, like Childers's novel, merely warn of the war's imminence and its likely broad shape, but imagined the details and development of the war, was unavoidably a kind of science fiction. The future could be close and readily imaginable, as in novels by Robert Cromie and M. P. Shiel. However, even if the perspective were political, there was scope for unmoored fantasy, as other novels of those two writers demonstrate.[16] Very real fears and prospects of an Anglo-German,

European, or even world war could, when commended to writing, inhabit the large-scale scenario sponsored by evolutionism (immense struggles for survival among nations and races that we would now call geopolitics) and even compose the endgame scenario we find in the eschatological or apocalyptic fantasies by Cromie and others we have already encountered.

To the future war tradition, the Ulster writer Robert Cromie contributed *For England's Sake* (1889), in which he imagines the coming struggle between Russia and England in Asia (the outcome of the 'Great Game'), and then *The Next Crusade* (1896). The latter is a novel that begins with some country-house matter and its associated romance, and quickly becomes an account of what is in effect a pre-play of the future Great War. Our two heroes, Cameron and Jackson, enlist for different reasons (Cameron to forget his financial ruin, the impoverished Jackson to persuade Miss De Courcy that he is a worthy suitor), and they ship out to the Mediterranean. Austria has declared war on Turkey, the 'Sick Man of Europe', the originator of the 'great international imbroglio which for three fearful months convulsed Europe and finally altered its map' (the narrator tells of events that have already taken place, but in the contemporary reader's future). Russia joins Turkey, England will join Austria so that 'the late struggle in Asia' (the real-life Great Game and Cromie's 1889 fictional war) will be 'repeated on a larger and altogether a grander scale in Europe'. Austria is determined to thrust Turkey out of Europe after atrocities perpetrated by the Turks; it will be 'a fight to the finish'. Like England, other countries—Rumania, Serbia, Bulgaria, Montenegro, Albania, Greece, and Egypt—join behind Austria while Germany's navy offers itself on the Russian and Turkish side. The largest army ever shipped from England departs to the cries of soldiers: 'It is for England! Ay! It is for England.' It is 'a New Crusade, the grandest that had ever sailed from the West unto the East'.[17]

Cromie follows the notion of the Crusades far enough to write a grim and exciting account of the 'White Company', soldiers disfigured by Turkish atrocities who form themselves into an elite and cruel company who then wreak savage revenge on the Turks before disbanding by committing suicide. This is an allusion to the 'White Company' of the Crusades, referred to by Eleanor Alexander in *The Lady of the Well* (1906). Cromie imagines a chiefly cavalry war that reaches climax in the battle for Byzantium and Cromie gives vent to some cultural triumphalism, even sadism, in his pleasure at the reckoning, at Armageddon. 'The Purple East would in the coming day witness a blaze which would burn its damnable conventions into something less than dust. And the fire would be cheap even if its flames were fed with dead men's bones. This was more than a milestone in the march of progress. It was an epoch in the history of humanity.' Austria flies her eagles over Saloniki, the English flag is run up in Stamboul, 'the Mediterranean was at last a British lake'. A last reference to Waterloo completes this patriotic bout of delirium inside which Cromie has written some page-turning adventures.

A similar contemporary racism mars the lively writing of the egregious M. P. Shiel in *The Yellow Danger* (1898), one of Shiel's twenty-six novels. *The Yellow Wave* appeared in 1905 and in 1929, *The Dragon* (1913) was lightly revised and republished as *The Yellow Peril*, betraying a racial fixation.

Shiel (1865–1947) was born in the West Indies of Irish parentage (his father was a Matthew Dowdy Shiell) and his obituarist thought he had the 'fertile imagination of an Irish Dumas *père*.'[18] Since his father, a Methodist lay preacher and ship owner, was himself born in Montserrat, and his mother was of mixed race (Shiel himself lived much of his life in England), the claim for Shiel's Irishness is tenuous.[19] However, he earned a place in Katharine Tynan's 1902 revision of Charles A. Read's *The Cabinet of Irish Literature* in which he is represented by a story from *Prince Zaleski* (1895), a volume of three detective stories published by John Lane in his famous Keynote series. Zaleski has been called 'the most decadent and imperial detective in fiction', an impression enhanced by the opulence, at times overheated opulence, of Shiel's prose in stories that are heavily influenced by Poe. (A 'tropical luxuriance', a contemporary reviewer called Shiel's linguistic inclination.) The extract Tynan gives her readers confirms another reviewer's description of Shiel's detective Zaleski as 'a kind of sublimated Sherlock Holmes, who solves problems, not so much by more vulgar inductive reasoning as by intuition and a certain hyper-sensitiveness to impressions'.[20] The literary Eastern-cum-Gothic stage properties of the stories (gems, trances, chalices, gravestones, fevers, drugs, dreams, vaults, etc.) are as alien to the stories of Freeman Wills Crofts as it would be possible to get, and link Shiel not only to Poe but to the decadent Nineties of *Dorian Gray* and *À Rebours* by Huysmans, and the early twentieth-century tales of Lord Dunsany. So although, if we admit Shiel to the Irish syllabus, we might place him alongside Bodkin, Meade, Conyers, and Crofts as a detective writer, we would be more realistic in placing him beside other Irish practitioners of decadent fiction.[21] Shiel is also remembered by aficionados as a writer of thrillers and supernatural stories (e.g. *The Pale Ape*, 1911) and proved himself a popular master of category fiction,[22] casually crossing and recrossing the borders between detective fiction and supernatural tales and what we might call decadent fiction. Tynan praised his workmanship and thought his novels of mystery and terror 'very remarkable'. He ventured into science fiction as well, and *The Purple Cloud* (1901), said to be his masterpiece, has been claimed as 'one of the few works of science fiction of its period not overshadowed [as Cromie's clearly were] by the achievements of H. G. Wells'.[23]

But it is as the writer of a coming war novel that I mention Shiel here. *The Yellow Danger* both inhabits and promotes the race fear that gripped many

Westerners around the turn of the twentieth century.[24] It is a febrile emulation of Wellsian fiction, midway between science fiction and would-be cautionary realism (actually dark romance), propelled by a vicious Sinophobia and enlivened by an unpleasant sadism in the descriptions of torture and atrocity. Although it heatedly imagines the Great War as a global assault by the hordes of the 'heathen Chinee', with mighty naval battles like Armageddon (with the promise of 'boats of the air' to come) and an attempt at a worldwide League of Yellow Races, it is nevertheless set in its own day, 1898–9. It is full of the geopolitics of its time, with real politicians as characters, including Sir Robert Hart (Inspector General of the Chinese Imperial Maritime Customs), Lord Curzon, and Lord Charles Beresford. In 1900, the latter anxiously pondered 'The Future of the Anglo-Saxon Race' in the pages of the *North American Review* before deciding that the race would resist following previous nation-alities down 'the path of degeneracy' (the new plutocracy was a larger threat than the 'angry waters of the Latin races') and once again triumph through its cool, phlegmatic, critical stance amid crises.[25] Shiel's hero and redeemer, a perfect Englishman named John Hardy, reads like a combination of Lord Nelson and the future Lawrence of Arabia. Like Cromie and other writers of coming war fiction, Shiel 'spoke for England' even though he was no more English than they were.

PATRICK MACGILL AND LORD DUNSANY

Then the war so often imagined broke out. The maritime war Childers envis-aged in *The Riddle of the Sands* became chiefly a land war, and the cavalry war he envisaged in his Imperial trilogy (one of essential motion, like the maritime warfare he foresaw) became static trench war when cavalries were stymied in virtually frozen fronts after the early neutralizing clashes of infantries. But he was right to claim that England would have to turn its amateurism into professionalism to have a chance at victory, and quickly, and this speeded-up transformation is acted out for us in the first volume of Patrick MacGill's Great War trilogy, *The Amateur Army* (1915). It is unlikely MacGill conceived his three books as a trilogy, for the first started life as a series of articles dashed off in his spare time while he underwent military training with the London Irish Regiment in England in order to become part of the British Expeditionary Force. Thereafter his experiences as a rifleman and then stretcher bearer provided the material for two more books, *The Red Horizon* (1915) and *The Great Push: An Episode of the Great War* (1916) which take his story from embarkation for France to action at Loos. Full of characters, incidents, and easy transitions like his fiction, these volumes have the readability and forward momentum of his popular novels; they exhibit by turns painful realism, casual comedy (even in war), and at length a kind of war romance, to set beside the other kinds of romance we have encountered in Irish fiction.

MacGill in all his writing is a *faux naif*, an affable storyteller, chiefly concerned it seems with keeping up a brisk pace (like an infantryman at a quick march) and keeping the reader amused; he transfers his sympathy for down-and-outs to sympathy for private soldiers—this also serves to connect his fiction with his wartime nonfiction—and appears to be writing modest literature for the common man. It helps in this regard, then, that he is an enthusiastic soldier, cheerfully boasting that the British Army is 'the most democratic army in history' and that 'we British are one of the most military nations in the world' ('we British' despite his boast that there are only two *'real* Irishmen' in the battalion, he and another).[26] He respects his fellow Tommies, including the junior officers with whom he comes into contact, and clearly enjoyed his minor celebrity as the author of the articles that compose the book and of his popular Kiplingesque poems. He writes: 'There are three things in military life which make a great appeal to me; the rifle's reply to the pull of the trigger-finger, the gossip of soldiers in the crowded canteen, and the onward movement of a thousand men in full marching order with arms at the trail', before going on to describe a night march and manoeuvres with memorable panache (p. 71). The rookie rifleman is in fact a literary man, having read Daudet, de Maupassant, and Balzac before setting foot in France and reading Montaigne in the trenches when he gets there. He is a sharp and humorous observer, and obviously nobody's fool, and if he is loyal it is certainly through no false consciousness or innocence. *The Amateur Army* is a fine journal of enlistment and training and one feels on the strength of it alone that were more wartime experiences to come, they would be recorded with MacGill's usual upbeat energy even if they were to record the disillusion and disabuse that inevitably followed the early optimism of the War.

And indeed, *The Red Horizon*, which takes MacGill's story from embarkation with the BEF through billetings in French villages, train journeys towards the front, marches to the trenches, to action in the neighbourhoods of Givenchy, Souchez, and the Hills of Lorette, and is not stinting with portraits of painful deaths on 'the slaughter line', nonetheless ends with a chapter entitled 'Romance' that is only lightly (and perhaps inadvertently) mocking in its surrealistic and allegorical suggestiveness. MacGill sings the romances that follow the young soldier, from the romance of his mission at the outset, through the distant line of battle ('a red horizon'), the mystery and glamour of the watching, waiting, and warring, 'the romance of the long night marches', the throbbing heart when the star-shell-lit scenes of battle come into view, to the glorious fatigue of the weary in some musty barn lit by candles and cigarettes: 'There is romance, there is joy in the life of a soldier', the memoir ends, and it seems a literal affirmativeness.[27]

MacGill does not describe the trajectory of romance followed by disillusionment, disgust, and anger so familiar from Great War poetry, but his relentless eye for detail and his fearlessness in telling truth prevents our calling him naive. For Rifleman No. 3008, London Irish, earned whatever vantage-point he chose from which to remember a war still raging even as he wrote. There are splendid passages and episodes: the Irishman Feelan singing 'The Wearing of the Green' the night before the trenches; the description of a march to the front that is almost Shakespearian ('All individuality is lost, the thinking ego is effaced, the men are spokes in a mighty wheel, one moving because the other must, all fearing death as hearty men fear it, and all bent towards the same goal'); a strange dream of Donegal fields MacGill has whilst standing sentry; the re-creation of a German charge and the 'wild fascination' such danger inflames.[28] And there are brisk disquisitions on trenches and dugouts that prove MacGill an intelligence to some extent out of its element in the animal conditions where soldiers attempt to duplicate conditions of home. His writing reached a lot of people hungry for what was virtually news from the front, so punctual was MacGill in his reportage: a fifth printing of *The Red Horizon* in its year of publication completed over 39,000 copies.

At one point in *The Red Horizon* MacGill comes across months-old corpses of French soldiers, fallen before the German trenches, and adds a footnote: 'The London Irish charged over this ground later, and entered Loos on Saturday, 25th September, 1915' (p. 254). This charge, its run-up, and its immediate outcome, are the subject of *The Great Push*. The author claimed in his Introduction that most of the book was written at the scenes of action, the eve of battle account written in the trenches, and the last chapter in the hospital at Versailles after his wounding at Loos. There are purplish passages as in all of MacGill's writing, but the reality he records has in any case its almost surrealistic vividness. If there are themes, they are, first, 'man's ingenuity for destruction',[29] though MacGill wastes no time on arid moralizing, and, second, the extent to which trench warfare developed its own routine and weird semblance to ordinariness despite the relentless bloodletting. The foot charge of the London Irish Rifles became famous overnight because London Irish rugby-playing infantry kicked a football towards and into the first line of German trenches; the ball bounces irregularly through MacGill's book, a symbol of Irish insouciance and one which fits MacGill's own great good temper and *joie de vivre* in the midst of carnage.[30] The legendary football rush was verified by Michael MacDonagh in his account of the advance on Loos (the London Irish captured the front line of German trenches, a section of the second, and Loos itself, before being relieved during the German counter-attack and sent behind the front lines) in *The Irish at the Front* (1916), written before the deeds of the 36th (Ulster) Division at the Somme.[31]

Perhaps the literary impulse in MacGill's Great War trilogy is the absorption of its otherwise dreadfully realistic events and characters into the impersonality of comedy and romance that derives as much from literature and the prior writing of the author himself as from personal experience. The literary impulse is there too in Lord Dunsany's *Tales of War* (1918), thirty-two short narratives that incline towards folk legend and romance because those are Dunsany's natural genres. Some are a Dunsanian kind of reportage: 'A Famous Man' concerns a makeshift cinema in Behagnies where soldiers came to watch Charlie Chaplin and ends with a daydream of Chaplin returning to humiliate the Kaiser in a revenge of his little tramp; 'The Oases of Death' recounts the burial of Baron Von Richthofen by British airmen during the 'battle of dull Prussianism against Liberty' and ends with the figure of Death stalking France but sparing the cemetery because it is his own garden.[32]

Dunsany joined the Royal Inniskilling Fusiliers during the Great War but it was in Dublin during the Easter Rising that he was wounded when seeking to help crush the rebellion; on his recovery he went to France and saw combat. Despite this personal experience, and despite their topical references, his stories become tales that aspire to an existence independent of the author. This does not preclude moving work, witness 'Last Scene of All', the death of a soldier convincingly imagined from his own point of view. But the tales compose a generalized portrait of a Waste Land. In one chapter, 'A Walk to the Trenches', that could be set beside 'The Night Side of Soldiering' from MacGill's *The Amateur Army*, Dunsany writes: 'You come to the trenches out of strangely wasted lands, you come perhaps to a wood in an agony of contortions, black, branchless, sepulchral trees, and then no more trees at all.' The infertility has been caused by the Kaiser, 'a man who was only an emperor and wished to be something more...a shallow, clever, callous, imperial clown...the All-Highest War Lord...the sinister originator of the then impending holocaust', the source of the woe of France, a malevolent and sick Fisher King. Among the questing heroes to redeem the wasted land are the pilots; what poets have anything more romantic 'than these adventurers in the evening air, coming home in the twilight with the black shells bursting below?' Incredibly, 'we live in such a period of romance as the troubadours would have envied'. The chief questing hero is England, launched on the latest of her benign crusades, as the last tale of all, 'Old England', tells us.[33] The vilification of the German emperor is balanced by the hymning of England, a rural England of immemorial landscape with figures, Dunsany's spiritual and cultural home. Dunsany simply could not see the War in any but the broadest political terms any more than he could see Ireland in any but the broadest political terms; his writing tries to emancipate itself from conditions and contingencies and does so but at a cost, though it was not only Dunsany whose vision of a waste land was generated out of the devastated French landscapes of the Great War.

GOSSAMER

It is a puzzle where precisely to place for discussion a quietly industrious, perceptive, witty, and refreshing Irish novel by George A. Birmingham (Revd James O. Hannay, 1865–1950).[34] *Gossamer* opens in MacGill's crucial year of 1915 just after the narrator has seen action, been wounded, received the DSO, and resigned his commission. The bulk of *Gossamer* (1915) is told in retrospect, however, and concerns events between the autumn of 1913 and the outbreak of the Great War in autumn 1914. Only gradually and towards the end of his story does the looming war demand the lion's share of the narrator, Sir James Digby's, attention, which is engaged on several fronts besides the run-up to continental hostilities: the contest between Irish unionists and Home Rule nationalists; the allure and complexity of banking and finance (particularly the potent mystery of credit); the more dubious aspects of the Irish Literary Revival; the extraordinary possibilities of applied science; the endangered ethic of the gentleman. The novel updates Riddell's vision of business, including the technology of commerce; it offers an acerbic version of the Irish Revival; and it anticipates that cleavage in Irish loyalty created when Easter 1916 erupted in the midst of the Irish Great War effort and that will command our attention in the next chapter.

Birmingham had, and has, a reputation for comic writing of frothy popularity but *Gossamer* proves that he could be a thinking novelist, for it is a novel about competing value systems in a turbulent civilization that is yet far less dispiriting than Ireland, about which the worldly narrator is affably cynical. Even today, many Irish could sympathize with Digby's wan reflection that the Irish Question has dogged him all his life: 'It has been the great misfortune of my life that I have never been able to escape from the Irish question. It was discussed round my cradle by a nurse whom my parents selected for her sound Protestant principles. The undertaker will give his views of the Irish question to his assistant while he drives the nails into the lid of my coffin.'[35] It is a fate of almost existential ubiquity and intensity.

Birmingham (i.e. Hannay) earned his worldliness and had good reasons for his cynicism. Born in Belfast and educated at Trinity College Dublin, he became, variously, Church of Ireland rector in Westport, Co. Mayo (resigned), canon of St Patrick's (Dublin), rector in Kildare, chaplain to the viceroy and to the British legation in Budapest, incumbent of a small parish in Carlow, Church of England rector in Somerset, and vicar in Kensington, London. Although he was an early member of the Gaelic League he offended nationalist sensibilities. Some kinds of nationalism at the time were unable to bear very much reality—whether it was Synge's in 1907 or, later, Brinsley MacNamara's or Sean O'Casey's—and those nationalisms were prepared to deny it, by physical force if necessary.[36] Two years before *Gossamer* appeared, a play of Birmingham's caused an uproar in Westport and resulted in the author's being burned in effigy and, a year later, being expelled from the League. When Digby muses on Irish nationalism, his creator knows whereof he speaks, yet his narration displays on the whole a good-natured equanimity. Birmingham's prose style, too, displays a plain lucidity reminiscent of H. G. Wells.

To speak of Digby's attention being 'engaged' is rather paradoxical since Digby is a man of almost mid-twentieth-century philosophical posture; he is self-effacing if worldly, companionable yet guarded, a sceptic by experience and an outsider by caste. Yet Digby is the product of the Irish times recorded in the country-house novels we have looked at, in which the decline of the household and estate has been due to the succession of land acts that reduced acreage and community fiefdom and therefore power and, at last, esteem. (As one observer wrote in early 1920, 'The old landocracy is gone, or is fast disappearing.')[37] The novel offers an unusual study of the more cultivated Anglo-Irish mind, however imaginary. Digby is for the most part resigned and fatalistic, even drolly so (his wit, perhaps, insulating him from the pain other landed gentry suffered), but on one occasion he thinks of the loss as nationalist depredation, a species of legalized robbery, though he is aware of the irony of his interest in a current business venture that might engage in a depredation just as legal and unjustified. A landless baronet now, having sold his small Co. Cork estate to his tenants, he cannot escape what ownership of the land had largely concealed: that most native Irish never regarded him as truly Irish at all. He doesn't demur. 'No definition of the Irish people has yet been framed which would include me' (p. 3). Exposed at last by his landlessness is his status as 'a man of no country' (p. 3); he is 'de-nationalized', his Irish nationalist friend Gorman says (p. 299) and Digby is almost relieved that such is the case.[38]

We will meet below in a later novel by Edith Somerville an Anglo-Irishman (also a war hero) who shares Digby's plight and who attempts to extricate himself by embracing a kind of local nationalism, whereas Digby simply extricates himself, full stop. In the months leading up to what began increasingly to look like imminent war in Ireland and in Europe, the narrator in his customary distance is besieged by pressures from without to support this or that cause. He enjoys his 'immunity from the fever of patriotism' (p. 1) but if his friend Carl Ascher suffered from the onset of patriotism at the outbreak of the Great War (we learn of these 1914 events later), Digby too has suffered, if only in body, having enlisted, despite his refusal of the idea that he was fighting for his country. He may have merited decoration but he cannot savour the consolation of feeling like a hero; still, in the midst of lethal Irish and European questions, he insists that he is a disinterested spectator 'of a game which my ancestors played and lost' (p. 47).

But he knows that this cannot be entirely true. Although his father was an active unionist, he himself has no political opinions of any sort, he claims, but in fact has what must surely be an Anglo-Irish suspicion of democracy, and he finds his Home Ruler friend Gorman's faith in parliamentary majorities 'extremely touching'; he may have next to no religion but does nurse a dislike of the Roman Catholic Church; he may be landless but he describes himself as an 'unrepentant landlord' nevertheless—no hand-wringing ingratiation or apologies for him, none of the 'desperate submission of a remnant' that a character in Rickard's *The Fire of Green Boughs* (1918) sees among the Kerry Anglo-Irish;[39] and he tries to cleave to the mindset of the gentleman, that species (he may be the last remaining specimen) whose extinction in Ireland he attributes to Gorman and his nationalist colleagues.[40] Like Riddell's Bernard Kelly in *Struggle for Fame*, Digby believes that Ireland's real desire is to be left alone and free from meddlesome 'solutionism' and that the thing to do is nothing, yet admits that were Gorman and his Home Rule friends to advocate such an abstentionist policy, he in turn would advocate some strenuous course of action, the obligation of the Irish gentleman being to thwart, ignore, or mock the 'notoriously corrupt and unscrupulous professional class' that politicians constitute (p. 25). By the same token, he cheerfully admits that his class is not cultured nor wishes to be (p. 24), and his relative philistinism allows him to defend the so-called materialism of the Belfast merchants and Ulster unionists (but with cultivated panache) and ponder the class-based self-deception of the Irish Literary Revivalists. He admits, moreover, that although he belongs 'by birth and education to an aristocracy, a class which is supposed to justify its existence by its altruism' (p. 26)—we have come across copious examples in the fiction of altruistic nobility—he has retreated into a courteous self-interest. Yet, in fact, he worries more than he admits and is engaged in the affairs of others, though strictly, he claims, in a personal capacity, showing interest in individuals but not in causes.

In short, Birmingham's personable narrator may be a man of no country but he is a man of two worlds: comporting himself outside the borders of Society but knowing he has the right of entry and prepared to exercise it once in a while. He declares in upper-class tones what is a 'Protestant' and 'unionist' equivalent of Stephen Dedalus's *non serviam* though without the melodrama of young Dedalus's earnest declaration, melodrama not being an option in Digby's cultural repertoire.

Digby's lengthy retrospection begins on board a Cunard steamer to New York en route to Montreal and thence Vancouver to examine the companies in which he has invested. His financial portfolio has superseded the management of his estate, but in fact apart from a brief side trip to Canada, the first half of the novel takes place in New York, because Digby meets on board an Irish Nationalist MP (going to the United States to drum up support for Home Rule) and an apparently Jewish–English (but in reality German) millionaire financier based in New York and whose activities in that city detain Digby when he becomes fascinated by business and banking. Ascher's firm, it turns out, weaves a worldwide web of investment and credit and when he learns of its extent, Digby thinks it composes a romantic epic and that

neither the wanderings of Ulysses nor the discoveries of a traveller through Paradise and Purgatory make so splendid an appeal to the imagination as this vastly complex machine which Ascher and men like him guide. The oceans of the world are covered thick with ships. Long freight trains wind like serpents across continents. Kings build navies. Ploughmen turn up the clay. The wheels of factories go round. The minds of men bend nature to their purposes by fresh inventions. Science creeps forward inch by inch. Human beings everywhere eat, drink, and reproduce themselves. The myriad activities of the whole wide world go profitably on. They can go on only because the Aschers, sitting at their office desks in London or New York, make scratches with their pens on bits of paper. (p. 31)

Since the key to Digby's character is his freedom from illusion and anachronism, it would make little sense for his hymn to finance to be ironic, and it is repeated thrice more (pp. 99, 135, 299), even more eloquently. Indeed, although Digby countenances Gorman's view of financiers as mysterious tyrants whose extensions of international credit give them 'untempered power' he yet claims that an epic can be written round a devil as greatly as round a hero, Milton having shown us that. But Digby cannot accept Gorman's opinion. In any case, Gorman becomes involved in the commercializing of his own nephew's brilliant cash register invention, Gorman (nationalist MP, playwright, journalist) having in him, according to Digby, a mixture of the religious soul, artistic soul, and business soul. For bankers and financiers do for Digby have a soul as well as constituting in the aggregate a great profession on a par with ecclesiastics, surgeons, dentists, and lawyers, all with their own mysteries, argot, and accoutrements.

The romance of international financiers grows on Digby as he muses on how 'coded telegrams fluttered from their hands and went vibrating across thousands of miles of land or through the still depths of the oceans, over unlighted tracts of ooze on the sea-bottom. In London the words were read and men set free pent-up, dammed streams of money. In Hong-Kong the words were read and some steamer went out, laden, from her harbour. Gold was poured into the hands of tea-planters in Ceylon. Scanty wages in strange coins dribbled out to factory workers in Russian cotton-mills. Gangs of navvies went to work laying railway lines across the veldt in Bechuana Land.'[41] Native Ireland in *Gossamer* has pretty much escaped the coils of finance as it escaped the coils of Roman law and the coils of Renaissance culture, though even the prices that bullocks from lonely bogland vicinities fetch, or do not fetch, at local markets for Irish farmers depend, at the end of a long chain, on 'what the Aschers in their offices said and did' (p. 100). Digby muses on the curious and mysterious complexities of gossamer threads that floated and webbed the gorse and grass of his former fields in autumn and begins to see their usefulness as metaphors for Ascher's activities, 'covering every civilised land with a web of credit, infinitely complex' (p. 132), a web that the outbreak of the Great War tears before spinners of the threads were at work again, mending and fastening. When war is declared, Ascher faces the dilemma of returning to Germany to fight for the Fatherland or remain at his desk, ensuring that the gossamer of international finance remains intact. When he decides against a return to Germany from London (where the second half of the novel is set), Digby supports him, believing that the business Ascher is engaged in is human and not merely English or German, the white man's or the yellow man's, the Christian's or the Mohammedan's, and that such business exacts loyalty and requires its own ethic.

Ascher's demotion of patriotism is in contrast with Gorman's promotion of it, since for the latter patriotism is, or affects to be, all-demanding. Digby tells him that were Gorman as thoroughgoing a nationalist as he makes out, he would style himself O'Gorabhainm or at the very least, O'Gorman. But despite an obsessive patriotism that has curtailed his career as a playwright or novelist, and despite his liking nothing better than talking about Ireland as an oppressed and desolate land, Gorman is in fact a constitutional nationalist, a Home Rule campaigner of the Redmondite variety (though John Redmond, historical leader of the Irish Nationalist Party, goes unmentioned in the novel). Gorman deplores what became known as the the Curragh Incident and the gunrunning by Ulster unionists, both of which are recorded in the novel, and although like many nationalists he thought that the Ulster resisters to Home Rule had set a paramilitary example for nationalists to follow, he supports what was Redmond's attempt to convert the National Volunteers to the constitutional cause of Home Rule (p. 213). In the end, Gorman proves himself a democrat and realist, for on the outbreak of war he is content to accept the committing of Irish troops to the war effort and postponement of the application of the Home Rule Bill, in return for the expected English gratitude after the War in the shape of complete and immediate Home Rule.[42] (In the historic event, rejectionist ringleaders among the National Volunteers, who renamed themselves the Irish Volunteers, diverted nationalist energy into republicanism and the Easter rebellion of 1916, thereby, it is arguable, violently rupturing Irish constitutional progress.)

Digby is amiably disposed towards Gorman, despite the clash of their respective philosophies, and it is two different but related kinds of nationalism for which Digby reserves a sharper mockery and derision. Musing on Mrs Ascher's contempt for money, Digby is sure that 'it is only those who are very rich indeed, or those who are on the outer fringe of extreme poverty, who can despise money in this whole-hearted way' (p. 92). Mrs Ascher falls into the first category but Digby has overlooked W. B. Yeats and his fellow Revivalists who were not rich yet despised money, at least as a goal if not as a means of advancing their cause. (Some Revivalists of high social standing, such as Lady Gregory, Douglas Hyde, and Horace Plunkett, were hardly impoverished.)

Mrs Ascher, a sculptress, is a foreign Celtophile and aggressive enthusiast of strenuous Irish republicanism of a kind that even nowadays is not extinct; had the novel continued she would no doubt have been ecstatic over Easter 1916. She exults that Rome and the Renaissance passed Ireland by and that Ireland 'has not bowed the knee to our modern fetish of education'. She believes it is Digby, not she, who is the foreigner in the land of Irish spirit; like many such enthusiasts, then and now, she despises Belfast that in its materialism 'stands for all that is vilest and most hateful in the world. It is worse than Glasgow, worse than Manchester, worse than Birmingham'. Digby with all the irony of a faint and courteous effort attempts to defend the honour of Belfast and its manufacturing accomplishments but for Mrs Ascher the whole Irish Question is a struggle 'between a people to whom art is an ideal and a people who have accepted materialism and money for their gods, an atheist people'. She shows Digby her sculpture of a female figure with her foot on a hairy, prick-eared, pig-like creature that Gorman deems 'emblematic' and 'symbolical', and Digby mischievously guesses its subject: 'The Irish party trampling on Belfast'; it is in fact 'The spirit of poetry in Ireland defying materialism'. Both the sculptress and Gorman believe that the Ulster unionists are bluffing in their threat to defy Home Rule and must be weak because they are contemptible. Digby's acquaintance, Malcolmson is such a unionist and an organizer of imminent military resistance, so when Gorman insists that Ulster will not be allowed to exclude itself from Home Rule, the narrator replies sardonically: 'Well, it's your affair, not mine. I mean to stay in London and keep safe; but I warn you that if the spirit of poesy attempts to triumph utterly over

Malcolmson he'll shoot at it. I know him and you don't. You think he's a long-eared pig but that ought to make you all the more careful. Pigs are noted for their obstinacy.'[43]

Mrs Ascher wishes to intervene with her money and her art in a fashion that recalls Yeats's Countess Cathleen, of whom Mrs Ascher is a kind of *nouveau riche* satirical embodiment. (There's a touch of Kathleen Ni Houlihan and Maud Gonne about her, too.) At one point, Countess-like, she unclasps her necklace and takes the rings from her fingers and flings them on the ground before Gorman: 'More', she cries, 'you must have more.' She sings the praises of the Irish Players and sees its theatre as 'the single example in the modern world of peasant art, from the soil, of the soil, redolent, fragrant of the simple life of men and women, in direct touch with the primal forces of nature itself. There is nothing else quite like those players and their plays. They are the self-revelation of the peasant soul. From the white-washed cabins of the country-side, from the streets of tiny, world-forgotten villages, from the islands where the great Atlantic thunders ceaselessly, these have come to call us back to the realities of life, to express again the eternal verities of art.' Digby replies, but in weariness only to himself, that it is silly to talk about white-washed cottages and the self-revelation of peasant souls. 'Neither the dramatists nor the players are peasants, or ever were. They are very clever, sometimes more than clever, members of the educated classes, who see the peasants from the outside just as I see them, as Mrs Ascher would see them if she ever got near enough to what she calls the soil to see a peasant at all.' And when, still in a white heat of enthusiasm, she praises the splendid efforts to rescue and preserve the national language in defiance of materialism and in pursuit of a purely spiritual ideal, Digby is forced to speak aloud: 'Nobody ever heard of the Irish-speaking peasants taking the smallest interest in the language. The whole revival business is the work of an English-speaking middle class, who never stop asking the Government to pay them for doing it.'[44]

Digby describes himself as 'a plain man. The only thing I really admire is common sense' (p. 88). This assertion would normally signal an ironic gap between novelist and narrator, and one's suspicion might be deepened when Digby tells us that he and Gorman find art, drama, and music far less interesting than banking, 'a fascinatingly interesting subject' (p. 24). Yet Digby's gradual understanding of what we now call globalism and the virtuality of credit and other financial transactions through technology is genuine and convincing. (When Ascher explains the inherent dangers of credit and the vital importance of market confidence, he anticipates the Wall Street crash that occurred fifteen years later.) Moreover, Digby's understanding was in contemporary Irish terms dissident, since the thrust of the Irish Revival was anti-capitalist, nationalistic and protectionist economically, culturally, and politically (Sinn Fein: 'Ourselves'). It has also proven to be prescient, globalism and virtuality having expanded extraordinarily in the late twentieth century developed world. Ironically, the recent economic 'miracle' witnessed in the Republic of Ireland from the middle 1990s has been attributed to the wholesale extension of credit, technological access to the global market, and the profitable near-fetishizing of education that Mrs Ascher deplores.[45] Birmingham's novel is another example of a fictional Ireland that has closer relations in reality to the multifarious Ireland of the present than that of the otherwise justly celebrated literature of the Revival. Digby's tempered treatment of the Great War, being fought even as Birmingham was commending it to paper, also anticipates more faithfully the equable attitude to the conflict that is emerging in Catholic Ireland today.

NOTES

1. Symons, *Bloody Murder: From the Detective Story to the Crime Novel* (London: Faber and Faber, 1972), p. 221. He believes Childers's novel was the 'first spy story with any literary pretensions' (p. 224).

2. Erskine Childers, *The Riddle of the Sands: A Record of Secret Service* (London: Sigwick & Jackson, 1927 [reset 1931]), p. 2. The original subtitle was *A Record of Secret Service Recently Achieved,* but the adverbial phrase was dropped as time went on, and editions of the novel have appeared without any subtitle.

3. Shane Leslie, *The End of a Chapter* (London: Constable, 1918), pp. 120, 189–90. In fact, criticisms of the Admiralty were routine as early as 1898 (see 'The British Ship of War', *Contemporary Review,* vol. 73) and in that same year an article in the *Contemporary Review* (vol. 74), identified 'The Arch-Enemy of England' as the German Emperor (or Kaiser). Rivalry in armaments between the two powers heated up after 1908 and by 1910 an article entitled 'The Danger of an Anglo-German War' was no longer provocative; E. M. Forster wove the theme into his reconciliatory novel, *Howards End,* published that same year.

4. See T. J. Binyon's review of Jim Ring's *Erskine Childers* (1996), *Times Literary Supplement,* 24 May 1996: 32; see also Preface to *The Riddle of the Sands,* pp. vii–viii.

5. Hugh and Robin Popham (eds.), *A Thirst for the Sea: The Sailing Adventures of Erskine Childers* (London: Stanford Maritime, 1979), p. 7.

6. According to Binyon, Childers back in London turned his letters home from South Africa into the book (*Times Literary Supplement,* 24 May 1996: 32), whereas according to Hugh and Robin Popham, the letters he wrote to his sisters were turned by a Mrs Thompson (with the sisters' complicity) into a book without his knowledge: *A Thirst for the Sea,* p. 2. Childers later wrote the fifth volume of the *Times History of the War in South Africa.*

7. Erskine Childers, *In the Ranks of the C.I.V.: A Narrative and Diary of Personal Experiences with the C.I.V. Battery (Honourable Artillery Company) in South Africa* (London: Smith, Elder & Co., 1900), pp. 249, 129, 226.

8. Two years before *The Riddle of the Sands* appeared, Arnold White took to task the British powers that be for running an inefficient empire, including a flabby navy, while 'German efficiency has already secured a formidable and homogeneous fleet': *Efficiency and Empire* (1901; Brighton: Harvester Press, 1973), p. 275. According to White's 1973 editor, it was a sequence of three British defeats at the hands of Boer irregulars in December 1899 that provoked a debate in Britain on 'National Efficiency' (p. vii).

9. Childers, *German Influence on British Cavalry* (London: Edward Arnold, 1911), p. iv.

10. Such circumstances repeated themselves in the 1930s when many well-born Englishmen (or Britons)—including the real-life Lord Londonderry and Kazuo Ishiguro's fictional Lord Darlington (in *The Remains of the Day*, 1988)—found that their admiration for German regeneration through efficiency after the humiliation of Versailles slid into pro-Germanism and even blindness to Hitlerite ambition.

11. Childers, *The Riddle of the Sands*, pp. 72, 112–13. The Irish would become such a race, and he could claim to be an Anglo-Irishman. But as to his love of sailing and the sea, Childers thought the race relevant to himself was the English, and he thought he saw in himself 'some hereditary predisposition to the sea' peculiar to Englishmen: Hugh and Robin Popham, *A Thirst for the Sea*, p. 8.

12. Hugh and Robin Popham, *A Thirst for the Sea*, pp. 19–20.

13. Binyon, *Times Literary Supplement*, 24 May 1996: 32.

14. In some cases the direction of allegiance reversed itself, as in the cases of Charles Gavan Duffy (later *Sir* Charles) and D'Arcy McGee who became prominent constitutional politicians and representatives who disavowed their prior revolutionary participation.

15. A sizeable collection of such stories can be found in I. F. Clarke (ed.), *The Tale of the Next Great War, 1871–1914: Fictions of Future Warfare and of Battles Still-to-Come* (1995). The idea of Germany as the threat and aggressor had its early beginnings in the German successes in the Franco-German war of 1870. The invasion of England was both a fictional and nonfictional spin-off from the German preoccupation. Max Nordau, in the words of Bergonzi, considered 'a preoccupation with the future as symptomatic of the *fin de siècle* mentality', which strengthens Bergonzi's classification of 1890s science fiction as end-of-the-century work: *The Early H. G. Wells* (Toronto: University of Toronto Press, 1961), p. 35. If the coming war was imagined to be in the distant future, then the writer was writing science fiction; if it were imagined as imminent, the writer was writing a kind of cautionary realism.

16. A bizarre political fantasy which has the apparatus of science fiction is the slightly earlier *A Modern Daedalus* (1887) by the Co. Down writer, Tom Greer. The war in this case is the Anglo-Irish war and the time is the present which, however, is

'futurized' by the depicted fantasy. The story purports to be the reminiscences of one John O'Halloran, whose discovery of the means of flight enables him to lead the Irish to total victory over the English in 1886, interrupting Parnell's parliamentary struggle in order to do so. The wish-fulfilment of O'Halloran's physical-force nationalism and his introduction to the world of aerial warfare and to Ireland of guerilla warfare (learned from the Boers) sit strangely with Greer's Anglophile Preface and the confessed unionism of O'Halloran himself. According to Stephen J. Brown (*Ireland in Fiction*, p. 119), Greer was a Liberal Home Ruler who unsuccessfully contested North Derry in 1892. The novel is anti-Tory and pro-Parnell but otherwise unstable in poltical viewpoint.

17. Robert Cromie, *The Next Crusade* (London: Hutchinson, 1896), pp. 13, 45, 46, 49, 70, 73. In the wake of 11 September 2001, the novel has a grim relevance it would not have had since 1945.

18. 'M. P. Shiel: Master of Fantasy', obituary (attributed to John Gawsworth) in *The Times*, 20 February 1947: see http://www.alangullette.com/lit/shiel/essays/ShielO-bituaryTimes.htm

19. So delighted was Shiel's father in the birth of his first son that he crowned him King of Redonda, an uninhabited West Indian island. Shiel was succeeded as King by John Gawsworth (King Juan I); the present King is the Spanish novelist Javier Marias who has used his throne to raise A. S. Byatt, Pierre Bourdieu, John Ashbery, and others to the Redondan peerage: see Phil Baker, 'The Apostle of Wonder', *Times Literary Supplement*, 29 April 2005: 25.

20. See the previously cited review, and in addition the *Manchester Guardian* review of *Prince Zaleski*, transcribed at http://www.alangullette.com/lit/shiel/essays/guardian_prince_zaleski.htm

21. Shiel recalled that when he began as a writer in London he got to know 'the literary people' who included Wilde, Ella D'Arcy, George Egerton, Henry Harland, and Ernest Dowson, all associated with *The Yellow Book*: 'Of Myself' in Shiel, *Science, Life and Literature* (London: Williams and Norgate, 1950), p. 21. One wonders if another essay in Shiel's volume, 'Of Writing', written around 1909 and 'Originally addressed to a Mrs. Meade of Kensington' (p. 58) was in fact written first to L. T. Meade.

22. See his entry in John M. Reilly (ed.), *Twentieth-Century Crime and Mystery Writers* (New York: St Martin's Press, 1985).

23. David G. Hartwell, Introduction to *The Purple Cloud* (Boston: Gregg Press, 1977), p. v.

24. I discuss the novel more fully inside that context in *The Age of* Titanic, pp. 126–33.

25. Lord Charles Beresford, 'The Future of the Anglo-Saxon Race', *North American Review*, 171 (1900): 802–10. The much decorated and honoured Sir Robert Hart (1835–1911) was born in Portadown and the family moved soon after to Lisburn. He was educated at a Wesleyan school in Somerset and (from the age of 15) at Queen's College Belfast. He left for China in 1854 when he was 19 and did not return for good until 1908, though he returned for a visit to Lisburn and Portadown. He married Hester Bredon of Portadown. He was made baronet in 1893.

In the 1960s when I was an impoverished student at Queen's University (as Queen's College had become), I was grateful to receive the Sir Robert Hart scholarship, not knowing until recently to whom I was indebted for this modest life-saver. Like Hart, I read English literature and philosophy at Queen's which may have been a term of the scholarship.

26. Patrick MacGill, *The Amateur Army* (London: Herbert Jenkins, 1915), p. 15. MacGill refers to 'God Save the King' as 'our' anthem (p. 41).

27. MacGill, *The Red Horizon* (1916; London: Caliban Books, 1984), pp. 300–6.

28. Ibid., pp. 61, 176–82, 252.

29. Patrick MacGill, *The Great Push: An Episode of the Great War* (London: Herbert Jenkins, 1916), p. 85.

30. The poem of MacGill's that serves as epigraph to Chapter 1, 'In the Advance Trenches', echoes in its beginning the poignant, nostalgic, yet jaunty and carefree note of A. E. Housman: 'Now when we take the cobbled road | We often took before, | Our thoughts are with the hearty lads | Who tread that way no more.'

31. Michael MacDonagh, *The Irish at the Front* (London: Hodder and Stoughton, 1916), pp. 123–4.

32. Lord Dunsany, *Tales of War* (Boston: Little, Brown and Company, 1918), p. 120.

33. Ibid., pp. 26, 44, 45, 57, 72, 75, 107.

34. For bringing to my attention *Gossamer* as well as *The Golden Rose* by Katharine Tynan and *The Ladies' Road* by Pamela Hinkson, I am grateful to Keith Jeffrey's article, 'Irish Prose Writers of the First World War', in Kathleen Devine (ed.), *Modern Irish Writers and the Wars* (Gerrards Cross: Colin Smythe, 1999), pp. 1–17.

35. George A. Birmingham, *Gossamer* (London: Methuen, 1915), p. 164. *Gossamer* appeared in Methuen's 'Popular Novels' series, along with Conrad's *Victory*, Wells's *Bealby*, Bennett's *A Great Man*, and Lawrence's *The Rainbow*.

36. The riotous behaviour of the audience during a staging of Synge's *The Playboy of the Western World* in 1907 is notorious. Brinsley MacNamara's novel *The Valley of the Squinting Windows* (1918) was publicly burned and the author's family boycotted and harassed. Sean O'Casey's *The Plough and the Stars* provoked a riot at the Abbey Theatre in 1926. Yeats famously defended O'Casey, but later exercised his own nationalist censorship when he rejected O'Casey's play *The Silver Tassie* (1926) on the trumped-up grounds that O'Casey did not know his material (the Great War) intimately, when it is more likely that Yeats simply did not wish Irish artists to deal sympathetically with the War (or perhaps any artists, recalling his attitude to Wilfred Owen in his Oxford anthology of 1936). Later occasions of nationalist fury at Irish artists were reduced by the precautionary supervision of the Irish Censorship Board set up in 1929, itself a bureaucratically nationalist body. That did not prevent John McGahern's suffering harassment and dismissal from his position as a schoolmaster when his novel, *The Dark* (1965) slipped through the loosening censorship net.

37. 'Ignotus', 'Irish Realities', *Blackwood's Edinburgh Magazine* 207 (March 1920): 347.

38. *Gossamer*, pp. 3, 299. Digby's landlessness in a sense reduces him to the status of the Northern or Ulster-Scots Protestants: besieged by nationalists, deprived of the

common name of Irishmen—not that most of them have wished it—men and women of no real country. Digby seems in this regard like a mouthpiece for Hannay, the Northern Protestant.

39. Mrs Victor Rickard, *The Fire of Green Boughs* (1918; New York: Dodd, Mead and Company, 1919), p. 158.

40. Birmingham, *Gossamer*, pp. 145, 3, 17, 47.

41. Ibid., pp. 99–100. I discuss the contemporary convergence of technology, finance, and romance in *The Age of* Titanic, especially in chs. 1 and 6.

42. For a succinct history of the background to this portion of the novel, see R. F. Foster, *Modern Ireland 1600–1972* (London: Penguin, 1989), pp. 461–76.

43. Birmingham, *Gossamer*, pp. 126, 161, 164, 206, 208. On the belief of some politicians that Ulster unionists were bluffing, see Patrick Maume, *The Long Gestations: Irish Nationalist Life 1891–1918* (Dublin: Gill & Macmillan, 1999), p. 132.

44. Birmingham, *Gossamer*, pp. 209, 166, 166, 167.

45. See David McWilliams, *The Pope's Children: Ireland's New Elite* (2005).

14

'This Sharp, Bitter Cleavage': War and the Rising

CHANGING FORTUNES

It would have been impossible for, say, Lord Dunsany to have transferred his allegiance from the British Army to Sinn Fein, but this is what Harold Firbank does in *The Fortune: A Romance of Friendship* (1917) by Douglas Goldring. Firbank's conversion loosely resembles Goldring's own experience. Goldring was born in 1887 in Greenwich and spent his early years in Brighton before entering Oxford after which he went to London in 1907 where he became an editor with *Country Life* and a sub-editor under Ford Madox Ford at the *English Review*. He enlisted in 1914 but was invalided out, and turned conscientious objector. He became a 'propaganda novelist' (someone who wrote problem-novels with a forthright ideology) and travelled to Dublin to investigate the events of Easter Week. He set out to meet the Irish, met his future wife, discovered Irish nationalist sympathies, and wrote *The Fortune* which was published by Maunsel. He traced his Irish connection in *Odd Man Out: The Autobiography of a 'Propaganda Novelist'* (1935) and in a chapter, 'Irish Influences', in *The Nineteen Twenties: A General Survey and Some Personal Memories* (1945), which begins with his going to live in Yeats's old apartment in London on his return to England after his Irish sojourn.

In his Introduction to its 1931 republication, Goldring called *The Fortune* 'this amateurish, outmoded novel', but it is a sprawling *Künstlerroman* of genuine interest, and Aldous Huxley, who supplied a Preface to the 1931 edition, claimed that it is 'the earliest, indeed the only contemporary, fictional account of War-time pacifism'.[1] Goldring identified two of Wells's pre-War novels as 'coming war' novels that foresaw the Great War—*In the Days of the Comet* (1906) and *The World Set Free* (1914)—but was disappointed that whereas Wells in those works condemned the imminent conflict (in the first novel specifying the war between Germany and England), he changed his tune when the real conflict began. Wells is one of the writers (Chesterton is another) Goldring took to task in 'After Fourteen Years', his 1931 Author's Introduction to *The Fortune*.

Towards the end of the novel, when Harold Firbank is a British soldier in Dublin putting down the rebellion and exhausted in the midst of battle, he recalls the chief events of his life, from English public school onwards, a useful summary for the critic: 'beginning with Stannington, all the various stages of his life came before his mind—Oxford, his home at Wesport [Lancashire], his failure in the Civil Service Examination, his "Bohemian" period with Violet Falconer, his years of waiting in Brussels while he was writing his play, then London and Peter [Petronella, the Irish girl whom he married], the success of *The Fortune* [his play], his marriage, the war, the birth of his son' (p. 341). And always, the presence and influence of James Murdoch from the Irish country house in Rathfarnham, Mount Dore, with whom he attends school and Oxford, and clearly the fictional representative of 'The Influence', an unidentified figure recalled in *Odd Man Out*. The relationship between James and Harold is the deepest in the novel and beyond Murdoch's political sway (he is a conscientious objector and at his tribunal in England waived the exemption his Irish residence would have entitled him) there would seem to be a suppressed sexual attraction on Harold's unilateral side.

Goldring almost inevitably retraces the steps of the mainstream novelists. The novel opens in Mount Dore which looks towards another eighteenth-century Big House, Weston Park, nicknamed 'The Fortune'—so-called because Murdoch's great-grandfather married an Irish heiress called Lucretia O'Reilly—which the Murdoch family left when it burned down. Firbank in Ireland means that the novel joins the 'English-visitor-to-Ireland' sub-genre. Firbank himself lives in a suburban villa in Lancashire, the son of The Revd Pennington Firbank and whose sister Agatha is a Girton College, Cambridge graduate and feminist. At Oxford Firbank runs with the 'Decadents', a group of neo-Aesthetes, examples of the *rechauffé* Nineties Aesthetes Shane Leslie remarked on, and which warming-over we have already met in the novels of Filson Young, James Douglas, Ella MacMahon, Katherine Cecil Thurston, and W. M. Letts.[2] In London, while writing his play and his novel, Firbank meets Petronella (Peter) Stapledon and the Irish connection is strengthened.

The Stapledons are unionists but 'Peter' has an aunt of Home Rule persuasion under whose sway Harold gradually falls. Meanwhile Firbank, who had been a member of the OTC (Officers Training Corps) at Oxford (he suffers split allegiances), becomes a captain in the 'Hallamshires' on the outbreak of the war and is posted to the front where he sees action, is wounded by a sniper, and is sent to London and then Somerset to convalesce, finding himself in the process becoming a conscientious objector. (Like Siegfried Sassoon in convalescence, Firbank assails the 'hidebound boobyism' of the ruling caste that is running, and ruining, the War; they are Victorians, at sea in the warfare of the modern world, despite their gentlemanliness, courage, and unselfishness.) There is an illuminating depiction of the Tribunal Appeals Court Murdoch appears at (after which he returns to Ireland), a scene marred by the kind of casual anti-Semitism that is routine in many of the novels we have looked at.

The culture of World War I conscientious objection is well evoked and if we wish to fill out Goldring's picture, we might read *After Ten Years: A Personal Record* (1931) by Constance Malleson (1895–1975), who grew up as Lady Constance Annesley in Castlewellan House, Co. Down, daughter of Hugh, 5th Earl Annesley. Malleson was the mistress for many years of Bertrand Russell (one of the few intellectual contemporaries to escape Goldring's retrospective wrath) and a friend of Lady Ottoline Morrell and Gilbert Cannan. Although her husband Miles Malleson joined the City of London Fusiliers on the outbreak of the Great War, and though her brother Brongie joined the Naval Air Force (and was shot down over Belgium), she opposed conscription and moved in pacifist circles while her sister Clare was a Suffragist; her husband was invalided home from abroad and later faced a Tribunal as a conscientious objector.[3] Goldring claims that the theme of anti-War sentiment caused *The Fortune* to be suppressed, though he does not say how it was suppressed.[4]

Mended, Firbank arrives in Ireland in 1916 to visit James and take up a War Office posting in the Curragh. He is under the familiar spell of Ireland and though Firbank becomes an officer engaged in suppressing the Easter Rebellion, his heart is not in it; 'He was part of a machine which he had come to hate.'[5] He has caused his own misfortune by not following James in conscientious objection; the title of his play, *The Fortune*, now rings ironically; but there is no way back: 'He was part of the machine now, he would never be able to get out of it till peace was declared.' The rebellion itself is 'crack-brained' but could be quelled amicably through English magnanimity even as it was waging; once again, brutal English stupidity was losing the day (pp. 339–40). He himself is shot by one of his own men as a rebel spy. The last chapter includes references to 'the saintly Pearse, poor Joseph Plunkett' and Firbank's widow as a result of what happens rediscovers the depth of her own Irishness, so that Firbank's conversion is posthumously completed. Although Goldring's pro-Irishness seems firm, he is not otherwise easy to pin down, despite George Orwell's naming of him as a suspicious crypto-Communist. He described himself variously as 'a libertarian, Little Englander, pacifist and someone with leftwing views'.[6] The sprawling nature of his novel accords with the instability of its political angle of view, but it is indisputably a 'modern' novel, a novel of the twentieth century, like the novels of Filson Young, despite its promiscuous use of themes, settings, and motifs we have already encountered.

Changing Winds (1917) by St John Ervine is also a modern novel, despite its bagginess and essentially three-decker structure, and crosses some of the same turbulent terrain as *The Fortune*. A group of young talented friends are buffeted by the cross-winds of public events, ideas, and movements, which have their violent double-headed apotheosis in the Great War and the Easter Rebellion. Henry Quinn, an Ulster Protestant, makes three close friends at an English public school and after attending Trinity College Dublin resumes their friendship in London where he becomes a successful novelist (and his friend Gilbert a successful playwright). Since Quinn writes a novel entitled *The Wayward Man* (the title of an Ervine novel published ten years later) we are tempted to see a good deal of personal fact in *Changing Winds*. Clouds gather in Ireland: the resistance to Home Rule by the drilling UVF, the Curragh Mutiny, the rise of Sinn Fein and the National Volunteers. At first these do not impinge on Quinn, buffeted as he is more immediately by his love affairs and bedevilled by his anxious fear that he is a coward (for which his first serious lover, Sheila Morgan, an Antrim farm girl, repudiates him). The 'sex-question' preoccupies him—how can one practise 'sex-equality'? Shouldn't one seek infinite variety in women and love? How emotionally open ('sloppy') should one be, or how 'close'? (Really, how should one live? And—as it transpires—die?)[7]

Ervine has accurately captured in Quinn the deep ambivalence and way-wardness of the Ulster Protestant, who loves England and Ireland, but does not always love England and does not always love Ireland, who is a unionist whose love of Ireland can nonetheless become support for Home Rule. (And who is not the missing but the ever-present link between England and Ireland.) But the Home Rule Quinn envisages is very different from that of his old tutor John Marsh, Sinn Fein republican and Gaelic revivalist. Quinn's admiration for Tom Arthurs of Harland & Wolff shipyard—likely a portrait of William (Lord) Pirrie—and Belfast's engineering achievements suggests one more among the practical reforms of the island Quinn has in mind: the improvement of elementary education; The encouragement of trades union-ism; the broadening of community service; the reorganizing of the railways and communications; the combatting of the priests ('Catholicism is Death'), publicans, politicians, and poets (i.e. seeking freedom from the bondage of religion, drink, history, and romance), reforms of the kind the all-Irelanders Pirrie and Filson Young, another Protestant from Ulster, envisioned.[8] It is a kind of Home Rule in practice that does not entirely nullify Irish unionism and it was a common, if now forgotten, position of the time.

But such reform, no doubt stimulated into life in any case by the advance of Sinn Fein, is pre-empted by the Easter Rising which Quinn witnesses in Dublin where he has gone to get his papers in order before marriage to an

English girl, and which Ervine gives us a lively depiction of at the close of the novel. But all along, Quinn's ideas and resolutions are dogged by his fear of cowardice. In contrast is John Marsh who is killed as a leader of the rebellion, deluded but brave. Then there are Quinn's friends Gilbert Farlow and Ninian Graham (the latter from a Devonshire country house, Boveyhayne Manor, where scenes of the novel take place) who enlisted when War broke out and are killed. The War has transformed almost everyone and made heroes democratically of the least likely, such as Lady Cecily's husband and Gilbert and Sheila Morgan's husband. His friends have sacrificed themselves to something bigger than themselves, and this is what Quinn has always been unable to do, splashing about as he has done in the shallows of life.[9] In the end, returning from Dublin to England, he resolves to marry and then enlist and is sure he will be killed. It is a literary touch suggestive of bravado that Ervine might not have intended and does not quite capture the bravery or determination the ending might seem to require.[10]

Ervine has brief portraits of Dublin and London slums and assigns some harsh words on the Charity Organisation Society with its Care Committees to Rachel Wynne, who sees hard women badgering the poor and who would have been 'Inquisitors if they'd been born in Spain when there were Inquisitors'; she'd like to 'inquisit' Mrs Smeale, the Devonshire Mayor's wife.[11] But the Great War represented a momentous climax, crowning years, for the (chiefly female) philanthropic movement, to which an interesting novel by David Lyall set partly in Ireland, *An English Rose* (1918), testifies. This novel, like *The Fortune* and *Changing Winds*, draws on the Easter Rising to provide an exciting climax as well as a crucible for national and emotional allegiance.

ROSES AND LIME

Although published a year after those two novels, *An English Rose* is clearly an Edwardian, not a post-War novel, even though it also drew upon the insurrection at Easter 1916 to provide a found climax. But in the case of *An English Rose*, the reader is induced to regret the insurrection and to hope that Irish energy will be redirected to the allied cause in the Great War and that 'the spell of Ireland', that 'witchery, an enchantment, something in the air of Ireland', prove to be a benign one. Lyall reverses the direction of sentiment in *The Fortune* through the redemptive grace, the beauty, good nature, and capacity for love of the English girl-rose of the title.[12] *An English Rose* is a popular romance subjected to the strains of the First World War, a charming story that lacks Goldring's ambitious, nervous seriousness, and it comes as no surprise to learn that the author's real name was Annie S. Swan (1859–1943), a popular Scottish novelist of startling prolificness and contemporary middle-brow reputation.

Like *The Fortune* and other works we have looked at, *An English Rose* is a country-house novel in which there are no fewer than five houses that function, as we now realize they do in these novels, as themselves crucibles for social identities, for the tension between conservatism and change. The English rose herself, Cicely Marsham, is of a family that had to leave its family estate in Hertfordshire, Lesterford Park, and has slid down the social scale into comfortable Streatham suburbia ('Suburbans of the suburban!' Cicely calls her family), that social metathesis that Forster dissected with distaste in *Howards End*, observing London's creeping suburbia with alarm and locating the country house of his title likewise in Hertfordshire, for him the symbolic heart of England. But before *An English Rose* is over, Cicely—having become Lady Steering under peculiar circumstances—sets about the regeneration of Steering Hall and Deverills Manor (amalgamated country seats) also in Hertfordshire, and indeed of Mullamore as well, an Irish country house neglected by its absentee owner, The O'Rourke, too busy fighting for the Foreign Legion and planning Irish rebellion to care for his estates in Ireland.

The peculiar circumstances are these: Cicely Marsham, a 22-year-old rest-less beauty, unversed in love and eager to contribute to the war effort, accompanies her aunt, Lady Winyard, to France as a Volunteer Aid worker, tending the wounded in a French country house, the Chateau Coeur la Reine, on behalf of the Red Cross. Here is the real and fictional adaptability of the country house, its ready assimilation by the popular novelists to war fiction. Marsham begins as an amateur volunteer but quickly becomes one of the 'experts at wounded heroes' whom Goldring describes in *The Fortune*. In the chateau she meets two convalescing French Foreign Legionnaires, one Irish ('Dennis Kane' who turns out to be The O'Rourke) and one English ('Steering' who turns out to be Lord Steering). Cicely is wounded alongside Steering in a stray German aeroplane attack; before he dies he asks her to marry him, and though she feels nothing for him that way she consents out of self-sacrificial compassion of the kind war nurtures; she discovers on his death that she has become Lady Steering. It seems Steering has engineered his death bed marriage to redeem his previous dissoluteness; he has been a family black sheep with 'all the bad blood of his race in his veins without the courage to fight it'; by the time Cicely meets him, his jaw lacks strength and his face the lineaments of moral fibre despite the fact that his body movements suggest 'public school games strenuously played, hard riding to hounds, all the virile sports of a race whose youthful training the war has justified (pp. 90, 25).

Cicely's consent is an unwitting intervention in the downward trajectory of the Steering heredity (Cicely's three brothers have all enlisted and are splendid fellows) and the mechanism of inheritance is dramatically telescoped into a quarter of an hour during which time Cicely has to decide whether she will become the wife of a dying man about whom she knows next to nothing.[13]

Peacetime fictional forces and themes beyond the country-house setting were conscripted by novelists responding to the Great War. One is the connection of self-sacrifice with the essential nature of a woman. Under the circumstances of the War this connection had to be extended to incorporate young men, whose daily and often lethal self-sacrifice was only too apparent. Familiar female charity continues (Cicely's sister Ann is secretary to a rich Streatham woman 'who has a regular organised system of giving to charities'), but the War represented a vivid culmination of Victorian and Edwardian philanthropic endeavours at home and in France, and women were fully active.[14] Cicely is a volunteer nurse thirty miles from the front, tending the wounded soldiers who are brought back by convoy, and when she travels to Steering Hall and Deverills Manor to meet her sudden family, she discovers a crooked bailiff, manoeuvres him into enlisting, and sets up a headquarters for the women's Land Army, with herself as commanding officer and the bailiff's wife as quartermaster.

The familiar tension between Victorianism and post-Victorianism is also played out in the novel. The now dowager Lady Steering is 'very Victorian'; when she hears of Giles's death, her daughter Caroline brings her 'vinaigrette, with which the Victorian woman always fortified herself in moments of weakness'. But weak she is not, acting on the assumption that 'women have great powers behind the throne' that do not need the legal acknowledgement of the vote. Her concept of strong womanhood is poles away from Caroline's and Cicely's, but Caroline, a vigorous young modern woman who nevertheless cannot stand up to her mother, knows that the contemporary notion of Victorian women having no power is a false one; rather, capable women of the previous generation affected 'clinging, womanly ways, an outward deference to masculine superiority which the masculine mind finds it impossible to resist'. The bailiff's wife, Mrs Barnacle, stealthily controls her would-be bullying husband ('He generally does come to my way of thinking when I really lay myself out. It's all a matter of arrangement with them.') And Aunt Georgie, Lady Winyard, hardly a suffragette, is intent on bringing modern efficiency to the Red Cross station at the chateau.[15] No doubt in the figures of the old Lady Steering and Lady Winyard (who can resemble Forster's Ruth Wilcox and Mrs Plynlimmon), Swan (Lyall) was defending women of her own generation, of which she herself was a particularly capable example, marrying a schoolmaster but encouraging him to resume medical studies and support- ing him financially through her writing while he did so.[16] Swan herself was a noted lecturer in the cause of temperance and during the Great War worked for the Ministry of Food as well as visiting soldiers' camps at home and abroad, and working in munitions factories. Her husband served with the Black Watch during the War.[17]

Reacting to the emergency of the War, Cicely is even more womanly in her philanthropy and self-sacrifice than Lady Steering; indeed, the War 'has opened countless doors for the unattached female, and she need never be at a loss'. War is liberating for woman (and Lyall hints too at the breakdown of the social class system the War is already beginning to cause). Rather than hindering female growth and fulfilment patriotic service actually allows it; Cicely plans to establish a school as part of her Land Army activities and to revolutionize agriculture; she tells her new sister-in-law that 'We are the New Age knocking at the door, Joyce. Don't you feel it?' (The phrase 'New Age' was used by MacMahon when portraying her young violinist Victoria in A New Note, 1894.) Cicely is a second-generation New Woman but devoid of ideology and political purpose beyond self-realization and productiveness. And it seems that love is essential to her worldview. This familiar theme is once again paramount. She conceives for Kane (The O'Rourke) a 'deathless love which, understanding all, forgives all, and she was lifted by it clean above the awful and momentous issue of the hour'—the carnage in Dublin during the Easter Rising.

But her understanding and forgiveness do not extend to The O'Rourke's patriotic fervour which on his side is endangered by his love for Cicely, the English rose. When he visits Steering Hall but cannot promise to enlist in the British Army or even promise not to fight England, they part. Yet he has been rocked. 'It is not the first time a woman's smile, the lure of her face and voice, have played havoc with a man's plan for life.' Indeed, it turns out that for Cicely's love he refrains from joining Sinn Fein and taking up arms at Easter. He is wounded as an observer on a Dublin street and is tended by Cicely before she too is slightly wounded (she has crossed to Ireland to look for him). She recovers and falls under the spell of Ireland, while The O'Rourke returns to Mullamore to convalesce, and Cicely joins him there. He will join the British Army in England and fight for the Empire and the Union Jack (not quite enough for Cicely: she suggests the Irish Guards so that he can combine Irish and English patriotism). When the War is over, they will marry and live at Mullamore and regenerate an estate decayed through The O'Rourke's long absence, since Cicely feels that in Ireland she has found home. She has redeemed The O'Rourke from Sinn Feinism and absentee landlordism and will redeem his country house, as though redeeming Ireland by keeping the island in the Empire and United Kingdom and bringing to productive fulfil-ment the present constitutional and political arrangement.[18] It is a plan many in Ireland as well as England would have applauded, though in the end the greater self-sacrifice would seem to be Ireland's since in Swan's novel the New Age woman gets her own way in every department.

The larger theme of *An English Rose* is the ambiguity of one's life in wartime. Cicely is conscious by a kind of 'prevision' of the intimation of destiny and plan in her life ('Something told her... that henceforth her destinies were to be irrevocably bound up with the low green island dipping down into the sea'), of the workings of fate which can employ miracles. On the other hand, she can feel that she is the mere 'sport of fate', and find herself simply waiting for her life to unfold, vulnerable in this 'world of sorry chance'.[19] Had Lyall-Swan devoted more time to the War and thought more about the front, the balance may have settled more obviously on the side of chance, for the lethal chanciness of active service was a firm theme in Great War writing originating in trench experience.

The Fire of Green Boughs (1918) by Mrs Victor (Jessie Louise) Rickard is a novel, the action of which like that of *The Fortune* and *An English Rose* crosses from England to Ireland (as the action of many pre-War Irish novels did), and likewise depicts the smaller Irish–English war inside the Great War (the plot-notion of the internal and external fronts), and through the mechanism of a mixed Irish–English marriage attempts to enact a desirable reconciliation between the old foes and (were it only realized) natural allies. We would be inclined ever since the setting up of the Irish Free State and, more to the point, the founding of the Irish Republic, to regard this as wishful thinking, but during the Great War there was plenty of apparent social and even political justification for the optimism. There are other resemblances among the three novels. Like *An English Rose*, Rickard's novel portrays women's war work that had its origin of impulse and organizational prowess in female Victorian philanthropy in Britain and Ireland. And like *The Fortune*, *The Fire of Green Boughs* explores the effect of the Great War on the home front, creating as it does everything from hardline anti-Germanism to pacifism, and playing havoc with the lives not just of men but also of women, especially women, in this novel's case.

Before the novel ends, the war has reached across the channel to London, and there is a description of an air-raid:

Searchlights were feeling swiftly over the sky, and every now and then a Very light soared up languidly into the darkness, and threw its blinding flare over the whole visible expanse. The dull red blur of exploding shrapnel made dim, bloody-looking stars overhead, and the sound of soaring shells sang their queer anthem to the night. Through all, the heavy boom of the guns rolled on with a roar of strong defiance, and the throb of the engines of the invisible invaders was persistent and steady.[20]

But Rickard's chief concern is the re-evaluation, one might even say transvaluation, that the war is effecting at home, and Dominic Roydon carries the novel's responsibility for this transvaluation. He is a soldier invalided home (to the regret of his gung-ho father Sir Jasper, who is sorry his son missed the Somme and whose death in battle would have been compensation) who renounces war, and becomes an Anglican curate and a renowned preacher. (Named by Rickard, no doubt, after St Dominic who returned stray sheep to the fold.)[21] He does good in the deprived areas of London: 'I have asked him over and over again', says Lady Roydon in exasperation, and unwittingly quoting Thoreau, 'why he could not *do* good by just *being* good.' The War has created in Dominic the dilemma of reconciling the obstinate world of individual experience that the War has clearly made more obstinate, and the 'hypothesis of an unseen world' of the spirit. Siegfried Sassoon-like, he rounds in rage upon the men past military age who encourage the War: 'It was as though all the resuscitated old men had some vampire joy in sucking the life out of the young...Age was conquering with a completeness which turned his heart sick.' He sees a terrible idea sweeping the earth: 'the awful determination of age that youth should be its vassal.' His soldier friend Archie is even more ferocious in an anger that would have done D. H. Lawrence justice, raging against 'the greybearded muddlers' who should be hanged on gibbets all over Europe 'and there would be a clean world again'. Rickard's title derives from a passage in which Dominic recalls his saddest memory: the fire his father Sir Jasper tried to ignite with the fresh remains of a lime tree he cut down on his Irish estate (Roydon Lodge in Kerry, originally called Ballina-dree) and which sputtered and failed and merely sent up 'wreaths of bitter smoke' and which Rickard intends to signify the bitter harvest of young deaths during the War and the absence of the flames of 'romantic self-sacrifice' that Archie says has died.[22]

The old order has ended but the 'ruling classes' do not realize it. Dominic, Willie Kent (a Kerry MP), and Sylvia Tracy are described as 'moderns who owed nothing to the past', moving about with blank misgivings in a world not realized. And Sylvia Tracy—Dominic's cousin who has been brought up by Sir Jasper and Lady Roydon in their London town house on the death of her mother, Lady Roydon's sister, and the disappearance of her father into the American Midwest—is Rickard's chief modern. Sylvia wants to join the vast army of workers engaged in helping their country in its hour of need, many of them women; indeed, women dominate the streets 'and out of every ten, six or eight wore uniforms of some kind.' Oddly, this saddens Dominic in its acute irony:

Women were everywhere and their preponderance depressed him in spite of himself. Old women, women of middle age and young women, all walled in with their own restrictions, and yet capable of high courage and long endurance. Before the war they had wanted everything to and for themselves, and he recalled the violent articles which the Women's Suffrage papers had published in their noisy attack upon his own sex. Now they had their wish, and they knew that it did not give them one tithe of what they desired to receive.[23]

Tracy is Rickard's case study. She is described as 'the direct inheritress of the Victorian fiction which now turned her into a sort of island in the flood; cut off from the resources of a former civilization' (p. 104). She is typical of the 'artificially surrounded beings' (p. 47) of the higher classes, Society girls faced during the War with a blank life or else dull work in an office or hospital, 'or the further distraction of weeding turnips and learning how to cart manure' (p. 48), distraction, that is, from the bigger issue of what to do with their lives. Sylvia goes to work in a government ministry and quits; she has to leave the Roydon town house when Lady Roydon dies and the house is to be shut up; she is offered the refuge of Roydon Lodge in Kerry and drifts there at the suggestion of Willie Kent. Who is Sylvia? Is she an adventuress, profiteer, coward, traitor, opportunist? Or is she someone of courage? Is she a victim of wartime circumstances? These are the terms used of her by other characters, and the ambiguities of character are deepened rather than resolved when she goes to Ireland, one more Visitor to Ireland from the pages of a popular novel. The answers are important because she is the pivotal figure of the story.

In keeping with the cultural formula of these novels, Sylvia falls under the spell of Ireland: 'A kind of delirium of appreciation swept her...Softness was over all things, and a definite brooding spirit...the far older and greater spirit of the country itself laid its magic hand upon her and brought to her a feeling which was like the touch of inspiration' (p. 124). She communes with the spirit of the Lynches, former owners of Ballinadree (renamed Roydon Lodge by Sylvia's in-laws). One fears Rickard might be complicit in Tracy's formulaic Celtophile fantasy: 'She knew that they had danced, and sung, and talked copiously; they had lived with a superb reality which knew nothing of the false joys of a town. She was sure that they had never grown tame or really old, for they had left traces of their free vitality in all the rooms of the rambling, battered, steadfast old house' (pp. 126–7). Sylvia Tracy is 'home' again, 'a sense of peace had fallen over her spirit which she had never before known or dreamed of' (p. 130).

Yet Tracy has landed amidst gathering Sinn Fein menace. Once, the house-keeper says, the gentry were against the nationalists; now the gentry *are* nationalists (surely Rickard's fond illusion) and the 'boys' are against the troops (p. 128). But along with the Sinn Fein threat is the fear of German invasion. Katharine Tynan remembers the talk in Ireland of invasion from around Christmas 1914 onwards, while Thomas Kettle believed a German victory could result in an invasion of Ireland.[24] It is not collusion with Sinn Fein rebels that lands Sylvia in trouble, but instead her flouting of the Defence of the Realm Act by harbouring a dying German submariner whom she hides from the local District Inspector Ambrose Boyne who considers her a rotter, a coward, and a traitor, and no doubt in league with the Shinners ('Women were coming gradually into the Sinn Fein movement, to an extent which he condemned with all his heart', p. 219).

Tracy is spirited away to England by Willie Kent but encounters Boyne at a London dinner party and is exposed; most of the diners shrink from her and she becomes 'homeless' once more. Again she is saved by Kent whom she loves and whose proposal of marriage she accepts. To the 'moderns', love had seemed improbable. For Dominic 'the word "love" was scored through on the book of Life with a deep mark of erasure'; for her part, Sylvia tells him that she thinks that their wartime generation has lost the art of love. 'It used to be the main profession for the daughters of the house, but now it isn't, and we can't do it easily.' Rickard could be commenting here on the plots of innumerable popular country-house novels. Yet her own novel ends by redeeming both love and marriage; Lord Carfax proposes to Sylvia and is refused, before she and Kent plan for their future. Sylvia, it seems, is courageous after all, yet somehow, it is intimated, Sylvia Tracy is not unlike Kent. The Irish, he explains, 'are opportunists like all conquered races' and this might explain any Irish pro-German sentiment, since England is fighting to resist becoming under a victorious Germany what Ireland is under a victorious England. What a pair of moderns, exclaims Dominic to Kent and Sylvia in exasperated admiration, when Sylvia claims that her happiness dwarfs any accusation of pro-Germanism (and no doubt, pro-Sinn Feinism).[25] But it is unclear at the end of this interesting novel precisely where Rickard stands on the issue of Irish separation from the United Kingdom. This is perhaps because Rickard was both an Irish patriot and an English patriot and a believer in the Empire. This dual allegiance muddied the waters but was something enjoyed, or endured, by countless Irish men and women of the period.[26]

There is no such lack of clarity in a popular novel by Annie P. Smithson (1873–1948), a Protestant who converted to Catholicism in 1907 and actively embraced republicanism during the Troubles and civil war. Her Irish Heritage (1917, claimed by Mercier Press in its 1988 republication to have been an Irish best-seller at the time, like several other novels by Smithson) is the story of the circumstances and events of a similar religious and political conversion. Since district nurses play a prominent role in the novel and Smithson herself was a district nurse, one can presume a good deal of autobiographical matter. In which case, one might be tempted to see a surprisingly intimate connection between the motifs of the county-house novel that exploits concurrent political events and the lives of the authors. For if Her Irish Heritage culminates in a choice the heroine must make between supporting British troops in the

Great War and Irish rebels in Dublin at Easter 1916, the story that explains the choice she makes requisitions almost all the plot motifs we have identified, upending them when republican politics requires it. Smithson's deployment of the motifs in the service of her political agenda is almost admirable and makes her novel culturally intriguing if regrettable as literature.[27]

Clare Castlemaine is the motherless daughter of an apparently wealthy Londoner who is found on his death to have lost most of his money in the stock-market. The newly orphaned young woman is invited to live in Ireland with her uncle and cousins, the Blakes, they being (in a reversal of the usual premiss) rich by comparison. The Blakes, a motherless Catholic family of nine children and a father, are, in fact, of the Dublin professional middle class, allowing Smithson to present the multifarious faces of nationalist Ireland in 1913, the grown children being involved in a variety of educated pursuits, from the Gaelic League to social work in the Dublin slums. Before long, the cousinly Visitor to Ireland falls under the spell of the island and begins to discover the Irish Catholic heritage of her dead mother which will eclipse the English Protestant heritage of her father, the novel being firmly wedded to the notion not only that heredity will out but that Irishness in terms of 'cultural genetics' is a dominant allele (conversion being a kind of mutation). It is, however, the 'dominant' environment of the Blake household that permits the release, as it were, of Clare Castlemaine's dormant cultural traits, nurture helping nature to self-realization.

Castlemaine's turn to Catholicism is made easier by the fact that Protestantism is, it seems, essentially schismatic whereas Roman Catholicism is unified and universal. Unity is seen as innately superior to dissidence and individuality, from self through family to nation: Ourselves, never Myself. (Self-sacrifice in the novel, meaning charitable social work, is a form of active community awareness and communal effort.) Clare herself has been brought up as an agnostic, which is at once very Protestant and irreligious. However, one plot-strand of the novel is Clare's 'testing' of Catholicism: if her new friend Mary Carmichael, an Ulster-Scots Presbyterian convert to Rome and a district nurse among the poor (perhaps Smithson's self-portrait), successfully leans on the Church during her personal crisis that Castlemaine shrewdly anticipates, then she, Castlemaine, will convert. Carmichael's trial, being jilted by a 'bad' Catholic when she thought she was engaged, is a second plot-strand which also 'Catholicizes' the novel's 'Harlequin-type' romance. Carmichael's suffering, because it affects friends and family, is seen as a communal and unifying predicament; it is, in a strange way, 'offered up' to those around her. In the event, the Church sees Carmichael through and Clare converts.

The primary theme of *Her Irish Heritage* is the syndrome (favourable in the author's eyes, not pathological) of beliefs and values of which Irish

Catholicism is but one. This slight novel is surprisingly steeped in the populist biology and race-consciousness of its time, which fuelled Irish nationalism as it did other nationalisms and racialisms. Castlemaine stops seeing herself as of the Anglo-Saxon race and sees herself as of the Celtic race. (The spiritual Irish peasant is described as vastly superior to the plodding and merely sensuous English farm-worker, the Irish colleen to the English hussy.) She is initiated into the 'Story of Ireland' about which she has been taught nothing, and converts to republicanism. She converts at the same time to a proud sympathy for the Irish language movement. All in all, Irishness is seen as a natural and even supernatural existential terminus. For above all, Clare realizes the essential spirituality of the Irish, glowing against the dull materialism of the English who, like the Ulster Scots, are acceptable only as converts. (One of the Blake sons is a cheerful anglophobe.) Indeed, clearly Castlemaine herself is only truly acceptable when she marries a Celt, and she does so, converting from Clare Castlemaine to Mrs Anthony Farrell, a variant use of the venerable marriage device as cultural unification.

The wonderful Irish landscape (Co. Clare in this novel), inhabited by the fortunate peasants, offers Mary Carmichael a chance to heal and it is where she is recuperating when her friend Clare marries the proper Celt. One chapter, 'In the Slums', follows Bride Blake and Mary Carmichael into the Coombe, the slum area of Dublin we have already encountered. The characters' use of the term 'slumming' is balanced between embarrassed self-consciousness and brazen daily usage among the self-sacrificing middle class. In any case, compared to those in Mulholland and Edelstein, the slum-denizens are in Smithson's novel rather jolly, having amidst their poverty the company of each other and their religion to keep them afloat, even buoyant. After all, in the interests of unity, no one who embraces the constituent elements of the Irish organism must be left out.

Easter 1916 is one of those constituents, and *Her Irish Heritage* is dedicated 'to the Memory of the Men who Died, Easter, 1916'. When the Great War breaks out, Clare, by unwise reflex, as it turns out, supports the Allied cause whereas Mary Carmichael smiles condescendingly (this would not be Smithson's adverb), expresses impatience with any reference to the British Empire, and claims that her anti-Britishness is due to the absence of English blood in her veins: '"—some Scotch is mixed with the Irish certainly, but that", with a little laugh—"is a very decent mixture!".'[28] She is sorry Clare cannot yet see the War 'from an Irish standpoint', even when Clare mentions alleged Hun atrocities, the only detail from the War that Smithson mentions. Soon, Castlemaine is won over to the incontrovertible justice of the rebel cause in Dublin in Easter week and the Great War fades from view.

BETWEEN TWO SHADOWS

A transitional Ireland pivoting on Easter 1916 and concurrent episodes of the Great War is pictured, then, in several Irish novels. Outside literature, the twin opposing attractions of the Great War and Sinn Fein Ireland impacted directly on the lives of Childers and Lord Dunsany. Before the Great War broke out, Childers opted for republicanism whereas Dunsany opted for service in the British army. More interesting, however, is the contrast between Childers and Tom (T. M.) Kettle, both Irish nationalists. Kettle—essayist and journalist, but Robert Lynd also called him a mathematician, economist, barrister, philosopher, bohemian, and scholar—was something of a reverse Childers.[29] In the summer of 1914 Kettle crossed to Belgium to purchase guns for the Irish Volunteers; Childers's yacht *Asgard*, engaged in the same mission, was on the seas. While Kettle was in Belgium, war was declared. The ironic parallel with Childers is that the desire to make an impact proved in the end, after the search for guns, fatal for each man. However, whereas Childers ultimately attached greater importance to Irish independence than to the War (which ended with the Irish Question still unanswered), Kettle stayed on in Belgium as a war correspondent, believing that Prussian aggression in Europe far outweighed English sins in Ireland. His despatches were often heated, purplish, and memorable. In one, 'Under the Heel of the Hun', he sized the situation up like this: 'It is as simple as it is colossal. It is Europe against the barbarians'.[30]

According to Lynd, Kettle regarded Pearse and Connolly as having in Spring 1916 'all but destroyed his dream of an Ireland enjoying the freedom of Europe'.[31] J. B. Lyons tells us that Kettle referred to 'the Sinn Féin nightmare'.[32] Yet he raged against the manner of British suppression of the Rising.[33] Like John Redmond and many others, Kettle thought of enlisted Irish soldiers as forming the first Home Rule army and insisted that they would be fighting not for England and the colonies but for Ireland and Europe. He hoped joint experience of the War would reconcile Ulster with Ireland, Ireland with England. For his part, Redmond believed that as a combatant, Ireland would 'help to bend the British Empire to a mission of new significance for humanity'.[34] Kettle's anthology, *Irish Orators and Oratory* (1916) concludes with Redmond's eloquent intervention in the British House of Commons debate upon the declaration of war, 3 August 1914, offering Britain the opportunity to withdraw troops from Ireland, leaving defence of the island to the two bodies of Volunteers, Irish and Ulster. Events after Easter 1916, however, contorted Redmond's and Kettle's positions into terrible irony. When he debated the anti-recruiting campaigners, Pearse and Yeats, Kettle,

Lyons tells us, turned up in the uniform of a British soldier, Lieutenant, 9th Royal Dublin Fusiliers.[35] Wearing that uniform, he was killed at Ginchy, at the Somme, in September 1916. He would not have allowed that his self-sacrifice was any less for Ireland than Pearse's at Easter in the same year.

The difference in physical scale between the Easter Rebellion and the Great War was of course immense. Even inside Ireland the events were monumentally disproportionate. Robert Lynd pointed out that 'there were not enough Irishmen in the Dublin insurrection of 1916 to make up even one battalion of the Irish Guards ... For every Irishman who shouldered a rifle on the insurgent side, nearly a thousand Irishmen bore weapons on the side of the Allies.'[36] Nevertheless, through the power of symbolism, the Easter Rising took its place alongside the War to complete a potent emblem of duality, one that inspired and troubled writers of the time (including Rickard, Goldring, Ervine, Swan, and Tynan) or at the very least offered fascinating plot-forces (the plot was, in Childers's case, his own life).

For a few years it seemed a roughly equal struggle and no stark crossroads had been reached.[37] But an Ireland torn between loyalty and rebellion was unstable and it is caught without fanfare in Ella MacMahon's often humorous and poignant *Irish Vignettes*. These nineteen pieces—the earliest published between 1920 and 1921—were first published in serial form under the title 'Vignettes' and then in book form as *Irish Vignettes* in 1928. They exist appropriately somewhere between short stories and essays. There are references to both the Zeppelin air raids on London and Easter 1916. One character with marvellous duplicity (or is it merely doubleness?) shouts 'Up the Irish Fusiliers! Up the Rebels!' The characters are suspended between 'a bygone day' and a 'new Ireland' of the period 1914 to 1918; Sinn Fein is on the rise but the Troubles have not begun. Among the 'peasants' (her word) whom MacMahon writes of in the guise of a travelled and cultivated Irishwoman there is a new 'impidence' (as one of the country cast calls it); there is an increasing dislike of England and a discernible pro-Germanism.[38] The rural Irish are caught between 'purely feudal predilections' and 'modern democratic opinions' but the latter could themselves—though this is only implied—favour either Sinn Fein populism or continued unionism. The author herself seems similarly suspended in sympathy and opinion between two Irelands but retains an alert ironic detachment. But the Great War/Easter 1916 duality lost its potency quite soon after the War which, astonishingly, the Rising all but erased in the Southern Irish popular and even literary imagination.[39] There is evidence that the erasure of the Irish Great War experience is nowadays being reversed.

In Tynan's novel, *The Golden Rose* (1924), that potency is lost *before* the Great War is half over and her novel takes as one of its themes the supersession of the War by the Rising in the hearts and minds of Tynan's farmers and peasants in

Connaught even while Irishmen were fighting and dying in France and Belgium. Before she wrote her novel, Tynan remembered her deeply mixed feelings about the two events in *The Years of the Shadow* (1919). She recalled one sunny Sunday morning in April 1915, while in the company of a captain in the Royal Irish Regiment, encountering a group of casualties from St Vincent's Hospital, and the captain addressing two soldiers wounded at Ypres. In the afternoon she watched 500 Irish Volunteers going for a route march in the Dublin mountains, 'where they acquired their deadly skill at markmanship. Easter Week, 1916, was yet more than a year away'.[40] Her sympathy was equally divided between the past and future combatants. The 'Rebellion' preoccupied her for many weeks after it happened but she neither condemns it nor lauds it; it is as if she was stunned by it into neutrality. In her country house, Brookhill, Co. Mayo, where she was living when the Rising took place, she went on writing a book that, ironically, became *Lord Edward: A Study in Romance.* 'I was Rebellion-ridden,' she writes. It pained her that her belief that 'affection for England and love of Ireland could quite well go hand in hand' was urgently brought into question. 'I was enthusiastically pro-Ally . . . To me any bloodiness between England and Ireland was unthinkable . . . We had grown up to the love of Ireland and now came this sharp, bitter cleavage, in which, with incredible rapidity, the great body of the Irish were massing themselves in a hostility against England—and England, a great part of her, against Ireland' (pp. 204–5).[41] Tynan's reluctance to give an opinion of the rightness or wrongness of the rebellion suggests that neither the affection nor the love were affected by it and that both remained intact, balanced, unreconciled into one emotion. She visited Dublin in June and felt for the first time menace and fear in the city that had not left her by the time she wrote her memoir.

Clearly the depth of her emotional engagement with the War strengthened her feeling for England. Her feeling for the soldiers was already strong, and Brookhill was abustle with soldiers from the nearby camp, the men drying their rain-sodden uniforms in the big laundry, the officers visiting, the stables occupied by horses belonging to Major-General Percy and his Staff.[42] During the conflict she became a sought-after war poet, consoler, and 'mother-confessor' after a poem of hers opened a floodgate of letters and was quoted from pulpits; she was soon writing a hundred letters per week to the bereaved.[43] Her elder son fought in Palestine and her younger in France, whose experiences open *The Wandering Years* (1922), in which she relates her younger son's account of the Armistice and excerpts his letters from Germany which he entered as part of the Army of Occupation. She also reproduces from notes and memory stories that came to her fireside during and immediately after the War but makes no claims for them, calling them 'flashes from the War' and one senses she chooses stories that highlight the terribleness of what young men endured.[44] She heard a young soldier 'say one day that the happenings of the War were only bearable because they were real happenings. In imagination they would have been intolerable, if one could have imagined them.' Hers is the perspective of a mother: 'Things we shall never have to suffer happened to these children of ours' (pp. 73, 72). But the Irish mother whose son is away fighting for Britain and the Empire (and, according to some, for Ireland) is as perdurable a figure as the Shan Van Vocht or Kathleen Ni Houlihan whom the Revivalists were championing, but she has been largely overlooked in literature outside her dubious representation in O'Casey's *The Plough and the Stars* (1926).

The Golden Rose registers early signs of the massing of the Irish in hostility against England and those Irish who were fighting for her in Europe and does so from a preponderantly female perspective.[45] Whatever its modest literary merits, it is a brave and illuminating novel that is honest in its implied narrator's confusion when caught between, on the one hand, the imperatives of instinctual love of son and brother and traditional loyalty to the Irish soldier fighting for the British cause, and, on the other hand, the imperatives of Irish patriotism and social need of neighbour. At first no choice is necessary, when the War effort, and the Irish boys who helped make it, are supported by all but diehard Sinn Feiners, but even before the Easter Rising in 1916 the waters are muddier than they seem. Tynan has a Joycean if politer cynicism towards those Irish opportunists who made profit by the War and supported its continuance on that score, and hypocrites who were two-faced, 'running with the hare and hunting with the hounds' as one character is described as doing.[46] But the gradually waxing tide of popular sentiment is clear and, of course, writing from the perspective of 1923 or 1924, Tynan knew that the Irish heroes-in-making of the Great War had been prematurely expelled from the nationalist pantheon.[47]

As is commonly the case with the popular novelists, Tynan's recreation of Great War rural Ireland is couched within a romance whose familiar plot constituents are a love affair, an apparent jilting, revelation of the truth, a reunion, and an imminent marriage. It is the variables of the formula that earn our attention. The true love is that between the beautiful daughter of a Catholic dispensary doctor and the son of the local (Protestant) peer (Lord Creeslough); that is to say, between the child of the professional middle class and the child of the Big House (Castle Molyneux). Given the reservations about the middle class (certainly the mercantile middle class) that we have met in Tynan, it is hardly surprising that the O'Reilly family in fact originated in this remote rural west (as though honorary peasants), have a redeeming impoverishment—not helped by the doctor's penchant for whiskey—*and* are remote descendants of a native aristocracy.[48] At the same time, the poverty is clearly relative, since the daughters are sent to convent school in England, and one of them to Roehampton, while the sons attend Trinity College Dublin and Sandhurst, the fees required for these apparent extravagances receiving no mention. Tynan's intention, though, is clearly to depict with sympathy educated Catholic Irish who willingly sent their boys to the war or went themselves; Dr O'Reilly goes out himself in 1915 and is invalided home almost two years later; four of his boys go out, one of them being killed serving with the 10th (Irish) division at the Suvla landing (Gallipoli) in August 1915, one wounded but winning the DSO and MC, one taken prisoner in Germany.

The novel opens in early 1917 with the daughter Carmel trimming a hat by the window of her family home in Cahirmore and remembering what has happened to her, chiefly since the rhapsodic summer of 1914 before the declaration of war when she met and fell in love with Beaufoy (Beau) Molyneux and he with her. Most of the events occur in her memory but at times the third-person narrative is no longer indirect first-person and we are present at scenes at which Carmel was not. It is more than three-quarters through the novel before events catch up on that day by the window and then proceed until a few weeks after, in May 1917, with Beau home wounded and the lovers re-engaged to marry. It is unfortunate that Tynan repeats from *A Girl of Galway* the device of amnesia to explain Beau's apparent jilting of Carmel: he was wounded at the front and in his shell shock only vaguely recalled a girl he once knew.[49] This time, however, the amnesia is not merciful or redemptive but rather a baffle in the path of love and one reinforced by his mother, the snobbish Lady Creeslough who wants her son to marry above Carmel's station. While in hospital Beau understandably falls for his attractive nurse and becomes engaged to her (promising the recurring safe marriage of the popular romances) though she steps aside when hearing of a true love back in Connaught. Tynan also reprises the figure of the kindly Anglo-Irish landlord, though acknowledges historical reality by making Lord Creeslough's immediate forebears rackrenting landlords. Beau, the heir to Castle Molyneux, is a Redmondite, as are the O'Reilly family and, one can be sure, Tynan herself: she would have seen Redmond's position as culturally and politically a reconciliatory one.

It is the course of the War as it is received in the west of Ireland that lends *The Golden Rose* its interest for us. Carmel is the reader's custodian of the friendly and talkative pre-war Ireland, which she keeps alive in her memory, though recalling how soon after the War's outbreak Ireland grew darker and tenser. Yet at first the exploits of the doctor's sons thrill his patients and neighbours and the tidings of his son's death fills them with apparent sorrow. Carmel remembers the days 'when, before a soldier, the heart melted, the hands went out'.[50] But, in fact, ever since the War began 'there had been a steadily growing distaste and dislike of it among the people. It was too early yet to call it hostility. That was to come: but a good many things had happened in Ireland since civil war threatened in

1914 to break up the peace, which some people thought sluggish, of the years before the war.' Tynan alludes here to Ulster's resistance to Home Rule. By early 1916 the people, very few of whom had been touched by the War, are 'oddly indifferent, almost hostile' to the O'Reillys, the War, and the Irish soldiers fighting it. Ireland's temper is obscure, uncertain. The change in the people is 'subtle ... they were less friendly, less respectful.' The unfriendliness is 'strange', the hostility is 'mysterious'.[51]

In Dublin, however, even as late as March 1916, 'there was everywhere the friendliness of the war' (p. 146). Then happened the definitive watershed of the Easter Rising, from the other side of which Carmel in early 1917 is recalling events. She and her mother are in France visiting the dangerously ill doctor,[52] and into this strangely beautiful weather and spring flowers 'there came something violent and terrible hurtling into the peace as though a shell had dropped upon them. It was the news of the Dublin Rebellion' (p. 169). The latest crossroads has been reached. Carmel takes it hard; she breaks down and weeps 'for Ireland, for the Irish soldiers in the war, betrayed and deserted as they would see it, for the madness of it all and for what was going to happen' (p. 170). Her father too thinks the rebellion a wicked betrayal. Back home he claims that the rebellion had corrupted the kindly people, and this is remembered against him. Even before the Rising, his neighbours had decided that he had been wrong, not heroic, in abandoning his patients to a *locum tenens* in order to join the War. Now in the wake of the Rising, the Royal Irish Constabulary (RIC) become the enemy and some families are split in their loyalty, one brother in the War, one in the Rebellion ('the same spirit in both of them', p. 188), a kind of Irish civil war of the affections.[53] The Irish soldiers are no longer heroes, or even victims, but misguided fools, even traitors: 'There was no heroism now but that of 1916', Carmel realizes in early 1917. She could not have known, but her creator did, that the course of Irish history had been redirected, with immeasurable consequences.

If this is one theme of *The Golden Rose*, an associated theme is the War's emotional toll, especially on women keeping vigil at home, a theme that would be explored at greater length and subtler insight by Tynan's daughter Pamela seven years later, in a novel the title of which identifies the theme: *The Ladies' Road*. But Tynan herself captures economically the mixed emotions that underlay the political ambivalences and polarities of the Irish at the time. Having grieved alone for her brother Pat, a grief that sometimes superimposes itself on that for her missing fiancé, Carmel suddenly requires 'a kinship of suffering' (p. 138). She finds it at first in those uncommon cabins and farmhouses of the west with a son in the War, alive, wounded, or dead; her grief isolates her more than it binds her to the people, the War inserting a wedge into the Irish heart. At the French hospital, where she experiences 'the comradeship of the war' among the women, she notes how their faces had 'that aching look of a high uplifted patience, the look of martyrdom', a martyrdom that defeats 'the solitude of suffering' (p. 167). Only Beau's eventual return to her, and her half-sexual, half-maternal embracing of him, resolves her feelings into something like unity and purpose at the end of the ladies' road.

Tynan and her heroine keep faith with the Irish soldiers in acknowledging the gravitational pull of Easter 1916 without succumbing emotionally to its force. When Irish readers and critics think of the vigils kept by women, they would most likely think of Pearse's adulation for such vigils and of Synge's Maurya in *Riders to the Sea*, the very embodiment of female vigilance, patience, mourning, steadfastness, and stoicism. The alternative figures to these need not be Percy Barron's daughters of Empire, silently bearing their losses in contrast to the unseemly keening of bereft Irish women. Tynan, like her daughter Pamela, demonstrates that those ambiguous virtues were recordable, and recordable with eloquence and feeling, in a very different cultural and political context.

BETWEEN THE DEVIL AND THE RIC

Both Easter 1916 and the Great War have already receded in importance in Edith Somerville's *An Enthusiast* (1921), concerned as the author is with the later and euphemistically named 'Troubles' (in truth, insurrection, counter-insurrection, reprisal, murder, and mayhem) that heated up once the Government of Ireland Act (1920) provided for the partition of the island and the establishment of two governments. The Troubles were a subject that attracted fiction writers with a bent for action stories but also those sympathetic to the unionist cause who wished to dramatize what they regarded as the republican terror abroad in the land. A congenial host for such fiction was *Blackwood's Edinburgh Magazine*. 'Maga', as the magazine was affectionately known to subscribers, was an organ of Tory politics, as a 1917 retrospective article in the magazine had it.[54] It was begun by William Blackwood in 1804, and the editor in the late Victorian period, William Blackwood III, saw it as 'an essential part of the British colonial social life' (as Finkelstein observes), arguing as it did for an expansionist foreign policy and publishing stories of exotic locations, often in the Empire. According to Finkelstein, 'the death of the British Empire also signalled the slow death of *Blackwood's Magazine*'. The magazine's editorial interest in the exotic presumably made the travel writing of Hannah Lynch appeal to readers of *BEM*, where she often appeared despite her nationalist proclivities expressed in other forums.

The Blackwood family had strong connections with the East India Company, and on this ground Andrew James's *Ninety-Eight and Sixty Years After* (retitled *The Nabob* for republication in 2006) would surely have had an immediate if minor appeal, given the tales' imperial connections.[55] The 1798 setting of *Ninety-Eight* would have added for *Blackwood's* the desired exoticism to more recent and familiar Irish violence and brutality. The strong Scots dimension of the tales must also have made the Edinburgh house of Blackwood a natural home for them, a dimension signalled from the start by the echo in their title of Sir Walter Scott's *Waverley, or, 'Tis Sixty Years Since* (1814) and justified by the use of Ulster Lowland Scots speech in *Ninety-Eight* and the dominance in the whole work of Northerners of Scottish ancestry.

I have discussed *The Nabob* as supernatural fiction but its immediate impact rests on its depiction of cruelty, sectarian hatred, and brutal political violence in Co. Antrim in the months leading up to the 1798 rebellion. Although *The Nabob* is historical fiction, James was writing at a time when it was imaginable that such a state of affairs could return to Ulster; Irish unrest involving military and paramilitary action was familiar in the years between 1907 and 1911, years when respectively the tales were written and published. If James's composition of *The Nabob* was indeed stimulated by contemporary Irish unrest, his concern was justified when the Troubles began in earnest. When they did, they provoked from James, writing under his real name, a sustained fusillade of essays in *Blackwood's Magazine* between August 1919 and May 1922, written from an increasingly sharp unionist and anti-nationalist angle.[56]

Andrew James was in fact James Andrew Strahan (1858–1930), born like Mrs J. H. Riddell in Carrickfergus, Co. Antrim, the son of a Belfastman. From Queen's College he was called to the English bar and became Reader of Equity, Inns of Court, London 1897–1929 and was Professor of Jurisprudence and Roman Law at Queen's University, 1909–26. He was the author of a versatile series of well-distributed legal textbooks, some going into as many as six editions.[57] By 1919 Strahan was writing essays for *Blackwood's*, all of them brief cultural histories, and several of them in their descriptive and reflective powers qualifying him for the same title of essayist that was already won by Robert Lynd, another Protestant Ulsterman, though one of republican leanings. The speed of publication accelerated during the Sinn Fein crisis and the Troubles. Some of the essays adverted to historical events he had already drawn on in *The Nabob* but this time around he grew increasingly impatient and affronted by rebellion, by Sinn Fein separatism, and IRA violence, and struck a more strident pro-Union note. By June 1921 he saw the Troubles as war between the gunmen and the Government, between lawlessness and law, and he was a lawman by training and profession. He thought the unionists were at the end of their tether and he could even contemplate discriminating reprisals when aimed at those guilty of crimes or of harbouring the criminal, but not vigilante action or reprisals against a population or community from which the guilty came. The '98 he had depicted so graphically in *The Nabob* had indeed come round again, as though demonstrating the tales' darker themes and validating the thrust of the first set of tales, *Ninety-Eight*, rather than the sequel set, *Sixty Years After*. In the midst of the most recent Troubles it was difficult to adopt the healing, peacetime mindset of his character Michael Macdonnell or enjoy without heated editorializing the narratorial pleasures of the the old schoolmaster. The Nabob, and his counterpart on the rebel side, had returned to his picture frame from which his portrait had disappeared when his ghost had been exorcised. He was to disappear once more in the middle of the 1920s or so, as though into the vault of history, but he or his like then, alas, reappeared half a century later and over the course, not of a week as in 1798 or a few years as in the original Troubles, but of thirty years, the graves opened, ghosts were made, and the horror was sustained.

Blackwood's, we are told, drew its readership from military and civil service ranks, at home and abroad, and this would account for the allure of action stories as well as essays about civil unrest in Ireland, an island in any case both exotic to most English and of at least secondary interest to British students of the Empire. 'Vignettes' by Ella MacMahon, for example, appeared in *Blackwood's*, sketching the unstable and simmering Irish years during the Great War. Chiefly, though, *Blackwood's* favoured real action seen and engaged in from the point of view of the established authority, a viewpoint unfamiliar to most students of literature that has come out of Ireland since the Irish Literary Revival. Many of these fictions depict an Ireland of deceiving daylight and violent nighttime, a country of spurious loyalties, intimidation, and secret allegiances, and are written from a loyalist perspective, with the police as sympathetic if often ineffectual and besieged figures. (*The Nabob* depicts a similar countryside, though set a hundred years and more before.) 'A Foretaste' by 'An Irishwoman' (*BEM*, May 1920)—which like MacMahon's vignettes reads like autobiographical fiction—is a story set in the autumn of 1919 (perhaps in Co. Meath) during martial law prompted by the Sinn Fein war against the British. The independent-minded young narrator's family suffers a 'strike' by their servants which is a cover for the anti-loyalist, anti-Big House motives of a Sinn Fein-inspired boycott and plan of sabotage and the family receives protection from the Royal Irish Constabulary. The determination of the young narrator wears down the Shinners and the boycott collapses.

We could see this plot resolution on hindsight as in the larger historical picture a species of wish-fulfilment, but for a couple of years the constitutional fate of Ireland hung in the balance and from the loyalist angle the story combines, like several of the Troubles fictions, a sense of doom with an oblique exhortation to hopeful and courageous resistance. 'The Terror by Night' (*BEM*, July 1920) by the same anonymous author (the placename of 'Dunreagh' recurs) is likewise set during the Troubles and recounts the narrator's frightening experience of a car breakdown at night in the countryside, during which she hears about a young countryman who joined the British Army and fought with distinction, only to find on his return a very different Ireland in which Sinn Fein is a power. He is subjected to a persistent and relentless persecution by shadowy Sinn Feiners for his loyalty to the monarchy, boycotted, and then his farm sabotaged. In his room he displays a portrait of King George V topped with a Union Jack. He is told by masked gunmen it must go; he removes it and bears his wife and child off to England in disgust. In the story's propaganda mode, the narrator claims 'similar cases occur continually all over the country', and not just involving ex-British soldiers.[58] An RIC man claims that Irish soldiers returned from the War are enduring 'a reign of terror'.[59] The narrator during her car breakdown stumbles in the dark to the police barracks only to find dereliction and a message written in pebbles: DEATH TO THE R.I.C.

One imagines that 'Tales of the R.I.C.', by another anonymous author, were exactly to the taste of Blackwood and his readers, being action stories about the tribulations and escapades of the constabulary as they battled Sinn Fein/IRA in 1920, written from pro-unionist, anti-republican, and anti-bolshevist perspectives. Appearing in *Blackwood's* in 1921, *Tales of the R.I.C.* was republished as a book by William Blackwood and Sons the same year, the author still unidentified, perhaps for reasons of his personal security at a time of frequent assassinations.[60]

These twenty-one readable tales set in the far west (Clare and Galway) narrate violent episodes in the Anglo-Irish war waged on the ground between the RIC, 'Black and Tans', Auxiliaries, and regular British soldiers on one side and on the other side the Volunteers, who came to be called the Irish Republican Army, the armed wing of Sinn Fein.[61] The plots of the tales are literally that: Volunteer plots to attack rural RIC barracks, assassinate Resident Magistrates, soldiers, and police where possible, burn courthouses, and raid country houses for arms, murdering landowners if necessary. The Volunteers drive cattle and shave the heads of girls fraternizing with policemen or soldiers; they intimidate opponents among their own people by extorting money, beating, killing, or expelling them from Ireland. The RIC, who bear the brunt of the Volunteers' war against British authority,[62] their members and families suffering boycotts as well as physical assault, are the main force of counter-terror and engage in their own plots of reprisal. Meanwhile, Sinn Fein have set up courts and internment camps to replace British mechanisms of justice, which latter continue to function as best they can, creating an absurd doubling of government, a grotesque illusion of choice for the people that merely confuses and terrifies them, caught as they are between the devil and the deep blue sea.[63] 'Probably very few people in England have the remotest idea', contends the narrator, 'to what extent anarchy was rife throughout the South and West of Ireland, even in parts of loyal Ulster, during the year 1920' (*BEM* 210: 314).

The tales variously recount the murder of an informer (a British Army deserter conscripted as an agent by the RIC); the capture and escape of a rebel leader; the foiling of a gun-running plot; the shooting then drowning (by burial in sand up to the neck) of a Resident Magistrate; the rescue of a new English owner of a fishing-lodge from the clutches of the Volunteers; the failure to rescue an Irish landowner, member of an old-established family, from the determination of members of the Transport Union (James Con-nolly's followers—Bolsheviks, the narrator calls them) to have his land and the IRA's determination to burn him out; the discovery of an IRA rifle-range; the rupture of a family through divided loyalties and the killing in a gunfight of one IRA brother by a police force that includes another RIC brother; the driving back to America of an idealistic Irish-American nurse who arrives to aid the independence movement only to find out the reality of the IRA and their designs on the land she has inherited; the bravery of a Catholic priest who denounces IRA violence; the kidnapping and murder of an Anglo-Irish hero of the Great War, now a Resident Magistrate, and his clever burial beneath a dead Volunteer in a bog cemetery to prevent the discovery of his body (the discovery is made, however, in an equally clever manner); the late but earnest attempt by the massed forces of authority, in something at last resembling conventional warfare, to capture a force of one thousand Volun-teers on a western peninsula, only to have a truce declared by the British government and the soldiers and police recalled to barracks.[64]

In one tale, 'The Bog Cemetery', the narrator remarks that Irish public opinion is no longer relevant because the people have become mere spectators of the criminal violence, 'like the younger generation in England, who waste a large part of their lives in picture-houses, gazing at films of vice and crime' (*BEM* 210: 304). Besides being a very early observation on the power of cinema (later, television) to inure viewers to violence (indeed, the power of violence itself to stupefy), this is an inadvertent irony since *Tales of the R.I.C.* has a similarity to contemporary serial cinema. The narrator is clearly offering his tales as grim entertainment in the form of adventure stories and directing them at English readers, many of them, no doubt, assumed to be military personnel in the Empire; numerous brand names of warfare stud the narrative to amuse them: Crossley, Colt, Mills, Lewis, Mauser, Zeiss, Thompson, Ford, Vickers. But the narrator at times reveals himself as author in order to break the 'gaze' of the reader as spectator: for the tales are also propaganda, tales with a purpose, that purpose being to break the malignant (rather than romantic) spell Ireland casts on English politicians, to warn, to stir to indignation—perhaps to the extent of their protesting to those politicians—English readers at home or abroad in the Empire. At moments, the author's essayism is heated and irate: on Bolshevism and Germany and the Irish peasantry but chiefly on Sinn Fein and British policy-makers. Sinn Feiners are likened to an anathematized trio of alliterated enemies: the Boche, Boers, and Bolsheviks.[65] Eamon de Valera, Countess Markievicz, James Connolly ('the prince of Irish Bolsheviks'), and Michael Collins are all pilloried.

The tales short-circuit the historical complexities and reduce the cast of players to the action formula of virtuous, steadfast, and besieged RIC versus the duplicitous, brutal, and Anglophobic Volunteers. Omitted from the author's picture of a wholly tyrannical and anarchic Sinn Fein is the growing popularity of the party after the British decision in 1918 to enforce conscription, the overwhelming success of the party in the general election of 1918 (gaining 73 out of 105 seats), the conservatism of the first Dáil Éireann (Irish parliament) and its avoidance of Bolshevist tendencies (Labour and trades union interests were not represented), the belief of the Volunteers that they were legitimated by popular support and the existence of the Dáil, and the repeat electoral success of Sinn Fein in the municipal elections of January 1920. The author likewise omits the extent of condemnation of Sinn Fein/IRA by urban and rural district councils and by the Catholic Church (he portrays one priest lonely in his courage amidst Church complicity).[66] On the other hand, the author has restricted himself on the whole to 1920 and John A. Murphy is of the opinion that condemnation by local politicians and the Church waned by that year because of the retaliatory measures by Crown forces. Murphy's account of the period also confirms that a late surge in the Crown's physical capacity in the summer of 1921 made IRA victory impossible, fewer than 3,000 Volunteers ranged against 50,000 British soldiers and several thousand RIC, and that the Truce in July 1921 came not a moment too soon for Sinn Fein. Moreover, he confirms the author's picture of IRA men swaggering in the immediate aftermath of the Truce, 'recipients', in Murphy's words, 'of an unhealthy degree of hero-worship'.

Anthony Blake is the hero of the tales, a young Irish subaltern who returns from the Great War and becomes a District Inspector in the Auxiliary Division of the RIC.[67] Several of the major figures in *Tales of the R.I.C.* are Great War veterans, and the theme of Irish ingratitude and hostility to their soldiers runs throughout the tales. Our hero, however, is in the end helpless amid the inimical circumstances that favour the Irish rebels and are created in part by what the opinionated narrator sees as the pusillanimity or indifference of the Liberal British government, culminating in the Truce that is merely the latest betrayal of Irish loyalists.

The loose interconnection of the largely free-standing tales through the figure of Blake, as well as similarities of plot, recall *The Nabob* and there is an outside chance that J. A. Strahan ('Andrew James') was the author. In each set of tales there are graphic descriptions of the parlous state of the country and brutality of the times, in each case a single year, 1798 and early 1920 to early 1921; both Strahan and the author of *Tales* recount atrocity intimately and unflinchingly in ways the celebrated novelists of the Troubles shied from. And in each set, it is the depressingly familiar Irish recourse to *reprisal* that is the motive force of the plots. Moreover, the abhorrence of Bolshevism that animates the narrator also animates the essays that Strahan wrote for *Blackwood's* under his own name. But on balance I think that another hand was responsible for the tales and that the similarities simply testify to shared attitudes among loyalists since, among other things, Strahan would surely have signed his own name to 'Irish Realities', an essay that appeared in the magazine in March 1920 over the name 'Ignotus' (i.e. unknown, unrecognized) and that could easily have been written by the author of *Tales of the R.I.C.* 'Irish Realities' reports the 'atmosphere of terror and nervous apprehension' in much of Ireland, the dispersal of the landed gentry ('the landlord is down and out, and there is no wholesome middle-class opinion in Ireland'), the popular animus against the RIC, the imminent abandonment of the police to the tender mercies of Sinn Fein, and the incapacity of the English to take the Irish bull by the horns—all of which are illustrated in graphically violent form in *Tales of the R.I.C.*

Although generally pessimistic, 'Ignotus' leaves open the possibility of a miracle to solve the intractable Irish Question, Ireland being a land of surprises; in a long shot, Irish realism becomes Irish fancy. Eschewing fancy, the author of *Tales of the R.I.C.* makes a few dour predictions which were in a manner borne out by events. He believes that were de Valera to relinquish his demand for an all-island Irish Republic in favour of something less, for example a partitioned island, he would be signing his own death warrant: the assassination of Michael Collins proved the author correct. He predicts that no settlement that would satisfy de Valera could satisfy or appease Ulster and again was proven right. He predicts that on the day an Irish Republic is announced a cleavage would open up between two emerging Irish parties that would fly at each other's throats. He believed that they would be Sinn Fein's petty bourgeoisie and Labour's proletariat; he did not foresee the Treatyites and the Diehards (anti-Treatyites), but was accurate in his sense of likely civil war in the event of independence coming to pass.[68]

As a sequel to his fiction, the author of *Tales* revisited Ireland in a lengthy report entitled 'Ulster in 1921' ('By the Author of "Tales of the R.I.C."'), published in *Blackwood's Magazine* in October 1922. There he realleged British desertion of Southern loyalists (and alleged their fresh attempt to desert

Northern loyalists) and deflated the last-ditch optimism expressed by 'Ignotus' in 'Irish Realities': the future did not look bright for Southern unionists and he himself, having considered England and the Colonies, had decided to cross the new border into Northern Ireland to begin again. (This would seem to rule the Ulsterman Strahan out as author of *Tales.*) These were the three favoured destinations of the Anglo-Irish who chose exile over Home Rule, and there were many of these.[69] Their departure constituted a diaspora unlamented in much of Ireland, brought country house society closer to negligibility, and facilitated the triumph of the Catholic lower middle class in Free State Ireland. As for the RIC, though members stationed in the six counties of Northern Ireland had stayed there when the force was disbanded in 1921, the author of 'Ulster in 1921' described it as in any case a force whose morale was essentially spent at the end: it was still disciplined but had no heart in the work.

DILEMMAS OF ALLEGIANCE

The author of *Tales of the R.I.C.* thought the portrait of the Irish peasant in the immensely popular *Some Experiences of an Irish R.M.* (1899) by Somerville and Ross was a true one but incapable of illuminating the life (and death) of the RM in the troubled Ireland of 1919–21 (*BEM* 209: 668). However, in the same year that the tales of the RIC were published, Edith Somerville, in the absence of her dead collaborator, took on Troubles Ireland in a long fiction. But action and violence are far more obliquely conveyed in *An Enthusiast* and only gradually occupy Somerville's foreground, remaining largely in the background until their inexorable advance to all but centre stage at novel's end. The novel establishes the familiar trajectory in Troubles novels that Elizabeth Bowen, Pamela Hinkson, and J. G. Farrell later finessed when they depicted in tragic and (when the reader closes the novel) elegiac fashion the melancholy long withdrawing roar of Anglo-Irish life, a kind of resignation in literature that the author of *Tales of the R.I.C.* would have despised from the haven of Northern Ireland.

The relatively calm part of south-west Munster in which *An Enthusiast* is set gives breathing space to Somerville's familiar gift for romance and humour but her self-imposed obligation to currency required fidelity (however perfunctory and reluctant one senses it to be) to a state of affairs in which violence of some sort was general all over Ireland.

Even though the district of which Eskragh was the centre was less 'disturbed' than others, there were not many days of that summer, and still fewer nights, when the peace that seemed to hold it was not broken; when the glory of the summer mornings was not smirched by the smoke of fires, outward and visible signs of inner fires of hatred, and the short stillness of the summer nights shattered by the hard, inhuman clamour of shots.[70]

Towards the end of the novel this characterization, like the seasons themselves, darkens, though the author's inveterate gift for humour cannot help but incongruously introduce the comic macabre:

There has not often been a time in Ireland when what is ambiguously spoken of as Unrest has not been an integral feature of the country's life, a skeleton in the cupboard, whose bones give an occasional disquieting rattle, whose moods are as incalculable as those of the weather. But in the year 1920 the skeleton had come forth, bribed, cajoled, flattered, persuaded of his wrongs. Slowly, at first, he had declared himself, but by the early autumn there were not many houses where he was not sitting, master of the feast, calling the tune, and making others pay for it. (pp. 225–6)

But there is still room for uncertainty in the direction of Ireland's immediate fate, which hangs in the balance, between the two shadows thrown by audacious republicanism in 1916 and by Anglo-Irish officer bravery on the fronts of the Great War, a bravery transposed back home into staunchness in the face of republican attack.

Daniel Palliser MC embodies that instinctive and traditional bravery, but although he has become master of a big house and estate that are legitimate republican targets by definition, he regards himself as a patriot and is indubitably a reformer, believing that the solution to Ireland's problem lies in prosperity which can best be achieved by modernization of land use (including mechanization), co-operative schemes in agricultural production, and improvements in education. In terms of his answer to the Irish Question, Palliser stands (though he would not be aware of it) in the tradition of Arthur Young, Robert Kane, Samuel Smiles, and Filson Young. But his perspective is deliberately narrow: his patriotism is less that of Anglo-Ireland, of Grattan and his parliamentary cohorts, than of locality, above which he believes the contest between unionism and nationalism as political positions is waged irrelevantly. (Still, one cannot help but see Palliser's reformism as an adaptation to changed circumstances of that upper-class philanthropy that Birmingham's Sir James Digby disavows and that several characters in the country-house novel enthusiastically embrace.) He is a fairly strict utilitarian and if he shares the idea of co-operation with AE, he does not share the latter's mysticism: he wants the creameries but not the dreameries. Palliser's chosen political context is the aftermath (though unidentified in the novel) of the Local Government (Ireland) Act of 1898 which introduced a network of county boroughs, county councils, urban district and rural district councils and which, like the Land Acts, lessened the power of the large landowners. These innovations encouraged local consciousness and the setting up of a variety of local bodies: Palliser becomes President of the Agriculture Society and Vice Chairman of the Farmers' Society, though the first of these is inherited on the death of his father, the old Colonel, veteran of the Crimean War.

Palliser is to a degree a realist. The novel opens with the narratorial observation that 'The position of the landless landlord is now a familiar one' (p. 3), echoing the same observation by Mrs Donovan in Croker's *Lismoyle* (p. 149), a contradiction in reality that Palliser is prepared to treat with—renting out his house and modernizing the cultivation of previously decorative gardens. But there is a dramatically more important element of idealism and naivety in Palliser's position. The novel opens with his conviction that the bulk of the Irish people know that the Palliser heart is Irish, despite what Sinn Fein might say. Later, we are told that Palliser was of those 'whose opinions, once formed, were of disastrous tenacity—disastrous because his strong will held them with a force that limited their power of growth. He was of the fiery company of enthusiasts' (p. 49) and is elsewhere called a 'zealot'. In 1920, Somerville added an essay for her miscellany of pieces by Ross and herself called *Stray-Aways* (1920) in which she identified Maria Edgeworth's father as 'a reformer and an enthusiast', and in contrasting his optimism with Sir Jonah Barrington's more realistic 'amused pessimism', Somerville connects Edgeworth with Palliser, though the latter is perhaps a more naive example.[71]

Palliser attempts what proves to be the impossible task in 1920 of rejecting (or accepting: the same thing) both unionism and nationalism. Lady Ducarrig (with whom he gradually falls in love) calls him 'Mr. Facing-both-ways' (p. 74) and he accepts the epithet. ' "I'm not a Unionist", he reflected, "and I'm certainly not a Sinn Feiner. I suppose I'm among the half-tones, what they call 'pastel tints'—'Mr. Facing-both-ways'? No, hang it! I'm nothing" ' (p. 80). But unlike Digby, another landless landlord, he want and tries to belong where Digby withdraws into wry spectatorship. However, in Ireland one is not permitted to be nothing unless one is either a unionist or a nationalist nothing, and when Palliser expresses the folly of his position—'An ass halting between two burdens, a Laodicean, neither hot nor cold!' (p. 138)—one might detect a degree of self-portraiture by Somerville. It is Palliser who cracks the Somervillean joke, when Father Hugh MacNamara tells him that he too is getting it from both sides, the authorities and the IRA: ' "between the devil and the R.I.C." said Dan, with a short laugh' (p. 177).

But at first Palliser seems to find supporters and success until, against the backdrop of growing Sinn Fein confidence and daring, he is thwarted by corruption among the local small farmers, jealous greed among businessmen, race dislike among nationalists, and (though it might be a card played by hypocrites) moral reservation about his friendship with Lady Ducarrig. Palliser launches a broadside against the cowardice of the farmers (who the reader may let stand for the plain people of Ireland) but Somerville lets her flawed hero revive the Joycean and Yeatsian Parnellite theme when she has Palliser, wrestling with the choice between love for Lady Ducarrig and his vow to help Ireland, wonder if he should renounce his lover for Ireland, 'a country that killed her prophets and stoned them that loved her' (p. 259). If *An Enthusiast* is a portrait of a zealot, it is also an indictment of Ireland itself.

Palliser seems to turn away from politics to love (as Yeats said the intelligent and cultivated Irish turned from politics to art in the wake of Parnell's fall), though this in turn seems to require him to confront the IRA when they attack his family seat, Monalour House. Somerville leaves Palliser's motivation ambiguous, for the sword he carries when he charges Monalour House might be Rossetti's Pilgrim's sword of love or his father's Crimean sword of Anglo-Irish battle; is he defending the house, and, if so, is he joining the 'guns' (Lord Ducarrig's shooting guests who resist an IRA that is unused to resistance in these circumstances) or fighting a gallant solo battle? Or has he finally collapsed mentally under the strain of his dilemma? My guess is that Somerville could not take her hero off the horns of his dilemma, any more than she could resolve her own dilemma of allegiance.

As for the historical and tonal instabilty of *An Enthusiast* to which I earlier drew attention, Ireland in 1920 was highly unstable; it was between shadows, and a realistic depiction of it had to capture its instability and volatility. Somerville's narrative wobbles between the familiar humour of *Some Experiences of an Irish R.M.* (1899)—see her portrait of the country Irish (p. 24), embarrassing in the circumstances of 1920, though it confirmed McDonnell Bodkin's assessment of Irish humour—and the realism (though here broadened) of *The Real Charlotte* (1894), not to speak of the romance of late Victorian fiction. But Somerville might have argued that at the same time it reflected aspects of changing Irish reality of the time. The perennial sabotage of one mode of expression by another (be it comedy, romance, or realism) reflected, she might have argued (adducing Joyce as proof), a very real, exasperating, and in the end tragic state of Irish affairs. Lamenting something that the most recent Irish Troubles confirmed, Palliser puts his finger on an Irish trait. 'It's the levity,' says Palliser, 'the mixture of levity and brutality in the people that breaks my heart' (p. 116).[72]

NOTES

1. Douglas Goldring, Introduction to *The Fortune* (1917; London: Desmond Harmsworth, 1931), p. xxiv; Aldous Huxley, Preface, p. viii. The 1917 subtitle was dropped in the 1921 and 1931 republications.

2. In *Odd Man Out*, Goldring (who attended a public school, followed by Oxford—the Catholic Pusey College) identified his early literary influences and models as James Elroy Flecker (with whom he became friends), Ernest Dowson, A. E. Housman, and Frances Thompson. He later met figures associated with Wilde: Reginald Turner and Robert Ross, as well as Norman Douglas and Ernest Thesiger.

3. Malleson's description of the bizarre variety of anti-War and anti-conscription types is similar to that provided by Goldring in the same year: *After Ten Years: A Personal Record* (London: Jonathan Cape, 1931), p. 100; Douglas Goldring, *The Fortune*, p. xiii. Malleson recounts her involvement in the pacifist movement on pages 98–109.

4. Douglas Goldring, *The Fortune*, p. xv. Goldring's 1931 premonition of the future was proven accurate: 'If the guns go off again, as they so easily may somewhere between 1936 and 1940, unless the very young take the trouble to do something to avert their own fate, we may look for a political landslide, which will give us Mr. Winston Churchill and his like to rule us': *The Fortune*, p. xxiii. But this was to apportion prospectively unilateral blame. By 1940 Churchill was incomparably preferable to Hitler to all but the dyed-in-the-wool Communists who made a pact with Herr Hitler.

5. The admission of being under a spell seems odd in a left-wing commentator, yet Goldring wrote of his stay in Ireland: 'no foreigner, certainly no Englishman, is ever "quite the same", after falling under the spell': *Odd Man Out: The Autobiography of a 'Propaganda Novelist'* (London: Chapman and Hall, 1935), p. 176.

6. The description is that of Goldring's granddaughter, Polly Bird, reacting to a *Guardian* article on Orwell's 'crypto-outing' of Goldring and others; his son Patrick Goldring reacted similarly: 'Letters', *Guardian*, 28 June 2003.

7. St John Ervine, *Changing Winds* (New York: Macmillan, 1917), p. 306.

8. Ervine, *Changing Winds*, pp. 502–3, 533–4. Quinn shares with Marsh the idea that Ireland must engage in 'self-regeneration' and leave behind her whining self-pity (what an historian recently christened the MOPE syndrome, standing for Most Oppressed People Ever).

9. This self-consciousness, even self-centredness, this provincialism, this absence of either England or Ireland as large beckoning Causes and Loves, are, Ervine seems to imply, an unfortunate characteristic of the Ulster Protestant. Ervine himself enlisted in the Dublin Fusiliers and was wounded, losing a leg in Flanders.

10. A volume of short stories that quietly celebrate the Ulstermen who enlisted and perished, many of them at the Somme or Suvla Bay, is S. Lindsay's *Sons of Ulster* (London: Stockwell, n.d.), the title a phrase Frank McGuinness the playwright was later to make famous. These modest little stories—often pious and often teaching the moral that we should count our blessings—try to validate ordinary experience and ordinary men, humble lives in neglected places. The stories are set not at the front but at home. In 'The House of Silence' three sons from County Antrim enlist, one in a Scottish regiment, two in the 6th Inniskillings. Their stories are told by a Presbyterian minister. Two of the sons are killed at the Suvla Bay landings, part of the Dardanelles expedition, one son earning a posthumous

VC. The surviving son takes part in the Big Push of July 1; he is wounded, has his arm amputated, is discharged, and returns home where he might get married. End of story. Religion and the Great War dominate these Protestant small-farmer country lives, as historically they would have done. Some of the dialogue is in Ulster Scots. There is a little humour. When a Mrs McCrum is told that 'We're beginnin' tae drive the Germans back tae Berlin,' she replies: 'Land-sakes! Wullie, drivin' them, ir they? Feth, an A'd jest let them walk.' Only in one story does politics intrude. In 'Home on Leave', a Capt Bob Wilson recounts the battle of the Somme and the gallantry of 'Carson's men'. At the close of the story one character says: 'A'm thinkin' Home Rule is killed, at least as far as Ulster is concerned. We wur aye united tae Englan', but noo the union has been cemented wi' bluid. Englan' is no' likely tae forget her freens' (p. 87). The Linenhall Library (Belfast) catalogue suggests the publication date of the volume is 1917.

11. Ervine, *Changing Winds*, pp. 313–14. Writing to Shane Leslie, F. Scott Fitzgerald called Ervine, on the strength of the 'semi-brilliant' *Changing Winds*, one of the contemporary 'gloomy half-twilight realists': *The Letters of F. Scott Fitzgerald*, ed. Andrew Turnbull (New York: Charles Scribner's Sons, 1963), pp. 373–4.

12. David Lyall, *An English Rose* (London, New York: Cassell and Company, 1918), pp. 301, 311.

13. By a peculiar error, Cicely's three brothers begin as Roger (the eldest), Dick, and Tony (pp. 8–9) and end as Jack (the eldest), Teddy, and Tony (p. 126); this error might be the price of Swan's astounding pace of composition.

14. The country house, too, which had incubated the philanthropic impulse, came into its own during the Great War. J. Johnston Abraham from Coleraine remembers (as 'James Harpole') the wounded soldiers he as a surgeon sent 'to convalesce at a country mansion run by one of those patriotic ladies with kind hearts and no experience who were such a feature during the Great War', James Harpole, *Leaves from a Surgeon's Case-Book* (1937; London: Cassell for the British Publishers Guild, 1941), p. 67.

15. David Lyall, *An English Rose*, pp. 127, 101, 125, 165, 224.

16. See *Scottish Authors: 'Annie S. Swan, Novelist, 1859–1943'*: www.slainte.org.uk/clips/publications/scotauth/swanadsw.htm

17. *Edwardian Fiction: An Oxford Companion*, ed. Sandra Kemp, Charlotte Mitchell, and David Trotter (Oxford: Oxford University Press, 1997), s.v. Swan, Annie.

18. David Lyall, *An English Rose*, pp. 186–7, 210, 160, 310.

19. Ibid., pp. 49, 186–7, 277, 278, 87, 110–11, 118.

20. Mrs. Victor Rickard, *The Fire of Green Boughs* (1918; New York: Dodd, Mead and Company, 1919), p. 141.

21. In Mary Maher's novel, *Fidelity* (1898), St Dominic is described as 'bringing back the straying sheep to the fold' (p. 78).

22. Rickard, *The Fire of Green Boughs*, pp. 24, 30–1, 33, 34, 67, 149, 150, 247, 146.

23. Ibid., pp. 238, 327, 73, 243.

24. Katharine Tynan, *The Years of the Shadow* (London: Constable, 1919), pp. 156–7. J. B. Lyons, *The Enigma of Tom Kettle: Irish Patriot, Essayist, Poet, British Soldier, 1880–1916* (Dublin: Glendale Press, 1983), p. 281.

25. Rickard, *The Fire of Green Boughs*, pp. 98, 263, 301, 327.
26. There were sincere attempts to combine Irishness with imperial obligations. Rickard was proud of the fact that her husband, Lieut.-Colonel Rickard, introduced the shamrock in February 1915 as part of the cap badge of the Second Battalion of the Royal Munster Fusiliers 'with the object of giving a distinctively Irish emblem to all ranks': Mrs Victor Rickard, 'Dedication' to her book *The Story of the Munsters at Etreux, Festubert, Rue du Bois and Hulloch* (London: Hodder & Stoughton, 1918). The first and second battalions of this regiment were originally regiments in the army of the East India Company and became part of the regular British Army when control of India passed from the Company to the Crown, and whose honours before the Great War were won chiefly in India, Afghanistan, Burma, and South Africa—in imperial service, in other words: Lord Dunraven (Hon. Col. 5th Batt. Royal Munster Fusiliers), 'Introduction' to *The Story of the Munsters*, pp. vii–xiii.

This short, poignant and well-written book (originally published in *New Ireland* magazine in 1915, as chapters and then as a book which sold out by the end of the year) is part history, part homage, and part epitaph. It is an account of several Great War battles in which the Munsters were engaged—losing some, winning some, fighting others to an all too familiar standstill; on balance it is a story of gallantry under fire—and includes the story of how Louise Rickard's husband fell while leading the 2nd Battalion at the Rue du Bois on 9 May 1915. Rickard suppresses her personal feelings in the account, diverting them instead into her story of a religious service on the eve of battle. 'When the Munsters came up the road, Colonel Rickard halted the Battalion. The men were ranged in three sides of a square, their green flags, embroidered with the Irish harp and the word "Munster", a gift from Lady Gordon, placed before each Company. Father Gleeson mounted, Colonel Rickard and Captain Filgate, the Adjutant on their chargers, were in the centre, and in that wonderful twilight Father Gleeson gave a General Absolution. To some present, very certainly, the "vitam æternam was intensely and beautifully manifest, the day-spring of Eternity very near...Miseratur vestri Ominpotens Deus, et dismissis peccatis vestris, perducat vos ad vitam æternam." The whole Regiment with their heads bared, sang the *Te Deum*, the great thanksgiving, the "Sursum Corda" of all the earth...The men who prayed there were, very few of them, the men of the original Battalion. Gaps had been filled again and again, and most of the Munsters who fought next day were newly come from Ireland and new to the life. Lads from Kerry and Cork, who, a year before, had never dreamed of marching in the ranks of the British Army' (pp. 35–6).

The Story of the Munsters is written with the empathy that could be mistaken for eyewitness recall: 'So the day passed, and the wounded lay out under the cruel lash of the sleet and bitter wind. Not one man returned to Headquarters, except some wounded who straggled in, dazed and bleeding. The chorus of the field guns, and the crack, crack of rifle fire went on persistently. Lyddite and high explosives rained through the murky evening, and still no orders were issued that reached the Munster Fusiliers. They had gone out, as is their way, to do their bit, and had disappeared into the vast nothingness behind the night. Darkness fell, and great flashes lit the dark; those pale, awful gleams of super-civilisation swept over the ghastly land. The enemy's search-lights were feeling after the mutilated and wounded, showing up the stretcher-bearers and Red Cross dressers . . .'.

At Festubert, 22 December, the Munsters were pinned down by a counter-attack and picked off, but the survivors held on and were located by Major Julian Ryan (shot a few weeks later), and brought in before daybreak revealed them fatally to the enemy. An Appendix of letters from officers to fathers, mothers, and widows deepens the poignancy of the book, and though Rickard permits herself a few purple passages, particularly when she is moved by the Irishness of the Regiment, this is a book with the feel of good if occasionally sentimental fiction.

27. This novel is discussed briefly in Lisbet Kickham, *Protestant Women Novelists and Irish Society 1879–1922* (2004).

28. Annie M. P. Smithson, *Her Irish Heritage* (1917; Cork: Mercier Press, 1988), p. 158.

29. Robert Lynd, 'The Work of T. M. Kettle', collected in Sean MacMahon (ed.), *Galway of the Races: Selected Essays* (Dublin: Lilliput Press, 1990), p. 101.

30. Professor T. M. Kettle, 'Under the Heel of the Hun', in *The Ways of War* (London: Constable, 1917), p. 106. (This volume is a collection of Kettle's war journalism, made by his widow Mary Sheehy Kettle.)

31. Lynd, 'The Work of T. M. Kettle', *Galway of the Races*, p. 105.

32. Lyons, *The Enigma of Tom Kettle*, p. 297.

33. Robert Lynd, 'T.M. Kettle', in *Essays on Life and Literature* (London: J. M. Dent, 1951), p. 53. According to Patrick Maume, Kettle may have developed some late doubts about his military involvement: *The Long Gestation: Irish Nationalist Life 1891–1918* (Dublin: Gill & Macmillan, 1999), p. 185.

34. John Redmond, Introduction to Michael MacDonagh, *The Irish at the Front* (London: Hodder and Stoughton, 1916), p. 5.

35. Lyons, *The Enigma of Tom Kettle*, pp. 271–2.

36. Robert Lynd, *Ireland a Nation* (London: Grant Richards, 1919), p. 118. Lynd himself is a case-study in deep Irish ambivalence. Although he was a Belfast Protestant who became well known as a practitioner of the classic English essay, he was also a literary propagandist for a vigorous Irish nationalism. He set out the wares of Sinn Fein in *Home Life in Ireland* (1909) and endorsed its programme of economic self-sufficiency. He remained a Sinn Fein supporter even after the Easter Rebellion, though admitting in *Ireland a Nation* (1919) that most Irish nationalists saw the Rising as a rebellion not against England but against Ireland. His exposition and defence of Sinn Fein seem lukewarm beside his fascination with the Great War and his great friend, Kettle ('the Hamlet of modern Ireland'), about whom he wrote four essays. 'The Irish Soldier', a chapter in *Ireland a Nation*, is full of Irish military pride, and like Redmond and Kettle, he believes that 'the war with Germany was the first war in history in which the Irish soldier fought *qua* Irishman on the same side as England' (p. 109).

37. We can find a vivid and satirical portrait of a confused, uncertain, and multiple Ireland on the eve of the Great War in Gerald Griffin's neglected *The Dead March Past: A Semi-Autobiographical Saga* (1937).

38. Ella MacMahon, *Irish Vignettes* (London: John Lane The Bodley Head, 1928), pp. 220, 75, 1–4, 74, 132.

39. A very different kind of Great War book is the fascinating *Leaves from a Surgeon's Case-Book* (1937; London: Cassell for the British Publishers Guild, 1941) by 'James Harpole' (J. Johnston Abraham). Abraham's medical reminiscences are dominated by the War. He discusses in sequence the diseases that broke out under conditions of the War in its various European and Middle East theatres: tetanus, diptheria, malaria, tuberculosis, typhus, and typhoid fever. He explains in an illuminating way the etiology of these diseases and the research they stimulated. He writes about the injuries soldiers sustained, including shell-shock (what we now call post-traumatic stress disorder) that caused functional rather than actual injury; paralysis due to spinal and head injuries; and heart-damage. The surgical and other treatments these injuries and diseases provoked are surprisingly modern: open-heart surgery, plastic surgery, including cosmetic surgery, inoculation and vaccination, biological engineering, hormonal injections (including Steinach's Operation that Yeats underwent and that enabled patients of poor physique—in an anticipation of steroids—'to accomplish feats worthy of Olympic champions', p. 123). Even seventy years after they were written, Abraham's reminiscences are educational. This is in part because Abraham sees disease as an expression of culture, and cultural history dates less quickly than medical technology; when discussing influenza pandemics and epidemics he reminds us of the devastating impact of disease on some civilizations of the past. He also remarks that the Great War was won less by armies than by the food blockade; 'but it is not yet appreciated except in scientific circles, that it was the lack of vitamin protective foods that really caused the physical deterioration of the Central Powers and led to their final surrender' (p. 166). It was fitting that someone who saw action in the Great War as a medical officer (there are glimpses of Lawrence of Arabia after the British captured Jerusalem in 1917) should see the medical campaign against incurable diseases and horrific injuries as a kind of warfare and his own role as medicine's war correspondent, someone waging his own war against people's fear of disease, which fear must have increased after the Great War. A year after the publication of *Leaves*, Abraham (again as 'James Harpole') made the metaphor literal when he titled a new set of reminscences *The White-Coated Army* (London: Cassell, 1938), seeing doctors as 'officers in a Health army fighting the long fight against disease' (p. ix). In this book he turns the cases he recalls into semblances of short stories. Abraham continued his project of popularizing medical advances in *Behind the Surgeon's Mask* (1940) and *A Surgeon's Heritage* (1953) with the occasional overlap of anecdote and cases among the four volumes. In *Lettsom: His Life, Times, Friends and Descendants* (1933), a biography of John Coakley Lettsom the famous physician, Abraham (and the book appeared above his own

name) provided us with nothing less than a medical history of the eighteenth and nineteenth centuries (and Quakerism and slavery into the bargain).

40. Tynan, *The Years of the Shadow*, pp. 174–5.

41. In *The Wandering Years* (London: Constable, 1922, pp. 34–5), Tynan remarks that 'Disaffection to England has been largely kept alive in Ireland by the ill-paid schoolteachers. A hungry man is a dangerous man, as Shakespeare knew.' She adds that the Easter Rising had in its ranks a good many ill-paid civil servants. She clearly prefers an economic to a cultural or political explanation of growing Anglophobia.

42. Tynan, *The Wandering Years*, pp. 4–5.

43. Tynan, *The Years of the Shadow*, pp. 175–6. She noticed that by December 1918 her famous poem, 'Flower of Youth,' had not been read from the pulpits of her own (Roman Catholic) faith.

44. Tynan (ibid., p. 146) recalls starting a war journal which she entitled 'A Woman's Notes of the Great War' and although she purported by the time she wrote her book to find it 'intensely depressing', it would be good to read it.

45. There is an excellent account of the waxing and waning of Irish commitment to the War, set inside the Home Rule-independence debate, in Maume, *The Long Gestation*, pp. 147–214.

46. Cf. Maume, *The Long Gestation*, p. 151.

47. Yeats helped in a small way to effect this expulsion. His poem, 'An Irish Airman Foresees his Death,' written after the death of Lady Gregory's son Robert (Major Robert Gregory, RFC, MC, killed on the Italian front in January 1918), identifies his friend's son's motives as local patriotism and 'A lonely impulse of delight' among the clouds, while denying that they included duty, law or loyalty to England. Since the local patriotism in question is love for the barony of Kiltartan, and given the significance with which Lady Gregory and Yeats invested Kiltartan, the poet in effect attributes Robert Gregory's motive in joining the Royal Flying Corps to Irish patriotism, even Irish literary revival. The poem seems like an extraordinary appropriation not just of voice but of mind and heart. I venture to suggest that the Great War, like the infinitely smaller but still iconic event of the *Titanic* disaster, was for Yeats a rival and threatening historical tragedy in which he had no part to claim and thus to be appropriated or ignored as the case might be. At first the Easter Rising was discountenanced (he thought the insurrection a mistake and fretted that he had not been warned of its imminence), but Yeats quickly recovered and in 'Easter 1916' gave the rebellion his own interpretation, one that became triumphantly influential.

48. Tynan thought that had the natural leaders of Ireland, the Irish Catholic aristocracy, not flown after the Siege of Limerick, the history of the island would have been entirely different: *The Wandering Years*, p. 34.

49. She also repeats a chronological problem from *A Mad Marriage*. Carmel is stated to be 26 in early 1917 but is said to be 20 in 1914, when of course she ought to be 23.

50. Katharine Tynan, *The Golden Rose* (London: Eveleigh, Nash & Grayson, 1924), p. 81.

51. Ibid., *The Golden Rose* (London: Eveleigh, Nash & Grayson, 1924), pp. 140, 138, 141–2, 143, 138.
52. Tynan rarely forgets her tremendous interest in Catholic charity and good works. Carmel and her mother stay in a convent (the YMCA hostel being full) amidst nuns who want to go abroad helping the people and dispensing beneficence but who cannot because they belong to an enclosed order. The nuns 'burnt for France, perhaps more than the most ardent patriot outside' (p. 166).
53. Tynan had a personal acquaintance with such a family, the older brother (a solicitor) being arrested for Sinn Fein activity, the younger brother being killed as a British soldier in France: *The Wandering Years*, p. 56. On her journey to Co. Cork to find out for the owner, her cousin Lady Ardilaun, how badly Macroom Castle has been burned, Katherine Everett meets a woman one of whose sons is out with the IRA and one with the Free Staters, her eldest having been killed as a British soldier during the Great War: *Bricks and Flowers: Memoirs* (1949; Bungay, Suffolk: Reprint Society, 1951), pp. 179–80.
54. Quoted by David Finkelstein, 'The Rise and Fall of the House of Blackwood's Magazine', http://mcdept.qmuc.ac.uk/Blackwoods/blackhist.html Finkelstein is the author of *The House of Blackwood: Author-Publisher Relations in the Victorian Era* (2002).
55. I discuss the tales' background of imperial India in my Afterword to *The Nabob: A Tale of Ninety-Eight* (2006).
56. I discuss these forceful essays in my Afterword to *The Nabob*.
57. See my Afterword to *The Nabob* for further details of Strahan's career.
58. 'An Irishwoman', 'The Terror by Night', *Blackwood's Edinburgh Magazine* 208 (1920): 38.
59. Katharine Tynan referred to the Troubles more generally as 'the Reign of Terror' and 'the Terror', still at its full height in May 1921: *The Wandering Years*, pp. 336, 338. For an account of 'The Terror in Ireland' by someone who considered the Crown forces, particularly the 'fascist' Black and Tans, to be the aggressors, see Douglas Goldring, *Odd Man Out*, Part II, ch. 5.
60. The tales ran in *BEM* (vols. 209, 210) between April and November 1921. An earlier series, *Tales of the Royal Irish Constabulary*, by Michael Brophy, appeared in 1896, published by Bernard Doyle in Dublin.
61. Katharine Tynan offers readers her experiences, first-hand and second-hand (through anecdotes), of the Troubles up until the Truce, in *The Wandering Years*, pp. 195–9, 203–8, 234–44, 336–86. These corroborate a good deal of what appears in *Tales of the R.I.C.* However, although it might seem odd that she emphasizes the human, homely, and humorous in her account (though of course it would have been the case that Irish humour was not killed even in an Ireland under curfew), she explains in a brief Afterword dated May 1922 that she removed certain chapters of serious treatment of 'the Irish struggle' because they would be more appropriate in a later volume, since the future of the country is still in grave doubt.
62. According to R. F. Foster, the army were a less popular target for IRA squads than the RIC and by the time of the Truce, 400 policemen had been killed as compared

with 160 regular soldiers: *Modern Ireland 1600–1972* (1988; London: Penguin Books, 1989), p. 497. An attempt to humanize, as well as quantify, RIC casualties is made by Richard Abbott's *Police Casualties in Ireland 1919–1922* (2006). Abbott provides an alphabetical list of the RIC dead and it has a mute poignancy, unavoidably reminding us of the compilation of the dead in the Northern Ireland troubles of 1969–98: *Lost Lives*, eds. David McKittrick et al. (1999).

63. This doubling was repeated after the Anglo-Irish Treaty when for a time there were Provisional Irish Government courts and Irish Republican courts. Irish cultural bifocalism, therefore, lasted from 1916 until the end of the Irish civil war in 1923.

64. The burial alive of the Resident Magistrate is recounted by Richard Bennett in *The Black and Tans* (London: Edward Hulton, 1959), p. 98. Bennett retails similar atrocities, reprisals, and counter-reprisals to those in *Tales of the R.I.C.* but since he includes the tales in his bibliography, caution should be exercised; there are factual errors in his book.

65. One understandable distortion in the narrator's political perspective, one oddly shared by some Irish liberation nationalists in the nineteenth and twentieth centuries, is his idea that the Irish Question is essentially an imperial question. He seems to believe that the British Empire must be defended on its contested western European flank. His use of 'kopjes' to describe small Irish hills and 'wallah' to describe certain Irish officials betrays his imperial outlook. On the other hand, his use of imperial vocabulary may be an attempt to familiarize Ireland for readers in imperial Africa and India.

66. These are all observations made by John A. Murphy in *Ireland in the Twentieth Century* (Dublin: Gill and Macmillan, 1975), chapter 1.

67. There was in real life a Cecil Arthur Maurice Blake, an Englishman who had served with distinction in the Royal Artillery during the Great War, who joined the RIC and became a District Inspector. He and his wife (and two soldiers) were ambushed and murdered by the IRA in May 1921 as they were leaving Ballyturin House, a country house in Gort, Co. Galway. See Abbott, *Police Casualties*, pp. 241–2. Abbott reminds us that there are no memorials to the RIC in Ireland.

68. The force of the narrator's contempt for British Liberal policy in Ireland (shared by Strahan) implied a chronic malfeasance in the British government's handling of Ireland. The author alleges that British Prime Ministers could fulminate against Sinn Fein/IRA at the very moment secret meetings were going on between the two parties (210: 631); that Sinn Fein propaganda in the United States and England was clever, persuasive, and unanswered (210: 625); that British government assurances to loyalists coincided with plans to desert loyalists (210: 623); that loyalists could be ignored by the British government when they had no vote to exercise on the mainland (210: 636); that an anti-unionist agenda could be maintained by citing the supremacy of the peace process ('the "peace atmosphere" was the important factor': see 'Ulster in 1921' by the same author (212: 439). Every one of those allegations was repeated by unionists during the Troubles, 1970–98. Moreover, the paramilitary pattern established in *Tales of the*

R.I.C. re-emerged after 1970: the IRA carried out sustained attacks on Royal Ulster Constabulary barracks; the IRA intimidated its own population; the young emigrated when they could; there were IRA assassinations of members of the judiciary; the English government attempted time and again to surrender through face-saving truces, only to be held to their public assurances by loyalists. To complete the picture, there were police excesses and collusions while reprisals carried out by loyalist organizations and gangs were often atrocities.

69. By 1930, the population of Protestants in the new Irish Free State fell by 3 per cent, down to 7.4 per cent: Foster, *Modern Ireland*, pp. 533–4. However, because of the social and professional status of the remainder, Foster reminds us that a modest, unofficial form of 'Ascendancy' lingered on.

70. Edith Somerville, *An Enthusiast* (London: Longmans, Green & Co., 1921), p. 126.

71. 'Ireland, Then and Now,' in Somerville and Ross, *Stray-Aways* (London: Longmans, Green & Co., 1920), pp. 203–4.

72. A far more optimistic statement in fiction on the future of Ireland, if not its present, is a novel by Miriam Alexander, *The Green Altar* (1924), which is set in Munster and spans the years between the 1890s and September 1922 when the Irish civil war was not many months old. This is a country-house novel; there are two houses involved, both feeling the rising tensions of rivalrous sects and national allegiances (there is swelling patriotism and loyalist reversions), one house declining into bigotry. In the lives of the houses, star-crossed romances and marriages are played out. Despite the late appearance of the Black and Tans and the enormities of the Anglo-Irish war, the novel is low-intensity fiction. A kind of right-thinking Protestant nationalism informs the novel, and there are many spurts of essayism devoted to the character and reality of Ireland. The novel shakes down to the idea that Ireland, with luck, will turn out all right, contemporary appearances to the contrary.

Postscript. 'The Ladies' Road': Women Novelists 1922–1940

RUPTURES AND CONTINUITIES

The confused period between the end of constitutionally British Ireland and the inauguration of the Irish Free State and constitutionally British Northern Ireland is easy to mark off: it was between December 1920 when the Government of Ireland Act became law and January 1922 when the new Free State parliament, the Dáil, ratified the Anglo-Irish Treaty of 1921. However, there are various candidates for those years of cultural ferment straddling this high constitutional watershed, starting anywhere from the 1890s when the Irish Cultural Revival got into stride and ending when two largely separate if connected cultures emerged in the two parts of Ireland during the 1920s. Between times, there were, of course, candidate years waymarking the 'punctuated disequilibrium' of Irish political life.[1] A watershed is also known as a 'water parting' and the Irish division was geographical as well as temporal, with a border now between the two parts of the island. (To some extent there had been two cultures on the island already—this made partition thinkable, feasible, and even necessary, if not universally wished for—but after 1922 they were given official recognition and encouragement in the two respective jurisdictions.) Indeed, Northern Ireland as a separate region of the United Kingdom began in certain regards to grow away from the nation state of which it was a unique and anomalous 'province'—this, ironically, made reunification of the island (this time outside the UK) the more thinkable for those who had opposed partition.

The political rupture inside the southern twenty-six counties caused by the Anglo-Irish Treaty had its social and cultural fallout, when many Anglo-Irish voted with their feet and left the South either for the new Northern Ireland or England or elsewhere in the United Kingdom or in the Empire, drastically changing the social make-up and internal power relations of what now composed the Free State. The Anglo-Irish had constituted a third culture on the island, chiefly in the South, but after partition and democratization in that

Catholic part of Ireland, the Anglo-Irish could not cohabit there except in a severely reduced form. Writers were among those who personified the break with the past. The ideals of the Revival project could be said to have guttered out around the time when the new Free State announced itself as essentially Catholic and insular, implicitly in 1922 (since the 1922 constitution was a liberal document), explicitly in 1937 with the new constitution.[2] It was in 1925 that Yeats the Free State senator protested against the introduction of such a sectarian law as the proscription of divorce; censorship, and other mechanisms of proscription were to follow before too long. The Revival was unwinding. Sean O'Casey, AE (George Russell), Patrick MacGill, Oliver St John Gogarty, Stephen MacKenna, James Stephens, John Eglinton (W. K. Magee), and Eimar O'Duffy—all chose to live outside Ireland, following literally in the footsteps of Moore and Joyce. O'Casey, AE, MacKenna, Eglinton, Stephens, and O'Duffy all chose England. The 'Residency Requirement' had clearly expired.

These writers were in fact tracing the steps of many popular Irish novelists, but by then it was too late for those who had not been part of the Revival to be rehabilitated and the popular writers continued as marginalized or forgotten figures. Meanwhile, Northern Ireland exacerbated the sense of rupture, starting out as reasonably tolerant like the Free State but soon becoming as overtly Protestant as the Free State was Catholic, though Catholics tended to stay rather than leave, constituting a minority who kept a low profile while keeping their grievances warm.

Partition, civil war in the South, a powerful and unsophisticated Catholic Church, an understandable official chauvinism and isolationism after centuries of English and Anglo-Irish domination, censorship by both Church and State, a new 'flight of the earls' (i.e. of the gentry, Catholic and Protestant) leaving in prominence an uncultivated petty bourgeoisie—by the 1930s these represented for Catholic Free State writers a deadening rather than inspiriting adversity. Frank O'Connor bemoaned a new establishment of Church and State that thwarted the imagination and encouraged emigration by its very mediocrity; he claimed that national dignity had disintegrated like much else in Ireland, leaving the field to sectarianism, utilitarianism, vulgarity, and provincialism. Sean O'Faolain pictured Ireland as a broken society the parts of which were flung around like *disjecta membra* of the wheel of life. They regarded the Irish novel as a casualty of the times that were out of joint and they turned instead to the short story. Historically, they thought, the realistic Irish novel had barely been possible; now it most certainly wasn't.[3]

There were, however, some ironic continuities after 1922. It was the cultural nationalism of the Revival, like the political nationalism that had achieved partition and the Free State and at the same time was vigorously contesting these achievements, that had established the terms of the argument by which

O'Connor and O'Faolain framed their literary response to the rupture. They did not look beyond those terms to acknowledge literary accomplishment by writers outside the Revival or in works set outside the island; the Residency Requirement of the latter was for them still in force. Revival ideals had not materialized any more than nationalist ideals, and a disillusionment pervades their fiction. But in another sense, their disillusionment, their dissent, had been inherited from the diverse counter-Revival of Moore, Joyce, Brinsley MacNamara, and Daniel Corkery. Fictional realism may have originated in all of these writers from the hollowness and failure of Irish romanticism (and thus was a kind of reactive disappointment rather than a temperamental disdain for romanticism), but the net result was a realism that tried to but could not sustain itself over the course of what we might call the English novel. Corkery was hostile to the Revival because it was an *Anglo-Irish* Revival whereas he wished to see a native literary Revival, the natural capital of which was by default Cork, rather than Dublin, and since O'Faolain and O'Connor were Cork writers like Corkery who was their mentor, it is not surprising that their counter-Revival had a more significant strand of nativist disappointment than the counter-Revival of Moore or Joyce, both of whom had international cultural horizons and a firmer adherence to the independent aesthetics of fiction.

Yet there were other more obvious literary continuities despite the cultural disjunctions of the 1916–1922 period, and they might have been of some stabilizing cultural utility had they been paid attention. The Ulster writers, Bullock, Ervine, Reid, and Birmingham continued to publish novels in the 1920s and even into the 1930s and 1940s that did not show the formal stigmata of political turmoil (though by then the North was in any case sliding off the Irish critical map) any more than they made stylistic acknowledgement of the formal experiments being carried out by Eliot, Pound, Wyndham Lewis, Woolf, Joyce or any other modernists.[4] The Ulster writer Alexander Irvine also continued to publish fiction. *The Man from World's End and Other Stories of Lovers and Fighting Men* was written in 1926 in France when Irvine was a naturalized American. The eleven stories recount love stories told to him by soldiers in the Great War into whose company Irvine had been sent by Lord Rhondda, the Food Commissioner, as a morale-booster—'mind-sweeping', Irvine called it in his autobiography, *A Fighting Parson* (1930). In the chapters relating Irvine's experiences on the Somme and other killing fields of the War, we can find the origins of many of the incidents in the stories. In their narrative pace and buoyant candour, the stories associate Irvine with the earlier work of Patrick MacGill, another populist writer whose experiences at the front blurred and overlapped the fictional and first-hand. Like the Donegal man, Irvine's chosen modes are brass-tack realism and unlikely sentiment less cloying than that of *My Lady of the Chimney Corner* because the lethal circumstances of the War lend the humanity of the sentiment a found dignity. All the stories are readable but 'The Mystic Lovers' is a superb story of love and miracle amidst carnage that ought to be in the Irish anthologies.[5]

The avoidance of literary experiment was true for other established Irish novelists whose work straddled independence and partition. Edith Somerville's country-house novel, *The Big House of Inver* (1925), is a familiarly told tale of the declining fortunes of a Big House in the west of Ireland from the early eighteenth century until the novel's present—1912—by which time Inver has been severed from both its demesne and its lodge. But perhaps this saga is darker and less edifying than it might have been in earlier novels. The Prendeville family through dissipation and debt has brought dereliction to the house, and the novel's plot involves the family's attempt to wrest the house from the custody of the Weldons, a family of agents and 'land-grabbers' that has accompanied, or dogged, the Prendevilles through the decades. In fact, the Prendevilles themselves were in the beginning land-grabbers, Norman adventurers whose motto became 'Je Prends'. Their comeback is solely and tellingly in the hands of an illegitimate daughter of the dynasty, Shibby Pindy (Isabel Prendeville), a schemer of mixed native and settler blood and whose ancestress in the Somerville and Ross canon is the titular anti-heroine of *The Real Charlotte* (1894). The once beautiful house of Inver becomes by the end a shoddy prize and in any case meets fire at the moment an English baronet and his bride, the daughter of the land-grabbers, enter the spurious joy of possession. Inver stands nonetheless in silent reproach for the way in which it has been betrayed by owners and inhabitants who have not met its own tacit standards of cultivation.

The careless feudal relationship the sons of the Prendevilles have maintained through the centuries with their tenantry, at times exercising a casual *droit de seigneur* (of the concept of which they are in fact ignorant), results in illegitimate offspring, liaisons outside wedlock, strategic matches, contested wills and legacies, and blackmail. The community preoccupation with blood and heredity— 'What's bred in the bone will come out in the meat!' could be the theme[6]—is at odds with (we have seen it before) the curious, un-English, on balance mutually demeaning intimacy and curious equality between landowners and tenants that one imagines was greater in the west of Ireland than elsewhere. It is a disturbingly dishevelled society, filled with unprepossessing characters, so unsalubrious as to confirm in a different key Stephen Gwynn's conviction that the whole system was rotten from top to bottom; Somerville's gentry is but a parody of a ruling class. Shibby is a Mass-going Catholic, but in fact religion is of no account in the novel, the life depicted in it existing beneath religious sensibility. Yet instead of an admirable hybridity, we have a mongrel and unlovely society.

The semblance of social order depends on ingrained social and racial habits, providing a shaky foundation for a tottering edifice.

Barely hidden beneath the velvet of Somerville's humour is the metal of her anger and impatience, enabling her to engage in a narratorial duplicity, just as Shibby Pindy hides her own steely will beneath, when necessary, her actressy and congenial wiles. Somerville's is an avenging realism, almost delighting in exposing the reality beneath the hypocrisy. The author's impatience shows in the pace and perspective of her narration, the way she takes the story and characters by the scruff of the neck, as one might the several dogs that frequent the narrative. Shibby embodies Somerville's own hearty ambivalence towards this frayed and degenerate version of her own society—fully engaged in it yet standing outside it at the same time. She is a formidably strong woman, capable of manhandling a human obstacle in her path, yet condemned by her sex as well as her breeding to be at best 'fifth business': 'Shibby's contempt for her own sex was characteristic of her time and her class. Daughters were only pawns in the game of life, cyphers that required a masculine figure in front of them to give them value' (p. 54). Charmless throughout, like her society, Shibby's failure bestows pathos on her at the end, that failure coinciding with a larger end: 'The story of the Big House of Inver is finished', its demise nonetheless profiting John Weldon who while effecting the sale to the English baronet had insured Inver in his own name, the hated middle-man triumphing, as though a sign not just of the past but also of the future.

Just as *An Irish Cousin* was, during its composition, 'Gothicized' by the authors' visit to the lonely country house of a relative in a remote part of Cork, so Edith Somerville got her inspiration for Inver and demesne from a letter which she had received from Martin Ross in March 1912, the year Somerville set *The Big House of Inver*. By 1925 Ross had been dead a decade but Somerville credited her as co-author—'An established Firm does not change its style and title when, for any reason, one of its partners may be compelled to leave it', she wrote in her 'Author's Note'—and this cleaving to the past through loyalty to her dead collaborator may have prevented Somerville from ever breaking the mould of her fiction: the established Firm does not change its tried and tested product. In any case, she appends an excerpt from Ross's letter which describes a house and a way of life that allowed her collaborator to revisit illegitimacy, degeneration, madness, suicide (or murder), dilapidation, and other Gothic appurtenances when she was stirred to write *Inver*: 'Yesterday I drove to see X—House. A great cut stone house of three stories... Perfectly empty... It is on a long promontory by the sea, and there rioted three or four generations of X-s, living with country women, occasionally marrying them, all illegitimate four times over... Yesterday, as we left, an old Miss X, daughter of the last owner, was at the door in a little donkey-trap. She lives near in an old castle, and since her people died she will not go into X- House, or into the enormous yard, or the beautiful old garden. She was a strange mixture of distinction and commonness, like her breeding, and it was very sad to see her at the door of that great house.' In *The Big House of Inver*, it is the house, not its occupants, that is the tragic hero of this tawdry Anglo-Irish story.

Like Somerville, Beatrice Grimshaw wrote obliviously across the divisive events in Ireland. *Victorian Family Robinson* (1934) is a witty novel set in the 1860s but in terms of its women's rights theme is set really in the days of Grimshaw's own girlhood when her independence was thrusting into view, i.e. in the 1890s. The novel opens with a mock-tribute to the wonderful days of mid-Victorian Britain and to the happy domestic lives of a modest Victorian country house, especially the lives of girls, clearly drawn from Grimshaw's own girlhood in Ulster. But these mock-halcyon days are ended when one daughter appears to be 'Coming to a Bad End'.[7] We are offered two kinds of revolting daughter. There is Adeline Robinson who becomes entangled with a married officer, Captain Charlie Chaine, of the 999th Lancers, who is sent about his business by her Anglican vicar father, but who alas for the vicar soon shares the family's fate as castaways on a coral island. (The vicar is supposed to be a descendant of the model for the father in *Swiss Family Robinson* of which Grimshaw's tale is a lightly satirical rewrite.) However, it is her sister Eleanor's revolt that is radical in its possibilities.

Eleanor suddenly awakes to the 'wild gipsy fancies' and 'passion for far travel that had been hopelessly frustrated in her mother' (pp. 12, 27). Eleanor is a mid-Victorian precursor of the author herself. Eleanor reads about those intrepid high Victorian women travellers, Ida Pfeiffer, Constance Cumming, and Isabella Bird (Grimshaw's predecessors), but it is too early in cultural time for her to forget the need to be 'nice' and emulate their feats, and as for 'the wild queer passions that were to lure the girls of forty, fifty, seventy years later [i.e. 1900s, 1910s, 1930s] away from their proper occupations of marrying and having babies' (steering 60 h.p. cars, piloting planes to San Francisco or the South Pole) . . . 'no one yet had dreamed of such monstrous improprieties' (pp. 29–30). Eleanor's foresight matches the narrator's hindsight, and she predicts that in fifty or sixty years (i.e. around the time the novel is being written), girls will know what they want and how to get it, and many of them will not want marriage, darning, cooking, arranging flowers, and visiting the poor (p. 95). Meanwhile, Eleanor herself can merely exclaim: 'I wish—I wish I were a man' (p. 93). She is not quite 'fast', a word, we are told, that in the 1860s and 1870s meant 'doggy, horsy, athletic, outdoor-ish to excess; in fine, a feeble imitator of the inimitable Man', though she is a young woman of her day ('the Girl of the Period', as some called her, caricatured as a cigar-smoking, swimming, polka-dancing, hard-riding flirt) who furtively longed for adventure (p. 28).

She gets her adventure willy-nilly when the ship carrying her family to Australia (where her father, now a widower, has been appointed a bishop) founders mercifully close to a South Sea island on which the eight survivors fetch up. Primarily, the novel asks itself what happens when mid-Victorian respectability is cast out of its element, with 'Society a dead letter' (p. 275). One result is a threat to social hierarchy and order. Soon after their establishment on the island, a sailor asks for Eleanor's hand in marriage, claiming that although he is beneath her in class, 'There's no class here'. Lady Gilliland begs to differ: 'I totally disagree. Class is indestructible' (p. 103). Another result is the sudden relativizing of cultural values, something with which Grimshaw had long been familiar. Yet another is an outbreak of island romances that threaten Victorian morality, including the sanctity of marriage. 'James Robinson', the narrator tells us mischievously, 'had never heard of the theory, so popular in later times, that classed all desert islands as dangerous to morals' (p. 65), but even he begins to entertain hopes that he might inherit the hand of the beautiful Lady Gilliland who had been en route to Australia to join her Governor husband. Eleanor even contemplates a 'safe' marriage with the sailor, but the wedding is interrupted by the arrival of 'white natives' from another island, descendants of the survivors of a shipwreck in the Regency period, seventy years before. The newcomers, feral Englishmen, want wives and carry everyone back to their own island where they draw lots for the four women on the island and intend to marry them by island custom. Meanwhile, a local strong woman, Rizpah, a kind of natural feminist, leads a revolt on behalf of women's rights, and insists that the captive males be grooms to island women. Grimshaw entertains us with a festival of pairings; there are over a dozen liaisons and island marriages (Eleanor herself falls in love with a young islander, Malachi) that appear to mock the Victorian sanctity of Christian marriage.

But in fact, as in her earlier novels, Grimshaw draws back from doing so and offers in the end no daring or even realistic agenda for female self-fulfilment. Eleanor marries her young man in a ceremony conducted by the island pastor that resembles that of the English Prayer Book, but young Malachi is almost immediately killed; a rescue ship arrives before Gerald Black can ignore his wife and marry Rizpah; once the rescue ship arrives, Lady Gilliland decides to go to her husband while James Robinson decides to remain on the island as a minister; Charles, who is dead set against divorce, receives word through a rescuing sailor that his wife has died in another shipwreck and only then is he free to marry Adeline. No marriage is entered into or survives that is not Christian, respectable, and lawful. Eleanor chooses to remain on the island with her father, becoming one of those formidable women of the religious missions, like Deborah Alcock, or of the imperial outposts, like Lady Gilliland herself, devoting herself to the kind of strenuous service that requires strength and initiative. After all, Eleanor's time has not come, but when it did come for Beatrice Grimshaw, she had converted to Catholicism and she chose carefully the ways in which she would flout contemporary standards. True, Grimshaw's own trajectory through the South Seas was very different to Eleanor's. She, rather than her character, fulfilled the gypsy fancies of Eleanor's dead mother. Yet she did so by combining the Victorian vice of being 'fast' with some ultimate proprieties of a familiarly Victorian kind. It may have been the case that after the immense real-life decision to go abroad, travel for Grimshaw was in some respects an escape from, rather than a challenge to, Victorianism, even perhaps a sublimation of a freedom both sought for and, in her fiction at least, denied for herself.

Novels by Katharine Tynan appeared as late as 1933, though she died in 1931, making the publication of half a dozen books posthumous. *An International Marriage* (1933) conveniently gathers for the reader all the preoccupations of the Victorian, Edwardian, and Georgian Irish country-house and Society-novel and extends them, in fidelity to the best of the genre, into new social conditions, including the effects of the Great War. In this novel Tynan is coming to renewed terms with the War, Anglo-Catholicism, Englishness, love, marriage, philanthropy—and age, Tynan being in her seventies when this novel about an ageing wife was published.[8] In several ways, then, *An International Marriage* is a fortuitous bridge between pre-1922 and post-1922 women novelists. Once again Tynan depicts the vicissitudes in love and marriage, but in the novel setting of a Europe torn and disorientated by the Great War. The War itself lasts only briefly in the novel and in the soft focus of the narrative it becomes a largely emotional and sentimental affair. It is the aftermath of the War that consumes the bulk of the novel, though the emotional focus robs references to unemployment, social unrest, and socialism of what force they might have had; events are, shall we say, *philanthropized*.

Yet the conflict is seen as a world-changing watershed, this side of which religion, love, marriage, and social responsibility can no longer be the same. The War is claimed as having changed England where the returning soldiers have lost their narrowness of view and where the old prejudices, including anti-Catholicism, have died.[9] The returning men behave strangely, however; they are 'inflammable' and expect the cool Englishwomen to run after them, suffering from what one characters identifies as '*cafard*, sickness of life' (pp. 82, 91). But the women who stayed behind behave strangely, too, or Tynan's very English heroine, Amelia Jay, would not have reversed her celibacy and marriage avoidance at the age of 38 when she marries in haste an Austrian fifteen years her junior, a marriage unequal in age and financial resources, but not in social station. Jay has been from a young age the mistress of Charlecote Manor, a country house at the heart of English squirearchy, whilst Franz is Count von Ludolph, godson to 'the old Emperor,' though because of the War his family has lost its wealth and the dilapidation of its country seat is reversible only through Amelia's money, an interesting transposition of a familiar country-house motif.

The age gap allows Tynan to explore an unusual marriage, there being two other such marriages in her story. This union, the reverse of the lopsided marriage of rural Ireland—old husband, young wife—faces prejudice in affluent rural England; the difficulty is intrinsic, too, since as Jay acknowledges, Franz is like her son as well as being her husband. She had never felt young until she met Franz but now she must 'do everything that should keep age at bay' (p. 152). She recalls older rich women who kept their young husbands by leashing them (p. 130) and determines instead always to yield to Franz. Some years and two children later, with Franz lying gravely ill, she comforts herself that the age gap will become irrelevant and her idyll achieve perfection on his death, that their children would be with her down the long vista of the years until she rejoined her young husband 'somewhere at the end' (p. 246). All this lends pathos to the life of an otherwise strong woman that might have raised the ire of a Sarah Grand but also deepens the psychology of what might have been, where this theme is concerned, a simple marriage romance. Amelia recognizes that her marriage is in the eyes of others, and even herself, a 'mad marriage' (pp. 38, 253), a phrase Tynan borrows from her earlier novel of that title. Moreover, the marriage has its larger historical role since Amelia and Franz can comfortably stand respectively as personifications of pre-War and post-War societies, capable, however, of fertile conjunction.

But the marriage between Franz and Amelia is also an 'international marriage'. 'I am afraid of international marriages,' says one character (p. 81), whilst Lady Marcia is altogether against them (p. 83). Amelia Jay sees the English as xenophobic, unimaginative, and hidebound, and English husbands are nowhere as uxorious as the Austrians, or as given to dancing and chivalry. Yet because she is so English, a kind of female squire who must remember to discover and maintain her nimbler European self, national differences weigh on Amelia Jay and threaten the success of her marriage, though in these circumstances, too, love triumphs. This is the more remarkable because Franz and Amelia marry in Vienna just after the War, and this alliance of recent enemies provokes her English (but not Franz's Austrian) friends and relations. Her friend Mrs Donne sees Jay as no longer British but instead 'cosmopolitan' (p. 64).

If love is the agency of cosmopolitanism in *An International Marriage*, love is also inseparable from suffering. Penury among the post-War Austrians is ennobled as 'My Lady Poverty'; the country people are very poor 'but it was such poverty as was bearable, almost beautiful' (p. 149). Suffering pervades *An International Marriage* and amounts to a virtue, though a still higher virtue is the pity that suffering excites. For example, the English, Amelia thinks, are 'Very ordinary dull people beside the brilliant Viennese, *who were more delightful because they had known calamity*' (p. 147, my italics), and Franz and his young associates are embodiments of suffering, having been mistreated by the Russians. (Oddly, suffering in the novel is the preserve of soldiers of the Central Powers, as though Tynan's philanthropic drive had skewed her political, and even humanitarian vision.) Before the War, Amelia had been 'a centre of beneficence' in her manor house (p. 205), her 'beneficent instincts' prompting her to become a Poor Law Guardian at the age of 21 when her father died. On the outbreak of War she offers Charlecote Manor as a hospital and she herself travels to London to accompany her friend Everard Southwell, an Anglican Archdeacon, as he conducts his parish work in the East End among 'the submerged poor' (p. 25), a strand of the novel that recalls Tynan's friend Rosa Mulholland's *Father Tim*, Meade's *A Princess of the Gutter*, Letts's *The Rough Way*, and Rickard's *The Fire of Green Boughs*.

In Tynan's novel, it is the aftermath of the Great War that permits the transformation of an English 'Lady Bountiful of the villages. There were many such in England of the Victorian days' (p. 252). The War has created the devastating conditions under which suffering has been internationalized and pity unleashed across the borders: Victorian philanthropy, we might say, has found a world adequate to its own prodigious appetite. And so, too, has the Irish novel of philanthropy. By no mere coincidence, the War has released Amelia Jay's pent-up love, offered her marriage, awakened her maternal instincts (p. 23), and given her youth: all indistinguishable from her pity and sensitivity to suffering. Amelia Jay brings the philanthropic female to fulfilment at a time when socialism is in the air and organized charity is losing its social prominence; she becomes a bridge over troubled international waters, the very 'spirit of the world' (p. 254) that will prevent a future European war and help bring about through a wonderful hybridity—of which her marriage was an example—a utopia of transnational peace and rejuvenation. She is meant to be the precursor of a new world order the other side of sectarianism, prejudice, racism, national rivalry, and conflict.

All the while, Everard Southwell, an impassioned preacher of sermons, whom Amelia was widely expected to marry, is on the road that leads to Rome, being already a 'shining light of Anglo-Catholicism' (p. 58), and he soon 'goes over' in a critical movement of faith that echoes MacMahon and Letts. In Tynan's novel the War may have loosened ties and dissolved barriers but Archdeacon Southwell, soon to be plain Father Southwell, leaves the Church of England because 'my old Church gives too much liberty. It is good to have things fixed for one' (p. 128). Although Tynan depicts Jay as firmly Anglican, her heart is not in it; she has Amelia haunting Catholic churches in Italy before the War, marrying an Austrian Catholic just after it, and lobbying for a Catholic church back in Charlecote. She seems like an instrument of Tynan's wish for Catholic redress in Protestant England. Indeed, one might see in the novel a kind of Newmanism, the retrieving of England for Rome through the Trojan horses of ecumenism and cultural *métissage*.

Like Amelia's mixed marriage and the mixed nationality of her son and daughter, Southwell's Anglo-Catholicism ought to be a kind of hybridity that heralds Tynan's post-War cosmopolitan world. We are assured that the War has breached the barriers of mutual suspicion and dislike between the denominations as well as the social classes. But just as a squirearchy and cultivated nobility remain respectively at the necessary centre and top of Jay's ideal world, so is a certain kind of ritualized religious nobility also essential at the top: Anglicanism may be a kind of religious squirearchy, but Roman Catholicism is the noble denomination. One senses the drag towards Catholicism and deep reservations about England that an Irish Catholic novelist would entertain. Catholic Austria rather than Catholic Ireland is the proposed necessary counterweight to English laxity, and though young Franz is a fervent and chivalrous dancer, he is a teetotal, vegetarian, hard-working man of discipline, practitioner of a kind of Catholic puritanism that Tynan warms to in depicting.

Tynan's cosmopolitanism in *An International Marriage* takes her far from the cultural nationalism of the Irish Revival. But Catholicism, through the lens of which all Irish Catholic writers in our period must have viewed Protestant England, sets a limit to identification with the neighbouring island. Perhaps this perspective explains the puzzling pro-Austrianism of the novel, and also what reads like naivety about the European situation and the likelihood of a new European order. It appears Tynan believes internationalism is close and real, that the Austrians are splendid people, somehow innocent of wrongdoing, mere sufferers and casualties, and the English the greatest threat to peace through their prejudices. Southwell even believes— presumably with Tynan's approval—that if Jay makes her son a good English squire *and* a good Austrian nobleman, she will help to prevent another war (p. 128). The date of these opinions may be the early 1920s, but they are being commended to paper at the start of the 1930s, late enough, one might think, for Tynan to get wind of what was happening in Germany, a country entirely ignored in *An International Marriage*.

NEW WOMEN WRITERS

The cultural malaise of the Free State appeared to affect the male Catholic writers more than the female, perhaps because for one reason or another male Catholic writers took internal Irish politics and culture more to heart than their female colleagues, having for much longer had, as voters and workers outside the home, a direct and personal stake in political structures. Morever, the apparent lack of fuss with which Catholic and Protestant women writers left Ireland (or returned to it) emulated that of their female predecessors. *Exile* as a post-Joycean or post-1922 theme and course of action would be melodramatic if applied in their cases, so some other cultural explanation should be sought for the fact that Elizabeth Bowen, Pamela Hinkson, Kate O'Brien, Helen Waddell, Constance Malleson, and Margaret Barrington all lived in England for lengthy periods (O'Brien also lived in Spain and Hinkson in Germany) and that Kathleen Coyle lived in Paris before leaving for the United States.[10] Perhaps they were at ease in the old pre-1922 dispensation; certainly their fiction is less of the Free State than of another Ireland, part Anglo-Irish, part-English, part upper-middle-class (or even upper-class) ex-patriate. In any event, these women writers kept obliquely alive the larger Ireland while the deliberate and creative insulation of Revival Ireland was succeeded by the repressive and uncreative Free State.

This generation of Irish women novelists—born between 1883 and 1904, their first novels appearing, with one exception (Barrington was a latecomer to fiction), between 1923 and 1933—disprove the thesis that contemporary Irish society could not produce novels in the English manner. Moreover, they main-tain continuity of style and theme with their predecessors and do not illustrate any fracturing or rupturing that is amenable to easy political and cultural explanation. However, they wrote the kinds of novel that modernism and Irish nationalism induced critics to neglect, which gave free rein to the hernial diagnosis. On the whole, they depict a social world more elevated than their male counterparts and several of them, moreover, have an international per-spective through education and travel rather than the agenda (or political necessity) of exile. They inherited a traditional subtlety for the intricacies of social relationship (Jane Austen and Maria Edgeworth rather than Moore and Joyce are their ancestors) and if this reflects the marginal role in constitutional politics women have historically played in Ireland, it also permits a social objectivity missing in so much male Irish fiction. Sean O'Faolain thought that the Irish writer in the Free State must turn inwards, 'for there alone in his own dark cave of self can he hope to find certainty of reality'; such a metaphor would be entirely unsuited to the social convexities that characterize the best Irish women's fiction of our period.[11]

Several of the women writers contribute to the Irish country-house novel. Bowen and Malleson knew the country house from the inside, as did M. J. Farrell (Molly Keane, who continued to reside in Ireland) and, to cite a female Ulster novelist who puts the country house to other kinds of use, D. G. Waring.[12] Of course, beyond the boundaries of the demesne lay at a distance not only the demesnes of relations and friends in Ireland but also one's own town house in

London and the town houses of relations and friends, and, farther yet, the estates in England belonging to friends and relations, and, two bodies of water away, hotels and apartments in fashionable European resorts. Society was stretched thinly but toughly across the political and constitutional divisions of Britain and Ireland. As Miss Pym says of the Italian riviera resort at the start of *The Hotel* (1927), the first novel by Elizabeth Bowen (1899–1973): 'Gratifying how one's intimate world contracted itself, how one's friends wove themselves in! Society was fascinating, so like a jigsaw puzzle!'[13] Strangers are welcomed and absorbed, too, if of the right sort (or rejected if of the wrong, i.e. vulgar sort), and Bowen's hotel unites (or reunites) families, cousins, and new acquaintances in a scale model, not just of the country house, but of Society, just as the ocean liner and hotel do in Woolf's first novel, *The Voyage Out* (1915), with which *The Hotel* has something in common.

ELIZABETH BOWEN

It is as if in *The Hotel* the country house has floated free from its familiar and historic moorings and yet has permitted Society to keep its integrity, though the novel's plot requires a temporary shaking of the rigging. Like Tynan in *An International Marriage*, Bowen thinks of her most travelled characters not merely as holidaymakers (the country house set at summer play) but as cosmopolitans (p. 166)—updated twentieth-century versions of Victorian tourists—and in the hotel, moreover, *everyone* is that visitor so familiar in the country house novel, out of his or her element. In Bowen as in Woolf, and many of the country-house novelists, there is sardonic wit at the expense of selected characters, sporting mischievously in the gap the narrator maintains between herself and what she is narrating, though Society will survive even this, with the plot's end constituting a resumption of calm water after disturbances. Miss Pym, closing, as she opened, *The Hotel*, thinks that 'Friendship is such a wonderful basis in Life—or has such a wonderful basis in Life; either, she thought was true' (p. 268). But by then, this truth rings hollow in the light of what has befallen young Sydney Warren, who rejects a marriage proposal from the Revd James Milton, thinks better of it and accepts, then calls her engagement off, in part, it seems, under the subtly meddlesome influence of her friend, the older Mrs Kerr to whose wiles Miss Warren seems to tumble at novel's end.[14] Mrs Kerr is the familiar strong woman of the Irish novel: 'I'm not a Feminist', is her mock-admission, 'but I do like being a woman' (p. 21). Sydney's would have been a 'safe' marriage but better than nothing and perhaps capable of growth.

While orchestrating familiar musings on love, engagements, and marriages in the transposed setting of a country-house romance, Bowen establishes like a bass line a malice and self-servingness subdued in their expression both by the outward cultivation of the characters and the outward cultivation of the narrative voice. I am reminded of what Lady Cotswold says in *A Woman-Derelict* (1901) by May Crommelin, that 'in polite society, expression is used to conceal our thoughts. So is speech.'[15] Bowen's is a more acute ear even than Somerville's for the kind of cruelty that might be a side-effect of an ingrown social set with too much power, too much time on its hands, and insufficient constructive outlets for its intelligence. They are 'cruel—in a leisurely sort of way', as Milton describes the Italians whose fortified villages faced the Saracens (p. 57).

The reader's overall impression is of disappointed or betrayed lives or lives soon to be so. Sydney Warren is the serious centre of the novel and through her Bowen explores the elusiveness and unreality of happiness. When Sydney thinks of the whole Past as being merely in abeyance, capable of coming to life again, before thinking of her fellow guests as 'undesired, secure and null' (p. 57), it is hard not to think of the lives of Bowen's characters as themselves deferred and in abeyance, with Sydney their inarticulate and unconscious spokeswoman. *The Hotel* might concern exclusively English characters in Italy, but the sense of desuetude, dislocation, or of an ending must surely have been deepened by Bowen's post-1922 Anglo-Irishness.

Bowen's is a socially narrow canvas but densely enough populated and, in compensation for its narrowness, nuanced and delicately if confidently painted. The narrator parses so finely everything from motive through feeling and gesture to dress that the result resembles dissection. It is devastating on a Lilliputian scale. An almost random example might be our introduction to the self-composed Mrs Kerr in the company of Miss Pym who in some agitation through a falling out with Miss Fitzgerald has attached herself to this superior being (pp. 14–15). The focus in this scene is on the immediate foreground, and a picnic or an out-of-order lift can be significant events. (These indeed are chief dramas in the novel.) It is a species of realism recognizable from women's fiction, founded in social and personal relations and which we might call emotional realism, since the term 'psychological' seems too harsh and scientific. But when the camera draws back, it mock-heroically invests the narrow canvas with the bigger familiar brushstrokes of drama to suggest a storm-in-a-teacup satire. It is a distortion of perspective that lends cosmic significance to 'moments'. Miss Pym is recalling her tiff with Miss Fitzgerald: 'She could not remember how it began; she could not remember anything leading up to it; just that there had been something intolerable about Emily from the moment she came to the door... That is the worst of anger, that terrible clarity. They had had, at that moment when everything tottered, worse than a sense of destruction: they had felt the whole force of a doubt in that moment. . . .' (p. 15). It might be a cataclysm being described, yet the friendship of Emily and Miss Pym is silently repaired and closes *The Hotel.* As Mrs Kerr alleges: 'You know, women's lives *are* sensational' (p. 21).

But the novel's perspective does not rest with a mock-heroic inflation. The microcosmic function of the hotel and its guests is not only social but existential. On the picnic, Veronica and her fiancé Victor scramble down a hill and engage in flirtatious horseplay. Sydney, 'disappointed in her own society', looks down and sees the faraway couple 'gesticulating soundlessly below her in the sunshine . . . as in some perfect piece of cinema-acting, emotion represented without emotion', and wonders whether if she were to arrive at that point (Veronica's abandon) 'she would be cut off from herself, as by her other emotions. She watched the miniature Veronica toss back her hair and walk away' (p. 68). It is a perspective that might remind us of the way Woolf's narration in *The Voyage Out* periodically zooms out to dwarf her characters.

Bowen takes the theme of the self farther than any Irish woman novelist before her. Having been turned down by Sydney the first time, Revd James Milton a little later has a grave doubt about Sydney but it is 'that most profound concern possible for another human being, when it becomes a question no longer of the extent of one's possession of them, but, transcending this, of what in their untouchable selves they *are*' (p. 189). It is ironic, then, that having accepted him, Sydney in a moment of awareness after a near car accident on the mountain, 'for the first time felt life sharply, life as keen as death to bite upon the consciousness' (p. 245) and moments later tells Milton she can't marry him because 'I had had no idea we were as real as this' (p. 247), that (by allusion to her earlier sight of Veronica and Victor) we are more than mere spectators at our own cinema-acting. But though she calls off the marriage there is no sense of liberation, and later it is implied that she attributes the failure to Mrs Kerr's malign influence on her. It is one character's theory that 'for everybody there seems to be just one age at which they are *really* themselves' (p. 195); the horror of this is not just that the one age passes, making one obsolescent, but that one might miss even that one age and with it the possibility of self-realization (self-development, self-culmination). Sydney may have passed the age of real selfhood or may never reach it. Miss Pym and Miss Fitzgerald seem to be luckier and end the novel hand in hand, reunited and secure. But from where they sit up the mountain, the hotel is as small as a doll's house, the final and terrifying perspective that, even in her absence, is Sydney Warren's.

The chief Bowen character seems to live not in the centre but to the side of her life in a state of dissociation the harder to discern and make sense of (for character and reader alike) because her life is so sociable, and almost ritually so. But in fact, the mannered sociability is a source of the dissociation. The Anglo-Irish may have been a highly sociable people but in the context of Ireland rather than their social class on either side of the Irish Sea, they could appear as a caste, living not in the centre but to the side of real Irish life. In *The Last September* (1929) it is as if the Anglo-Irish collectively become a Bowen character. In this novel the country-house setting is 'resumed' and a connection established by default with many of the Irish novels I have discussed.

Behind the screen of trees around their demesne, the Anglo-Irish of Bowen's stories feel safe from the vulgar drama being played out in Ireland. But they are a community in denial, islanded and distracted in part by their obsession with right behaviour, and increasingly vulnerable to the emboldened native Irish. Bowen's characters, remnants of the Protestant nation, live in a maroon world 'the colour of valediction',[16] and when danger obtrudes on them, they turn bleakly but gracefully to face the consequences, the time long past for the breezy remedies and hopeful reformism of many earlier country-house novels. *The Last September* gives us life at Danielstown, a country house in County Cork whose days are numbered during the 'war of independence'. It is 1920 and only a few sense danger or the incongruity of dances while British soldiers are ambushed and neighbouring country houses are put to the torch. (The soldiers, fresh from the Great War, some with shell-shock, are dismayed by Irish guerilla tactics that are 'not cricket'.) Only the young nephew and niece of Sir Richard and Lady Naylor are aware of a central emptiness and an irrelevance to the 'violent realness' beyond the demesne. But perhaps the endless passage of visitors to the country house, life in transit, with absence almost as real as presence, insulated the Anglo-Irish, as well as distracting them, from trouble until it could no longer be denied. In any case, Lois Farquar and Lawrence (the novel's Visitors to Ireland) have 'a sense of detention, of a prologue being played out too lengthily, with unnecessary stresses, a wasteful attention to detail.'[17] Nephew and niece even express a wish to witness the house burn and at novel's end they just miss having their wish come true, having left for England. The IRA, shadowy realities throughout the novel, fire Danielstown with two other country houses in February 1921, the door of which, while the 'executioners' depart, 'stood open hospitably upon a furnace'.

The adverb has been delicately chosen, reminding us, beyond the cruel irony, of the 'social idea' embodied in the country house. Bowen thought that ideally the country house enabled its inhabitants and guests to escape from egotism, instability, and greed into impersonality and the 'steady behaviour' that she saw etched into every line of her own ancestral home.[18] The modern alternative was love, which is merely a source of grievance to Lady Naylor's late-Victorian generation; because it often portends the wrong kind of marriage, love is an irritant and complication in the life depicted in later Irish country-house novels. Lois is offered love by someone who is not to the manner (or manor) born, before Lady Naylor (playing the role of Mrs Kerr in *The Hotel*) destroys her love for Gerald Lesworth, the English soldier who dies at the hands of the IRA but as if at the behest of Lady Naylor. Although she must once have embodied the wholeness of life—the social idea—at Danielstown, Lady Naylor is snobbish, hypocritical, and tyrannical, embodying instead the rancid afterlife of the Big House. Lady Naylor may have had her day (like the Irish country house) but Lois, though love is at present impossible, may yet have hers after this last September of girlhood. It is implied that she will in the future join the search for romantic love (but outside Ireland) that is the goal and compensation for those who have never known the more venerable and steadier pleasures of Big House life.[19] It is as if Bowen translates the imagery of the Irish country-house novel into its own insubstantial after-imagery. But those who do not find even love in Bowen's stories often find instead a psychic derangement,[20] a condition that mirrors the social derangement in their world, a malaise of which the fate of the Anglo-Irish can seem like the provenance.

M. J. FARRELL

It was Bowen's belief that from a broad perspective the lives of the Anglo-Irish, 'like those of only children, are singular, independent and secretive'.[21] This is Lois Farquar's profile and the implication is that she represents the last and lost childhood of the Ascendancy, and when she leaves for Europe, she enacts the small diaspora that accompanied the passing of that childhood. That young Easter Chevington in *Mad Puppetstown* (1931) by the long-lived M. J. Farrell (1904–96) is an only child and is, moreover, motherless, entirely fits the genre of the country-house novel set during the Great War and Irish Troubles. Taking place in Co. 'Westcommon' (read Kilkenny and/or Waterford) between 1908 and the early years of the Free State, the novel offers for its first eighty pages Easter's idyllic childhood in a family devoted to horse-riding and fox-hunting; these years are the symbolic heyday of the Ascendancy. Then 'the Great War in Europe and the little bitter, forgotten war in Ireland' obtrude.[22] Easter's rather remote father, Major Chevington, is killed in the Great War, repeating a thematic and symbolic motif in this fiction; one symptom of the malaise in Bowen's fiction world is the ineffectuality of the men she creates, as though the Ascendancy had somehow been widowed or emasculated, and in *Mad Puppetstown* this is made literal. The remoteness of the father, like the intensity of the country-house pleasures, testifies to the obliviousness of the Anglo-Irish as, closer at hand, the Troubles creep closer. In one splendid, twenty-page scene, a rural fishing idyll ends in horror when Easter's Aunt Brenda's suitor, Major Grey, is murdered by the IRA. (The merry widow Aunt Brenda plays Lady Naylor's part in her shallowness and self-centredness, the careless reprehensible heart of the Irish 'Raj'.) The proximity of the native tenant class outside the Big House is the 'Achilles' heel' of the Ascendancy, while the native servant class within allows a kind of 'Trojan horse' tactic on the part of Sinn Fein. The Anglo-Irish diaspora is enacted by Easter's family who decamp to England and only Aunt Dicksie's refusal to leave Puppetstown House (she represents the rump Ascendancy who stayed at their post during the Troubles) prevents the house from going the fiery way of Danielstown and other country houses.

When young Easter, more Irish than English and heir to the house, returns at her age of majority in 1921 with her cousin Basil to claim the house, times have changed in Ireland and at Puppetstown. Aunt Dicksie's custodianship, described in mildly Gothic scenes reminiscent of Farrell's contemporary William Faulkner and assorted Irish predecessors, has caused Puppetstown to shrink within itself: the house is the novel's main character and on the murder of Major Grey and flight of Aunt Brenda, in Aunt Dicksie's eyes it has lost its honour—betrayed, forsaken; like Somerville's Inver, desolate in shame and sin. The efforts of Easter and Basil to restore life to the house, despite the contempt of the newly insulting native Irish, is an oblique form of accommodation to the new dispensation. Easter and Basil who love each other only as kin—bringing the recurring figure of the cousin in the country house novel to a kind of completion—need not wed as long as Aunt Dicksie is alive, so it is an uncertain future that they, like their class, have: temporary, reduced, and doubtless infertile, but happy in its individual homecoming and triumph of the spirit.

So well have the remnant Anglo-Irish accommodated themselves in the Ireland of 1933 that in Farrell's superbly dark and comic *Devoted Ladies* (1934), George Playfair, a fox-hunting ex-British officer who has come into his inheritance in Co. 'Westcommon', can claim that 'the country is in great order now' as he tempts his boyhood friend Sylvester back to Ireland.[23] Playfair's Catholicism is irrelevant in the high social circumstances of the novel, and Anglo-Irish accommodation allows them to live a semblance of their old lives of hunting and visiting untroubled by the native Irish who are, extraordinarily, entirely out of Farrell's picture. But all is not well. The novel is in the beginning the portrait of a successful English writer of popular West End plays, Sylvester Browne, by turns romantic and cruel, in whom doubt about the value of his work has set in, accompanied by a loss of enthusiasm and growing cynicism. The description of the end of his London party that opens the novel recalls the self-disgust of Eliot's Prufrock and the wider disgust of portions of Eliot's *The Waste Land* (1922); 'disgusted' and 'disgusting' are among the commonest words of the novel. Sylvester's venom-tongued misanthropy is generating enough surplus to suggest a playful and nearly motiveless malignity, rivalled by that of Jessica, the English lesbian lover of the hapless and sexy American widow, Jane, whom the egregious Jessica bullies viciously. 'She sat twisting her great white hands (their painted nails had an obscene quality half flower half animal)' (p. 15). Jessica brains Jane at the party with a bottle of tonic water for flirting with George and yet the intimidated Jane creeps back obediently to her lover.

If Farrell is trying like Eliot to capture the malaise of a generation, she yet offers us a richer example of mischievous idleness and unmoored intelligence than slightly 'iffy' London cosmopolitans when Sylvester, Jessica, and Jane all become visitors to Ireland. Jane has been seduced fitfully (she has an attention disorder) by a clutch of Irish sporting novels that Playfair has sent her, and they happen to include Farrell's second novel, *Young Entry* (1928), which Jessica conveniently summarizes and dismisses for us: 'Girlish friendship and fox-hunting—now they're eating soda-bread—what's that? Oh, we're in Ireland I see. And never a silver cup but its *engraved with a good horse's name*. What a revolting bit of camp' (p. 60).[24] *Young Entry* charted the escapades of Prudence Lingfield-Turett, a wild Irish girl who would be at home in the pages of Conyers and Meade and who maintains the tomboy element of the Irish country-house novel. Camp the novel may have been, but still, another (fictional) novel, *The Wanderings of William*, is judged to be not 'suggestively sporting like *Young Entry*' (p. 61). 'Sporting' seems ambiguous in the light of girlish friendship. 'Girlish' is another common word in *Devoted Ladies*, usually applied maliciously by character and author to the sad and disgusting Viola (Piggy) Browne; the novels' titles can appear like lesbian jokes: *The Girl Who Gave, Joan Whips-in*... Farrell might easily have had George Playfair send Jane her first novel, *The Knight of Cheerful Countenance* (published in 1926 but written when Farrell was 17), a novel that belongs to what we might call the 'open-air' branch of the country house novel, here set in the first months of the Free State. Like Conyers, Farrell writes too eloquently and knowledgeably about riding and hunting for the novel's own good. 'Grouse, girls and guns' is the telling title of one chapter, though since a reference is made to 'Irish sporting novels', the book attempts to exempt itself from the strictures applied to the genre. Yet here, too, genre trumps realism. The deadly political events, the civil war and the poisoned relations between landlords and tenants, are backgrounded too distantly for the novel to escape into seriousness, a criticism that one could level even at the far superior *Mad Puppetstown*.[25]

The familiar magical spell of Ireland can be used shamelessly by novelists hoping it will be a leg-up in the task of enthralling their readers, but in

Devoted Ladies it is something Sylvester regards as the stuff exclusively of the fox-hunting novel by 'some hysterical Irish novelist writing her seventy-thousand words' (p. 28) before he himself delights ridiculously in the 'rich sentimentality of his thoughts about mountains unseen in the rain and ugly roads and drenched sheep' (p. 30). Even Jessica's and Jane's manservant, the nasty Albert, thinks 'there's something *about* Ireland, I don't know what it is' (p. 66), which ought to be enough to discredit the notion of Irish magic. At the very least, Farrell has isolated it as by now a tired motif in the country-house novel. For the reality is very different from the magic. The visitors to Ireland stay with cousins (who else?) of Sylvester's, Hester and Piggy Browne, in a small country house, Kilque, down at heel and like its owners in need of money, the constant motif of life there. Piggy is poor but overflowingly hospitable, a familiar 'tradition of wasteful jollity behind her' (p. 124).

Although she is destined to become the novel's heroine, Piggy is sidelined by everyone, unattractive, occasionally infatuated with George Playfair and Robin Nuthatch (yet another cousin of Sylvester's), but constantly infatuated with Robin's wife, the beautiful Joan, who bullies and uses Piggy without compunction, the two of them forming a second set of ironically denominated 'devoted ladies'. There is pricelessly witty description, narration, and dialogue, the funnier because of its almost idle cruelty. Sylvester in a jesting manner cannot stand Piggy. 'Usually Sylvester would regard her from out a dark and disgusted silence, but now and then he would talk to her with savage playfulness or honeyed spite. And not always honeyed. And he could not bear to look at her. She inspired him with a definite hostility both mental and physical' (p. 101).

The bullied bully in turn. Jane, who in one comic scene bullies one of the ubiquitous dogs, is under the ruthless sway of Jessica. Jessica plays in the novel an even darker version of Bowen's Mrs Kerr and Lady Naylor: the older woman as spoiler. The benign strong woman of the Irish country-house novel is revealed in Farrell and Bowen as not so benign after all, though perhaps we met her already in M. Hamilton's Doodie Fenchurch. Although Sylvester sets out to thwart Jessica's scheme to prevent the marriage of Jane and George even if it means her destroying Jane's reputation and even Jane herself, Sylvester has insufficient investment in the outcome to be ruthless in his counter-scheme. It is left to Piggy to save the impending marriage by an act of murder and a fatal act of self-sacrifice, though it is a grotesque, parodic version of the female altruism we have encountered in the Irish novel. Piggy acts because she has been bullied into turning service into her life's point, since she knows she is 'outside love for ever' (p. 170) and unmarriageable. Yet this allows her in one swift action to bully the odious Jessica once only but terminally, and Piggy is happy to pay the ultimate price. To the cumulative image in the novel of an Anglo-Irish gentry ingrown and back-biting, exercising hollow power on each other now that they have lost power in the larger Ireland, and their lives having dwindled from utility to futility, we can add the terrible significance Piggy might have for us: the turning of the ertswhile masters of Ireland into a queer kind of service, Anglo-Irish mastery into subservience, the downward trajectory traced in generations of the country-house novel almost complete.[26]

And yet there is a wicked survivors' humour in it all—and even poetry. Just as Farrell engages in self-parody in order to escape the strictures on Ireland's 'Lady Novelists' (p. 53) she has herself recorded in *Devoted Ladies* (and the title might well itself be a literary in-joke)—creating along the way an interesting meta-fiction we don't associate with her kind of fiction—so it is as if yesterday's gentry parody themselves in their persistent obsession with field sports and what the rest of us regard as the frills of life, not the substance.[27] Farrell typically achieves part of her effect—how deliberately is not clear—through the incongruity between her prose stylishness on the one hand, and, on the other, the seemingly trivial matter on which such stylishness seems to be wasted. But even Farrell cannot resist what she sincerely regards as the poetic call of the hunt, and when she describes Sylvester a-hunting in a scene that one might have thought should be witty at his expense, instead the prose tautens into a brief aria, poetry at once modern and old-fashioned, in intention beyond parody and scorn:

A fox slipped out of the covert—a little fox, monstrously visible in the thin greyness of the light. Sylvester rode at him, heading him back into the covert, a strong pulse of excitement breaking through his bandage of watchfulness.

He waited again. Hounds were hunting another fox. Further failed their voices. His horse ate grass; midges persecuted Sylvester with assiduous attention. He lit a cigarette. Wan light about him. Pallid the propped corn-sheaves. Silent all birds. Heavy and waxen are the opening eyelids of the morn. (p. 274)[28]

PAMELA HINKSON

The big house in flames has generated powerful images in Irish fiction. Somerville's Inver burns, eight or so years too 'previous' in Irish historical terms. For if the images gathered pace in Irish fiction, that is because of the terrible reality of the 1920s. Both Ballyrankin, Co. Kildare where Farrell grew up and Woodrooff, Co. Tipperary where she spent much time, were burned in the Troubles.[29] In her country-house memoir, *Bricks and Flowers* (1949), Katherine Everett describes the immediate aftermath of the burning of Macroom Castle (her cousin Lady Ardilaun's old home in Co. Cork) during the civil war when the Free Staters fired it to force the IRA to abandon their stronghold. As soon as she and her cousin hear of the blaze, Everett volunteers to bicycle sixty miles after a train ride to Limerick to check on the Castle's fate and arrives after a miniature epic journey to hear from a witness what happened and to see for herself the great door still smouldering, wrought-iron balustrades writhing through a collapsed stone staircase, and furniture piled outside which the local woman caretaker (an Irish touch) had forced the Free Staters to carry out before they torched the Castle.[30]

The Ladies' Road (1932) by Pamela Hinkson (1900–82), daughter of Katharine Tynan to whom she dedicates the novel, closes like *The Last September* with the IRA burning of a country house that had always been surrounded by the mysterious, protective, and in the end dangerous woods: 'That night Cappagh lit a torch for the countryside.'[31] (The suggestion of the House's altruism echoes Bowen's 'hospitably': grace under fire.) The inhabitants of neighbouring country houses watch, waiting their turn, but with a composure and resignation born of the depredations that the Great War has already committed against their families. 'Such a holocaust... of one family' (p. 294) remarks one character, referring after the War to the Mannerings of the Sussex country house, Winds, and who are related to the Creaghs of Cappagh (cousins abound in the novel). The Great War has insulated or inoculated the Anglo-Irish to some extent against the pettier (but epoch-making) war of the IRA launched under cover of darkness. Together, the Troubles and the Great War bring the decline of the country house to a climactic end; though it survived the greater, it cannot survive the lesser. This is one of the larger themes of *The Ladies' Road*, another being the rapid remoteness of 'that other life before the War' (p. 185), a world remembered for us in the novel chiefly by young Stella Mannering, the yearly visitor from England who recalls Cappagh, where she spent her childhood summers, as set in a magical land of uncertainty and adventure. Edmund Urquhart, another visitor with nationalist sympathies, may be disappointed that Cappagh isn't really Ireland, 'yet it had the indefinable magic of the country about it' (p. 32). By novel's end, the magic spell of Ireland has dimmed, and the land is rather too adventurous.

The artistic equal of *The Last September*, and like it showing the influence of Virginia Woolf, Hinkson's is the best Irish novel about the effects of the Great War at home in Ireland and one of the best Irish novels of its day. It is a work of sustained empathy that sponsors acute observations by characters and narrator alike. The insulation of the characters' lives, the emotional reticence of their class, the subjective, Woolfian blurring of sharp distinctions between the recent and more distant past in the memories of the characters, and the divided loyalty of the novelist herself about the Troubles that she shares with Bowen (though Hinkson was a Catholic)—these fuse into elegy, touched with that pathos and sentimentality that the Great War sanctioned and that the highly politicized Troubles were reluctant to sanction. It seems that staging the Great War at the centre (even though it is seen obliquely through Stella Mannering) precluded the witty malice we find in the novels of Bowen and Farrell. In the end, the pathos in both *The Last September* and *The Ladies' Road* is the irrelevance of the attitudes of the big house inhabitants to their tenants, to Ireland, to politics: history was overtaking them and they were powerless. This elegiac note sounds through many of the novels by the new women writers.

The Ladies' Road explores with delicacy other themes: the predicament of that lost generation who like Stella Mannering came into youth during the War (she was born around 1900) and who faced a future of uncertainty and compelling memories; both her brothers are killed in the War. Also, the suffering and dwindling of those girls and women too attentive to others, or too engrossed in another, and who are forced to wait too long for their return, or his return, causing loyalty to warp love and love itself to fall victim to estrangement. As well, the cruelty with which the War allows the dead to remain unchanged while the survivors-in-arms or family members at home change and age. And the way the War sponsors at home a kind of self-absorption and an exclusiveness of grief; there are innumerable references to characters feeling shut-out or standing in doorways looking in. Shifting its scenes between Sussex, Ireland, London, and the battlefields of France, between the years 1915 and 1923 when Ireland and the world change forever, poignantly attentive to the months and seasons and the dates of battles and deaths, and entwining two related landed families, one English, one Irish, *The Ladies' Road* is a novel generous in spread and rich in theme.

In the matter of the War's transvaluation of society at home, Hinkson is at once more restricted in field of view and more intimate than Rickard. But they share a woman's perspective (though Hinkson is the better writer) and among the roads that thread their way through Hinkson's novel (they compose a motif), the most important is the imaginary, barely consoling 'Ladies' Road' of the title down which Stella might yet go, retracing her brother David's footsteps into France and the nameless villages he passed through and the nameless wood where he had lain since May 1918.[32] But of course, the Irish Troubles supervene, foreground occluding background: Langfield burns, Mallagh burns, Castle Shaw and Cooperstown wait their turn, the arsonists sometimes mere boys, sometimes workers on the estates, sometimes apologetic, sometimes halfhearted, but the houses burn in any event. The mistress of Cooperstown believes that after it all there would be only Ireland, not a world between two worlds, and after all, her generation had spent everything in the War and were condemned to watching the stream of life from the bank.

The novel ends on that puzzling yet convincing languorous note of resignation that seems to have accompanied the end of country-house power in Ireland in the 1920s.[33]

KATE O'BRIEN

Because the inhabitants of the country house and the upper-middle-class house primarily constituted in Ireland a social caste, and only secondarily a religious minority, the deep cultural and political changes that threatened the Protestant inhabitants threatened likewise Catholic inhabitants, as the novels of Kate O'Brien (1897–1974) demonstrate. While her characters are typically from the wealthy professional middle class, the novels maintain features of the country-house novel. For example, the malaise of the Mulqueen family of Roseholm House in *The Ante-Room* (1934),[34] hardly differs from what afflicts the Protestant gentry. However, O'Brien did not always set her novels in Ireland, and although they have Irish characters, her novels, like those of many of her female Irish predecessors, took advantage of expatriate experience, in her case as a governess in Spain, a journalist in England, and a traveller and sojourner in Europe, particularly, like Hannah Lynch, in Spain. (O'Brien spent her last years in England where she died.) Hers was the broadened horizon of the Catholic and Protestant middle and upper middle classes, but specifically it was Catholic Europe (France, Belgium, Spain) that gave Irish middle-class Catholic girls, as pupils in convent schools or as governesses, the chance, at least, to escape the introversions of nationalist Ireland.

If the conflict between freedom and Catholic faith, love and Catholic conscience is a master theme in O'Brien, the issue is not as clear-cut as it is in Joyce, in part because O'Brien chooses unlike Joyce to dwell on various characters torn in their desires and choices who are nevertheless not simply the author disguised. The explicit Catholic cruxes distinguish O'Brien's novels from those of Mulholland, Francis, and other unwavering believers, but not from those by Thurston, Grimshaw, or MacMahon. And like the best of her predecessors, O'Brien uses as background—a background that occasionally ruptures the foreground—contemporary social and political upheavals, in her case usually war or the threat of war.

Indeed, love, Catholic faith, family, and war (offstage) form a matrix of experiences in O'Brien out of which freedom of some sort must if possible be achieved. Of these, woman's love, and perhaps its impossibility, comes close to being the supreme goal and reality. For example, behind Aunt Hannah's family pride and strategizing in *The Last of Summer* (1943)—set during the days running up to Britain's declaration of war against Germany in 1939—lies personal disappointment in love. Like a Bowen villainess, she seeks to prevent the attachment between her son Tom and her niece Angèle, ostensibly so as not to endanger the proper continuance of the Kernahans of Waterpark House, but in truth because Angèle's father jilted her years before. 'This country is Heaven's anteroom', remarks one character cynically, but Heaven is never reached; love appears to be the ultimate reality and good whose anteroom merely, Aunt Hannah has been forced to inhabit all these years. A comparable wound has lifelong repercussions in the partly autobiographical *The Land of Spices* (1941), a novel banned by the Irish Censorship Board, apparently for a homosexual allusion. This is a rich, meditative novel of two women's flight from love, warmth, and emotional attachment into *la pudeur et la politesse* of religious vocation, as though to ratify the observations of Riddell, Tynan, Grimshaw, Hart, and both Thurstons on the religious life as a form of emotional rebound for women. Life in the Belgian convent is meticulously rendered, and though it is a kind of illusory retreat from Irish and European upheavals of O'Brien's childhood (Home Rule agitation, the Gaelic revival, the suffragette movement, European nationalism, and an imminent Great War), it also permits the growth into womanhood of Anna and Helen, both intellectually inclined and both psychologically wounded by early emotional experiences: Helen discovering her father in a sexual relationship with his friend Etienne, Anna losing through death the only person she ever loved.

But in O'Brien, love is no straightforward good. It often invites—as it does in Bowen and Hinkson—compunction, detachment, and loneliness. This is due in part to the 'chauvinism' of the ineffectual men, whose patronizing attentions O'Brien's women, like Bowen's, have to endure, as must Agnes Mulqueen in *The Anteroom*, who is torn between her Catholic conscience and desire for her brother-in-law, Vincent. Her love, while strong enough perhaps to quell religious conscience, is not in the end stronger than love for another woman, in this case a sister. She finally renounces Vincent's love, primarily not because he wishes merely to avoid the reality of his marriage, or even because of her conscience, but because of her sisterly devotion. Rejected, Vincent turns a shotgun on himself, one of the uncommon instances of suicide in an Irish Catholic novel.

Agnes's self-denial may not be quite on a par with the more overt instances of female altruism in the Irish novels; when it is read alongside the actions and experiences of other O'Brien heroines, it might be thought to share with them, as with those of heroines in her contemporaries, Bowen and Farrell, a suspicion of men and occasionally lesbian undertow that seems to me to characterize a significant strain of Irish female fiction. But the qualification of the undertow as lesbian is too narrowly precise, excluding as it ought not to, elements of the sororal, androgynous, and existential. This becomes clearer when we read the excellent *Mary Lavelle* (1936), another partly autobiographical work that was banned in the Free State. This coming-of-age novel records the experiences of a young Irish provincial Catholic girl working as a governess in northern Spain between June and October 1922.[35] Her father is a doctor, of 'indolent "squireen" stock' who married the daughter of a medical man; he wanted to get his son a commission in the Munster Fusliers but instead Jimmy Lavelle joined the IRA and is out with them during the civil war that is being waged while Mary is in Spain. She is engaged to a pleasant young Irishman (demobbed from the Munsters with whom he fought in the Great War, becoming a Major and DSO) and on her way to a 'safe' Irish middle-class marriage on her return. The novel paints a picture of the Irish governesses, or 'misses', in her Spanish town, who compose an expatriate and sisterly enclave—their dreams, illusions, and fates. They come out, as Lynch said they did, because their parents will not or cannot subsidize their education or foresee Irish husbands for them. Many have no alternative but to stay, often sinking socially, marrying natives below the level of their employers, becoming nuns, or disappearing. As a group in exile without power, they exist in tacit contrast to the overt clamouring for economic or political self-government in 1922 Spain, with the rising restlessness of the Communists and in 1922 Ireland, with the ongoing battle between republicans and Free Staters.

But if the heart of the novel is Mary Lavelle's first sexual passion, nonetheless her own sudden discovery of the possibility of, and immediate search for, a kind of self-government connects Mary, one of the 'misses', with Mary, the passionate individual liberated (or so it seems) from her Irish Catholic constraints and the altruism of female service. She becomes infatuated with Spain, not least because of a bullfight she attends. The corrida has a deferred impact by planting in her an acknowledgement of the power and vitality of 'the moment of truth',[36] and this comes to crux when, as she falls in love with Spain, she also falls in love with Juanito, the married son of the family of her employers, a passionate young Communist whose kisses awaken her senses, as her fiancé's has never done. It is her first crush, her first love, her first passion, her first sex, all in one accelerating duet. Their growing relationship advances on the crucial 'moment' during their assignation in Toledo, in the more southerly warmth, and achieves it.

And yet, it is not so crucial. O'Brien describes how at the climax the lovers see 'almost dully the full, great curve of their unattainable love' (p. 256). It is described immediately as only 'one kind of consummation'. For Mary has not merely anticipated the passion but put it rather coolly in the context of her life. She has already told Juanito that their infatuation 'is simply an uncomplicated pain which we must get over' (p. 254). She has never been in love

before, she tells Juanito, yet knows that 'it's a perfectly unreasonable illusion—and must be borne as that. It's of no use. It's not suitable or manage-
able. It blurs things, puts everything out of focus. It's not a thing to live with.
It's a dream' (p. 247). The narrator from 'her' point of view reiterates the
illusory nature of love (p. 305) and smiles on both its absurdity and its
necessity at the time. And even before Juanito and she make love, she has
felt 'regrets and griefs and faithlessness' (p. 253), as though the illicit relationship is following a prescribed course towards some disillusionment the
other side of love. It is the narrator on Mary's behalf who recognizes the well-
trained Irish Catholic's acceptance that human nature, undisciplined, can be
both incredibly sinful and incredibly foolish (pp. 180–1), but the folly seems
as important to O'Brien as the sinfulness. And it is less the sinfulness of her
fornication that bothers Mary than the effect on her poor fiancé the tame
version of the story of her Spanish escapade will have. Little wonder O'Brien
has Juanito think of 'their love's fantastic, heavy anticlimax' (p. 338). Mary
sins with a married man without real compunction or the consequences of a
spiritual crisis, and the Catholic Church is no more rejected outright than
Irish nationalism; although this shows a female pragmatism, it would surely
be from the Church's point of view a more serious lapse than Dedalus's
double sin of fornication and announced apostasy (with intervals of confession and contrition).

Moreover, one feels that Lavelle's is less a heterosexual awakening than an
awakening into self-consciousness and individuality by someone whose life
has been prescribed by group values—those of a provincial town, of the
Catholic Church, of the conventions of female service, of the traditions of
romance. As young as 12 or 13, 'her main idea had been to be free and lonely',
an ideal of 'perpetual self-government' (p. 27). Her love affair seems like a
necessary but insufficient vehicle for her awakening into the possibility of
autonomy, which is the possibility of essential loneliness. There is an inescap-
able hint of callousness in her attitude, a combination of residual deep
Catholic suspicion of romantic sexuality, lesbian or at least androgynous
reservation, and painful existential realism. When one of the misses, Agatha
Keogh, confesses her love and desire for Mary, the latter does not recoil; she is
understanding but confused, seeing Keogh's confession as arriving out of 'this
tangle of our longings' (p. 286). Lavelle is ambivalent in her emotions, and
this is of a piece with her sexual presentation. Juanito feels (an anticipatory?)
loneliness when he looks at the 'androgenous (*sic*), speckless beauty of her
head . . . and bony, vigorous hands' (p. 243); a little later, her 'composed,
braced attitude of meditation gave her for the moment the non-voluptuous,
introverted air of a boy' (p. 248); later still, good, simple, 'without wile
or coquetry,' she is 'almost androgenous (*sic*) in her friendly detachment'

(p. 320).[37] The narrator, like Mary herself, is hedging her bets. And since the notion of personal self-government is a political metaphor, it is not surprising to read of Mary's ambivalence in the matter of the Irish civil war. After all, her fiancé is an ex-British soldier, her brother an IRA man. She hears in the speech of a Basque nationalist the names 'Arthur Griffith' and 'Patrick Pearse'. When a Spaniard proclaims support for de Valera and Irish republicanism, Mary asks: 'Do you then sympathise with the nationalist ambitions of the Catalans and the Basques?' (p. 152) and receives a dusty answer. Mary herself is unsure which side to support in the civil war; self-government, yes, but what kind? The novel ends with Mary Lavelle returning to Ireland to face the almost certain end of her engagement; she is sure that she will go into exile; she will be free like Stephen Dedalus from the various threats from every quarter to her goal of self-government but, like Dedalus, risk loneliness. Sexual desire is but a stage; if there is infatuation in O'Brien's novels, lasting passion is impossible because of 'the fatuous egotism of love ... the final impenetrability of one mind by another'.[38]

KATHLEEN COYLE

Love, altruism, and marriage are subjected to politely harsh scrutiny in the newer women writers. Expectations in love have risen unfulfillably as the society that once kept them in check has collapsed. Moreover, to the extent that they accept a final subjectivity—one flagged by deepening interiority in the Irish country-house novel—these women novelists are realists in a special sense, making necessity into some kind of virtue, turning anteroom into living room, but without entirely surrendering the goal of freedom, however ill-defined that was in the decades before the clarifying wave of feminism of the 1960s and after. We find Ulster-born women novelists with much the same difficult agenda. Middle-class and upper-middle-class female identity and experience antedated and largely overrode in art the newly constituted differences between England and Ireland, North and South. Religious differences, too, which were virtually constitutionalized in the predominantly Catholic Free State and predominantly Protestant Northern Ireland, were likewise largely overridden. The net result is that in the name of the emotional complexities of person and gender, the women writers blur all the hard cultural and political lines of male fiction.

In *Liv* (1929) by Londonderry-born Kathleen Coyle (1883–1952), the title heroine is a young, restless woman who leaves her Norwegian village and her fiancé and travels to Paris, where she fetches up among a community of bohemian artists. There she finds 'Love' with Per Malom, a half-Norwegian, half-Spanish painter against whom Liv is warned and for whom she falls like all the other women who have met him. Their love is true but he is married, and answering a drive as unignorable as that which brought her through the mountains, Liv returns to Norway. Is it her disappointment in love, her fear of bohemianism and conventional obligation to her fiancé? Or is it her Norwegian soul that does not require physical presence? Malom's Norwegian mother had told him that 'In the South you love with the body, in the North we love with our souls!' and he recalls this before Liv deserts him. Her aunt Sonja tells her that they are 'the daughters of Ibsen' but also 'the daughters of the Vikings,' restless when young but drawn back to the white country: 'Here we ... preserve our pride. When we go south, into warmer lands, we lose something of ourselves.'[39] Rebecca West, who predicted Coyle's emergence as 'an extremely distinguished writer', praised Coyle's earlier novels but thought they displayed a shadowy quality that *Liv* escaped, yet the startling brightness of the Norwegian landscape in *Liv* is still overshadowed by the emotional interiority of Coyle's heroines that is her hallmark as a novelist. West was right, however, to see Coyle as 'a writer of great subtlety' who reminded her of Katherine Mansfield, a writer who 'for our own sakes we must watch her (*sic*) eagerly'.[40]

That interiority we see again in *A Flock of Birds* (1930) in which the Ladies' Road is travelled single-mindedly by Catherine Munster, the widowed mother of a boy condemned to death in Belfast for murder during an IRA ambush. The Munsters are wealthy and travelled Protestants who live outside Dublin in a country house called Gorabbey, and the novel registers the collision between the Protestant wealthy, the Great War and the Catholic populace mobilizing for independence.[41] However, the collision is muffled almost beyond our hearing by the Nietzsche-reading Catherine's intense introspections. As in O'Brien, political events are background and pretext. The gaoling and sentencing of her son Christy is the occasion for Munster's painful examination of her life and life itself, the emotional meaning of motherhood, marriage, love, the profound differences between women and men. The theme of self-sacrifice we have often noted in women's fiction is transmuted here into a suffering at once more personal and transcendent. Appropriately, Coyle like Hinkson achieves deep, almost Woolfian interiority yet without a comparable stylistic innovation beyond a distinctive obliquity of presentation. The geography of the novel is obscure and is replaced by a detailed landscape of intense feeling. And whereas the publisher's blurb on the original edition dates the action to 1919, one bibliographer dates it to somewhere between 1919 and 1922; but the Great War is still in progress in the novel, to which the references to Marshal Foch testify, and 1917 or more likely 1918 appears to be the year the events occur. Catherine's decision to vacate Gorabbey on the eve of her son's execution and her other son's announcement that he will soon marry a girl from a social class beneath him quietly repeat the familiar theme of the decline of the country house.

The novel explores psychologically Pearse's contention that "'tis women that keep all the great vigils' and tries to reconcile it with Stephen Dedalus's contention, quoted by Munster's well-read and Europeanized daughter, Kathleen, that Ireland is a sow that eats its own farrow, Christy being one of Ireland's farrow in this case. Christy's girlfriend Cicely believes she understands why Christy did what he did and Kathleen accuses her of being a stupid idealist; Cicely and Christy's siblings become engaged in an emotional tussle for Christy's love and attention. Even Catherine is a rival of her daughter and Christy's fiancée for her son's affections. Yet she is also a self-sacrificial figure who belongs to 'that communion of mothers who have given their sons; whose sons have been taken'; she discovers that what she feels for her son is 'something greater than love'.[42] Her emotional reality lies beyond idealism and realism, certainly beyond politics; it is as if the Cathleen Ni Houlihan of the Revival were subjected to genuine psychological scrutiny and, like that symbolic figure, Catherine Munster has a core of implacable self beneath the self-sacrifice; she thinks: 'Pity is the feeblest force on earth. It melted as you used it' (p. 159); for, after all, it is neither Cathleen nor Catherine who is going to meet her death for the Cause.

Catherine's love transcends, but also compensates for, an unrequited love that might remind us of O'Brien's Agnes Mulqueen: the love Catherine bore for her cousin Mitchell, a man who did not marry her (her own marriage seems to have been a disappointment); it is 'something that might have been Mitchell's centre, a consummation, a fire in which her own heart answered flame for flame' (p. 39). Her son's doom is a catalyst for her own pilgrimage to the far side of love. Despite the rather heavy-handedness by which Christy Munster is Christ and Catherine is Mary, the novel is a fine achievement in emotional realism that occasionally cloys but does not lapse into the utter pathos of Pearse's and O'Casey's suffering mothers; Coyle finely charts Munster's difficult passage through love to the grace that lies the other side. The chief success of the novel lies in Coyle's creation of the tense courteous maintenance of outward composure by Catherine—related to her social class—behind which she keeps her inner turmoil.

CONSTANCE MALLESON

Lady Constance Malleson (1895–1975) remains entirely overlooked as an Irish artist, though she was a daughter of the well-known Annesley family of Castlewellan, Co. Down; she described her girlhood there in her autobiography,

After Ten Years (1931) and mentions her family's involve.
cause during the gun-running days of the final Home Rule
sister, Lady Mabel, emigrated to New Zealand in 1940 where
famous artist. Constance was educated in Dresden and Paris and a.
Royal Academy of Dramatic Art. She became a well-known actress (as
O'Niel) and a pacifist, one of the 'old advanced crowd', as D. H. Law.
stingingly called them. It was her open marriage to Miles Malleson that allowe.
her to become Bertrand Russell's mistress and perhaps the most important
woman in his life.[44] A radical descendant of the female philanthropic activists of
the generation before her, she also became a Labour Party advocate and social
reformer (specializing in mental hospital and blood supply reforms) who
travelled and lectured in Scandinavia in the 1930s and 1940s.[45]

Back in Castlewellan, the various Land Acts of the late Victorian period had
taken their familiar toll, according to Constance shrinking the Annesley hold-
ings from 70,000 to 9,000 acres.[46] The Northern Ireland Land Purchase Act of
1925 delivered a wounding blow, while military requisitioning of the house in
World War II delivered the *coup de grace*; in *After Ten Years* there are some
poignant paragraphs on the decline Malleson finds when she returns home
some time in the 1920s, a real-life version of recurring passages in the novels.
Amidst the decay and untended overgrowth she found wire entanglements left
over from the Troubles—all speaking of 'lean years and of a hard struggle: of self
denial and meagre living'.[47] Given this and Malleson's politics and experience, it
is no wonder that in her hands the country-house genre went feral.

The advanced crowd ('our lot')—intellectual bohemians and on the whole,
a wealthy set—makes up the cast of *The Coming Back* (1933), set in Cambridge, Devonshire, London, and Dublin and which concerns the emotional
life of Konradin Waring, an Irish–Finnish woman. Her odyssey begins in
Dublin and at first she values independence more than love, but quickly
that is subverted by her intense affairs. Waring is a would-be novelist; her
beauty attracts men and she readily responds, emotionally and sexually. But
from the beginning she wishes for passionate love with freedom ('without lies
or deception'; 'she *must* be free'), for intensity without marriage (Malleson's
own position on the subject, as she explains in *After Ten Years*). 'Love' and
'freedom' ('it was the cry of the age') are chanted mantra-like throughout the
novel whose theme they are and which represent the highest good and are
almost independent of the human beings concerned.[48] The main man in her
series and her soul-mate is the Cambridge astronomer, Gregory del Orellano
(modelled in part on Russell) but in the end she loses him; these entanglements and disentanglements form the plot of the novel.

The time of the novel is unclear and presumably it is just after the Great War
but there is a very 1930s *fin-du-globe* assumption at work that supports no

political discussion in the novel; it is as if the multiple political positions of the Twenties and Thirties have been transposed into emotional positions, with Waring's freedom representing political egalitarianism but never spelled out beyond a vague idealism. One lover reflects that 'She prided herself on being democratic—but she was, in fact, merely promiscuous.'[49] Sexual jealousy is the equivalent of some oppressive political system, but freedom may be a kind of hypocrisy and double standard, egotism disguising itself as self-giving, a desire for free (complimentary) love disguising itself as pure self-expression. There is also, as in Bowen, O'Brien, and Coyle, the probability that solitariness, not love, is the ultimate reality, yet Waring ends the novel defiant in loss, still hopeful, as one might retain belief in a system despite political setbacks.

In *Fear in the Heart* (1936), Konradin Waring's counterpart is Auriel, Lady Mallory. Lullington Castle in the west of England has come to Auriel because her father has 'barred the entail', just as Castlewellan came to Malleson's sister because their father 'had broken the tail male'. (Her half-brother, Francis, the 6th Earl, was killed in the Great War.) Auriel may therefore be based in part on Malleson's sister, just as Auriel's sister, Jenny (who wants a baby but despises marriage and has Parisian leftist friends), may be based in part on the author. Jenny sees no salvation in any of the contemporary 'isms' on offer, including Mussolini's and Hitler's fascism and Moscow's communism, but the pessimism seems privileged, as it does in *The Coming Back*, though it might explain through a kind of short-circuitry the absence of political discussion in Malleson's novels. Yet the older (if still youthful) Auriel has a deeper pessimism, having lived through the Great War and lost her husband (killed at Ypres) and a baby as well as her father. (Malleson's own father died in 1914 when she was 19 and her brother was shot down over Belgium.) The lost generation of those who survived the War as youngish adults (one thinks of Hinkson's Stella Mannering)—'a damaged lot: scrap left over from the war'—is a secondary subject of the novel.[50] And as though criticizing Waring from the previous novel, Auriel reprimands Jenny: 'I'm tired of all this talk of love...Your interest in it seems to me melodramatic and morbid' (p. 84). Jenny like Konradin is of the new generation of New Woman, though Auriel thinks her a common egoist, theory-ridden like the intellectuals she despises, and selfishly bearing an illegitimate child.

Yet the novel's primary theme, that one should in all respects live boldly and without fear, especially when in love, is Jenny's philosophy, and Auriel herself, having suffered a breakdown on the death of her husband, responds to the love of Hilary Barnes, a married artist, and begins to reawaken, to discover fearlessness again. Barnes's wife Clare tumbles to her husband's love for Auriel and in a pre-emptive strike throws them together as friends; but Auriel grows angry with

Clare, believing her responsible for the husband's artistic drought, while Clare blames the War, out of which Hilary was invalided, for her husband's post-War sterility. Auriel decides to act and theirs becomes an unconventional west-country romance, reminiscent of Malleson's affair with the married Russell.[51] But Clare is a Catholic and no divorce is possible; Barnes's love becomes ingrown and he has a severe breakdown (another of the damaged generation); when he recovers sufficiently, he writes to tell Auriel he is going to Japan and will be gone for some time; when he returns he will live with his wife. Yet he writes that Auriel has not gone away from him, and at the end of the letter the narrator asks herself: 'Wasn't that, perhaps, something very like love?'

Hilary Barnes disbelieves in the 'Lawrentian philosophy' of the 'crudely physical' and in the 'rapturous union' in which his heroes and heroines lose themselves (p. 182). Yet this does not prevent Malleson writing in a Lawrentian vein, in which, for example, 'the flame of life was in her' (p. 183) and in which Auriel Mallory describes her desire: 'I want to have the core of love, the hard kernel that is without beautiful sensuous trappings' (p. 204). But it is true that Auriel and Barnes are in search of a love more ideal than the Lawrentian variety, and more akin to the idea of love we have seen in earlier romances, but with greater equality of the sexes. Hilary early associates Auriel with Héloïse: 'he thought of *la très sage Helloïs*—and her image became one with the image of Auriel Mallory' (p. 63). Perhaps the equation was suggested to Barnes by the way Auriel's surname recalls the author of *Morte d'Arthur* (a suitably French romance), and allows the novelist to insert herself through the first two syllables of her own married surname. Using the Héloïse connection, Malleson advances the theme of love with freedom from convention, morality, and dogma. Auriel lends Hilary the story of Héloïse and Abélard. She sees herself as Héloïse and quotes: 'I would rather be called your harlot than be empress of Christendom', and marks up for Barnes passages promoting Héloïse's fearless love (p. 242).

HELEN WADDELL

Auriel might have lent Barnes George Moore's version, but instead it is a contemporary one. 'He looked at the spine of the book to read the lettering. *Peter Abelard. A Novel. Helen Waddell. Constable.* It seemed strange to him that he had not happened upon the book before. Years back he had read George Moore's. A different form of perfection' (p. 246). Since *Peter Abelard* was published in 1933, it might be thought unsurprising that Barnes has not come across it, but in fact the novel was immensely successful from the start, and there were sixteen impressions before the year was out, and by 1935 there had been twenty impressions before Constable put out a popular edition in 1939 and reprinted it in 1940. *Peter Abelard* was written by Helen Waddell (1889–1965), born in Tokyo, the daughter of Hugh Waddell, an Irish Presbyterian missionary who died when she was 12. Back in Belfast where like Beatrice Grimshaw she attended Victoria College, she spent some years after her graduation in English from Queen's University, Belfast in selflessly caring for her widowed stepmother (shades of Deborah Alcock) before studying in Oxford and Paris, after which she worked at literature (scholarship, translation, editing) in London. She demonstrated self-sacrifice again in caring for others during World War II and in the last ten years of her life was selfless in the most literal and cruel way, suffering from some version of Alzheimer's disease.[52] Between times, Waddell gave evidence for being the most brilliant Irishwoman of her generation.

Peter Abelard followed Waddell's brief scholarly ruminations on Abelard in *The Wandering Scholars* (1927), a work of prose brilliance, however sound or original the scholarship. She called Abelard 'the scholar for scholarship's sake ... one of the makers of life, and perhaps the most powerful, in twelfth-century Europe' and declared that 'His personality, no less than his claim for reason against authority, was an enfranchisement of the human mind.'[53] Since he can appear as an Alcockian proto-Protestant, this dimension of Abelard may have appealed to the Presbyterian in Waddell as well as to the scholar, and provided one strand of the novel: the negotiations, accommodations, and confrontations between the mundane and the cloistral, between heresy and dogma, reason and faith, authority and individuality. Here was matter enough, with Abelard's intellectual pride and the suggestion of a tragic flaw. But the other dimension, Abelard's capacity for a fateful passion and the lyric gift his passion wrung from him, must have appealed to the hidden romantic novelist in this trained scholar; the 37-year-old Abelard neglected scholarship 'for a windflower of seventeen growing in the shadow of Notre Dame'. By the time the story had played itself out, 'Their love had been a street-song in Paris; the outrageous vengeance of the girl's uncle on her love and tardily made husband had been a blazoned scandal' (pp. 130–1).

In fact, Waddell manages to lend Abelard's brilliance as a philosopher something of the substance of bodily passion, as though exemplifying T. S. Eliot's nostalgia for a time before the dissociation of sensibility; early on, Gilles, Canon of Notre Dame, thinks of himself as a sensualist of the mind as well as body, and Abelard as an ascetic of the mind but sensualist of the body who has not found opportunity; yet Abelard knows, having met Heloise, that the mind will supply the body's desiderata, and he understands 'the rich temptations of the Desert Fathers. Lord, what an orgy of the mind they had!'[54] Soon the body's desiderata are supplied and Abelard even learns like Heloise that lust is the root of love, a proposition Auriel Mallory underlines for Hilary Barnes (cf. Yeats: 'for love must go to bed with lust'). They marry, endorsing Gilles's observation that lust is the root too of marriage. The terrible revenge of castration by Fulbert, Heloise's uncle and Canon of Notre Dame, and the later years of Heloise and Abelard are *sui generis* yet *Peter Abelard* as a Christian and philosophical romance with love at its centre and martyrdom at its terminus harks back to Boyle's *Theodora and Didymus* (1687). Its theme of suffering for one's belief and individual conscience might also recall for us Alcock's cruder narratives from Christian history, but as a novel about love and marriage and what Heloise with impatience calls 'this spider's web of woman's life, with its small panic fears and caution and obsequiousness' (p. 205), *Peter Abelard* takes its place among those novels whose heroines sometimes fly above these nets, on principle in the New Woman novels, through temperament in other novels.

AFTERWORD

Elizabeth Bowen continued writing fiction through the 1940s and 1950s and into the 1960s. Pamela Hinkson had begun publishing fiction in the early 1920s (both adult and schoolgirl fiction) and continued into the early 1940s. Kate O'Brien wrote on into the 1950s. Kathleen Coyle published at least one novel after 1940. Many of the connections I have made between culture and fiction stayed relevant, *mutatis mutandis*, long after that date. M. J. Farrell's fiction career was extraordinary since whereas eleven novels published between 1926 (*The Knight of Cheerful Countenance*) and 1952 (*Treasure Hunt*) would have constituted a considerable career in novel-writing, Farrell in fact ceased publishing novels until 1981 when she resurfaced as Molly Keane with *Good Behaviour*. Farrell began, in other words, during the early, pinched years of the Free State and ended (there was a novel in 1983) when the Irish Republic was maturing and the Anglo-Irish Agreement, a milestone during the Northern Ireland Troubles, was in the offing. Before Farrell's hiatus, Margaret Barrington had published *My Cousin Justin* (1939), one familiar theme of which is the collapse of society around the inhabitants of the country house.[55] Olivia Manning (1908–80), born in Portsmouth but whose mother was an Ulsterwoman who often took Olivia and her siblings to stay in Bangor, Co. Down, had published her first novel, *The Wind Changes* (1937), a story set in Galway, Dublin, Belfast, and the Aran Islands about an Ulsterwoman caught up both in the Troubles of 1921 and in the lives of several men, and which could readily be set for discussion beside Barrington and many of the women novelists I have mentioned, and especially, perhaps, Malleson.

And to prove the surprising stamina of the country-house novel, there is *Tea at Crumbo Castle* (1949) by Magdalen King-Hall (1904–71), author of sixteen long fictions between 1925 and 1962, most of them historical novels. A seventeenth novel, *The Well-Meaning Young Man* (1930), was co-written with her sister, Louise King-Hall. Born in London and spending time as a girl in Australia, Brighton, Scotland, Portaferry (Co. Down), and Cobh (Co. Cork), Magdalen (Madge) King-Hall was of an illustrious seafaring family (her father was an admiral and her brother a naval commander). After the publication of her first novel, she was for a time a journalist in London. She married Patrick Perceval Maxwell and lived in the Sudan and London before returning in the 1930s to Co. Down, Northern Ireland where her husband farmed near his family home.[56] According to a *Time Magazine* review of her best-known book, King-Hall had spent much of her girlhood at Quinton Castle, near Portaferry.[57] In 1952 she and her family moved to Headborough, Co. Waterford where she lived until her husband died in 1968 and where she herself is buried.

Two of King-Hall's novels were striking public successes. *Life and Death of the Wicked Lady Skelton* (1944) was filmed twice, in 1945 and 1983. But King-Hall had already achieved fame, even notoriety, with her first novel, *The Diary of a Young Lady of Fashion in the Year 1764–65* (1925) by 'Cleone Knox', written when King-Hall was 19.[58] It was published in London with the help of an 'editor', 'her Kinsman Alexander Blacker Kerr'[59] and on its appearance was greeted as a discovery of great, even Pepysian historical interest, but was later exposed as a 'forgery'. In either guise, it saw nine American editions within two months, having been much talked about in London the previous year. The elaborate 'hoax' of this sprightly and titillating *faux* eighteenth-century country-house novel and Grand Tour novel would nowadays raise no post-modernist eyebrow.

The diary is that of a 20-year-old woman—part flibbertigibbet, part shrewd enough observer—whose family lives at Castle Kearney, Co. Down (a fictionalized Quinton Castle, Kearney being a fishing village nearby). Cleone's attachment to a young lover is frowned upon, and she is banished on holiday to Ballywiticock House, to reach which she and her escorts pass through Portaferry and Newtownards. While she is there, she and her lover attempt an elopement which is discovered at the eleventh hour and she is returned to Castle Kearney in disgrace. Her father's remedy for his daughter's behaving like a 'slut' is to whisk her off on a Grand Tour of Europe, and off they set, travelling via Belfast and Derbyshire to London, Bath, Paris, Lausanne, and Venice, all the while the Revolting Daughter keeping her lively and convincing journal of sights, incidents, fashions, escapades, and personalities.

Three topics command Cleone Knox's attention. One: the distinction between the modish and the natural, between the beauties of the 'beau monde' (especially fashion) and the beauties of nature (especially Swiss landscape). Two: the licentiousness of Venice and Paris ('this Gay Cruel City'). Three: the new radical notion of liberty and 'the Rights of Individuality' abroad in France and Switzerland.[60] The editor's 'footnotes' allow King-Hall to express contrary opinions on these topics, while never permitting the views to stiffen into seriousness. The diary ends with the release of Cleone's brother Ned from gaol in Venice where he had been lodged for trying to elope with a 14-year-old Venetian nun, daughter of an illustrious family, and with the news that her lover had arrived from Ireland. We are told by the 'editor' in an 'Envoi' that Knox and her beau eloped successfully this time, and that she left behind her journal which turned up among her family's papers in 1904. The lovers marry in Geneva and return to Co. Down in 1766 where the diarist eventually has twelve children and a happy marriage.

It is amusing to regard *The Diary of a Young Lady of Fashion* as a wayward contemporary ancestor of the country-house novels that have populated this book. If so, *Tea at Crumbo Castle* is a tardy and rather frayed descendant, however readable. This novel is of the neo-Gothic and murder-mystery subgenre of the country-house novel, set within sight of the plains of Tipperary in 1931 and the late 1870s. The frame narrator who opens and closes the novel is the familiar English Visitor to Ireland, who arrives in 1931 to keep her hostess company in her modest country house, Naphir, while the latter's husband is off with the army in Egypt. The narrator is aware that the attitude of a previous English visitor, now resident in Ireland, is itself hackneyed: 'like all English people . . . [she] had quickly succumbed to the charms of the scenery and the agreeable manners of its inhabitants.'[61] By 1931 the decline of the Protestant population 'of late years in the rural districts of Southern Ireland' (p. 1) has resulted in the local Church of Ireland service, which opens the novel (complete with a sermon), attracting a congregation of merely nine souls. By this observation, King-Hall keeps the country-house novel abreast of current social developments in Ireland.

Early in her stay, the narrator visits nearby Crumbo Castle, a gloomy 'Early Victorian Gothic pile' filled with amazing lumber of the past,[62] where she finds old Mrs Toye as the last survivor. She turns out to be the late Frederick Toye's second wife who came into sole possession of Crumbo when Toye died in 1879, his first wife, Lady Charlotte, having died under mysterious circumstances.

There is a lengthy third-person flashback to 1878, the year before Lady Charlotte's death after an illness, Toye's own death, and the death of their daughter Blanche, and the flashback narrative solves the puzzle of the three close deaths. A dark story emerges of grievance, cruelty, greed, and power. Before her death, Lady Charlotte was nursed by Emily Hogan, who had been raised in 'a poky, dreary little house, smelling of boiled cabbage, in a Dublin suburb ' (p. 26) and was detested by the other staff. She it is who becomes the second Mrs Toye. The behaviour of the equally dislikable Toye goes some way to explain the decline of the gentry. Blanche's father 'had raged terribly when Mr Gladstone disestablished the Protestant Church of Ireland' (p. 42), but this was not all. 'Far worse in its effects on Mr. Toye than the Disestablishment of the Church was Gladstone's Land Act of 1870. Now it seemed that the end of everything had indeed come. The words "ruin", "anarchy" and "scoundrelly legislation", boomed out in Mr. Toye's deep angry voice, sounded like a bell tolling for the passing of the "landlord and his class"' (pp. 42–3). At first Crumbo Castle prospers despite Parnell and the Home Rule movement and despite some tenant evictions, but Land League and Fenian agitation intensifies and a year after his wife's death, he is murdered by disaffected tenants with the last-minute complicity of his daughter who suspected him of murdering her mother. The lonely Blanche, thwarted in her one romance by the class snobbery of her family and who might have stepped from the pages of *Jane Eyre*, which she is reading at one point, takes drastic action to punish herself when she finds the answer to the murder mystery. The novel's reflective implication is that what happened after 1879 was a long humiliating epilogue for the Anglo-Irish, a symbolic dissolution being subliminally visualized by the reader in the very name of the Castle and title of the book.

NOTES

1. R. F. Foster has taken issue with the orthodox view (Yeats's own, expressed in a 1932–3 address to American audiences) that politics were largely in abeyance between the fall of Parnell and the rebellion of Easter 1916. Foster regards Irish politics as having been radicalized around 1900 in opposition to the Boer War and again at the outbreak of the Great War in 1914: *Modern Ireland 1600–1972* (1988; London: Penguin Books, 1989), pp. 431, 456. To the timeline we could also add 1912 with the introduction of the third Home Rule Bill and Ulster resistance to it, and 1914 (again) when the Home Rule Bill passed. Before and immediately after the ratification of the Anglo-Irish Treaty there were, of course, the Anglo-Irish war of 1919–21, the Government of Ireland Act of 1920, and the split in the South of Ireland when the Treaty was signed, which resulted in a civil war, 1922–3.
2. The constitution of the Free State was strong on rights and freedoms: see Foster, *Modern Ireland*, p. 516 n. One Revival writer, Darrell Figgis, had a hand in the 1922 constitution. The 1937 constitution entrenched the Catholic nature of Irish society.
3. For O'Connor and O'Faolain, their novels, and their literary response to the Free State, see John Wilson Foster, 'The Irish Renaissance, 1890–1940: Prose in English' in Margaret Kelleher and Philip O'Leary (eds.), *The Cambridge History of Irish Literature* (Cambridge: Cambridge University Press, 2006), vol. II, pp. 156–60.

4. Reid provided his own personal continuity across the decades of rupture, by rewriting *The Bracknels* (1911) as *Denis Bracknel* (1947) and *Following Darkness* (1912) as *Peter Waring* (1937).

5. If only a fraction of what Irvine tells of his life is true, it would still be impressive. The variety of his military, civilian, philanthropic, evangelical, and union experiences in Ireland, Scotland, Egypt, England, the United States, and Germany is astonishing. He was a remarkable man.

6. E. Œ. Somerville & Martin Ross, *The Big House of Inver* (London: Heinemann, 1925), p. 218.

7. Beatrice Grimshaw, *Victorian Family Robinson: A Novel* (London: Cassell & Co., 1934), p. 11.

8. According to John Kelly and Eric Domville, editors of *The Collected Letters of W.B. Yeats*, vol. 1 *1865–1895* (Oxford: Clarendon Press, 1986), p. 516, Tynan was born in 1859 and not 1861 as she always claimed.

9. Katharine Tynan, *An International Marriage* (London: Ward, Lock, 1933), pp. 72, 89, 137.

10. The biographical explanations are both diverse and individual, having mostly to do with education and the movement of family. Bowen, for example, was sent to England from Co. Cork at the age of 7 because her father entered a home with mental problems; she was educated in England and lived there a great deal, merely summering in Ireland (a visitor in her own country house) until she inherited Bowen's Court in 1930. Hinkson was Katherine Tynan's daughter and knew England intimately. Waddell was born in Tokyo, the daughter of an Ulster Presbyterian minister and Orientalist and was taken to Belfast when she was 10; she was educated at Oxford and taught in England. O'Brien was educated abroad and developed a taste for Spain. Malleson like most of the others regarded England as a natural place to travel to, visit relations, likely meet a partner, write and publish. Barrington, daughter of an RIC district inspector, was educated at Alexandra College, Dublin, and only moved to England when she separated from her husband, the historian Edmund Curtis. Politics seems not to have played a large role in these expatriations.

11. O'Faolain is quoted by John Nemo, *Patrick Kavanagh* (Boston: Twayne, 1979), p. 57.

12. D. G. Waring (1891–1977) published at least eleven novels between 1936 and 1942. They can readily occupy the country-house genre, the romance genre, and the spy genre. *Nothing Irredeemable* (1936) is a rather thin love-and-marriage romance conducted against the background of a country house in decline and the 'betrayal' of Irish unionists by the English government during the Troubles. *Fortune Must Follow* (1937) is a thicker text that also exploits the country-house set; it concerns a Northern Irish ex-British spy who returns to Ireland when his cover is blown. Having once infiltrated the IRA, he uses his connections to crack a cross-border smuggling ring. Waring tackles Irish politics in thriller mode with her eye also on worrying international political developments on which she has a wavering right-wing international Unionist 'take'. Dorothy Grace Waring was born in England but her family had occupied Lisnacree House, Co. Down since

the late eighteenth century. She served in the Red Cross during the Great War, during which she married (later divorcing). She became controversially embroiled in the Troubles on the Unionist side. In the late 1920s she was a member of the British Fascists, becoming District Officer, Women's Unit, then member, HQ Staff Ulster Women Fascists. She began to write after the dissolution of British Fascism but in the early 1930s she was involved with the anti-Catholic Ulster Protestant League. She reinvented herself in the 1940s as a BBC Northern Ireland radio personality. The year after she entered a home, Lisnacree House was burned down in time-honoured Irish fashion. See Gordon Gillespie, 'The Secret Life of D. G. Waring', *Causeway* (Spring 1998): 43–8. Gillespie rightly points out the Kiplingesque influences on her writing and thinking and her affinity in fiction to John Buchan. See also Gillespie's entry for Waring in the *Oxford Dictionary of National Biography* (2004).

13. Elizabeth Bowen, *The Hotel* (1927; London: Jonathan Cape, 1950), p. 12.
14. In 1921, Bowen's own engagement foundered on the Italian Riviera where her Aunt Edie was staying in a hotel; her fiancé came to see her (as Milton comes late to the hotel) and it seems that her aunt was less than encouraging and the engagement was broken off. See Victoria Glendinning, *Elizabeth Bowen* (1977; New York: Avon Books, 1979), pp. 42–3. Incidentally, Bowen's father in 1918 married a sister of Stephen Gwynn's.
15. May Crommelin, *A Woman-Derelict* (London: John Long, 1901[?]), p. 110.
16. The phrase occurs in 'The Happy Autumn Fields', reprinted in *Elizabeth Bowen's Irish Stories* (Dublin: Poolbeg Press, 1978), p. 96.
17. Elizabeth Bowen, *The Last September* (1929; London: Jonathan Cape, 1960), p. 163.
18. Bowen later explained and justified 'the social idea' that animated life in the country house: her 1940 essay, 'The Big House,' is reprinted in *The Mulberry Tree: Writings of Elizabeth Bowen*, ed. Hermione Lee (London: Virago, 1986), pp. 25–30. See also Elizabeth Bowen, *Bowen's Court* (London: Longmans, 1964), p. 26.
19. Barbara Brothers has shown how in a 1949 novel Bowen depicts egotism and new, somewhat shabby romantic love as the only comfort to those who are outside the world of the novel's Anglo-Irish estate, Mount Morris: 'Pattern and Void: Bowen's Irish Landscapes and *The Heat of the Day*', *Mosaic* 12 (1979): 129–38.
20. For example, Valeria in 'Her Table Spread' and Mary in 'The Happy Autumn Fields'.
21. Quoted by Glendinning, *Elizabeth Bowen*, p. 10.
22. M. J. Farrell (Molly Keane), *Mad Puppetstown* (1931; London: Virago, 1985), p. 23. Farrell (born Molly Skrine) was the daughter of Moira O'Neill (Nesta Skrine, née Higginson) and grew up in a country house in Co. Waterford but spent a good deal of time with a wealthy family in a big house in Co. Tipperary where she met habitués of London's literary and intellectual life.
23. M. J. Farrell, *Devoted Ladies* (1934; London: Virago Press, 1984), p. 28.
24. 'Entry' is a fox-hunting term, referring to a young fox's initiation into the sport but like much else in fox-hunting can for the sporting novelists have human application. Towards the close of *Devoted Ladies*, Jane is likened to a fox seeking a covert from the jealous and lethal advances of Jessica.

25. True to genre, in *The Knight of Cheerful Countenance* an English cousin visits Ballinrath House and initiates the love entanglements.

26. Farrell had already darkened considerably the formulas of the Irish country-house novel in *Taking Chances* (1929), a novel that includes most of the elements of the genre—country-house sporting life, the tragicomic dynamics of the landowning family, the Visitor to Ireland figure, the Ascendancy and orphanhood connection, the themes of love and marriage. But the English Visitor to Ireland, Mary Fuller, plays the wild Irish girl role, being indeed the serpent in paradise, the alien newcomer who is no mere catalyst but hurts others as well as being herself hurt. 'Mary was a factor for disturbance.' And the exploration of the kinds and consequences of love and marriage is deeper and darker than usual, with pregnancy, illegitimacy, miscarriage, abortion, and adultery as terms of the equation. 'Why wasn't love a thing like hunting?' Mary Fuller wonders in pain and with unwitting humour: *Taking Chances* (1929; London: Virago, 1987), pp. 30, 136.

27. In describing Sylvester, the narrator likens him to 'the eldest son in a Conversation Piece' (p. 38). Farrell had published a novel of just that title, *Conversation Piece*, in 1932. The Conversation Piece suggests all of Farrell's novels: small-scale group portraits (the heyday of which was the eighteenth century) in elegant social settings, depicting a hunting, dining, or musical scene, and often with dogs and horses.

28. *The Rising Tide* (1937) is yet another Farrell country-house novel that includes an impressive poetic memory of fox-hunting (Virago Press, 1984), pp. 215–17. This novel, that opens in 1900 and follows a family through the 1920s, exhibits most of the expected motifs of the genre. Familiarly, the Great War is a greater watershed (the man of the house is killed) than the Anglo-Irish war and the Irish civil war, though all are off-stage and muffled by perspective. If one theme is the difference between pre-War and post-War Anglo-Irish life, another is the country house itself, which could be called 'sad Garonlea' to set beside 'mad Puppetstown', biding its time in the exertion of its melancholy influence. The native tenants love the novel's heroine, Cynthia, but are entirely out of earshot, and it is a purely internal generational power struggle waged between the tyrannical Lady Charlotte French-McGrath (the embodiment of the pre-War order) and her daughter-in-law, the soon widowed Cynthia French-McGrath, between Cynthia and the brooding spirit of Garonlea itself, and in the end between Cynthia and her own embittered son, inheritor of the house who rejects his fox-hunting mother's ruthless gaiety and wishes to return Garonlea to its disciplined sad self. *The Rising Tide*, beautifully written but oddly hollow, narrates the intestinal wars, and fortitude, of a family and caste, registering continuity with the past amidst the characters' increasing irrelevance to the present.

29. See 'Molly Keane: An Interview with Polly Devlin', *Conversation Piece* (1932; London: Virago, 1991), n.p.

30. Katherine Everett, *Bricks and Flowers: Memoirs* (1949; Bungay, Suffolk: Reprint Society, 1951), pp. 176–83.

31. Pamela Hinkson, *The Ladies' Road* (London: Gollancz, 1932), p. 319. The Penguin 1946 edition sold over 100,000 copies.

32. Pamela Hinkson, pp. 217, 309.

33. Perhaps this derives from Hinkson's religious quietism that we see in a later novel with a title virtually identical to that of her mother's earlier novel: *Golden Rose* (1944). This novel is set among the professional classes (soldiers, engineers, doctors) in India and (in flashback) France some time after the Great War. Its chief figures are the Nursing Sisters of a Catholic religious Order. In particular, the story is that of the lives of two women, both confused and disappointed in love, one achieving happiness in religious service, the other caught between the love of two men. Sister Françoise (who was Diane de Préaux, one of whose grandmothers was country-house Irish) carries the novel's themes: the burden of the world's pain carried by those such as she who are 'out of the world', and the ultimate relationship between love of God (and God's love) and love of humanity (including love of one man). The story is told with Hinkson's characteristically close attention to foreground and with her familiar contemplative memories and flashbacks. Although in style and subject-matter the novel can most readily be set beside Kate O'Brien's fiction, the themes of philanthropy, Catholicism, sexual and romantic love, marriage, and the Irish and British in the Empire, relate it to innumerable earlier novels by Irishwomen, including some by her mother.

34. In the United States, this novel was entitled *The Anteroom*. O'Brien was born in Limerick.

35. Lavelle hails from Mellick, a fictional town that occurs in O'Brien's earlier historical novel, *Without My Cloak* (1931).

36. Kate O'Brien, *Mary Lavelle* (London: Heinemann, 1936), p. 344.

37. Since 'androgenous' means 'of or pertaining to production of male offspring', O'Brien must surely mean 'androgynous'.

38. Kate O'Brien, *The Anteroom* (New York: Doubleday, Doran & Co., 1934), p. 265.

39. Kathleen Coyle, *Liv* (London: Jonathan Cape, 1929), pp. 183, 216, 101–2, 252.

40. Rebecca West, Introduction to *Liv*, pp. 8, 13, 14. Coyle's previous novels were *Picadilly: A Novel* (1923), *The Widow's House: A Novel* (1924), *Youth in the Saddle* (1927) and *It is Better to Tell* (1927).

41. Coyle's own religious affiliation is pleasingly ambiguous. According to Ann Owens Weekes, citing John Cronin, Coyle's mother was Catholic and her father 'secretive about his religion' (which in Ireland sounds like a variety of Protestantism): 'Women Novelists, 1930s–1960s' in John Wilson Foster (ed.), *The Cambridge Companion to the Irish Novel* (Cambridge: Cambridge University Press, 2006), pp. 194–5.

42. Kathleen Coyle, *A Flock of Birds* (New York: E. P. Dutton, 1930), pp. 242, 39.

43. Constance Malleson [Colette O'Niel], *After Ten Years: A Personal Record* (London: Jonathan Cape, 1931). Two other chapters are called 'Return to Ireland' and 'Ireland Again'. Her father was a veteran of the Kaffir Wars in South Africa (1851–53) and the Crimean War (1853–56) and was wounded in both. Lady Mabel and Francis (later 6th Earl) were the children of his first marriage, to Mabel Markham; Clare and Constance were the daughters of his second marriage, to Priscilla Moore, an Irishwoman.

44. Malleson appears at length in Ronald W. Clark's *The Life of Bertrand Russell* (1975).

45. In 1947, Malleson published *In the North: Autobiographical Fragments in Norway, Sweden, Finland: 1936–1946.* Malleson's papers are housed at McMaster University, Hamilton, Ontario, Canada.

46. However, *Land Owners in Ireland 1876* (Baltimore: Genealogical Publishing Company, 1988), lists Annesley ownership in Co. Down at 23,567 acres (the third largest estate in Northern Ireland and thirteen acres larger than Mountstewart!), though the family perhaps owned land elsewhere.

47. Constance Malleson, *After Ten Years*, pp. 12, 186–9.

48. Constance Malleson, *The Coming Back* (London: Jonathan Cape, 1933), pp. 180, 158, 176, 100.

49. Constance Malleson, *The Coming Back*, p. 138.

50. Constance Malleson, *Fear in the Heart* (London: Collins, 1936), p. 79. '... was she to be for ever no more than scrap thrown aside from the war?' (p. 173).

51. The idyllic portion of the Hilary–Auriel romance echoes the 'few idyllic days' Russell and Malleson spent at Lulworth (cf. Lullington) in Dorset during the war and the 'idyllic meetings in Somerset and Cornwall' they contrived in the late 1920s: see Clark, *The Life of Bertrand Russell* (London: Weidenfeld and Nicolson, 1975), pp. 381, 441.

52. Useful biographies of Waddell are Monica Blackett, *The Mark of the Maker: A Portrait of Helen Waddell* (1973) and Dame Felicitas Corrigan, *Helen Waddell: A Biography* (1986). See also Norman Vance, *Helen Waddell: Presbyterian Medievalist* (Belfast: Presbyterian Historical Society, 1997).

53. Helen Waddell, *The Wandering Scholars* (1927; Harmondsworth: Pelican Books, 1954), pp. 129–30.

54. Helen Waddell, *Peter Abelard: A Novel* (1933; London: Constable, 1939), pp. 12–13, 93. Waddell published *The Desert Fathers: Translations from the Latin* in 1936 (completing a decade of extraordinary output) and one of the themes of her Introduction is the danger to the spirit that passions of the flesh were taken to represent; the warfare between spirit and flesh animates *Peter Abelard.*

55. The love in this novel between Loulie (Anne-Louise Delahaie), the novel's narrator, and her cousin Justin Thorauld, an orphan, exists midway between cousinage and desire and implies the withdrawal, infertility, and endurance of the Anglo-Irish after the series of blows to their esteem and position. I discuss *My Cousin Justin* briefly in 'The Irish Renaissance, 1890–1904: Prose in English,' Margaret Kelleher and Philip O'Leary (eds.), *Cambridge History of Irish Literature* (Cambridge: Cambridge University Press, 2006), vol. 1, pp. 164–5.

56. See the biographical and bibliographical information on King-Hall on the County Waterford Museum website.

57. *Time* review of *The Diary of a Young Lady of Fashion*, 14 June 1926, which summarizes a press conference (presumably in London) which King-Hall gave to announce her authorship of the pseudonymous work. See the *Time Magazine* website, Vignette StoryServer series.

58. The County Waterford Museum website lists 1924 as the first publication date of the *Diary* whereas the Thornton Butterworth (London, 1925) edition gives 1925

as the date of first publication. D. Appleton & Co. of New York published the novel in 1926.

59. King-Hall was a cousin of Winston Churchill through the Ker family.
60. 'Cleone Knox', *The Diary of a Young Lady of Fashion in the Year 1764–1765* (London: Thornton Butterworth, 1925), pp. 169, 182.
61. Magdalen King-Hall, *Tea at Crumbo Castle* (London: Peter Davies, 1949), p. 5.
62. Said on the County Waterford Museum website to be modelled on Strancally Castle on the Blackwater, near Knockanore, Co. Waterford.

APPENDIX:

A Note on Joyce and Popular Fiction

British fiction before *Dubliners* (1914) had depicted the mundane lives of the lower orders, but what distinguished Joyce's stories was the thrifty eloquence by which his fellow citizens are exhibited. The stories are popular in the sense of depicting ordinary lives and commonplace thoughts, even if the economic prose style, plot irresolutions, and terse character presentations are hardly those of popular fiction, and worked against commercial success. Joyce's lower middle class is without coherence or solidarity; its culture is scrappy—half-English, half-Irish, inherited from above and below—and without integrity. Yet Joyce, whose own family descended to the bottom of the middle class, made himself at home with the rich but motley popular culture of his Dubliners, their sayings, jokes, anecdotes, gossip, songs, rumours, half-baked knowledge: like a parody of the wisdom and culture Yeats, Lady Gregory, and others sought amongst the peasantry.

Joyce claimed that his was a tactical and preparative realism, an impassive fidelity to the surfaces of Dublin life, a 'nicely polished looking-glass' held up before Dubliners as a first step in their civic reanimation and even 'spiritual liberation'.[1] But in the meantime, the realism of *Dubliners* amounted to a painful truth; indeed, Joyce's realism is deeper than ground-clearing; like Moore's in *The Untilled Field* (1903) it implies a moral and spiritual rot too entrenched to be reversed, certainly by a rural-romantic revival. In 1906, while Joyce was writing the stories in Rome and trying to place them as a volume, he saw a review of *The Realist and Other Stories* (1906) by the popular Cork writer, E. Temple Thurston. Joyce told his brother Stanislaus that he had ordered Thurston's book from England, having been drawn to the reviewer's description of the stories as 'daring'. Several weeks later he sent Stanislaus the book, presumably having thought it worthwhile to do so.[2] The title story of Thurston's collection has less in common with Joyce's work in progress than with Poe's stories, the 'apocalyptic stories' of Yeats, or *The Picture of Dorian Gray*, telling the story as it does of a painter who in pursuit of a complete realism arranges the actual death on the cross of the young man who is modelling Christ for the painter's 'Crucifixion', turning a living being into a perfectly achieved still life (or death). But Joyce must have been interested in Thurston's Prologue to the fifty-page story in which he claims a greater contemporary need for truth than for love and reminds readers of the popular search for truth being conducted in science and art. Thurston believed that 'we are passing into the adolescence of intellect', finding ourselves between the infantile acceptance of fairy tale and allegory and the adult demand for unvarnished truth.[3] Joyce's stories, in implicit contrast to the folk-work of the Irish Revival and depicting varieties of intellectual adolescence, might have been adduced to support Thurston's claim. The Cork writer distinguished two kinds of realism—'that which uplifts and that which casts down' (p. 6)—and *Dubliners* engaged in the second, of necessity, Joyce argued, his realism re-creating (to quote Thurston) 'the valleys of darkness that must be passed through' (p. 7).

The actual and figurative darkness in the lives of Joyce's Dubliners is ineffectively lit by the chief characters' guttering pseudo-romantic daydreams. In *Dubliners* and *Ulysses* (1922) these can derive from or resemble the popular fiction that offered romantic plots and encouraged in its readers extra-textual daydreaming.[4] In the Nausicaa episode of *Ulysses* Leopold Bloom and Gerty MacDowell—introspective or dreamy readers of popular stories—sexually converge for the reader. Gerty has read Maria Susanna Cummins's *The Lamplighter* (1854)—the heroine of which bears Gerty's name—which sold 40,000 copies in a week and was reprinted as late as 1906. Bloom reads *Tit-Bits* and picks up soft pornographic romances for his wife, Molly, on this occasion *The Sweets of Sin*, the title and swift perusal of which provides Bloom with intermittent sexual arousal during his day. The Nausicaa episode is narrated in part in the sentimental-romantic language of such popular fiction and affectionately parodies the motifs of female self-sacrifice, female romantic sexual longing, and male caddishness found in it, as well exploiting the popular Irish genre, the 'Temperance' story, as Stephen J. Brown named it.[5]

Sexual sin is more seriously treated in *A Portrait of the Artist as a Young Man* (1916). When Stephen Dedalus visits Dublin's brothel neighbourhood, the nether world of the slums, it is a scene familiar from popular romantic-realist fiction in Victorian Britain and Ireland (including novels by Mulholland, Meade, and Letts), though narrated with greater subjective intensity. (In *Ulysses* the brothel scene is a more self-consciously nightmarish and modernist affair.) It is also a scene that belongs in a belated *fin-de-siècle* work of fiction, and the author of *A Portrait* and creator of the febrile novice poet Stephen Dedalus would surely have agreed with Wilde's Gilbert in 'The Critic as Artist' that contemporary writers desired 'to realize our own age in all its weariness and sin', a sentiment as applicable to *A Portrait* as to *Dorian Gray* or *The Sands of Pleasure*. He would also have agreed with Gilbert that there is more to be learned from the sinner than from the saint.[6] As we have seen, slums and sin were often coupled in episodes of Victorian and Edwardian novels that charted the hero's growth (and lapses) and *A Portrait* is very much of its time in this regard. Irish novels of spiritual crisis had likewise already appeared; Joyce's daring lay both in the spirituality in question—Irish Roman Catholicism—and in the implied finality of the apostasy.

In short, whereas Joyce's artistic priorities were early beyond the remit of the Irish Revival, it was some time before his fiction outgrew the preoccupations of Victorian and Edwardian fiction, popular or no. Even in *Ulysses*, the temperate and sober Bloom ponders in the Eumaeus episode the Irish drink plague ('drink, the curse of Ireland') as well as the value of the Contagious Diseases Acts of 1864, 1866, and 1869 in controlling the spread of venereal disease, though he is equitably aware that 'some man is ultimately responsible for [the prostitute's] condition'.[7] Bloom inhabits at least the mental world of philanthropic impulse, whereas Dedalus is a stranger to it. Just as he shrugs cynically when Bloom confides his social concerns, Dedalus in *A Portrait* extends the purview of his 'non serviam' to social and charitable action: he will look first to his own interests, take part in no campaign of social reform, entertain no self-sacrifice or perform no philanthropy. 'Dedalus,' MacCann tells him, 'I believe you're a good fellow but you have yet to learn the dignity of altruism and the responsibility of the human individual.'⁸ Joyce did not simply have Dedalus refuse to serve; he also demonstrated that refusal through perspective, an increasing reliance on the sense-impressions and cognition of individual minds. It is the sustained prose equivalence of Dedalus's thoughts (and in *Ulysses*, of Bloom's and Molly's as well) that constituted Joyce's break with the popular and mainstream Victorian and Edwardian novel.

For his part, Bloom, despite his philanthropic impulse and concern for social purity, entertains many impure thoughts during his day, pondering the pleasures as well as the wages of sin. He daydreams of living the arousing excerpt of *The Sweets of Sin*, either as cuckolder (in the case of Martha Clifford) or cuckold (in the case of Molly).⁹ Bloom, after all, out of prurience as well as empathy, lives others' lives, and these include the lives of characters in popular fiction. (Later in the novel, Joyce will attribute thoughts to Bloom and develop his character in linguistic and rhetorical ways that promote him well beyond the world of popular fiction.) A major preoccupation for Joyce is the nature of the Blooms' marriage, and although its secret and rich infidelities of thought and deed make it an unusual union among the legion of fictional marriages in the 1890–1922 period, *Ulysses* can nevertheless be added, in that respect, to the long list of marriage novels of the time.

NOTES

1. The mirror metaphor can be found in a letter of 23 June 1906, quoted in Richard Ellmann, *James Joyce* (Oxford: Oxford University Press, 1983), p. 222. By 'civic reanimation' I mean a reversal of the 'hemiplegia or paralysis' which Joyce diagnosed in Dublin in a letter of 1904: see Ellmann, p. 163. 'Spiritual liberation' was to be achieved only after Ireland had acknowledged the truth of Joyce's chapter of 'moral history' that *Dubliners* composed: letter to Grant Richards the publisher, 13 May 1906: see Ellmann, p. 221.

2. *Letters of James Joyce*, ed. Richard Ellmann (New York: Viking Press, 1966), vols. 2 and 3, pp. 201, 205. Ellmann includes Thurston's book as part of Joyce's library left behind in Trieste when he moved to Paris in 1920, though he points out that the book was not among the surviving collection (having of course been in the possession of Stanislaus Joyce): *The Consciousness of Joyce* (London: Faber & Faber, 1977), pp. 97, 130.

3. E. Temple Thurston, *The Realist and Other Stories* (London: Sisley's Ltd., 1906), pp. 5–6.

4. This aspect of *Dubliners* appears to have influenced Hugh A. MacCartan (b. 1885) whose volume of sketches and stories, *Silhouettes* (1918), includes two studies of quiet desperation, unfulfilment, and negative epiphanies reminiscent of the lives of Litter Chandler and other Dubliners: "Life: A Study in Timidity" and "James Fenelon, Bachelor", both set in lower-middle-class Dublin. The author, a civil servant, was born in Co. Down, and moved to Belfast and then Dublin—all three places providing settings in *Silhouettes*. MacCartan depicts Dublin slums,

unromantic marriage, and the aftermath of Easter 1916, but in the Joycean attempt to create literary rather than popular fiction, succeeding only fitfully.

5. I discuss this episode more fully in 'The Irish Renaissance, 1890–1940: Prose in English' in Margaret Kelleher and Philip O'Leary (eds.), *The Cambridge History of Irish Literature* (Cambridge: Cambridge University Press, 2006), vol. 2, pp. 151–2.

6. *The Portable Oscar Wilde,* ed. Richard Aldington and Stanley Weintraub (1946; New York: Viking Penguin, 1981), pp. 99, 104. I discuss sin in Joyce in 'The Irish Renaissance, 1890–1904: Prose in English', pp. 147–50.

7. James Joyce, *Ulysses* (1922; Harmondsworth: Penguin Books, 1969), p. 553.

8. James Joyce, *A Portrait of the Artist as a Young Man* (1916; New York: Penguin Books USA, 1992), p. 215.

9. A recent critic claims that Joyce set out to provoke the Social Purity advocates (which included Sarah Grand) and that much of his fiction is in conscious reaction against them as he sought notoriety for his depictions of impurity: Katherine Mullin, *James Joyce, Sexuality and Social Purity* (2003).

Index